THE LETTER
TO TITUS

VOLUME 35

THE ANCHOR BIBLE is a fresh approach to the world's greatest classic. Its object is to make the Bible accessible to the modern reader; its method is to arrive at the meaning of biblical literature through exact translation and extended exposition, and to reconstruct the ancient setting of the biblical story, as well as the circumstances of its transcription and the characteristics of its transcribers.

THE ANCHOR BIBLE is a project of international and interfaith scope. Protestant, Catholic, and Jewish scholars from many countries contribute individual volumes. The project is not sponsored by any ecclesiastical organization and is not intended to reflect any particular theological doctrine. Prepared under our joint supervision, THE ANCHOR BIBLE is an effort to make available all the significant historical and linguistic knowledge which bears on the interpretation of the biblical record.

THE ANCHOR BIBLE is aimed at the general reader with no special formal thinking in biblical studies; yet, it is written with the most exacting standards of scholarship, reflecting the highest technical accomplishment.

This project marks the beginning of a new era of co-operation among scholars in biblical research, thus forming a common body of knowledge to be shared by all.

William Foxwell Albright
David Noel Freedman
GENERAL EDITORS

THE ANCHOR BIBLE

THE LETTER TO TITUS

◆

A New Translation
with Notes and Commentary
and An Introduction to Titus,
I and II Timothy, The Pastoral Epistles

JEROME D. QUINN

THE ANCHOR BIBLE

Doubleday
New York   London   Toronto   Sydney   Auckland

THE ANCHOR BIBLE
PUBLISHED BY DOUBLEDAY
a division of
Bantam Doubleday Dell Publishing Group, Inc.,
666 Fifth Avenue, New York, New York 10103

THE ANCHOR BIBLE, DOUBLEDAY, and the portrayal of an anchor
with the letters AB are trademarks of Doubleday, a division of
Bantam Doubleday Dell Publishing Group, Inc.

NIHIL OBSTAT:
David A. Dillon S.T.D.

IMPRIMATUR:
†John R. Roach, D.D.
Archbishop of Saint Paul and Minneapolis
February 29, 1988

The *Imprimatur* states simply that the material contained in a book has
been read, and that nothing contrary to Catholic doctrinal or moral
teaching has been found in it.

LIBRARY OF CONGRESS CATALOGING-IN-PUBLICATION DATA

Bible. N.T. Titus. English. Quinn. 1990.
    The letter to Titus : a new translation with notes and commentary
and an introduction to Titus, I and II Timothy, the Pastoral
Epistles / by Jerome D. Quinn. — 1st ed.
        p.   cm. — (The Anchor Bible ; v. 35)
    Bibliography: p.
    Includes index.
    1. Bible. N.T. Titus—Commentaries.   2. Bible. N.T. Pastoral
Epistles—Introductions.   I. Quinn, Jerome D.   II. Title.
III. Series.   IV. Series: Bible.   English.   Anchor Bible.   1964 ; v.
35.
BS192.2.A1 1964.G3 vol. 35
[BS2753]
220.7'7 s—dc20
[227'.85077]   89-33818
                                                            CIP

ISBN 0-385-05900-0

*Dedicated
to
The Most Reverend John R. Roach
Archbishop of Saint Paul and Minneapolis
and to
William O. Brady
Leo Binz
and
Leo C. Byrne
former archbishops in Saint Paul
who encouraged and supported the studies
that have produced this work*

CONTENTS

♦

CONTENTS

PREFACE

♦

In January 1965, after W. F. Albright and D. N. Freedman had extended their invitation to me to contribute the volume on Titus, 1 Timothy, and 2 Timothy to the Doubleday Anchor Bible series, I discussed the matter with the late Leo Binz, then my archbishop in Saint Paul. At that time the final form of the II Vatican Council's Constitution on Divine Revelation (November 18, 1965) could not simply be presumed. The archbishop cautioned me about the stormy theological seas into which I was venturing. It was a moment in which scriptural discussions about original sin and the grace of Christ, justification by faith, the relations of believers with their Lord and with one another, and similar hardy theological perennials occupied many. I observed to the archbishop that the materials that I had been asked to analyze were rather more modest and uncontroversial, hardly the center of the New Testament. With his blessing I accepted the job.

The events of the intervening score and more years disproved my contention that the letters to Titus and Timothy were academic pleasances. This correspondence has become intensely controversial, theologically, sociologically, even politically. The personnel of the institutional church, their qualifications and authority, the relation of all of this to Paul and thus to the apostles of the risen Jesus are all somehow at stake for the author of these letters. The roles of believing women in the churches pose questions that are not marginal or simply speculative. Questions about worship, particularly sacramental worship (baptism, ordination, marriage), are again at the center of Christian debate, not to mention the demands of a Christian ethic on individual men and women, husbands and wives, widows, even to some extent on children. The relation of Christians, Jewish as well as Gentile, to their Jewish contemporaries is never far from the surface of these ancient texts; for it was their understanding of and relation to the Law and the Scriptures themselves (which for them coincided roughly with what we call the LXX Old Testament) that reinforced their Christian identity. What I thought was relative calm almost twenty-five years ago has proved to be the eye of the Christian hurricane.

A word is in order about the arrangement of this volume on the Letter to Titus. That specific title presupposes a much later characterization for the

PREFACE

Letters to Titus and 1 and 2 Tim as "the Pastoral Epistles" (PE hereafter). A separate volume (35A) is being devoted to 1 and 2 Tim.

The INTRODUCTION that follows here is devoted to all three of these letters. The full-dress bibliography appears as an appendix in the second volume. This volume can stand separately, and it has a bibliographical appendix that will serve as a key to the ancient and modern authors cited.

The translation of Titus offered piecemeal in the body of the commentary can be referred to easily and read through as a whole on pages 25–29 before the NOTES and COMMENTS begin. The Anchor version of 1 and 2 Tim has been added to Titus (pp. 30–47) to facilitate reference, for this correspondence is cited at every turn in the INTRODUCTION as well as in the body of the commentary contained in this volume.

Five excursuses have been appended to the NOTES and COMMENTS. They draw together the materials about faith, knowledge (of the truth), religion, life, and salvation in the PE as a whole and forestall some repetition in commenting on a terminology that is critical to the concerns of the Letter to Titus and of those to Timothy.

A prefatory comment is in order about the rationale of this philological and historical commentary. I have used the text of Titus as a staging point. Matters from Titus that reappear in 1 and 2 Tim have regularly been explained on their first appearance, though some details are reserved for the later references.

The sections titled NOTES are intended to give the modern reader some insight into the linguistic worlds, secular and religious, Jewish and Christian, from which the readers of the PE came and which the PE influenced. Text-critical questions have been confined, by and large, to these NOTES, which are intended also to furnish philological documentation for the arguments that are advanced in the sections called COMMENT, where the nets are cast farther into the seas of linguistics and history. If the NOTES tend to be more narrowly focused on the words of the text, more objective and technical, and consequently more forbidding, the COMMENTS are more provocatively argued, are more individual and hypothetical, and are, I venture to hope, of interest to a broader spectrum of readers.

I have not suggested further readings for the student apart from the citations in the NOTES and COMMENTS, which have that purpose among others. The *TWNT/TDNT* is rarely cited because I presume everyone reads it religiously, with critical consciousness of the date of a particular article. The case is otherwise with Ceslaus Spicq's *Lexic.* and *Supp. Lexic.* and with the as yet incomplete *TWAT/TDOT.* Hence the reader is alerted to their entries regularly.

I have of set purpose avoided giving lists of names of my predecessors who have adopted one or another position in explaining the PE. My dependence on the scholars, ancient and modern, who have explained these letters will be readily identified; failures to see the force of their arguments surely will be (and ought to be) scored. Nevertheless, these scholars all would contend, as I do, that their reasons and not their names are what count. Academic succession, the pedigree of authority, even the raw numbers of proponents and opponents of a particular interpretation are sociologically interesting phenomena. Scholarship advances, however, with the individual insights and analysis of its practitioners, not by majority vote. There evidently is a place for a history of scholarship; for the PE one by W. Schenk, "Forschung," has been promised. I have not furnished one with this commentary.

A most onerous task for the author is to acknowledge adequately his obligations and gratitude to the multitude of men and women who made his book possible. I must gratefully acknowledge first of all the academic institutions that nurtured, supported, and encouraged me: the Saint Paul Seminary, School of Divinity of the College of Saint Thomas, in Saint Paul; the University of Minnesota, particularly William A. McDonald, classicist and archaeologist; the Pontifical Biblical Institute in Rome, which twice welcomed me as a guest professor; and the North American College in Rome, which invited me to be its scholar in residence. For their timely subventions in this work, I am grateful to the Knights of Columbus and to the Catholic Biblical Association of America.

Then I must thank the librarians of the institutions named above as well as those of the seminaries, Protestant and Catholic, in our local consortium, and a multitude who cannot be numbered from all the Earth.

I cannot let this occasion pass without recording my gratitude to the skillful physicians and medical personnel of Alice Springs, Australia; Oxford, England; and of this State of Minnesota, who four times, since 1976, kept my heart beating against all the odds.

I am grateful to the typists who lightened my labor and to those who helped by proofreading, verifying references, and the like. In particular I must thank Father Dimitri Cozby, whose bibliographical assistance with the ancient Fathers has been invaluable, along with Phillip Boelter and many others who have been indefatigable research assistants in the final draft of this commentary. The first draft of this whole work on the PE was read, corrected, and annotated by Michael Patrick O'Connor, then of Doubleday, who has retained an active interest in the book as it has taken shape. David Noel Freedman edited the final text with his proverbial thoroughness and efficiency. Both editors saved me from many a blunder; many a telling point I owe to their observations. The administrative editors at Doubleday over the years have been unfailing in patience and kindness. I am grateful to Eve Roshevsky, formerly of the Doubleday Religion Department, and to Theresa D'Orsogna, who currently coordinates the Anchor Bible project.

Finally, and with some trepidation, I want to thank a host of colleagues, friends, and family for bearing with (or without) me in the many years I have devoted to this commentary. I am grateful especially to my students as well as to my brothers in the presbytery of the Archdiocese of Saint Paul and Minneapolis.

PREFACE

In particular, Karl M. Wittman, Patrick J. Ryan, and Patrick D. Lannan were unremitting in stimulating me to finish the job.

January 26, 1988
Feast of Saints Timothy and Titus

Jerome D. Quinn
Professor of New Testament
The Saint Paul Seminary
School of Divinity of the
College of Saint Thomas,
Saint Paul, Minnesota

Following Monsignor Quinn's death in September 1988, I was asked by Doubleday to bring the completed manuscript of *The Letter to Titus* to publication. With this task accomplished, a few additional prefatory notes are in order.

1. Translations of biblical passages are Monsignor Quinn's own, unless otherwise noted.
2. Citations of biblical manuscripts follow the system used in the twenty-sixth edition of the Nestle-Aland *Novum Testamentum Graece*.
3. Most citations of classical authors refer to the Loeb Classical Library editions. Only the exceptions are noted, with editions, if known, cited in the body of the commentary.

This volume, and the companion one on 1 and 2 Timothy, represents Jerome Quinn's final and perhaps greatest work in this life. The preparation and completion of it occupied him for nearly twenty-five years. My association with this man of God spanned only a short while at the end of that time. However, I am sure all those who knew Jerome Quinn as brother, teacher, priest, or friend will join together with me and with those who will read and use his work in a simple prayer, which was also Quinn's own:

> Give me Wisdom, the attendant at your throne,
> and reject me not from among your children;
> for I am your servant.
> —Book of Wisdom, Chapter 9

September 30, 1989
Feast of Saint Jerome

Phillip Boelter
Student
Luther-Northwestern
Theological Seminary,
Saint Paul, Minnesota

PRINCIPAL ABBREVIATIONS

◆

AGJU	Arbeiten zur Geschichte des antiken Jundentums und des Urchristentums
AnBib	Analecta biblica of PBI
ANRW	*Aufstieg und Niedergang der Römischen Welt*
Ap. Frs.	Apostolic Fathers
AzT	Arbeiten zum Theologie
BAGD	W. Bauer, W. F. Arndt, F. W. Gingrich, and F. W. Danker, *Greek–English Lexicon of the NT* (2d ed.; Chicago: University of Chicago, 1979)
BAT	*Biblical Archaeology Today: Proceedings of the International Congress on Biblical Archaeology, April 1984, Jerusalem* (Jerusalem: Israel Exploration Society, 1985)
BDF	F. Blass, A. Debrunner, and R. W. Funk, *A Greek Grammar of the NT* (E.T. Chicago: University of Chicago, 1961)
BSGRT	Bibliotheca scriptorum graecorum et romanorum teubneriana
CAC	Corpus apologetarum christianorum saeculi secundi (ed. J. Otto)
CC	Corpus Christianorum
CIG	*Corpus inscriptionum graecarum*
CII	*Corpus inscriptionum iudaïcarum*
CIL	*Corpus inscriptionum latinorum*
CSEL	Corpus scriptorum ecclesiasticorum latinorum
D-C	M. Dibelius and H. Conzelmann, *Die Pastoralbriefe*, HNT 13 (E.T., P. Buttolph and Y. Yarbro; Hermeneia series; Philadelphia: Fortress, 1972)
DELG	P. Chantraine, *Dictionnaire étymologique de la langue grecque* (Paris: Klinksieck, 1968–1980)
DJD	Discoveries in the Judaean Desert (of Jordan) (Oxford: Clarendon)
E.T.	English translation
FRLANT	Forsuchungen zur Religion und Literatur des Alten und Neuen Testaments

PRINCIPAL ABBREVIATIONS

GNT[3corr]	*Greek New Testament* of UBS, third edition (corrected; eds., K. Alard et al.)
HNT	Handbuch zum NT
H-R	E. Hatch and H. A. Redpath, *A Concordance to the LXX* (3 vols.; Grand Rapids, Mich.: Baker, 1983, repr. of 1897 ed.)
ICC	International Critical Commentary
IDB	G. A. Buttrick, ed., *Interpreter's Dictionary of the Bible* (Nashville: Abingdon, 1962)
IDBSup	*IDB Supplementary Volume* (Nashville: Abingdon, 1976)
LCL	Loeb Classical Library
LP	E. Lobel and D. Page, eds., *Poetarum lesbiorum fragmenta* (Oxford: Clarendon, 1955)
LSJ	H. G. Liddell, R. Scott, and H. S. Jones, *A Greek–English Lexicon* (9th ed., with Supplement by E. Barber; Oxford: Clarendon, 1940, 1968)
LXX	Septuagint
MM	James H. Moulton and George Milligan, *The Vocabulary of the Greek NT* (Grand Rapids, Mich.: Eerdmans, 1930, repr. 1972)
MT	Masoretic Text
NAB	*New American Bible*, successor to Confraternity Version
NCBC	New Century Bible Commentary
NEB	*New English Bible*
NHL	*Nag Hammadi Library*, ed. J. M. Robinson (New York: Harper & Row, 1977)
NOAB	*New Oxford Annotated Bible*
NovT	*Novum Testamentum*
NovTSup	Supplements to *NovT*
NT	New Testament/Neue Testament/Nouveau Testament
NTD	Das Neue Testament deutsch
NTG[26corr]	*Novum Testamentum Graece* (ed. K. Aland et al.; Stuttgart: Deutsche Bibelgesellschaft, 1983)
OCD	*Oxford Classical Dictionary* (ed. Max Carey; Oxford: Clarendon, 1949)
OGIS	*Orientis graeci inscriptiones selectae*, second edition (ed. Wilhelm Dittenberger)
OL	Old Latin
OLD	*Oxford Latin Dictionary*
OT	Old Testament/Alten Testament/Ancien Testament
OxyP	Oxyrhynchus Papyri
PBI	Pontifical Biblical Institute (Rome)
PE	the Pastoral Epistles: Titus, 1–2 Timothy
PG	*Patrologia graeca* (ed. J. Migne)
PL	*Patrologia latina* (ed. J. Migne)

PRINCIPAL ABBREVIATIONS

PSI	Pubblicazioni della Società Italiana: Papiri greci e latini
RAC	*Reallexikon für Antike und Christentum* (ed. T. Klausner)
RSV	*Revised Standard Version*
SBL	Society of Biblical Literature
SBLDS	SBL Dissertation Series
SBLMS	SBL Monograph Series
SBLSBS	SBL Sources for Biblical Studies
SBT	Studies in Biblical Theology
SC	Sources chrétiennes
SCBO	Scriptorum classicorum bibliotheca Oxoniensis
SCS	Septuagintal and Cognate Studies
SFG	*Synopsis of the Four Gospels,* ed. Kurt Aland (second edition, repr. Stuttgart: UBS, 1972)
TDNT	*Theological Dictionary of the NT* (E.T. by G. W. Bromiley of *Theologisches Wörterbuch zum NT,* ed. G. Kittel and G. Friedrich; 10 vols.; Grand Rapids, Mich.: Eerdmans, 1964–1976)
TDOT	*Theological Dictionary of the Old Testament* (E.T. of *Theologisches Wörterbuch zum Alten Testament,* ed. G. J. Botterweck and H. Ringgren; 5 vols. to date; Grand Rapids, Mich.: Eerdmans, 1974–1986)
Theod.	Theodotion's Greek translation of the OT
THKNT	Theologischer Handkommentar zum NT
TSMAO	Typologie des sources du Moyen Âge occidental
TU	Texte und Untersuchungen
TWAT	original of *TDOT*
TWNT	original of *TDNT*
UBS	United Bible Societies
VL	*Vetus latina* (ed. H. Frede)
VTSupp	*Vetus Testamentum Supplement*

BIBLIOGRAPHICAL KEY

◆

Aland, *Repertorium*
  Aland, K. *Repertorium der griechischen christlichen Papyri: Biblische Papyri* (Patristische Texte und Studien 18; Berlin: de Gruyter, 1976).
  ——. *Synopsis of the Four Gospels.* See *SFG* in Principal Abbreviations.
Aland, *Konkordanz*
  ——. *Vollständige Konkordanz zum griechischen Neuen Testament* (3 vols.; Berlin: de Gruyter, 1978–1983).
Andersen and Freedman, *AB Hosea*
  Andersen, Francis I., and David Noel Freedman. *Hosea* (AB 24; Garden City, N.Y.: Doubleday, 1980).
Arnim, *SVF*
  Arnim, Hans F. A. von. *Stoicorum veterum fragmenta collegit Joannes ab Arnim . . .* (4 vols.; Leipzig: Teubner, 1903–1924; Dubuque, Iowa: Brown Reprint, no date).
Audet, *Didaché*
  Audet, J. P. *La Didaché: Instructions des Apôtres* (Études bibliques; Paris: Gabalda, 1958).
Aune, *Prophecy*
  Aune, David E. *Prophecy in Earliest Christianity* (Grand Rapids, Mich.: Eerdmans, 1983).
Balch, *Code*
  Balch, D. L. *Let Wives Be Submissive: The Domestic Code in I Peter* (SBLMS 26; Chico, Calif.: Scholars, 1981).
Bammel, "Rom 13"
  Bammel, Ernst, and C. F. D. Moule, eds. *Jesus and the Politics of His Day* (Cambridge: University Press, 1984), pp. 365–383.
Barr, *Words for Time*
  Barr, James. *Biblical Words for Time* (SBT 33, second series; Naperville, Ill.: Allenson, 1962).
Barrett, *Signs*
  Barrett, C. K. *The Signs of an Apostle* (the Cato Lecture, 1969; London: Epworth, 1970).

Barrett, "Titus"
———. "Titus," in *Neotestamentica et Semitica: Studies in Honor of Matthew Black* (eds., E. E. Ellis and M. Wilcox; Edinburgh: Clark, 1969), pp. 1–14.

Bartchy, *Slavery*
Bartchy, S. S. *Mallon Chrēsai: First-Century Slavery and the Interpretation of 1 Corinthians 7:21* (SBLDS 11; Missoula, Mont.: University of Montana, 1973).

Barth, *AB Eph.*
Barth, Marcus. *Ephesians* (AB 34 and 34A; Garden City, N.Y.: Doubleday, 1974).

Barth, "Traditions"
———. "Traditions in Ephesians" *New Testament Studies* 30 (1984), pp. 3–25.

Barthélemy and Rickenbacher, *KHS*
Barthélemy, D., and O. Rickenbacher. *Konkordanz zum hebräischen Sirach; mit syrischen–hebräischen Index* (Göttingen: Vandenhoeck and Ruprecht, 1973).

Bauer, *Rechtgläubigkeit/Orthodoxy*
Bauer, W. *Rechtgläubigkeit und Ketzerei im ältesten Christentum* (Beiträge zur historischen Theologie 10; Tübingen: Mohr, 1934). E.T., *Orthodoxy and Heresy in Earliest Christianity* (eds., R. A. Kraft and G. Krodel; Philadelphia: Fortress, 1971).

Bauer, Walter, W. F. Arndt, and F. W. Gingrich. *A Greek–English Lexicon of the New Testament and Other Early Christian Literature* (E.T. and adaptation of W. Bauer's fourth revised and augmented edition, Chicago: University of Chicago, 1957). The second edition (1979) is a revised and augmented E.T. of Bauer's fifth edition of 1958, by F. Gingrich and F. W. Danker. See BAGD in Principal Abbreviations.

Beasley-Murray, *Bapt. NT*
Beasley-Murray, G. R. *Baptism in the New Testament* (Exeter: Paternoster, 1962).

Benko, "Criticism"
Benko, Stephen. "Pagan Criticism of Christianity During the First Two Centuries A.D.," in *ANRW* II.23/2 (eds., H. Temporini and W. Haase; Berlin: de Gruyter, 1980), pp. 1055–1118.

Benko and O'Rourke, *Catacombs*
——— and John J. O'Rourke, eds. *The Catacombs and the Colosseum: The Roman Empire as the Setting of Primitive Christianity* (Valley Forge, Penn.: Judson Press, 1971).

Berge, "Savior"
Berge, Paul. "Our Great God and Savior," unpublished thesis from Union Theological Seminary, Richmond, Va., 1973 (copyright, 1974).

Bernard
Bernard, J. N. *The Pastoral Epistles* (Cambridge: University Press, 1899; Thornapple reprint from Grand Rapids, Mich.: Baker, 1980).
Betz, *Gal.*
Betz, H. D. *Galatians* (Hermeneia; Philadelphia: Fortress, 1977).
Bib. Pat.
Biblia Patristica (eds., J. Allenbach et al.; Paris: Éditions du Centre National de la Recherche Scientifique, 1975–).
Biblical Archaeology Today: Proceedings of the International Congress on Biblical Archaeology of April, 1984, in Jerusalem. See *BAT* in Principal Abbreviations.
Bieber, *Theater*
Bieber, Margarete. *The History of the Greek and Roman Theater* (second edition; Princeton: University Press, 1961).
Bisbee, "Acts of Justin"
Bisbee, Gary A. "The Acts of Justin Martyr: A Form-Critical Study," *The Second Century* 3 (1983), pp. 129–157.
Blass, F., A. Debrunner, and R. W. Funk. *A Greek Grammar of the New Testament and Other Early Christian Literature.* See BDF in Principal Abbreviations.
Böhlig and Wisse, *G. Egypt.*
Böhlig, A., and F. Wisse, eds. *The Gospel of the Egyptians* (Grand Rapids, Mich.: Eerdmans, 1975).
Boismard, *Hymnes*
Boismard, M.-E. *Quatre Hymnes baptismales dans la première Épître de Pierre* (Paris: Cerf, 1961).
Bömer, *Religion der Sklaven*
Bömer, Franz. *Untersuchengen über die Religion der Sklaven in Griechenland und Rom* (4 vols.; Mainz: Akademie der Wissenschaften und der Literatur, 1958–1963).
Bonner, *Education*
Bonner, Stanley F. *Education in Ancient Rome: From the Elder Cato to the Younger Pliny* (Berkeley: University of California Press, 1977).
Bornkamm, *Paul*
Bornkamm, Günther. *Paul* (E.T. by D. M. G. Stalker; New York: Harper & Row, 1971).
Botterweck, G. J., and Helmer Ringgren. *Theological Dictionary of the Old Testament* (5 vols. to date; E.T. by J. T. Willis). See *TDOT, TWAT* in Principal Abbreviations.
Bradshaw, *Canons Hipp.*
Bradshaw, Paul, ed. *The Canons of Hippolytus* (E.T. by C. Bebawi; Bramcote, Notts.: Grove Books, 1987).

Bratcher, *Translator*
  Bratcher, R. G. *A Translator's Guide to Paul's Letters to Timothy and to Titus*
  (New York and London: United Bible Societies, 1983).
Bromiley, Geoffrey W., E.T. and ed. *Theological Dictionary of the New
  Testament* (orig. eds., G. Kittel and G. Friedrich). See *TDNT, TWNT* in
  Principal Abbreviations.
Brown, *Birth*
  Brown, R. E. *The Birth of the Messiah: A Commentary on the Infancy
  Narratives in Matthew and Luke* (Garden City, N.Y.: Doubleday, 1977).
Brown, *"Episkopē"*
  ————. *"Episkopē* and *Episkopos:* The New Testament Evidence,"
  Theological Studies 41 (1980) 322–338 in *The Critical Meaning of the
  Bible* (New York: Paulist, 1981).
Brown, *AB Epistles*
  ————. *The Epistles of John* (AB 30; Garden City, N.Y.: Doubleday, 1982).
Brown and Meier, *Antioch/Rome*
  ———— and J. P. Meier. *Antioch and Rome: New Testament Cradles of
  Catholic Christianity* (Ramsey, N.J.: Paulist, 1983).
Brownlee, *Qumran*
  Brownlee, W. H. *The Meaning of the Qumran Scrolls for the Bible* (New
  York: Oxford University, 1964).
Brox
  Brox, N. *Die Pastoralbriefe* (Regensburger Neues Testament 7; Regensburg:
  Pustet, 1969).
Bruce, "Tacitus"
  Bruce, F. F. "Tacitus on Jewish History," *Journal of Semitic Studies* 29
  (1984), pp. 33–44.
Bultmann, *Primitive Christianity*
  Bultmann, R. *Primitive Christianity in Its Contemporary Setting* (Cleveland,
  Ohio: World, 1956).
Bultmann, *Th. NT*
  ————. *Theology of the New Testament* (2 vols.; London/New York: SCM/
  Scribners, 1955).
Burnett, "Philo"
  Burnett, F. "Philo on Immortality: A Thematic Study of Philo's Concept of
  Palingenesia," *Catholic Biblical Quarterly* 46 (1984), pp. 447–470.
Campbell, *Greek Lyric*
  Campbell, D. A. *Greek Lyric* (LCL; Cambridge, Mass.: Harvard University
  Press, 1982).
Campenhausen, "Polycarp"
  Campenhausen, Hans von. *Polycarp von Smyrna und die Pastoralbriefe*
  (Heidelberg, 1951, as reprinted in *Aus der Frühzeit des Christentums:*

Studien zur Kirchengeschichte des ersten und zweiten Jahrhunderts (Tübingen: Mohr, 1963), pp. 197–252.

Carcopino, *Cicero*

    Carcopino, J. *Cicero: The Secrets of His Correspondence* (E.T. by E. O. Lorimer, 2 vols.; London: Routledge and Kegan Paul, 1951; repr. New York: Greenwood, 1969).

Carcopino, *Rome*

    ———. *Daily Life in Ancient Rome* (E.T. by H. T. Rowell; New York: Penguin, 1956).

Carr, *Angels*

    Carr, W. *Angels and Principalities: The Background, Meaning, and Development of the Pauline Phrase "hai archai kai hai exousiai"* (Cambridge: University Press, 1981).

Cavallin, *Life*

    Cavallin, H. C. C. *Life After Death: Paul's Argument for the Resurrection of the Dead in I Cor 15* (Lund: Gleerup, 1974).

Chadwick, *Chr. Thgt.*

    Chadwick, H. *Early Christian Thought and the Classical Tradition: Studies in Justin, Clement, and Origen* (New York: Oxford University, 1966).

Chadwick, "Gewissen"

    ———. "Gewissen," *RAC* 10.1025–1107.

Chantraine, Pierre. *Dictionnaire étymologique de la langue grecque: Histoire des mots.* See *DELG* in Principal Abbreviations.

Charles, *AP*

    Charles, R. H., ed. *Apocrypha and Pseudepigrapha of the Old Testament in English: With Introduction and Critical and Explanatory Notes to the Several Books* (2 vols.; Oxford: Clarendon, 1913).

Charlesworth, *OT Pseud.*

    Charlesworth, J. H., ed. *The Old Testament Pseudepigrapha* (2 vols.; Garden City, N.Y.: Doubleday, 1983–1985).

Charlesworth, *Pseud.*

    Charlesworth, J. H. *The Pseudepigrapha and Modern Research with a Supplement* (Missoula, Mont.: Scholars, 1976).

Clark, "*Spes*"

    Clark, M. E. "*Spes* in the Early Imperial Cult," *Numen* 30 (1983), pp. 80–105.

Collins and Nickelsburg, *Ideal Figures*

    Collins, J. J., and G. W. E. Nickelsburg, eds. *Ideal Figures in Ancient Judaism: Profiles and Paradigms* (Missoula, Mont.: Scholars, 1980).

Constable, *Letters*

    Constable, Giles. *Letters and Letter Collections* (TSMAO 17; Turnhout: Brepols, 1976).

Conzelmann, *1 Cor.*
  Conzelmann, H. *First Corinthians* (Hermeneia; Philadelphia: Fortress, 1975).
Coppens, "L'Élu"
  Coppens, J. "L'Élu et les élus dans les écritures saintes et les écrits de Qumrân," *Ephemerides theologicae lovanienses* 57 (1981), pp. 120–124.
Corbett, *Marriage*
  Corbett, Percy E. *The Roman Law of Marriage* (Oxford: Clarendon, 1930, repr. 1969).
Corriveau, *Liturgy*
  Corriveau, R. *The Liturgy of Life: A Study of the Ethical Thought of Saint Paul in His Letters to the Early Christian Communities* (Brussels: Desclée, 1970).
Cranfield, *Rom.*
  Cranfield, C. E. B. *A Critical and Exegetical Commentary on the Epistle to the Romans.* (ICC 32; 2 vols.; Edinburgh: Clark, 1975–1979).
Cremer, *BW*
  Cremer, H. J. *Biblisch-theologisches Wörterbuch des Neutestamentlichen Griechisch* (Gotha: L. Klotz, 1923).
Crouch, *Haustafel*
  Crouch, J. E. *The Origin and Intention of the Colossian Haustafel.* (FRLANT 109; Göttingen: Vandenhoeck and Ruprecht, 1972).
Crum, *CD*
  Crum, W. E. *A Coptic Dictionary* (Oxford: Clarendon, 1962).
Cullmann, *Christ and Time*
  Cullmann, O. *Christ and Time: The Primitive Christian Conception of Time and History* (third edition; E.T. by Floyd B. Filson; Philadelphia: Westminster, 1964).
Cullmann, *Christology*
  ————. *The Christology of the New Testament* (London: SCM, 1959).
Cullmann, *Worship*
  ————. *Early Christian Worship* (London: SCM, 1953).
Cullmann, *Peter*
  ————. *Peter: Disciple, Apostle, Martyr* (second edition; E.T. by Floyd Filson; Philadelphia: Westminster, 1962).
Culpepper, *School*
  Culpepper, R. A. *The Johannine School: An Evaluation of the Johannine-School Hypothesis Based on an Investigation of the Nature of Ancient Schools* (Missoula, Mont.: Scholars, 1975).
Cuming, "EYCHĒS"
  Cuming, Geoffrey J. "DI' EYCHĒS LOGOU," *Journal of Theological Studies* 31 (1980), pp. 80–82.

Cuming, *Essays*
———, ed. *Essays on Hippolytus* (Grove Liturgical Study 15; Bramcote, Notts.: Grove, 1978).

Cuming, *Hippolytus*
———. *Hippolytus: A Text for Students* (Grove Liturgical Study 8; Bramcote, Notts.: Grove, 1976).

Cumont, *ORRP*
Cumont, Franz. *Oriental Religions in Roman Paganism* (E.T. of 1911 by New York: Dover, 1956).

Dagens, "Velatio"
Dagens, Claude. "À propos du cubiculum de la 'velatio,'" *Revista di archeologia cristiana* 47 (1971), pp. 119–129.

Dahl, "Particularity"
Dahl, Nils. "Particularity of the Pauline Epistles as a Problem in the Ancient Church," in *Neotestamentica et Patristica; eine Freundsgabe O. Cullmann* (eds., W. C. van Unnik et al.; Leiden: Brill, 1962), pp. 261–271.

Daniel, "Faux Prophètes"
Daniel, Constantin. " 'Faux Prophètes': Surnom des Esséniens dans le sermon sur la Montagne" *Revue de Qumran* 7 (Dec. 1969), pp. 45–79.

Daniélou, *TJC*
Daniélou, Jean. *The Theology of Jewish Christianity* (Chicago: Regnery, 1964).

Deer, *"Hina"*
Deer, D. S. "Still More about the Imperatival *Hina,*" *The Bible Translator* 30 (1979), p. 148.

Deissmann, *B St*
Deissmann, G. Adolf. *Bible Studies: Contributions, Chiefly from Papyri and Inscriptions, to the History of the Language, the Literature, and the Religion of Hellenistic Judaism and Primitive Christianity* (second edition; E.T. by A. Grieve; Edinburgh: Clark, 1909).

Deissmann, *LAO*
———. *Light from the Ancient East; The New Testament Illustrated by Recently Discovered Texts of the Greco-Roman World* (second edition; E.T. by L. Strachan; London: Hodder & Stoughton, 1911; New York: G. H. Doran, 1927).

Deissmann, *Paul*
———. *Paul: A Study in Social and Religious History* (E.T. by W. E. Wilson; New York: Harper & Row, 1957, repr. of the 1927 edition).

Derrett, "Palingenesia"
Derrett, J. D. M. *"Palingenesia* (Matthew 19.28)," *Journal for the Study of the New Testament* 20 (1984), pp. 51–58.

Dibelius, *James*
   Dibelius, M. *James* (Hermeneia; E.T. by Michael A. Williams [revised by
   Heinrich Greeven, ed. Helmut Koester]; Philadelphia: Fortress, 1976).
   —— and H. Conzelmann. *Die Pastoralbriefe.* E.T., *The Pastoral Epistles.*
   See D-C in Principal Abbreviations.
Diels, *Vorsokratiker*
   Diels, Herman, and W. Kranz, eds. *Fragmente der Vorsokratiker* (Zurich:
   Weidmann, 1966).
Di Lella, *AB Dan.*
   Di Lella, A. A., and L. F. Hartman. *The Book of Daniel* (AB 23; Garden
   City, N.Y.: Doubleday, 1978).
Di Lella, *AB Sir.*
   Di Lella, A. A., and P. W. Skehan. *The Wisdom of Ben Sira* (AB 39; Garden
   City, N.Y.: Doubleday, 1987).
Dittenberger, *Syll.*
   Dittenberger, Wilhelm. *Sylloge inscriptionum graecarum* (4 vols.; repr.
   Hildesheim: G. Olms, 1986; orig., 1915–1924).
Dockx, *Chronologies*
   Dockx, S. *Chronologies neotestamentaires et vie de l'Église primitive:
   recherches exégetiques* (Gembloux: Duculot, 1976).
Dodd, *Acc. Scr.*
   Dodd, Charles H. *According to the Scriptures: The Substructure of New
   Testament Theology* (New York: Scribners, 1953).
Dodd, *More NT*
   ——. *More New Testament Studies* (Manchester: University Press, 1968).
Donelson, *Pseudepig.*
   Donelson, Lewis R. *Pseudepigraphy and Ethical Argument in the PE*
   (Tübingen: Mohr, 1986).
Donfried, "Paul"
   Donfried, K. "Paul and Judaism," *Interpretation* 38 (July 1984), pp. 242–253.
Donfried, *Setting*
   ——. *The Setting of Second Clement in Early Christianity* (*NovTSup* 38;
   Leiden: Brill, 1974).
Dover, *Morality*
   Dover, K. J. *Greek Popular Morality in the Time of Plato and Aristotle*
   (Berkeley: University of California, 1974).
Dumézil, *ARR*
   Dumézil, Georges. *Archaic Roman Religion, with an Appendix on the
   Religion of the Etruscans* (2 vols.; Chicago: University of Chicago, 1970).
Dunbabin, "*Invida*"
   Dunbabin, K. "*Invida rumpantur pectora . . .*" *Jahrbuch für Antike und
   Christentum* 26 (1983), pp. 7–37, pls. 1–8.

Dupont, *Gnosis*
Dupont, Jacques. *Gnosis: la connaissance religleuse dans les Épîtres de Saint Paul* (Louvain: E. Nauwelaerts; Paris: J. Gabalda, 1949).
Dupont-Sommer, *EWQ*
Dupont-Sommer, A. *The Essene Writings from Qumran* (E.T. by G. Vermes; Cleveland, Ohio: World, 1962).
Durham, *Voc. Men.*
Durham, Donald B. *Vocabulary of Menander* (Amsterdam: Aakkert, 1969, repr. of 1913).
Easton
Easton, B. S. *The Pastoral Epistles* (New York: Scribners, 1947).
J. K. Elliott, *Greek Text*
Elliott, James Keith. *The Greek Text of the Epistles to Timothy and Titus* (Salt Lake City: University of Utah, 1968).
J. H. Elliott, *Home*
Elliott, John Hall. *A Home for the Homeless: A Sociological Exegesis of 1 Peter; Its Situation and Strategy* (Philadelphia: Fortress, 1981).
Ernout and Meillet, *DELL*
Ernout, Alfred, and Antoine Meillet. *Dictionnaire étymologique de la langue latine* (2 vols.; third edition; Paris: Klincksieck, 1951).
Falconer, *PE*
Falconer, Robert A. *The Pastoral Epistles* (Oxford: Clarendon, 1937).
Fears, "Virtues"
Fears, J. Rufus. "The Cult of Virtues and Roman Imperial Ideology," in *ANRW* II. 7/2 (1981), pp. 887–948.
Fee
Fee, G. D. *1 and 2 Timothy, Titus* (Good News Commentary; San Francisco: Harper & Row, 1984).
Ferguson, *Values*
Ferguson, John. *Moral Values in the Ancient World* (London: Methuen, 1958).
Fiore, *Function*
Fiore, Benjamin. *The Function of Personal Example in the Socratic and Pastoral Epistles* (AnBib 105; Rome: PBI, 1986).
Fischer, *Concordantiae*
Fischer, Bonifatius. *Novae concordantiae bibliorum sacrorum iuxta vulgatam versionem critice editam* (5 vols.; Stuttgart: Frommann-Holzboog, 1977).
Fitzmyer, "Divorce"
Fitzmyer, Joseph A. "Divorce Among First-Century Palestinian Jews" (H. L. Ginsberg vol. of *Eretz Israel*, 14; Jerusalem: Israel Exploration Society, 1978), pp. 103–110, 193.

Fitzmyer, *ESBNT*
———. *Essays on the Semitic Background of the New Testament* (London: Chapman, 1971).
Fitzmyer, *Gen. Apoc.*
———. *The Genesis Apocryphon of Qumran Cave I: A Commentary* (second edition; Rome: Biblical Institute, 1971).
Fitzmyer, *AB Lk*
———. *The Gospel According to Luke* (2 vols.; AB 28–28a; Garden City, N.Y.: Doubleday 1981–1985).
Fitzmyer, "Office of Teaching"
———. "The Office of Teaching in the Christian Church According to the New Testament," *Lutheran Catholics Dialogue VI: Teaching Authority and Infallibility in the Church* (eds., Paul C. Empie, T. Austin Murphy, and Joseph A. Burgess; Minneapolis, Minn.: Augsburg, 1980), pp. 186–212.
Fitzmyer, *Aramean*
———. *A Wandering Aramean: Collected Aramaic Essays* (Missoula, Mont.: Scholars, 1979).
Forkman, *Limits*
Forkman, Göran. *The Limits of the Religious Community* (Lund: Gleerup, 1972).
Frede, Josef Hermann. *Vetus Latina* (vol. 25; Freiburg: Herder, 1979). See *VL* in Principal Abbreviations.
Friberg and Friberg, *Analytical GNT*
Friberg, Barbara, and Timothy Friberg, eds. *Analytic Greek NT: Greek Text Analysis* (Grand Rapids, Mich.: Baker, 1981).
Friedrich, *Aphrodite*
Friedrich, P. *The Meaning of Aphrodite* (Chicago: University of Chicago, 1978).
Funk, "Parousia"
Funk, Robert W. "The Apostolic Parousia: Form and Significance," in *Christian History and Interpretation: Studies presented to John Knox* (eds., W. R. Farmer, C. F. D. Moule, and R. R. Niebuhr; Cambridge: University Press, 1967), pp. 249–268.
Furnish, *AB 2 Cor*
Furnish, Victor Paul. *II Corinthians* (AB 32A; Garden City, N.Y.: Doubleday, 1984).
Gaster, *DSS*
Gaster, T. H. *The Dead Sea Scriptures, in English Translation with Introduction and Notes* (third edition used unless second or first is noted; Garden City, N.Y.: Doubleday, 1956, 1964, 1976).
Gelston, *"Euchēs"*
Gelston, A. *"Di' Euchēs Logou,"* *Journal of Theological Studies* 33 (1982), pp. 172–175.

BIBLIOGRAPHICAL KEY

Gernet, *AAG*
Gernet, L. *The Anthropology of Ancient Greece* (E.T. from the French of 1968 by J. Hamilton and B. Nagy; Baltimore: The Johns Hopkins University, 1981).
Giverson, *Apoc. Joh.*
Giverson, S. *Apocryphon Johannis* (Copenhagen: Munksgaard, 1963).
Goldstein, *AB 1 Macc, 2 Macc*
Goldstein, Jonathan A. *1 Maccabees* (AB 41; Garden City, N.Y.: Doubleday 1976); *2 Maccabees* (AB 41a; Garden City, N.Y.: Doubleday, 1983).
Gomme and Sandbach, *Commentary*
Gomme, Arnold W., and Francis Henry Sandbach. *Menander: A Commentary* (London: Oxford University, 1973).
Good, *Sheep*
Good, Robert M. *The Sheep of His Pasture: A Study of the Hebrew Noun 'Am (m) and Its Semitic Cognates* (Chico, Calif.: Scholars, 1983).
Goodspeed, E. J. *Index apologeticus sive clavis Iustini martyris operum* (Leipzig: J. Ninrich, 1969, repr. of 1912 edition).
Goppelt, *Typos*
Goppelt, Leonhard. *Typos: The Typological Interpretation of the Old Testament in the New* (E.T. by Donald H. Madvig; Grand Rapids, Mich.: Eerdmans, 1982, from the German of 1939 and 1965).
Gordon, *Epigraphy*
Gordon, Arthur Ernest. *Illustrated Introduction to Latin Epigraphy* (Berkeley: University of California, 1983).
Grayston, "Meaning of *parakaleo*"
Grayston, Kenneth. "A Problem of Translation: The Meaning of *parakaleo, paraklesis* in the NT," *Scripture Bulletin* 11 (1980), pp. 27–31.
Griffiths, "Isis"
Griffiths, J. Gwyn. "Isis and *Agape*," *Classical Philology* 80 (1985), pp. 139–141.
Guelich, *Sermon*
Guelich, Robert. *The Sermon on the Mount: A Foundation for Understanding* (Waco, Tex.: Word, 1982).
Guthrie
Guthrie, D. *The Pastoral Epistles: An Introduction and Commentary* (Tyndale New Testament Commentaries 14; Grand Rapids, Mich.: Eerdmans, 1957).
Haelst, *Catalogue*
Haelst, Joseph van. *Catalogue des papyrus litteraires juifs et chrétiens* (Paris: Publications de la Sorbonne, 1976).
Haenchen, *Acts*
Haenchen, Ernst. *The Acts of the Apostles: A Commentary* (E.T. by Bernhard Noble and Gerald Shinn; Oxford: Blackwell, 1971).

Haft, "Cretan Lies"
Haft, Adele J. "Odysseus, Idomeneus and Meriones: The Cretan Lies of
Odyssey 13–19," *The Classical Journal* 79 (April–May 1984), pp. 289–306.
Hagner, *Use*
Hagner, Donald A. *The Use of the Old and New Testaments in Clement of
Rome* (*NovTSup* 34; Leiden: Brill, 1973).
Hall, *Melito*
Hall, Stuart George, ed. *Melito of Sardis on Pascha and Fragments: Texts and
Translations* (Oxford: Clarendon, 1979).
Hammond, *Epirus*
Hammond, N. G. L. *Epirus* (Oxford: Clarendon, 1967).
Handley, *Dyskolos*
Handley, Eric W., ed. *Dyskolos* (Cambridge: Harvard, 1965).
Hanhart et al., Göttingen LXX
Hanhart, Robert, et al., eds. *Septuaginta: Vetus Testamentum graecum* (19+
vols. available; Göttingen: Vandenhoeck and Ruprecht, 1983).
Hanson, "Domestication"
Hanson, Anthony Tyrell. "The Domestication of Paul: A Study in the
Development of Early Christian Theology," *Bulletin of the John Rylands
Library of Manchester* 63 (1981), pp. 402–418.
Hanson, *PE*
——. *The Pastoral Epistles* (NCBC; Grand Rapids, Mich.: Eerdmans,
1982).
Hanson, *Studies*
——. *Studies in the Pastoral Epistles* (London: SPCK, 1968).
Harnack, *Mission*
Harnack, A. *The Mission and Expansion of Christianity in the First Three
Centuries* (E.T. by J. Moffatt; New York: Harper & Row, 1968, repr. of
1908 edition).
Harris, "Titus 2:13"
Harris, Murray J. "Titus 2:13 and the Deity of Christ," in *Pauline Studies:
Essays Presented to F. F. Bruce on his 70th Birthday* (eds., Donald A.
Hagner and Murray J. Harris; Grand Rapids, Mich.: Eerdmans, 1980), pp.
262–277.
Harrison, *Paulines*
Harrison, Percy N. *Paulines and Pastorals* (London: Villiers Publications,
1964).
Harrison, *Problem*
——. *The Problem of the Pastoral Epistles* (Oxford: Humphrey Milford;
Oxford University, 1921).
Hasler, *Timotheus*
Hasler, Victor August. *Die Briefe an Timotheus und Titus: Pastoralbriefe*
(Zürcher Bibelkommentar 12; Zurich: Theologischer, 1978).

Hatch, Edwin, and Henry A. Redpath. *A Concordance to the LXX and the Other Greek Versions of the OT*. See H-R in Principal Abbreviations.

Heal, "Canterbury"
Heal, Felicity. "The Archbishops of Canterbury and the Practice of Hospitality," *Journal of Ecclesiastical History* 33 (1982), pp. 544–563.

Hemer, "Name of Paul"
Hemer, Colin J. "The Name of Paul," *Tyndale Bulletin* 36 (1985), pp. 179–183.

Hengel, *Atonement*
Hengel, Martin. *The Atonement: The Origins of the Doctrine in the New Testament* (E.T. by John Bowden; Philadelphia: Fortress, 1981).

Hengel, *BJP*
————. *Between Jesus and Paul: Studies in the Earliest History of Christianity* (E.T. by J. Bowden; London: SCM, 1983).

Hengel, *Charismatic*
————. *The Charismatic Leader and His Followers* (E.T. by James Grieg; New York: Crossroad, 1981).

Hengel, *Hellenism*
————. *Judaism and Hellenism: Studies in Their Encounter in Palestine During the Early Hellenistic Period* (2 vols.; E.T. by John Bowden; Philadelphia: Fortress, 1974).

Hengel, *Zeloten*
————. *Die Zeloten: Untersuchungen zur jüdischen freiheits bewegung in der Zeit von Herodes I. bis 70 n. Chr* (AGJU 1; Leiden: Brill, 1961, second edition 1976; E.T. from Edinburgh: T. Clark, 1988).

Hill, "False Prophets"
Hill, David. "False Prophets and Charismatic: Structure and Interpretation in Matthew 7:15, 23," *Biblica* 57 (1976), pp. 327–348.

Hill, *Greek Words*
————. *Greek Words and Hebrew Meanings: Studies in the Semantics of Soteriological Terms* (London: Cambridge University, 1967).

Hinson, "Essene Influence"
Hinson, E. "Evidence of Essene Influence in Roman Christianity: An Inquiry," *Studia Patristica*, ed. E. A. Livingston, 17 (1982), pp. 697–701.

Hitchcock, "Latinity"
Hitchcock, F. R. M. "Latinity of the Pastorals," *Expository Times* 39 (1927–1928), pp. 347–352.

Holtz
Holtz, G. *Die Pastoralbriefe* (THKNT 13; Berlin: Evangelische, 1965–1972).

Horbury, "False Prophecy"
Horbury, W. "1 Thess 2:3 . . ." *Journal of Theological Studies* 33 (1982), pp. 492–507.

G. Horsley, *NDIEC*
Horsley, G. H. R. *New Documents Illustrating Early Christianity* (4 vols.; North Ryde, Australia: Macquarie University, 1981–1987).

R. Horsley, "Zealots"
Horsley, Richard A. "The Zealots: Their Origin, Relationships, and Importance in the Jewish Revolt," *NovT* 28 (April 1986), pp. 159–192.

R. Horsley and Hanson, *Bandits*
——— and John S. Hanson. *Bandits, Prophets, and Messiahs: Popular Movements in the Time of Jesus* (Minneapolis, Minn.: Winston, 1985).

Hort, *James*
Hort, F. J. A. *The Epistle of Saint James* (London: Macmillan, 1909).

Hultgren
Hultgren, Arland J. *I and II Timothy, Titus* (Augsburg Commentary; Minneapolis, Minn.: Augsburg, 1984).

Huxley, *Greek Epic*
Huxley, George Leonard. *Greek Epic Poetry from Eumelos to Panyassis* (London: Faber and Faber, 1969).

Isaksson, *Marriage*
Isaksson, Abel. *Marriage and Ministry in the New Temple: A Study with Special Reference to Mt 19:3–12 and 1 Cor. 6:3–16* (E.T. by Neil Tomkinson; Lund: Gleerup, 1965).

Jaeger, *Paideia*
Jaeger, Werner W. *Paideia: The Ideals of Greek Culture* (3 vols.; New York: Oxford University, 1945).

Jaekel, *Sententiae*
Jaekel, Siegfied. *Menandri sententiae: Conparatio Menandri et Philistionis* (BSGRT; Leipzig: Teubner, 1964).

Janzen, "ʾAšRÊ"
Janzen, Waldemar. "ʾAšRÊ in the OT," *Harvard Theological Review* 58 (1965), pp. 215–226.

Jeremias, *NTD*
Jeremias, Joachim, and A. Strobel. *Die Briefe an Timotheus und Titus; Der Brief an die Hebräer* (NTD; Göttingen: Vandenhoeck and Ruprecht, 1975).

Jeremias, *Prayers*
———. *The Prayers of Jesus* (Philadelphia: Fortress 1978).

Jervell, *Paul*
Jervell, Jacob. *The Unknown Paul. Essays On Luke–Acts and Early Christian History* (Minneapolis: Augsburg, 1984).

Jewett, "Conscience"
Jewett, Robert. "Conscience," *IDBSup*, pp. 173–174.

Jewett, *Anthropological Terms*
———. *Paul's Anthropological Terms: A Study of Their Use in Conflict Settings* (Leiden: Brill, 1971).
Johnson, *"Topos"*
Johnson, Luke Timothy. "James 3:13–4:10 and the *Topos peri Phthonou,*" *NovT* 25 (October 1983), pp. 327–247.
Johnson, *Writings*
———. *The Writings of the New Testament: An Interpretation* (Philadelphia: Fortress, 1986).
Jonge, *T. 12 Patr.*
Jonge, M. de. *The Testaments of the Twelve Patriarchs: Critical Edition of the Greek Text* (with cooperation of H. W. Hollandes et al.; Leiden: Brill, 1978).
Karris, "Polemic"
Karris, Robert. "The Background and Significance of the Polemic in the PE," *JBL* 92 (1973), pp. 549–564.
Käsemann, *Rom.*
Käsemann, Ernst. *Commentary on Romans* (E.T. by Geoffrey W. Bromiley; Grand Rapids, Mich.: Eerdmans, 1980).
Katsouris, *Tragedy*
Katsouris, A. G. *Linguistic and Stylistic Characterization: Tragedy and Menander* (Dodone, Supplement 5; Joannina: University Press, 1975).
Kelly
Kelly, J. N. D. *A Commentary on the Pastoral Epistles: I Timothy II Timothy Titus* (Black's New Testament Commentaries; London: A. Black, 1963).
Kenny, *Stylometric*
Kenny, Anthony. *A Stylometric Study of the NT* (Oxford: Clarendon, 1986).
Keresztes, "Imperial Government"
Keresztes, Paul. "The Imperial Government and the Christian Church," in *ANRW* II.23/1 (Berlin: de Gruyter, 1979), pp. 247–315.
Kilpatrick, "Possessive"
Kilpatrick, G. D. "The Possessive Pronouns in the NT," *Journal of Theological Studies* 42 (1941), pp. 184–186.
Kim, *Recommendation*
Kim, Chan-Hie. *Form and Structure of the Familiar Greek Letter of Recommendation* (SBLDS 4; Missoula, Mont.: Scholars, 1972).
Kittel, *Hymns*
Kittel, Bonnie. *The Hymns of Qumran* (SBLDS 50; Chico, Calif.: Scholars, 1981).
Knight, *Sayings*
Knight, George W. *The Faithful Sayings in the PE* (Grand Rapids, Mich.: Baker, 1979 [Kok, 1968]).

Koester, *HLEC*
   Koester, Helmut. *History and Literature of Early Christianity* (Hermeneia; Foundations and Facets, 2 vols.; Philadelphia: Fortress, 1982).
Kraable, *"Hypsistos"*
   Kraable, A. Thomas. *"Hypsistos* and the Synagogue at Sardis," *Greek Roman and Byzantine Studies* 10 (1969), pp. 81–93.
Kraft, *Clavis*
   Kraft, Henricus. *Clavis patrum apostolicorum* (Munich: Kösel, 1963).
Krause, *Essays NH*
   Krause, Martin, ed. *Essays on the Nag Hammadi Texts in Honor of Pahor Labib* (Leiden: Brill, 1975).
Kretschmar, "Glaube"
   Kretschmar, Georg. "Der paulinische Glaube in der Pastoralbriefen," in *Glaube in NT: Studien zu Ehren von Hermann Binder anlässlich seines 70 Geburtstags* (eds., F. Hahn and H. Klein; Neukirchen-Vluyn: Neukirchener, 1982), pp. 115–140.
Kuhn, "Epheserbrief"
   Kuhn, K. G. "Der Epheserbrief im Licht der Qumrantext," *New Testament Studies* 7 (1961), pp. 334–346.
Lampe, *PGL*
   Lampe, Geoffrey W. H. *Patristic Greek Lexicon* (Oxford: Clarendon, 1961).
Lash, "Hymn-Hunting"
   Lash, C. J. "Fashionable Sports: Hymn-Hunting in I Peter," in *Studia Evangelica Vol. VII: Papers Presented to the Fifth International Congress on Biblical Studies*, held at Oxford, 1973 (ed., E. A. Livingston, TU 126; Berlin: Akademie, 1982), pp. 293–297.
A. Leaney, *RQM*
   Leaney, A. R. C. *The Rule of Qumran and Its Meaning* (London: SCM, 1966).
R. Leaney, *"Nomikos"*
   Leaney, Robert. *"Nomikos* in Luke's Gospel," *Journal of Theological Studies* (1951), pp. 166–167.
Le Déaut, *Nuit*
   Le Déaut, Roger. *La Nuit paschale: Essai sur la signification de la Paque juive à partir du Targum d'Exode xii,42* (Rome: PBI, 1963).
Lee, "Epimenides"
   Lee, G. M. "Epimenides in the Epistle to Titus (I 12)," *NovT* 22 (1980), p. 96.
Leivestad, "Meekness"
   Leivestad, Ragnar. "The Meekness and Gentleness of Christ," *New Testament Studies* 12 (1965–1966), pp. 156–164.

Lestapis, *L'Enigme*
Lestapis, Stanislas de. *L'Enigme des Pastorales de Saint Paul* (Paris: Gabalda, 1976).
Liddell, Henry George, Robert Scott, and Henry Stuart Jones. *A Greek–English Lexicon* (ninth edition with Supplement, ed. E. Barber). See LSJ in Principal Abbreviations.
Lieu, "Greeting"
Lieu, Judith, " 'Grace to You and Peace': the Apostolic Greeting," *Bulletin of the John Rylands University Library (of Manchester)* 68 (1985) 161–178.
Lifshitz, *Donateurs*
Lifshitz, Baruch. *Donateurs et fondateurs dans les synagogues juives* (Paris: Gabalda, 1967).
Lifshitz, "Cesarée"
———. "Inscriptions de Cesarée," *Revue biblique* 74 (1967), pp. 50–59.
Lightman and Zeisel, "Univira"
Lightman, Marjorie, and William Zeisel. "Univira: An Example of Continuity and Change in Roman Society," *Church History* 46 (1977), pp. 19–32.
Lock, *Commentary*
Lock, W. *A Critical and Exegetical Commentary on the Pastoral Epistles (I and II Timothy and Titus)* (ICC; Edinburgh: Clark, 1924).
Lohse, *Col.*
Lohse, Eduard. *Colossians and Philemon* (Hermeneia; E.T. by William R. Poehlmann and Robert J. Karris; Philadelphia: Fortress, 1971).
Longenecker, *Christology*
Longenecker, Richard N. *The Christology of Early Jewish Christianity* (London: SCM, 1970).
Lucchesi, "Précédents"
Lucchesi, E. "Précédents non bibliques à l'expression néo-testamentaire," *Journal of Theological Studies* 28 (Oct. 1977), pp. 537–540.
Lührmann, *Glaube*
Lührmann, Dieter. *Glaube im Frühen Christentum* (Gütersloh: Mohr, 1976).
Luther, *Lectures on Titus*
Luther, Martin. *Lectures on Titus, Philemon and Hebrews*, vol. 29 of *Luther's Works* (St. Louis: Concordia, 1968), p. 57. The German edition is *D. Martin Luthers Werke* (Kritische Gesamtausgabe: Weimar edition, 1883ff.).
Malherbe, "Theorists"
Malherbe, Abraham J. "Ancient Epistolary Theorists," *Ohio Journal of Religious Studies* 15 (1977), pp. 3–77.
Malherbe, *Cynic Epistles*
———. *The Cynic Epistles* (SBLBS 12; Missoula, Mont.: Scholars, 1977).

Malherbe, "Inhospitality"
———. "The Inhospitality of Diotrephes," in *God's Christ of His People: Studies in Land of Nils A. Dahl* (eds., Jacob Jervell and Wayne Meeks; Oslo: Universitetsforlaget, 1977), pp. 222–232; repr. in his *Social Aspects* (second edition).

Malherbe, "Medical Imagery"
———. "Medical Imagery in the PE," in *Texts and Testaments: Critical Essays on the Bible and Early Church Fathers* (ed., W. Eugene March; San Antonio, Tx.: Trinity University Press, 1980), pp. 19–35.

Malherbe, *Social Aspects*
———. *Social Aspects of Early Christianity* (second edition, enlarged; Philadelphia: Fortress, 1983).

Mansoor, *Hymns*
Mansoor, Menahem. *The Thanksgiving Hymns* (Grand Rapids, Mich.: Eerdmans, 1961).

Marrou, *Education*
Marrou, Henri I. *A History of Education in Antiquity* (E.T. by George Lamb; New York: Sheed and Ward, 1956).

Marshall, *Luke*
Marshall, I. Howard. *The Gospel of Luke* (Exeter: Paternoster, 1978).

Marshall, "Review"
———. "Review of S. G. Wilson, *Lk PE*," *Journal for the Study of the New Testament* 10 (1981), pp. 69–74.

Martin, *Carmen*
Martin, Ralph P. *Carmen Christi: Philippians 2:5–11 in Recent Interpretation and in the Setting of Early Christian Worship* (London: Cambridge University, 1967).

Martin, "NT Hymns"
———. "An Early Christian Hymn (Col 1:15–20)," *Evangelical Quarterly* 36 (1964), pp. 195–205.

McKenzie, "Knowledge"
McKenzie, J. "Knowledge of God in Hosea," *Journal of Biblical Literature* 74 (1955), pp. 22–27.

Meeks, *Urban*
Meeks, Wayne. *The First Urban Christians: The Social World of the Apostle Paul* (New Haven, Conn.: Yale University, 1983).

Meijer, "Philosophers"
Meijer, P. "Philosophers, Intellectuals, and Religion in Hellas," in *Faith, Hope, and Worship: Aspects of Religious Mentality in the Ancient World* (ed., H. S. Versnel, Studies in Greek and Roman Religion 2; Leiden: Brill, 1981), pp. 216–263.

Meineke, *FPCN* 4
Meineke, August. *Fragmenta poetarum comoediae novae* (Berlin: Reimer, 1841).

Menxel, *Elpis*
Menxel, François van. *Elpis, espoir, esperance: Études sémantiques et théologiques de l'esperance dans l'Hellenisme et le Judaisme avant le Nouveau Testament* (Frankfurt am Main, New York: Peter Lang, 1983).

Merk, "Glaube"
Merk, Otto. "Glaube und Tat in der Pastoralbriefen," *Zeitschrift für die neutestamentliche Wissenschaft* 66 (1975), pp. 91–102.

B. Metzger, *Canon*
Metzger, Bruce M. *The Canon of the NT: Its Origin, Development, and Significance* (Oxford: Clarendon, 1987).

B. Metzger, "Early Fragment"
———. "A Hitherto Neglected Early Fragment of the Epistle to Titus," *NovT* 1 (1956), pp. 149–150.

B. Metzger, *TCGNT*
———. *Textual Commentary on the Greek NT* (New York: United Bible Societies, 1975).

W. Metzger, *Christushymnus*
Metzger, Wolfgang. *Der Christushymnus 1 Timotheus 3, 16; Fragment einer Homologie der paulinischen Gemeinden* (AzT 62; Stuttgart: Calwer, 1979).

W. Metzger, *Die letzte Reise*
———. *Die letzte Reise des Apostels Paulus. Beobachtungen und Erwagungen zu weinen Itinerar nach Pastoralbriefen* (AzT 59; Stuttgart: Calwer, 1976).

Meyer, *"Mithras"*
Meyer, Marvin W. "The *Mithras* Liturgy" (edition with E.T. in Graeco-Roman Religion Series 2; Missoula, Mont.: Scholars, 1976).

Milik, *Enoch*
Milik, Joseph T. *The Books of Enoch: Aramaic Fragments of Qumran Cave 4* (Oxford: Clarendon, 1976).

Milik, "Melki-sedeq"
———. "Melki-sedeq et Melki-rěsaᶜ dans les anciens écrits juifs et chrétiens," *Journal of Jewish Studies* 23 (1972), pp. 95–144.

Minear, "Apoc. Adj."
Minear, P. S. "An Apocalyptic Adjective," *NovT* 12 (1970), pp. 218–222.

Mohrmann, "Epiphania"
Mohrmann, Christine. "Epiphania," in *Études sur le latin des Chrétiens* (4 vols.; Rome: Edizione d'Istoria e Letteratura, 1958–1977) 1.245–275.

Momigliano, *Quarto contributo*
Momigliano, Arnaldo. "Time in Ancient Historiography," in *Quarto*

contributo alla storia degli studi classici e del mondo antico (Rome: Edizioni di Storia, 1969), pp. 13–41.

Monsengwo, *Nomos*
Monsengwo, Pasinya L. *La Notion de Nomos dans le pentateuque* (Rome: PBI, 1973).

Moore, *AB Dan. add.*
Moore, Carey A. *Daniel, Esther and Jeremiah: The Additions* (AB 44; Garden City, N.Y.: Doubleday, 1977).

Morton, *Concordance*
Morton, A. Q., S. Michaelson, and J. D. Thompson. *A Critical Concordance to the PE* (Wooster, Ohio: Biblical Research Associates, 1982).

Mott, "Deliverance"
Mott, Stephen Charles. "The Greek Benefactor and Deliverance from Moral Distress," unpublished 1972 Ph.D. dissertation; see *Harvard Theological Review* 65 (1972) 601 for summary.

Mott, "Ethics"
————. "Greek Ethics and Christian Conversion: The Philonic Background of Titus 2:10–14 and 3:3–7," *NovT* 20 (1978), pp. 22–48.

Mott, "Benevolence"
————. "The Power of Giving and Receiving: Reciprocity in Hellenistic Benevolence," in *Current Issues in Biblical and Patristic Interpretation: Studies in Honor of Merrill C. Tenney* (ed., Gerald F. Hawthorne; Grand Rapids, Mich.: Eerdmans, 1975), pp. 60–72.

Moule, *Birth*
Moule, C. F. D. *Birth of the NT* (third edition; Harper's NT Commentaries; San Francisco: Harper & Row, 1982).

Moule, *Essays*
————. *Essays in NT Interpretation* (Cambridge: University Press, 1982).

Moule, *Idiom*
————. *Idiom Book of NT Greek* (Cambridge: University Press, 1959).

Moulton, *Grammar*
Moulton, James Hope. *Grammar of NT Greek* (2 vols.; Edinburgh: Clark, 1908–1919).

———— and George Milligan. *The Vocabulary of the Greek NT*. See MM in Principal Abbreviations.

Mullins, "Benediction"
Mullins, Terence Y. "Benediction as a NT Form," *Andrews University Seminary Studies* 15 (1977), pp. 59–64.

Murphy-O'Connor, *PQ*
Murphy-O'Connor, J. *Paul and Qumran* (ed., J. Murphy-O'Connor; Chicago: Priory, 1968).

Mussier, *Dio Chrys.*
  Mussier, G. *Dio Chrysostom and the New Testament, Parallels* . . . (Leiden: Brill, 1972).
Muszynski, *Fundament aus Qumran*
  Muszynski, Henry K. *Fundament, Bild, und Metaphor in den Handschriften aus Qumran* (AnBib 61; Rome: PBI, 1975).
Musurillo, *Acts*
  Musurillo, Herbert A. *The Acts of the Christian Martyrs* (Oxford: Clarendon, 1972).
Musurillo, *Pagan Martyrs*
  ———, ed. *The Acts of the Pagan Martyrs* (Oxford: Clarendon, 1954).
Nautin, "Rituel"
  Nautin, Pierre. "Le Rituel de mariage et la formation des sacramentaires 'léonien' et 'gélasien,' " *Ephemerides Liturgicae* 98 (1984), pp. 425–457.
Nickelsburg, *Ideal Figures*
  Nickelsburg, George W., and J. J. Collins, eds. *Ideal Figures in Ancient Judaism: Profiles and Paradigms* (SCS 12; Chico, Calif.: Scholars, 1980).
Nock, *Conversion*
  Nock, A. D. *Conversion: The Old and the New in Religion from Alexander the Great to Augustine of Hippo* (Oxford: Clarendon, 1933).
Nock, *EGC*
  ———. *Early Gentile Christianity and Its Hellenistic Background* (New York: Harper & Row, 1964).
Nock, *ERAW*
  ———. *Essays on Religion and the Ancient World* (ed. Zepheniah Stewart; 2 vols.; Cambridge, Mass.: Harvard University, 1972).
Nolland, "Grace"
  Nolland, J. "Grace as Power," *NovT* 28 (Jan. 1986), pp. 26–31.
Nordheim, *Das Testament*
  Nordheim, E. von. *Die Lehre der Alten: I. Das Testament als Litteraturgattung im Judentum der hellenistisch-römischen Zeit* (Arbeiten zur Literatur und Geschichte des hellenistischen Judentums 13; Leiden: Brill, 1980).
O'Connor, *Verse*
  O'Connor, Michael Patrick. *Hebrew Verse Structure* (Winona Lake, Ind.: Eisenbrauns, 1980).
Oldfather and Daly, "Menander"
  Oldfather, W. R., and W. L. Daly, "A Quotation from Menander in the Pastoral Epistles," *Classical Philology* 38 (1943), pp. 202–204.
Ong, *Presence*
  Ong, Walter J. *The Presence of the Word: Some Prolegomena for Cultural and Religious History* (New Haven, Conn.: Yale University, 1967).

Owens, *"Kalon"*
Owens, J. "The *Kalon* in Aristotle's Ethics," in *Studies in Aristotle* (ed.,
Dominic J. O'Meara, Studies in Philosophy and the History of Philosophy
9; Washington, D.C.: Catholic University of America, 1981), pp. 261–277.

Palmer, *RRRE*
Palmer, Robert E. A. *Roman Religion and Roman Empire* (Philadelphia:
University of Pennsylvania, 1974).

Pardee, "Overview"
Pardee, Dennis. "An Overview of Ancient Hebrew Epistotography," *Journal
of Biblical Literature* 97 (1978), pp. 321–346.

Penella, *Apollonius*
Penella, Robert J., ed. *The Letters of Apollonius of Tyana* (Leiden: Brill,
1979).

Penna, "Configurazione"
Penna, Romano. "Configurazione Giudeo-Cristiana della chiesa de Roma nel
I secolo," *Lateranum* 50 (1984), pp. 101–113.

Penna, "Juifs/Ebrei"
———. "Les Juifs à Rome au temps de l'apôtre Paul," *New Testament
Studies* 28 (1982) 321–347; corrected and enlarged in "Gli Ebrei a Roma al
tempo dell'Apostolo Paole," *Lateranum* 50 (1983), pp. 101–113.

Perdue, "Parenesis"
Perdue, Leo G. "Parenesis and the Epistle of James," *Zeitschrift für
neutestamentliche Wissenschaft* 72 (1981), pp. 241–256.

Petrolini, "Valenza *Kairos*"
Petrolini, Enrica. "Valenza filosofica dell'antico termine *Kairos*," *Sapienza*
30 (1977), pp. 346–362.

Places, *"Tempora"*
Places, Edouard des. *"Tempora vel momenta,"* in *Mélanges E. Tisserant*
(Vatican City: Bibliotheca Apostolica, 1964) 1.105–117.

Plumpe, *Mater*
Plumpe, Joseph. *Mater Ecclesia* (Washington, D.C.: Catholic University of
America, 1943).

Porter, "Adjectival Attributive"
Porter, Stanley E. "The Adjectival Attributive Genitive in the NT: A
Grammatical Study" *Trinity Journal* ns 4 (Spring 1983), pp. 3–17.

Potterie, "Mari"
Potterie, Ignace de la. " 'Mari d'une seule femme': Le Sens théologique d'une
formule paulinienne," in *Paul de Tarse: Apôtre du Notre Temps* (Rome:
Abbaye de S. Paul, 1979), pp. 619–638.

Potterie, "Truth"
———. "Truth," in *Dictionary of Biblical Theology* (ed., Xavier Leon-
Dufour; second edition; New York: Seabury, 1973), pp. 618–621.

Potterie, *Ver. S. Jn.*
––––––. *La Vérité dans Saint Jean* (2 vols.; Rome: PBI, 1977).
Preisigke, *Wörterbuch*
Preisigke, Friedrich. *Wörterbuch der griechischen papyrusurkunden . . .* (Berlin: Grete Preisgke Grohzig, 1927).
Prior, *Paul*
Prior, Michael Patrick. *Paul the Letter-Writer and the Second Letter to Timothy (Journal for the Study of the New Testament* supplement series; Sheffield: JSNT, in press).
Pritchard, *ANEP*
Pritchard, James. *The Ancient Near East in Pictures* (Princeton, N.J.: Princeton University, 1954).
Qimron and Strugnell, "Halakhic Letter"
Qimron, E., and J. Strugnell. "An Unpublished Halakhic Letter from Qumran," in *BAT,* pp. 400–407.
Quinn, "Ap. Ministry"
Quinn, Jerome D. "Apostolic Ministry and Apostolic Prayer," *Catholic Biblical Quarterly* 33 (1971), pp. 479–491.
Quinn, "Holy Spirit"
––––––. "The Holy Spirit in the Pastoral Epistles," in *Sin Salvation and the Spirit: Commemorating the Fiftieth Year of the Liturgical Press* (ed., D. Durken; Collegeville, Minn.: Liturgical, 1979), pp. 345–368.
Quinn, "Jesus as Savior"
––––––. "Jesus as Savior and Only Mediator (1 Tim 2:3–6): Linguistic Paradigms of Acculturation," in *Fede e cultura/Foi et culture* (Torino: Elle di Ci, 1981), pp. 249–260.
Quinn, *Perspectives*
––––––. "The Last Volume of Luke: The Relation of Luke–Acts and the PE," in *Perspectives on Luke–Acts* (ed., C. Talbert; Macon, Ga.: Mercer, 1978), pp. 62–75.
Quinn, "Ministry"
––––––. "Ministry in the New Testament," *Biblical Studies in Contemporary Thought* (Somerville, Mass.: Grerno, Hadden, 1975), pp. 130–160.
Quinn, "P46"
––––––. "P46—the Pauline Canon?" *Catholic Biblical Quarterly* 36 (1974), pp. 379–385.
Quinn, "Parenesis/Settings"
––––––. "Parenesis and the Pastoral Epistles," in *Semeia,* forthcoming; the first part is a revision of H. Cazelles, *Mélanges: De la Tôrah au Messie* (eds., J. Doré, P. Grelot, and M. Carrez; Paris: Desclée, 1981), pp. 495–501.

Quinn, "Captivity"

———. "Paul's Last Captivity," *Studia Biblica* 3 (1978) (ed., E. A. Livingstone; Sheffield: JSOT, 1980), pp. 289–299.

Quinn, "Seven Times"

———. "Seven Times He Wore Chains (*I Clem. 5.6*)," *Journal of Biblical Literature* 97 (1978), pp. 574–576.

Quinn, "Terminology"

———. "On the Terminology for Faith, Truth, Teaching, and the Spirit in the PE: A Summary," in *Teaching Authority and Infallibility in the Church: Lutherans and Catholics in Dialogue VI* (eds., P. Empie, T. A. Murphy, and J. A. Burgess; Minneapolis, Minn.: Augsburg, 1980), pp. 232–237.

Rad, *Hexateuch*

Rad, Gerhard von. *The Problem of the Hexateuch and Other Essays* (E.T. by E. W. Trueman Dicken; Edinburgh: Oliver & Boyd, 1966).

A. Rahlfs, *Septuaginta*

Rahlfs, Alfred, ed. *Septuaginta* (fifth edition; Stuttgart: Württembergische Bibelanstalt, 1952).

Rahner, "*Theos* in NT"

Rahner, Karl. "*Theos* in the New Testament," in *Theological Investigations* (Baltimore, Md.: Helison, 1961), pp. 79–148.

Räisänen, "Werkgerechtigkeit"

Räisänen, Heikki. "Werkgerechtigkeit eine frükatholische Lehre?" *Studia Theologica* 37 (1983), pp. 79–99.

Reicke, "Chronologie"

Reicke, Bo. "Chronologie der Pastoralbriefe," *Theologische Literaturzeitung* 101 (1976), pp. 81–93.

Renehan, "Quotations"

Renehan, Robert. "Classical Greek Quotations in the NT," in *The Heritage of the Early Church* (eds., David Neiman and Margaret Schatkin; Orientalia Christiana Analecta 195; Rome: Pontificale Institutum Studiorum Orientalium, 1973), pp. 17–45.

Renehan, *Notes*

———. *Greek Lexicographical Notes: A Critical Supplement to the Greek–English Lexicon of LSJ* (Göttingen: Vandenhoeck and Ruprecht, 1975).

Renehan, *Text. Crit.*

———. *Greek Textual Criticism: A Reader* (Cambridge, Mass.: Harvard University, 1969).

Reumann, "Jesus the Steward"

Reumann, John N. P. " 'Jesus the Steward': An Overlooked Theme in Christology," in *Studia Evangelica* 512 (ed., F. L. Cross; *Texte und Untersuchungen 103;* Berlin: Akademie Verlag, 1968) 21–29.

Reumann, *Righteousness*
———. *"Righteousness" in the NT*, with responses by Joseph A. Fitzmyer and Jerome D. Quinn (Philadelphia: Fortress, 1982).

Riesenfeld, *"Arneisthai"*
Riesenfeld, H. "The Meaning of the Verb *Arneisthai*," in *Coniectanea Neotestamentica* (Lund: Gleerup, 1947), pp. 207–219.

Ringgren, *Faith*
Ringgren, Helmer. *The Faith of Qumran: Theology of the Dead Sea Scrolls* (E.T. by Emilie T. Sander; Philadelphia: Fortress, 1963).

Roberts, *Manuscript*
Roberts, Colin H. *Manuscript, Society, and Belief in Early Christian Egypt* (London: Oxford University, 1979).

Roberts, "P. Yale I"
———. "P. Yale I and the Early Christian Book," in *American Studies in Papyrology*, vol. 1: *Essays in Honor of C. Bradford Welles* (New Haven, Conn.: American Society of Papyrologists, 1967), pp. 25–28.

Roberts and Skeat, *Birth*
——— and Theodore Cressey Skeat. *The Birth of the Codex* (London: Oxford University Press for the British Academy, 1983).

Robinson, "Hodayot-formel"
Robinson, James M. "Die Hodayot-formel in Gebet und Hymnus der Frühchristentums," in *Apophoreta: Festschrift für Ernst Haenchen zu seinem 70 Geburtstag* (ed., W. Eltester; Berlin: Toepelmann, 1964), pp. 194–235.

Robinson, *NHL*
———, ed. *The Nag Hammadi Library* (San Francisco: Harper & Row, 1977).

Romaniuk, "L'Origine . . . pour nous"
Romaniuk, Kazimierz. "L'Origine des formules pauliniennes 'Le Christ s'est livré pour nous,' 'Le Christ nous a aimés et s'est livré pour nous,' " *NovT* 5 (1962), pp. 55–76.

Sachot, "Salut"
Sachot, M. "Pour une Étude de la notion de salut chez les Pères Apostoliques," *Recherches de science religieuse* 51 (1977), pp. 54–70.

Sampley, *Two/One*
Sampley, J. Paul. *And the Two Shall Become One Flesh: A Study of Traditions in Ephesians 5:21–33* (Cambridge: University Press, 1971).

Sandbach, *Menandri*
Sandbach, Francis Henry. *Menandri Reliquiae selectae* (Oxford: Clarendon, 1972).

Sandmel, "Myths"
Sandmel, Samuel. "Myths, Genealogies, and Jewish Myths and the Writing

of the Gospels," in *Two Living Traditions: Essays on Religion and the Bible* (Detroit: Wayne State University Press, 1972), pp. 158–165.

Sass, *"Doulos"*

Sass, G. "Zur Bedeutung von *doulos* bei Paulus," *Zeitschrift für neutestamentliche Wissenschaft* 40 (1941), pp. 24–32.

Schadewaldt, "Humanitas Romana"

Schadewaldt, Werner von. "Humanitas Romana," in *ANRW* I.4 (ed., Hildegard Temporini; Berlin: de Gruyter, 1973), pp. 43–62.

Schenk, "Forschung"

Schenk, W. "Die Pastoralbriefe (I und II Tim. und Tit.) in der neueren Forschung (1945–1985)," in *ANRW* II.25/4 (ed., W. Haas; Berlin: de Gruyter, 1988).

Schiffman, "Non-Jews"

Schiffman, Lawrence H. "Legislation Concerning Relations with Non-Jews in the *Zadokite Fragments* and in Tannaitic Literature," *Revue de Qumran* 11 no. 43 (December 1983), pp. 379–389.

Schiffman, "Testimony"

———. "The Qumran Law of Testimony," *Revue de Qumran* 8 (December 1975), pp. 603–612.

Schmidt, "Interpolation"

Schmidt, Daryl. "1 Thess 2:13–16: Linguistic Evidence for Interpolation" *JBL* 102 (1983), pp. 269–279.

Schoder, *Hellas*

Schoder, Raymond V. *Wings over Hellas: Ancient Greece from the Air* (New York: Oxford University, 1974).

Schramm, *Fest/Festival*

Schramm, Tim, and Otto Eckert. *Fest und Freude* (Stuttgart: Kohlhammer, 1977). E.T. by James L. Blenins, *Festival and Joy in the NT* (Nashville: Abingdon, 1980).

Schürer, *HJP*

Schürer, E. *History of the Jewish People in the Age of Jesus Christ* (second edition; Edinburgh: Clark, 1973–1986).

Selwyn, *1 Pet*

Selwyn, Edward G. *The First Epistle of Saint Peter* (London: Macmillan, 1961).

Silk, *Imagery*

Silk, M. S. *Interaction in Poetic Imagery* (Cambridge: University Press, 1974).

Skeat, "Vaticanus"

Skeat, T. C. "The Codex Vaticanus in the Fifteenth Century," *Journal of Theological Studies* 35 (October 1984), pp. 454–465.

Skeat, "On 2 Tim 4:13"

———. "Especially the Parchments: A Note on 2 Timothy 4:13," *Journal of Theological Studies* 30 (1979), pp. 173–177.

Smallwood, *Jews*
 Smallwood, E. Mary. *The Jews Under Roman Rule from Pompey to Diocletian* (Leiden: Brill, 1976).
Spicq, *Agape*
 Spicq, Ceslaus. *Agape dans le NT/Agape in the New Testament* (E.T. by Marie A. McNamara and Mary H. Richter, 3 vols.; St. Louis: B. Herder, 1963–1966).
Spicq, *EP*
 ————. *Les Épîtres Pastorales* (Paris: Gabalda, 1969).
Spicq, *Lexic./Supp. Lexic.*
 ————. *Notes de Lexicographie Neotestamentaire* (2 vols. and Supplement; Göttingen: Vandenhoeck and Ruprecht, 1982).
Spicq, "Religion"
 ————. "Religion (vertu de). Nouveau Testament," in *Dictionnaire de la Bible, Supplément*, vol. 10; (Paris: Letouzey & Áne, 1987), pp. 223–228.
Staden, "Hairesis"
 Staden, Heinrich von. "Hairesis and Heresy: The case of the *hairesis ioctrikoci,*" in *Jewish and Christian Self Definition* (eds., Ben E. Meyer and E. P. Sanders, vol. 3; Philadelphia: Fortress, 1980), pp. 76–100.
Stenger, *Christushymnus*
 Stenger, W. *Der Christushymnus I Tim 3,16: Eine Strukturanalytische Untersuchung* (Regensburger Studien zur Theologie 6; Frankfurt: Peter Lang, 1977).
Stern, *Authors on Jews*
 Stern, Menahen, ed. *Greek and Latin Authors on Jews and Judaism* (3 vols.; Jerusalem: Israel Academy of Sciences and Humanities, 1974).
Stillwell, *PECS*
 Stillwell, Richard, ed. *Princeton Encyclopedia of Classical Sites* (Princeton, N.J.: Princeton University, 1976).
Stowers, *Letter Writing*
 Stowers, Stanley K. *Letter Writing in Greco-Roman Antiquity* (Library of Early Christianity 5; ed., W. A. Meeks; Philadelphia: Westminster, 1986).
Strack-Billerbeck
 Strack, Hermann and Paul Billerbeck. *Kommentar zum Neuen Testament aus Talmud und Midrasch* (6 vols.; Munich: Beck, 1922–1961).
Strobel, "Schreiben des Lukas?"
 Strobel, A. "Schreiben des Lukas? Zum sprachlichen Problem der Pastoralbriefe," *New Testament Studies* 15 (1969), pp. 191–210.
Strugnell, "Notes"
 Strugnell, John. "Notes en marge du Volume V," *Römische Quartalschrift für christliche Altertumskunde und Kirchengeschichte* 1 (1970), pp. 163–276.

Sudhaus
  Sudhaus, Siegfried. *Philodemi: Volumina Rhetorica* (2 vols. and Supplement; Leipzig: Teubner, 1892).
Sutcliffe, "Hatred"
  Sutcliffe, Edmund. "Hatred at Qumran," *Revue de Qumran* 2 (1960), pp. 345–355.
Swete, *Theodore*
  Swete, Henry B., ed. *Epistolas B. Pauli comentarii, the Latin Version with the Greek Fragments* . . . (2 vols.; Cambridge: University Press, 1880).
Theissen, *Setting*
  Theissen, G. *The Social Setting of Early Christianity: Essays on Corinth* (E.T. ed. with an introduction by J. H. Schotz; Philadelphia; Fortress, 1982).
Therrien, *Discernement*
  Therrien, Gerard. *Le Discernement dans les écrits pauliniens* (Paris: Galenda, 1973).
Thompson, *Origin*
  Thompson, Thomas L. *The Origin Tradition of Ancient Israel*, vol. 1: *The Literary Formation of Genesis and Exodus 1–23* (*Journal for the Study of the Old Testament* Supplement 55; Sheffield: Sheffield Academy Press, 1987).
Throckmorton, *"Sōzein"*
  Throckmorton, B. N. *"Sōzein, sōtēria* in Luke–Acts," in *Studia Evangelica: Papers Presented to the Fourth International Congress on NT Studies Held at Oxford, 1969* (ed., Elizabeth A. Livingstone, vol. 6; Berlin: Akademie, 1973), pp. 515–526.
E. Turner, *Typology*
  Turner, Eric G. *The Typology of the Early Codex* (Philadelphia: University of Pennsylvania, 1977).
N. Turner, *Words*
  Turner, Nigel. *Christian Words* (Nashville, Tenn.: Nelson, 1981).
N. Turner, *Grammar*
  ———, ed. *A Grammar of NT Greek* (vols. 3 and 4 ed. by James Hope Moulton; Edinburgh: Clark, 1963–1976).
N. Turner, *Insights*
  ———. *Grammatical Insights into NT Greek* (Edinburgh: Clark, 1965).
N. Turner, "NT Vocab."
  ———. "New Testament Vocabulary," *NovT* 16 (April 1974), pp. 149–160.
Unnik, *Sparsa*
  Unnik, W. C. van. *Sparsa Collecta, the Collected Essays of W. C. van Unnik* (3 vols.; Leiden: Brill, 1973–1983).
Unnik, *Tarsus*
  ———. *Tarsus or Jerusalem: The City of Paul's Youth* (E.T. by George Ogg; London: Epworth, 1962; repr. in his *Sparsa* 1.259–320).

Vaux, *Israel*
Vaux, Roland de. *Ancient Israel* (E.T. by John McHugh; New York: McGraw, 1961).
Vermes, *DSS*
Vermes, Geza. *The Dead Sea Scrolls in English* (Baltimore: Penguin, 1962).
Verner, *Household*
Verner, David C. *The Household of God: The Social World of the PE.* (SBLDS 71; Chico, Calif.: Scholars, 1983).
Wallace, "Adjective"
Wallace, Daniel B. "The Relation of Adjective to Noun in Anarthous Constructions in the NT," *NovT* 26 (April 1984), pp. 128–167.
Walsh, *"Spes"*
Walsh, P. G. *"Spes Romana, Spes Christiana,"* *Prudentia* 6 (1974), pp. 33–42.
Walzer, *Galen*
Walzer, Richard. *Galen on Jews and Christians* (London: Oxford University, 1949).
Weiss, "Pagani"
Weiss, Herold. "The *Pagani* Among the Contemporaries of the First Christians," *Journal of Biblical Literature* 86 (1967), pp. 42–52.
Welles, *Correspondence*
Welles, Charles Bradford. *Royal Correspondence in the Hellenistic Period* (Chicago: Ares, 1974, repr. 1934).
C. Westermann, *Blessing*
Westermann, Claus. *Blessing in the Bible and the Life of the Church* (E.T. by Keith Crim; Philadelphia: Fortress, 1978).
W. Westermann, *Slave*
Westermann, William L. *The Slave Systems of Greek and Roman Antiquity* (Philadelphia: American Philosophical Society, 1955).
Whitaker, "Baptism"
Whitaker, Charles. "Baptism," in *Hippolytus* (ed. G. Cumming; Bramcote, Notts.: Grove, 1978), pp. 52–60.
Whitaker, "Formula"
———. "The History of the Baptismal Formula," *Journal of Ecclesiastical History* 16 (1965), pp. 1–12.
White, "Epistolary Literature"
White, John L. "NT Epistolary Literature in the Framework of Ancient Epistolography," *ANRW* II.25/2 (eds., Wolfgang Haase and Hildegard Temporini; Berlin: de Gruyter, 1984), pp. 1730–1756.
Whittaker, *Tatian*
Whittaker, Molly, ed. and trans. *Oratio ad Graecos and Fragments* (Oxford: Clarendon, 1982).

Wiedemann, *Slavery*
  Wiedemann, T. *Greek and Roman Slavery* (Baltimore: The John Hopkins University, 1981).
Wikgren, "Problems"
  Wikgren, Allen. "Some Problems in Jude 5," in *Studies in the History and Text of the New Testament in Honor of Kenneth Willis Clark* (eds., B. L. Danniels and M. J. Suggs; Studies and Documents 29; Salt Lake City: University of Utah, 1967), pp. 147–152.
Wilken, *Christians*
  Wilken, Robert L. *The Christians as the Romans Saw Them* (New Haven, Conn.: Yale University, 1984).
R. Wilson, "Sōtēria"
  Wilson, R. McL. "Sōtēria," *Scottish Journal of Theology* 6 (1953), pp. 406–416.
S. Wilson, *Lk PE*
  Wilson, Stephen G. *Luke and the PE* (London: SPCK, 1979).
Winston, *AB Wisd.*
  Winston, David. *The Wisdom of Solomon* (AB 43; Garden City, N.Y.: Doubleday, 1979).
Wolff, *Hos.*
  Wolff, Hans Walter. *Hosea* (Hermeneia; E.T. by Gary Stansell; Philadelphia: Fortress, 1974).
Wright, *Midrash*
  Wright, Addison. *The Literary Genre Midrash* (Staten Island, N.Y.: Alba House, 1967).
Yadin, *War*
  Yadin, Yigael, ed. *The Scroll of the War of the Sons of Light Against the Sons of Darkness* (E.T. by Batya and Chaim Rabin; New York: Oxford University, 1962).
Yadin, *Temple*
  ———. *The Temple Scroll* (3 vols.; Jerusalem: Israel Exploration Society, 1983).
Zimmer, "Lügner"
  Zimmer, C. "Die Lügner-Antinomie in Titus 1,12," *Linguistica Biblica* 59 (1987), pp. 77–99.
Zuntz, *Text*
  Zuntz, Günther. *The Text of the Epistles: A Disquisition upon the Corpus Paulinum* (The Schweich Lectures of the British Academy, 1946; London: Published for British Academy by Oxford University, 1953).

THE LETTER
TO TITUS

INTRODUCTION

◆

NOMENCLATURE

Thirteen letters in the NT have been transmitted under the name of the apostle Paul. Three of them, one entitled since the second century "To Titus" and a pair "To Timothy," are the concern of this commentary and its INTRO-DUCTION. Several centuries have passed since German NT studies began to call these letters "the Pastoral Epistles," that term implying a certain theological as well as literary unity that is proper to them. The eighteenth-century phrase had its precedent already in Thomas Aquinas, who had characterized 1 Tim as "a rule, so to speak, for pastors" (see Fiore, *Function*, p. 3, n. 7, and Thomas Aquinas, *Commentaria* 2.184D; *Super I Epistolam ad Timotheum, lectio ii in 1:3;* Turin: Marietti, 1929).

The three short letters are, like Phlm, addressed to individuals, and their individuality as letters ought not to be overlooked (see Johnson, *Writings,* p. 389). The PE are "pastoral" in a way that Phlm is not; that is, these three letters are concerned with "shepherding" the church of the living God. Already around the turn of the second century the Muratorian Fragment (lines 60–63) justified their position in the Christian canon because of their contribution to ecclesial discipline in the church universal, a case made in the name of Paul the apostle (see B. Metzger, *Canon,* p. 196). In the last analysis they are concerned with what believers do. The PE certainly are exercised at every turn about what Christians believe (and what their neighbors believe about them); but these letters emphatically have no time for speculative thinking or theoretical research, and they little appreciate Christians who pursue such activities (Titus 3:9; 1 Tim 1:4; 2 Tim 2:14; 3:7; regularly the data and arguments for the assertions of this INTRODUCTION about the PE are found in the NOTES and COMMENTS on the texts cited). These three letters are "pastoral" because they are *practical,* in other words, they are ordered to a Christian *praxis,* to the activities of believers.

DOCUMENTS AND DATA

The varied hypotheses about the origin and purpose of the PE have been extrapolated from the facts about the tangible documents of which the original text remains extant in Greek. A review of the concrete and observable phenomena of that text will precede a survey of those matters which are inferred with more or less certainty from the observable data. The text of the PE is the first, basic reality to be analyzed; then the literary form in which this text has been composed and transmitted; third, the literary and nonliterary materials that the author incorporated into this form. Finally, the data referred to by the PE will be surveyed, to glean some of the information that they give about the secular and ecclesial milieus that once packaged these compositions. From that vantage one can then review, in the next main section of this INTRODUCTION, the varied hypotheses about and reconstructions of the origin and purpose of the PE. The final section precedes a translation of all three letters, which in turn is followed by the NOTES and COMMENTS on Titus.

The Greek text of the PE, like the rest of the NT, has been transmitted in numerous ancient codices, that is to say, on leaves of papyrus or parchment bound together into what we call a "book." But before 100 c.e. practically all Hellenistic literary compositions were copied on rolls (Roberts and Skeat, *Birth;* see 2 Tim 4:13; Skeat, "On 2 Tim 4:13"). It was in Rome in the latter part of the first Christian century that secular authors began to experiment with the codex for literary compositions (though Julius Caesar may have used a codex notebook before this time for his letters to the Roman Senate [Suetonius, *Iulius* 1.56.6]). The innovation was attractive to late first-century Christians, again probably those in Rome, and by the end of that century Christians (in distinction from their Jewish and pagan contemporaries) had transferred their sacred literature, the LXX Greek OT and the compositions that came to be called the NT, from the rolls on which they had been copied originally into codices or books. The very earliest scraps of Christian documents, including a papyrus page of the Letter to Titus, are already in "book" form. This innovation gave a visible identity to the Christian writings; it was also in every sense a pastoral, that is, practical, measure that met a need in the second-century churches: for the codex was an efficient way of gathering several compositions under one cover for easy consultation in public reading or private study.

From the earliest papyrus, all of the manuscripts of the PE are in codex form. Yet the Greek text of the PE was originally composed, in all probability, on one or more rolls (depending on whether the letters were originally written together as a collection or were composed and dispatched separately). The reconstruction of any intervening process has its repercussions for every hypothesis about the origin and purpose of these letters. Certain features of the process can be discerned in the arrangement of the compositions within the extant NT codices; thus the gospels and Acts are always separate from the epistolary literature and within the latter a Pauline collection, dating from about the year 100 (Zuntz, *Text*, p. 279; see pp. 216–283), can be distinguished from a collection of seven other epistles (or eight if Heb is included). Within these epistolary collections the length of an individual letter appears generally to have determined its place within the collection (thus, among the Paulines, Rom first and Phlm last; see *VL* 24[2].290–303). The PE appear to mark a new beginning within the extant Pauline codices, for 1 Tim is notably longer than 2 Thess. Probably this point marks the seam where two second-century collections of Pauline letters were joined, a collection of letters to churches (at times including Heb, as in P[46] and the archetype of B) and a smaller collection of Pauline letters addressed to individuals (also arranged in almost all extant codices with the longest first and Phlm, the shortest, last; see Quinn, "P[46]"; Roberts, *Manuscript*, pp. 60, 62). An alternate and perhaps even earlier order, attested in the Muratorian Fragment and the fourth-century Latin commentary on the Paulines called Ambrosiaster, reads Titus before 1 and 2 Tim. This oldest attested order has been adopted for this commentary.

The Greek text of the PE (*NTG*[26corr] and *GNT*[3corr]) has been transmitted in many manuscript codices since the fourth century (see especially S, A, C, D), and P[32] may be as early as 200 (Aland, *Repertorium*, p. 253; Haelst, *Catalogue*, p. 189, §534; E. Turner, *Typology*, p. 147). The absence of the PE from B still provokes questions (Skeat, "Vaticanus," pp. 464–465). J. K. Elliott, in *Greek Text*, has studied every significant variant in the PE with a variety of principles for textual criticism. The PE are alluded to or cited by many ancient Christian writers, and for the second Christian century alone *Biblia Patristica*, 1.507–518, offers about 450 references. In the mid-second century Marcion refused the PE a place in his canon, according to Tertullian (*Adversus Marcionem* 5.21). Tatian rejected Timothy while retaining Titus, according to Jerome (*PL* 26.556; cited also in Whittaker, *Tatian*, pp. 82–83). But Polycarp almost certainly quoted the Letters to Timothy in his *Phil.* 4.1, perhaps as early as 120 c.e. Whether Ignatius and *1 Clem.* knew the text of the PE is more problematic but seems on the whole more likely now than it did a generation ago (Spicq, *EP*, pp. 162–163; Hagner, *Use*, pp. 236–237; Quinn, "Seven Times").

The language of the PE (their actual vocabulary, syntax, and style) has a certain homogeneity throughout the small corpus. These letters somehow sound different from the rest of the Paulines, including the other "private" letter, to Philemon (see the tables assembled and revised by Harrison, *Problem* and *Paulines*). As A. D. Nock (*ERAW* 1.342–343) noted, "it is clear that as we pass from the Pauline Epistles to the Pastorals . . . there is an approximation to the phraseology of the world around, a lessening of the feeling of isolation, and an increase in intelligibility to the ordinary contemporary man, had he happened upon these books." Roughly one-third of the words in the PE (names of persons and places aside) do not appear in the other Paulines; almost one-fifth do not appear elsewhere in the NT (though the overwhelming majority of them do appear in Greek documents that predate 50 c.e., including Philo and the LXX). The language of the PE has notable resemblances to that of Luke–Acts (Strobel, "Schreiben des Lukas?"; Quinn, *Perspectives;* S. Wilson, *Lk PE;* Marshall, "Review"; Moule, *Birth,* pp. 264–265, 281–282; idem, *Essays,* pp. 113–132). Moreover, in their narrow compass the PE coin about half a dozen terms (N. Turner, "NT Vocab.," pp. 149–150) and use some terms in a quite unusual sense (thus *themelios* in 1 Tim 6:19). Granted the ineradicable exuberance of ancient Greek and that no author then had an unabridged dictionary to consult, such coinages are not only "spontaneous and unconscious creations." They also "may represent an attempt to convey ideas which seemed to need new expressions" as well as devices for "stylistic emphasis or dramatic effect" (Nock, *ERAW* 2.642–643).

Computer analyses of linguistic data from the PE have become available (Aland, *Konkordanz;* Friberg and Friberg, *Analytical GNT;* Morton, *Concordance;* Kenny, *Stylometric,* with further bibliography). It becomes feasible with their aid to analyze in precise detail the use and distribution of the Greek particles and the length of the words and sentences in the compositions before us. Earlier and more narrowly based studies appeared to confirm that the PE were quite homogeneous internally and different from the rest of the Paulines. Anthony Kenny in his recent and more broadly based study finds scarcely any significant difference between the PE and the rest of the Paulines, Titus alone excepted. He sees "no reason to reject the hypothesis that twelve of the Pauline Epistles are the work of a single, unusually versatile author" (*Stylometric,* p. 100). The relatively limited word pool in the individual letters (not to mention the limitations imposed by our lack of precise knowledge of the processes of composition and authorship in the ancient world) restricts the certitude of the inferences that can be drawn from stylometric data (N. Turner, *Grammar,* pp. 102–104).

The large number of terms that are peculiar to the PE in biblical Greek already alert the reader to their affinities with the more literary traditions in Hellenistic Greek. Their vocabulary generally is less biblical (i.e., Septuagintal) than Paul's, though there are notable contacts with sapiential and other ethical compositions of Hellenistic Judaism (e.g., 4 Macc; *T. 12 Patr.*). One hears some language typical of the popular Epicurean, Cynic, and Stoic philosophers (e.g., Philodemus of Gadara; Epictetus; see N. Turner, *Grammar,* p. 102). The language of the Greek drama (staged everywhere in the Hellenistic world for the public at large)—particularly the tragedies of Euripides and the comedies of Menander—had its effect on ordinary people and their speech. Philo has a still moving description of the enthusiastic standing ovation that he saw given in response to Euripides' encomium of freedom in a performance of the *Auge,* a

4

tragedy now lost (*Quod omn. prob.* 141). With a language thus formed the PE sought to address such people.

The fifty-five proper nouns and adjectives of the PE belong to the total working vocabulary of the author: some of them are unique to these letters (thus "Jewish" in Titus 1:14); some occur otherwise only in the other Paulines ("Luke" in 2 Tim 4:11 and Col 4:14; Phlm 24); still others are found elsewhere only in the Lukan corpus (thus "Crete" in Titus 1:5 [see 1:12]; "Antioch," "Iconium," and "Lystra" in 2 Tim 3:11; and the double name "Pontius Pilate" in 1 Tim 6:13). Other cities and places are mentioned too: Nicopolis in Titus 3:12; Ephesus in 1 Tim 1:3; 2 Tim 1:18; 4:12; Rome in 2 Tim 1:17; Thessalonika in 2 Tim 4:10; Troas in 2 Tim 4:13; Corinth and Miletus in 2 Tim 4:20; in addition, the areas or provinces of Macedonia (1 Tim 1:3), of Asia (2 Tim 1:15), of Galatia or Gaul, and of Dalmatia (2 Tim 4:10). Together they suggest the geographical world presupposed by this correspondence. Of the personal names none occurs more often than that of Jesus, and thus the christological concerns of these compositions are telegraphed.

Particularly in two areas the vocabulary of the PE already reflects specialized patterns of use. The first falls in the area of Christian conduct or ethics, and the terminology is that for distinguishing good from bad acts (Donelson, *Pseudepig.* pp. 171–183). The second area (and it intersects with the first) is that of particular Christian ministries and the vocabulary for designating those who shoulder specific roles in the service of the body of believers, a vocabulary still notably uncultic (see Johnson, *Writings*, p. 385). In both areas the PE share some of their emerging technical vocabulary with other first-century Christian documents (such as the terminological clusters around faith and love or apostle and presbyter). Other terminology is almost unique to the PE (*chera*, the term for widow; the clusters of words built around *sōphrōn* [sensible] and *eusebēs* [godly]; see Excursuses III and V).

The second major consideration about the language of the PE is their syntax: that is, the way in which the words are ordered into sentences, their patterns in the use of coordinating and subordinating particles (note computer analyses mentioned above), their characteristic ways of employing the Greek moods and tenses (thus the optative, a mood rarely used in the NT, almost certainly appears several times in 2 Tim [e.g., 1:16, 18]). The influences of the LXX, of Hellenistic Judaism, and of Latin surface regularly. A striking and hardly appreciated syntactical phenomenon in the PE is the periodic breakdown of syntax, ranging from inordinately rough, abrupt transitions (thus Titus 2:6–8; 1 Tim 3:1a–b), through inexplicable shifts in the inflection of verbs (1 Tim 2:15), to sentence fragments that are without a verb or object to weld their endless phrases together (thus Titus 1:1–4; 1 Tim 1:3–7). All of this belongs to the individual character of the PE as Greek compositions.

With the question of the style in which the PE are written one is beyond issues of vocabulary and syntax as such and at the utmost verge of the data about their language (see N. Turner, *Grammar*, pp. 101–105, 172). When their text is read aloud in Greek, the author's use of sound to accent his thought is often notable. The reader hears alliteration, assonance, rhyme, paronomasia, polysyndeton (for abundant expressiveness), asyndeton (for a vivid, impassioned effect, adding a certain brilliance to epistolary style; see BDF §460 and 1 Tim 1:8–10). Poetic citations ornament the composition (Titus 1:12; 1 Tim 3:16; 2 Tim 2:11–13), and the prose has at times distinctly poetic rhythmic structure, particularly when prayers are alluded to or cited (thus 1 Tim 1:12–17). A predilection for unusual, even unique terminology has already been observed. By and large, the style of the PE is Hellenistic (note the compound words) rather than Hebraic and lacks the energetic versatility that characterizes other parts of the Pauline epistolary. The PE read in a calm, slow, colorless, monotonous fashion. Their tone is sententious, stern, didactic, sober, stiff, domesticated, with an occasional striving by means of unusual terminology for literary effect and an atmosphere of erudition. Their style is by and large paraenetic, that is, the author urges his points rather than argues them (Quinn, "Parenesis/Settings").

The PE stand before us both in the form of three individual "letters" and as a part of a small group of Pauline letters that were addressed to individuals (including beside the PE only Phlm). These in turn stand in the NT after a larger collection or epistolary of Pauline letters to Christian congregations or churches. In the current order of the NT collection, still another eight letters follow the Pauline collection. The epistolary constitutes about one-third of the NT.

Compositions in epistolary form represent the oldest surviving Christian literature, though the form (unlike that of the gospel genre) was a borrowing from the contemporary, first-century world, where the letter already had a long and instructive history in Roman, Hellenistic, and Semitic cultures. The epistolary form was relatively little used for literary composition (in contrast to everyday communication) in Palestinian Judaism, though one must note 4QEn^g and the "polemic-halakic letter" of 4Q 394–399 (MMT), edited by Qimron and Strugnell ("Halakhic Letter"). The authors call attention to the similar character of some Pauline letters. First Timothy comes to mind. Still, the popularity of the letter form in Greek-speaking Judaism appears in the epistolary compositions cited in LXX Esth, Bar, and Macc, not to mention *Enoch*, the *Ep. Arist.*, and the *Apoc. Bar.*

Current studies of epistolary theory in the ancient rhetoricians (Malherbe, *Cynic Epistles*, "Theorists," *Social Aspects*, pp. 13–17, 57–58, 101–107; White, "Epistolary Literature," pp. 1730–1756; Stowers, *Letter Writing*), not to mention the innumerable texts that the ancient world called "letters" or "epistles," are making it clearer what early Christians expected when they read or heard a composition in an epistolary form. They did not look for a technical, scientific treatise; and letters were felt to be a limited, even an inadequate substitute for personal, face-to-face communication (see 1 Tim 3:14; 4:13). Spontaneity and confidentiality were not considered to belong to the essence of an ancient letter (though evidently sometimes these characteristics occur). Still, the ancient reader probably made the distinction immediately between personal, private letters and those which were intended to be read by anyone who was interested in picking them up (not unlike the distinction between first- and second-class mail in the United States). A letter was received as a gift, a sign of personal, individual attention and care for the recipient, a part of a conversation between friends. In a letter the recipient expected to see the character of the sender, "an icon of the soul"; and thus in ancient rhetorical schools letters were written as exercises in characterization of famous persons, mythical or historical (see Ovid, *Heroides*). Just as the ancient author of a history composed the kind of speech that a certain person would and could have given (sometimes using sources, sometimes not), so a letter or letters could be written to depict the personality and character of a philosopher or statesman or literary figure (see Malherbe, *Cynic Epistles;* and Horace, *Epistles,* passim).

When ancient Christians began to read a letter "To Titus" or "To Timothy," they expected in virtue of the epistolary form to hear (or overhear) a Pauline conversation in writing, to receive an icon of the apostle's soul and a convincing characterization that conveyed his heartfelt personal care as well as his teaching, directives, and requests. The readers expected all of this whether the letter was originally a piece of private correspondence originating before the apostle's death, or a "characterization" composed after his martyrdom, or a combination of the two (i.e., an originally private correspondence got up for publication in an expanded form).

As noted above, the PE have not come down to us simply as separate letters. They are proposed (perhaps with Phlm) as letters to individuals, an epistolary collection, already distinct from the collection of Pauline letters to churches in the second century, when they were being read in the order Titus–1 Tim–2 Tim. The opening of the Letter to Titus (1:1–4), which is out of all proportion to the letter that follows, is an internal indication that it headed such a collection (see Quinn, *Perspectives,* pp. 63–64, 72).

A letter collection is itself a literary genre that enjoyed a limited popularity in Greek philosophical circles but came into its own in Roman political life (see Carcopino, *Cicero,* 1.4–37) and only later among poets and philosophers. Thus collections of the "letters" by persons as diverse as Cicero, Augustus, Horace, Ovid, Seneca, and Pliny were published (or in Augustus's case available in the archives; see Suetonius, *Augustus* 2.71, 76; *Claudius* 5.4), whether in prose or poetry, whether on personal or literary matters, whether on political or philosophical (i.e., ethical) questions, whether edited by themselves while they were still alive or published by others after their deaths. The premise of all such collections is that there are letters worth saving for the education, instruction, and enjoyment of the next generation, for individuals and groups to whom they were not originally addressed. The actual authors or their admirers assembled such collections because they were convinced of the enduring importance of the one who wrote the letters and the importance and permanent interest of the matters that had been discussed in the individual epistolary "conversations."

The epistolary genre was used not only for letters, separate or in freestanding collections, but also for letters in other genres of composition. Sometimes a letter or an epistolary collection was prefixed to another work (thus the seven letters that open Rev, the pair that open 2 Macc, and perhaps the "Edict" from Cyrus at the beginning of Ezra); sometimes they are given within the composition (as is the correspondence with the exiles in Jer 29; 1 Macc 10:22–45; 12:5–23; the LXX Esth 3:13a–g; 8:12a–x [RSV 13:1–7; 16:1–24]; Acts 15:23–29; 23:25–30); sometimes they are added at the end (examples in Quinn, Perspectives, pp. 68–69; see the LXX Esth 10:3l [RSV 11:1]; additions to Justin, Apology 1.69–71). The appearance of compositions in the epistolary form within a larger work of instructive history signaled the genuineness, the credibility, and the authority of what was going to be or had been narrated. A cluster of letters intensified these impressions. From another point of view letters within a narrative served to satisfy with edifying biographical notices the questions in a community about outstanding and yet controversial personalities whose past teaching and acts were still appreciated.

Accordingly, the PE were opened and read as a collection in the second century, and perhaps even in the first (regardless of whether the letters had also an individual preexistence). The collection offered an authoritative message from the past, a message from a significant personality, a message containing (at least in the judgment of the collectors) observations and instructions the significance of which was meant to transcend the setting presupposed in their text. The collected letters thus come as a "prophecy" from the past to a new generation (see Pliny citing M. Cato's letter to his son in Naturalis historia 7.51.171; 29.7.14; Ovid occasionally describes his elegiac letters Ex Ponto as containing prophecies). The original addressees of such correspondence tend to sink below the historical horizon, while the author (genuine or putative) remains the polestar around which a new public revolves. Thus Titus and Timothy in the PE are less actual historical individuals than paradigmatic persons, models with which the new public is expected to identify (Fiore, Function; see also Nickelsburg, Ideal Figures). "The essence of the epistolary genre, both in antiquity and the Middle Ages, was not whether the letter was actually sent but whether it performed a representative function" (Constable, Letters, p. 13). The PE incontrovertibly aim to represent Paul as herald, apostle, teacher (1 Tim 2:7; 2 Tim 1:11), instructing and directing the men who shared his apostolate. These men in turn, as Paul's true children (cf. Titus 1:4 with 2:15; see 1 Tim 1:2) and his heirs, transmit the apostle's doctrine and directives to "God's house, which is the church of the living God" (1 Tim 3:15). They also see to it that this household has managers (see Titus 1:7), presbyters as well as bishops with their deacons, whose lives and teaching represent Paul (note also the "faithful men" of 2 Tim 2:1–2).

Other recent studies have more closely specified the paraenetic—in other words, hortatory—character of the PE as the ancient world understood paraenesis (Perdue, "Parenesis"), namely, as traditional ethical exhortation, universally applicable to individual persons, addressed to an audience that is paradigmatic and typical rather than genuinely individual and historical, and often an admonition that does not envision or admit contradiction (Quinn, "Parenesis/Settings"). Such letters expect not answers but action from the recipients. The epistolary form of 2 Tim has attracted special attention because it has many characteristics of the testamentary genre in the ancient world (Nordheim, *Das Testament*). Paul becomes the illustrious, dying patriarch, leaving his goods, his wisdom, and his wealth to his children who carry on his name, his plan, his hopes. The dead man's paraenesis is endowed with a prophetic thrust, weight, and authority as the last words of a very important person. The *topos* is a commonplace in the OT, as the testament or last will of Jacob (Gen 49), of Moses (Deut 33), of Joshua (Josh 23–24), and of David (2 Sam 23:1–6 [or 7]) illustrate. The Johannine speech of Jesus at the last supper shows the adaptable tenacity of the rhetorical figure (Aristotle, *Rhetoric* 1.2.21 [1358a14]; 2.22.10–23.30; and see Philodemus, *Volumina rhetorica* 1.226).

At every turn in the PE there appear quotations of and allusions to compositions that served as sources for this paraenetic epistolary. Greek versions of the OT are quoted (1 Tim 5:18a) as well as an oracular line from a pagan poet (Titus 1:12); there is a saying in 1 Tim 5:18b which Luke 10:7 places on Jesus' lips. An allusion to an apocryphal composition about Jannes and Jambres appears in 2 Tim 3:8 (see Charlesworth, *OT Pseud.*, 2.427–442). There are citations of archaic Christian hymns (1 Tim 3:16; 2 Tim 2:11–13; see W. Metzger, *Christushymnus;* Stenger, *Christushymnus;* Quinn, "Holy Spirit," pp. 353–355) and prophecies (1 Tim 1:18; 4:1; Quinn, "Holy Spirit," pp. 346–347, 356–360) and possibly some short dispatches that originated at the end of Paul's life (thus Titus 1:1, 4–5; 3:12–15; 2 Tim 1:1–2, 15–18; 4:9–15). Although the case has been argued (Hanson, "Domestication"), there is no convincing evidence that the PE quote from the other Pauline letters, unless perhaps Rom.

If the foregoing compositions were already in relatively fixed texts, there appear to be sources cited in the PE that were in more plastic forms, relatively open to redactional activity. Such are the Christian domestic codes (*Haustafeln*) of Titus 2:2–10 (see Sampley, *Two/One*, pp. 18–30; Verner, *Household*, pp. 13–25, 83–111; Donelson, *Pseudepig*, pp. 171–183) and 1 Tim 5:1–2 (to be read with 6:1–2). Similarly, there are more than a few lists that specify good and bad ethical qualities as well as bad and good persons (e.g., Titus 1:6–10; 1 Tim 1:9–10; 2 Tim 3:2–5). The lists of bad qualities appear to use more archaic, catechetical materials that aim to identify the Christian in contrast to the unbeliever; the lists of virtuous qualities are not addressed to the whole believing community but to particular classes or orders of believers. Relatively specific conduct is demanded, often with an apologetic if not a missionary goal. Also among the more plastic materials cited by the PE are those which contain directives for the Christian life, particularly for those who engage in liturgical worship, materials that we classify as church orders. They occupy 1 Tim 2–3 and 5:3–25. The former, perhaps from a congregation of predominantly Gentile origin, begins with directives for the public prayer of the church; then treats the liturgical conduct of men and women (with an added note on the role of the Christian wife in public teaching, 1 Tim 2:11–3:1a); finally it turns (1 Tim 3:1b–13) to the qualifications and regulations for the specific ministries of men (bishop, deacons) and women (a group without title who parallel the deacons in 1 Tim 3:11). Sacral language is conspicuously absent in describing any of these persons. The other church order of 1 Tim, perhaps from a house church of predominantly Jewish origin, is enclosed within a household code (5:1–2; 6:1–2) and deals with widows (1 Tim 5:3–15) and presbyters.

Prayers abound in the PE. The briefest are in the opening and closing epistolary blessings (twofold in 2 Tim 4:22; there was originally perhaps no blessing in 1 Tim 6:21b [note the way Irenaeus, *Adversus haereses* 3.3.3 (SC 211.34) cites the correspondence with Timothy]). Other prayers appear too, brief and spontaneous (thus 2 Tim 1:16–17) as well as long and solemn (thus 1 Tim 1:12–17; 2 Tim 1:3–14). Flexible as these compositions are, they often appear to contain traditional elements and to move formulaically from an opening address to the body of the prayer, which then concludes in a doxology. Another type of prayer that verges on the creedal is the acclamation form preserved in 1 Tim 2:5–6 (Quinn, "Jesus as Savior," pp. 253–257).

Of the materials cited or redacted by the author of the PE the most difficult to bring into precise focus are those which may be characterized as ecclesial paraenesis (as distinct from the epistolary paraenesis noted above). An authoritative teaching office seems to be presumed which articulates Pauline apostolic doctrine through creed, cult, and catechesis, and it is to be received in faith. Compositions of various types, cited under the rubric *pistos ho logos*, "this is the Christian message meant to be believed" (indicated with an asterisk among the following references), also figure in this kind of paraenesis (Knight, *Sayings*).

Creedal formulas in the PE are relatively rare, brief, and closely identified with Paul's gospel and his prayer (1 Tim 1:15*; 2 Tim 2:8). The paraenesis characteristic of the public worship of believers, the sacramental cult in the widest sense, including liturgical orations and homilies, appears frequently in the PE. See Titus 2:4–5 for a citation from a marriage charge; 2:11–14 for a baptismal confession; 3:4–7* for a didactic baptismal oration; 1 Tim 2:13–15* for another citation from a marriage homily; and 1 Tim 6:11–16 for an ordination charge. The previously noted hymn of 2 Tim 2:11–13* could have been used in a baptismal liturgy. Various types of ethical catechesis also appear to draw on previously existing materials and redact them in an authoritative way for a particular purpose. Thus Titus 2:7 adapts the household code with the qualities it demands of believers of various ages and classes to make it apply to the apostolic minister himself; in 1 Tim 4:8* the teaching on godliness is particularly applied to the figure of Timothy; in 1 Tim 6:6–10 and 17–19, the wealthy believers are the object of what seems to be partially traditional exhortation.

After surveying the text of the PE, their literary form, and the previous compositions on which they drew, one broaches the methodologically delicate task of disengaging from these materials a sketch of the world, geographical and social, to which the PE refer. The places and the persons, named and unnamed, that figure explicitly in the text suggest materials for a societal profile of ecclesial life as the PE conceive it, that is to say, the ways in which believers are to relate to their God, to one another, and to those who do not share their faith.

Titus and 1 Tim profess to come from Paul en route to Macedonia and Nicopolis in northwest Greece; 2 Tim comes from Rome (Quinn, "Captivity"). The island of Crete is the destination for Titus; the metropolis of Asia Minor, Ephesus, for the correspondence with Timothy. In the whole correspondence a total of perhaps fifteen places and areas are mentioned that are found from modern Italy and France through Yugoslavia and Greece into central Turkey. Within this theater of action one encounters almost forty persons by name, a few of whom belong to OT traditions (Adam and Eve, Moses, Jannes and Jambres, David). Jesus Christ, God, the Spirit, angels, and the devil are discussed below. In the "present" that the PE presuppose, Paul and more than a dozen of his current and past coworkers, along with some members of the churches, are explicitly named; more surprisingly, some opponents of the apostle and his mission are also noted by name (1 Tim 1:20; 2 Tim 1:15; 2:17; 4:14). Beyond these names the reader gets a glimpse of other "brothers," the "faithful" of the Christian generation being addressed (1 Tim 4:6; 6:2; 2 Tim 4:21; 1 Tim 4:3, 10, 12), as well as unfaithful and unnamed opponents of the Pauline teaching, some of whom are Jewish Christians (Titus 1:10, 14–16; 1 Tim 1:3–7; etc.). A secular society, its rules, and even its rulers are in the author's peripheral vision (see Titus 1:12; 3:1; 1 Tim 1:9; 2:1–2; 6:15), and he senses their pressure on and scrutiny of Christian marriages and ministries (Titus 2:5, 8; 1 Tim 3:7), even of the conduct of Christian slaves (1 Tim 6:1).

A social description of the ecclesial communities presupposed by the PE indicates a clearly stratified social structure within them, a structure that the author generally perceives (on the model of the extended family in the Hellenistic and Roman world) as the household of the living God (1 Tim 3:15; Verner, *Household*), in other words, as the family to which God as Father gives life. Within that extended family (which need not be numerically large) are old and young; male and female; free and slave; married and single (including the widowed); parents and children; rich and poor; Jewish and pagan, all who have accepted faith in Christ and worship the one God through him. That faith and the worship it engenders are the keys for understanding the life of the church as the PE present it.

The adage has it, "The rule for praying is the rule for believing." The rule of faith in the PE is rooted in the liturgical acclamation and confession of the one and only God of Israel, "who wills that all human beings be saved" (see 1 Tim 2:3–7; Quinn, "Jesus as Savior"). God is seldom called Father in the PE (only in the opening blessing of each letter), and Jesus is never called the Son.

Still, what specifies the articulation of the faith in the PE and differentiates it from normative forms of Judaism is its attitude to Jesus, "risen from the dead, from the line of David" (2 Tim 2:8), who receives (as God does) the titles "our savior" and "Lord" (thus Titus 1:3–4; 1 Tim 1:2; 6:15; 2 Tim 1:18). He can be addressed directly in prayer (1 Tim 1:12; 2 Tim 1:18). In Titus 2:13 he is, almost certainly, "our great God" (Harris, "Titus 2:13"). As previously observed, no name occurs more often in the PE (thirty-two times) than Jesus Christ or Christ Jesus (Christ alone in 1 Tim 5:11).

From this faith in "the Man, Christ Jesus, who gave himself as a ransom for all" (1 Tim 2:5–6) derives the vision of the church's mission in the PE and their intense concern for prayers by believers for the unbelieving society around them (1 Tim 2:1–2; 4:10). In this setting of ecclesial prayer and mission a doctrine about the Holy Spirit has begun to take shape in the PE (Quinn, "Holy Spirit"). The Spirit appears to be involved in the words of prophecy (1 Tim 1:18; 4:1, 14), in the transmission of the words of apostolic teaching (2 Tim 1:14), and especially in the inspiration of the sacred written words of all scripture (2 Tim 3:15–16). Yet the only person to receive the title "prophet" is the pagan poet Epimenides (Titus 1:12). The liturgical actions of what we call baptism and ordination are more or less explicitly linked with the Spirit (Titus 3:5; 2 Tim 1:6–7; Reumann, *Righteousness*, pp. 234–235, 237–238 [J. Quinn]). Fragmentary citations of compositions that may have emanated from liturgies of marriage, reconciliation (2 Tim 2:25–26), and possibly even the Eucharist (1 Tim 2:1; 4:4–5; Hanson, *Studies*, pp. 97–109), though they contain no reference to the Spirit, witness to the inclusive ecclesial vision that inspired the liturgical texts cited by the PE.

This ecclesial vision of the PE includes an eschatological aspect, which is also revealed by the Spirit; these days are the last days (1 Tim 4:1; 2 Tim 3:1). The prayers of these letters set one's hope on life eternal, which has begun in this last age (Titus 1:2; 2:12; 1 Tim 4:8) but will reach its consummation on "that Day" (2 Tim 1:12, 18; 4:8) when Jesus appears in glory (Titus 2:13; 1 Tim 6:14) as judge of "the living and the dead" (2 Tim 4:1). Paul prays for the Lord's mercy on that judgment day upon a fellow Christian, apparently deceased, who had been kind to him (2 Tim 1:16–18; see 4:19); he leaves a still living coppersmith called Alexander to the Lord to be judged according to his works, which are bad (2 Tim 4:14–15). Belief in the final judgment is closely linked to that in the final resurrection (cf. Titus 3:5 with 2 Tim 2:17–19), though the PE do not emphasize the latter as such. Eternal life will consist in living with Christ, sharing his reign (2 Tim 2:10–12), and thus receiving "the crown of the upright life" (2 Tim 4:8) from him.

The PE have passing references to the angelic orders (1 Tim 3:16 may refer to the apostolic "messengers" of the resurrection). "The elect angels" of 1 Tim 5:21, loyal to God, stand in contrast to spirits and demons that inspire false doctrines (1 Tim 4:1). The devil or Satan is perceived as implicated in certain activities for which believers face condemnation (1 Tim 1:20; 3:6–7; 5:15; 2 Tim 2:26).

This rule for faith expresses itself in the order for public worship that the PE presume. A strong sense of community pervades the correspondence (first-person plural pronouns are frequent), and the directives about assemblies for worship emphasize the groups involved. Thus the men are distinguished from the women in 1 Tim 2:8–10; the wives from women in general in verses 11–15. Various groups of ministers can be discerned (see below). The place for worship is not described. One infers from the paraenesis addressed to well-to-do believers (1 Tim 6:6–10, 17–19) that the wealthy man or woman, married or widowed, offered his or her house for the liturgical assemblies and perhaps hospitality to itinerant apostolic ministers as well as to some indigent Christians (Titus 3:13–14; 1 Tim 5:10, 16; 2 Tim 1:18; 4:13, 19). Such a "house church" might be limited to one (extended) family; it could scarcely accommodate an assembly of more than a few dozen persons for worship. As numbers increased, more homes would be the sites for separate assemblies. It is conceivable that a group of believers who were wholly of Jewish origin might have retained their own Jewish place of liturgical assembly, a larger home or a small building (*proseuche*), for their Jewish prayer, which was now in the process of becoming identifiably Christian.

If the place for worship, as the PE envision it, is elusive, the setting in time is irrecoverable. There is no evidence for the hour of the day or the day of the week favored by these congregations for their public worship, though the silence could be taken as willingness to tolerate worship on the Sabbath (because other Jewish practices are explicitly criticized). "The widow proper . . . stays on night and day in entreaties and prayers" (1 Tim 5:5), a turn of phrase that suggests the Jewish way of reckoning the day from sunset to sunset. A hint at a ritual order for worship in 1 Tim 4:13 evinces no concern that it be observed by all congregations. The only ceremonial observance that the PE proffer as specific to their (Pauline) practice is that a wife does not teach or direct her husband in the liturgical assemblies (1 Tim 2:12).

The practical, day-to-day conduct of all believers is, for the PE, an integral part of their faith and worship, to such an extent that "the rule for praying" is the rule for action. The faith that expresses itself publicly in worship to God also expresses itself publicly in "fine works," *erga kala,* by which is meant not simply good deeds (*agatha;* 1 Tim 2:10) but visibly and attractively good actions (Titus

13

2:7, 14; 3:8, 14; etc.). From these actions unbelievers can get a glimpse of the power of the gospel and its grace, delivering from bad acts (Titus 2:11–12; 3:3–7), enabling believers to take their share in the suffering and death of Jesus (2 Tim 1:8; 2:11–12) and "to live in a sensible, honest, godly way in this present age." As there is a strong accent on the community in worship in the PE, so there is a corresponding emphasis on the exemplary conduct of the baptized as "a people of his [God's] very own, enthusiastic for fine deeds" (Titus 2:14) and on the conduct of people in various groups or classes or orders within the body of the faithful. The household codes urge certain types of action upon various age groups, both according to their sex and according to their legal status as slave or free (thus Titus 2:2–10; cf. 1 Tim 5:1–2; 6:1–2). Similarly, the conduct of the aspirants to the presbyteral, diaconal, and widow's ministries is prescribed with a view to the group or order to which they will pertain. In contrast, the qualifications for the candidate for bishop are always in the singular and envision him as an individual (1 Tim 3:1b–7 and perhaps Titus 1:6–9). Yet even he is in his class a typical figure, as are the Paul, the Titus, and the Timothy of this correspondence (2 Tim 3:10–11; Titus 2:7–8; 1 Tim 1:16; 4:12).

Ethical conduct is urged on believers (whether addressed as individuals or as members of the orders or classes of persons within the community) as an essential part of their missionary witness to the ambient Hellenistic world. Ethical questions attracted popular interest in that society, and philosophers lectured about moral issues on the streets and in the baths. The ancient Greek drama had a powerful popular influence often overlooked in this regard: the plays, particularly those of Euripides and Menander, kept ethical debates constantly before the eyes of the populace. Thus when the PE observe "that law is not laid down for an upright person" (1 Tim 1:9), they are speaking not only the language of the Greek philosophical tradition but also that of the Greek New Comedy (Reumann, *Righteousness*, p. 236 [J. Quinn]; see the bibliographical key at the end of these volumes under Menander). The list of vicious persons that follows (1 Tim 1:9–10) reminds the reader not only of the decalogue but also of the acts that destroy the characters in Greek tragedy.

Finally, for the PE, "the rule for praying" is the rule for leadership. The approach of these letters to the conduct of apostolic ministers is typological. It is significant that, in this typology, persons (in the fullest sense of that term, which designates not only what an individual is but also what he has done) precede what we call "office" or "function." Paul is a "model of" and a "model for those who are going to believe in him [i.e., Jesus] for eternal life" (1 Tim 1:16; see 2 Tim 1:13). His individual teaching, his experience of the will of Christ, his sufferings, his way of living define what it means to be an apostle. He does not fit an a priori abstract definition of an apostle; he personally defines what the term signals. As Paul is the apostle for the PE, so he is the teacher with one coherent teaching about how the believer lives according to the word of God. In contrast, the PE hear the plurals "teachers" and "teachings" (2 Tim 4:3; 1 Tim

14

4:1) in a bad sense (Quinn, "Terminology," p. 235). Paul also functions as a prophet without being named as such, as he builds up, exhorts, and consoles his correspondents (see 1 Cor 14:3). Still, there is no evidence that the author of the PE remembered (much less tried to perpetuate) a tripartite local leadership called apostles, prophets, and teachers (1 Cor 12:28).

Titus and Timothy are in a true sense Paul's "children" (see Titus 1:4, 1 Tim 1:2, 18; etc.), and the dying patriarch directs his last will and testament to the latter as his heir. He who, by Paul's choice (and that choice appears to be the all-important factor) shared Paul's ministry during the apostle's life, will continue to do so after Paul's death. For the PE Titus and Timothy are paradigmatic persons who furnish the pattern (Titus 2:7; 1 Tim 4:12) of what the continuing Pauline apostolate is and does. They are models of Paul and models for believers as they are designated to carry on the apostle's work, carry out his commands, imitate his sufferings, teach his gospel and practice it themselves, preside at the liturgy, receive material support for their ministerial work, and choose other men who will in their turn share their apostolic ministry (see Titus 1:5; 1 Tim 1:3–6, 18–19; 4:12–16; 6:11–14; 2 Tim 1:6–14; 2:1–8; 3:10–17; 4:2–5).

Even the opponents envisioned by the PE (Karris, "Polemic") have a typological character, for to the extent that they are "anti-Paul" they are also "anti-Christ" (2 Tim 4:14); to the extent that their doctrines are opposed by the Holy Spirit they belong to unholy demons (1 Tim 4:1–2). The designation of some of the opposition by name in the PE (1 Tim 1:20; 2 Tim 1:15; 2:17; 4:14)—an unusual phenomenon in ancient Jewish and Christian polemic, which regularly demurred at granting that limited acknowledgment of existence to opponents (see Ign. *Smyrn.* 5.3)—underscores their typological function. The Pauline cadre of ministers and their teaching contrast sharply with the mob of competitors who have been making inroads on the house churches, perhaps particularly through wealthy patronesses (see Titus 1:11; 2 Tim 3:6–7) who shared their strong Jewish interests in "myths and endless genealogies" (cf. 1 Tim 1:4 with Titus 1:14; 3:9) as well as their quite un-Jewish rejection of marriage (1 Tim 4:3). Interest in emancipation from the constraints of domestic life seems to have played its part (see Titus 2:3–5; 1 Tim 2:11–15; 5:13–14). The key contention, however, of the opponents is "that the resurrection has already occurred" (2 Tim 2:18), a collapsed eschatology in which the future resurrection of all believers has been simply identified with Jesus' resurrection. A form of this oversimplified eschatology had already been bruited about Corinth in the mid-fifties (1 Cor 15:12).

Behind the figures of Paul, Titus, and Timothy in the PE stand the unnamed leaders of the churches, leaders whose prerequisite qualities, particularly in verifiably good conduct, are spelled out in lists of vices and virtues. Presumably the congregation participates in verifying such conduct and presenting suitable candidates to Titus and Timothy who, in virtue of the apostle's order, designate them for a Pauline ministry as they once were themselves designated (see Titus 1:5; 1 Tim 5:22; 2 Tim 1:6; 2:2). Prophetic oracles appear to have been traditional in the liturgical action surrounding some appointments (1 Tim 1:18; 4:14). Those appointed lead the worship of the community, teach, care for the temporalities, provide for the needy (see Titus 1:7–9; 1 Tim 3:2–10, 12–13; 5:17). Unmarried women (1 Tim 3:11) and widows (1 Tim 5:3–16) have their own qualifications to collaborate in some of these ministries. From the two church orders in 1 Tim the names of four groups or classes of ecclesial ministers appear (a representative of each in the Roman church may be sending a greeting in 2 Tim 4:21). A hint at the archaic Jewish-Christian origins of the ministers called "widows" and "presbyters" is that they are expected to receive financial support from believers, whereas the sources for the income of "bishop" and "deacons" are ignored (though they are not to be money-minded [1 Tim 3:3, 8; Titus 1:7] like the teachers who belong to the opposition [Titus 1:11]; see Theissen, *Setting*, pp. 27–67).

Titus envisions the establishment of Pauline ministers on Crete, perhaps combining the titles "presbyter" and "bishop" in order to designate them (no deacons or widows are mentioned). They are God's stewards (see Titus 1:7) for communities that appear to be small, independent house churches, dispersed throughout the many towns of the island (but not in the rural areas as such; Titus 1:5). If their members were of predominantly Jewish origin, with strong Jewish ties and interests, the enticements of anti-Pauline teachers "from the circumcision" (Titus 1:10) with consequent controversies about the function of the Mosaic Law in Christian life become understandable (Titus 3:9; see 3:13). Perhaps one should think of these congregations as typologically as one does "Titus" and the "presbyter-bishop." They represent in this construction the more archaic, Jewish-Christian congregations of the Christian movement being updated according to a Pauline model.

First Timothy envisions its text being read in a large metropolitan center, Ephesus (1 Tim 1:3). Apparently a significant number of the congregations are of predominantly Gentile origin, for Paul in the first church order in this letter (2:1–3:13) is emphatically "the Gentiles' teacher in faith and truth" (1 Tim 2:7; contrast 2 Tim 1:11). A bishop with deacons and women assistants presides over a house church with this background. The Qumran *mebaqqer*, "overseer," and his assistants offer a possible explanation of the quarter of the Jewish community in Palestine that gave rise to the Christian titles of bishop and deacon and their original functions. By contrast, the second church order of 1 Tim (5:1–6:2) envisions house churches of predominantly Jewish origin, in which the registered widows and ordained presbyters, who constitute a presbyteral body, a "presbytery" (1 Tim 4:14), are the key ministers. The abuses that have arisen in these orders and the set procedures for dealing with them give the impression that the Jewish-Christian house churches have been in existence somewhat longer than the predominantly Gentile congregations (though these too have their members of long standing; see 1 Tim 3:6). Again, like Crete with a congregation in each large town, Ephesus may be understood typologically: but it is any large, Greek-speaking metropolis of the latter first century in which more or less established congregations of Jewish and Gentile Christians live close to one another. First Timothy proposes a Pauline symbiosis for the different ways in which these groups of believers receive their guidance from those who direct their worship and works of charity.

HYPOTHESES TO EXPLAIN THE DATA

The PE, even in translation, differ notably from the other ten letters of the Pauline collection in the NT in their vocabulary and style, in their subject matter, in the development of their thought, in the settings presupposed. The other Paulines appear to be earlier, some of them much earlier, than the PE. If, however, the PE are approached from the very end of the first and beginning of the second centuries, from the ecclesial world of Clement, of Ignatius and Polycarp, of Hermas, the same documents appear to be very close indeed to the other Pauline letters (thus the commentaries of Barrett versus Kelly; but contrast Brox with Jeremias).

The PE tend to resist questions about their background and origin, about when they were composed, and by whom; from what place they were sent, to whom and where. The historical critical method gives these questions an urgency for present-day commentators that was not always present. All scholars of the PE draw inferences from practically the same concrete data in and about the letters, analyzing the linguistic, historico-sociological, and theological components of the correspondence. Yet these data have provoked the most dramatically different hypotheses to explain the origin and purpose of the PE.

The preceding overview of materials about the text, genre, and contents of the PE was arranged in a roughly descending order of the historical accessibility and certainty of the data. Now, in the light of these varied materials one can review the hypotheses that modern students of the PE construct to answer questions about the origin and purpose of these letters. Basically, these questions are five: Who was the author of the PE? When were they written? From what place were they dispatched? To whom and where were they sent? The answers to these questions have their part to play in understanding the purpose of the PE; why were they written?

"Who wrote the PE?" If one answers simply from what the text of the letters says, Paul is as much the author of them as he is of the other ten letters that begin with his name (thus the commentaries of Bernard, Guthrie, Spicq, and many more). Yet the language of this correspondence is notably different from that of the rest of the Paulines. On this basis, some have proposed that these letters were actually written by a member of the Pauline entourage and dispatched under Paul's authority at various times in the fifties and early sixties of the first Christian century (thus, in various forms, Jeremias, Kelly, Holtz, and Fee; see also the special studies by Dockx, *Chronologies;* Lestapis, *L'Enigme;* Reicke, "Chronologie"; W. Metzger, *Die letzte Reise;* and Prior, *Paul*). When an interest in gathering the apostle's correspondence began at the end of the first century, the PE were copied in a codex of Paul's letters to individuals along with Phlm, a letter with considerable similarities to other Pauline texts and a few to the PE. On this construction Paul is author of the PE because they were *authorized* by the apostle during his own ministry.

Other students of the PE submit that this hypothesis does not adequately account for the church orders and domestic codes cited in Titus and 1 Tim or for the ministerial orders discussed in the correspondence (not to mention the differences of language). Such phenomena seem to presume that a generation of Christian development and reflection has intervened between Paul's time and that of the PE.

The ancient conception of authorship was rather wider than ours. Even the epistolary genre and particularly the genre of the letter collection were not always taken as written by the person whose name stood at the head of these compositions. If the origin of the PE before the death of Paul is in fact indefensible, then it is conceivable that the letters were written in the second (70–100 c.e.) or even the third (100–130 c.e.) Christian generation.

Hypotheses have been advanced for each time frame. Walter Bauer (*Orthodoxy,* pp. 222–224) has even argued that the PE were written as a riposte to Marcion (see also F. Gealy, *Interpreter's Bible* 11.358–360). Helmut Koester (*HLEC* 2.305, 308) probably also sides with him. A date in the early second century and the third Christian generation is proposed (or presupposed) in the commentaries of Easton, Barrett, Dibelius and Conzelmann (D-C), Hanson, and Hultgren. A similar dating is found in other works from Harrison, *Problem,* through Campenhausen, "Polycarp," to Donelson, *Pseudepig.* There is a tendency to favor an origin at the turn of the first Christian century. The ecclesial ministries envisioned by the PE, described without sacral imagery, appear less clearly organized and rather less developed than those in *1 Clem.* and second-century Christian documents. Moreover, at least some, perhaps all (see Zuntz, *Text,* p. 279) of the other Pauline letters had been collected and were for the first time being cited as such by the authors in this third generation (beginning with *1 Clem.* in 96 c.e.). If the PE originated in the second century, it is striking that they, intent on transmitting the Pauline heritage, do not quote the apostle's own words. At most one reads in several places two or three words running that appear to be slogans from a Pauline tradition; none of these slogans is a proper citation of one of his letters. Thus Titus 1:15 has "For the clean, all things are clean"; this is cited as if it were a proverb already in Rom 14:20.

The years from about 70 to 100 c.e. offer a time frame that allows for post-

Pauline ecclesial developments as well as some linkage with the Paul of history and his apostolate (including perhaps short dispatches that he had sent to his coworkers); thus W. Lock (*Commentary*, xxii, "between 60 and 90 is probable"; see Falconer, *PE*). This commentary favors 80–85 for the letters as we have them.

Some authors have been impressed by the linguistic and theological links between the PE and Luke–Acts. The NOTES and COMMENTS that follow call particular attention to the parallels in the Lukan corpus, so that the reader may judge for himself whether these links might reflect two different authors, both drawing on common first- and/or second-generation traditions; or, it may be—depending on the date assigned to Luke–Acts—whether the author of the PE had access to Luke–Acts or vice versa. Some scholars have hypothesized that one author was responsible for both Luke–Acts and the PE. Some moderns suggest that the author of Luke–Acts was Paul's amanuensis for the PE (Lock, *Commentary*, p. xxix; Moule, *Essays*, pp. 113–132; *Birth*, pp. 281–282; Strobel, "Schreiben des Lukas?"); another argues that they are quite separate compositions of the same author, written well into the second Christian generation (S. Wilson, *Lk PE*, with Marshall, "Review"); another has submitted that the PE were written by the author of Luke–Acts as the "third roll," intended to be read after the two volumes of Luke–Acts as an epistolary appendix that carried the narrative up to Paul's death (Quinn, *Perspectives*).

Those positing an author for the PE in the second Christian generation point to a variety of data. The emphatic apologia for Paul offered by the PE fits the decades immediately after his execution. The apostle had died as a Roman citizen subject to Roman law. There was an understandable tendency among believers, due to the shame of his end as a criminal, to play down the person of the apostle, his ministry, and his teaching (which had been controversial in the first place). Whoever wrote the PE wants to counter that tendency. Moreover, for the PE, Jewish Christianity is still a live option. House churches are still being established for Jewish Christians and are growing. Their relation with the Pauline apostolate and doctrine must still be worked out in practice. By the end of the first century, however, large-scale conversion from Judaism had dwindled and Jewish-Christian house churches were withering on the vine.

Still, if this correspondence was composed in the second Christian generation, why are there three letters? One might have sufficed. The genre of letter collections suggests the answer. Various churches in the second generation knew they had received letters from Paul. This correspondence as a whole was yet to be collected (Dahl, "Particularity"; B. Metzger, *Canon*, pp. 257–261). The PE as a collection would have been received and read not as individual letters from the Paul of history but as a "characterization" of the great apostle and his teaching for the new generation.

The original order of the letters within the collection is probably that in which Titus leads off, followed by 1 Tim and then 2 Tim. The elaborate, sixty-six-word epistolary prologue of Titus 1:1–4 sounds like a preface to the collection, not only to the short letter that follows. At the same time, 1 and 2 Tim complement each other, and a final position for the epistolary testament of 2 Tim is evidently appropriate (Quinn, *Perspectives*, pp. 63–64). Titus does more in its initial position than introduce on a small scale the themes that 1 Tim then expands at length. The house churches envisioned by Titus take first place in this collection not because they are small and relatively isolated but because they are predominantly Jewish-Christian. The Pauline proclamation of the gospel in the previous generation had been "to everyone who believes"; but that universal proclamation involved a divinely willed priority, "to the Jew first and also to the Greek" (Rom 1:16 [*RSV*]; see 2:9–10). The PE preserve this priority in their positioning of Titus before 1 Tim (where the house churches appear to be of predominantly pagan origin and Paul is explicitly "the Gentiles' teacher" [1 Tim 2:7]).

Where were the PE composed? Titus and 1 Tim profess to have been sent while the apostle was on a journey that extended from the island of Crete past Ephesus, with Macedonia and eventually Nicopolis in Epirus as his goal; 2 Tim claims a Roman setting. If the letters originated as a collection in the second Christian generation, the data admit of several reconstructions. Some have proposed that Asia Minor and specifically Ephesus, the destination proposed by the text of the PE for the correspondence with Timothy, were actually the letters' place of origin (most recently, the commentaries by Hanson and Hultgren). On this hypothesis an Ephesian leader with a deep attachment to the Pauline apostolate of the previous generation wrote the PE in the name of Paul to the Ephesian Christians. It is significant that, in this reconstruction, the author of the correspondence proposes that this collection comes not only from Paul but from Rome.

It is also possible that the PE actually derive from the Roman church, where an author composed the collection to rehabilitate the apostle martyred in that city of which he was legally a citizen and to propose him as a teacher for the urban churches of the whole central Mediterranean area, whether the congregations be Jewish or pagan in origin. This proposal emphasizes the elements in the PE that reflect the archaic, Jewish-Christian organization of the Roman church, its Greek language, and its interests as they are documented from Rom and Acts through *1 Clem.* and Hermas (see Brown and J. Meier, *Antioch/Rome;* Penna, "Juifs/Ebrei" and "Configurazione"). The Pauline apostolate had been an urban mission, not a rural one (Meeks, *Urban,* 9–50). The roads that he had traversed all led to the *Urbs* of late antiquity, the city of Rome, its influence palpable in every other city of the empire. If the imperial *Urbs* had executed Paul, the Roman Christians were determined to keep his apostolate alive. It is appropriate on this hypothesis that Rome was the place in which letter collections had become popular and the codex had its origin.

To whom were the PE sent and to what destination(s)? Possible answers were implicit in the preceding discussion. Now they can be marshaled explicitly. According to the hypothesis of the origin of the PE before Paul's martyrdom, the Titus whom we know from Gal and 2 Cor and the Timothy whom we encounter in the rest of the Paulines as well as in Acts are the recipients of these letters, on the island of Crete and in Ephesus, respectively.

If the PE appeared after Paul's death, not only Titus and Timothy but also the places to which the letters are addressed may have a typical or representative function. Thus the many small congregations on "Crete" seem to be conceived of as comparatively new Jewish-Christian churches, and accordingly "Titus" transmits and represents what Paul has to contribute to the organization and formation of such congregations. In 1 Tim, Paul is emphatically "a herald and apostle—it is a fact though it sounds incredible—the Gentiles' teacher in faith and truth" (2:7). In this perspective, "Ephesus" stands for the result of the great Pauline mission in the metropolis of Asia Minor; some of these metropolitan congregations have a majority of members who are of pagan origin, others are predominantly Jewish-Christian house churches; "Timothy, his [Paul's] true child in faith" (1:2), visibly joins these groups of congregations within a large urban center with the Pauline family of churches. In the Pauline last will and testament of 2 Tim, the addressee is heir to the apostolic inheritance, the "deposit" (1:11–12) of Paul's teaching as well as his mission to "all of the pagans" (4:17). One might hazard that the Christian congregations in Rome, whether of Jewish or of pagan origin, were the actual models for the paradigmatic congregations of the PE.

THE PURPOSE OF THE PE

Why were the PE written? Although one would have to nuance the purpose differently according to each hypothesis submitted above, whether one or all of these letters originated at the end of the first Christian generation or at the beginning of the second generation they aim at providing continuity in the apostolic and ecclesial mission of bringing *all* persons, Jew and Gentile, slave and free, male and female, old and young to faith in and worship of Jesus. They emphasize the links of Christians with their past, with the Scriptures of the OT, with Jewish ethics and family practices, with the Pauline apostolate and its teaching, with the ambient Hellenistic and Roman culture from which they all came. The letters also emphasize the links among Christians and the symbiotic unity that ought to characterize believers here and now. They not only score divisive persons but also positively urge a common Pauline faith and worship, a Pauline ethic, and Christian ministries that accord with Pauline precedents. The PE further intend to prepare Christians for the future, a future that in fact found the "catholic church" and the catholic canon of Scripture pitted against the gnostics and the followers of Marcion. But the PE have their eye on a present Christian continuity with another future. " 'Godliness is useful for everything, because it contains the promise of a life that is now and that is going to be.' This is the Christian message, meant to be believed and worth welcoming wholeheartedly" (1 Tim 4:8–9).

THE ANCHOR BIBLE TRANSLATION OF

TITUS, 1 TIMOTHY, AND 2 TIMOTHY

◆

To Titus

◆

I. An Apostle's Greeting (1:1–4)

1 ¹Paul, slave of God, yet apostle of Jesus Christ, for the faith of God's elect and for full and godly knowledge of the truth, ²in hope of life eternal which the God who is without deceit promised from all eternity ³(in due time he made his message clear of course in a proclamation I was entrusted with, at the order of our savior, God) ⁴writes this to Titus, his true child, for the faith all share. Grace and peace from God the Father and Christ Jesus, our savior.

II. The Apostolic Commission to Titus (1:5–3:11)
II.A. For Ministry and Magisterium (1:5–16)
II.A.1. The Appointment of Ministers (1:5–9)

1 ⁵The reason that I let you remain on Crete was to set right the remaining matters and to establish presbyters in every city as I myself commanded you. ⁶Every one of them ought to be

> unimpeachable,
> a husband to one wife,
> with children who are believers,
>> who cannot be charged with debauchery,
>> who are not refractory.

⁷Indeed a bishop has to be

> unimpeachable
>> (God's steward, so to speak),
> not arrogant,
> not irritable,
> not a drinker,
> not a bully,
> not money-minded.

[8]Rather he must be one who likes guests,

> likes goodness,
> who is sensible,
>> upright,
>> devout,
>> self-controlled,

[9]who sticks to the message that is meant to be believed, according to the teaching, so that he can both encourage with wholesome apostolic instruction and refute opponents.

II.A.2. True and False Teaching (1:10–16)

1   [10]Indeed there are many, particularly among the Jewish Christians, who are refractory, spouting nonsense and seducing minds: [11]these people must be muzzled, for they are the kind who teach things they ought not and overturn entire households, for their own financial gain, shame to say.

[12]A countryman of theirs, a prophet of their own, said:

> Liars ever, men of Crete,
> Nasty brutes that live to eat.

[13]This is truthful testimony, and good reason to refute them sharply, so that they may recover their health in the faith [14]instead of doting on Jewish tales and commandments of people who are abandoning the truth. [15]For the clean, all things are clean. For the polluted and the unbelievers, however, nothing is clean. Rather, their very way of thinking and their conscience have been polluted. [16]God they profess to know but by their deeds they disown him. They are disobedient abominations, counterfeiters of all excellent deeds.

II.B. For the People of God (2:1–3:11)

II.B.1. Teaching for Diverse Groups of Believers (2:1–10)

2   [1]Now you, Titus, are to speak of matters that suit our wholesome instruction.

[2]Thus older men are to be

> temperate,
> serious,
> sensible,

robust in faithfulness,
>in charity,
>in steadfastness.

[3]Older women, similarly, are to be as reverent in demeanor as priests, not devils at gossip, not slaves to drink. They are the right teachers [4]for spurring on younger women

to love their husbands,
to love children,
[5]to be sensible;
>chaste;
>tending the hearth;
>considerate;
>subject to the authority of their own husbands;

so that the message of God not be defamed.

[6]Encourage the young men, similarly, to use common sense [7]in all matters (given that you proffer yourself as

a pattern in fine deeds;
openhanded with the instruction;
a reverent man,
[8]wholesome in preaching,
irreproachable,

so that the opponent, able to muster nothing bad to say about us, will be embarrassed).

[9]Slaves are to be subject to their masters in all matters, aiming to please them, not to oppose them, [10]not to pilfer. Rather they are to give such good evidence of complete reliability that they add luster in every way to the instruction of our savior, God.

II.B.2.   The Faith, Matrix of Christian Living (2:11–14)

2   [11]Revealed was the grace of God for the rescue of all human beings. [12]It disciplines us to disown godlessness and worldly lusts, and to live in a sensible, honest, godly way in this present age [13]as we wait for the blessed hope revealed in the glory of Jesus Christ, our great God and savior. [14]He laid down his life for us, to set us free from every wrong and to cleanse for himself a people of his very own, enthusiastic for fine deeds.

II.B.3.   The Baptismal Life (2:15–3:11)

II.B.3.a.   Obedience Versus Disobedience: Present
Versus Past (2:15–3:2)

2   ¹⁵These are the things to speak of, Titus, in as commanding a way as possible, whether you are encouraging or refuting. Let no one slight you. 3   ¹Remind these Jewish Christians

to be subject to government authorities,
to accept direction,
to be ready to take any honest work.
²They are not to insult anyone,
    not to be argumentative.
They are to be gentle,
    to show every consideration to every person.

II.B.3.b.   The Baptismal Event (3:3–8a)

3   ³After all, we were once

fools ourselves,
disobedient,
deluded,
slaving for diverse lusts and pleasures,
in malice and jealousy spending our days,
detested,
hating one another.

⁴"When the humane munificence of our savior, God, was revealed, ⁵he saved us, no thanks to any upright deeds that we performed ourselves but because of his own mercy, saved us through a washing of regeneration and of renewal by the Holy Spirit ⁶that he poured out lavishly on us, through Jesus Christ, our savior. ⁷God's was the grace that made us upright, so that we could become heirs with a hope of life eternal." ⁸ªThat is the Christian message, meant to be believed.

II.B.3.c.   True and False Instruction (3:8b–11)

3   ⁸ᵇI wish you, Titus, to insist on these matters, so that those who have put their faith in God will be intent on "taking the lead in fine deeds." Activity like that is fine and useful for people.
⁹On the other hand, steer clear of foolish speculations, of genealogies, of

controversies, of wranglings about the Law. Such activities are useless and fruit-less. ¹⁰Give the divisive man one warning, then a second. Don't see him again, ¹¹for you can be sure a man like that has turned sour and keeps on sinning as he brings on his own condemnation.

III. Personal Notes (3:12–15a)

III.A. Decisions and Directives (3:12–14)

3 ¹²As soon as I send Artemas to you, Titus, or perhaps Tychicus, do your best to come to me at Nicopolis, for I have decided to spend the winter there. ¹³Do all you can to speed the journey of Zenas the lawyer, and Apollos, with all their needs satisfied. ¹⁴Thus let our own people too learn what it means "to take the lead in fine deeds" with regard to the urgent necessities of life, so that they will not be fruitless.

III.B. Greetings (3:15a)

3 ¹⁵ᵃAll who are here with me join in greeting you affectionately, Titus. Greet those who in faith are friends of ours.

IV. Final Prayer (3:15b)

3 ¹⁵ᵇGrace be with all of you.

To Timothy (1 Tim)

♦

I. An Apostle's Greeting (1:1–2)

1 ¹Paul, apostle of Christ Jesus, at the order of God, our savior, and of Christ Jesus, our hope, ²writes this to Timothy, his true child in faith. Grace, mercy, peace from God the Father and Christ Jesus, our Lord.

II. The Apostolic Commission to Timothy: Part One (1:3–3:13)
II.A. Apostolic Commands (1:3–20)
II.A.1. Heterodoxy (1:3–7)

1 ³It was at my explicit encouragement while I was en route to Macedonia that you, Timothy, stayed on in Ephesus. My purpose was that you charge certain people not to propound strange teachings, ⁴not to dote on tales and endless genealogies that can only proffer lucubrations instead of God's own plan that one receives in faith. ⁵The goal of your charge and mine is, rather, charity arising from a clean heart and from a clear conscience and from a faith unfeigned. ⁶Some people, once they have deviated from these, have slipped off into mere chattering. ⁷They want to be "rabbis" but they have no idea either of what they are saying or of the things that they insist on.

II.A.2. Orthodoxy (1:8–17)
II.A.2.a. Paul on Law (1:8–11)

1 ⁸Fine as we know the Law is, there is still the question of one's using it lawfully. ⁹That involves knowing that law is not laid down for an upright person; rather it is for lawless and refractory persons,

for godless people and sinners,
for the unholy and profane,
for patricides and matricides,
for murderers,

¹⁰for the incestuous,
for homosexuals,
for slave traders,
for liars,
for perjurers;

—and anything else that stands opposed to the wholesome instruction ¹¹that accords with the gospel I was entrusted with, the good news of the glory of the blessed God.

II.A.2.b. Paul at Prayer (1:12–17)

1   ¹²I give thanks to Christ Jesus, our Lord,

who put his strength in me
  because he regarded me as trustworthy
    and placed me in his ministry,
      ¹³a man who was formerly
      a blasphemer
      and a persecutor
      and insanely arrogant.
But mercy found me out
  because I did not know what I was doing
  in my unbelief.
¹⁴Still the grace of our Lord superabounded
  along with that faith and charity,
    which come from union with Christ Jesus.
¹⁵The Christian message,
  meant to be believed
  and worth welcoming wholeheartedly,
    is "Christ Jesus came into the world to
    save sinners."
    Among them I have first place.
¹⁶But for this very reason mercy found me out,
  so that Christ Jesus could evidence patience
  to the utmost,
    using me as a model of those who are
    going to believe in him for eternal life.
¹⁷So to the king of eternity,
  the immortal, invisible, only God,
    are the honor and glory for all eternity.
    Amen.

THE LETTER TO TITUS

II.A.3. Timothy's Task (1:18–20)

1 ¹⁸This is the charge I am setting out before you, Timothy, my child, a charge that accords with the prophecies that conducted us to you in the first place. They were given to help you campaign the fine campaign, ¹⁹with faithfulness and a clear conscience. Certain people, once they spurned their conscience, went on to shipwreck in their faith. ²⁰Among their number were Hymenaeus and Alexander, whom I handed over to Satan to teach them a lesson for having insulted God.

II.B. Apostolic Exhortations (2:1–3:13)
II.B.1. Prayer and Worship (2:1–3:1a)
II.B.1.a. For Whom and Why (2:1–7)

2 ¹Now I urge, first of all, that entreaties, prayers, intercessions, thanksgivings be made for all human beings, ²for kings and all in high station. Our purpose is to spend a tranquil and quiet existence in an altogether godly and reverent way. ³This is an excellent thing and welcome in the eyes of our savior God, ⁴who wants all human beings to be saved and to come to full knowledge of the truth, ⁵which amounts to this:

> God is one;
> One also is the mediator of God and human beings;
> the Man,
> Christ Jesus,
> ⁶who gave himself as a ransom for all;
> The testimony to this has occurred in due time.

⁷For that testimony I was appointed a herald and apostle—it is a fact though it sounds incredible—the Gentiles' teacher in faith and truth.

II.B.1.b. By Whom and How (2:8–3:1a)

2 ⁸Now my wish is that the men take part in the prayer "in every place" of worship, that they lift up hands that are holy, that they be without wrath and resentment.

⁹Similarly, I also wish the women to make themselves attractive in a becoming costume, with sensible discretion. Their beauty is not in their coiffure and gold ornaments, or in their pearls or extravagant clothing, ¹⁰but it comes through their excellent deeds—that suits women who are professing real godliness.

[11]Let a married woman quietly learn in the assemblies for worship and quite obediently. [12]Moreover I do not allow a wife to teach in the public worship and to boss her husband. That is learning "quietly." [13]The reasons for my directive are that God fashioned Adam first, then Eve; [14]and furthermore that Adam was not fooled [by the serpent] but his wife was made a fool of and she turned to sin. [15]"A person will be saved rearing children, provided they persevere in faithfulness and charity and a sensible holiness." **3** [1a]That is the Christian message, meant to be believed.

II.B.2.　On the Ministers (3:1b–13)
II.B.2.a.　The Bishop (3:1b–7)

3　[1b]If anybody aspires to the episcopate, he sets his heart on fine work. [2]Thus a bishop has to be

> irreproachable,
> a husband to one wife,
> temperate,
> sensible,
> urbane,
> one who likes guests,
> a skilled teacher
> [3]not a drinker,
> not a bully,
> > but gentle,
> not argumentative,
> not one who likes money.

[4]He is to be outstanding in his direction of his own home, with children who are obedient and quite reverent. [5](For if anybody does not know how to direct his own home, how will he take care of God's church?) [6]He must not be a neophyte lest, inflated with vanity, he fall under the devil's condemnation. [7]But he must enjoy also a fine recommendation from outsiders, lest he fall into disgrace and a snare of the devil.

II.B.2.b.　The Deacons and Women Ministers (3:8–13)

3　[8]Similarly, deacons have to be

> serious persons,
> > not retailing gossip,
> > not addicted to heavy drinking,
> > not money-minded,

⁹but persons who hold the mystery of the faith with a clean conscience. ¹⁰Let them first be put to the test; then let those who are unimpeachable serve as deacons. ¹¹(Similarly, the women who are ministers have to be

> serious persons;
> not devils at gossip;
> temperate;
> believers in every sense.)

¹²Deacons are to be husbands of one wife, outstanding in the direction of their own children and homes. ¹³For men who give outstanding diaconal service gain a fine standing for themselves and a right to speak out for the faith that is theirs in Christ Jesus.

III. A Piece in Pause (3:14–4:5)
    III.A. Pauline Introduction (3:14–15)

3 ¹⁴I am putting these matters in writing for you, Timothy, though I still hope to come to you before long. ¹⁵Still, if I do delay, this letter will let you know how a person has to behave in God's house, which is the church of the living God. [There you, Timothy, are] a pillar and pedestal for the truth.

    III.B. Hymn (3:16)

3 ¹⁶And great is the mystery of godliness. There is no denying it!

> . . . He who was revealed in human flesh,
>   Was made victorious in the Spirit:
> He who was seen by God's messengers,
>   Was heralded to the pagans:
> He who was received in faith, in the world,
>   Was taken up in glory.

    III.C. Prophecy (4:1–5)
        III.C.1. Oracle (4:1)

4 ¹Here is the Spirit expressly declaring, "In these latter times some people, who dote on seductive spirits and demonic doctrines, will apostatize from the faith."

III.C.2. Interpretation of Oracle (4:2–5)

III.C.2.a. Doctrines of Opponents (4:2–3)

[2]These lying frauds, with their cauterized consciences, [3]interdict marriage and demand abstinence from foods, things that God created for believers and persons who have recognized the truth, to share in thankfully.

III.C.2.b. Refutation from Scripture (4:4–5)

[4]For everything in God's creation is fine and none is despicable when received with thanksgiving. [5]Every one of them is hallowed by God's word in Scripture and intercessory prayer.

IV. The Apostolic Commission to Timothy: Part Two (4:6–6:21a)

IV.A. As Apostolic Teacher (4:6–16)

IV.A.1. Personally (4:6–10)

4 [6]When you suggest matters such as the preceding to your brothers, Timothy, you will be a fine minister of Christ Jesus, yourself nourished on the words of the faith and of that fine instruction with which you are quite familiar. [7]Have nothing to do with profane old wives' tales. Train for action that aims at godliness. [8]"Whereas physical exercise is useful for a little, godliness is useful for everything, because it contains the promise of a life that is now and that is going to be." [9]This is the Christian message, meant to be believed and worth welcoming wholeheartedly. [10]Ultimately this promise is the reason for our job and our contest, that we have fixed our hope on the living God, savior of all, particularly of believers.

IV.A.2. For the Faithful (4:11–14)

4 [11]These are the matters, Timothy, to charge and to teach. [12]No one is to disdain you for your youth. Rather keep on being a pattern for believers—

in word,
in behavior,
in charity,
in faithfulness,
in purity.

[13]Until I arrive, concentrate on your public reading of the Scriptures, on your preaching, on your instruction. [14]Neglect not that gracious gift within you, the

one given to you under prophetic direction, with an imposition of the hands of the presbytery.

IV.A.3. Summary Exhortation (4:15–16)

4 ¹⁵Let these matters be your study. Be absorbed in them, so that your progress can be perceived by all. ¹⁶Pay attention to yourself and to your instruction. Persevere in these activities; for, if you do this, you will save both yourself and the persons listening to you.

IV.B. As Apostolic Supervisor (5:1–6:2)
IV.B.1. Domestic Code: Part One (5:1–2)

5 ¹Never scold an elderly man but keep encouraging him as if he were your own father. Encourage young men as if they were your own brothers; ²older women as mothers; young women as if your own sisters, in complete purity.

IV.B.2. The Order of Widows (5:3–16)

5 ³Honor the claims of widows who deserve that title.

⁴Thus, in the case of a widow who has children or grandchildren, they should be the first to learn the meaning of reverence for one's own home and of giving recompense to their forebears. For this is a welcome thing in the eyes of God [the Father].

⁵(The case is otherwise with the widow proper, one who is a completely destitute woman who has fixed her hope in God and stays on night and day in entreaties and prayers. ⁶A widow indulging herself voluptuously has died while still living. ⁷And charge them on these matters, so that they will be irreproachable.)

⁸In the case of a man who does not provide for his own people and particularly his immediate family, he has disowned the faith and is worse than an unbeliever.

⁹Follow these rules for enrolling a widow on the official roster: she must have lived no less than sixty years; she must have been a wife to one husband; ¹⁰she must have public attestation of fine deeds. Thus,

did she rear children?
did she welcome guests?
did she wash traveling Christians' feet?
did she come to the help of the oppressed?
did she set out to do every excellent deed possible?

[11]On the other hand, have nothing to do with the younger widows. The reason is that they want to remarry whenever they feel attractions that are incompatible with their commitment to Christ. [12]They stand condemned because they broke their previous pledge to him, [13]not to mention that, at the same time, they also learn how to be lazy while circulating from house to house, and not just lazy but gossips as well, saying what they have no right to say. [14]Now my wish is that younger widows remarry, rear children, run their homes, offer no pretext for reviling to the adversary, [15]for some of them have already slipped off after Satan.

[16]In the case of a woman who is a believer and who welcomes widows into her home, let her continue to come to their help and the local church not be burdened but free to help the widows proper.

IV.B.3.   The Order of Presbyters (5:17–25)

5   [17]The presbyters who have given outstanding direction deserve to get double pay, particularly those whose jobs are preaching and instruction; [18]for the Scripture says, "You shall not tie shut the mouth of the ox that is threshing grain" and "The workman is deserving of his wage."

[19]Do not give a hearing, Timothy, to a charge against a presbyter, unless the evidence comes from two or three witnesses. [20]Those who are sinning you are to refute while all of the presbyters look on, to put fear of wrongdoing into the rest of them.

[21]As God [the Father] and Christ Jesus and the elect angels look on, I adjure you, Timothy, to keep these directives without prejudice, that is, not doing anything out of partisanship.

[22]Be in no hurry, Timothy, to impose hands on anyone.

Incur no responsibility for the sins of others.
Keep yourself chaste.

[23]Drink only water no longer, but take wine, moderately, for your bad stomach and your frequent bouts with illness.

[24]The sins of some people are obvious enough, escorting them to judgment; others trail their sins behind them.

[25]Similarly also, fine deeds are obvious, and those that are not obvious cannot stay hidden always.

IV.B.4.   Domestic Code: Part Two (6:1–2)

6   [1]Those Christians who are bound in slavery are to regard their masters as deserving all esteem. Thus God's name and the instruction will not be defamed. [2]Moreover, slaves that have masters who are believers are not to disdain them.

After all, they are brothers. Instead they are to be even better slaves because they have masters who practice kindness as men who are believers and beloved.

These are things, Timothy, for you to teach and encourage.

IV.C.   In Relation to Problems (6:3–21a)

IV.C.1.   The Heterodox (6:3–5)

6   ³In the case of a man who propounds strange teachings and has no recourse to the wholesome sayings that come from our Lord, Jesus Christ, or to the godly instruction, ⁴one can only conclude that he has become a conceited ignoramus with a morbid craving for speculations and quibbling about terminology. These in turn produce

jealousy,
controversy,
vituperations,
vicious insinuations,
⁵the incessant bickerings of men
whose minds are a shambles and
who have been robbed of the truth;
they think godliness is a means
for gain.

IV.C.2.   Riches: Part One (6:6–10)

6   ⁶No question of it. Godliness brings gain, great gain—for someone contented with what he has. ⁷The reason is that we brought nothing into the world; as a result we cannot take anything out of it. ⁸So then if we have keep and covering, with them we shall be content. ⁹Those, however, who want to be wealthy topple into a temptation and a trap and multiple lusts, senseless and injurious, the kind that engulf people in utterly ruinous destruction. ¹⁰The root that lies under all evils is the love of money. Certain persons who have craved it have strayed off from the faith and have skewered themselves with multiple tortures.

IV.C.3.   An Ordination Charge (6:11–16)

6   ¹¹You, O man of God, must shun these things. Instead pursue

upright conduct,
godliness,
faithfulness,

38

charity,
steadfastness,
gentleness.

[12]Contend in the fine contest, the contest in the arena of faith. Lay hold on eternal life. You were called into that life and for it you made that fine profession before the eyes of many witnesses. [13]Before the eyes of the God who keeps all things alive and of Christ Jesus who publicly attested to the fine profession before Pontius Pilate I charge you [14]to keep the apostolic command beyond blemish, beyond reproach, until the revelation of our Lord, Jesus Christ. [15]That revelation God will make in due time, he who is

the blessed and only suzerain;
the king of those who act as kings
    and lord of those who act as lords;
[16]the only one who possesses immortality,
    who inhabits inaccessible light;
the one whom no human being ever saw
    or can see
to whom belong honor
    and might eternal.
Amen.

IV.C.4. Riches: Part Two (6:17–19)

6   [17]Timothy, charge the wealthy of the present age

not to be snobbish,
to have set their hope not on precarious wealth,
but on the God who lavishly provides
    everything for our satisfaction;
[18] charge them to do good;
to become wealthy in fine deeds;
to be munificent,
    sharing all around,
[19] making their deposits in an
        excellent fund for the future,
        so that they can lay hold
        on the life which deserves
        that name.

V.   Closing Summary (6:20–21a)

6   20O Timothy, keep what has been deposited with you. Keep your distance from the profane drivel and dialectic of so-called knowledge. 21aSome, who profess to have this at their disposal, have in fact deviated in their faith.

VI.   Final Prayer (6:21b)

6   21bGrace be with you all.

TO TIMOTHY (2 TIM)

◆

I. An Apostle's Greeting (1:1–2)

1 ¹Paul, apostle of Christ Jesus, by the will of God and for the sake of the promise of life that is in Christ Jesus, ²writes this to his dear child, Timothy. Grace, mercy, peace from God the Father and Christ Jesus, our Lord.

II. Thanksgiving Prayer (1:3–14)
II.A. The Past (1:3–5)

1 ³I give thanks to the God whom I, like my forebears, worship with a clean conscience, as I make unceasing mention of you in my entreaties, night and day. ⁴When I remember your tears, I yearn to see you and so to have my fill of joy. ⁵I have a reminder of your unfeigned faith, the very same as that which first dwelt in your grandmother, Lois, and in your mother, Eunice, and in you too, I am convinced.

II.B. The Present (1:6–12)

1 ⁶So I, with good reason, remind you, Timothy, to rekindle that gracious gift of God the Father, which is within you through the imposition of these hands of mine; ⁷for God gave us not a dastard spirit but one of dynamic strength and of charity and of discretion. ⁸May you not be ashamed about the testimony to our Lord or about me, his prisoner. Instead, along with me take your share of suffering for the gospel, as God gives the strength, ⁹the God who saved us and called us for a holy life. That saving call did not correspond to our deeds. It corresponded with his own design, his own grace, given us in Christ Jesus from all eternity. ¹⁰That gracious design, however, has now been made clear through the revelation of our savior, Christ Jesus. He broke the power of death. He made life and immortality shine forth through the gospel, ¹¹for which I in turn was appointed herald and apostle and teacher. ¹²Thus I, with good reason too, am undergoing these afflictions; but I am not ashamed of them, for I know the one

in whom I have put my faith and I am convinced that he has the power to keep for that Day what has been deposited with me.

II.C.   The Future (1:13–14)

1   ¹³With that faith and charity which are yours in Christ Jesus, stick to the model of the wholesome words that you heard from me. ¹⁴Keep that fine deposit, Timothy, through the Holy Spirit who dwells in us.

III.   Personal Note One (1:15–18)

1   ¹⁵You know this, of course, that all in the province of Asia—to name only Phygelus and Hermogenes—abandoned me. ¹⁶May the Lord, however, grant mercy to the family of Onesiphorus, for time and again he revived my spirits and was unashamed about this manacle on me. ¹⁷Instead, when he came to Rome he hunted for me right away and he found [me]. ¹⁸So may the Lord grant him to find—indeed he will find mercy from the Lord on that Day. And you know well enough how many services he provided in Ephesus.

IV.   Testament of Paul (2:1–4:8)
IV.A.   The Legator (2:1–13)

2   ¹Now, my child, find strength in that grace which is in Christ Jesus; ²and those things that you heard from me, through many witnesses, set out for trustworthy men, the kind who will also be competent to teach others. ³As a fine soldier of Christ Jesus take your share of suffering along with me. ⁴No one on active duty in the military gets involved in the business of civilian life. He avoids this to please the man who called him to arms. ⁵Moreover, take the case of a man who competes in the public games: he does not get the winner's crown if he does not compete according to the rules. ⁶Or again: the farmer on the job ought to be the first to have his share of the crops. ⁷Consider what I am saying here, Timothy; for in every way the Lord will grant you insight.
⁸Keep in mind Jesus Christ,

> risen from the dead,
> from the line of David.

That corresponds to my gospel ⁹for which I am being wronged, put into chains as though a wrongdoer—but the word of God has not been chained. ¹⁰For this very reason, that is, for the sake of the elect, I am submitting to everything. My purpose is that they too reach the salvation which is in Christ Jesus with eternal glory.

[11]The Christian message, meant to be believed, is this:

". . . for if we shared in his death,
  we shall share in his life.
[12]If we submit now,
  we shall share in his reign.
If we ever disown him,
  he is the one who will disown us.
[13]If we are faithless,
  he is the one who stays faithful,
  for he cannot possibly disown himself."

IV.B.   The Challengers Challenged (2:14–3:9)
      IV.B.1.   The Errors (2:14–26)

2   [14]Bring these matters to mind, Timothy, I adjure you, as God looks on. Shun quibbling over words—good for nothing except the utter ruin of the listeners. [15]Do your best to make yourself a fit offering to God, a workman who has no reason for shame, one who clears the way for the message of the truth. [16]Steer clear, however, of "profane drivel," for it progresses ever more deeply into godlessness [17]and its message spreads like gangrene. Take Hymenaeus and Philetus as examples. [18]It is men like those who have deviated in the truth when they say that the resurrection has already occurred, and so they overturn some people's faith.

[19]God's solid foundation stands, nevertheless, bearing this seal:

"The Lord knows those who are his,"
and
"Let everyone who names the Lord's name abandon wickedness."

[20]Still in any great house there are not only the utensils of gold and silver but also wooden ones and earthenware, for noble and ignoble purposes. [21]So if a person will only purge himself of that drivel, he will be a utensil for a noble purpose—

hallowed,
useful to the master,
ready for any excellent deed.

²²Shun juvenile desires. Rather, pursue

upright conduct,
faithfulness,
charity,
peace,

in company with those who invoke the Lord from a clean heart. ²³Steer clear, however, of foolish and undisciplined researches; as you are well aware, they breed only wranglings. ²⁴The Lord's slave ought not to wrangle. Instead, he has to be

gentle with all,
a skilled teacher,
forbearing,

²⁵considerate in correcting the unmanageable, just in case God may grant them a change of heart that will lead back into full knowledge of the truth. ²⁶Then their heads would clear and they would find their way "out of the snare of the devil in which he has been keeping them alive" and into the will of God himself.

IV.B.2. The Erring (3:1–9)

3 ¹Realize this, however, that in the last days rough times will be at hand; ²for then people will be

intent on themselves,
intent on money,
pretentious,
arrogant,
blaspheming;
to those who bore them,
   undutiful,
   ungrateful,
   irreligious,
   ³unaffectionate,
   irreconcilable;
devils at gossip,
   uncontrolled,
   uncouth,
   uncaring about goodness;
   ⁴renegade,

reckless,
conceited,
intent on pleasure
rather than intent on God.

⁵These people hold onto the appearance of godliness but they have repudiated its dynamic. Keep people like that at a distance too. ⁶For from their ranks come those who are worming their way into homes to captivate the little ladies,

loaded with sins
and driven by diverse cravings,
⁷ever learning
and never turning to full knowledge
of the truth.

⁸Just as once Jannes and Jambres defied Moses, so too these numbskulled counterfeiters of the faith are defying the truth, ⁹but they will not progress far. Their own stupidity is going to become just as obvious to everyone as the stupidity of those two.

IV.C.   The Legatee (3:10–4:8)
IV.C.1.   Paul's Life (3:10–13)

3   ¹⁰You, however, Timothy, were quite familiar

with the instruction,
with the approach to living,
with the design,
with the faithfulness,
with the patience,
with the charity,
with the steadfastness

that were mine, ¹¹along with the persecutions, with the sufferings, such as happened to me in Pisidian Antioch, in Iconium, in Lystra. What persecutions I bore! Still, from all of them the Lord delivered me. ¹²Moreover, all who want to live in a godly way in Christ Jesus will be persecuted. ¹³However, vicious people and charlatans will progress—from bad to worse, deluding and deluded.

IV.C.2.   Timothy's Imitation of Paul (3:14–4:4)

3   ¹⁴You, however, Timothy, persevere in the things you learned and became sure of. You are well aware of the people you learned from ¹⁵and that from your

45

tenderest years you have known the sacred letters which have the power to make you astute in attaining salvation through faith which comes from union with Christ Jesus. [16]All the Scripture is inspired by God and useful

> for instruction,
> for censuring,
> for straightening people out,
> for giving training in upright conduct,

[17]so that the man of God may be complete, that is, completely equipped for every excellent deed.

4 [1]As God the Father looks on, and Christ Jesus who is going to judge the living and dead, I adjure you, Timothy, while bearing witness to his revelation and his kingdom:

> [2]herald the message;
> stand on the alert, when convenient,
>   when inconvenient;
> refute;
> reprove;
> encourage—

with the utmost patience in the task of teaching. [3]For there will come a time when they will not put up with this wholesome instruction. Instead, they will load themselves with teachers who answer their craving to get relief for their itchy ears. [4]Furthermore, as they turn a deaf ear to the truth, they will slip off after tales.

IV.C.3. Paul's Death (4:5–8)

4 [5]You, however, Timothy,

> keep calm, in every sense;
> accept being wronged;
> do the work of one who announces the gospel;
> carry out fully the ministry that is yours.

[6]For now my own blood is to spill as a wine-offering. The time set for my embarkation has come. [7]I have contended in the fine contest. I have run the whole track. I have kept faith. [8]Whatever happens there lies in store for me the crown of the upright life with which the upright Judge, the Lord, will recompense me on that Day—and of course not only me but all who have their hearts set on his revelation.

V.   Personal Note Two (4:9–21)

   V.A.   News for Timothy (4:9–15)

4   9Do your best to come here soon; 10for Demas, his heart set on this present world, left me helpless and set out for Thessalonika. Crescens has gone to Gaul; Titus, to Dalmatia. 11Only Luke is with me now. Pick up Mark and bring him along with you, for he can be helpful to me in my ministry. 12I have appointed Tychicus to go to Ephesus.

   13When you come, bring along that cape which I left behind in Troas at Carpus's home—and bring the books, too, particularly the notebooks. 14There in Troas Alexander, the coppersmith, brought many false charges against me. (The Lord will give him the recompense that corresponds to his deeds.) 15Watch out for him yourself now, because his defiance of our words was frenzied.

   V.B.   Paul at Law (4:16–18)

4   16At my first appearance in court no one was on my side; instead, all left me helpless. (May it not be held against them!) 17Still the Lord stood by me and put his strength in me, so that through me the proclamation would be carried out fully, or, in other words, so that all the pagans would listen to it, and I was delivered "from the lion's mouth." 18The Lord will deliver me from every one of these vicious attacks and he will save me for his kingdom, in heaven. To him, the glory for all eternity. Amen.

   V.C.   Pauline Greetings to Ephesus (4:19–21a)

4   19Greet Prisca and Aquila and the family of Onesiphorus.   20Erastus stayed on in Corinth. I had to leave Trophimus behind in Miletus when he fell ill. 21aDo your best to come here before winter.

   V.D.   Roman Greetings (4:21b)

4   21bEubulus sends along greetings to you, Timothy, as do Pudens and Linus and Claudia and all our brothers.

VI.   Final Prayers (4:22)

4   22The Lord be with your spirit, Timothy. Grace be with you all.

Notes and Comments on the Letter to Titus

♦

OUTLINE OF TITUS

SUMMARY OF THE LETTER

The PE come to us as a collection of correspondence that opens with a letter under the name of Paul to his collaborator, Titus. The individual, personal relation of the apostle to his coworker is the frame within which is sketched a Pauline policy and program for predominantly Jewish-Christian congregations, of which the churches on Crete are paradigms (see the INTRODUCTION to this volume).

The long, solemn greeting and blessing for Titus, which serves to open not only this letter but also the whole roll of correspondence, contains a descriptive definition of the apostolic task divinely imposed on Paul (Titus 1:1–4). The body of the letter (1:5–3:11) then articulates the apostle's commission to the colleague who shares in and carries out the Pauline apostolate, as a man's son carries on the name and work of his father.

The first series (1:5–16) of orders from Paul centers on the establishment of presbyteral-episcopal ministers in the cities of Crete. The qualifications of candidates for this work are sketched through catalogs of vices and virtues (1:5–9). The list concludes pointedly with the requirement that these men be responsible, convincing teachers. The description that follows (1:10–16) offers the reason for that insistence. Certain Jewish-Christian teachers are perverting the consciences of their fellow believers. The new Pauline teachers must stop them.

The second part of the body of this letter (2:1–3:11) again addresses Titus explicitly, giving him Pauline directives for the whole people of God. A domestic code (2:2–10) supplies the grid for instructing various groups within the Jewish-Christian congregation: older men and women, younger women and men (including Titus himself), the Christian slaves.

The visibly good and attractive lives of God's household are a revelation to all people of the blessing that the crucified savior has in store for those who put their faith in him (2:11–14).

Titus must confront the present Jewish-Christian troublemakers (2:15–3:11) with their disobedience and the reminder that they have relapsed into the vicious life that preceded baptismal rebirth. That event, as it was interpreted by the Pauline teaching, is to be the center of gravity in Titus's instruction. His time is to be spent encouraging the faithful to live out what they believe; he is to waste no time on theological cavils and quibbles. Two warnings for the troublemaker are enough.

As the composition closes (3:12–15a), a letter of introduction appears for the pair of missionaries who bear it, commending their cause to the support of their fellow Christians on Crete, whom the apostle greets through Titus. He is summoned to meet Paul at Actium (Nicopolis) as soon as his replacement from the Pauline entourage appears.

The plural address of the final prayer (3:15b) directly refers to all Cretan Christians. Paul's commission to one of his collaborators is intended to be "overheard" by the Cretan churches. The personal and the public aspects of this letter can be distinguished but not separated.

TO TITUS
I.   AN APOSTLE'S GREETING (1:1–4)

1   ¹Paul, slave of God, yet apostle of Jesus Christ, for the faith of God's elect and for full and godly knowledge of the truth, ²in hope of life eternal which the God who is without deceit promised from all eternity ³(in due time he made his message clear of course in a proclamation I was entrusted with, at the order of our savior, God) ⁴writes this to Titus, his true child, for the faith all share. Grace and peace from God the Father and Christ Jesus, our savior.

NOTES

1:1.   *Paul.* In the NT 128 out of 158 occurrences are in Acts, which also uses the name once for a person other than the apostle (Acts 13:7; see Haenchen, *Acts,* pp. 64, 398–400). Every document in the Pauline epistolary, including each of the PE, uses the name at least once. The only NT mention of Paul outside of Acts and the Pauline epistolary links his name with the apostle Simon Peter (2 Pet 3:15). The Ap. Frs. use the name only of the apostle, sometimes mentioning his correspondence too (thus *1 Clem.* 47.1; Ign. *Eph.* 12.2).

Neither the LXX nor *CII* contains the name "Paul," but it is frequently documented as a Roman surname (never a praenomen) in the Hellenistic world (see BAGD, s.v.; Preisigke, *Wörterbuch,* s.v.; MM s.v.; Hemer, "Name of Paul," pp. 179–183). For a Jewish use of the name in what are now entitled the *Acta Alexandrinorum,* see Musurillo, *Pagan Martyrs,* pp. 49–59, 179–194; Schürer, *HJP,* pp. 39–40; and Deissmann, *B St,* pp. 313–317, with his observations on the double form of the name *Saulos/Paulos* in Acts (BDF §53.2).

slave of God. Of the 124 NT uses of *doulos,* "slave," 30 are in the Pauline epistolary, including Titus 2:9; 1 Tim 6:1; and 2 Tim 2:24. *Doulos* occurs 29 times in Luke–Acts (compare 30 times in Matt, 5 in Mark, 11 in John). On the three NT uses of the feminine, *doulē,* see below.

The NT uses *theos* for God more than 1,300 times. With the article (see 1:2–3 below) it is regularly but not always understood as a personal name for the Father (see Rahner, "*Theos* in NT," pp. 79–148, esp. 143–144). The PE have

48 out of the 548 Pauline uses of *theos,* with 13 in Titus, 22 in 1 Tim, and 13 in 2 Tim. The occurrences cluster in Titus 1:1–4 and 2 Tim 1:1–8. The relative frequency of *theos* in Luke–Acts (almost 300 times) is notable.

The actual phrase, "slave of God," is used in the Paulines only here as a self-designation. Otherwise in the NT it occurs as a self-designation in Jas 1:1 (see Dibelius, *James,* pp. 65–66). For its use as a title bestowed by a divining spirit on Paul, Silas, and Luke (?), see Acts 16:17. It designates Christians in general in 1 Pet 2:16 and Rev 7:3, and Moses in Rev 15:3. The feminine *doulē kyriou* occurs in the NT only as Mary's self-designation (Luke 1:38; 48, where *autou* = *kyrios/theos* of 46–47). The only other NT use of the feminine is in Acts 2:18 (see LXX Joel 3:2), where the plural is parallel to the masculine *doulous* in a passage that explains why all God's people, regardless of sex, receive the Spirit. The LXX seldom uses the phrase.

The phrase *ʽbd ʾl* (*ʾlhym*) has not thus far turned up in Qumran. Philo uses the phrase *ton tou theou doulon* (*Quis her.* 7; see *Mig.* 45; *Mut.* 46) with a certain sense of inevitability that derives from his Jewish belief in creation and a reluctance that derives from the Greek ideal of human freedom. In Josephus, *Ant.* 11.90 and 101, the Jews and their leaders are described as *douloi tou (megistou) theou,* "slaves of (the greatest) God."

In the Ap. Frs. before Hermas, the persecuted people of God are on a single occasion designated *tous tou theou doulous* in 2 *Clem.* 20.1 (see *Mart. Pol.* 20.1).

yet apostle of Jesus Christ. For the omission of "yet" (*de*) in a few manuscripts see J. K. Elliott, *Greek Text,* p. 216; for the weak adversative nuance, BAGD, s.v.

The noun *apostolos,* "apostle" (seventy-nine times in the NT; thirty-four in the Paulines) occurs below in 1 Tim 1:1; 2:7; and 2 Tim 1:1 and 11. There are six uses in Luke and twenty-eight in Acts, versus one in each of the other gospels. The only use in the LXX is 3 Kgdms 14:6, of Ahijah as *apostolos* "a harsh messenger" (= MT *šalûaḥ*) to Jeroboam's wife.

Of the more than thirty uses of *apostolos* in the Ap. Frs. the term certainly applies to or includes Paul in *1 Clem.* 5.3; 44.1; 47.1 (with the definite article), 4; Ign. *Rom.* 4.3; and Pol. *Phil.* 9.1.

Forms of "Jesus Christ" occur thirty-two times in the PE but only half a dozen times in the order here. Only at 1 Tim 5:11 does "Christ" alone occur. The name "Jesus" alone is not employed in the PE. The name occurs only three times in the nominative in the PE, always as "Christ Jesus" (1 Tim 1:15–16; 2:5), and once in the accusative, as "Jesus Christ" (2 Tim 2.8). Titus uses "Jesus Christ" in 2:13 and 3:6 but "Christ Jesus" in 1:4, where the order of the name involves the meaning of the whole phrase in which it occurs. The preference for the order "Jesus Christ" may signal a Jewish-Christian emphasis, for Heb uses "Jesus Christ" three times, but never the reversed order. Similarly, the Catholic Epistles always use "Jesus Christ."

On the manuscript variants in transmitting "Jesus Christ" here and elsewhere in the PE, see Appendix I of J. K. Elliott, *Greek Text*, pp. 198–202. Some variants may be traceable to the abbreviations of the *nomina sacra* in oblique cases (see 1 Tim 1:12). "Jesus Christ" is certainly the regular form in Titus; however, in the letters to Timothy, "Christ Jesus" becomes the regular form (twenty-four times) and "Jesus Christ" appears only three times (see Knight, *Sayings*, pp. 32–33). Again perhaps one encounters a signal of a change in audience, from predominantly Jewish-Christian congregations to Pauline congregations containing significant numbers of converts from paganism.

for the faith of God's elect. The preposition *kata* (471 times in the NT), here translated "for," occurs six times with the accusative in Titus 1:1–9; it recurs in 3:5 and 7. There are thirteen further occurrences in the PE: 1 Tim 1:1, 11, 18; 5:19 (the only use in the PE with the genitive), 21; 6:3 and 2 Tim 1:1, 8, 9 *bis;* 2:8; 4:3, 14.

For the sense of goal or purpose reflected in the version of Titus 1:1, 4 see the COMMENT below.

the faith. See Excursus I, *"Pistis* Terminology in the PE."

of God's elect. Of the twenty-two NT uses of *eklektos,* there are two further ones in the PE: 1 Tim 5:21 and 2 Tim 2:10, of which the latter is also nominal, as here in Titus. Of the three other Pauline occurrences (Rom 8:33; 16:13; Col 3:12), the first and last are in the phrase *eklektoi (tou) theou,* which is otherwise not documented in the NT. Yet the language of Luke 18:7 is notable. "And will not God (*ho . . . theos*) vindicate his elect (*eklekton autou*)?" and perhaps also Luke 23:35, where "the Christ of God" is "the elect (*ho eklektos*)." *Eklektos* is not found in Acts.

Although *eklektos* occurs more than one hundred times in the LXX, the actual phrase "God's elect" is never used and only once "the Lord's elect" (LXX 2 Kgdms 21:6, of Saul). Yet on occasion the possessive pronoun refers the elect to God (see LXX Isa 42:1; 45:4; 65:9, 15, 23; Sir 46:1; 47:22).

The phrase *bḥyry 'l* appears in 1QpHab 10:13, speaking of the judgment in store for those who have "insulted and outraged *the elect of God*" (Dupont-Sommer, *EWQ*, p. 266), in other words, the Qumran community, as well as in 4Q 171:pPs 37.iv.14 (DJD 5.45). See 1QpHab 5:4; 9:11–12; and 1QH 14:15; as well as 4Q 164:pIsaᵈ; 4Q 171:pPs 37.ii.5; iii.5 ("the community [*ꜥdt*] of his elect"); and iv.11–12 (DJD 5.27–28, 43–45), where the possessive refers to God. See Fitzmyer, *ESBNT*, p. 155; Lohse, *Col.*, p. 146 n. 92; Coppens, "L'Élu," pp. 120–124.

The Qumran fragments of the Aramaic Enoch (cited as in Milik, *Enoch,* with page references to his edition) do not employ the phrase "God's elect," though there are references to the righteous and to Enoch himself as "elect"; see 4QEnᵃ 1:1, pp. 141–142; 4QEnᵍ 1:ii.23, p. 260; 4QEnᵍ 1:iv.12, pp. 265–266.

Of the twenty-eight occurrences of *eklektos* in the Ap. Frs. (including *Mart.*

Pol. 16.1; 22.1), twenty-two are plural, and most of these are in *1–2 Clem.* and Hermas. The phrase "God's elect" occurs only in *1 Clem.* 1.1; 46.4; and 59.2 (all with *tou theou* or *autou*), as well as in *Herm. Vis.* 3.8.3 (of faith through which *God's elect* are saved) and 4.3.5 (also with *tou theou*). *Eklektos* with a possessive referring to God occurs occasionally.

and for full and godly knowledge of the truth. Literally, "and [for] recognition of truth (*epignōsin alētheias*) which (*tēs*) accords with godliness (*kat' eusebeian*)." For the philological analysis of *alētheia, epignōsis,* and *eusebeia,* see Excursuses II and III.

The use of the article *tēs* for the relative pronoun is found also at 2 Tim 2:20 and 3:9, and its attraction here into the genitive of its antecedent is characteristic of the LXX and Luke–Acts (BDF §294).

2. *in hope of life eternal.* This translates *ep' elpidi zōēs aiōniou.* For the whole unusual phrase, see Excursus IV, "The Terminology for Life in the PE."

In the NT the phrase *ep' elpidi* is found only in the Paulines (Rom 4:18; 5:2; 8:20; 1 Cor 9:10 *bis*) and in Acts 26:6. In the LXX there are fewer than a dozen uses of the phrase *ep' elpidi.*

The noun *elpis* "hope" occurs fifty-three times in the NT, though never in the gospels or Rev. In the NT epistolary 36 out of 45 occurrences are in the Paulines (including Titus 1:2; 2:13; 3:7 and 1 Tim 1:1); eight are in Acts. For the verb *elpizein* in the PE, see 1 Tim 3:14; 4:10; 5:5; and 6:17.

Among the Ap. Frs., *1 Clem.* 57.5 takes it up in citing Prov 1:33. Moreover, *1 Clem.* 27.1 writes of "this hope" of bodily resurrection (see "the common hope" of 51.1).

In Ignatius, *elpis* is emphatically identified with Jesus Christ as well as linked to the resurrection that all share with him (Ign. *Eph.* 1.2; 21.2; *Magn.* 7.1; 9.1; 11.1; *Trall.* inscr.; 2.2; *Phld.* 5.2; 11.2; *Smyrn.* 10.2). In Pol. *Phil.* 8.1 the hope is similarly identified with Jesus.

Barnabas, which uses *elpis* seven times, seems to cite Titus 1:2 when he writes in 1.4 about the faith and love that dwell in the recipients of his teaching "in the hope of his [the Lord's] life," *ep' elpidi zōēs autou* (see 1.6, "the hope of life," *zōēs elpis*). Hermas, in *Sim.* 9.26.2, writes of greedy church ministers who "have no hope of life."

For the terminology for "hope" in the Hellenistic world and in the Jewish world before the NT period, see van Menxel, *Elpis.*

which the God who is without deceit promised from all eternity. The verb *epaggelesthai* "to promise" is used of God in eleven of fifteen occurrences in the NT, including Rom 4:21; Gal 3:19; and Acts 7:5. This verb when it describes human beings making promises occurs in uncomplimentary contexts (Mark 14:11; 2 Pet 2:19). In 1 Tim 6:21, some "profess to have at their disposal" a "so-called knowledge," and even in 1 Tim 2:10 there is some irony in counseling the extravagantly spangled worshiper how one actually "professes" godliness. This usage is Septuagintal, where in nine of eleven instances the verb refers to human promises, usually of money in unsavory context (1 Macc 11:28; 2 Macc 4:8, 27, 45; 3 Macc 1:4; Esth 4:7) and otherwise of presumably empty professions (LXX Prvb 13:12; Wis 2:13; Sir 20:23). See the COMMENT below for the instances in which God is the subject: 2 Macc 2:18; 3 Macc 2:18; 3 Macc 2:10.

In the Ap. Frs. a trace of the uneasiness with human promises and professions remains in Ign. *Eph.* 14.2, "no one who professes (*epaggellomenos*) faith sins," and then, "so they who profess to be of Christ (*hoi epaggellomenoi Christou einai*) shall be seen by their deeds (*di' hōn prassousin;* cf. *di' ergōn agathōn,* 1 Tim 2:10). For the 'deed' (*to ergon*) is not in the present profession (*nyn epaggelias*) but is shown by the power of faith, if a man continue to the end."

the God who is without deceit. In Greek, *ho apseudēs theos. Apseudēs,* "without deceit," occurs only here in the NT. In the LXX it is found only in Wis 7:17 of God's gift to Solomon of "unerring knowledge (*gnōsin apseudē*) of what exists," including times (*chronōn*) and seasons (7:18). In secular Greek, the adjective particularly describes oracles: thus Pausanias, *Description of Greece* 9.23.6 and Euripides, *Orestes* 363–364, calling the Nereid Glaucus not only the sailors' seer and prophet (*mantis . . . prophētēs:* cf. Horace, *Carmina* 1.15) but also *apseudēs theos.* Plato's *Republic* 2.383B cites Aeschylus on Apollo's *theion apseudēs stoma,* "divine mouth without deceit."

In the Ap. Frs., *1 Clem.* 27.1–2 links the divine promise with God's inability to lie, and *apseudes* occurs in Ign. *Rom.* 8.2, where Jesus is "the mouth without deceit (*to apseudes stoma*) by which the Father has spoken truly (*alēthōs*)." In *Clementine Homilies* 11.33 (*PG* 2.300) Jesus is *ho apseudēs.* In *Mart. Pol.* 14.2, the last prayer addresses "the God who is without deceit and true (*ho apseudēs kai alēthinos theos*)," who has prepared ahead of time, manifested (*proephanerōsas*), and fulfilled what his martyr servant undergoes. The prophetic connotations of the phrase surface again in the Syriac *Odes of Solomon* 3.10, "This is the Spirit of the Lord which is not false, which teaches the sons of men to know his ways."

from all eternity. Literally, "before eternal ages," *pro chronōn aiōniōn.*

The preposition *pro* occurs in this phrase in 2 Tim 1:9 and in *pro cheimōnos* in 2 Tim 4:21. In the LXX and the Ap. Frs. this particle never governs *chronos.*

For the reversible phrase, "times and/or seasons," *chronoi kai/ē kairoi* (1 Thess 5:1; Acts 1:7), cf. LXX Dan 2:21; 4:37; 7:12 (singular and note Theod.); and Wis 8:8. On Philo, *Quaestiones et Solutiones in Genesin* 1.100 see E. Lucchesi, "Précédents," pp. 537–538. For gnostic speculations on the aeons, see *Gos. Eg.* passim and *Eugnostos* 73, 81–89 (*NHL,* pp. 195–205; 211, 217–224).

The *pro chronōn aionion* here in Titus and in 2 Tim 1:9 takes the form in Rom 16:25 *chronois aioniois,* in the description "of the mystery that was kept secret *for long ages"* (*RSV*). The LXX (like the Ap. Frs.) does not write *chronoi aionioi* but prefers *eis ton aiona chronon* (e.g., Isa 9:6; 13:20; 14:20; etc.).

See Excursus IV, "The Terminology for Life in the PE," for the analysis of *aionios.*

The plural *chronoi,* usually for separate dates or periods, can designate a single period (Menander, *Kitharistes* 44–45; BAGD s.v.; cf. Luke 8:29 with 20:9). Of the fifty-four NT uses of *chronos,* twenty-four are in the Lukan corpus, where seven of them are plural.

3. (*in due time he made his message clear of course*). The parentheses mark the anacoluthon commented on below, and the "of course" represents the slightly adversative force of *de* after *ephanerōsen,* "he . . . made clear" (see 2 Tim 1:9–10, . . . *pro chronōn aiōniōn, phanerōtheisan de nyn* . . .). *Phaneroun* occurs once more in the PE at 1 Tim 3:16. This verb is documented in pre-Christian Greek only in LXX Jer 40:6 (MT 33:6) and a handful of secular documents, almost all Hellenistic (BAGD, s.v.). The forty-nine NT uses are concentrated in the epistolary, esp. in the Paulines.

in due time. With the non-Septuagintal *kairois idiois* the other member of the bound phrase, *chronoi kai kairoi,* emphatically broken by the anacoluthon, now appears. In the PE *kairoi* are always modified (1 Tim 4:1; 2 Tim 3:1; and contrast 2 Tim 4:3, 6). In the NT only the PE use the plural phrase *kairois idiois* (1 Tim 2:6; 6:15); Gal 6:9 has the singular. In the Ap. Frs. only *1 Clem.* 20.4 uses the phrase, writing of the earth, in accord with God's will (*thelēma*), teeming "at its proper seasons (*tois idiois kairois*)" and producing "food in full abundance" for all living creatures (cf. 20.10 and *Test. Solomon.* 6.3). The closest Septuagintal parallel to the usage of *kairois idiois* in the PE appears in LXX Dan 7:25; 9:27; 12:7 (= *ʿdn, mwʿd*), where the *kairoi* are the "times" that can be counted off in the last days.

(*his message*). *Ton logon autou,* the possessive referring to "the God who is without deceit." This is the first of twenty appearances of *logos* in the PE, four of which are in the plural (1 Tim 4:6; 6:3; 2 Tim 1:13; 4:15). Another five occur in the phrase *pistos ho logos* (Titus 3:8 q.v., and 1:9 below). "God's word," *logos* (*tou*) *theou,* occurs in Titus 2:5; 1 Tim 4:5 (anarthrous); and 2 Tim 2:9, with the article adding perhaps the nuance of the personal name, Father. Three anarthrous uses of the singular, *logos,* in the PE—in Titus 2:8 and 1 Tim 4:12; 5:17 —all specify an oral activity of persons who share the Pauline apostolate. The further uses of the articular *logos* (singular) in 2 Tim 2:15, 17 and 4:2 closely parallel the usage here in Titus. "The message of the truth," *ho logos tēs alētheias,* is a condensed formulation of "the message" of "the God who is without deceit." This *logos* stands in contrast to *ho logos autōn,* that is, the word of the false teachers who empty the resurrection (and thus eternal life) of its reality. Timothy then (in 2 Tim 4:2) is directed, *kēryxon ton logon,* "herald the message," which here in Titus is formally placed *en kērygmati,* that is, in the Pauline proclamation.

(*in a proclamation I was entrusted with, at the order of our savior, God*). The *kērygma,* "proclamation," and its cognates *kēryx* and *kēryssein* are analyzed at 1 Tim 2:7.

First Timothy 1:11 writes of "the gospel that I was entrusted with (*ho episteuthēn egō*)." For the analysis of *pisteuein* see Excursus I, "*Pistis* Terminology in the PE."

(*at the order*). The noun *epitagē* began to appear in the second century B.C. Hellenistic Greek and the LXX use it of royal and divine orders (1 Esd 1:16; Wis 14:17; 18:15; 19:6; Dan 3:16; 3 Macc 7:20). See also the Greek *Enoch* 5.2 (4QEnᵃ 5:2; Milik, *Enoch,* p. 146); 21.6 and *Pss. Sol.* 18.12.

All seven NT uses of *kat' epitagēn* are in the Paulines. In the PE, *epitagē* recurs in Titus 2:15 (with *meta pasēs*) and 1 Tim 1:1, with *kat'*. Except for 1 Cor 7:25, the remaining examples are also with *kat'* and refer to God's (Rom 16:26) or to Paul's (1 Cor 7:6; 2 Cor 8:8) commands. See G. Horsley, *NDIEC* 2.86, §49.

(*of our savior, God*). On *ho theos* see 1:2; on *sōtēr,* see Excursus V, "The PE on Salvation."

4. *writes this to Titus, his true child, for the faith all share.* The first two words are not in the Greek. The native Latin name "Titus" (from *titus,* "a wild dove," Ernout and Meillet, *DELL,* s.v.) occurs once again in 2 Tim 4:10. The whole letter to Titus is to be heard as Paul's direction for a person who otherwise is named in the NT only in Gal and 2 Cor. In the LXX only 2 Macc 11:34 employs this name in citing a letter from Roman envoys, one of whom is Titus Manius. As the silence of *CII* suggests, Jews did not use the name, though it was common enough among pagans outside of Italy (Preisigke, *Wörterbuch,* p. 439). Naturally the name was a byword among Jews after the events of A.D. 66–70 and the accession of the Flavian Titus to the imperium thereafter. By then in Jewish communities the name may have sounded the way the name of Hitler does now.

his true child. The epithet *gnēsiōi teknōi* is used again, of Timothy, in 1 Tim 1:2, but nowhere else in the NT, LXX, or Ap. Frs.

The adjective *gnēsios* occurs otherwise in the NT only in the Paulines. In Phil 4:3 Paul's *gnēsie syzyge* is to help reconcile a disagreement between two Christian women in Philippi. The only other use (2 Cor 8:8) is nominal. The LXX employs the term in Sir 7:18, where a friend is synonymous with a "true brother."

Teknon as early as Homer is used by an older person addressing any younger adult, as *phile teknon* in *Odyssey* 2:363, and see Menander, *Geōrgos* 25, 63, 84, 109. The noun is very frequent in the LXX, and the singular is used figuratively, especially in Sir. In the PE, the singular refers only to Titus and Timothy (1 Tim 1:2, 18; 2 Tim 1:2; 2:1; and see 1 Cor 4:17; Phil 2:22). The occurrences in the plural in the PE are, with one exception (1 Tim 3:12), the object of *echein* (Titus 1:6; 1 Tim 3:4; 5:4), and all refer to natural progeny. In the Ap. Frs. the singular occurs in a figurative sense only in *Did.* 3.1, 3, 4, 5, 6; 4.1 (but note the singular of the human embryo in *Did.* 2.2 = *Barn.* 19.5).

for the faith all share. The adjective *koinēn*, translated as "all share," occurs only here in the PE; for the cognates *koinōnein* and *koinōnikos*, see 1 Tim 5:22; 6:18. The only other Pauline uses of *koinos* are in Rom 14:14 (*tris*), and there with the sense of "ceremonially impure." Acts 2:44 and 4:32 (see *Test. Abr.* A 1:10) use the term of Christians sharing all of their material goods. The closest parallel to the usage here is Jude 3, "writing . . . of the salvation that we all share (*graphein . . . peri tēs koinēs hēmōn sōtērias*)." The expression *koinē pistis* is not documented in the LXX, the NT, or the Ap. Frs., but Ignatius refers to "the common hope" (*hē koinē elpis*) of believers (see Ign. *Eph.* 1.2; 21.2, *Phld.* 5.2; 11.2).

Grace and peace from God the Father and Christ Jesus, our savior. Charis kai eirēnē is found in S, C*, D, G, and others; *eleos* appears between these nouns in A, C², K, and so on (see appendix in *GNT*³ᶜᵒʳʳ). The late Ethiopic versions reverse the order of the two in a way reminiscent of the *pax et gratia a domino nostro Iesou redundet* of Tertullian, *De virginibus velandis* 17.5. See B. Metzger, *TCGNT*, p. 653, and J. K. Elliott, *Greek Text*, pp. 173–174 on the reading adopted here.

Outside of the PE, all of the Pauline letters open with *charis hymin kai eirēnē* (see also 1 Pet 1:2; 2 Pet 1:2; Rev 1:4), and the second-person plural for the addresses is regularly balanced by the addition of the first-person plural to the following *apo theou patros hēmōn*. The LXX never pairs *charis* with *eirēnē*, and in the Ap. Frs. only *1 Clem.* inscr. opens with the pair and then in the full Pauline phrase, *charis hymin kai eirēnē*.

The 155 NT uses of *charis* are concentrated in the epistolary, with 13 in the PE, 87 in the other Paulines. Outside of the 25 occurrences in Luke–Acts, the term is found in the gospels only in the Johannine prologue. In the PE the anarthrous *charis* opens each letter (1 Tim 1:2; 2 Tim 1:2), and the articular form closes each one (Titus 3:15; 1 Tim 6:21; 2 Tim 4:22). Another anarthrous formulaic usage is that with *echein* opening the prayers at 1 Tim 1:12 and 2 Tim 1:3. These formulas are not to be divorced from the regularly articular confessional texts of Titus 2:11; 3:7; 1 Tim 1:14; 2 Tim 1:9 (anarthrous); and see 2 Tim 2:1. The *charis* of these texts is that of God and/or Christ.

Eirēnē occurs in the opening blessing formula of 1 Tim 1:2 and 2 Tim 1:2. The one other appearance in the PE, at 2 Tim 2:22, is in a list of virtues. Of the eighty-seven remaining NT uses of this term, thirty-nine are in the other Paulines and twenty are in Luke–Acts (see the greetings of Luke 10:5; 24:36, s.v.l.). The Hebrew equivalent was part of an introductory greeting in a conversation and for delivering a message (Judg 6:23; 2 Sam 18:28; 2 Kgs 4:26) and thus passed into the opening salutation of the written conversation that a letter transmits (Theod. Dan 4:1; also the opening of the letter of ben Kosiba, during the second Jewish revolt, in DJD 2.159–161: Lohse, *Col.*, p. 5). For *šālôm* and congeners as a greeting in ancient Aramaic and Hebrew letters, see Fitzmyer, *Aramean*, pp. 191–192 and 219–221, and Pardee, "Overview," pp. 338–339. In

2 Macc 1:1 the epistolary salutation invokes *eirēnēn agathēn* on the Jews in Egypt.

None of the Ap. Frs. uses the term *eirēnē* more often than *1 Clem.* from the opening cited above through the closing prayer. The closest parallel to the PE in the Ignatian usage is his *Smyrn.* 12.2, which draws to a close praying, *charis hymin eleos eirēnē hypomenē dia pantos*. Polycarp (*Phil.* inscr.) opens his letter with *eleos hymin kai eirēnē; Barn.* 1.1 also begins with a greeting "in the name of the Lord who loved us in peace," and *Mart. Pol.* init. opens as a letter with the prayer *eleos eirēnē kai agapē . . . plēthyntheiē*.

from God the Father. The PE use the title *patēr* of God only in this phrase and as part of their opening blessing (1 Tim 1:2; 2 Tim 1:2). Otherwise *patēr* occurs only in 1 Tim 5:1 of a human father. The rest of the Paulines use *patēr* of God in thirty-eight of fifty-nine occurrences; Luke–Acts, by contrast, designates God as *patēr* in twenty of ninety-one uses. In Acts God is Father only in 1:4, 7; and 2:33. The Hebrew Bible seldom explicitly entitles the God of Israel "Father," but see Ps 89:27 (= LXX Ps 88:27) and Sir 51:10 (Hebrew and Greek). The mockers of Wis 2:16 say that the just man boasted that God was his father (*patēra theon*). See H. Ringgren, "*'ab*," in *TDOT* 1.16–19.

The phrase *apo theou patros* (regularly with *hēmōn*, as noted above) belongs to the standard opening of a Pauline letter, and it also occurs in the concluding blessing of Eph 6:23 but not elsewhere in the NT, though in Paul forms of *(ho) theos (kai) (ho) patēr* are frequent enough. The closest NT parallel to this phrase is 2 John 3, *charis eleos eirēnē para theou patros*.

Although *1 Clem.* inscr. adds the phrase *apo pantokratoros theou* to the salutation already noted, the phrase *apo theou patros* is not documented in the Ap. Frs. Ignatius regularly writes of "God the Father," but even that phrase does not recur in the Ap. Frs.

and Christ Jesus, our savior. The name "Christ Jesus" reverses the order of the elements in v 1. "Our savior" in v 3 referred to the Father; it is now a title for Jesus, who is not styled Son in the PE and who is not called Lord in Titus. This omission is all the more striking when one notes that *kai kyriou Iesou Christou* concludes the salutation of eight of the ten remaining Paulines (1 Thess 1:1 phrases it *en theōi patri kai kyriōi Iesou Christōi*, while Col omits the phrase). Both 1 Tim and 2 Tim have the more Pauline vocabulary at this point, but even then with a difference, for they both write *kai Christou Iesou tou kyriou hēmōn*, using a different word order for names and title as well as adding the first-person plural possessive (see the variant in Gal 1:3).

COMMENT

1:1–4. See the INTRODUCTION to this volume for the position of the Letter to Titus at the head of this correspondence and for the relation of Titus 1:1–4 to all three PE. There, too, reasons for reading these opening verses of Titus in conjunction with the close of Luke–Acts are suggested.

1. *Paul.* The superscription for this correspondence identifies first a man named Paul who, in gradually expanding phrases, is described as "a slave of God" and finally as "an apostle of Jesus Christ." This epistolary collection comes *in persona Pauli.* To that extent, it resembles the rest of the Paulines and shares the interest of Acts (see NOTES). That Paul alone is mentioned differentiates the PE from most of the other Paulines and reminds one of Jas, 1–2 Pet, and Jude instead of the NT letters that come under no name (1 John; Heb) or simply a title (2–3 John).

For the PE the person of Paul actually belongs to the teaching that this correspondence aims at transmitting. Paul does not simply give a definition of an apostle; he is part of the definition. The historical Paul had used letters as an extension of his person, enabling him to transcend the limitations that physical distance placed on his apostolic ministry in word and action (see 1–2 Cor passim). Those letters were instruments for a powerful, personal meeting with an apostle (Barrett, *Signs*, p. 74), an encounter that his physical presence would simply reinforce (see 2 Cor 10:3–11; 13:10; White, "Epistolary Literature," pp. 1739–1750). If the Pauline correspondence had spanned physical separation from his churches during the first generation, a new generation sought to ensure that the Pauline apostolate would also span time. To have made the person of Paul the point of departure for the PE is to have said in principle that there is an ultimately irreconcilable diversity or variety in that which will be called "apostolic."

This correspondence proposes for the second-generation believer what it conceived to be the irreducibly individual and characteristic witness of the man named Paul. There was only one Paul. But was there only one apostle? Were there not other equally individual and authentic witnesses to Jesus Christ? The phrases following Paul's name in this superscription are the beginning of the answer that the PE submitted to those questions. The Paul who writes the PE does so first of all as "slave of God." The unabashed assertion of individuality, of the freedom that a personal name implies, is immediately and paradoxically qualified. Paul is a slave, a nonperson in the view of the Hellenistic world, a chattel that belonged totally to its owner, a "living tool" without rights, without power, without family, without property (cf. Aristotle *NE* 8.11.6; 10.6 *EE* 7.9; *Pol.* 1.2; Bartchy, *Slavery*, pp. 37–82; Spicq, *Lexic.*, pp. 211–217). Yet one must recall that even in the Greek world the religious sphere was precisely where one could in a good sense say "I am called the god's slave" (Euripides, *Ion* 309; cf. *Bacchae* 366; *Orestes* 418; *pace* Rengstorff, in *TDNT* 2.264), or "I live in no sense as a slave (*doulos*) of yours but of Loxias [Apollo]" (Sophocles, *Oedipus Rex* 410). The "prophetic" context in these passages is notable. Moreover, the Roman slave was considered a *persona* in such religious matters as his oaths, his curses, and the inviolability of his grave (J. G. Gager in Benko and O'Rourke, *Catacombs*, p. 111). On the sociological institution see Titus 2:9; 1 Tim 6:1.

The OT authors used the sociological institution as a paradigm for the relation of their nation to Yahweh. As an official in the royal court was proud to identify himself as "slave of the king" (see the seals in Pritchard, *ANEP*, nos. 276, 277 [pp. 85, 280]), so king and commoner alike called themselves "slaves of Yahweh." It was particularly in its worship service (*ʿbd:* see Quinn, "Ap. Ministry," pp. 481–482) that Israel saw itself, communally and individually, as the Lord's slave (see LXX Pss 18:12, 14; 26:9; 30:17; the plural in 33:23; 104:6; etc.), and this was the title par excellence for the venerable leaders and founders of the nation, including some of the kings (LXX Ps 104:26, 42 of Moses, Abraham; Judg 2:8 of Joshua; LXX Pss 77:70; 88:4, 21, 40; 143:10; and often elsewhere of David; 2 Chr 32:16 of Hezekiah; Haggai 2:23 of Zerubbabel [cf. Zech 3:8 with 6:12]), as well as for the prophets as God's messengers and spokesmen (LXX Jer 7:25; 25:4; Jonah 1:9). Yahweh himself calls Nebuchadrezzar, pagan king of Babylon and destroyer of Judah, "my slave" in Jer 25:9 (which the LXX piously dropped at that point; see also 27:6; 43:10). Thus, before the God of Israel, every human being can have only one basic role, that of the slave, the instrument, the utensil, the vessel of the only God (2 Tim 2:20).

The worship of the first Christian believers hymned one who "emptied himself, taking the form of a slave" (Phil 2:7), and thus a terminology that had been sociological and, in Israel, theological became christological. The Christology in turn determined the application of the same *doulos* terminology and similar concepts to Christians themselves and particularly those whom they considered their founders and leaders; spokesmen for and messengers of their Lord (see *SFG* §263 for the way in which the Synoptic and Johannine traditions use the *diakon-/doul-* terminology to explain the relationship of Jesus with his disciples). Already in the Pauline tradition every believer is "a slave of Christ" (1 Cor 7:22–23), and Paul entitles himself "a slave of Jesus Christ" (Rom 1:1) and shares that title with other men (Phil 1:1 of Timothy; Col 4:12 of Epaphras, who in 1:7 is *syndoulos hēmōn;* in Col 4:7 Tychicus is *syndoulos en kyriōi*).

The PE open on this Pauline note but transpose it into a new key with the unusual turn of phrase, "a slave of God." The expression would be congenial to Jewish Christians (see Jas 1:1) and signal the sector of the community of believers for which the subsequent Pauline directives were ultimately intended. In contrast, the PE call Timothy "the Lord's slave" (*doulon . . . kyriou:* 2 Tim 2:24 q.v.), a phrase the LXX employs of Jonah (1:9) and Theod. of priests (Dan 3:85). Otherwise it is undocumented in the NT or the Ap. Frs., though, in Phil 1:1, Timothy and Paul are "slaves of Christ Jesus," and Phil 2:22 reads, "But Timothy's worth you know, how as a child with his father he has slaved (*edouleusen*) with me for (*eis*) the gospel." In the light of the other uses of *kyrios* in the PE, along with various forms of the phrase "slave(s) of Jesus

Christ" in the NT epistolaries, it is all but certain that *doulos kyriou* here refers to Jesus as Lord. With these unusual and distinctive phrases the PE are already tentatively probing the difference between the apostle and his coworker.

The author of Luke–Acts can speak of the slave in both a sociological and a theological sense (cf. Luke 7:2–10; 22:50 with 1:48; 2:29; Acts 2:18, and the slave parables of Luke 12:35–48; 14:16–24; 17:7–10; etc.). Moreover, the prayer of the Jerusalem Church calls the apostles the slaves (*tois doulois sou:* Acts 4:29) of the Lord (*kyrie = theon, despota* of Acts 4:24). In Acts 16:17, Paul and his entourage are similarly hailed by a "divining spirit" as "slaves of the God most high" (*douloi tou theou tou hypsistou:* see Kraable, *"Hypsistos"*), a pagan prophecy that bears comparison with Titus 1:12 and recalls the texts cited above from the Greek authors.

The strongly Jewish and theological background for this title makes it both sweet and sour, a fragile combination of the free and the necessary. It is basically a self-designation for articulating total commitment to another person. Yet the confession has grown out of the realization of one's total dependence on that person. If the slave must obey the master who has dispatched him with his word, it is with the satisfaction that the master has put his trust in him (see Sass, *"Doulos"*).

yet apostle of Jesus Christ. First God's slave, Paul is still an apostle of Jesus Christ. Humiliation is the setting for his distinction and the slightly adversative "yet" (*de*) balances one with the other. As Paul is *God's* slave, not man's, the *Lord's* prisoner, not Nero's (see 2 Tim 1:8), so he is an apostle for the PE because he belongs to and has been sent by Jesus Christ (1 Tim 1:1, 12–17; 2 Tim 1:1). If before God he is a slave, before men he is an apostle (Rengstorff in *TDNT* 2.277) by God's own institution (cf. the use of *tithenai* in 1 Tim 1:12; 2:7; 2 Tim 1:11 with the use in 1 Cor 12:28). As the Greek term *apostolos* means "one sent," Paul comes on the scene as a herald dispatched by a victorious king announcing a triumphal appearance (see *kērygma* in both verse 3 and 2 Tim 1:11, and *kēryx* in 1 Tim 2:7), as a teacher sent to the pagans (*didaskalos*, 1 Tim 2:7).

for the faith of God's elect. The author has formally signaled his compositional structuring with the fourfold repetition of the versatile Greek preposition *kata*, which governs *pistin*, then *eusebeian*, in verse 1; and later, in verses 3–4, *epitagēn* and again *pistin*. The next section of Titus, the apostolic commission for the appointment of ecclesial ministers (1:5–9), is again framed within *kata polin* and *kata tēn didachēn*. The only other use of this particle in Titus is in the baptismal paraenesis cited in 3:5, 7.

The meaning, however, of the preposition *kata* cannot be caught with a single English particle (see BDF §224; BAGD s.v.). Here in Titus 1:1, 4, *kata* (*koinēn*) *pistin* most probably describes both "apostle" and his "child" in terms of their purpose and goal, namely, "for the faith (all share)," a sense of *kata* documented elsewhere in the Paulines (2 Cor 11:21; Phil 3:14) that may be suggested by the movement in a certain direction implied by the governing verb (see Luke 10:32–33; Acts 27:7–8, 12). In Titus the verbal force in *apostolos* would still be sensed, as if that term were translated as "the one sent" (see John 13:16). For other commentators who have opted for the sense "marked by," "in the sphere of," "corresponding with," see Spicq, *EP*, p. 592 and R. Bultmann in *TDNT* 6.213–214.

As the PE conceive the apostle, he has been sent first of all "for the faith of God's elect and for full and godly knowledge" (literally, "a recognition of truth that corresponds with godliness"). The phrase gathers into a dense cluster a series of terms that focus the doctrinal concerns of this correspondence (faith, knowledge, truth) and the moral response that corresponds to them (godliness). For the details of the usage of this language in the PE see Excursus I, *"Pistis* Terminology in the PE"; Excursus II, "Truth and *epignōsis alētheias* in the PE"; and Excursus III, *"Eusebeia* and Its cognates in the PE." The belief "of God's elect" is described in 1:4 as "the faith all share (*koinēn*)," in other words, the belief of a community (see Jude 3; 2 Pet 1:1; Spicq, *EP*, pp. 594–595) that is described as "God's elect." Thus members of the Qumran community designated themselves among their Jewish contemporaries, though the usage here and in 2 Tim 2:10 has its closest affinities with the Pauline tradition (see Rom 8:33; 16:13; Col 3:12; and Excursus I).

The phrase "God's elect" is by no means stereotyped in Jewish Greek, though probably it has been hewn from that quarry for its apocalyptic coloring and its suggestion of the divine initiative and choice that have manifestly and finally separated out the good from the evil. The terminology for the elect appears particularly in texts associated on one or another count with the church in Rome, the Jewish antecedents of which would make it a likely site for such a transplant. Yet the language did not catch on generally in early Christian literature (but note Hippolytus, *Apostolic Tradition* §20, where the Roman practice is to call the candidates for baptism *electi;* see also Minucius Felix, *Octavius* 11.6) and even its rare appearance in the gnostic documents is still in eschatological contexts (see *NHL*, pp. 230, 420). The reluctance to use it may reflect missionary concerns. The language of election was heard by unbelievers in an obnoxiously exclusive, elitist sense that exposed the Christian flank to the mocking sarcasm of a Celsus (see Origen, *Contra Celsum* 4.23; 5.14, 41–42, 50; and Chadwick, *Chr. Thgt.*, pp. 25–26). Such terminology was certainly not to be flaunted. Yet it was no less certainly "according to the Scriptures" and thus was not to be discarded but rather defended.

and for full and godly knowledge. The use of the phrase "the faith of God's elect" in the opening of the PE, along with Paul's suffering for the sake of the elect in 2 Tim 2:10, may again link this correspondence with the church in Rome, which witnessed Paul's execution. If, as suggested in Excursus III, *eusebeia* is to be heard as the Roman *pietas,* then the whole phrase here in Titus

1:1 about the faith of God's elect, and genuine, godly knowledge has a peculiarly Roman ring to it.

2. *in hope of life eternal.* The PE open by explicitly linking the apostolic work for Christian faith and godliness with "hope of life eternal" (see 1 Tim 4:8). The Paul of Acts 26:6 speaks out of such a background before Agrippa. "And now I stand here on trial for hope (*ep' elpidi*) in the promise (*tēs epaggelias:* see *epēggeilato* in Titus 1:2) made by God to our fathers." He continues, "For this hope (*peri hēs elpidos*) I am accused by Jews . . . [cf. 28:20]. Why is it thought incredible (*apiston*) by any of you that God raises the dead?" (Acts 26:7–8). Although Acts has no scruple about using *elpis* in a secular sense (16:19; 27:20), it is usually employed in connection with the witness of Peter and Paul to the resurrection of the dead and specifically to that of Jesus (2:26 [citing LXX Ps 15:9, *ep' elpidi*]; 23:6; 24:15). In the first of Paul's speeches in Acts to the Jewish community of Rome, he is quoted as saying, "it is because of the hope of Israel that I am bound with this chain," a hope that is then defined in terms of God's kingdom and Jesus himself (28:20, 23; cf. 1 Tim 1:1). In the light of the previous usage, "the hope of Israel" here must refer to the resurrection of the dead, to which Paul bears witness in the person of the risen Jesus.

The Paul of history had written about promise, resurrection, and hope in Rom 4:16–18; in that letter are four out of five of his uses of the phrase "life eternal." Acts and Titus have not quoted the text of Romans. They have taken up the language that the Roman church had learned from an apostolic teacher (see Acts 13:46, 48). Thus Titus 2:13 transmits a baptismal confession that refers to (literally) "the blessed hope and manifestation of the glory of our great God and savior, Jesus Christ." Here, unmistakably, hope is targeted at the eschatological consummation of history in the glorious appearance of the risen Jesus. This more dramatic formulation becomes, in Titus 3:7, "life eternal." In 1 Tim 1:1 Paul's apostleship is "at the order of God, our savior, and of Christ Jesus, our hope." Here a formula of remarkable density focuses all that has previously been articulated about hope into the person of the risen Jesus, at whose royal order the Pauline apostolate had originated. *First Clement* explicitly links hope and resurrection of the dead; the Ignatian correspondence besides often identifies hope with the person of Jesus; still the whole phrase in Titus, about "hope of life eternal" remains unused in the Ap. Frs., though variants on it, if not actual allusion to it, have been noted in *Barn.* and *Herm.*

life eternal. See Excursus IV, "The Terminology for Life in the PE."

which the God who is without deceit promised from all eternity. The adjectival clause plays on the term *aiōnios,* comparing and contrasting the description of the goal *ep' elpidi zōēs aiōniou* with that of the origin of that life in the divine promise "from all eternity," *pro chronōn aiōniōn.* A similar play on *zōē aiōnios —basileus ton aiōnōn* occurs at 1 Tim 1:16–17. Invoking that which had been in the beginning to explain that which is to characterize the present end of creation is not only an exegetical procedure at Qumran (see 1QH 12:8) but also one attributed to Jesus (see Mark 10:6; *SFG* §252) and found in Paul (Rom 5:12–21) and 1 Tim 6:7. The phrase "hope of life eternal" is unusual; the descriptive clause that follows seeks to clarify it, using traditional concepts and terminology, including the phrase *pro chronōn aiōniōn* (2 Tim 1:9). Because that phrase is formulaic, its use of the adjective *aiōnios* does not quite coincide conceptually with the use of the same word in the phrase *zōē aiōnios*.

The meaning of the *aiōn/aiōnios* terminology and the biblical language about time (*chronoi* and *kairoi* are also in Titus 1:2–3) takes one into the controversy between Barr, *Words for Time*, and Cullmann, *Christ and Time*. Barr has carried the day against Cullmann's contention that in the NT *aiōn* (*aiōnios*) refers to an infinite expanse of *time*, that is to say, a *temporal* succession without beginning or end. He has also shown that Cullmann's complete separation of a chronological, abstract *chronos* from a realistic, "filled" *kairos* is not linguistically justified (see Momigliano, *Quarto contributo*, p. 18). With Barr, one can make a persuasive case for the biblical authors presupposing (if not explicitly affirming) that time began with the rest of creation (see Eph 1:4; John 17:24), a position that Philo certainly voiced in this period (Barr, *Words for Time*, p. 75; Philo, *Op. mund.* 26). Against that background, the phrase *pro chronōn aioniōn* of Titus 1:2 and 2 Tim 1:9 (cf. *NEB*) refers to the timeless order in which God himself lives in contrast to the *chronoi aiōnioi*, the countless ages through which his creatures have come and gone (see 1QS 3:15–18). To that timeless order *zōē aiōnios* belongs. It is more difficult to fix the precise sense in which *aiōnioi* qualifies *chronoi*. In 2 Tim 2:10, *aiōnios* does indeed describe God's glory as perpetual and unchanging (Barr, *Words for Time*, p. 77). In 1 Tim 6:16, where man's doxological response to God is described, it is not so clear that *aiōnios* refers to the unending divine order. Certainly with *chronoi aiōnioi* the divine reality is not being described. These *chronoi* are measurable, limited periods of time, and *aiōnioi* certainly seems to qualify each of them as lasting "an age." In this connection, as Barr has noted (*Words for Time*, pp. 123–124), some early Latin versions render this phrase in the PE with *ante tempora saecularia* (see *VL* 25 [2].851–853) taking up the term *saeculum*, which referred to a period that would extend just beyond the longest human lifetime in a single generation, a period of more than a century (cf. Lucretius, *De rerum natura* 2.1153; 5.791, 805, 988, 1169, 1238, where *mortalia saecla* refer to living human beings whose lives are limited, in contrast to that *aeterna vita* which is attributed to the gods, 5.1175). *Saeculum* designated a period of time in this world, as the use of *saecularia desideria* to translate the *kosmikas epithymias* of Titus 2:12 illustrates (cf. *VL* 25 [2].905 with the Vulgate Heb 9:1). Thus for the old Latin versions the plural *chronoi aiōnioi* of the PE mean the countless centuries of history, however many they might be. Antedating all such ages was the design, the grace, the promise of God for a life that belonged to the divine order, that was *aiōnios*, in the way that God's life was endless (see Excursus IV, "The Terminology for Life in the PE"). Thus Titus 1:2 deliberately contrasts the lasting life of an age to come (*aiōnios:* see Luke 18:30) with the periods of time, however long (*aiōnioi*), that constitute this age (see Hill, *Greek Words,* pp. 186–189).

which the God . . . promised. Life eternal, according to the PE, is grounded in the divine promise. The verbal phrase here in Titus 1:2 becomes "the promise of life" in 1 Tim 4:8 and 2 Tim 1:1, an unusual expression. The ancient Greek world almost never spoke of the promise of a god; the later strata of the LXX, however, do furnish precedents for such terminology in Jewish circles. Thus in 2 Macc 2:17–18, the Palestinian Jews are described as saying, "It is God who has saved all his people, and has returned the inheritance to all, and the kingship and priesthood and consecration, as he promised (*epēggeilato*) through the law (*dia tou nomou*)" (*RSV*). The expectations for the future are grounded on the texts of the promises past. "For we have hope (*elpizomen*) in God that he will soon have mercy upon us and will gather us from everywhere under heaven into his holy place" (see 3 Macc 2:10, of God's promise to hear prayers from the Jerusalem temple). Moreover, although LXX Ps 55:9 certainly mistranslated MT Ps 56:9, it is notable that the human tears in God's "book" (*beSiprātekā*) were understood as being somehow in his "promise" (*epaggeliai*). That is to say, Greek-speaking Jews conceived of their scriptures as intimately linked with the divine promise to the nation and to individuals (see Josephus, *Ant.* 2.219; 3.23–24, 77).

The terminology of divine promise first appears among Christians in Rom, Gal, and 2 Cor; and it designates, among other things, the Spirit (cf. Gal 3:14) and life from the dead (cf. Rom 4:13–21), but these are proposed within the Pauline dialectic of promise versus law (cf. Gal 3:21–22). In 2 Cor 7:1, which is not set in that dialectical horizon, it becomes clear that the divine promises give shape not only to the eschatological goal but to the daily life of the believers. The relation of hope and the promises with the Scriptures of Israel is taken up in Rom 15:4–13.

Of the gospels, only Luke 24:49 has Jesus use *epaggelia* of "the promise of my Father," which in Acts 1:4; 2:33, 39 is associated with the Holy Spirit. The divine promise to the "fathers" of Israel figures in Acts 7:5, 17; 13:23, 32; 26:6–8. When Acts 23:21 uses the noun of a human promise, it is of an act that was to have fatal consequences for Paul.

The *epaggel-* terminology in Acts indicates, on the whole, the realities with which Paul had associated the promises (the Spirit, the resurrection, the Scriptures) but without the Pauline dialectic. A similar absence of dialectical vigor can be noted in the use of the *epaggel-* terms in the PE, with the verb referring to the divine promise as well as to human professions that permit even considerable slippage between what is professed and the ensuing reality (see Wis 2:13; 1 Tim 2:10; 6:21).

Because the promise of life eternal preceded all of the ages of history, the promise itself is essentially future in its orientation and thus ultimately pertains to the only one who knows the future, God. If he shares that knowledge with others, who are in the historical order, it comes as prophecy, that is to say, a revelation, and the assurance of its truth is grounded ultimately in the divine nature of the trustworthy God who cannot deceive or be deceived (see Num 23:19; 1 Sam 15:29; Rom 3:4; 2 Cor 1:18; Heb 6:18; *1 Clem.* 27.1–2). The teaching on the two spirits, of truth and perversity, in 1QS 3:13–4:26, ultimately proceeds from this conviction that God cannot deceive.

The adjective *apseudēs* had in the Hellenistic world the connotation of a prophetic knowledge that only a divinity could give, a truth that was beyond simply human verification. When Ignatius called Jesus the Father's "mouth," he was explaining the relation between Jesus and the Father by alluding to those passages in Exodus in which Aaron was to be for Moses as a mouth and a prophet are for God (Exod 4:16; 7:1); to describe that "mouth" as "without deceit" suggests precisely that prophetic assurance with which the revelation had come through Christ.

Out of this prophetic certitude about a revelation from the God who cannot deceive comes the certitude of the apostle whom that God and his Christ have sent (1 Tim 1:12; 2:7). The PE, moreover, explicitly associate the ministry that Paul has shared with Timothy with prophetic interventions and the activity of the Spirit (1 Tim 1:18; 4:14; 2 Tim 1:6, 13–14), again grounding the trustworthiness of his witness to eternal life in the trustworthiness of the God who has promised it.

3. (*in due time he made his message clear of course*). The parentheses around Titus 1:3 mark an anacoluthon, where the carefully spun out thread of thought snaps. If the author had continued his period, the previous adjectival clause modifying eternal life would now have been balanced by a second contrasting (*de*) adjectival clause that would have described the revelation of life eternal in the historical order. Instead the previous two verses are left hanging without a main verb, and what amounts to a new sentence comments parenthetically on the immediately preceding clause by comparing and contrasting the *chronoi* of 1:2 with the *kairoi* of 1:3. Each of these terms is qualified in the text: *chronoi* as *aiōnioi*, *kairoi* as *idioi*. These adjectives, along with the drastic anacoluthon, have driven a wedge into a hendiadys *chronoi kai kairoi* (or the reverse), which occurs as early as LXX Dan 2:21; 4:37; Wis 8:8 and which recurs in the Pauline epistolary in both 1 Thess 5:1 and Acts 1:7 (in the form *chronoi e kairoi*). In Acts 17:26, 30 the two terms are completely separated, as here in the PE, and each is given a distinct sense. The reason for taking the phrase apart and reinterpreting its elements may be that it suggests for Christians a forbidden apocalyptic calendar (see Matt 24:36; Mark 13:32, *SFG* §293; Augustine, Letter 197.2 [*PL* 33.899–900]; and Barr, *Words for Time*, pp. 44–46). Both Acts and Titus have completely defused it by taking quite literally as separate elements words that were originally understood as synonyms and united in a hendiadys (BDF §446). The method was not original with these documents, for already Rom 15:8–13 interpreted the key covenant phrase "truth and love" by

dividing it up between Jews and pagans. The distinction between a quantitative *chronos* and a qualitative *kairos* was certainly felt in classical Greek (Ammonius, cited by Places, *"Tempora,"* p. 105). Although LXX Eccl 3:1–8 (versus MT) exploited the distinction, biblical Greek no longer adverted regularly to it (cf. 2 Tim 4:2; Barr, *Words for Time*, pp. 33 n. 1, 39, 46, 122 n. 2, 124 n. 2). The regular practice, however, furnishes the background for the downplaying of that phrase in Acts and Titus, for these authors knew the qualitative connotation in *kairos*.

Here in Titus 1:3, as in 1 Tim 2:6 and perhaps in 6:15, the understanding of the *kairoi* as appointed or appropriate times is determined by the possessive *idioi*, just as the preceding *chronoi* were defined quantitatively as *aiōnioi* (see Barr, *Words for Time*, p. 43, cf. 41). Although elsewhere in the NT only Gal 6:9 uses *idios* with *kairos* (see NOTES above), Luke 1:20 uses *eis ton kairon autōn* of the appointed fulfillment of the angel's words about the birth of Zechariah's son (cf. the Matthean addition [21:41] of *tous karpous en tois kairoi autōn* to the vinedresser parable of Mark 12:9 [*SFG* §278]). In Acts 14:17 the harvest times (*kairous karpophorous*) are by God's appointment, and in Acts 17:26 God has fixed "allotted times" (*prostetagmenous kairous*) for all persons on earth. If the divinely established "order" of nature is here being appealed to, it is precisely because that order is a paradigm for the historical order within which human beings too have their "seasons" (see *1 Clem.* 20.4, 10 in NOTES). Edouard des Places (*"Tempora,"* p. 115) has acutely noted that the compound in **tag-* is part of the key to understanding the *kairoi*. All *kairoi*, whether natural or historical, are at the divine command, and precisely as such they resist the attempts of human reason to gain control over them, to order them, or to predict them rationally. Men can construct a chronology; a "kairology" is inconceivable (see Petrolini, "Valenza *Kairos,*" pp. 351–356). Thus here in Titus 1:3 the *kairoi idioi* are linked with the divine order (*kat' epitagēn*) that had been issued to the apostle whose work has its set seasons, as does the agricultural world around him (cf. 2 Tim 2:6 with 1 Cor 3:5–9; 9:7–11; as well as John 4:35–38).

In a description of the apostolate as *to martyrion kairois idiois*, "testimony in due time" (1 Tim 2:6), the PE designated a witnessing not only to Jesus' sufferings for all but also a complementary testimony to Paul's own humiliating arrest (2 Tim 1:8) and the *kairos* of his return to his Lord (2 Tim 4:6). In both Hellenistic and LXX usage the plural *kairoi* can mean *time* in general "with no element of either decisiveness or plurality in meaning" (Barr, *Words for Time* p. 62 n. 1, cf. pp. 32–34). The PE use the term *kairoi* in this generic sense (1 Tim 4:1), but they also use it with a genuinely plural meaning (2 Tim 3:1). Moreover, *kairois idiois* is an unusual phrase that is part of a conscious analysis in Titus 1:3 (as distinct from the traditional material of 1 Tim 6:15). First Timothy 2:6 is to be heard in the light of that analysis. If in fact the "times and/or seasons" of the apocalyptic phrase were heard in a generic sense, there is all the more reason for the author of the PE to "overinterpret" the plural and thus further deapocalypticize the terminology as he introduces it into his description of the apostolate. There are as many *kairoi* as there are occasions given by God for the apostolic ministers to bear witness before unbelievers (cf. the *martyrion hēmōn*, of Paul, Silvanus, and Timothy, in 2 Thess 1:10). If, indeed, it is not for apostles to know "times or seasons" in an apocalyptic sense (Acts 1:7), they are to be "my witnesses (*martyres*) . . . to the end of the earth" (Acts 1:8; cf. 4:33). The revelation (*logon autou*, 1:3) has its God-given seasons, which are complemented by the seasons given to heralds for its proclamation (*en kērygmati*, 1:3).

he made his message clear. The schema for developing the thought is the contrast between the divine promise of life, hidden in the eternal order and revealed (*ephanerōsen*) in the apostolic proclamation. Because the verb here for causing revelation is by no means common in pre-Christian Greek and becomes frequent in the Paulines (see NOTES), where it is associated with the antitheses between light and darkness and between concealment and revelation, some have suggested a pre-Pauline apocalyptic and gnostic origin for the schema (R. Bultmann and D. Lührmann in *TDNT* 9.4–5), whereas others have made a case for its being a nongnostic development of thought within the first-century Pauline tradition (Conzelmann, *1 Cor.*, p. 58). That part of the tradition documented by the PE supports Conzelmann's view. The use of the schema here in the opening of the correspondence is already dependent in its language and its method of theological reflection on the traditional materials that are cited in 1 Tim 3:16 and 2 Tim 1:10. The former is part of a first-generation, Jewish-Christian, prophetic hymn confessing the mystery of the Son "who was revealed (*ephanerōthe*) in human flesh" and proclaimed (*ekērychthē*) by the apostolate to the pagans. The historical revelation, prophetically mediated, furnishes the precedents for the terminology and the method of conceptualization that appear in these opening verses of the PE. The passage of 2 Tim is also in the general context of the apostle's prayer, which in 1:9–11 exploits a liturgical confession that had summarized the Pauline creed in terminology that time and again reappears in Titus 1:1–3. Here too, in apostolic prayer and worship, the revelation past is conceived as becoming present to and for the one who believes what the Pauline apostolate proclaims and celebrates. The PE do not draw this schema of concealment/darkness versus revelation/light directly out of the texts of the earlier Pauline letters. They do employ a tradition of community worship that had been previously influenced and formed by the Pauline apostolate, including one or another of his letters, particularly Rom.

Behind all schemata, however, is "the God who is without deceit," and he has revealed "his (*autou*) message (*logon*)" in the apostolic proclamation, "the message of the truth" (2 Tim 2:15) in contrast to "the message" of men who controvert the resurrection (2 Tim 2:17). For the PE that message has been entrusted for oral proclamation and teaching to Paul, to his coworkers, Titus and Timothy, and to the presbyter-bishops whom they designate or supervise (see Titus 1:9; 2:7–8; 1 Tim 4:12; 5:17; 2 Tim 4:2, 15). The message corresponds to the Scriptures of Israel (see Titus 2:5; 1 Tim 4:5) and contains not only the words (*logoi*) of Jesus but those of his apostle also (see 1 Tim 6:3; 2 Tim 1:13), wholesome words that are to be assimilated in faith by the apostolic minister himself, not only set out for the faith of others (1 Tim 4:6, 12; 2 Tim 1:13). The message of God that his messengers have articulated cannot be chained down (2 Tim 2:9), and it is now proposed for belief and action in the catechetical summaries; the prayers, hymns, and creedal professions; the preaching and teaching of those who have shared and still continue the Pauline apostolate (see Titus 1:9 and the five *pistoi logoi* of the PE noted at 3:8a).

(*in a proclamation*). The PE open and close with a reference to Paul's *kērygma* (2 Tim 4:17), that is, the result of the act of proclamation (BDF §109.2), and they link "the message" of God with the *kērygma* of which Paul is *kēryx* (1 Tim 2:7) and which Timothy is to proclaim at the Lord's command in still other seasons (*kēryxon ton logon:* 2 Tim 4:2). The *kērygma* apparently coincides largely with "the gospel that I was entrusted with" at 1 Tim 1:11 (see 2 Tim 1:10–12; 2:8–9), and the Pauline proclamation of the message of God is here traced back to the historical moment of his conversion-vocation by the risen Jesus (1 Tim 1:12–18). In that setting Paul had been entrusted with a commission from the Lord who had found him trustworthy (see Excursus I, "*Pistis* Terminology in the PE"). The revelation of the risen Jesus was the setting for Paul's call by the Father to bring the good news about his Son to the pagans, as Gal 1:1, 15–16 described it (cf. Rom 1:1). The PE here and in 1 Tim 1:1, 12–16 employ a quite different terminology to describe the same event.

(*[that] I was entrusted with, at the order of our savior, God*). Paul wrote often enough of his apostolic vocation as "by will of God (*dia thelēmatos theou*)," and 2 Tim 1:1 uses precisely that phrase. Here in Titus 1:3 and 1 Tim 1:1 the Pauline mission fulfills or corresponds with (*kat'*) the divine order (*epitagēn*). This strong phrase had appeared in Hellenistic Greek, and the LXX had used it of the commands of God and of kings (see NOTES). The Paulines, outside the PE, used the phrase of God's as well as the apostle's own orders. The PE similarly use the term of the commands of God and of the apostolic minister (Titus 2:15). The God who has given the apostle this order is himself *basileus* ("king"; 1 Tim 1:17; cf. 6:14–15), and the suggestion of royal power may be heard here.

(*our savior, God*). The anarthrous designation of God with which this prologue began has gradually expanded. In 1:2 God was "without deceit"; now in the final expansive phrase he is "our savior, God" *tou sōtēros hēmōn theou.* For the meaning of the phrase, see Excursus V, "The PE on Salvation."

4. *writes this to Titus.* The emphatic Pauline *ego* of Titus 1:3 eases the transition out of the anacoluthon and to the name of the addressee of this first letter in the collection. If the preceding verses are to be read as a prologue to the correspondence as a whole, 1:4 sharply narrows the field to Titus and the Pau-

line directives to this man whose Roman name, utterly abhorrent to the Jewish people of the empire after A.D. 70, evokes that turning to the Gentiles with which Acts had concluded. A pagan named Titus had in the first Christian generation joined the congregation at Antioch and, apparently at Paul's initiative, had been coopted into that ministry which he and Barnabas exercised there (see Gal 2:1, 3; Quinn, "Ministry," pp. 148 n. 83, 151). The irritation and eventual confrontation that this event generated were still being rehearsed and justified a decade after the fact, when Paul between the years 50 and 55 wrote to the Galatian churches (Gal 2). Titus had been Paul's liaison with the refractory Corinthian converts (see NOTES), and Paul called him "my brother" (2 Cor 2:13) and "my partner and fellow worker" (koinōnos . . . synergos: 2 Cor 8:23). The first-generation documents contain no further references to this trusted collaborator in at least a decade of the Pauline apostolate. For the second-generation materials, the disturbance in the text of Acts 18:7 may indicate that the copyists (if not the author) wanted to distinguish Titus Justus from a person with a similar name (Barrett, "Titus," pp. 2–3, who reviews also the variant at 13:1 and other surmises; E. Haenchen, Acts, p. 535). The only indisputable occurrences of Titus in the second-generation documents are in the PE, which here begin and will eventually conclude (2 Tim 4:10) with his name. The silence of Acts concerning his previous career may be due to the painful controversies with which he was associated, controversies that Acts muted or omitted altogether (Barrett, "Titus," p. 2). On the hypothesis that the PE are to be read as a conclusion to Acts, the figure of Titus was accordingly saved for the concluding roll. In any case, the author of the PE had received an authentic tradition that a man named Titus had held a key position in the Pauline mission. Although his career in the previous generation (as known from Gal and 2 Cor) is not adverted to in the PE, it is suggestive that the letter here addressed to him is particularly exercised about the relation of Jewish Christians to the Pauline apostolate (Titus 1:10–16; 2:15–3:3; 3:9), a problem that certainly engaged the "historical Titus" in his collaboration with the apostle.

his true child. That collaboration with Paul is explained in the unusual appositional phrase, gnēsiōi teknōi (see NOTES), which proposes the father–son relationship as a paradigm for explaining the relationship of the apostle with his coworkers, Titus and Timothy. The anachronistic comparisons of these figures with "apostolic delegates" or "metropolitans" or "monarchical heads" or "coadjutors" are seductively charming, but the text of the PE employs the father–child model for expressing the way in which the apostolic task was shared and transmitted. This familial paradigm will surface, in one form or another, almost whenever this correspondence addresses itself to questions of ecclesial ministry by men or women (e.g., Titus 1:6; 1 Tim 1:18; 3:4–5, 12; 5.9–10; etc.). Even where tekna refer to the physical offspring of a mother or father (e.g., Titus 1:6; 1 Tim 5:4), the references are intended to furnish the visible criteria for choosing a person for a ministry in the church, which in its turn is explicitly compared to the family (1 Tim 3:5). The familial comparison is frequent in the OT, particularly in the Hebrew sapiential tradition, to describe the transmission of a wisdom accumulated from long experience, and Qumran illustrates the usage (CD 2:14; 13:9; 1QH 7:20–21).

The *teknon* was the one to be benefited by what we would call a catechesis, an education for living (see Audet, *Didaché*, pp. 302–304). The genius of the comparison lies in its combination of elements: living, individual persons appear but in a basic, universal social structure; both external, physical and inner, moral relationships are presumed; both authority and obedience can be seen in a horizon of love and loyalty; the role of parent as primary teacher can be exploited; present possession and subsequent transmission of (or succession to) the goods of the family can be explained. It is not accidental that this correspondence is explicitly addressed to Paul's "children" and that it closes with the last will and testament of 2 Tim, in which the dying patriarch bequeathes the divinely bestowed inheritance to his children.

In what sense are Titus and Timothy Paul's children? There is a polemical edge in *gnēsios*. There is obviously a sense in which Titus and Timothy do not owe their physical birth to Paul. At the same time, there are persons who claim the apostle as their father but who have, in comparison with a Titus or a Timothy, no legitimate right to do so. The term *gnēsios* suggests qualities of an internal, moral order that correspond with more tangible realities (see NOTES). They are really his children because they have believed in and acted on the message that the apostle proclaimed. They have learned from their father. Does this suggest that Paul had brought them into the family of believers? Was Paul's apostolate, in the mind of the author of the PE, immediately linked with the conversion of the pagan, Titus, and the Jew, Timothy? The other Paulines do not affirm this interpretation. An immediate link between Paul and Timothy's conversion does not appear in Acts 16:1–2 or 2 Tim 1:5; 3:14–15. The "genuineness" of the relation of Titus and Timothy to Paul, as the PE envision it, is grounded on their sharing in his apostolic work. Already in Phil 2:20, 22, Timothy's work with Paul for the gospel was like that of a child with his father. The comparison suggests the apostle's initiative and choice in the relationship, but without excluding other elements (1 Tim 1:18; 4:14). Paul (the Jew), Timothy (half Jewish, half pagan), Titus (the pagan) are, regardless of their former religious histories, now united in one family for the apostolic ministry. For their one, real "Father," see below on the source of the blessing with which this apostolic greeting ends.

for the faith all share. United by their belief in the revelation given by the infallible, savior God, Paul and Titus share (cf. *koinōnos* and *synergos* in 2 Cor 8:23) the apostolate "for the faith all share," *kata koinēn pistin.* For *kata pistin*, see 1:1 above and Excursus I. The adjective here makes explicit the public and communal character of the belief to which the apostolate is ordered, a faith that belongs to and is the concern of not only the apostle and his collaborators but also the body of believers who, with Paul and Titus, confess "our savior God." Moreover, the whole relation between Paul and Titus unfolds in the subsequent pages, in the apostle's "conversation" with his colleague that begins with the second-person singular forms of 1:5. The *teknon* of this greeting certainly suggests that Paul's colleague was his chronological junior, just as does the exhortation given to him along with the younger men in Titus 2:6–7 (and perhaps the word of encouragement in 2:15). The term is not used to satisfy modern biographical and psychological interests but rather for the ecclesial purpose of this correspondence. As Paul himself became an apostle "for the faith of God's elect" (1:1), so now the relation between him and his "real child" exists to serve the community of believers in the minister established for them (Titus 1:5–16) as well as in their formation as God's people (Titus 2:1–3:11). The "historical Titus" on the island of Crete (1:5) comes back into focus as this letter concludes (3:12–15), but the probably authentic memories of his relationship with Paul in the mid-sixties of the first century (see INTRODUCTION) now serve to remind the reader of this correspondence of the historical phases through which congregations of believers have passed from the appearance of an apostle, through the continuation of his work by collaborators and colleagues, into the situation in which they become local churches under a leadership that is authenticated not by its having existed for some time but by its relation to the apostolic founders of the congregation. Titus himself is remembered as being on the move, at Paul's behest, to the very last lines of the PE, when he has gone to Dalmatia (2 Tim 4:10). His pagan background and Roman name made him an appropriate addressee to lead off a correspondence assigned to the apostle to the pagans. The memory of his sharing in Paul's care for newly founded congregations, and particularly for a troubled one like Corinth, suggested him as a fitting model for the way Paul would guide newly founded, young churches, the first fruits of a missionary journey and visit (cf. Jeremias, NTD, p. 2). The second part of this correspondence then turns, through a paradigmatic Timothy, to Paul's relationship with a church that has already begun to have a history, the Ephesian congregation.

The continuing tensions in even newly founded congregations between the traditions of the Jewish Christians and the practices of the converts from paganism lie behind the text of Titus, which envisions churches that are experiencing problems as they come to terms with their Jewish heritage (and its direct heirs) in their communities (see Titus 1:10, 14; 3:1–3, 9). In such a situation, a document transmitting Paul's instruction for Titus (who in the previous generation had been at the very center of a similar inner-Christian crisis) would have additional impact. In 1–2 Tim this tension has relaxed somewhat.

Grace and peace. With the direct greeting, "grace and peace," the second member of the epistolary address, Semitic in its omission of a verb, is begun. The first member had provided names of the writer and recipient (see Lohse, *Col.,* p. 5 for the literature). The typically Greek letter (also illustrated in the

NT by Acts 15:23; 23:26) used only one member (thus, *X* greets [*chairein*] *Y*). The *charis* of the Pauline formula is a nominal echo of the absolute infinitive in the Greek formula, but the meaning of the term in the PE is rooted in what the Christian traditions exploited by the PE meant by it (Titus 2:11; 3:7); in the meaning that it has in tandem with *eirēnē* (also with *eleos,* as in 1 Tim 1:2; 2 Tim 1:2), the bound phrase here; and finally the meaning that it receives in the genre of a blessing.

The form of the opening epistolary benediction in the Paulines, apart from the PE, normally contains three elements: a wish for a blessing; a recipient for the wish; and the divine source of the blessing (not in 1 Thess 1:1 s.v.l.). The elements admit both expansion and repetition. In one instance the third element does not appear, but the first two always do and in the order noted (see Mullins, "Benediction," pp. 59–60). Mullins's analysis (pp. 61–64) has traced the structure of this genre into the benediction formulas of the LXX and has noted that the NT is distinctive not in its use of the genre but in putting a blessing prayer at the opening (and closing) of a letter. See 3:15 and C. Westermann, *Blessing,* pp. 96–98 for further observations on the origin and purpose of these NT epistolary blessings.

The PE resemble the rest of the Paulines in prefixing a blessing to each of these letters, a blessing that to a great extent uses the terminology of the other opening Pauline benedictions (see Notes) and that has formal elements reaching back to Septuagintal sources. The PE differ in that the second formal element, the recipient, is not mentioned in any of these letters; the structure for their opening benediction is simply "wished-for blessing/divine source." Considering the loyalty of the PE to the work and words of Paul, it is difficult to conceive of this difference as an arbitrary alteration of language and form known to be Paul's. Rather, the simpler form is drawn from the same LXX genre that Paul had taken up and modified structurally (following Mullins rather than Lieu, "Greeting," pp. 167–172). To mention the recipient of the blessing at this point would call for the second-person singular, which in turn would give the impression that this was simply the correspondence between two individuals. But, as the closing blessings of the entire PE make clear, the letters are expected to be heard by the whole congregation of believers, who are addressed in the "Grace be with all of you" of Titus 3:15; 1 Tim 6:21 (s.v.l.); and 2 Tim 4:22. The use of the second-person plural, in the opening blessing, would obscure the very pattern for the transmission of the Pauline inheritance that the PE sought to inculcate. Thus, it was better to omit altogether mention of recipient(s) of the benediction. The resulting laconic formula would still be quite unmistakable in meaning, and its telegraphic character would convey an appropriate sense of insistent urgency. Its very brevity would invite the kind of expansion that already occurs in the opening blessing of 1–2 Tim, where *eleos* appears between *charis* and *eirēnē.*

In this setting of a blessing prayer, the gift that is sought is "grace and peace." The phrase is practically a hendiadys, a single reality designated by terms in a bound phrase. The *charis* emphasizes precisely the gift aspect of that which is urgently sought. The second term, *eirēnē*, has a strongly Hebraic background. *Charis* would remind Greek readers of the well-worn *chairein* of their standard epistolary greeting; *eirēnē* would not carry a similar resonance. But a reader coming from the Jewish tradition would hear the echo of the Hebrew *šālôm* (with its basic meaning of bodily soundness or health) behind *eirēnē*, and this would be for him a more familiar conversational introduction than *chairein*. Because neither Jew nor Greek hears the actual terms with which he is familiar, the hendiadys *charis kai eirēnē* has still a certain freshness and force in it. The free gift that the apostle prays for is a peace—a soundness and health—that has a divine origin. The language and concepts of the benediction from this point on remind one of the hymn for the savior's birth (see Luke 2:11) that Luke has the shepherds hear, "on earth peace to those favored (by him)" (*epi gēs eirēnē en anthrōpois eudokias:* Luke 2:14b, as in Brown, *Birth*, p. 393, see 403–405; 425–427). The divine goodwill (*eudokia*) or grace (*charis*) that was "revealed . . . for the rescue (*sōtērios*) of all human beings" (Titus 2:11; cf.3:4–5) is from the point of view of its effect "peace." Mercy, another complement for *charis* (1 Tim 1:2 q.v.), brings salvation (as Titus 3:5) in the form of deliverance from sins, forgiveness; and this issues ultimately in peace between God and men (it is not accidental that *eirēnē* has the final position both in the benedictions of the PE and in the list of virtues in 2 Tim 2:22).

from God the Father and Christ Jesus, our savior. The peace that is from one aspect God's gift is from another point of view the peace that came through the healing works and forgiving words of Jesus (see Acts 10:36). Both of those aspects are elaborated as this benediction moves into its second phase, to specify the divine origin of the blessing that is being invoked—"from God the Father and Christ Jesus, our savior." As Excursus V has contended, the savior title now explains the name of "Christ Jesus," which is so written (note the chiastic envelope formed with 1:1) that the apposition of *Iesou* with *tou sōtēr* stands out sharply. As Jesus now receives the title that the previous verse gave to God, the personal title, Father, is now given to the One who has progressively been characterized as *theos, ho apseudēs theos,* and *tou sōtēros hēmōn theou* in 1:1–3. The name "Father" for God is not only in the emphatic final place in this series, but it is also the most characteristically Christian title, with roots in the highly individual usage of the historical Jesus, who invoked God as *'abba'* (see Jeremias, *Prayers,* and the literature cited there). The PE all use the phrase *apo theou patros* in their opening benedictions; in the rest of the Paulines this phrase occurs (with *hēmōn*) regularly in such benedictions. The short form in the PE may derive from a more archaic one, which the other Paulines regularly "personalized" with *hēmōn* (1 Thess 1:2 and 2 Thess 1:2 s.v.l. would then witness to similar short forms that Paul was taking up earlier in his ministry). Unlike the rest of the Paulines, the PE entitle God as "Father" only in these initial blessings. The name was too important, too critical to miss altogether; hence the emphatic position it has in opening each letter. Yet it was not to be overemphasized in a correspondence that never calls Jesus the "Son." The appropriateness of the appearance of the title "Father" is bestowed on the person who has given life to his children. Again, the family and household imagery, noted above, come into sharp, personal focus in this title. Titus has just been called a true child of Paul, as Timothy will be. Yet he is not their father in this relationship. God is, and he explicitly receives the title. He alone stands at the ultimate origin of life eternal, for which the apostle and his "children" work. The corrective given implicitly here, which appropriately "relativizes" the description of the apostolate that has dominated this whole preface, is similar to the peculiarly Matthean saying, "And call no man your father on earth, for you have one father who is in heaven" (Matt 23:9).

The expansive description of the divine source of the "grace and peace" being prayed for in turn implies that from one aspect the free gift is eternal life (from the Father) and that, from another aspect, the peace (*šālôm*-health) is that which comes from Jesus' healing mercy.

II. THE APOSTOLIC COMMISSION TO TITUS (1:5–3:11)
II.A. FOR MINISTRY AND MAGISTERIUM (1:5–16)
II.A.1. THE APPOINTMENT OF MINISTERS (1:5–9)

1 ⁵The reason that I let you remain on Crete was to set right the remaining matters and to establish presbyters in every city as I myself commanded you. ⁶Every one of them ought to be

unimpeachable,
a husband to one wife,
with children who are believers,
    who cannot be charged with debauchery,
    who are not refractory.

⁷Indeed a bishop has to be

unimpeachable
(God's steward, so to speak),

76

not arrogant,
not irritable,
not a drinker,
not a bully,
not money-minded.

⁸Rather he must be one who likes guests,

likes goodness,
who is sensible,
upright,
devout,
self-controlled,

⁹who sticks to the message that is meant to be believed, according to the teaching, so that he can both encourage with wholesome apostolic instruction and refute opponents.

NOTES

1:5. *The reason.* On the Hellenistic prepositional *charin*, which recurs in 1:11 and 1 Tim 5:14, see BDF §160; 216; 456.4. The usage, infrequent in biblical Greek, occurs in both the Pauline (Gal 3:19; Eph 3:1, 14) and the Lukan literature (Luke 7:47).

I let you remain. For the second aorist *apelipon* (S*, D*, Psi, 81, 365, 1739, and 1881), the apparent imperfect, *apeleipon*, is a variant by itacism (A, C, F, G, 088, 0240, 33, and 1175): see B. Metzger, "Early Fragment," p. 150; J. K. Elliott, *Greek Text,* pp. 162–163. The *katelipon/kateleipon* of S², D², L, P, 104, and 326 would conform the usage of the PE (2 Tim 4:13, 20) with the other Paulines as well as Luke–Acts.

on Crete. See the INTRODUCTION on the world of the PE.

was to set right. The *epidiorthōsēi* of S*, C, D², 088, and 0240 could be either third-person singular active or second-person singular middle of the aorist subjunctive; the *epidiorthōseis* of A, D*, F, G, Psi, 1881, and 2495 opts for an unambiguous second-person singular active form that is parallel to the following *katastēseis* (see J. K. Elliott, *Greek Text,* p. 174). *Epidiorthoun* is not otherwise attested in the LXX, NT, or Ap. Frs. In pre-Christian Greek it appears only in a second-century B.C.E. inscription from Hierapytna on the southeast coast of Crete, *CIG* 2555.9 = *Inscriptiones Creticae* 3, pp. 49–52. The uncompounded cognate *diorthoun* occurs with the same sense, notably in the inscriptions about laws and treaties; see Dittenberger, *Syll.* 283.4, fourth century B.C.E., of lawgivers writing and revising laws in Chios; and 581.85, second century B.C.E., of revising treaties with Cretans.

the remaining matters. Ta leiponta, literally, "the things lacking," from the verb *leipein,* which will recur in Titus 3:13 and four times elsewhere in the NT. Thus in Luke 18:22, "One thing is lacking in you"; in Jas 1:4–5, "that you may be complete, lacking in nothing. If any of you lacks wisdom"; and Jas 2:15, about Christians who "lack daily food." In the Ap. Frs. Ignatius writes, "For many things are lacking to us, so that we may not lack God" (*Trall.* 5.2; see *Herm. Vis.* 3.1.9; *Sim.* 9.9.4), and he urges Polycarp to pray that he may "lack nothing and abound in every charism" (*Pol.* 2.2). In the latest strata of the LXX there are eight uses of *leipein,* a few somewhat parallel to the Christian usage outlined here. See Spicq, *Lexic.,* pp. 472–474.

to establish presbyters. On the presbyters of the PE, see 1 Tim 5:17–25. The phrase *kathistanai presbyterous* occurs only here in biblical Greek; then *1 Clem.* 54.2 writes of "Christ's flock with its established presbyters (*meta tōn kathestamenōn presbyterōn*)," also uses the verb regularly of installing bishops and deacons (*1 Clem.* 42.4–5; 43.1; 44.2–3). Even *1 Clem.* 4.10 (citing Exod 2:14) is part of the case against the Corinthian rejection of their presbyters. The only other use of the verb in the Ap. Frs., *Herm. Sim.* 5.6.2, is also of Roman provenance.

The verb *kathistanai* occurs elsewhere in the Paulines only in Rom 5:19 (*bis*). Of the eighteen other NT uses, eight are in Luke–Acts. Hebrews (5:1; 7:28; 8:3) employs this verb for the appointment of (high) priests, a usage that belongs to the Maccabean stratum of LXX (1 Macc 10:20; 2 Macc 14:13; 4 Macc 4:16).

in every city. The distributive *kata polin,* meaning "in every single city" (see 2 Macc 4:36; 3 Macc 4:4; 6:41), occurs otherwise in the NT only in Acts 15:21; 20:23 (cf. 15:36). The usage is Lukan (BAGD, s.v. *kata,* § II.l.s), and reappears in Ign. *Rom.* 9.3.

(*as I myself*) *commanded* (*you*). *Diatassein,* occurring only here in the PE, is regularly found in the rest of the Paulines and the Lukan corpus. Otherwise in the NT only Matt 11:1 uses the verb.

6. *Every one of them.* Greek *ei tis* occurs only here in Titus, as well as in the lists and codes of 1 Tim 3:1, 5; 5:4, 8, 16; 6:3; *ei ti heteron* concludes the catalog of vices in 1 Tim 1:10, which *ean tis* in 1:8 introduces (see 2 Tim 2:5, 21 for the only other occurrences of *ean tis* in the PE). G. W. Knight (*Sayings,* p. 55) has observed that *ei tis* is never used in the LXX to introduce casuistic laws; and it is rare in the Lukan literature. By contrast, Paul uses *ei tis* frequently, perhaps because it already belonged to the catechetical language and materials that both he and the PE utilized in different ways (see COMMENT).

ought to be. For the nuance of obligation, note, in the parallel position in v 7, *dei* (see 1 Tim 3:2).

unimpeachable. Anegklētos belongs to legal and forensic language; it appears a single time in the LXX (3 Macc 5:31) and never in the Ap. Frs. All five NT uses are in the Paulines: here, in the following verse, and then in 1 Tim 3:10 the term appears among the requisites for the ecclesial ministries of presbyter-bishop and deacon. On 1 Cor 1:8 and on the short list of virtues in Col 1:22, see Conzelmann, *1 Cor.*, p. 28 and Lohse, *Col.*, p. 65.

a husband to one wife. Literally, "a man of one woman." This phrase will recur in the lists of virtues for the bishop and the deacon in 1 Tim 3:2, 12. The closest parallels in profane Greek are the epigram of Carphyllides (second century B.C.E.: *Greek Anthology* 7:260; cf. 324), "I enjoyed one wife (*miēs apelausa gynaikos*) who grew old with me," and the astrological papyrus (third century C.E., PSI 3.6, §158.25–26) that notes a planetary configuration that makes men blameworthy for "not staying with one wife (*me epimenontas miai gynaiki*)."

The actual phrase of the PE, however, is not documented in biblical Greek or in the Ap. Frs., though see Clement of Alexandria, *Stromata* 1.5; 3.1 (O. Stählin; Leipzig: Hinrichs, 1906, 2.20.8; 197.12). First Timothy 5:9 contains a mirror image of the expression, in which the woman admitted to the order of widows is to be the wife of one husband. In the PE, *anēr* always refers to those of the male sex; in the singular it always designates a married man (1 Tim 2:12); in the plural it may refer to men, whether married or unmarried (1 Tim 2:8), or to husbands in particular (Titus 2:5). Almost the same pattern is found with the uses of *gynē* in the PE: the singular designates a wife (1 Tim 2:10, 12, 14); the plural refers to women, regardless of their married state (1 Tim 2:9–10 and 3:11, where the reference may be to wives or to unmarried women).

with children who are believers. See Excursus I, "*Pistis* Terminology in the PE."

who cannot be charged. Literally, it reads "not under accusation," *en katēgoriai*, a term that will recur in the *ordo* for presbyters in 1 Tim 5:19. Otherwise in the NT this word occurs only in John 18:29, for the formal accusation lodged with Pilate against Jesus; it is not otherwise documented in the LXX or the Ap. Frs., though its cognates cluster in Acts and in the Maccabean corpus.

with debauchery. Greek *asōtia* designates a variety of vices, though Aristotle remarks that the *asōtos* is properly speaking one who wastes his own substance, "for he who is ruined by his own agency is indeed *asōtos*" (*NE* 1119b35–1120a1; cf. 1120a30–1121b11). A Roman heard the term as equivalent to *nequam*, for an unimportant and worthless person (Aulus Gellius, *Noctes atticae* 6.11.1–2). The etymological pun on *asōtos* (not to be saved/prodigal) is untranslatable but not to be ignored here in Titus, where the *so(s)-* terminology occurs at every turn (see Excursus V, "The PE on Salvation"). In Eph 5:18, *asōtia* is drunkenness; in 1 Pet 4:4 a list of pagan vices is summarized with the term. Luke 15:13 (cf. 30) uses the adverb *asōtos* of the prodigal's style of living. The only occurrences in the LXX are of gluttony (cf. LXX Prov 28:7 with MT) and fornication (2 Macc 6:4). The Ap. Frs. do not employ the term. See Spicq, *Lexic.*, pp. 154–156.

who are not refractory. The *anypotaktoi* will recur in 1:10 and 1 Tim 1:9; see *hypotassein* in 2:5, 9; 3:1. The LXX and the Ap. Frs. do not employ the Hellenistic *anypotaktos*, and its one other NT use, in Heb 2:8, is in a favorable sense.

7. *Indeed a bishop has to be unimpeachable.* On the bishop, *episkopos*, see the INTRODUCTION, and 1 Tim 3:2 for a variant on the phrasing here. For the eight other uses of *dei* in the PE, see 1:11 (*bis*); 1 Tim 3:2, 7, 15; 5:13 (*deonta*); 2 Tim 2:6, 24. Almost half of the remaining NT occurrences are in Luke–Acts.

(*God's steward, so to speak*). The LXX uses *oikonomos* of men who are delegated to administer the property of a higher (*royal*) authority, but never figuratively. See 2 Tim 4:20 on the Erastus who, in Rom 16:23, is "the city treasurer" of Corinth. The nine other NT uses of *oikonomos* are in parabolic and figurative contexts, all Lukan or Pauline, except for 1 Pet 4:10 (see Ign. *Pol.* 6.1 for the only use in the Ap. Frs. and *T. Jos.* 12.3 about Joseph as *oikonomos*). For the secular texts and the literature, see Spicq, *Lexic.*, pp. 606–613 and the articles of John N. P. Reumann cited at 1 Tim 1:4.

not arrogant. Authadēs occurs otherwise in the NT only of the defiant opponents in 2 Pet 2:10; LXX Prov 21:24 is closest to the NT usage (otherwise only in LXX Gen 49:3, 7). The Corinthian troublemakers are thus characterized in *1 Clem.* 1.1 (cf. 30.8; 57.2). The use in the negative paraenesis of *Did.* 3.6 resembles this passage of Titus. Theophrastus, *Characters*, 15, offers a trenchant profile of the surly.

not irritable. Orgilos does not occur otherwise in NT, but, as with *authadēs*, see LXX Prov 21:19 (also in 22:24; 29:22, and LXX Ps 17:49) and *Did.* 3.2.

not a drinker, not a bully. The phrase recurs in 1 Tim 3:3. The vulgar *mē paroinos*, practically equivalent to the English "not a drunk," is, like *plēktēs*, "bully" otherwise undocumented in the NT, LXX, or Ap. Frs. See Menander (Sandbach, *Menandri*) *Perikeiromenē* 1022 (444), for *paroinos* and the verbal forms in *Epitrepontes* 473 (296) and *Aspis* 386 (41). The latter passage illustrates the conceptual link between intoxication and verbal abuse which in the PE is reinforced by the alliterative pairing of *paroinos* with *plēktēs*, an unusual adjective in secular Greek that can be applied not only to men but to wine (Plutarch, *Moralia* 2.132D).

not money-minded. Mē aischrokerdēis qualifies the deacons of 1 Tim 3:8; it is not found otherwise in the NT, LXX, or Ap. Frs., but see 1 Pet 5:2 for the cognate adverb. Theophrastus, *Characters* XXX is devoted to the avaricious. See Polybius, *Histories* 6.46.1–4 for the proverbial *aischrokerdeia* of the Cretans.

8. *Rather he must be one who likes guests, likes goodness.* The alliteration intensifies with this pair of compounds in *philo-*, of which the former, *philoxenos*, will recur in 1 Tim 3:2 but elsewhere in the NT only in 1 Pet 4:9 (of all believers). The LXX does not use this term, which belongs to an inscriptional terminology that is practically undocumented in the papyri (Spicq, *Lexic.*, pp.

932–935) but which is regularly found from Rom and Heb through the PE to *1 Clem.* and Hermas. The *philagathos* of this catalog is found only here in the NT (but see the unique *aphilagathos* of the vice list in 2 Tim 3:3). Its only LXX occurrence is in the list of the virtues of the spirit of wisdom in Wis 7:22. This usage appears also in *Ep. Arist.* 124, 292 and Philo, *Mos.* 2.9, suggesting that Alexandrian Judaism found the term congenial. For a full survey of the ancient data, see Ceslaus Spicq's *Supp. Lexic.,* pp. 671–673.

who is sensible, upright. For *sōphron* see Excursus V, "The PE on Salvation." For the "upright," *dikaios,* elsewhere in the PE, see 1 Tim 1:9 and 2 Tim 4:8. The cluster of *(a-)dik-* words in the PE is treated at Titus 3:5, 7.

devout, self-controlled. Hosios, which appears eight times in the NT, occurs once again in the PE of the hands of men raised in prayer (1 Tim 2:8); the antonym *anosios* in the lists of 1 Tim 1:9; 2 Tim 3:2 does not recur in the NT. The other Paulines do not use the adjective, but they once use the cognate adverb (1 Thess 2:10) and once a cognate noun (Eph 4:24) in short lists. Luke 1:75 has the priest Zechariah use the noun; Acts 2:27 and 13:34, 35 employ nominal forms of the adjective but only in citing the LXX, where the term appears with some regularity, but only once in the phrase *dikaios kai hosios,* and there referring to the Lord. *Hosios* appears in the Ap. Frs. only in *1–2 Clem.,* once in the phrase *dikaios kai hosios* (*1 Clem.* 14.1). The *T. Benj.* 3.1 speaks of Joseph as *agathos kai hosios anēr* (cf. 5.4). Josephus, *Ant.* 15.138 has a nominal use in the phrase "holiness and justice," *to hosion kai dikaion.*

Egkratēs, not documented elsewhere in the NT, is the antonym of the *akratēs* in the list of 2 Tim 3:3. Paul uses the cognate nouns in the catalog of Gal 5:23 and in 1 Cor 7:5; the verb in 1 Cor 7:9 and 9:25. For the other uses of the noun, see Acts 24:25 and the list of virtues in 2 Pet 1:6 (*bis*). The LXX contains as many as twenty uses of the *egkrat-* cluster, particularly in the later strata, but generally with the wider sense of having power over other persons, places, and things. Sirach, especially in 26:15, closely parallels the NT usage for self-control. *First Clement* and Hermas use the *egkrat-* cluster regularly, but its appearance in the lists of Pol. *Phil.* 4.2; 5.2, as well as in *2 Clem.* 4.3, is notable.

9. *who sticks to the message that is meant to be believed.* The paraenesis of 1 Thess 5:14 uses *antechesthai* with a different nuance; the only other NT use of the verb, in the Q logion of Luke 16:13 (= Matt 6:24), has the sense found here (see Guelich, *Sermon,* p. 334). The LXX, like the NT, always uses the verb in the middle, but with a wider range of meanings. The closest parallels are in the prophetic and sapiential traditions (see LXX Isa 56:2, 4, 6; Jer 51:10 [MT 44:10]; Prov 3:18; 4:6). In the Ap. Frs. only *Herm. Vis.* 1.1.8 employs this verb. On "the message" see 1:3.

meant to be believed. See the COMMENT below and 3:8a.

according to the teaching. With *didachē,* which will reappear in 2 Tim 4:2, the cluster of eight **dida-* terms begins in the PE. They recur thirty times. In the LXX only the title of Ps 59 uses *didachē,* as the prayer that follows is said to be "by David for teaching." While the NT employs *didachē* thirty times, there are fewer than half that number of uses in the Ap. Frs.

so that he can both encourage with wholesome apostolic instruction and refute opponents. For the PE *didaskalia* is a technical term in the singular, and thus the translation "apostolic instruction"; it is *hygiainousā* here as well as at 2:1; 1 Tim 1:10; and 2 Tim 4:3. This term otherwise in the PE applies to faith (Titus 1:13; 2:2) and to words (*logoi:* 1 Tim 6:3; 2 Tim 1:13), as the cognate *hygiēs* refers to *logos* in Titus 2:8. Luke uses *hygiainein* of physical health (5:31; 7:10; 15:27). Otherwise in the NT only the epistolary greeting of 3 John employs the term. The LXX Prov 13:13 grounds health in respect for God's command but comes no closer to the usage of the PE. The Ap. Frs. do not employ *hygiainein* and use the cognates of physical health, though Hermas's parabolic use of *hygiēs* is notable. The reference to wholesome instruction does not appear in A, which reads *parakalein tous en pasē* [sic] *thlipsei,* "encourage them in every trial," a phrase from 2 Cor 1:4 (contrast *T. Gad* 4.4, "whenever difficulty arises, it [hatred] plots how he [the master] might be killed," *en pasei thlipsei, epicheirei kat' autou*).

encourage . . . and refute. Parakalein and *elegchein* are paired again in 2:15; the closest NT parallel is Luke 3:18–19. The similar list of 2 Tim 4:2 separates these verbs and reverses the order. *Parakalein,* which occurs more than a hundred times in the NT, recurs in the PE in Titus 2:6 as well as in 1 Tim 1:3; 2:1; 5:1; and 6:2. In the LXX the uses of this verb are concentrated in Sir and the Maccabean corpus. In the Ap. Frs., Ignatius favors the term. See Grayston, "Meaning of *parakaleo,*" pp. 27–31. *Elegchein* recurs in the PE at Titus 1:13 and 1 Tim 5:20. There are only a dozen other NT uses. This verb is characteristic of the LXX's sapiential and prophetic traditions (see the citations in *1 Clem.*) but infrequent in the Ap. Frs. After the short lists of vv 7–8, the expansive text of v 9 invited scribal expansion at this point; thus the medieval cursive 460 added, "Do not appoint those who have been married twice, making them deacons, nor those who have wives from a second marriage. Let them not approach to perform the divine liturgy at the altar. As a minister of God reprove the leaders who are unjust judges and robbers and liars and ruthless" (see *NTG*[26 corr] for the text). This scribe also glossed the text at 1:11 and 2 Tim 4:19 (J. K. Elliott, *Greek Text,* pp. 176–177 and 171).

opponents. The *antilegontas* are literally those who contradict, a term that will recur in 2:9. Elsewhere in the Paulines only Rom 10:21 employs this verb in quoting LXX Isa 65:2 (see *Barn.* 12:4). Five of the six remaining NT uses are in Luke–Acts. Of the seven other LXX occurrences, Sir 4:25 is notable: "Never speak against the truth but be mindful of your ignorance" (*RSV*). The only other use in the Ap. Frs. is Ign. *Smyrn.* 7.1. of "those who deny the gift of God (*antilegontes tei dōreai tou theou*)," the risen Jesus in the Eucharist.

COMMENT

1:5. *The reason that I let you remain on Crete was to set right the remaining matters.* The opening of the Pauline commission to his coworker is marked by the shift from the third-person address used in the apostolic greeting to Titus to the four-times-repeated second-person address of this verse, introducing the directives for the appointment of ecclesial ministers. The second-person address will reappear, again with a reference to Crete, at 1:12–13, when the subject shifts to true and false teaching. The emphatic repetition of the first-person singular, three times in this verse (and not to reappear until 3:8), links all that is to follow with the repeated first-person singular of 1:3, the text of which ("I . . . at the order [*ego kat' epitagēn*]") is also taken up in "as I myself commanded (*ego . . . dietaxamēn*)" at 1:5. An untranslatable and faint link exists between the *charis* of the greeting and opening *toutou charin* of this verse. The play on "remain . . . remaining" (*apelipon . . . ta leiponta*) within v 5 is a third illustration of a stylistic device for facilitating transitions favored by the PE. The device was favored in transitions from scene to scene in Greek drama; see Katsouris, *Tragedy,* pp. 137–140 and Menander, *Dyscolos* 520–521. The repetitions of similar sounds and terms, not necessarily related conceptually, serve as a kind of decorative sheath around the author's developing thought (see Silk, *Imagery,* pp. 175–176).

The divine command had sent Paul into the apostolate; now the apostolic command sends Titus to carry on the Pauline task. The first-person singular emphasizes that this was in fact Paul's own intent and purpose; the second-person address underlines a particular, historical coworker who continued what had begun with the apostle present. This man and his task are seen as indissolubly linked in the apostolic commission (*apelipon se . . . hina ta leiponta*) that fills the body of this letter. The Cretan scene for the Pauline intervention may go back to a source that the author of the PE introduced at this point: the opening scene of an apostolic coworker settled in his task certainly belongs to the overall schema that develops through the rest of this correspondence. The particularity of person and place are in contrast to the generic "to set right the remaining matters." The verb, *epidiorthoun,* is not only Cretan but also suggests an intervention conceived as public and legal (see NOTES). The PE favor the **ortho-* compounds (2 Tim 2:15; 3:16), but the closest parallel to the sense here is the lawyer's reference in Acts 24:2 to the "reforms" (*diorthōmata*) of the Roman procurator Felix (cf. Heb 9:10). The Pauline paraenetic intervention on the Cretan scene is for the reformation of an existing body of believers, not for the conversion and formation of a new church from the pagans. This Pauline reform turns first to prospective leaders and their teaching, then to the conduct of all classes of Christians (see the outline of this letter).

and to establish presbyters in every city as I myself commanded you. The Pauline role of Titus is specified without prejudice to the part that Cretan believers would play in presenting the candidates for the presbyteral work and testifying to the qualifications that are listed through v 9. The liturgical means that Titus would employ to make presbyters on the Pauline model are left unspecified (in *Constitutiones apostolorum* 7.46.10, Paul ordains Titus himself as bishop of Crete). The regular Lukan usage of *kathistanai* (see NOTES) best illustrates what the language here in Titus leaves one free to infer: a superior appoints another as judge, arbitrator, steward, governor, ruler (Luke 12:14, 42, 44; Acts 7:10, 27, 35, citing LXX Exod 2:14). In Acts 6:3, the Seven, chosen by the full body of Jerusalem believers, are to be appointed to their duty by the twelve as a body (*katastēsomen epi tēs chreias tautēs*), an appointment that involves presenting the candidates to the apostles and the imposition of hands in a setting of public prayer (Acts 6:6).

The language of Titus, however, remains generic; the means of making the presbyters are not the matters to be discussed. The concern is with their mission and their Pauline character. Thus presbyters are to be appointed "in every city" on an island that was proverbial for its numerous cities. The urban character of the Christian movement becomes explicit here. The emphasis on putting presbyters in every single town (but not in every single house church, as noted by Malherbe, *Social Aspects*, second edition, pp. 70, 101) presumes not large numbers of Christians in each community but the sharpening of the missionary focus for believers. Christian congregations, even with few members, make the work of their savior visible and attractive to a surrounding populace that could come to belief (1:6–7; 2:5, 8, 10–14; 3:1–2, 8). An influential part of the congregations envisioned by Titus are converts from Judaism (1:10), and thus in all probability from the middle class who plied the crafts, manned the workshops, and tended the stores of the urban centers. They were accustomed to living as a self-sufficient religious enclave within paganism. To such Jewish-Christian churches the Pauline missionary experience is proposed, the vanguard of which will be a body of new presbyters on the Pauline model, "as I myself commanded you." The position of the last clause and the emphatic *ego* (not to recur in Titus) bring the verb into the tradition of the Pauline orders for his churches in 1 Cor 7:17; 11:34; and 16:1, a tradition known to Ign. *Rom* 4.3; *Trall.* 3.3; and *Eph.* 3.1. The Lukan usage, even in Acts 20:13, does not correspond with it.

6. *Every one of them ought to be unimpeachable.* A Pauline conjunctive, *ei tis estin* (literally, "if anyone is"), relates this verse to the previous and makes it descriptive of the presbyters, whose visibility in the wider community is now specified in terms of their personal daily conduct as believers. The primary and indispensable qualification for the new Pauline presbyters is a tangibly and recognizably good life. The emphasis on the visible and verifiable aspects of a believer's life in grace is comparable with the Lukan heightening of the palpable

character of the divine interventions in the acts of Jesus and the Holy Spirit (see Luke 3:22; 24:39; Acts 2:2–3).

All sectors of the Christian community would concur in requiring good conduct from their leaders. That consensus would vanish when one asked what virtues would be looked for and what was their relative importance. The repeated Pauline "unimpeachable" of vv 6–7 suggests that the PE have combined two previously existing lists of qualifications for ecclesial ministers, the former titled "presbyters," the latter, "a bishop." For the purposes of the author at this point they were practically synonymous, though the different terms emerged originally from different Jewish milieus (see 1 Tim 3:1b–7), and the different qualifications reflected different expectations for ministers. For the PE, the lists are complementary, not contradictory. Yet it is instructive that the author gave priority to the list of v 6, where both the title "presbyter" and the qualifications seem to derive from a Jewish-Christian tradition from Jerusalem (see Brown, "Episkopē," pp. 326–327; Meaning, pp. 131–132). Just as this correspondence as a whole leads off with a letter to predominantly Jewish-Christian congregations, so a Jewish-Christian set of qualifications from Jerusalem heads the requisites for leaders in these churches. The primary characteristic of the presbyteral candidate is to be the integrity of his individual conduct, which offers no convincing evidence for wrongdoing. The characteristics of the candidate's life with his wife and finally with his children are to be reviewed. The forensic tone of the list and its strong emphasis on the home and family would be compatible with such a Jewish-Christian origin and destination.

a husband to one wife. The phrase in the PE always describes persons with a public ministerial role among believers. In every instance it qualifies a man or woman in his or her marital status and thus implies some manifest form of sexual control. The emphatic "one" contains the key to the specific relationship that the PE envisioned. The phrase as a whole is technical, at least in limited circles; yet it must have been so well entrenched that explanation seemed otiose.

Interpreters propose a variety of situations that could be relevant here (see Potterie, "Mari," pp. 620–623, for the literature). Not all are mutually exclusive. It is possible that the virtue described here could be exercised in several ways, but one must not forget that what is being proposed is intended to be an obviously verifiable quality.

The emphatic position of "one" here and in the other three occurrences of the formula practically eliminates the notion that marriage is here proposed as a prerequisite for those who exercise the Christian ministries. If such an idea were being put forward, the children mentioned next would also be required.

Polygamous relations, though regularly documented in the ancient world, are hardly being referred to, for the comparable formula in 1 Tim 5:9 would require positing polyandry, whereas polygamy and polyandry are not symmetrical in the same culture. Thus the phrase must apply to the marital status of a person to his or her one spouse. Here again interpreters have proposed that the phrase refers to fidelity to one partner and excludes concubinage, adultery, and other promiscuous sexual acts. Others submit that it refers to a person's sexual conduct after his one and only marriage, whether it has ended by death, divorce, or some other form of separation.

It is difficult to interpret the phrase simply in terms of marital fidelity and avoidance of sexual promiscuity. Greek had adequate terminology available, both positive and negative, for denoting such conduct (see 2:4–5; 1 Tim 5:11–14). Moreover, this interpretation ultimately places more value on the invisibility of vice than on the visibility of virtue in a presbyter.

The interpretations that place this quality in a person's sexual conduct after his one marriage give the most promise for understanding what this phrase denotes. But even here one must account for several possibilities. There is no question that the ancient world, pagan and Jewish, placed a high value on a person's remaining unmarried after the death of his only spouse. The literature and funerary inscriptions praising the *monandros* and *univira* are demonstrative on that score (see the texts in Spicq, *EP*, pp. 402, 430–431, and Lightman and Zeisel, "Univira," pp. 19–32). Yet such a person was never described with the phrase "husband of one wife/wife of one husband." Is the primary reference, then, to those in any way separated from their spouses? Surely the phrase is not meant to exclude those who had divorced and remarried, for divorce was ruled out by the Pauline and gospel traditions (1 Cor 7:10–11; Mark 10:11–12 par.). In fact the Qumran materials (see 11QTemple 57:17–19; CD 4:12b–5:11) indicate that divorce and remarriage were under fire from some quarters in first-century Palestinian Judaism (see Fitzmyer, "Divorce," pp. 103–110, with its bibliography, as well as Yadin, *Temple* 1.353, 355–357; 2.258).

It is possible, however, that the phrase of the PE refers to one now separated from his spouse, who has not remarried. That separation might be due to divorce or desertion or to still another circumstance, to which the Qumran documents advert. Young aspirants to the community were to marry at twenty years of age and to live five years with their wives (1QSa 1:6–13), apparently to fulfill the command of the Torah to increase and multiply. Afterward they were to separate from their wives and live as soldiers subject to the prescriptions of sexual continence for those who fought in the Holy War (cf. 1QM 7:2–4 with 1 Sam 21:4–5). For such men there was no question of returning to their domestic life before the final victory. As Abel Isaksson (*Marriage*, p. 65) has observed, the rules for sexual contact at Qumran are an inseparable part of their eschatology. It is conceivable that Essenian converts to Jewish Christianity brought this practice with them and that the phrase of the PE is unusual because it is meant to designate those persons who are separated in any way from their spouse and who intend no second marriage.

But where would such a phrase originate? Is this in some sense a specifically Christian qualification for ministry? The most convincing suggestion to date is that of Ignace de la Potterie ("Mari," pp. 628–636), who has noted the way in which Paul, in 2 Cor 11:2, reminds his Corinthian congregation, "I betrothed you to Christ to present you as a pure bride to her one husband (*heni andri*)." The marriage of Christians is a visible expression of the relation of Christ to his church, as the marriage between Jews was a sign of the covenant union of the one God with his people (LXX Mal 2:10). Paul appears to be arguing in the Corinthian passage from already accepted materials (see 1 Tim 2:14). A reasonable surmise is that these materials included a traditional paraenesis that took formulas used in the celebration of Christian marriages (see Eph 5:21–33). In that case, the formula cited in these lists of the PE comes out of a liturgy for Christian marriage (see Quinn, "Parenesis/Settings"), which saw in the marital union of one man and one woman an image and sign of the union between the one Christ and his one church. The list of virtues appears in a passage identified formally as the ordination charge of a presbyter in 1 Tim 6:11–16.

What about a second marriage for a Christian, after the death of the first spouse? The question surfaces very early in the Pauline tradition (1 Cor 7:39–40). There are circumstances in which a second marriage is advisable (1 Tim 5:11–14 specifies one set; there may be others). There is a circumstance in which it is not to be countenanced, namely, in a candidate for the public ministries. The presbyters, the bishop and his deacons, the widows have specific roles for the community of believers, roles that publicly and permanently shape their whole way of living. One of those roles is their witness by their one Christian marriage to the permanent union of Christ and the church.

The origin proposed for the unique phrase in the celebration of Christian marriages in one ancient congregation, perhaps in Rome, explains why these lists of virtues and the PE themselves take the meaning of the expression for granted. In this community the terminology would be a quite familiar, though technical, expression, as certain phrases in the marriage vows are in English today. The phrase may have been particularly adapted for Roman ears, for Dionysius of Halicarnassus notes the ancient Roman preference for marriage "to one wife" (2.24.5 and note context; the Augustan *lex Julia* of 18 B.C.E. and *lex Papia Poppaea* of 9 C.E., attempting to discourage Roman widows and bachelors from remaining thus, are from a different point of view signs of the times [Corbett, *Marriage*, pp. 118–121]). Statius, *Silvae* 5.3.240–241 extols his father to whom "was known only one wedding torch, one love"; see also Ovid, *Fasti* 5.528. The later prophetic linking of monotheism with monogamy may indicate a strong Jewish background within the constituencies that used this phrase, an emphasis that appears in another form in 1 Tim 2:5.

with children who are believers, who cannot be charged with debauchery, who are not refractory. The first qualification in this list had been a single adjective; the second, a three-word phrase; now a third and final qualification expands into three phrases that evaluate the presbyteral candidate in terms of qualities, positive and negative, that can be observed in his children (see 1 Tim 3:4).

The point at issue is not that he must have children but that all whom he does have must, in the first place, be Christians who have been reared in or have accepted the faith of their father. One infers that the man who has educated his own sons and daughters in the faith will be able to teach it to another household, the church (see v 7 below). In antithesis to children who are believers are those guilty of public profligacy, whose intemperance in matters of food and drink and sex, because it is common knowledge, belies the faith that the family professes. Such a criterion presupposes that the children are well into adolescence, if not beyond it. Thus their father, the prospective presbyter, ought to be into his thirties. As damaging as dissolute offspring are to a man's candidacy, this list also excludes from the presbyteral ranks a father whose children are rebellious and disobedient. One is encountering here not the willfulness of mere youngsters but the rebelliousness of young adults in public opposition to the social and political orders. For the author of the PE the term "refractory" particularly stigmatized Jewish-Christian troublemakers whose political alienation (see 1:10; 3:1–3) would in turn make their father's sympathies suspect and thus his teaching less credible.

7. *Indeed a bishop has to be unimpeachable (God's steward, so to speak).* With a transitional phrase that is both Pauline (1 Cor 11:19; 15:25, 53) and Lukan (Luke 21:9) in its suggestion that every human act must belong to God's will, a second set of qualifications begins for the leader, now called an *episkopos*, a term probably to be taken collectively. The *presbyteroi* of 1:5 are in the plural; even the singular "every one of them" in v 6 does not ease the appearance of the new title in the singular. The author of the PE evidently considered the terms as somehow equivalent at this point. The awkward expression that could easily have been ironed out indicates that he did not consider them completely synonymous. The actual term *episkopos* probably goes back to the origin of the subsequent list of qualifications in a church in which the members had been influenced by a different Jewish background (see COMMENT on 1 Tim 3:7 and the Qumran *mebaqqer*). The author of the PE leaves the title for their leader unchanged as if to emphasize that, whatever the titles for Christian ministers in different congregations, the qualifications for the task were compatible, if not identical. To that same end the "unimpeachable" of the Jewish-Christian list is allowed to stand as part of the transition into the catalog of episcopal qualifications.

The parenthetical description of a bishop as "God's steward" takes up the familial or household paradigm, implicit in the preceding catalog, and explicitly compares a bishop to an *oikonomos*, a Greek compound referring literally to house regulation. The church is a family in which God is Father; a bishop is compared to the man, often a slave, who administered the property of the head of the house. Paul had once described Cephas, Apollos, and himself as "stewards of God's mysteries," with emphasis on the trustworthiness demanded of such persons (1 Cor 4:1–2). A similar emphasis appears in the reference to the trustees for an heir during his minority (Gal 4:2). In the Lukan parables a sharp but dishonest manager (Luke 16:1, 3, 8; note *phronimōs* and *adikias*) figures in a lively illustration of the economic facts of life in the ancient world. In Luke 12:41–42, Peter inquires about the identity of the watchful servants who have just been described. Jesus opens a parabolic reply with, "who then is the trustworthy steward, shrewd as well (*ho pistos oikonomos, ho phronimos*), whom the master will set (*katastēsei ho kyrios*) in charge of his servants?" The answer is inescapable: the leaders (see Reumann, "Jesus as Steward," p. 28). As in the Pauline tradition, they are to be in the first place trustworthy; but the Lukan tradition asks too for that shrewdness which the worldly also value (see Luke 16:8 above). A contrast follows between this kind of manager-slave (*doulos;* Luke 12:43, see Titus 1:1) and the one who, in the master's absence, cudgels his fellow servants and indulges his appetites for food and drink, as though he would never have to answer for his actions to the master and endure the fate of the untrustworthy (Luke 12:45–46).

The conduct of the vicious manager in the Lukan parable corresponds to the five vices that are listed in Titus 1:7b. This catalog could well have been mined originally from the Lukan parabolic tradition used as a "narrative ethics" (see Schramm, *Festival*, pp. 151–154). All five vices, including avarice, are illustrated in the conduct of the parabolic stewards in Luke, though a quite different terminology appears in the list in Titus. A process of reflection upon and application of Jesus' parables has reduced their wisdom teaching into pointed prerequisites for the daily life of Christians. This list was used in turn for church leaders. Because none of this terminology for vice in Titus 1:7b coincides with either Luke or Paul, one infers that the author of the PE composed the interpretation of "unimpeachable" in terms of a parabolic and trustworthy manager. He proposed it in the process of adapting an already existing Christian list of vices transmitted through a liturgical charge that had perhaps in turn been developed from the dominical parables.

The vices listed at this point serve to make explicit what the initial, generic "unimpeachable" did not specify. Whereas the list of 1:6 had confined itself to this generic adjective for the conduct of the individual and had expanded on the family relationships of the prospective presbyter, this list of vices that disqualify an aspirant to episcopacy, along with the list of virtues in the next verse, all refer to individual, personal qualifications and do not advert to the interpersonal familial relationships as such. There is no evidence that the catalog was to be applied legalistically. The catalog functions rhetorically (noted the quintuple *mē* and repeated medial and final *-on*) as epistolary paraenesis; the vices are marshaled as simply irrefutable examples of the kind of conduct that disqualifies a candidate for a Pauline episcopate. The virtues that follow in 1:8 are proposed in similar fashion as beyond contradiction (see Quinn, "Parenesis/Settings").

Precisely because their arrangement and function is primarily rhetorical (see Horace, *Epistles* 1.1.38), there is no internal logical nexus that binds these catalogs together, and there is no further ethical analysis of the relations be-

tween the qualities listed. An ethically more sophisticated list is exemplified in
T. Judah 16.1, 3, where overindulgence in wine has within it "four evil spirits, of
lust, of feverish desire, of debauchery (*asōtias*), of money-mindedness (*ais-
chrokerdias*)," not to mention all sorts of violence. The list here is more like the
ancient physician's list of symptoms for an illness (thus Hippocrates, *Epidemion*
1.19 lists the *orgiloi* among others subject to the plague). A catalog of observable
phenomena that de facto signal health or disease is the purpose of such a list;
explanation and analysis belong to a later stage.

   8. *Rather he must be one who likes guests, likes goodness.* The adversative
particle *alla* again pertains to the rhetorical framework in which the author of
the PE set the positive section of his list, a contrasting catalog of the virtues
expected in a bishop. The emphatic opening with a reference to the candidate's
hospitableness may belong to the author's redaction of a previously existing
quintet of virtues. In that case a special circumstance in the congregation from
which the list derives would have given hospitality primacy over the other qualities. The reference is not simply to a generic love of neighbor, whether believer
or unbeliever. One is dealing with an ungrudging provision of food and shelter
to Christian missionaries (see 1 Tim 5:10), such as those who bore this letter of
recommendation in Titus 3:12–15. As A. J. Malherbe has suggested ("Inhospitality," pp. 222–232; *Social Aspects* with its addendum, pp. 92–112), such NT
passages reflect the prevalence of travel in the Roman Empire at large as well as
the mistrust of the local inns, a factor that led those en route to seek private
accommodations. These travelers and those who received them were evidently
not poor. Against this background one recalls that it was well-to-do converts who
opened their homes for corporate Christian worship, the "house churches"
glimpsed in the background of the PE and in other first-century Christian texts.
The host was responsible before Roman law for the group gathered in his or her
home (see Acts 17:5–9), which presupposes a certain discernment and objectivity. Into such assemblies came the traveling missionaries of the Christian faith,
bringing news, giving moral encouragement and theological instruction, receiving hospitality and supplies for the next stage of their trip. The host or hostess
for such an assembly was a person of means and evidently generous. As Malherbe argues at length, such generosity does not as such bestow office and
authority; it is, however, a positive qualification and, in this list, a primary one.

   What would have led the author of the PE to give hospitality top priority
among the episcopal virtues? There is no gainsaying the high value that the
ancient world, pagan and Jewish, placed on hospitableness. Cicero, taking his
cue from Theophrastus, remarked, "For it seems to me at least, it is most proper
that the homes of distinguished men should be open to distinguished guests.
And it is to the credit of our country also that men from abroad do not fail to
find hospitable entertainment of this kind in our city. It is, moreover, a very
great advantage, too, for those who wish to obtain a powerful political influence
by honourable means to be able through their social relations with their guests

to enjoy popularity and to exert influence abroad" (*De officiis* 2.64). The high valuation continued into the Renaissance (see Heal, "Canterbury," pp. 544–563).

Yet hospitality was one virtue among others (see Job 31:32; Rom 12:13; Heb 13:2; 1 Pet 4:9; *1 Clem.* 35.5 s.v.l.), even later in the PE (1 Tim 3:3; 5:10). The primacy here is probably not dictated by a speculative ethics but by the pressure of the practical situation (see Gen 18:1–8; 19:1–3) in the Jewish-Christian congregations that these directives address. From the early sixties of the first Christian century the leaders in such churches outside of Palestine would have found on their doorstep, regularly, in numbers, and in ever greater distress, refugees from the decimated Jewish-Christian churches of a Palestine in revolt against Rome. The task of hospitality was imperative, for the refugees were brothers in faith. The generosity was not without risk, for those being received were members by blood of the people in revolt. Moreover, the strain placed on the material resources of Jewish-Christian churches on the routes from Palestine must have been formidable. There was every reason in the practical order for insisting that the presbyter-bishop on the Pauline model had to be hospitable. The qualification here is no thoughtless repetition of a rhetorical *topos* (the thirty-odd qualifications for a general in Onosander do not advert to anything that corresponds to hospitality). The author of the PE gave this virtue top rank because the predominantly Jewish-Christian churches outside of Palestine to which Titus is addressed had pressing problems in caring for their Palestinian brothers. Such congregations ought to have no qualms about a Pauline *episkopos* whose primary qualification was that he welcomed displaced Jewish Christians.

The *philagathos*, "one who likes goodness," which opens the five-point catalog that the author of the PE was taking up at this point, is not as banal as it sounds in English. In Alexandrian Judaism this was the name of the virtue that was appropriate for a ruler who had to lay down the law, and for Philo *to philagathon* meant "to approve of things naturally excellent (*kala*) and to supply them without reserve to all who are worthy of them for their unstinted use." The word suggests not only a personal orientation but also an ability to discern.

who is sensible, upright, devout, self-controlled. The first and last qualities designated here were highly valued in Hellenistic society at large, and the Christian circles in which this list originated may have chosen them so that their bishop would "enjoy also a fine recommendation from outsiders" (1 Tim 3:7). About 50 C.E. Onosander opened his list of dozens of qualities requisite in a general with these same two terms. His comment on *egkratē* was that a general is "to be self-controlled because his is to be a surpassing position of leadership; for uncontrolled (*akrateis*) impulses issue in unchecked satisfaction of the passions when authority grants them the power to do anything they like" (*De imperatoris officio* 3: text in D-C, p. 159). The self-mastery envisioned extends beyond sexual self-control, but that precise form of self-mastery is the most visible sign of the quality sought. What "a husband to one wife" sought to insure in the Jewish-Christian list of v 6, "self-controlled" suggests in a Hellenistic terminology here.

A Jewish origin as well as a Hellenistic pagan appeal at the origin of this list may be heard in its describing the candidate as an "upright, devout" man (see NOTES). The latter term suggests one who has identified himself with the public worship of believing men, as "they lift up hands that are holy" (1 Tim 2:8). To require the candidate to be "upright" is, in the Jewish use of the whole cluster of terms related to *dikaios*, to have asked for an all-inclusive integrity of life before God and man; for the Christian this integrity could not be considered apart from what had occurred in baptism (see Titus 2:12; 3:5, 7).

9. *who sticks to the message that is meant to be believed, according to the teaching.* With a final recurrence, in *antechomenon*, of the -*on* sound that has been woven through the last two verses, the list ends with an expansive, rhetorical coda that is typical of the PE. As with 2:11–15 and 3:4–8 below, the preceding catalog has its climactic point and ultimate *raison d'être* in an elaborate, leisurely conclusion that contrasts sharply with the laconic series of entries that precede. In this verse of Titus, moreover, the vocabulary becomes notably like that of the PE generally, and one infers that here the reader encounters the point that the author himself intended to underscore with this form of exposition. That point is in fact the central concern of this whole correspondence, continuing and securing an authoritative, unmistakably Pauline teaching in second-generation Christian churches. Thus in this correspondence Paul's immediate collaborators hear his explicit command to teach (cf. Titus 2:1, 15 with 1 Tim 4:11; 6:2). Not only Timothy but all bishops are to be skilled teachers (*didaktikos* in 1 Tim 3:2; 2 Tim 2:24). By the same token, the teaching role of the cadre of presbyter-bishops (who are being constituted under Paul's mandate here in Titus) is articulated at length (see 2 Tim 2:2), and their teaching stands in contrast to that of an opposing group to be described in 1:10–16 (see 1 Tim 1:3; 6:3).

The candidate for becoming a Pauline presbyter-bishop is himself to be completely attached to God's message, that is, to the *logos* of 1:3 that was entrusted to Paul and proclaimed by him. An original and creative teaching is not the aim of the PE. The language employed here and elsewhere in the PE in connection with teaching suggests that it was to take place orally, in face-to-face encounter (thus, in this verse, "encourage," "refute"; in 2:1, "speak," *lalei;* in 3:1, "remind," *hypomimnēiske;* in 1 Tim 1:3, "charge," *paraggeilēis;* etc.). The unique mention of writing in this correspondence, in 1 Tim 3:14, proposes it as a makeshift for a personal meeting. One place for such an oral activity is the assembly of Christian men and women for their public worship, where only the men have the Pauline authorization to teach (cf. 1 Tim 2:12 with 4:13; 5:17). Another place is the Christian home, and there the wife and mother is to teach her children (cf. Titus 2:3 with 1 Tim 2:15; 5:10; 2 Tim 3:14–15). The presbyter-bishop here in Titus is certainly meant to teach in the Christian liturgy.

But what is he to teach? Precisely *the message* that God and his apostle had presented for Christian faith, that *pistos logos* which furnished the materials articulated in *pistoi hoi logoi* that begin to occur in Titus 3:4–8 (see Excursus I, "*Pistis* Terminology in the PE"). "The message that is meant to be believed" is exemplified by but not confined to such materials. The PE are themselves, as a whole, the *pistos logos* that a Pauline apostolic ministry is to teach. They present (as their author conceived it) "the center" of Paul for a new generation.

The message of the PE and of the Pauline presbyter-bishop is according to *the teaching.* The paraenesis for Timothy in 2 Tim 4:2 has taken up the terminology of this opening section of Titus, using an anarthrous *didachē* to mean "the task of teaching"; but there is no precise parallel in biblical Greek or the Ap. Frs. to *kata tēn didachēn* here in Titus. Precisely the opposite phrase does appear, however, in Rom 16:17, where Paul urges the Roman believers "to take note of those who create dissensions and scandals, in opposition to the teaching (*para tēn didachēn*) which you have learned (*hēn hymeis emathete*). Avoid (*ekklinete*) them." The articular usage here precisely parallels Titus 1:9, and the *didachē* comes into focus as an authoritatively transmitted communication in a recognizable form that resists alteration, a doctrine that recognized teachers gave and which believers were to learn (see Rom 12:6–7). With such a standard or pattern of teaching (*typon didachēs,* Rom 6:17) Paul presumes that Roman Christians have been shaped and molded after their baptismal deliverance. Such a *didachē* was concerned with the actual, everyday activities in which the Christian commitment expressed itself in the Christian way of living (Fitzmyer, "Office of Teaching," p. 193). It was the reflective, organized application of the faith out of a certain framework to the ongoing lives and problems of the baptized; it was not the spontaneous, creative, ad hoc guidance of the enthusiast. Prophets do not have to prepare their lessons; teachers ought to. In this connection, it is notable that when Paul describes the Corinthian assemblies for worship he distinguishes one who contributes a teaching (anarthrous *didachē;* 1 Cor 14:6, 26) from one who has a revelation or knowledge, a prophecy or a hymn, a tongue or an interpretation. This situation, with the variety of teachings that it implies, is not the one envisioned by the PE, in which *the* teaching is the formation offered by the Pauline directives for Christian life. From the men who have received and acted upon this Pauline catechesis are to be chosen the presbyter-bishops envisioned by Titus.

so that he can both encourage with wholesome apostolic instruction and refute opponents. From such a Pauline formation the presbyter-bishop derives his purpose and his power to carry it out. A Greek chiasmus describes that purpose with the antithetical *parakalein/elegchein.* The activities, which Titus and Timothy as coworkers with the apostle are to perform at Paul's command (see NOTES), are those that the presbyter-bishop is in turn to do. Indeed, the apostle himself in this correspondence is said to encourage (1 Tim 1:3; 2:1); he is never said explicitly to refute, but it is difficult to conceive of the paraenesis of

Titus 1:10–16 (to single out an example) as anything else. "To encourage" is, for the PE, to some extent synonymous with "to teach" (*didaskein*, 1 Tim 6:2 and cf. *lalein*, Titus 2:15). Can the context of this encouragement be specified further? The opening of the church order in 1 Tim 2:1–3:1ᵃ is instructive. The public worship of believers, the intentions for prayer and the faith that prompts it, the conduct of worshipers—these are the primary concerns of the Pauline encouragement (see 1 Tim 4:13). The conduct proper to various groups within the congregation is the only other content that the PE single out (see the context of Titus 2:6, 15; 1 Tim 5:1; 6:2).

The positive objects of encouragement are antithetically complemented by the apologetic capability of the candidate for presbyter-bishop to "refute opponents," literally, those who are contradicting, like the slaves in Titus 2:9 carping at their masters. Although unbelievers are not excluded as opponents, it is notable that the apostolic imperatives in the PE for Titus and Timothy have in mind the refutation of Christian opposition to the Pauline message and formation of Christian conduct. Even the presbyter is subject to public review (1 Tim 5:20) in this respect. What is the nub of the opposition, the point being contested? In the Lukan tradition it is not simply Jesus himself who is "a sign of contradiction" (Luke 2:34) and perhaps his teaching on the resurrection of the body against the "contradicting Sadducees" (Luke 20:27 s.v.l.); it is in addition the Pauline mission and the Christian way that are contradicted by their fellow Jews (Acts 13:45; 28:19, 22). Here in Titus 1:9 it is still the Pauline mission and teaching that are being controverted, but now particularly by Jewish Christians who must be refuted (Titus 1:10, 13). A procedure based on LXX Lev 19:17 (where *elegchein* translates Hebrew *ykḥ;* cf. Crum, *CD* 9.6–8) may be presumed here; see Forkman, *Limits*, pp. 124–125, 197–198 n. 42, and COMMENT below on 3:10–11.

For the PE there is no more important term for understanding what their author meant by teaching than *didaskalia*, as the fifteen explicit references (out of twenty-one in the NT) to "instruction" already signal. On its first occurrence Titus 1:9 qualifies it as "wholesome" (*hygiainousa*) and, as A. J. Malherbe has shown in "Medical Imagery," the suggestion of healthy and health-giving doctrine versus a diseased and pestilential one is what the author of the PE intends by this imagery. For him the Pauline gospel, the message of God, is in direct antithesis to the gangrenous message of false teachers (cf. 2 Tim 2:2, 8–9, 11–13, 15 with 17–18). These opponents are sick men who cannot stomach healthy words but suffer morbid cravings for the controversial (see 1 Tim 6:2b–5). The authors of D-C, pp. 24–25 note that this **hygi-* cluster of terms often suggested no more than what was reasonable, sane, and sensible; thus not only the philosophers but also the dramatists (Euripides, *Andromache* 448; Menander, *Misoumenos* 313; *Sycyonios* 81, 153; but contrast his *Samia* 417 and Euripides, *Phoenissae* 471–472). But, as D-C also observes, the health–disease imagery flares back to life too (cf. the banal usage of Philo, *Cher.* 36; *Det.* 10, 12 with the vivid *Abr.* 223, 275 or Clement of Alexandria, *Stromata* 1.8.40). It is arbitrary to contend a priori that the PE must use only a banal sense; in fact, their actual usage proves that for their author the health–disease figure was consciously exploited. The health included that of the mind, not just that of the body. The ancients indeed distinguished between the two, but realistically regarded them as inhering in each other in any human being: *mens sana in corpore sano.* The PE make that view their own (see 1 Tim 4:8) as they submit that the Pauline message and instruction bring health in another order to mind and body (see Excursus V, "The PE on Salvation"). That instruction can no more coexist with contradiction than disease can coexist with health.

That the "apostolic instruction" for the PE is emphatically Paul's *didaskalia* becomes clear when one observes that the use of the term in a good sense is always in the singular. The only use of the plural in the PE designates the devilish instructions of opponents (1 Tim 4:1). This singular instruction emanates from the one teacher whom the PE revere, Paul the apostle, for whom this correspondence reserves the term "teacher" (*didaskalos* in the singular, 1 Tim 2:7; 2 Tim 1:11). The plural of this title too is heard in a bad sense (2 Tim 4:3, along with the *nomodidaskaloi* of 1 Tim 1:7; in Titus 2:3 the compound *kalodidaskaloi* is needed to neutralize this connotation).

Can the technical sense of the Pauline instruction in the PE be more precisely determined? In the technical terminology of the ancient literary criticism, *didaskalia* was the word both for training the chorus of a drama and for the quasi-official written notice of the historical circumstances in which an author had produced (literally "taught," *edidaxen*) a particular drama (see Handley, *Dyskolos,* pp. 77, 123; Gomme and Sandbach, *Commentary,* p. 128); it accompanied the summary of the plot and (at least once) the text of the play. The connotation of the official and authoritative in such a technical usage matches the way in which the PE present the Pauline *didaskalia,* his own training (in well-known past circumstances) of a group of believers to act out his interpretation of what had occurred in Jesus' life, death, and resurrection. Even the rare Septuagintal uses of the term suggest authoritative guidance for action, with the singular used in a good sense (LXX Prov 2:17; Sir 24:33; 39:8), the plural in a bad one (LXX Isa 29:13). The latter passage is the one taken up in the gospel tradition (Mark 7:7; Matt 15:9) and alluded to in Col 2:22. In Eph 4:14 the distributive singular, "every wind of instruction," is equivalent to the pejorative plural. Outside of the PE, it is only Rom in the NT that employs the singular *didaskalia* in a good sense: in 12:7, referring to the product of the Spirit's charism for teaching, and in 15:4, of the Jewish scriptures as "written for our instruction." The usage of Rom and the PE is all the more striking when one notes that only Ignatius among the Ap. Frs. uses *didaskalia,* and then in the singular and pejoratively (*Eph.* 16.2; 17.1). The technical sense of *didaskalia* in the PE is of a piece with its meaning in Rom, where it was emphatically linked with the function of the OT Scriptures for believers now. That is precisely the meaning of *didaskalia* in 1 Tim 1:10–11, where Paul's gospel gives the right interpretation of the covenant commandments, the OT Law. Again in 1 Tim 4:13 Timothy, as Paul's collaborator, must "concentrate on your public reading of the Scriptures, on your preaching, on your instruction (*tēi didaskaliai*)," and his conduct is to conform to this *didaskalia* (1 Tim 4:6, 16). Finally, when Timothy's loyalty above all to Paul's own instruction is broached at 2 Tim 3:10, it is declared to be in harmony with "the sacred letters" that Timothy has known from his tenderest years, all of which are the gift of the divine Spirit and useful, above all, "for instruction" (2 Tim 3:14–16). The men who share his apostolate are committed to this wholesome Pauline application of the OT to conduct, despite all of the pressures on them to compromise (2 Tim 4:3; Titus 2:1, 7).

The *didaskalia* that a Titus and a Timothy gave at Paul's command (the imperative form of the vocabulary for teaching in the PE is notable) is the same instruction that is to engage the presbyter-bishop (Titus 1:9). In 1 Tim 5:17–18 there are presbyters "whose jobs are preaching and instruction." The immediate citation of a scriptural text (Deut 25:4) and a saying of Jesus (Luke 10:7) makes it reasonable to infer that the content of the preaching and instruction in which these men engage gives warrant for the support that they ought to receive. The earthy application of the OT text to the practical question about presbyteral salaries is an example of *didaskalia* that corresponds to the Pauline (and Roman) method of putting the OT into practice. The joining of the word of Jesus to that of the OT in this passage may illustrate what 1 Tim 6:3 refers to when describing the heterodox (see 1 Tim 1:3) who have "no recourse to the wholesome sayings (*logois*) that come from our Lord, Jesus Christ, or to the godly instruction." Here the *didaskalia* is distinguished from, though not contrasted to the words of Jesus (see also 1 Tim 4:6). The godly instruction is precisely Paul's gospel as it expounded the OT.

In Titus 2:10 and again in 1 Tim 6:1 one can verify that it is the Pauline exposition of the OT that is at issue. Both passages take up the question of the conduct of Christian slaves toward their masters. Respect, obedience, dependability characterize the course laid out. The reason is: they will "add luster in every way to the instruction of our savior, God" (Titus 2:10; cf. 1 Tim 6:1). Here, for the only time in the PE, the *didaskalia* is explicitly that of God, our savior (not of Jesus Christ), who "enspirited" all the sacred letters (see 2 Tim 3:15–16), in other words, the OT. These Scriptures did not reject slavery, and Paul's directives for slaves (e.g. 1 Cor 7:20–24) offered no basis for contravening them. There are no "words of our Lord, Jesus Christ" that directly address this question, though the parabolic teaching of Jesus took up the relation of slave to master as unhesitatingly as it did that of citizen to king or son to father. Thus the PE argue that when a refractory slave justifies his conduct as due to his Christian belief and formation he is misrepresenting the God of Israel and the

OT Scriptures as Paul understood them. A reliable slave, by contrast, enhances the apostolic *didaskalia*.

In this understanding of the apostolic instruction, Paul's interpretation of the OT is in no sense in competition with other interpretations, and he is not subject to the letter of Scripture. His *didaskalia* simply overwhelms those doctrines which are opposed to his. The wholesome Pauline instruction proceeds from the knowledge of the truth; the infected and infectious doctrines of his opponents are in the last analysis from unclean spirits (see 1 Tim 4:1). The apostolic instruction of Paul and his collaborators is validated by the Holy Spirit (cf. 1 Tim 1:18 with 2 Tim 1:14). To this wholesome *didaskalia* the presbyter-bishop in Titus 1:9 is to be totally committed.

II.A.2. TRUE AND FALSE TEACHING (1:10–16)

1   ¹⁰Indeed there are many, particularly among the Jewish Christians, who are refractory, spouting nonsense and seducing minds: ¹¹these people must be muzzled, for they are the kind who teach things they ought not and overturn entire households, for their own financial gain, shame to say.
¹²A countryman of theirs, a prophet of their own, said:

> Liars ever, men of Crete,
> Nasty brutes that live to eat.

¹³This is truthful testimony, and good reason to refute them sharply, so that they may recover their health in the faith ¹⁴instead of doting on Jewish tales and commandments of people who are abandoning the truth. ¹⁵For the clean, all things are clean. For the polluted and the unbelievers, however, nothing is clean. Rather, their very way of thinking and their conscience have been polluted. ¹⁶God they profess to know but by their deeds they disown him. They are disobedient abominations, counterfeiters of all excellent deeds.

NOTES

1:10. *Indeed there are many.* A textual problem is masked by *indeed.* The most important witnesses (S, A, C, 33, 81, etc.) begin the sentence with *Eisin gar polloi* (see Mark 2:15); after *polloi* an apparently pleonastic *kai* appears in D, G, I, K, Psi, 1739, and others. Classical literary usage, however, allowed *kai* after *polys* and before another adjective; Acts 25:7 exemplifies it (BDF §442.11). The elegant hendiadys *polloi kai anypotaktoi* may have struck the copyists of the former group of witnesses as superfluous and obscuring the meaning (B. Metzger, *TCGNT*, p. 653); thus their shorter, "corrected" text. J. K. Elliott (*Greek Text* pp. 177, 211) submits that the *kai* is original, arguing that it is perhaps a Semitism (see LXX Gen 47:9, *mikrai kai ponērai . . . hai hēmerai*).

particularly among the Jewish Christians. Malista may here specify who the *many* are, as would the English, "I mean namely" (see Skeat, "On 2 Tim 4:13"). "The Jewish Christians" are literally "the ones from [the] circumcision," *hoi ek [tēs] peritomēs*, in which the shorter reading without *tēs* is found in A, D', F, G, Psi, K, L, and P. The five other NT occurrences of the phrase (Acts; Paulines) do not use the article. The longer reading of the phrase in S, C, D*, 33, 038, and 442 is the more difficult because it is undocumented elsewhere in the LXX, NT, or Ap. Frs. The weight of the witnesses for this unharmonized reading makes it irresistible. The PE do not otherwise use *peritomē*, which is elsewhere typical of Paul (twenty-nine times) but which has only five other uses in the NT, in John and Acts. For the Paulines, *peritomē* can designate Jews who do not believe in Jesus (e.g., Rom 15:8; Gal 2:7–9); Jewish Christians (always with *ek*, Rom 4:12; Gal 2:12; Col 4:11); or all Christians, whether physically circumcised or not (Phil 3:3; see Col 2:11–13). Acts, like the Paulines, uses only forms of the phrase *hoi ek peritomēs (pistoi)* to designate Jewish Christians (10:45; 11:2). There are only four LXX uses of this term (in contrast to *aperitmētos*), and it never designates the Jewish people as such; in the Ap. Frs., Ign. *Phld.* 6.1 describes a Jewish Christian as "a man who has circumcision"; *Barn.* 9.4–7 uses the term four times but only once, mockingly, of a people, describing the Egyptians as *en peritomēi.*

who are refractory, spouting nonsense and seducing minds. See 1:6 on "refractory." "Spouting nonsense" represents a poetic, recherché adjective, *mataiologoi*, otherwise undocumented in the LXX, NT, and Ap. Frs., though see Titus 3:9 on *mataios* and 1 Tim 1:6 for *mataiologia*. A lyric fragment of Telestes (fourth century B.C.) speaks of "this report of the babbling (*mataiologon*) minstrels which flew without meaning or joy over Greece." A similar literary history lies behind "seducing minds," *phrenapatai*, which first appears in an anonymous erotic lyric (second century B.C.) complaining about a (self-?) deceiving former lover (D-C, text and version ad loc.). In BDF §119.2 the choice is "self-deceived," though "deceiver" (MM; LSJ; BAGD) appears to be the meaning in context. The term makes no other appearance in the LXX, NT, or Ap. Frs., though the cognate verb occurs in Gal 6:3.

11. *these people must be muzzled. Epistomizein* is not otherwise found in the LXX, NT, or Ap. Frs., though it is common enough in literary Greek.

for they are the kind who teach things they ought not. There are half a dozen other uses of "the kind who/which" (*hostis*) in the PE: in a positive sense in 1 Tim 3:15 (singular); 2 Tim 1:5 (singular); 2:2 (plural); in a derogatory sense, always plural, in 1 Tim 1:4; 6:9; and 2 Tim 2:18. On *didaskontes*, see 1:9; the content of their teaching is *ha mē dei,* an unclassical usage (BDF §428.4) that is probably equivalent to the *ta mē deonta* of 1 Tim 5:13.

and overturn entire households, for their own financial gain, shame to say. In 2 Tim 2:18 the false teachers "overturn" (*anatrepousin*) the faith; otherwise in the NT, John 2:15 uses this verb for Jesus' tipping over the money tables in the temple precinct. There are a dozen uses of the verb in the later strata of the LXX, but none in the Ap. Frs.

Only here does Titus mention households (*oikous*), but note the *oikonomos* in 1:7 and the *oikourgos* in 2:5. The term reappears in the singular in 1 Tim 3:4–5, 12, 15 (of God) and 2 Tim 1:16; 4:19, never of a physical structure as such but in the personal sense of the family (men, women, children, slaves) who constituted a home, whether that be a human home or a divine one. Ovid's elegiac puts it laconically; "tota domus laeta est, hoc est materque paterque / nataque: tres illi tota fuere domus" (*Fasti* 4.543–544; "The whole household was joyous, that is mother and father / and daughter; those three were the whole house").

In the remaining 105 NT uses of *oikos,* this personal sense appears in the other Paulines in 1 Cor 1:16, but it is farther from the surface in the other five Pauline occurrences. The meaning is rather more frequent in Luke–Acts, where 13 out of 58 uses of *oikos* have the personal sense (thus Luke 1:27; 19:9; Acts 2:36; 10:2; etc.). In the Ap. Frs. the personal sense predominates (thus Ign. *Smyrn.* 13.1–2; *Pol.* 8.2) but even *1 Clem.* once uses *oikos* of a physical structure (12.7). The LXX employs *oikos* often, in both senses noted, as do the *T. 12 Patr.*

"Entire," *holous,* though used more than a hundred times in the NT, occurs only here in the PE. The phrase *aischrou kerdous charin,* literally, "for the sake of disgraceful profit," stands in contrast to the *mē aischrokerdē* in 1:7 of the episcopal candidate. The cursive 460, in its expansive manner (see NOTES on 1:9), after the final *charin* of the text, has added, "Muzzle and refute and admonish children who are arrogant with or strike their parents. Do just as a father does with his children."

12. *A countryman of theirs, a prophet of their own, said.* Literally, "Some one of them, their very own prophet, said." The PE do not elsewhere employ **eip-* stem forms of *legein.* The author of the following hexameter is *prophētēs,* again only here in the PE, in contrast to 143 other NT occurrences; see 1 Tim 1:18; 4:14 for *prophēteia,* the only other term from the *prophēt-* cluster in the PE. In S*, F, G, 81, 1827, and others, *de* is added after *eipen* to relieve the asyndeton here (J. K. Elliott, *Greek Text,* p. 178).

Liars ever, men of Crete, Nasty brutes that live to eat. On the *Krētes,* see the INTRODUCTION on the world of the PE. "Liars" will recur in 1 Tim 1:10. On "nasty brutes," *kaka thēria,* see the uses of *kaka* in 1 Tim 6:10; 2 Tim 4:14.

"That live to eat" is literally, "lazy bellies," *gasteres argai* (see 1 Tim 5:13 on lazy young widows). On the *gastēr* as craving food, see *Odyssey* 6:133; perhaps

Menander, *Sycyonios* 43–45; on control of such craving, *egkrateia gastros,* Xenophon, *Cyropaedia* 1.2.8; see *Oeconomicus* 9.11; *Memorabilia* 1.2.1. Shepherds in Hesiod, *Theogonia* 26, are scored as *gasteres.* If such polemic seems rude from an Epimenides, one recalls that another of the Seven Wise Men of ancient Greece, Pittacus, was savagely mocked by Alcaeus as *kenon o* [*sic*] *physgon,* "that big gut" (LP, G 1.21, cf. Z 106).

   13.   *This is truthful testimony.* See Excursus II, "Truth and *epignōsis alētheias* in the PE." "Testimony," *martyria,* reappears in 1 Tim 3:7. All other uses of the **marty-* cluster are in the letters to Timothy: *martyrion* in 1 Tim 2:6; 2 Tim 1:8; *martyres* in 1 Tim 5:19; 6:12; 2 Tim 2:2; the verb *martyrein* in 1 Tim 5:10; 6:13; and *diamartyrein* in 1 Tim 5:21; 2 Tim 2:14; and 4:1.

   and good reason to refute them sharply. The strong, causal phrase *di' hēn aitian* (BDF §456.4) will recur in 2 Tim 1:6, 12 as well as in Luke 8:47; Acts 10:21; 22:24; 28:18 (negative), and 20 (with emphatic demonstrative). In the NT otherwise only Heb 2:11 uses the expression, which has been called a Latinism from *quam ob rem/causam* (Hitchcock, "Latinity," p. 350), but it already appears in the last strata of the LXX (esp. 2–3 Macc) and in Herodotus, *History* 1.1. In the Ap. Frs. the phrase appears (with an added *tauten* or *allen tina*) only in the documents linked with the Roman church, *1–2 Clem.* and Hermas's *Shepherd.* See 1:9 for "to refute"; for "sharply," *apotomōs,* cf. the only other NT use of the adverb in 2 Cor 13:10 and the nominal form, "God's severity," in Rom 11:22. Wisdom 5:22 uses the adverb; 5:20; 6:5; 11:10; 12:9; 18:15, the adjective, in contexts of divine and relentless judgment. Among the Ap. Frs., Pol. *Phil.* 6.1 uses the adjective in directing presbyters "not to be relentless (*apotomoi*) in judgment."

   so that they may recover their health in the faith. See 1:9 and Excursus I, "*Pistis* Terminology in the PE." S*, 122, and 1908 read *tēi pistēi* without the preposition *en.* P³² seems to have had it: the other major witnesses certainly do. J. K. Elliott notes how some scribes tended to thin out the proliferation of NT prepositions.

   14.   *instead of doting on Jewish tales and commandments of people who are abandoning the truth.* All other uses in the PE of *prosechein* ("doting" here) are in 1 Tim, usually in a pejorative sense (1 Tim 1:4, also with "tales" as its object; 3:8 of wine; 4:1 of evil spirits), but once in a good sense (1 Tim 4:13 of public worship; and note the variant in 1 Tim 6:3). There are no other Pauline uses of this verb; Luke–Acts account for ten of the nineteen NT uses (Acts 8:10–11 in a bad sense). The pejorative sense is rare in the many Septuagintal uses of the verb (Wis 14:30 of idolatry; cf. the rhetorical question of LXX Job 10:3) and practically unknown in the Ap. Frs. (cf. Ign. *Trall.* 4.1). In a striking parallel to this verse of Titus, *T. Asher* 7.5 writes of those who *mē prosechontes ton nomon tou theou all' entolais anthropon,* "are not doting on the law of God but on human commandments."

   "Jewish tales," *Ioudaikois mythois,* employs an adjective otherwise unattested in the NT. In the LXX only 2 Macc 13:21 (v.l. at 2 Macc 8:11) uses this term. In Ign. *Magn.* 8.1, "a life in accord with Judaism" has the variant reading "in accord with Jewish law (*nomon Ioudaikon*)." Galatians 2:14 uses the corresponding adverb of living in a Jewish style. Philo and Josephus employ the adjective; Plutarch, *Isis and Osiris* 31 writes of *Ioudaika eis mython parelkein,* that is, matters known in Jewish circles enter into the myth being discussed. *Mythoi* are mentioned in the NT only in the plural, in the PE (see 1 Tim 1:4; 4:7; 2 Tim 4:4) and in 2 Pet 1:16. The only LXX occurrence, in Sir 20:19, is in the singular, of a *mythos akairos*, "thought expressed at the wrong time." In *2 Clem.* 13.3, where pagans dismiss as "a myth and delusion (*mython tina kai planēn*)" what Christians proclaim without practicing, the meaning is "words only." Parallel to "Jewish myths" are literally "commandments of men," *entolais anthropon.* The *entalmasin* of F, G, and Theodoret is a harmonization with the citation of LXX Is 29:13 in Mark 7:7; Matt 15:9; and Col 2:22. The variant *genealogiais* of 1908 picks up 1 Tim 1:4. *Entolē* recurs in the singular in 1 Tim 6:14. Frequent in the NT otherwise (sixty-six times), there are a dozen other uses in the Paulines and five in Luke–Acts. The term is frequent in the LXX and usually refers to the commands of the God of Israel, particularly those of the Scriptures. See Monsengwo, *Nomos*, pp. 141–147. The Ap. Frs. also use the word often of the commands of Jesus, the apostles, and those who are charged with carrying on the apostolic ministry (e.g., Ign. *Magn.* 4.1; *Trall.* 13.2; *Smyrn.* 8.1). For the data on *anthropon*, "people" here, see 2:11.

"Who are abandoning the truth," *apostrephomenōn tēn alētheian:* see Excursus II, "Truth and *epignōsis alētheias* in the PE." The verb here recurs in 2 Tim 1:15 of abandoning the apostle himself and in 4:4 of those who turn their hearing from the truth. There are only half a dozen other NT uses, including Luke 23:14; Acts 3:26; and Rom 11:26, quoting LXX Isa 59:20. There are about five hundred uses of the word in the LXX but only eight in the Ap. Frs. Josephus, *Ant.* 8.245 writes of Jeroboam as "having wholly turned his thoughts away from God and from holy and righteous deeds (*apo tou theou kai ton hosion ergon kai dikaion*)."

15. *For the clean, all things are clean.* The PE contain seven of the twenty-six NT uses of "clean," *katharos*, which in 1 Tim 1:5 and 2 Tim 2:22 qualifies the believer's heart, and his conscience in 1 Tim 3:9 and 2 Tim 1:3. The only other Pauline use of the term is *panta men kathara* in Rom 14:20 (which may have provided the Byzantine tradition with its *men* at this point in Titus, to balance the *de* of the following clause). For the Lukan usage, see the COMMENT below. "All things" here and "all excellent deeds" in the following verse represent a distributive use of *pas*, a favorite adjective of the NT as a whole (more than twelve hundred uses) and one that will reappear more than fifty times in the PE.

For the polluted and the unbelievers, however, nothing is clean. This sentence develops through an antithetical chiasmus with an assonance on *a:*

panta kathara　　　　　　　　　*tois katharois*
tois de memiammenois　　　　　*ouden katharon*
　　kai apistois

The third and final *katharon* emphatically rounds off the statement of principle. "The polluted and the unbelievers," under one definite article in Greek, are mutually explanatory. For "the unbelievers" see Excursus I, *"Pistis* Terminology in the PE." "The polluted" (*memiammenois*) are explained with the repeated *memiantai,* "have been polluted," of the next clause. This verb, otherwise unattested in the Paulines, occurs elsewhere in the NT only in Heb 12:15; Jude 8, of moral failure; and John 18:28, of ritual stain. The LXX applies the verb not only to ceremonial irregularity but also to immoral worship and sexual conduct (e.g., LXX Job 31:11; Jer 2:7, 23, 33; 3:1–2; 7:30; Ezek 18:6, 11, 15; 22:11). This usage appears regularly in the *T. 12 Patr.,* for example, *T. Reub.* 1.6; *T. Levi* 14.6. *Testament of Issachar* 4.4 describes the singleminded man as one "who does not look upon feminine beauty lest he pollute his very way of thinking (*mianei ton noun autou*) with depravity."

Rather, their very way of thinking and their conscience have been polluted. Menander, Koerte 538/540K, "all that defiles is from within," is cited in context in the COMMENT on 3:3. The phrase just quoted from *T. Iss.* appears here in Titus with *nous* in tandem with *syneidēsis* (conscience). The parallel phrases in 1 Tim 1:5, 19 couple "a clean heart" and "faithfulness," respectively, with "conscience." *Nous* accordingly includes the inner moral disposition and character of human beings; thus already *Odyssey* 1.3 distinguishes the hero's sightseeing from his learning "the very way of thinking" (*noun egno*) of the many persons he encountered. Theognis, as cited by Xenophon's Socrates, says, "Noble things are taught by noble persons; if you mingle with the bad, you will destroy your native way of thinking (*ton eonta noon)" (Symposium* 2.4). In the LXX, where *nous* is not frequent, there are half a dozen instances in which it translates Hebrew *leb* (heart). The later strata of the LXX, particularly 4 Macc, favor the term, though Wis 4:12, "the giddy distraction of desire perverts the guileless mind" (*noun akakon:* Winston, *AB Wisd.,* p. 136) is very close to the usage of the PE (see J. Behm in *TDNT* 4.953). In the NT, beyond the twenty-one uses in the Paulines, only Luke 24:45 and Rev 13:18; 17:9 employ *nous.* The PE take up the term again in 1 Tim 6:5, describing "the incessant bickerings of men whose minds are a shambles," and 2 Tim 3:8 of opponents who are "numbskulled" (*katephtharmenoi ton noun*). The Ap. Frs. seldom use *nous,* but "the one mind" of believers in Ign. *Magn.* 7.1 (see *Herm. Sim.* 9.17.4 and 18.4), the internal attitude and frame of reference that Christian faith and worship provide, are in sharp contrast to the corrupt way of thinking that the PE score (cf. Eph 4:1–6 with 17–19).

"Conscience" (*syneidesis*) occurs only here in Titus, but five times in the correspondence with Timothy, where it is qualified with "clean" (*kathara*),

1 Tim 3:9; 2 Tim 1:3, or "clear" (*agatha*), 1 Tim 1:5, 19. In 1 Tim 4:2, as here in Titus, a conscience that has been polluted or cauterized is not qualified further. The fourteen other Pauline uses of *syneidēsis* are in the Roman and Corinthian letters. None of the gospels employs this noun, but Acts not only uses the term twice but also modifies it with *agatha* (23:1; cf. *aproskopos*, 24:16). Of the eight uses in Heb and 1 Pet, note particularly Heb 13:18 (*kalē*) and 1 Pet 3:16, 21 (*agathē*). The LXX Eccl 10:20 and Sir 42:18 use *syneidēsis* for thought and understanding, but Wis 17:11 alone illustrates the Hellenistic way in which the noun was understood of the conscience (see Winston, *AB Wisd.*, pp. 307–308 for the references, particularly the citations of Menander). This understanding appears also in *1 Clem.* 41.1; 45.7, *en agathēi/katharai syneidēsei* (see 1.3 and *2 Clem.* 16.4; Pol. *Phil.* 5.3), and Ign. *Trall.* 7.2 of a dissident as one who is not *katharos . . . tēi syneidēsei.* The "bad (*ponera*) conscience" appears in *Did.* 4.14; *Barn.* 19.12; and *Herm. Man.* 3.4. *Testament of Reuben* 4.3, "Even until now my conscience harasses me about my sin," may not be the first recorded Jewish use of *syneidēsis* for conscience as a moral faculty (Charles, *AP* 2.298), but it may represent a very archaic Jewish-Christian reworking of still older Jewish ethical paraenesis (see Charlesworth, *OT Pseud.* 1.783, with reference to *T. Judah* 20.1–2).

16. *God they profess to know but by their deeds they disown him.* The specious profession here contrasts with 1 Tim 6:12, the only other use of *homologein* in the PE. The cognate *homologia* also occurs in 1 Tim 6:12–13, and *homologoumenōs* introduces the hymnic fragment of 1 Tim 3:16. The cluster of terms is not characteristically Pauline, (*ex-*)*homologein* occurring only in the materials cited in Rom 10:9–10; 14:11; 15:9; and Phil 2:11; the noun only in 2 Cor 9:13. The wide use of *homologein* and *homologia* in law and commerce may explain their relatively rare appearance in the LXX (see O. Michel in *TDNT* 5.200, 204) as well as in the NT and Ap. Frs. The expression "to know God" is in the NT confined to the Paulines, where it always occurs with a negative to designate those who do not know the God of Israel, in other words, the pagans (1 Thess 4:5; 2 Thess 1:8; Gal 4:8). The OT roots of the phrase along with its suggestion of (false) worship appear in LXX Ps 78:6 and Wis 12:27 (s.v.l., and cf. 16:15–16).

but by their deeds. There are twenty occurrences of *ergon* in the PE. The term is almost always in the plural or is to be construed as thus, as in the *pan ergon* that follows in this verse (see also Titus 3:1; 1 Tim 5:10; 2 Tim 2:21; 3:17; 4:18). *Pros pan ergon* is further qualified in the PE with *agathon* (not *kalon*) in both this verse and 3:1; 1 Tim 5:10 (dative); 2 Tim 2:21 (with *eis*); 3:17 (likewise 2 Cor 9:8 [*eis*]; Col 1:10 [*en*]; and cf. 2 Thess 2:17 [*en*]). The antithetical formula, *apo pantos ergou ponērou,* appears in 2 Tim 4:18. In the PE the plural *erga* are usually qualified as *kala* (Titus 2:7, 14; 3:8, 14; 1 Tim 5:10, 25; 6:18) but once as *agatha* (1 Tim 2:10). *Erga agatha/kala* stand in contrast to the unmodified *erga* here in Titus 1:16 which, like the similarly unmodified *erga* of Titus 3:5

and 2 Tim 1:9, do not cause holiness and may be vicious (2 Tim 4:14). The PE employ *ergon* in a true singular only of the apostolic ministry of the bishop (1 Tim 3:1, with *kalon*) and of Timothy (2 Tim 4:5, "the work of one who announces the gospel"). This usage, relatively rare in the PE, corresponds to a regular Pauline and Lukan use of an unmodified *ergon* (thus 1 Cor 3:13–15; 9:1; 16:10; Acts 5:38; 13:2; 14:26; 15:38 and cf. the variant in 15:18). The characteristic emphasis of the PE appears when the plural *erga* are qualified as *agatha* or *kala.* The rest of the Paulines and the Lukan corpus never use *kalon* with *ergon* (but see Gal 6:9); half a dozen times the other Paulines qualify *ergon* with *agathon,* but only Eph 2:10 refers to *erga agatha.* Similarly, Luke only once writes of *erga agatha,* in Acts 9:36.

they disown him. Arneisthai recurs in 2:12; 1 Tim 5:8; 2 Tim 2:12–13; and 3:5 but not otherwise in the Paulines. Eight of eighteen other NT uses are in Luke–Acts. The LXX uses are rare and late, but Wis 12:27; 16:16 (of knowing God) and 4 Macc 8:7; 10:15 (of the Jewish religious tradition and the martyrs' brotherhood) are notable. The etymological link of this verb with terms that mean "pronounce a solemn formula" (*DELG* s.v.) is often discernible in biblical Greek and the Ap. Frs. Thus *2 Clem.* 17:7 notes "those who have denied (*arnesamenous*) Jesus by words or by deeds (*dia ton ergon*)."

They are disobedient abominations, counterfeiters of all excellent deeds. In Greek a polysyndetic *kai* binding three adjectives, *bdelyktoi* (abominable) . . . *apeitheis . . . adokimoi* (counterfeit) gives the final summary an expansive, even exhaustive sound (BDF §460.2–3). The assonance with *a,* now five times repeated (see v 15), reinforces the impression. *Bdelyktos,* not found elsewhere in the NT, is in the LXX only in Prov 17:15 (parallel to *akathartos*) and 2 Macc 1:27 (parallel to *exouthenēmenous,* rejected). Only *1 Clem.* among the Ap. Frs. employs the adjective, of schism (2.6), lust, and pride (30.1).

"Disobedient," *apeitheis,* recurs in the longer lists of vices in 3:3 and 2 Tim 3:2 (q.v. for the relation to Rom 1:30). Otherwise in the NT only Luke 1:17 and Acts 26:19 use the term. Almost all of the eight Septuagintal occurrences refer to the rebelliousness of God's people (thus LXX Num 20:10; Sir 16:6; 47:21; cf. *T. Dan* 5.11). The Ap. Frs. do not employ *apeithēs.* The uses of the cognate verb in Rom 2:8; 10:21 (= Isa 65:2) and *1 Clem.* 57.4; 58.1; 59.1 are notable.

"Counterfeiters," *Adokimoi* (literally, "untested" and so "unqualified"), will recur in the vice catalog of 2 Tim 3:8, as well as in that of Rom 1:28. Except for Heb 6:8, the rest of the NT uses are in the Corinthian correspondence (1 Cor 9:27; 2 Cor 13:5, 6, 7). In the LXX, *adokimos* refers to unrefined silver (Prov 25:4; Isa 1:22), whereas *dokimos* refers to pure silver and gold. The Ap. Frs. never use *dokimos,* and the single occurrence of *adokimos* appears to be based on 1 Cor (Ign. *Trall.* 12.3). For the positive *dokimazein* and *dokimos,* see 1 Tim 3:10 and 2 Tim 2:15.

COMMENT

1:10–11. *Indeed there are many, particularly among the Jewish Christians, who are refractory, spouting nonsense and seducing minds: these people must be muzzled, for they are the kind who teach things they ought not and overturn entire households, for their own financial gain, shame to say.* The preceding directives for the appointment of a Pauline ministry conclude with a reference to opponents of the apostolic instruction. Titus 1:10–16 describes a situation among Cretan believers in which an opposition flourishes that is numerically and religiously formidable. Its spokesmen are converts from Judaism; there may be converts from paganism in their party. Some are pictured as natives of Crete (1:12), but it is precisely their relation to Jewish tradition that puts them in opposition to the Pauline apostolate and his apostolic instruction. There is no evidence that all Jewish Christians belonged to the opposition described here. The Jewish character of the criteria for the new Pauline presbyters in 1:6 implies a Jewish background for some of the candidates. Paul's fellow workers, according to Col 4:11, included a few Jewish Christians; the Zenas and Apollos who come from Paul's entourage in Titus 3:13 appear to have had Jewish antecedents; it would accord with the strategy of this correspondence (cf. 1:12) to have Pauline Jewish Christians counter Jewish Christians' resistance to (or avoidance and ignorance of) the apostle's teaching.

A Jewish-Christian opposition to the Pauline apostolate was a notable phenomenon in the first Christian generation. But how could it have survived the debacle of the Palestinian revolt of A.D. 66–70? It is ironic that the most influential of Jewish Christians were those from the oldest Palestinian congregations, who had suffered already for decades at the hands of their countrymen (see 1 Thess 2:14–15; Gal 1:13, 23) and who came from the towns that had seen the ministry of Jesus himself forty years previously (see Luke 13:26). They were the displaced persons of the last third of the first century. They came to their Christian brothers outside Palestine trailing clouds of prestige but broken by persecution and war, homeless and poverty-stricken, even politically suspect. Their fellow believers, whether Jewish or Gentile, were bound in charity to receive them. The presbyter-bishop of a Jewish-Christian community in the diaspora had to be hospitable (see 1:8). From a Christian viewpoint these exiles had much to give. Their credentials and their origins were impressive, and they had to be formidable parties to reckon with when they opted for a cause or policy in the Jewish-Christian churches of the Mediterranean diaspora which had welcomed them. The text of Titus submits that there was an influential, articulate, and substantial number of them whose teaching and conduct were on a collision course with the Pauline apostolate and its appointed spokesmen.

It is no coincidence that the opposition is characterized as "refractory." The new Pauline presbyters have been chosen precisely with an eye to their having reared children who were not refractory (1:6); now they must deal with a group of fellow Jewish Christians who are locked for life in the cruel posture of immaturity. Adult Christian living involves willing subjection to authority; the admonition to be subject (*hypotassesthai*, 2:5, 9; 3:1) is conceptually and verbally in antithesis to the notion of *anypotaktoi*, who are both social and political misfits (3:1–2) as well as religious malcontents. Their "wranglings about the Law" are "useless and fruitless (*mataioi*)" in 3:9, and in 1 Tim 1:6, 9 their congeners surface again in the chattering (*mataiologia*) of those who want to be "rabbis" (*nomodidaskaloi*), but whose mistaken idolizing of the Law has actually made them "lawless (*anomoi*) and refractory."

The artful rhetoric of this passage appears in the plosive consonants as they erupt in the stream of *oi/ai* assonance, which runs through the exotic terminology translated as "spouting nonsense and seducing minds." With this flyting or poetical invective (see the INTRODUCTION) one encounters for the first time a regular feature of this correspondence. Because these documents are cast in epistolary form, we read only one side in a "systematic exchange of savage recrimination between opposed characters" (Ong, *Presence*, p. 197) that was a commonplace rhetorical device in the ancient world, a kind of intellectual wargame. The antagonists are dangerous beasts (see 1:12). The Pauline presbyter-bishops have received a divinely imposed duty (cf. *epitagē* and *diatassein* in 1:3, 5 with the *dei* here and in 1:7) to clamp shut the mouths that are fomenting rebellion (cf. Josephus, *Ant.* 17.251).

There are three aspects to their activity: teaching, an income, and intramural Christian strife. Each aspect has its antithesis in the activity of new presbyter-bishops, who are emphatically teachers (1:9), who are not preoccupied with their salary (1:7), and who have peaceful homes (1:6).

The opponents pretend to teach, but they lack an authentic commission and authoritative content (cf. *dei*). Hence what they teach is not "apostolic instruction" and is not graced with the terms *didachē* and *didaskalia* (1:9). The negative and vague designation of the content in the verbal *agon* here, as elsewhere, signals a contempt that is determined to leave no record at all of a rival instruction that was attractive enough to be a source of income and support for its proponents. These Palestinian-Christian displaced persons must have offered persuasive credentials to their Jewish-Christian hosts in the diaspora. But the teaching with which they paid for their living was, in the judgment of the author of Titus, counterfeit, and thus avarice becomes the single motive for their instruction, the subversive character of which appears in its effect. The greed of Cretans was almost as proverbial as their mendacity (texts in Spicq, *EP*, pp. 608–610; see 2 Tim 3:6–7 for a strategy that aimed at the women of the households and for another motive).

The small Christian congregations that gathered for worship in the roomy houses of their wealthier members (see the INTRODUCTION and 1 Tim 3:4) had offered hospitality to itinerant Jewish-Christian refugees from Palestine. They in turn have urged their practices and their theology upon the impressionable hosts. The latter were themselves of Jewish origin and particularly susceptible to teachings that appealed to their ethnic sympathies, national as well as religious. In the event, the house churches were now racked with dissension and controversy about the propriety and obligation of Jewish practices and beliefs among Christians. The evidence does not indicate a clean split on strictly ethnic lines, in other words, Jewish Christian versus converts from paganism. The debates are, however (the author of Titus holds), shattering to the belief (see 2 Tim 2:18) of all who ought to accept the faith as Paul taught it, and he intends to close the doors of the house churches to teachers without Pauline credentials (see Brown, *AB Epistles*, p. 748).

12–14. *A countryman of theirs, a prophet of their own, said:*

Liars ever, men of Crete,
Nasty brutes that live to eat.

This is truthful testimony, and good reason to refute them sharply, so that they may recover their health in the faith instead of doting on Jewish tales and commandments of people who are abandoning the truth.

The charges have been filed, and now the two witnesses to their truth (required by Jewish law, 1 Tim 5:19) appear. One is contemporary, one is ancient (see Aristotle, *Rhetoric* 1.15.13–16). The Paul who writes now is corroborated by a proverbial line from an ancient Cretan prophet-poet. Thus documentary evidence complements the quasi-oral epistolary genre; a pagan seer agrees with the Jewish-Christian apostle (see Quintilian, *Instituto oratoria* 5.7.32–36).

Where did the author of Titus find this testimony? He submits it as emanating from a native Cretan with indisputable prophetic credentials. As early as Clement of Alexandria (*Stromata* 1.59.1–2) this hexameter was attributed to Epimenides of Crete, who lived about the sixth century B.C.E. He used his diviner's talents to explain the past, not the future (Aristotle, *Rhetoric* 3.17.10). He had a disputed place among "the seven wise men" of Greece, and only a few dozen of his words and sayings survive (Diels, *Vorsokratiker*, nos. 1–26). Whether this text in fact goes back to that "very shadowy, half-legendary figure" (Renahan, "Quotations," p. 35) is indemonstrable. Theodore of Mopsuestia (Swete, *Theodore* 2.243–244) observed that the citation was a popular proverb rather than a quotation of an ancient poem as such. Already in the *Odyssey* a series of Cretan lies caps the portrait of Odysseus, the epic munchausen (Haft, "Cretan Lies," pp. 289–304; see Zimmer, "Lügner," pp. 77–99). Jerome in the fourth century knows only a report (*dicitur*) about a book of Epimenides' oracles that contained this verse (*PL* 26.572); the church historian Socrates asserts even less in the following century, when asked how Paul could have cited these words "unless he had read the oracles of Epimenides (*tous Epimenidou . . . chrēsmous*), the Cretan, a man initiated" (*PG* 67.421). The author of Titus is probably not citing from a composition that Epimenides had entitled "Oracles." He is rather quoting an anthology of sayings culled from the poems of the Cretan wise man and circulating in the schools of the Hellenistic world. The papyri have regularly contained such florilegia or gnomologies, collections of sayings, already proverbial and usually of an ethical character, plucked out of the poets, usually the dramatists, above all Euripides and Menander (see, e.g., OxyP 3004; 3005; 3214). Such anthologies sometimes noted the source of each proverb; sometimes they arranged them alphabetically, at other times according to subject matter. The original context, however, was not transmitted; the citation was for the sake of the meaning of the words quoted and no more. See H. Chadwick, "Florilegium," in *RAC* 7.1130–1160.

In the case of the devastating caricature in Titus 1:12, no small part of its effectiveness derives from the known nationality of the author. "This is how Cretans appear to the wise man who was their countryman" is certainly what the author of Titus wished to say and probably what the compiler of Epimenidean oracles wanted to say (because the mendacious character of the Cretans was a byword in the Greek language). It is quite conceivable that in its original context the judgment was placed on the lips of a character in one of his epics (cf. *PG* 103.621). G. L. Huxley (*Greek Epic*, pp. 81–83) suggests that the line is in fact an oracle from Delphi that replied to Epimenides' criticism of the claims of that shrine (cf. Diels, *Vorsokratiker*, no. 11). In that case, when the anthologist assembled Epimenidean oracles he also preserved the Delphic snub that put down the insolence of the Cretan diviner, perhaps signaling the insertion with *prophētēs* (which may have attracted the author of Titus) or with no more than a stroke of the pen to set it off from Epimenides' criticism (Lee, "Epimenides," p. 96). In any case, the hexameter became proverbial, more one suspects for the quality of its observation than for that of its poetic diction, just as certain limericks and other doggerel survive because their grotesque humor catches the popular fancy.

The hemistich *Krētes aei pseustai* may have been the original proverb to which Epimenides or another added the words that made it into a full-blown hexameter. The example of Callimachus's *Hymn to Zeus*, lines 8–9 (third century B.C.), is instructive in this respect, for the same opening hemistich there concludes with, "for the Cretans even built a tomb for you, O Lord" (cf. *Greek Anthology* 7.275 and Renehan, *Text. Crit.*, p. 53). The Epimenidean oracle takes another tack in its savage caricature of the Cretans as *kaka thēria*, literally, "evil wild animals," that is, beasts of prey: Crete was proverbial among the ancients for having no dangerous wild animals (see Plutarch, *De capienda* 86C; Pliny, *Naturalis historia* 8.83). The poet asserts that the human beings there give the lie to that belief. They are beasts of prey, not working for their food but idly prowling about for something to satisfy their hunger (see *Barn.* 10.4).

With deadly seriousness the author of Titus has Paul vouch for the truth of the cruel ancient jibe, thus solemnly joining the witness of an apostle to the oracle of the prophet-poet. The latter is cited as "a prophet" not only because the Hellenistic world so conceived him but also with an irony pointed at the Jewish-Christian troublemakers. Prophetic credentials were found and valued among the Jewish Christians, whether in Palestine or abroad (see Acts 13:1; 15:22, 32; 1 Cor 12:28–29; Eph 2:20; 4:11). The PE recognize prophetic phenomena among Christians (see 1 Tim 1:18; 4:1, 14); no Christian or Jew, however, receives the title. Its unique occurrence in the PE at this point serves to discredit native Cretan Jewish Christians who pretend to this charismatic title and order. Just because they are Cretans, they are liars. The bitter hyperbole of the argument at this point makes it difficult to believe that the author of Titus seriously envisioned the persuasion and conversion of Cretan opponents to the Pauline mission. Perhaps the theological and pastoral battle on the island had been lost by the time the PE were published, and the Cretan churches that had dead-ended into Judaism were warning examples of what happened to Christians who rejected Paul.

With the charges and witnesses marshaled, Titus is directly commissioned (note the singular address of the Greek) to lead the prosecution of the troublemakers. His refutation of them is to be the model for that of the presbyter-bishops of 1:9. The severity that Paul himself had shown in correspondence (see NOTES) is to live again in "his true child." It is, however, to be a therapeutic severity to produce a cure of mind and conscience, areas that will not admit anesthetics.

Jewish Christians who oppose Paul (see Dodd, *More NT*, pp. 44–45) have in fact become addicted to myths of emphatically Jewish origin and to merely human regulations. The chiastically parallel phrases appear to be a polemical description of the *haggadah* (the homiletic, narrative embellishment of the Pentateuchal history) and *halakah* (the "oral law" or further explanation of how to carry out the commandments of the Torah), both of which were components of contemporary Jewish explanation (midrash in the broad sense) of their sacred books for themselves. The Jewish-Christian opposition to the Pauline apostolate is attempting to bridge the gap between the Scriptures of Israel and the apostolic faith (which is *the truth*) by such haggadic and halakic commentaries. There is no escaping the contemptuous dismissal of these techniques and their products as merely human regulations and myths. Yet the PE are themselves a tissue of imperatives from a quite human Paul working through other men. Haggadic development appears in 1 Tim 2:13–15 and 2 Tim 3:8; halakic commentary, in 1 Tim 5:17–19; both are implied in 2 Tim 3:14–17. At what point does *haggadah* become myth? How does *halakah* become obligatory before God?

There is no question that a Christian use of the books of the OT is being debated at this point. Converts from Judaism and from paganism received as authoritative and holy a collection of documents that had expressed and determined Jewish life in previous generations (without prejudice to the questions about the limits of the collection that were still debated within Judaism of the first century C.E.). There is no question here of the wholesale rejection of these books (see 2 Tim 3:15–16); there is, moreover, no evidence that any Jew or Christian succeeded in making the classification *mythoi* stick to these documents. Philo in fact reacted vigorously against the thought (*Op. mund.* 1–3; *Gig.* 6–7). Thus one infers that the *mythoi* being scored at this point are Jewish or Jewish-Christian compositions about the sacred books that are revered in common. Are these the same kind of *mythoi* that reappear in the Timothy correspondence? The would-be Christian rabbis of Ephesus "dote on tales and endless genealogies" that are "lucubrations" (1 Tim 1:4). The language is reminiscent of Titus 1:14 and 3:9, which probably signals some coincidence in form and content. Timothy himself is told to "have nothing to do with profane, old wives' tales" (1 Tim 4:7) that are of a piece with the perverse interpretations of the Scriptures that have been refuted in 1 Tim 4:2–6. The Pauline apostolic instruction (*didaskalia*) about the OT is exactly the opposite of what these tales propose for believers.

The final reference in the PE to *mythoi* is in the testamentary paraenesis to Timothy to imitate Paul (2 Tim 3:14–4:4), where the exhortation to take "all of the Scripture" to heart and to "herald the message" of Paul concludes with the somber picture of those who "will not put up with this wholesome instruction" but "slip off after tales" (2 Tim 4:4). The Pauline method and its content (as the PE transmit both) are here the final criterion for discerning what are "Jewish tales" about the Scripture. A similar line of argument for the Petrine interpretation of the prophets contrasts "the cleverly concocted myths" of opponents with what the eyewitnesses of the glory of Jesus made known (2 Pet 1:16, cf. 19 of fixing attention [*prosechontes* in a good sense] on the prophetic message).

Can the content of the "Jewish tales" be further specified? With Samuel Sandmel, "Myths," one can agree that the text here presupposes a controversy among Christians, though at least some of the participants are converts from Judaism. The materials from the rabbinic *haggadah* and *halakah* that are adduced as illustrating the "Jewish tales" are, as Sandmel has also noted, sparse and unsatisfying (cf. D-C, pp. 16–17). Moreover, their dating is hard to establish. Yet Sandmel has too hastily called off the "search in Judaism and its literature" for the kind of compositions that a Christian (even of Jewish origin) could call *mythoi* if he disagreed with their teaching (though he might use them without qualm if they agreed). Particularly strong candidates are compositions that have a prophetic character and offer prophetic credentials, such as *Enoch*, the *T. 12 Patr.*, the *Book of Jubilees*, and the *Ascension of Isaiah* (see Daniel, "Faux Prophètes," pp. 64–65). The Qumran *Genesis Apocryphon* (1QapGen), an Aramaic amalgam of midrashic and targumic embellishments of the Genesis narratives about Lamech and Abraham (Fitzmyer, *Gen. Apoc.*, pp. 6–14), may well illustrate a sentimental piety that can verge on the erotic as it warms to its theme. The bodily charms of Sarai (1QapGen 20:2–17) are fabricated and exaggerated, so that the divine intervention that delivers her will appear all the more powerful. In Greek-speaking Judaism, LXX Esth 5:1a–d exploits the same device more discreetly, and LXX Jdt 10, not to mention *T. Jos.*, use it at greater length. All illustrate a tendency in the first century B.C.E. to incorporate materials with a sensual appeal into haggadic exposition.

This tendency in its turn would remind the Hellenistic reader of the sensual strain that often appears in the tales that the Greeks called *mythoi*. Just as the PE take a dim view of *mythoi*, so there is a Greek tradition that not only links tale telling with temptation but looks askance at the link. Already in Sappho, *Eros* is *mythoplokos*, a weaver of tales (LP §188), as Aphrodite is a weaver of wiles (LP §1.2). Plato scores the Cretans for their myth about Zeus's affair with Ganymede, asserting that they justified homosexual pleasure with this tale (*Laws* I.636C–D). Myths were not just stories, or just stories about what had never really occurred; they were stories in which, from one point of view, their authors foisted their own immoral conduct on the gods or, from another point of view, stories that enticed their hearers into evil acts on divine precedents. The Greeks themselves in their wiser moments pilloried such myths (Diels, *Vorsokratiker*, Xenophanes, fragment no. 11) and proposed their abolition from civilized society (Plato, *Republic* 2.376E–383C; *Laws* XII.941B). The Roman attitude is traced back to Romulus himself, who "rejected the traditional myths (*mythous*) about the gods in which there are insults or slanders against them, considering these tales as vicious, useless, and indecent, and unworthy not only of gods but even of good human beings" (Dionysius of Halicarnassus, *Roman Antiquities* 2.18.3).

From this complex of Jewish texts and Platonic and Roman critique of myths, one may infer something of the content of sentimental tales that gave "relief for their itchy ears" (2 Tim 4:3) and justified the polemical classification of some Jewish (and Jewish-Christian) devotional literature as *mythoi*. The PE have not the literary critic's or philosopher's concern for mythical form and content as such; they are concerned that the compositions thus branded can serve to excuse activities that are incompatible with the conduct that the Pauline tradition urged on believers. The same basic concern lies behind the practical directives about the candidates for baptism in the Roman church in the second century. There schoolmasters (who taught boys the pagan myths of classical literature) and actors (who played out the myths in tragedy and satyr plays) were not even admitted to the catechumenate, but were turned away like brothel keepers and artists who made idols (Cuming, *Hippolytus* §16). For a Jewish-Christian critique of the sensuality of Greek myths see the *Clementine Homilies* 4 and 5 (*PG* 2.157–195).

A further hint about the form and content of these tales takes one to Titus 3:8b–9, where the Jewish Christians (i.e., "those who have put their faith in

God") are bound in shallows "of foolish speculations (*mōras zētēseis*), of genealogies, of controversies, of wranglings about the Law." The pointless researches that are here paired with genealogies are parallel to the "tales and endless genealogies" of 1 Tim 1:4, and *zētēsis* seems to designate haggadic midrash (see the COMMENT below and Wright, *Midrash*, p. 40 n. 22) on the OT that runs counter to the Pauline interpretation of Scripture.

The "Jewish myths" of Titus 1:14 are paired with "commandments of people who are abandoning the truth" (as in 3:9 speculations and genealogies are complemented by controversies and wranglings about the Law). Just as there is midrash and midrash, so there are commandments and commandments. The singular *entolē* of 1 Tim 6:14 has the good sense of a whole life that corresponds to the apostolic faith; the plural *entolai* (like the plural *didaskaliai* of 1 Tim 4:1) already signals the uneasiness that is further articulated in "of people [literally, "of human beings] who are abandoning the truth." But the phrase is to be read as a whole.

The similarities to and differences from Mark 7:7–9 (Matt 15:3b, 9; *SFG* §150) are revealing. There a citation of LXX Isa 29:13 is aimed at Pharisees and scribes, "teaching as doctrines (*didaskontes didaskalias*—note the variant word order in the LXX) the commands of human beings (*entalmata anthrōpōn*)." This is defined as "the tradition (*paradosin*) of human beings (*anthrōpōn*)" and as the opposite of "the commandment (singular, *entolēn*) of God." The contrast of singulars with plurals, the divine with the human; the controversy with representative Jewish persons about putting the Scripture into practice; the occurrence of much of the key terminology in the Pauline tradition in Col 2:8, 22—all of these argue for the reappearance of the same concern in Titus 1:14. The Septuagintal phrase *entalmata anthrōpōn*, left unqualified and thus in sharp antithesis to the truth, is in Titus pointedly nuanced with the change to the cognate *entolai*, which is immediately modified; not all "commandments of people" are scored, but only those of people "who are abandoning the truth." "The commandments of men" are, according to the Scriptures and Jesus, contrary to the commandment of God. The commandments of men are not as such bad for the Pauline tradition, but they become so when they emanate from persons whose faith is atrophying as they give regulations that run counter to the Pauline gospel. As the Paul of history used haggadic and halakic midrash to teach the implications of his gospel for Christian conduct (e.g., 1 Cor 14:37), so the Paul of the PE makes regulations and interprets the Scripture with traditional Jewish techniques. The PE add that such interpretations are worthless and dangerous counterfeits on the lips of those who controvert the Pauline interpretation of the OT. The Pauline gospel is always "according to the Scriptures" (1 Cor 15:3–4); but the reverse is not true: not every interpretation of the Scripture in circulation in the churches of the latter first century is according to "my [i.e., Paul's] gospel" (2 Tim 2:8). In a word, the proclamation ultimately judges its hermeneutic and not vice versa.

15. *For the clean, all things are clean. For the polluted and the unbelievers, however, nothing is clean. Rather, their very way of thinking and their conscience have been polluted.*

The assonance on *a*, leading off the *alētheian* of v 14, binds this verse and the following together, as the repeated *oi/ai* did vv 10–11. The authoritative Pauline teaching for countering "commandments of people who are abandoning the truth" is offered in the laconic and already proverbial form in which it appeared in Rom 14:20. If Paul did not coin the phrase, he may have heard it in connection with the dietary issues debated between the house churches of Rome. Although the thought occurs in widely scattered ancient texts (see Spicq, *EP*, p. 612 for citations), this particular verbal formulation is undocumented previous to Paul, who understands its truth as guaranteed "in the Lord Jesus Christ" that "nothing is profane (*koinon*) in itself" (Rom 14:14). Although the Markan tradition expounds Jesus' teaching on what really makes persons profane (Mark 7:1–9, as above), it is only in the Lukan tradition of Jesus' woes over the Pharisees' purifications that Jesus teaches "Behold all things are clean (*panta kathara*) for you" (Luke 11:41). Then in Acts, during his Joppa vision, Peter three times declares, "I have never eaten anything profane and unclean (*koinon kai akatharton*)," and three times the voice of the Lord Jesus replies, "What God has cleansed (*ekatharisen*) you must not call profane" (Acts 10:14–15; see 11:8–9). Repercussions from this principle ripple out through the rest of Acts (see 15:7–11, 20–21, 29; 21:21, 28). In the PE the problem of putting into practice the Pentateuchal dietary laws reappears in 1 Tim 4:3. The way in which a solution was formulated could have drastic consequences. Apparently a party of Corinthian converts had summarized their position on the question as, "All things are lawful for me (*panta moi exestin*)" (1 Cor 6:12 and see 10:23) and then emancipated themselves from recognizably Christian conduct. The formulation in the Pauline and Lukan tradition forestalls such egotistical manipulation of Jesus' teaching. All visible creatures, including human beings precisely as palpable entities, are clean for those whose unseen heart is clean (see *T. Benj.* 8.2–3). The hungry human ego can profane and contaminate anything and anyone in the world. Persons whose "very way of thinking and . . . conscience have been polluted" cannot discern what pollutes and what purifies ecclesial life. Without the Pauline gospel and its principles for conduct, these persons have relapsed into the Judaism (*apistia:* 1 Tim 1:13) from which the risen Lord called the apostle. They have accordingly no title to be heard by the churches, for their understanding of the Scriptures is actually locked into a pre-Christian system of interpretation (cf. the singular use of *nous* in the gospel tradition in Luke 24:45 with *Barn.* 6.10). This understanding in turn cripples their consciences. In English "conscience" is the human faculty for making moral evaluation of both past and future acts. Ancient Greek employed *syneidēsis* and its cognates only of knowing something about one's past acts (Menander, *Samia* 272, 317, 478, 562, 584; *Aspis* 383) and often enough something of which the person felt ashamed (see Chadwick, "Gewissen," pp. 1026, 1066). The terminology suggested a certain internal, self-critical distance that a person could assume with respect to what he had freely done; in a proverbial line from Greek comedy, "Conscience is god for all of us / mortals (*brotis / hapasin hēmin hē syneidēsis theos:* Meineke, *FPCN* 4.357, 359, *Monostichoi* §597, 654; significantly, Menander says the same of *nous*, Koerte 13/11K, Koerte 64/70K, Koerte 749/762K). The popular Hellenistic usage (which is not a technical philosophical or theological one) appears in the first-generation Christian movement in Corinth, where questions about "conscience" and eating meat that had been sacrificed to pagan gods are submitted to Paul for settlement (see Jewett, *Anthropological Terms*, pp. 421–439 and idem, "Conscience"). The opening argument of Rom takes up the word in its description of the pagans who "show that what the law requires is written on their hearts, while their conscience also bears witness and their conflicting thoughts accuse or perhaps excuse them on that day" (2:15–16; see Ovid, *Fasti* 1.485–486); but the lengthy discussion of dietary scruples among Roman Christians is finally settled in terms of faith (Rom 14:22–23), not of conscience. The Roman believers may not have used the latter term in articulating their problems; Paul may have had no taste for exporting the Corinthian way of arguing the case. In the problematic of Rom 14 and here in Titus as well as in 1 Tim 1:19 and 3:9, the clear or clean conscience stands in immediate relation to faith. Thus one can confront the problem of the inviolable, individual conscience when that conscience has been radically polluted by superstition and aggressively entices others to adopt its criteria. "For all mortals conscience is a god," but when it becomes a false god, replacing the Pauline gospel "of the glory of the blessed God" (1 Tim 1:11) with "demonic doctrines" (1 Tim 4:1), it has nothing to offer a community of believers. Such a conscience no longer functions with an alternative Christian structure for judging conduct but actually conducts itself according to another gospel and as subject to another god (*pace* Jewett, "Conscience").

16. *God they profess to know but by their deeds they disown him. They are disobedient abominations, counterfeiters of all excellent deeds.* In Greek this is a single sentence, the rhetorical ornaments of which are an echo of those at the opening of this section (1:10). The opponents solemnly and explicitly align themselves, as Jewish Christians, with the one God of Israel (always anarthrous *theos* in the PE) and implicitly against the converts from paganism who do not carry out the dietary prescriptions of the Torah. The riposte of the Paul of the PE is drastic. These Jewish Christians are neither Christian nor Jewish. They have not "put their faith in God" (Titus 3:8, also anarthrous) but rather in a corrupted mind and conscience, which do not serve the true God and so cannot tell the saving truth about his creatures. They solemnly repudiate by their contemptible works (note the force of the Greek article) the person whom their lips confess. In the Greek here the person repudiated is not expressed, though *arneisthai* can take a personal object in Hellenistic and biblical usage (MM s.v.)

and does so in the *pistos logos* cited in 2 Tim 2:12b–13, where the Greek literally says, "If we *deny* (*arnēsometha*), he [the Lord Jesus] also will *deny us;* if we are faithless, he remains faithful, for he *cannot deny himself."* The initial *arnēsometha* evidently supposes *Christon* or *ton Kyrion* as its object, but the term is suppressed, as *theon* or *auton* is in this passage of Titus, for reasons of reverence that are not superficial. Neither the God of Israel nor his Christ can repudiate their promises to the persons who have repudiated them. The door has not been quite closed on Paul's opponents. Both their way of thinking and their judgment must change; only when they have admitted into their hearts the gospel of Paul and his apostolic instruction will they know and serve the one God. Meantime, not just one or another act of theirs is repudiated; everything they do is unclean and unholy before God because nothing proceeds from genuine faith in God. The crescendo of repudiation reaches its peak in the triple characterization of the opposition as abominable, contumacious, incompetent (*bdelyktoi, apeitheis, adokimoi*).

The rhetorical sting in this flyting lies in its programmatic reversal of the qualities vaunted by the Jewish Christian interlopers. They who belong to a people who abominated (*bdelyssomenos:* Rom 2:22) idols, have made an idol out of dietary laws (see Phil 3:19, "their god is their belly"). With shameful greed these abominable people have made common cause with "the Pharisees who were lovers of money" and so have fallen under the judgment of Jesus, "You are those who justify yourselves before men but God knows your hearts; for what is exalted among men is an abomination (*bdelygma*) in the sight of God" (Luke 16:14–15). This unique Lukan use of *bdelygma* also appears to psychologize (and thus "realize") the apocalyptic *bdelygma* of Mark 13:14 = Matt 24:15 (*SFG* §290), which in turn derives from LXX Dan 12:11 (cf. 9:27; 11:31) and the regular Septuagintal description of idols and even unclean creatures as *bdelygma* (Lev 11:10–42). Thus, ironically, those who claim to abominate idols and forbidden foods are themselves abominable.

Furthermore, those who present themselves as thoroughly obedient to the Scriptures and to Jesus are really *disobedient,* a rebellious faction whom ages of prophecy have never touched (Luke 1:17) and who refuse the obedience that Paul gave to the risen Lord (Acts 26:19).

The indictment reaches its climax in the expansive third member (see 1:9 above), where those who pride themselves on their superfluity of good works are radically deprived of every one of them. Any number multiplied by zero equals zero. The author of the PE is about to make his own case for the tangibly good lives of believers in the following chapters; all he is about to teach must be understood in function of the merciful munificence of the savior God. "All excellent deeds" of Christians are done by virtue of grace and faith (see 2:14; 3:4–7; 2 Tim 3:17). They may superficially coincide with some of the deeds of unbelievers or of "counterfeiters of the faith" (2 Tim 3:8). They are basically as different as gold and brass. The Jewish-Christian opponents of the Pauline tradition have, again ironically, been made targets for a withering critique that was originally aimed at pagans who, "because they did not see fit (*edokimason*) to recognize God, God delivered them over to an unfit way of thinking (*adokimon noun*), to do improper things" (Rom 1:28). Resistance to God's revelation perverts human knowledge (whether by pagan or by Jew) of God's creation, which in turn pollutes human conduct in relation to all creatures. See Therrien, *Discernement*, pp. 230–236.

II.B. FOR THE PEOPLE OF GOD (2:1–3:11)
II.B.1. TEACHING FOR DIVERSE GROUPS OF BELIEVERS (2:1–10)

2 ¹Now you, Titus, are to speak of matters that suit our wholesome instruction.

²Thus older men are to be

temperate,
serious,
sensible,
robust in faithfulness,
    in charity,
    in steadfastness.

³Older women, similarly, are to be as reverent in demeanor as priests, not devils at gossip, not slaves to drink. They are the right teachers ⁴for spurring on younger women

to love their husbands,
to love children,
⁵to be sensible;
    chaste;
    tending the hearth;
    considerate;
    subject to the authority of their own husbands;

so that the message of God not be defamed.

⁶Encourage the young men, similarly, to use common sense ⁷in all matters (given that you proffer yourself as

a pattern in fine deeds;
openhanded with instruction;
a reverent man,
[8]wholesome in preaching,
irreproachable,

so that the opponent, able to muster nothing bad to say about us, will be embarrassed).

[9]Slaves are to be subject to their masters in all matters, aiming to please them, not to oppose them, [10]not to pilfer. Rather they are to give such good evidence of complete reliability that they add luster in every way to the instruction of our savior, God.

NOTES

2:1. *Now you, Titus.* In Greek simply *sy de*, a regular signal in the PE for a significant shift in exposition (see 1 Tim 6:11; 2 Tim 3:10, 14; 4:5).

are to speak of matters that suit our wholesome instruction. For the closing phrase, see 1:9. "To speak" will recur in the transition at 2:15; the only other use of *lalein* in the PE is in the *ordo* for widows (1 Tim 5:3–16), of those younger women who circulate through the Christian community, "saying what they have no right to say" (v 13). With the "matters that suit" (*ha prepei*) a Pauline instruction here, compare the *ho prepei* of women in the order for worship (1 Tim 2:10). Outside the PE, the verb occurs in the Pauline directives for Christian women at worship (1 Cor 11:13) as well as in the catalog of vices of Eph 5:3. The link with prayer and good conduct is notable in the handful of Septuagintal uses. Of the Ap. Frs., Ignatius favors the term, employing it regularly of directives pertaining to a bishop (Ign. *Eph.* 2.2; 4.1; etc.).

2. *Thus older men are to be.* "Thus" reflects (and softens) a harsh transition into indirect quotation in Greek. The infinitive can also be taken imperatively (BDF §389; Moulton, *Grammar*, 1.179–180; Moule, *Idiom*, p. 126). The standard NT term for an old person is *presbyteros*, which also has the technical senses "(Jewish) elder" and "presbyter." The term *presbytēs* here occurs otherwise in the NT only in the singular, of Zechariah (Luke 1:18) and Paul (Phlm 9). *Presbytis*, the feminine of *presbytēs*, is used in 2:3; it is found otherwise in biblical Greek only in 4 Macc 16:14, in the singular (cf. *Herm. Vis.* 1.2.2). The line is thus firmly drawn between the ministerial *presbyteroi-episkopoi* of the previous chapter and the elderly men and women as a subgroup within the community of the baptized (see 1 Tim 5:1 for another way of handling the distinction). In a handful of minuscules cited by J. K. Elliott (*Greek Text*, p. 180), the reading *presbyterous* illustrates how the technical ecclesiastical usage

replaced and so explained the less usual term; there was hardly a similar pressure on the scribes with regard to *presbytides*.

temperate. Nēphalios recurs in lists of qualifications for the bishop and for the women whose ministry parallels that of the deacons in 1 Tim 3:2, 11. The term is otherwise undocumented in biblical Greek or the Ap. Frs. The cognate and similarly unusual *ananēphein* occurs in 2 Tim 2:26; *nēphein* in 2 Tim 4:5. In secular Greek this adjective describes sacrifices unmixed with wine (MM; LSJ; *DELG*); in Philo it retains this link with the sacred, and in Josephus (*Ant.* 3.279) it qualifies the priests personally. The cognate *nēptēs* occurs in the twelve-entry list of virtues for the general of an army in Onosander (D-C, pp. 158–159).

serious, sensible. On *semnos*, see Excursus III, "*Eusebeia* and Its Cognates in the PE"; on *sōphrōn*, Excursus V, "The PE on Salvation."

robust in faithfulness. See 1:9 on "wholesome instruction" and Excursus I, "*Pistis* Terminology in the PE." The triad *hē pistis, hē agapē, hē hypomonē*, in the same order, with the repeated article, is part of 1 Thess 1:3 (see also 2 Tim 3:10 for the repeated article and 1 Tim 6:11 for the triad, now anarthrous, embedded in a longer list). The articular triad surfaces again in Ign. *Pol.* 6.2.

in charity. Agapē occurs only here in Titus (see the variant in 2:10) but nine times in the Timothy correspondence (see 1 Tim 1:5), where the cognates *agapan* (2 Tim 4:8, 10) and *agapētos* (1 Tim 6:2; 2 Tim 1:2) are also found. *Agapē* is always coupled with one or more other virtues in the PE; if only one, that one is faith (1 Tim 1:5, 14; 2 Tim 1:13).

in steadfastness. Otherwise *hypomonē* occurs in the PE only in the lists of 1 Tim 6:11; 2 Tim 3:10. In the rest of the Paulines, Romans has six of the thirteen uses; in the gospels and Acts only Luke 8:15 and 21:19 contain this noun. For the cognate verb, *hypomenein*, see 2 Tim 2:10, 12. Most of the two dozen Septuagintal uses of the noun are in Pss, Sir, and especially 4 Macc. The *T. Jos.*, at 2.7 and 10.1–2, couples steadfastness with patience (*makrothymia*), prayer (*proseuchē*), and humility (*tapeinosis*) of heart. *Hypomonē* appears regularly in lists of virtues in the Ap. Frs. (thus *1 Clem.* 62.2) and is twice linked to Paul himself (*1 Clem.* 5.5, 7 and Pol. *Phil.* 9.1).

3. *Older women, similarly, are to be.* See the previous verse on the older men. *Hōsautōs*, "similarly," coordinates the descriptions of men and women in 2:6 and in 1 Tim 2:9 and 3:8, 11 (only in 1 Tim 5:25 are things coordinated thus). The verb *einai* is not repeated from the preceding sentence (BAGD, s.v.).

as reverent in demeanor as priests. The terminology is not found elsewhere in the NT and occurs only in the Maccabean stratum of the LXX (3 Macc 5:45; 4 Macc 9:25; 11:20). In the Ap. Frs. only Ign. *Trall.* 3.2 uses *katastēma* for a bishop's "demeanor" that "is itself a great lesson." In Hellenistic Jewish Greek the term can suggest an internal quality as well as external deportment (cf. *Ep. Arist.* 122, 165 with 210, 278; Josephus, *War* 1.40; 2.650; 4.287 with *Ant.* 15.236). *Hieroprepeis*, "reverent . . . as priests," is scarcely Attic or biblical

(Durham, *Voc. Men.*, p. 66). Xenophon, *Symposium* 8.40 thus describes persons, and for Menander's pretentious cook in *Dyscolos* 646 his art is sacrosanct (*hieroprepēs . . . hē technē:* Gomme and Sandbach, *Commentary,* p. 234); earlier he confides that one of his diplomatic ploys is to address a middle-aged woman who answers the door as *hieran* (i.e., "priestess," pp. 495–496). In first-century Jewish circles, Josephus, *Ant.* 11.329 uses *hieroprepēs* to refer to a "sacred encounter" involving the high priest and his colleagues (the adverb is used of towers in *Ant.* 10.225 and *Apion* 1.140). Philo often uses the adjective, and it appears in inscriptions (see Spicq, *EP,* p. 406; *Lexic.,* pp. 387–388, and the citations in D-C, p. 140).

not devils at gossip, not. The *mē . . . mēde* correlatives recur in 1 Tim 1:3–4; 6:17; and 2 Tim 1:8; the *mē . . . mē* of Sᶜ, D, F, G, H, and others. (*GNT* ³corr; *NTG* ²⁶corr) is probably an assimilation to 1 Tim 3:8 and other negative catalogs of the PE which, copied with Titus in last place, would have some impact (see J. K. Elliott, *Greek Text,* p. 137). "Devils at gossip" is simply *diabolous* in Greek. This anarthrous plural recurs in the ethical lists of 1 Tim 3:11 (of women associated with diaconal tasks) and 2 Tim 3:3 (of evil persons to come). The LXX does not use the plural, though the noun *diabolē* (slander) occurs ten times (see 2 Macc 14:27; 3 Macc 6:7). In the Ap. Frs., only Pol. *Phil.* 5.2, in a list of virtues for the deacons, prescribes that they "be not slanderers" (*diaboloi;* cf. 4:3 for *diabolē* of widows). The Greek verbal root *diaballein,* "to attack, to calumniate," underlies this adjectival usage for gossipy human beings (*DELG,* pp. 161–162), which appears already in Greek comedy in Aristophanes, *Knights,* line 45. Menander wrote, "There is not a gossipy old woman in the family" (*diabolos graus endon:* Koerte, 803/878K). Aristotle uses the term nominally, speaking of "sophist, or slanderer, or thief" (*Topics* 4.126a31–32: cf. Pindar, frag. 297; *Gnomologium Vaticanum* §337). Jewish-Greek usage went its own way, with the articular *diabolos* in the singular becoming a personal title (cf. LXX Job 1–2 passim; Zach 3:1–2; *T. Naph.* 3.1; 8.4, 6; *T. Asher* 3.2 with 1 Tim 3:6–7; 2 Tim 2:26). Josephus never employs *diabolos,* and the single use in Philo in a list of vicious qualities (*Sacr.* 32) is anarthrous, with the meaning being "slanderous."

slaves to drink. Literally, "who have been enslaved to much wine (*oinoi polloi*)." The latter phrase recurs in the ethical list for deacons in 1 Tim 3:8; see 1 Tim 5:23 for its contrary, "Take wine moderately (*oinoi oligoi*)." *Douloun* occurs only here in the PE (see 3:3 for the cognate *douleuein*), but five times in the other Paulines. Otherwise in the NT, 2 Pet 2:19 thus describes those who are slaves to moral corruption. Acts 7:6, quoting LXX Gen 15:13, uses the term in its sociological sense, of the Israelites serving the Egyptians as slaves (see LXX Prov 27:8; Wis 19:14; 1 Macc 8:11; as well as *T. Jos.* 18.3). The moral sense surfaces in the LXX only in 4 Macc 3:2; 13:2 (cf. *T. Jos.* 7.8 with *T. Judah* 15.2, quoted at 3:3). In the Ap. Frs., *Barn.* 16.9 describes those now believers as "those who had been enslaved to death."

They are the right teachers. This phrase is one anarthrous, compound term in Greek, *kalodidaskaloi,* otherwise quite unattested. Two meanings are possible: "Teachers of what is right," a predicative use that would be parallel to the use in *2 Clem.* 10.5 of *kakodidaskalein* (to teach evil), a verb almost as rare; or "the right teachers," an attributive use that corresponds with another rare noun, *kakodidaskalia* (evil teaching), in Ign. *Phld.* 2.1 (note how the variant reading in Ign. *Eph.* 16.2 opts for the attributive meaning).

4. *for spurring on.* The purposive clause may be *hina* with the subjunctive (as in S^c, C, and D and the majority of witnesses) or the indicative, *sōphronizousi(n)* (as in S*, A, F, G, H, P, and some others). J. K. Elliott (*Greek Text,* p. 181) submits that the variant is simply orthographic and opts for the subjunctive, which is practically always found with *hina* in the PE (see the v.1. in 3:8). Yet the pressure of standard NT usage may have ironed out an indicative expression that was original to this household code, in which the language is unusual at every turn. *Sōphronizein* itself is otherwise unattested in biblical Greek (except for Aquila, Isa 38:16) or the Ap. Frs., though common enough in secular Greek. Josephus employs this verb in *War* 2.493; 3.445; and 4.119; Philo often uses it (Spicq, *EP,* p. 620 for citations; *Lexic.,* pp. 870–871 for other data).

younger women. In Greek *tas neas,* "the new," with the meaning "the young," a sense not found elsewhere in the NT but often enough in the Maccabean literature (thus 2 Macc 5:13; 6:24, 28, 31) as well as in *1 Clem.* 1.3; 3.3; and 21.6 (see *2 Clem.* 19.1). In the NT *neos* regularly qualifies things, such as wine, but the Pauline usage of new dough and the new human being (1 Cor 5:7; Col 3:10) inserts the term into theological discourse (cf. Heb 12:24). On the comparative *neoteroi/-ai,* see v 6.

to love their husbands, to love children. In Greek this phrase consists of a pair of adjectives compounded with *philo-,* like the others in 1:8 and 2 Tim 3:2. *Philandros* is elsewhere unattested in biblical Greek or the Ap. Frs.; *philoteknos* appears only in 4 Macc 15:4–6 and *Herm. Vis.* 1.3.1 (of spoiling children). In Jewish Greek, Philo once uses *philoteknos* (*Abr.* 179), and in *Praem.* 139 describes wives as "sensible, tending the hearth, and loving their husbands (*sōphronas oikourous kai philandrous*)" (see v 5 here). Ceslaus Spicq (*EP,* pp. 392–393) has gathered numerous examples of these terms from the epitaphs of the Hellenistic world, some using both terms. Literary Greek preferred a rather different sense for *philandros* before the first Christian century, but *philoteknos* was familiar enough in the drama. Euripides, *Phoenissae* 356, writes "How all womenkind love their children (*philoteknon pos pan gynaikeion genos*)," a sentiment that appears with a proverbial character in *Heracles furens* 636, "All races love their children (*pan de philoteknon genos*)." Aristophanes, *Thesmophoriazusae* 752, has Euripides' father-in-law say to a woman, "by nature all you women love children (*philoteknos tis ei physei*)." In the time of the Roman republic, Porcius Cato is said by a Byzantine historian of the twelfth century (J. Zonaras, *PG* 134:761) to have called for women's ornaments that consisted in *sōphrosyne, philandria, philoteknia, peithos, metriotēs,* that is, temperance, love of husband, love of children, obedience, and moderation.

to be sensible; chaste. For *sōphrōn,* see Excursus V, "The PE on Salvation." *Hagnos* recurs in 1 Tim 5:22 and six times otherwise in the NT, in the epistolary only. The cognate *hagneia,* "purity," occurs in the list of 1 Tim 4:12 and in the domestic code that underlies 5:2. Of the eleven Septuagintal uses of *hagnos,* only 4 Macc 18:7–8 thus describes a woman (with a notable parallel to 2 Cor 11:2). Of the ten occurrences in the Ap. Frs., confined to *1 Clem., 2 Clem.,* and Hermas, only *1 Clem.* 1.3 thus describes a Christian woman's conscience (but see 21.7). The term originally belonged in Greek religious vocabulary, particularly that of prayer and sacrifice; but, as early as the seventh century, Alcaeus addressed not only the Graces but also Sappho as "dark haired, pure *(agna),* gently smiling" (cf. LP §384, with 386, as well as Sappho, 53 and 103.8: see *DELG,* p. 25). Internal ethical goodness as well as ceremonial propriety are suggested in the sharp Euripidean exchange *(Orestes* 1604) between Menelaus, "My hands are pure *(hagnos gar eimi cheiras),*" and Orestes, "But not your heart *(tas phrenas).*" At the entrance of a temple at Epidaurus there was an elegiac inscription that read, "Pure *(hagnon)* he ought to be who enters a fragrant temple, and purity *(hagneia)* is to think *(phronein)* holy things *(hosia)*" (in Clement of Alexandria, *Stromata* 5.1.13 [O. Stählin; Leipzig: Hinrichs, 1906, 2.334]).

Unlike Josephus, Philo employs the term of the virginal life of both men and women *(Jos.* 43), but especially of maidens *(Spec. leg.* 1.107; 2.30; cf. *Praem.* 159). Priests make offerings with pure hands in *Spec. leg.* 2.145; the number forty-nine is "pure and ever virgin" in *Vita cont.* 65.

tending the hearth. S^c, D², H and many Byzantine texts read the classical *oikourous* for the scarcely attested Hellenistic *oikourgous* of the major witnesses, S*, A, C, D*, F, G, I, 33, 81, 330, and 177, which have preserved the less elegant, original spelling (J. K. Elliott, *Greek Text,* pp. 181–182), not elsewhere documented in the NT, LXX, or Ap. Frs. *First Clement* 1.3 does employ the verb *oikourgein* of Christian wives in a similar context; but the adjective only appears in the second-century c.e. Soranus, *oikourgon kai kathedrion diagein bion,* "leading a domestic and sedentary life" *(Corpus medicorum graecorum;* Leipzig, 1908, p. 18, line 2, where it is a variant reading too; see LSJ, s.v. *oikourokathedrios* for J. Tzetzes).

considerate. Agathas is the sixth adjective in this list of seven, qualifying the "younger women" of v 4. The preceding and following adjectives explicitly give a context of home and marriage to the otherwise generic *agathas,* "good." In such a context this adjective means a good mistress, that is, considerate and kindly in dealing with her domestic help (thus the Vulgate's *benignas).* A similar sense appears in Matt 20:15 (see Mark 10:17–18 = Luke 18:18) and 1 Pet 2:18, as well as *1 Clem.* 56.16. As early as *Iliad* 3.179, when Helen calls Agamemnon *basileus t'agathos,* she means, in the context, a ruler who was good to her, in other words, considerate and kind. From Peshitta and Theophylact through *GNT*[3corr] and *NTG*[26corr] some have read *oikourgous agathas*, "good housekeepers"; but this sense alters the formal structure of the list, which is adjectival to *neai* and septuple. Only here in the PE does *agathos* directly qualify a person; usually works are so described (1:16), sometimes conscience (1 Tim 1:15), and once *pistis* (Titus 2:10). In thirty-seven other Pauline uses it never describes a person (though the nominal usage in Rom 5:7 is notable); the situation is different with the gospels and Acts.

subject to the authority. In the PE only Titus uses *hypotassein* (2:9 of slaves; 3:1 of political subordinates; cf. *hypotagē* of wife and children in 1 Tim 2:11; 3:4). There are twenty other Pauline uses of the verb, which in the gospels is peculiar to Luke. The verb begins to appear only in the Hellenistic period, and there are scarcely thirty uses in the LXX (concentrated in the Pss and 2 Macc), which never uses it of domestic relationships (Balch, *Code*, p. 98). Ceslaus Spicq has noted (*Lexic.*, pp. 913–916) that there is no parallel in secular Greek for a meaning that Jews and Christians expressed with *hypotassesthai*, the ready and reverent offering of oneself and one's service to God and to other persons. In the Ap. Frs. the relationship of the Christian congregation with its leaders is thus designated (*1 Clem.* 1.3), including the presbyters (*1 Clem.* 57.1–2); and Ignatius favors the verb for describing the relation of the believers to their bishop (*Eph.* 2.2 and cf. 5.3; *Magn.* 13.2; *Trall.* 2.1) as well as to their presbyters (*Magn.* 2.1; *Trall.* 2.2; 13.2) and even deacons (*Pol.* 6.1 and cf. Pol. *Phil.* 5.3).

of their own husbands. The Greek is *andrasin*, literally "men," as 1:6 and 1 Tim 3:12; see 1 Pet 3:1.

so that the message of God not be defamed. C, 623, 1827, 1845[c], Vg[ms], and Sy[h] add *kai hē didaskalia*, "and the instruction," from 1 Tim 6:1. For "the message," *ho logos*, see 1:3. In 1QS 1:14–15 the biblical laws, as understood by the Qumran community, are called "the words of God," *dbry 'l* (cf. 3:11; 5:14, 19); but the phrase does not recur. The earliest of the rare uses of *debar (ha) 'ĕlōhîm* in the MT seems to refer to an oracle (e.g., Judg 3:20; see W. Schmidt in *TDOT* 3.111–112). The LXX uses the phrase *logos (tou) theou* ten times— Judg 3:20; 2 Kgdms 16:23; 1 Chr 15:15; 25.5 (plural); 26:32 s.v.l. A; 2 Esdr 9:4; Prov 30:5 (plural) 31:8; and Jer 1:2; 9:19—and never the articular *ho logos tou theou* that occurs here in the PE and in 2 Tim 2:9. The articular form is regular in the other eight Pauline occurrences of the phrase (except for 1 Thess 2:13), as it is in Luke–Acts. The genitival "of God" emphasizes the divine origin of the message (subjective) more than its content (objective; see Fitzmyer, *AB Lk*, p. 565). In the Ap. Frs., *1 Clem.* 42.3 describes the apostles as "full of faith in (*pistōthentes en*) the Word of God" (see *Did.* 4.1; *Barn.* 19.4). These uses, along with the four anarthrous uses of the phrase in Ignatius, share a negative characteristic. None refers as such to the *written* Word of God, the Scriptures.

not be defamed. Blasphēmein will recur in the list of 3:2 as well as in those of 1 Tim 1:20 and 6:1. The cognate, *blasphēmos*, "blasphemer," appears in the lists of 1 Tim 1:13 and 2 Tim 3:2; and *blasphēmia*, "vituperation," in the list of 1 Tim 6:4. The verb is rare in the other Paulines. Three of its four uses are in Rom, where it describes verbal abuse from Paul's fellow believers for his teaching and ways of acting (Rom 3:8; 14:16; cf. 1 Cor 10:30). Romans 2:24, taking up LXX Isa 52:5 (MT *n's*), uses *blasphēmein* to mean pagan abuse for "the name" of the God of Israel. In Luke the verb refers to the act of reviling Jesus (22:65; 23:39) or the Spirit (12:10); in Acts Paul is, in one fashion or another, either defamed (13:45; 18:6) or the defamer (19:37; 26:11). In the eight Septuagintal uses of *blasphēmein* (contrast Theod. Bel 9) it refers to an insult to God; see, for example, 4 Kgdms 19:6, 22, translating MT *gdp* ("to hurl objects/ accusations," G. Wallis in *TDOT* 2.416–418). From Qumran, CD 12:6–8 admonishes the sectaries never to loot or murder the Gentiles "that they may not blaspheme (*ygdpw*)," and the vice catalog of 1QS 4:11 notes "a blaspheming (*gdwpym*) tongue." 1QpHab 10:13 predicts a fiery judgment for the man who "insulted (*gdpw*) and outraged God's elect." The root *n's* (Isa 52:5) is used of scorning God (CD 1:2) and his word (1QS 5:19) as well as the teacher of righteousness (1QH 4:22; 7:22). In *Mart. Pol.* 9.3, when the proconsul summons the old bishop to revile Christ, he replies, "How can I blaspheme (*blasphēmesai*) my king who saved me?" For the usage characteristic of the Ap. Frs., see 1 Tim 6:1.

6–7. *Encourage the young men, similarly, to use common sense in all matters.* For *parakalei*, "encourage," see 1:9; for *sōphronein*, "to use common sense," see Excursus V, "The PE on Salvation"; for *hōsautōs*, "similarly," see 2:3. A few witnesses (103, 1739, 424*, and Theophylact) omit the definite article before *neōterous*, "the young men." Although most other names of groups in this list are anarthrous (J. K. Elliott, *Greek Text*, p. 182), articular *tas neas*, literally, "the young (women)," in 2:4 is parallel to the articular reading offered here by almost all of the other witnesses. The anarthrous comparative *neōteroi* occurs in the domestic code of 1 Tim 5:1, parallel to the anarthrous feminine *neōterai* of 5:2. In the order for the widows *neōterai* is also anarthrous (1 Tim 5:11, 14). The rest of the Paulines do not employ this comparative; otherwise in the NT only in Acts 5:6 and 1 Pet 5:5 does it designate a group. In Pol. *Phil.* 5.3, "younger men are to be blameless in all things (*en pasin*)"; cf. *peri panta* here in Titus. For the *neōteroi* as a group contrasted with *presbytai*, see LXX Ps 148:12; LXX Susanna 64 is notable (though a satisfactory Greek text is beyond recovery): "Because of this the young (*neōteroi*) are beloved of Jacob— on account of their simplicity. And let us watch over the young (*neōterous*) that they be courageous sons. For the young (*neōteroi*) are idealistic, and a spirit of knowledge and understanding will always be with them" (Moore, *AB Dan. add.*, p. 113, cf. 115).

in all matters. The *peri panta* of v 7 is to be understood with the preceding *sōphronein* (thus *NTG*[26corr], D-C, and Spicq, *EP*, all *contra GNT*[3corr]). The problems of dividing words in uncial *scriptio continua* and distributing them appropriately caused such variants as *panta heauton/pantas heauton/pantas seauton/panton seauton* in witnesses such as (respectively), D*, 33, 104, and P (cf. *NTG*²⁶ᶜᵒʳʳ with J. K. Elliott, *Greek Text,* p. 182). *Peri* with the accusative is regular in the PE (otherwise in the Paulines, only Phil 2:23); the genitive in P is probably due to the influence of 2:8 and 3:8. *Peri panta* does not recur in the NT (but see Pol. *Phil.* 5.2 of deacons), whereas *peri panton* appears in Acts 1:1; 22:10; and 26:2, as well as 1 John 2:27 (cf. 3 John 2).

(*given that you proffer yourself as a pattern in fine deeds*). Classical Greek would have used *parechon* for the middle, *parechomenos,* "proffer" (BDF §316.3; cf. Menander, *Dyscolos* 286–287); but, as J. Moulton and C. F. D. Moule (*Idiom,* p. 24) have suggested, "the *form* of the Middle, as contrasted with the Active, calls attention . . . to the pronominal element" at this point the address to Titus to keep doing certain things *himself* over and above exhorting others. The translation expresses this concept with the parenthetical "given that you . . . yourself." The verb recurs in the PE in 1 Tim 1:4 and, with God as subject, in 6:17. In the rest of the Paulines *parechein* appears twice, notably in the household code of Col 4:1. Nine of the remaining eleven NT uses are in the Lukan corpus, including the middle voice in Acts 19:24. The Ap. Frs. use *parechein* nine times, including the middle in *1 Clem.* 20.10 and Ign. *Rom.* 2.2 s.v.l. Among the fifteen Septuagintal uses of this verb there is no close parallel to its use in Titus.

(*as a pattern in fine deeds*). See 1:16 on "fine deeds," noting that at this point the PE begin to qualify certain *erga* as *kala,* a usage otherwise documented in the NT only in Matt 5:16; 26:10 (Mark 14:6, both singular); John 10:32–33; Hebr 10:24; and 1 Pet 2:12. The phrase is found even more rarely in the Ap. Frs., where it appears in *2 Clem.* 12.4 and *Herm. Sim.* 5.2.7 (singular). The closest that the LXX comes to this expression is in Sir 39:16, "All things are the Lord's works (*ta erga kyriou*), for they are exceedingly fine (*kala*)," alluding to Gen 1:31.

"A pattern," *typos,* reappears in the PE in 1 Tim 4:12; in half a dozen other Pauline uses, persons present and past are *typoi* and function "typically" (1 Cor 10:11, except for the "pattern of teaching" in Rom 6:17). This usage corresponds with 1 Pet 5:3. Otherwise in the NT the term designates things: a form letter (Acts 23:25; see 3 Macc 3:30 and *Ep. Arist.* 34), pagan idols (Acts 7:43; see LXX Amos 5:26), the divinely revealed pattern for Yahweh's wilderness tent (Acts 7:44; see Heb 8:5 and LXX Exod 25:40), the scars left by nails and spear (John 20:25; cf. the cognate *typetein* designating a sudden, powerful blow, as in Luke 6:29; Acts 23:2–3). For *hypotyposis,* see 1 Tim 1:6 and 2 Tim 1:13. The *typos* comes with authority and obliges the recipient in secular Greek usage; it may involve a teaching (see Spicq, *Lexic.,* pp. 896–897). Thus in the Ap. Frs. the bishop and his presbyters (like the earthly masters of *Did.* 4.11) are *typoi* of the authority of God the Father (Ign. *Magn.* 6.1; *Trall.* 3.1) and they "preside . . . as a type and teaching (*didachen*) of immortality" (*Magn.* 6.2). The personal moral sense of *typos*, regular in the PE and the rest of the Paulines, appears once in the LXX, in 4 Macc 6:19, as the old Eleazar refuses to dissimulate and serve as "a pattern of godlessness (*asebeias typos*) to young persons in becoming an example (*paradeigma*) of eating unclean food." The *T. Zeb.* 3.6 and *T. Levi* 8.14 refer to the Pharaoh and the priests of the Gentiles with the phrase *kata ton typon.*

(*openhanded with the instruction*). See 1:9 for "instruction." The most influential witnesses, S*, A, C, D*, K, P, 33, and others, read *aphthorian*, a noun previously unattested in biblical or secular Greek and not found in the Ap. Frs. (but see Lampe, *PGL*, s.v. for later uses). The cognate *aphthoros*, "incorrupt," is used of young people, especially girls (LXX Esth 2:2; cf. Justin, *Apology* 1.15.6; *Dialogue* 100.5 [*PG* 6.349; 712]). As early as the second century, P³² reads *aphthonian* (as do F, G, L, 623*, and 1881), "ungrudging generosity," evidently taking the unique *aphthorian* with the preceding phrase about instruction and understanding "incorruption" in terms of curbing avaricious rather than sexual impulses. The unusual word order in Greek, with *en tēi didaskaliai* before *aphthorian*, indicates that some such specification was intended originally. The variant makes it explicit. The reading of the cognate but still unusual *adiaphthorian*, "sincerity, integrity," in S² and D² and most Byzantine witnesses is a less insightful attempt to paraphrase the difficult original. The same is to be said for the *hagneian*, "purity," which in C and Psi and many a minuscule glosses the preceding *aphthorian* (*contra* J. K. Elliott, *Greek Text*, p. 183). The translation "openhanded" understands the original, as did P³² and the others.

(*a reverent man*). Literally, "reverence," *semnotēs*, on which see 1 Tim 2:2; 3:4 and Excursus III, "*Eusebeia* and Its Cognates in the PE." Otherwise in biblical Greek, *semnotēs* occurs only in 2 Macc 3:12, of the Jerusalem temple. After *semnotēta*, D¹, K, L, and many Byzantine witnesses insert *aphtharsian*, probably with the meaning "incorruptibility" and thus still another gloss on the redoubtable *aphthorian.*

8. (*wholesome in preaching, irreproachable*). On "preaching," *logon*, see 1:3. "Wholesome," *hygies* (cf. 1:9 on the verb) is not found elsewhere in the NT epistolaries; in Acts 4:10 and in its ten occurrences in the gospels, physical health is designated, as is also the case with its nine LXX uses. In the Ap. Frs. only Hermas employs *hygies* of trees and stones, the soundness of which is to be interpreted allegorically (thus *Sim.* 8.1.3–4; 9.8.3, 5, 7). As early as Herodotus 1.8 a *logos ouk hygies*, "an unwholesome command," appears, and the negative formulation is commonplace thereafter (see D-C, p. 24 for related examples). *Akatagnōston*, "irreproachable," found only here in the NT, appears in 2 Macc 4:47 but not in the Ap. Frs. The term is not literary but belongs to the technical juridical language of inscriptions and later papyri (see Spicq, *EP*, p. 623, and *Lexic.*, p. 59).

(*so that the opponent, able to muster nothing bad to say about us, will be embarrassed*). "The opponent" is literally "the one (*ho*) from opposition (*ex enantias*)," a Septuagintal phrase used once elsewhere in the NT to refer to the centurion facing the crucified Jesus (Mark 15:39).

Enantios (used of contrary winds in Mark 6:48 [= Matt 14:24] and Acts 27:4) occurs once in the rest of the Paulines of the Jews who "oppose all human beings" (1 Thess 2:15), a usage that is similar to that in Paul's self-descriptions in Acts 26:9 and 28:17. Of the four occurrences in the Ap. Frs., Ign. *Smyrn.* 6.2 is notable when he writes of heterodox opinion about the grace of Christ and Christian charity, opinions that are "opposed to the will of God."

(*able to muster nothing bad to say about us*). Literally, "having nothing base (*phaulon*) to say *about us* (*peri hēmōn*)." For the first-person plural, A along with a few Byzantine and Western witnesses read the plural address, *hymōn*, "you," otherwise unattested in the body of the PE (see 3:15). The variant probably arose because the scribe took the first-person plural of Paul and Titus and respectfully adjusted the pronoun for addressing a congregation (*pace* J. K. Elliott, *Greek Text*, p. 123).

Legein, "to say," occurs only here in Titus and then half a dozen times in the Timothy correspondence, always with a suggestion of deliberate, formal announcement: by false teachers in 1 Tim 1:7 and 2 Tim 2:18; by Paul himself in 1 Tim 2:7 and 2 Tim 2:7; by the Spirit and Scripture in 1 Tim 4:1 and 5:18.

Phaulos, "bad," does not appear elsewhere in the PE. In the rest of the Paulines it is used twice in articulating the contrast between good and bad practices (Rom 9:11; 2 Cor 5:10), a usage that corresponds with its other NT appearances (John 3:20; 5:29, Jas 3:16) as well as with *1 Clem.* 28.1 (cf. 36.6), which alone among the Ap. Frs. employs the word. Of the ten Septuagintal uses, all in the sapiential books, four apply *phaulos* to human words and speech (LXX Job 6:3, 25; Prov 16:21; Sir 20:16), and in this respect they resemble the PE more than the other NT books.

(*will be embarrassed*). *Entrepein* appears only here in the PE but eight times elsewhere in the NT, including 1 Cor 4:14 and 2 Thess 3:14. Outside of the Paulines, the milder and more favorable middle sense of the verb prevails, "to have regard/respect for" (see Luke 18:2, 20:13). This is regularly the case also in the Ap. Frs. and the LXX, though Ign. *Magn.* 12.1 and 1 Esdr 1:45 use the verb to designate embarrassment.

9. *Slaves are to be subject to their masters in all matters.* On *doulos*, "slave," see 1:1; "to be subject," 2:5; "in all matters" is *en pasin*, which will recur in 2:10; 1 Tim 3:11; 2 Tim 2:7; 4:5. In all of these cases it modifies what precedes and thus uses the punctuation here (with *GNT*[3corr] and *NTG*[26corr]). See 1:15 on *pas*.

Despotai, "masters," appears in the domestic code of 1 Tim 6:1–2 (see 1 Pet 2:18 and the cognate *oikodespotein*, 1 Tim 5:14); the singular *despotēs* of 2 Tim 2:21 is parabolic and stands for the God of Israel, a usage that appears in the prayers, Jewish and Christian, of Luke 2:29 and Acts 4:24. The other NT uses are also in the singular and of God (Rev 6:10) or of Christ (2 Pet 2:1; Jude 4).

The title was a favorite in the Roman congregations, as the dozens of occurrences in *1 Clem.* and Hermas witness. *Didache* 10.3 in a prayer and *Barn.* 1.7 and 4.3 also entitle God *despotēs.* The LXX almost always uses the singular and that regularly as a divine title (see the prayers of Sir 23:1; Dan 9:8, 15, 16, 17, 19).

9–10. *aiming to please them, not to oppose them, not to pilfer.* Literally, "to be pleasing," [an imperatival *einai*] *euarestos,* only here in the PE. The rest of the eight NT uses refer to God or Christ, and seven are in the other Paulines. The Ap. Frs., among whom its frequency in *1 Clem.* and Hermas is notable, always use the term thus. The same can be observed in Wis 4:10 and 9:10, the only Septuagintal uses, as well as in *T. Dan* 1.3 and Philo. See COMMENT for *CII* 684.12.

See 1:9 on *antilegein,* "to oppose."

not to pilfer. For *mē,* some witnesses (D*, C², F, G, 33, 88, and a few more) read *mēde,* which may well be original, as at 2:3 (J. K. Elliott, *Greek Text,* p. 137). *Nosphizesthai,* "to pilfer," appears otherwise in the NT only in the story of Ananias and Sapphira (Acts 5:2, 3), where it refers to keeping back for one's own use things that had been dedicated to God (Goppelt, *Typos,* p. 119). A similar sense appears in *Herm. Sim.* 9.25.2, as well as in the only LXX uses of this verb in Josh 7:1 and 2 Macc 4:32.

Rather they are to give such good evidence of complete reliability that they add luster in every way to the instruction of our savior, God. Literally, "But evidencing (*endeiknymenous*) all good faith (*pasan pistin agathēn*)." The great cursive 33 omits *pistin* and then reads *agapēn* "charity" for *agathēn,* a usage that would, if original, be unique in the PE (see 2:2 on "charity"). For "good faith," see Excursus I, *"Pistis* Terminology in the PE." This phrase does not occur elsewhere in biblical Greek. Even though the LXX uses *endeiknymi* fourteen times, the closest it comes to this phrase of Titus is in Prov 12:17, "a just man reports openly the faith that has been shown (*epideiknymenen pistin*); the witness for unjust persons is crafty" (cf. 4 Macc 17:2). *First Clement* 26.1 writes of those who serve (*douleusantōn*) God "in confidence of good faith." For *hē agathē/kalē pistis* in the inscriptions and papyri, see Spicq, *Lexic.,* p. 703, who observes that even the unqualified *pistis* often means "good faith" as well as practical loyalty. "To give evidence," *endeiknysthai,* has "every consideration" as its object in 3:2; in 1 Tim 1:16 the risen Jesus gives evidence of patience in his calling Paul; and in 2 Tim 4:14 the coppersmith "brought many false charges" against the apostle. The seven other NT uses are in the Paulines and Heb 6:10, 11. In the Ap. Frs. only *1 Clem.* 21.7 and 38.2 use this verb for manifesting purity or wisdom in a public, verifiable fashion.

"That they add luster" is from *kosmein,* which will describe the function of feminine virtues in the Christian assembly for worship in 1 Tim 2:9 where the cognate adjective also appears. The verb does not appear elsewhere in Paul. Of its eight other NT occurrences, Luke 11:25 (= Matt 12:44) uses it of the parabolic house to which the unclean spirit returns, and Luke 21:5 thus describes the shining stones and trophies of the Jerusalem temple (cf. Rev 21:19 of the New Jerusalem and Matt 23:29 of adorning monuments and 25:7 of trimming lamps). Both 1 Pet 3:5 and Rev 21:2 figuratively designate feminine adornment by the verb. The closest parallel to the usage of the PE in the Ap. Frs. is when *1 Clem.* 33.7 writes of Christ and Christians as adorned with good works. Among more than two dozen Septuagintal occurrences those in 3 Macc 3:5 and 6:1, which describe lives adorned with good deeds and virtue, offer the closest parallel to the PE. For further data, see Spicq, *Lexic.*, pp. 440–445. See 2:9 for "in every way"; 1:9 for "the instruction of our savior, God," along with Excursus V, "The PE on Salvation." The recapitulating article (cf. 1 Tim 1:4; 3:13; 2 Tim 1:1; 2:1, 10) is only found introducing an attributive genitive in a handful of instances in the NT. The construction puts the emphasis on "our savior, God." A good many *koinē* texts omit this second article, which sounds awkward in NT Greek (see J. K. Elliott, *Greek Text,* p. 186: Porter, "Adjectival Attributive," pp. 12–13).

COMMENT

2:1. *Now you, Titus, are to speak of matters that suit our wholesome instruction.* The singular address, reinforced by the pronoun, clearly marks a new stage in the exposition, which will move through a domestic code into a description of the relation between the Christian faith and Christian living (2:11–14). The following stage is similarly introduced (see 2:15). This program and its rationale are submitted as a Pauline imperative that comes through the man who shares his apostolate. In the preceding stage Titus was to establish Pauline ministers and show them how to confound Jewish-Christian adversaries. Now, in contrast, the Paul of the PE prescribes a schema for the positive instruction of the Jewish Christians who remain loyal to his mission and to its ministers. This instruction is to assume an oral form and thus presupposes the personal presence of the Pauline minister in the setting within which his formal teaching is proposed (for this link between *lalein* and *didaskein/didachē,* see Acts 17:19 of Paul and 18:25 of Apollos, as well as 1 Cor 14:6). Because the instruction is, without further ado, proposed in the form of a domestic code, the setting implied for it is probably the house church assembled for worship and guidance. The code appears to have existed independently of the PE and to have been incorporated into the latter from another source, for the transition into its text in the following verse is harsh, its vocabulary is by and large unparalleled, and its syntax is, even for the PE, crabbed (see 2:7–8). This code must have come to the author of the PE with some notable history and authority in its own right that made it acceptable to the Jewish Christians to whom it was addressed while remaining credibly Pauline. As the code stands in the text, its infinitives all depend on "to speak," and the adjectives simply catalog qualities in a way that is formally parallel to the list in 1:6–8.

The contours of the preexisting composition can be discerned, however, when one recalls that the "essential imperative" of the domestic code called for imperatival verbs (Sampley, *Two/One,* pp. 22–23, 28; Crouch, *Haustafel,* p. 122; Balch, *Code,* pp. 97–98), and this is in fact the character of the infinitives in 2:2–10 when these verses are read without 2:1 and the editorial "encourage (*parakalei*)" of 2:6. In a word, the one Pauline command here and elsewhere in the *Haustafeln* of the PE has absorbed the multiple imperatives of the traditional code.

There are five divisions or classes presupposed in the paradigmatic household that is being addressed. Age and sex determine the first four, which are evidently paired into two corresponding sets, but in an order of persons not found elsewhere in the PE and with no explicit correlation of the virtues between the sets (Sampley, *Two/One,* pp. 19, 22):

A.   Males—older
B.   Females—older
B¹. Females—younger
A¹. Males—younger

The dividing line between older and younger is at about fifty years of age (see Philo, *Op. mund.* 103–105, citing Solon and Hippocrates on the various stages in human life). In the Roman world, Aulus Gellius noted three divisions by age for males: those less than seventeen are "boys" (*pueri*); those from seventeen to forty-six and subject to military conscription are "younger men" (*iuniores*); those beyond forty-six are "elders" (*seniores*) (*Noctes atticae* 10.28.1).

The unusual chiastic arrangement here in Titus, with the men in both first and last places, gives a certain precedence and distinction to age as such but not to sexual differentiation. Aesthetic and structural considerations are predominant here, and the chiasm has overruled the male, patriarchal sequence that would have been expected. Children, though obliquely noted (2:4), do not figure in the division. The fifth and final category consists of the nonpersons of ancient society, the slaves. There is no corresponding division for the virtues incumbent on masters and mistresses, though 2:5 gives a glimpse of the latter.

Specific virtues are urged on the members of the Jewish-Christian household, but the number of qualities varies for each class, as the layout of the translation illustrates. The young women are to cultivate a septet of virtues; the young men, only one. Derivatives of **sōphron-,* "sensible," found in each of the first four categories, illustrate the importance in this code of that common sense to which Greek ethics gave pride of place. The repeated urging of subordination upon wives and slaves (2:5, 9) ought itself to be subordinated to the common sense urged even more frequently. Conspicuous by its absence is any injunction to honor God or Christ, though "faithfulness" figures in the triad below. The author of the PE compensates for this omission by adding 2:11–14 on the faith as the matrix presupposed for all Christian living.

2. *Thus older men are to be temperate, serious, sensible, robust in faithfulness, in charity, in steadfastness.* The virtues incumbent on older Christian men divide into a group of four and then a distinct trio, which depends on the fourth item, "robust." The opening quartet proposes qualities as conspicuously Hellenistic and non-Jewish as the following trio urges virtues already traditionally biblical and Christian. The Christian homes that these "older men" established, led, and provided for offer the context for practicing the sober, respectable, prudent, and wholesome Christian life urged by this code. The extended and inclusive household of the ancient Semitic, Greek, and Roman worlds makes demands that are difficult to visualize in a society accustomed to the nuclear family. Both virtue and vice have a wider and more immediate social impact in the extended family. Virtues that seem banal and even pointless when only a handful of people are involved assume another aspect when many persons of different ages, sexes, and stations live together in a home.

The first virtue enjoined upon the "older men" is sobriety, particularly in alcoholic drink. The nuance of watchfulness was heard in the Greek (Jerome, *On Titus, PL* 26.598; see the *vigilantem* of some Latin versions, *VL* 25.483), but the Old Latin versions with their preference for *sobrii* indicate the meaning that was generally heard in the Western churches. Moreover, a similar injunction for older women appears in the next verse, which is a substantive parallel in the qualities urged here on this set of persons. The leaders of Christian homes are to conduct themselves no differently from the bishop-steward (see 1:7) of the house church. Antiphon's argument (fifth century B.C.) from the fact that "many old men are drunks" (*polloi de presbytai paroinountes, Third Tetralogy* 4.2) remained a credible observation on the leaders of both sexes in Hellenistic society, if Athenaeus (*Deipnosophistai* 10.423–448) and the epitaphs of the *Greek Anthology* are to be believed (see 7.348, 353, 355, 384, 398, 422, 423, 452, 454, 455, 456, 457, 533). The bibulousness of women was a commonplace of Greek comedy (see Aristophanes, *Clouds* 553–555; Menander, *Dyscolos* 946–953) and Menander's line, "All of us had know-how about cups and carousals" (Koerte 434/500K; see Koerte 743/554K), was proverbial. The cult of Dionysus apotheosized intoxication. And Israel was no more immune to the lure of the vine, as diverse traditions witness (see Gen 9:20–21 of Noah; 1 Sam 1:12–16 of Hanna; LXX Prov 20:1; 23:20–21, 29–35; Sir 19:1–2; 26:8 of a wife; 31:25–31; Tob 4:15; 1 Macc 16:15–16; 4 Macc 2:7; 1QpHab 11:2–15). Philo has a treatise *De ebrietate* that concludes with the observation that "the passion for wine is extraordinarily strong in mankind, and is unique in this, that it does not produce satiety. For whereas everyone is satisfied with a certain amount of sleep and food and sexual intercourse and the like, this is rarely so with strong drink, particularly among practised topers" (*Ebr.* 220). The indisputably Pauline paraenesis from 1 Thess 5:6–8 through Gal 5:21; Rom 13:13 and 1 Cor 5:11; 6:10; and 11:21–22 emphatically scores drunkenness as incompatible with a Christian ethic, and the same theme surfaces in Eph 5:18 and 1 Pet 4:3, as well as in the Roman paraenesis of *1 Clem.* 30.1 and *Herm. Man.* 6.2.5; 8.3; 12.2.1 and *Sim.* 6.5.5. Thus the temperance in drink to which the PE regularly return (though they never use the **meth-* cluster of terms) is certainly a biblical and Pauline theme and perhaps one characteristic of the Roman church as well.

The "older men are to be . . . serious, sensible," or, as the Greek suggests, "respectable, prudent." Old Eleazar is thus "serious" in 4 Macc 5:36; 7:15 (cf. 7:9). The Western churches, which heard the first virtue as temperance in drink, understood the following *semnous* of restraint in matters sexual, *pudici* (see *VL* 25.500, 503, where the same term becomes also *verecundi, casti, modesti*). The Latin version of Theodore of Mopsuestia (Swete, *Theodore* 2.246) goes on to translate *sōphronas* (sensible) as *castos* (chaste). The Roman contempt for sensually indulgent old men (see Cicero, *De officiis* 1.34 [§123]) left its mark, but the Greek here is more inclusive in its demand, and Jerome commented on a version that read *honestos* (honorable) at this point, "ut aetatis gravitatem morum gravitas decoret" (so that the weight of years would have the weight of good conduct as its ornament). The *gravitas* held at a premium by the ancient Roman was the high seriousness of a person not easily moved but who, when he did move, was deliberate and indeflectible. Of Q. Fabius Maximus, the famous Cunctator (i.e., the Delayer, in confronting Hannibal), Cicero writes, "Erat enim in illo viro comitate condita gravitas nec senectus mores mutaverat" ("There was about the man a seriousness seasoned with courtesy, and old age brought no change in his conduct"; *De senectute* 4.10). The "serious" older man, worthy of respect, is a "sensible" man (note the way in which the repeated sibilants and labials in the Greek bind these terms together). The suggestion of mental equilibrium and balanced practical judgment is conveyed by *sōphrōn.* The Vulgate *prudentes* reminds one that when a Roman like Cicero read Thucydides he could characterize the man and his history as *prudens, severus, gravis* (prudent, austere, serious)—and without popular appeal (*Orator* 30–32).

With the fourth and last quality for older men, "to be robust," this list moves from *sōphrōn* and mental health (note **sōs-*) to the physical health usually designated by *hygiainein.* If this quartet of qualities had a pre-Christian existence, the urging of good health upon the aging (if it is not just a cliché) has more the character of a prayer and fervent wish than the previous prescriptions. The list does not allow one to understand this robustness physically. The healthy vigor of Christian older men is to be "in faithfulness, in charity, in steadfastness." The expansion of the final member of a list with three phrases occurred before, in 1:6. In this case the triad is traceable into the earliest Pauline correspondence, where it appears to be already a customary and specifically Christian catechetical summary (see 1 Cor 13:13). The formula may perhaps have developed around an original binary phrase that formulated the whole Christian existence before the one God and all fellow men and women as living in faith and love (see Spicq, *Agape* 2.367 n. 7; the appendix on pp. 365–378 is to be consulted for the data and the debate about the origin of this triad; E.T. 3.205–214, but with truncated notes). The triad is by no means stereotyped in its seven Pauline occurrences outside the PE, for there is an oscillation between hope and steadfastness (cf. 1 Thess 1:3 with 5:8) as well as in the order of the terms. Already in Rom 5:1–5 the basic triad is being glossed with other virtues; here in Titus it serves as a codicil to the preceding list of four virtues, and in the correspondence with Timothy it surfaces within lists of six and nine virtues.

Rhetorically this specifically Christian and Pauline triad puts its cachet on the whole preceding list (and not just on "robust"). The repeated articles accent the importance of each virtue. The Christians know well enough that *hē pistis* designates their personal and total loyalty to God and Christ. For Greek and Roman eyes, however, this list appears deficient. No duties to the gods are specified (see texts in Crouch, *Haustafel*, pp. 37–46), and as Cicero put it, "prima dis immortalibus, secunda patriae, tertia parentibus, deinceps gradatim reliquis debeantur ("Our duties are owed first to the immortal gods, second to our native land, third to our parents, and then on a descending scale to the rest"; *De officiis* 1.160; see Epictetus, *Discourses* 3.2.4; Crouch, *Haustafel*, pp. 47–49; Balch, *Code*, pp. 2–3). From the decalogue to Sir 7:29–31, duties to the one God of Israel are explicitly urged on the house of Israel. In view of the apologetic motif in Titus 2:5, 8, and 10, why is the Christian meaning of *pistis* not unpacked? Perhaps this is a way to grasp the nettle of that objection. The Roman esteem for *fides*, their incorruptible loyalty to their pledged word, was a wonder of the ancient world, and Polybius ventured to suggest that this part of the native Roman religion had something to do with the survival of the *respublica* itself (Polybius, *Histories* 6.56.13–15; see Excursus III, *"Eusebeia* and Its Cognates in the PE"). If a Roman heard the *pistis* of this specifically Christian triad as the "faithfulness" that he valued (see 2:10 on "reliability"), believers would have an opening to explain that their faith put no less premium on loyalty and fulfillment of duties to the one God in whom they believed. In the view of the PE, this vigorous witness to faith and faithfulness is primarily incumbent on the senior men as leaders and representatives of the households that in turn constitute the house church.

To their faith, older men are to join "charity," to be taken in its technical Christian sense and thus not translated simply as "love." The term *agapē* itself underlines its specifically Jewish and Christian resonance, for, as Ceslaus Spicq has observed (*Lexic.*, p. 26), this noun has yet to be documented in a pagan source before the first Christian century (on the one, not altogether certain occurrence in reference to Isis in a first-century C.E. papyrus, see Griffiths, "Isis," pp. 139–141). On its LXX roots, see 1 Tim 1:5, for it is in the Timothy correspondence that the teaching of the PE on charity is elaborated.

The meaning of "steadfastness" in this triad is not articulated as clearly in the PE as is the significance of faith and charity. The triad is, of course, itself a context, and the link with hope (*elpis*) in the Pauline tradition (1 Cor 13:7) suggests itself. For the PE, however (see 1:2 above) hope designates the goal and reward of faith, Christ himself; accordingly the straits and strains of present expectation are accented with the *hypomen-* terminology. "If we submit (*hypomenomen*) now, we shall share in his reign" (2 Tim 2:12, and see 2:10). The Pauline tradition of interpreting the OT and particularly that of Rom 15:4–5 (see 2:7 and Käsemann, *Rom.*, pp. 134–135) lead one into the meaning of "steadfastness" for the PE. In the last centuries before Christ, Jewish authors used the *hypomen-* terminology more and more frequently for the trials that accompanied waiting for the Lord instead of for the waiting itself. In the latest strata of the LXX the *hypomen-* terms begin to appear with the sense "to endure" (see Sir 22:18; Wis 16:22; Dan Sus. 57). In the tense, persevering wait for God, the hope of Israel (cf. LXX Jer 14:8 with 22), there are trials to endure. The fourteen occurrences of the *hypomen-* terms in LXX Job are not fortuitous (as Jas 5:11 witnesses), and nowhere in the LXX are they more frequent than in 4 Macc, which has been called "a great hymn of praise to steadfastness" which the people of Israel showed as they were persecuted for their faith (F. Hauck in *TDNT* 4.585; see Spicq, *Supp. Lexic.*, pp. 658–665). As M. Dibelius (*James*, p. 73) has pointed out, *hypomonē* has an active nuance that suggests heroic steadfastness against evil. This in turn means that the Hellenistic world would understand such heroic resistance to trials as an aspect of what that society knew and admired as courage or fortitude (*andreia*, on which see Plato, *Republic*, 4.427E, 429A–430C; Aristotle, *NE* 3.1115a–1117b20; F. Hauck in *TDNT* 4.581–588). Hellenistic Judaism used the *andr(e)i-* cluster of terms for fortitude and occasionally joined them closely with *hypomen-* terminology (LXX Ps 26:14; 4 Macc 1:11; 15:30). In the PE along with the rest of the NT, the *andr(e)i-* terminology has completely disappeared, except for Paul's parting admonition to the Corinthians, "Be on the alert, stand firm in faith, be manly (*andrizesthe*), be strong" (1 Cor 16:13, taking up LXX Ps 26:14). In the Ap. Frs. only Hermas and *1 Clem.* 55.3 employ the words, and the latter may illustrate the reason for Christian reluctance to use such a term, for Clement observes that "many women have received power through the grace of God and have performed many manly deeds (*andreia*)." The etymological sense of manliness was evidently still heard in the Greek words for fortitude, and their eclipse in early Christian language precluded any hint that the steadfastness of Christians was a virtue for men only. A critical attitude about fortitude was in the air philosophically (see Plato, *Laches*; Cicero, *De officiis* 1.46, 50, 88; and Seneca, *Epistulae morales* 67.5–16; 85.24–29; Ferguson, *Values*, pp. 40–42), and the discreet choice of the *hypomen-* terminology by first-century Christian authors could have received a sympathetic hearing from those outside the churches as well as from the men and women within. In any case, faithfulness, charity, and steadfastness are not urged upon the senior Christian men exclusively but as leaders of and so examples for all of the believers in their households.

3–4ª. *Older women, similarly, are to be as reverent in demeanor as priests, not devils at gossip, not slaves to drink. They are the right teachers for spurring on younger women.* Thus far the language of this household code has often been unusual; it now gathers into a knot of terminology practically unexampled in this correspondence or in biblical Greek. Four attributes are urged on the elder Christian women, in a chiastic positive–negative (*mē*)/negative (*mēde*)–positive order in which the fourth entry expands into a purposive clause, which in its turn practically designates a fifth virtuous quality. The more expansive phrasing of these qualities, coupled with their at best partial coincidence with the virtues for older men and their obvious linkage with the virtues for young wives, all conspire to give vv 3–5 a unity of their own.

The "older women" (*presbytidas*) of this code correspond to the *presbyteras* of 1 Tim 5:2, but they cannot simply be identified with the group of women linked to the deacons in 1 Tim 3:11 or the widows of 1 Tim 5:3–16. A particular older woman might indeed be in one of these groups, but not just by virtue of age. As noted with the elder men, these women are presumed to be Christian wives and mothers within the extended households of the Hellenistic Roman world. The position of leadership that they share with their husbands by virtue of age explains why (apart from their being placed second in the list) there is no mention of the virtue of subordination for them. For the PE, moreover, it is inconceivable that they would not have to practice what they had to teach to the young women of the household.

The list of virtues urged on the senior women opens with a phrase about their reverent mien which reminds one of the seriousness previously urged on the elder men. The presence of these women in their homes is to be priestly, with the connotations of Jewish priestly worship suggested by such terminology. If in fact the households envisioned are Jewish-Christian, the terminology would be not only intelligible but also paradoxical, for it was not the Jewish practice to apply priestly language to women. The Christian description of conduct in terms of Jewish priestly worship is not irregular, however (see Bultmann, *Primitive Christianity*, pp. 48–51), and the Pauline correspondence not infrequently reminds believers, regardless of sex, "to present your bodies as a living sacrifice, holy and acceptable to God, which is your spiritual worship" (Rom 12:1, and see Corriveau, *Liturgy*, passim). On occasion priestly terminology describes the work of Paul and those who share his apostolic ministry (see Rom 15:16; 1 Cor 9:13–14). Here in Titus, however, only women are thus described, with a point that will become sharper with their designation at the conclusion of this chiasmus as "the right teachers."

The intervening negative injunctions continue to accent relational conduct within the home rather than character traits as such (see Bultmann, *Th. NT* 2.222). The lips of Christian women who transmit a priestly direction to their juniors (a veritable *Torah*) are not to be the lips of topers (see above) and talebearers. The Roman contempt for women who take wine was ancient (Ovid, *Fasti* 3.765–766) and not shared by Greeks (Dionysius of Halicarnassus, *Roman Antiquities* 2.25.6; cf. Aelianus, *Varia historia* 2.38). The secular Greek meaning of *diaboloi* does not distinguish between gossip about things that are true and gossip about those which are false. The Jewish-Christian hearer of this list would certainly understand *diaboloi* with the connotation (specific to those religious traditions) of "devilish" and perhaps with the suggestion of magical practices and sorcery (see Acts 13:10). Those who have just been called priests must have no part in rites and incantations that are radically diabolic (see Horace, *Epodes* 5 and 17, esp. "et Esquilini pontifex venefici / impune ut urbem nomine impleris meo?" "Are you, the pontiff of Esquiline sorcery, to fill Rome with talk about me and be unpunished?" [lines 58–59]; see the Pompeian mosaic of a scene from an unidentified Greek comedy in which young women are consulting an old witch.

The senior Christian women, who are to be slaves to God (see 1:1) and not "to drink," "are the right teachers" for the young women of the household. Just as the primary task of the Jewish priest was to transmit *torah*, revelation and the knowledge of God (see Deut 33:10; Hos 4:6; Mal 2:4–7), so the primary service that these matrons give to their households is imparting Christian teaching that they have received, "the message of God" of v 5 (see 1:3, 9). That message involves the scriptures of Israel, which they teach to youngsters, whether boys or girls (cf. 1 Tim 2:15 with 2 Tim 1:5 and 3:14–15). This household code presumes that role, however, and explicitly singles out the suitability of senior women "for spurring on younger women." The clause is so constructed that it links the directives for the older women with the younger while subordinating the latter to the former and at the same time enabling the apostolic minister to practice what he teaches. The "right teachers" for the "younger women" in the home are not Paul and Titus, just as in 1 Tim 2:12 a wife is not a suitable teacher for her husband in a liturgical assembly. What both this household code and the church order of 1 Tim presume is that Christian conduct can be taught and taught authoritatively. Because Paul teaches this conduct, it is seen as emanating from and being an inseparable part of the apostolic faith and to be received as such.

Already in the Hellenistic world, the mother's tasks of encouraging and counseling her daughter for the latter's domestic work could be taken for granted. In Xenophon's *Oeconomicus* 7.14, a wife tells her husband, "My mother said that my job was to be discreet (*sōphronein*)." In this context the husband and wife then work out just what such prudent conduct involves, and similarly in this code the content of the exhortation for the younger women is spelled out in the seven qualities that follow.

4ᵇ–5. *to love their husbands, to love children, to be sensible; chaste; tending the hearth; considerate; subject to the authority of their own husbands; so that the message of God not be defamed.* The septet of characteristics, with the opening pair of *philo-* compounds, the quartet of qualities opening with "sensible," and the expansive conclusion, reminds one formally of the qualifications for the bishop in 1:8.

A setting for the use (if not the origin) of such lists may be discerned in 1 Tim 6:11, where a sextet of virtues opens an ordination charge. If the liturgical celebration of what we call ordinations occasioned appeals to lists of virtues to be pursued and vices to be avoided, it is likely that the celebrations of marriage between Christians included a similar charge. Tantalizing fragments of such a liturgy have been discovered at Qumran (4Q 500(?), 502; DJD 7.78–105). A sample of the paraenesis from a Christian wedding appears in the church order cited in 1 Tim 2:13–15. It seems plausible that here in Titus the list of virtues for young wives also had, at some point, a place in the Christian liturgy of marriage in which traditionally (at least in the Roman rite) the bride was singled out for special blessing and instruction as she and her husband entered the order of married persons (see 1 Tim 2:13–15 and the appendix to the Gregorian Sacramentary, *PL* 78.261–264, esp. 263).

The opening pair of compound adjectives, with their reference to husbands and children, serves to specify the young women here as those bound for marriage. They are to cultivate affection for the persons closest to them. A shrewd insight into the psychology of married life puts the husband first (ahead of children) as well as last in the list. This household code (perhaps because of its more Jewish character) does not take into account younger women who would need encouragement and guidance for an unmarried life. In the light of 1 Tim 4:3 and 5:11–12, the omission may be deliberate.

The quartet of qualities that opens v 5 begins with "sensible," a characteristic that the young wives are to share with the older men of v 2 and the bishop of 1:8. With "chaste" and "tending the hearth," specifically familial, feminine virtues reappear. The first term, with its generic connotation of the holiness that one brings to divine worship, suggests that marital fidelity and the moral choices that it demands are an integral part of the young wife's faith and worship. The description of the older women in v 3 in priestly terms, along with the regular links of the **hagn-* root with ritual and cultic requirements, even in the NT (see Acts 21:24, 26; 24:18; Jas 3:17 and Dibelius, *James*, p. 213 n. 28), recommend a liturgical background for the usage here. If the suggestion at Titus 1:6 is correct, 2 Cor 11:2 takes up a first-generation Christian marriage liturgy with its reference to "one husband," and in such a liturgical setting the ceremonial as well as the ethical sense of "a chaste (*hagna*) virgin"—that is, determined to be faithful to her husband—would be appropriate. The household code at this point in Titus would thus reflect the cultic language of the Christian marriage ceremony, which because it is Christian cannot be merely cultic. If the Judaizers of Phil 1:17 camouflage Christ under cultic requirements and thus ironically do not proclaim him "purely" (*ouch hagnos*), still the Pauline paraenesis urges Christians to "appreciate whatever is pure" (*hosa hagna;* Phil 4:8).

"Tending the hearth" represents an unusual Greek compound, a feature that again may point to the already traditional language of a Christian marriage charge. The resemblances up to this point in terminology, concepts, and form to *1 Clem.* 1.3 make it tempting to propose that both Titus and *1 Clem.* are drawing on an already existing ecclesial formulation which, they were convinced, deserved apostolic if not Pauline authority (note in *1 Clem.* 1.3, "you [Corinthians] gave these instructions . . . and you taught" these ways of behaving). The list moves from the domestic work that the wife does herself to her considerate supervision of others who work for her (see 1 Tim 5:14). Although Luke–Acts and the rest of the gospels apply the term *agathos* to men, this passage in Titus is the only one in the NT in which women are so designated; again the application of an authoritative tradition is indicated.

Finally, the list turns to the tasks that wives undertake as they are themselves subject to the authority of a husband. The emphasis is unmistakable, as the single terms give way to a concluding phrase that expands into a purposive clause (see the parallel clause in v 4). The list, which began by noting the bond of affection that is to unite a young wife with her husband, now closes by accenting the bond of obedience. This whole section (2:2–10) reveals a concept of and a concern for order in the Christian home and in the lives of the individuals who constitute that household (see J. H. Elliott, *Home,* pp. 139–140). At this point and with this concern the paraenesis urges the wife with a quasi-imperatival participle (see Balch, *Code,* pp. 97–98) to be subordinate to her husband. The advice is thoroughly in the Pauline tradition (see 1 Cor 11:3; 14:34–36; Eph 5:21–24; Col 3:18); it recurs verbatim in 1 Pet 3:1; but there is no directive here, or elsewhere in the NT for that matter, for husbands to subject their wives to themselves (Col 3:19 indicates the contrary, in fact).

The older women are the ones who teach this virtue to their juniors, thus implying the practical advantages that accrue to such conduct. There is no appeal to its natural or legal necessity, though the language appears as early as the first century B.C.E. in pseudo-Callisthenes 1.22. ("A Narrative, Remarkable and Really Marvelous, of the Lord of the World, Alexander the King," in *Der griechische Alexander roman.* Ursala von Lauenstein, ed., Beitrage zur Klassischen Philologie 4. Meisenheim am Glan: Anton Hain, 1962) and later in Plutarch, *Moralia* 142E (see Balch, *Code,* pp. 98–99, 120), and it is plausible that the domestic code here takes up a phrase and a point of view popular in Hellenistic society at the time (see Selwyn, *1 Pet,* p. 434 and Balch, *Code,* pp. 143–149, esp. 147). On the Roman scene, Martial observed, "Let the married woman be subordinate (*inferior*) to the man she has married; in no other way do a woman and a man become equal (*pares*)" (8.12.3–4). Nonetheless, a specifically Christian motivation for these young wives is proposed. There is to be a ready and reverent offering of self and of Christian service to "their own husbands; so that the message of God not be defamed." This freely chosen subordination is to be motivated by the missionary character of Christian revelation. The concept surfaces again in 2:8 and in rather more positive form in 2:10. When the phrase recurs in 1 Tim 6:1, "God's name" replaces "the message of God"; in both cases God is distanced by this phrasing as well as by the passive verb from the insults that are envisioned (see G. Wallis in *TDOT* 2.418). The allusion to LXX Isa 52:5 is reminiscent of the Pauline argument with the typical Jew in Rom 2:24, but the PE do not cite the reference of the LXX and Rom to defamation "among the Gentiles." Possibly a missionary polemic that antedated Paul used this LXX text (see Käsemann, *Rom.*, p. 71), which had its scope considerably enlarged when believers applied it to their own households.

The expansion of an admonition in a domestic code by an allusion to or a citation of Scripture is common (Sampley, *Two/One*, p. 21). Thus at this point in Titus it is not only unbelievers who are to have no excuse for scoffing at the Pauline gospel; also other Christians, particularly Jewish Christians, must have no occasion to blame the apostle for the kind of insubordination that upsets homes and families (see 1:6, 10–11). The accent on order and thus on subordination is part of the *Haustafel* form itself. The vocabulary of subordination and obedience articulates that emphasis; the dramatic expansion of the code, which has been almost telegraphic up to this point, suggests that the relation of wife to husband was the object of some particularly searching criticism that merited an emphatic reply. The criticism would have emanated not only from pagan Roman contemporaries who were chronically allergic to Eastern cults and their novel customs (Balch, *Code*, pp. 65–80) but also from fellow Christians who detected a critical difference between missionary zeal and a pneumatic religious enthusiasm that simply bucked the whole ambient culture, including the Jewish one (see Crouch, *Haustafel*, pp. 120–145). "The only exhortations common to all N.T. *Haustafeln* are those directed to wives and slaves" (ibid., p. 149 n. 17), a good indication that in these two classes the stress and dissonance between their faith and the social order were most excruciating. The missionary motivation that is proposed for both groups puts the theological discussion of individual equality and freedom firmly in the speculative order and channels enthusiastic zeal into winning the goodwill if not the faith of their contemporaries.

6–7a. *Encourage the young men, similarly, to use common sense in all matters.* The abrupt, almost surely editorial, appearance of the imperatival address to Titus contrasts the advice that he is to give to young Christian men with the guidance that the older women transmit to their juniors. The domestic code is thus explicitly grafted again into a Pauline ministry and magisterium. All of the apostolic guidance for this group of men is focused into a single Greek verb, designating that same balance of judgment which has been referred to at every turn in this list and which here receives the widest conceivable extension. Still, one ought to recall that *sōphronein* suggested chaste conduct even for pagan men (see Aristophanes, *Clouds* 1060–1061, 1071). The correlative "similarly" suggests that the conduct just urged on the young women belongs also, other things being equal, to the moral equilibrium of men up to fifty. If in fact the hand of the editor appears with "encourage," it is possible that the original source of the domestic code at this point urged on the young men at least some of the qualities that follow in v 7b (D-C). As the text stands, the transition and further development are harsh and disjointed.

7b–8. (*given that you proffer yourself as a pattern in fine deeds; openhanded with instruction; a reverent man, wholesome in preaching, irreproachable, so that the opponent, able to muster nothing bad to say about us, will be embarrassed*). The basic schema underlying this passage is difficult to retrieve due to the abrupt shift in vv 6–7 into the singular address to Titus, not heard since 2:1. The *hina* clause at the end of v 5 certainly marked the end of the catalog of virtues for young Christian wives, as a similar clause in 8b marks the end of the list in vv 6–8a, and still another in 10b closes the directives for Christian slaves. Thus the formal division at this point includes Titus, to whom v 7 now turns as an individual. He is conceived as one of the young Christian men and as obliged "to use common sense in all matters" as they are. The remaining five virtues in this sestet are predicated of Titus as an individual. If the source that was being edited consisted of a locally accepted list of virtues for young Christian men in general, then the terminology that refers specifically to Titus's apostolic ministry ("a pattern . . . with instruction . . . in preaching") pertains to the redactor of the PE. The hypothetical source would be parallel in some of its requirements with the list for older men, urging the young men also to be sensible (2:2, *sōphronas*), to be fond of doing good (cf. 1:8, *philagathon* and 1 Tim 6:18, *agathoergein*), to be chaste (*aptharoi*), to be serious (2:2, *semnous*), to be robust (in faithfulness, etc. as in 2:2, *hygiainontas tēi pistei*, etc.), to be irreproachable.

The author of the PE adopted this list, retaining substantially an originally nominal construction (as contrasted with adjectives used in the previous lists) along with several terms unusual in Jewish and Christian Greek. Apparently the original catalog was already recognizably fixed in the catechesis of a local church, and the audible resonances from that congregation whose view this correspondence was transmitting exerted more influence on the redactor's program than did stylistic niceties. His editorial insertions become, on this reading, signals of his special emphases in articulating the teaching in the letter to Titus. Thus Titus is not only to develop the moral equilibrium that he urges upon his Christian confreres but also to be "a pattern in fine deeds." He is not only to do good along with the young men but also to perform deeds that will attract them to a like activity. Good works (*pan ergon agathon*) have already appeared in 1:16; now they become, in a phrase that is hereafter typical of the PE, "fine deeds" (*kala erga*), works that are both good and visibly attractive. The phrase is used only once in the LXX and then of God's works in creation. Wisdom 13 exploits the connotation of *kalos* when the author argues that the works (*erga*) of God can lead human beings to the God who did them, "because the things that are seen are beautiful" (*hoti kala ta blepomena,* 13:7; cf. 1 Tim 4:4). The innovative phrase of the PE marks a new stage in the understanding of the mystery of justification (see 3:5) and a new perspective on the Hellenistic world, which for centuries had proposed that there ought to be a deep union between the good and the beautiful in human activity (see Owens, *"Kalon,"* pp. 261–262). "For he that is beautiful (*kalos*) is beautiful so far as appearances go, while he that is good (*o de k'agathos*) will forthwith also be beautiful (*kalos*)" (Sappho, LP 50). Menander wrote, "To do no wrong even makes us handsome" (Koerte 790/568K). Another Greek writer of comedy puts it thus: "Virtue (*aretē*) alone is notable (*kataphainetai*) even in a beautiful body (*dia kalou tou somatos*)" (cited by Clement of Alexandria, *Paedagogus* 2.12.11 [O. Stählin; Leipzig: Hinrichs, 1905, 1.230]).

The "fine deeds" of the PE represent an opening to an attitude and estimate of such deeds among contemporary nonbelievers as well as a readiness to engage in dialogue with them about the origin and end of such conduct. But there must be no mistake about it, such "fine deeds" are presupposed in the Christian who enters such a dialogue. He comes to a discussion of what makes a person *kalos k'agathos* as one who is already, out of charity, doing good in a visible, attractive way to those who are in need (see Jeremias, *NTD,* p. 40). He has no illusions that the discussion as such will lead him or his questioners to "fine deeds." At its best, however, the dialogue will offer the opportunity to explain why and how the "fine deeds" of the Christian come into being (see 2:11–15; 3:4–7). The thoughtful pagan may have qualms about this procedure, for it ultimately raises the question about the relation of faith and reason, as Galen witnesses in the latter part of the second century. In the surviving Arabic version of his summary of Plato's *Republic,* the philosopher-physician further remarked, when discussing the need that most persons have for tales of recompense in a life to come, "we now see the people called Christians drawing their faith from parables (and miracles), and yet sometimes acting in the same way (as those who philosophize). For their contempt of death (and of its sequel) is patent to us every day and likewise their restraint in cohabitation . . . and they also number individuals who, in self-discipline and self-control in matters of food and drink, and in their keen pursuit of justice, have attained a pitch not inferior to that of genuine philosophers" (Walzer, *Galen,* p. 15, and see pp. 57–59, 75–79; also Wilken, *Christians,* pp. 68–93). Galen was at that time engaged in conversations with some of his compatriots, headed by Theodotus the tanner, who were members of the Roman Church (see Eusebius, *Church History* 5.28.6–19, esp. 14). He had seen and was impressed by the conduct of the Christians. Their actions were those urged by the philosophers of the day. Justin Martyr, who died in Rome about 165 c.e., had no qualms about retaining his philosopher's garb and occupation as a Christian. Aristides of Athens at the same time presented a similar picture (also Athenagoras and Melito of Sardis, fragment 1.7 in Hall, *Melito*). Accordingly, it is not astonishing that the earliest favorable pagan notice of the Christians treats them as philosophers. Yet those "fine deeds" enjoined upon Titus would, in Galen's view, be performed because of the "parable" of the appearance of Jesus in glory (2:13) to reward those who had obeyed this apostolic admonition and punish those who had disobeyed. The parting of the ways with the physician-philosopher would occur over his definition of a parable as a fable or myth. A Christian could not concede that the good he did was based on narratives that, however useful for teaching lessons in conduct, were about fictional realities that never had occurred and never would. Christian conduct was not that "middle-class morality," derived for the most part from natural disposition and habit (Epictetus, *Discourses* 4.7.6), which Plato had left to the nonphilosophers of his ideal society (cf. *Republic* 6.500D; 10.619C with *Phaedo* 82A–B; *Laws* 4.709E–710A; 12.967E–968A).

Titus is to be "a pattern," *typos*, of the attractive conduct that he urges on young Christian men. The Greek suggests the concentrated force of this living example, falling like a mallet (*typas*) or a punch upon the matrix of those whose lives it marks. An evocative parallel is Strabo's description of the Celts who "are barbarians no longer, but are . . . changed into the pattern (*typon*) of the Romans both in their language and their ways of living, and some of them even in their political organization" (*Geography* 4.1.12). Secular Greek seldom uses *typos* in the personal, ethical sense that appears regularly in biblical Greek, including the PE (but see Plato, *Republic* 4.443B–C for "the original principle and a kind of pattern [*typon tina*] of justice" and OGIS 383.212, "I have set forth a pattern of godliness [*typon de eusebeias*] for all my descendants," circa 50 B.C.E., MM, s.v.).

The author of the Letter to Titus chooses *typos*, however, for more than simply ethical reasons. He has placed Titus among the younger men of the congregation, conceiving him to be Paul's junior, perhaps by as much as twenty years. Whatever the popular misgivings about youthful leadership, not to mention converts from paganism in such a sensitive position (see 2:15; 1 Tim 3:6; 4:12; 5:1), Titus is emphatically Paul's "true child" (1:4), and children are *typoi* of their parents (Artemidorus Daldianus, *Onirocriticus* 2.45). Thus Titus is not only to leave "a pattern" on his peers but is also a living *typos* stamped out of the life and teaching of the Pauline model, *hypotyposis* (1 Tim 1:16; 2 Tim 1:13). In this analysis the apostolic succession in right conduct is refracted through the Christian life of Paul's coworker. The apostolic practice (i.e., tradition) is preeminently visible in the attractive deeds of the younger man who also delivers the Pauline instruction (*didaskalia*) and preaching (*logon*). With these editorial additions, the author of the PE has refocused a catalog for the good conduct of young men in the church into a catalog for young churchmen. The *Sitz im Leben* that suggested such a redaction may well be a liturgy of ordination, if 1 Tim 6:11 is indeed the opening of an ordination charge. In any case, the *typos*, looking simultaneously to the past and to the future, primarily personal and ethical, not purely mechanical and magisterial, is for the PE the key term for describing the apostolic ministry that Titus and Timothy share with Paul.

Second only to Titus's offering "a pattern in fine deeds" is that he be "openhanded with instruction." Deeds without words to explain them may be unintelligible; words without deeds are not credible. "Because the heathen cannot see our faith, they ought to see our works, then hear our doctrine, and then be converted" (Luther, *Lectures on Titus* (2:5), W, 25.46; E.T. 29.57). Those who have the responsibility for teaching Paul's gospel must be the first to live by it. Thus the arrangement of the virtues to be verified in the candidates for becoming presbyter-bishops in 1:6–9 culminates finally in a purposive clause that refers to their teaching. There is no gainsaying that Titus must teach, and the "instruction" is characterized with the neologism *aphthorian*, "incorruption," parallel with "pattern" and similarly the object of *parechomenos* (D-C). On the hypothesis that this noun belonged originally to a list of virtues for young Christian men, where it referred to sexual purity (see 1 Tim 4:12; 2 Tim 2:22), the redactor-author of the PE, prefacing the neologism by "with instruction," refocused it to mean incorrupt teaching. Corrupt doctrinal activity has overtones of sexual corruption in 2 Cor 11:2–3, and the PE appeal to the tradition behind that passage in 1 Tim 2:13–14 and perhaps 2 Tim 3:16–17. Already in 2 Cor 11:7–9 (cf. 2:17), the Pauline instruction is emphatically separated from material perquisites. The second-century reading *aphthonian*, "abundance," is an interpretive gloss that has displaced a difficult neologism. The interpretation, however, has correctly divined the author's meaning in the phrase as a whole. Incorruption in instruction refers to the abundant provision (thus Menander, Koerte 623/589K; Josephus, *Ant.* 12.133; *War* 3.505) of apostolic teaching without an eye to wages. The Pauline "instruction" is not for sale, neither is it strictly private stock; it has about it an incorruptible objectivity and is open to all, impartially shared by all, because it is authored by the savior of all (see 2:11–14).

The "reverence which Titus shows young Christian men ought to evoke the same attentive gravity in them, as the bishop in 1 Tim 3:4 has "children who are obedient and reverent." This reverence, both internal and external (D-C, p. 39), characterizes the life of the whole Christian community (1 Tim 2:2) and is cherished by the Roman Church (*1 Clem.* 41.1 and ten times in Hermas, but not elsewhere in the Ap. Frs.). In Maccabean times it was the Jerusalem Temple that evoked reverence (2 Macc 3:12); in the PE the noun begins to characterize Christian persons, whether individually or as a congregation. Christians are to inspire the respect and awe that the earthly dwelling place of God once excited.

Just as "with the instruction" was inserted before the noun translated "openhanded," so here the author of the PE redacts his source by prefacing *hygiē* (already anomalous on several scores) with *logon* to mean "wholesome in preaching" (as if it were an accusative of respect, BDF §160). Already in the second century it was unclear whether "irreproachable" referred to "preaching" or was only to be taken of Titus's conduct as a whole (cf. Irenaeus, *Adversus haereses* 4.26.4 with 5 [*PG* 7.1055–1056]). In light of the hypothesized list of virtues for young Christian men, along with the meaning of the purposive clause that follows immediately, this translation interprets "irreproachable" apart from "preaching" and with a wider reference to Titus's life as a Pauline minister.

The emphatic, inserted reference to preaching recalls 1:3, 9 on the spoken message (*logos*) of the apostle as the ground and root of the Pauline instruction. Wholesome "instruction" (1:9) grows out of healthy "preaching."

Finally, Titus is himself to be "irreproachable." In 2 Macc 4:47 this unusual adjective describes men "who would have been freed *akatagnōstoi* if they had pleaded their case even before Scythians." Thus the term suggests a judicial process that has resulted in complete vindication because of failure to substantiate charges. This final moral qualification, with its juridical overtones, leads smoothly into the expansive clause concluding this section of exhortation.

Titus himself is to give no grounds to "the opponent," who is presented as if he were preparing to bring charges "about us" that are bound to collapse for lack of verifiable evidence of anything "bad" done by Paul or his coworker. As these verses have centered on the Pauline address to Titus, the abrupt reappearance of the first-person plural (see 1:3, 4) is most naturally taken as referring to the apostle and his aide (see 3:15). The cluster of first-person plurals in 2:10, 12–14 and 3:3–7 (see below) have a broader reference to the church as a whole, including the apostolic ministers (see 3:14).

Can "the opponent" be specified further? The articular singular is emphatic, perhaps accenting the sporadic, atypical character of the slanders against the Pauline apostolate. In Gen 12:3 those who bless Abraham stand in contrast to the one who curses him (a nuance that the LXX does not reproduce). The singular may also allude to the requirement made in the *torah* for two or more witnesses in capital charges, a provision that is explicitly appealed to in 1 Tim 5:19, when there is a question about handling charges against presbyters. Such considerations (coupled with the usage of Paul and Acts) lead one to infer that "the opponent" is Jewish, probably Jewish-Christian (see Hanson, *PE*, for other proposals). If the latter, he is on the lookout for something "bad" in the conduct and teaching of Paul and Titus, something that contradicts the *torah* and that can be used to drive a wedge between the Pauline ministry and Jewish Christians. Paul himself had traced the Jewish-Christian opposition to his mission to Satan, the Adversary par excellence, backing the Judaizers (cf. 2 Cor 11:14 with Gal 1:8). The paraenesis in Titus is gentler and more discreet. The LXX does not use any forms of *enantios* to translate "Satan," and so the characterization here is more conciliatory in tone, though the satanic interpretation is not ruled out.

The "fine deeds" that Titus does himself and urges on others furnish no evidence to corroborate and no witness to substantiate the formal complaint that "the opponent" wants to lodge before his Jewish-Christian confreres. The

Greek verb for designating his consequent public embarrassment refers in the rest of the Paulines to believers who are (or ought to be) ashamed. This final clause as a whole, with its somewhat more Pauline vocabulary and conceptualization (see Rom 14:17–18; Phil 1:27–28), contrasts sharply with the preceding list, in which the terminology is quite non-Pauline and its studied obscurity is not unlike that produced by the abrupt insertion of technical medical or sociological vocabulary into more familiar discourse. The language of the list evokes an atmosphere of impressive magisterial authority transmitting a "preaching" and an "instruction" that are not totally self-evident, that have their technicalities, their own methodological demands, which are as unusual—even as unique —as the vocabulary chosen to articulate them. The final clause leads the reader back into a more familiar, more Pauline atmosphere.

9–10. *Slaves are to be subject to their masters in all matters, aiming to please them, not to oppose them, not to pilfer. Rather they are to give such good evidence of complete reliability that they add luster in every way to the instruction of our savior, God.* The previous section of this household code devoted most attention to the young churchman, Titus, and closed by including him with Paul in the phrase *peri hemōn*. The apostle and his coworker are thus the last free persons of the Christian household and the first of the slaves who now appear (see 1:1). This positioning of the apostolic ministers of the church is no accident, as the place of the bishops and deacons at the end of the church order in 1 Tim 2–3 and the place of the presbyters in 1 Tim 5:17–25 (just before that of the slaves in 1 Tim 6:1–2) illustrate. Here "slaves" and "their masters" appear in their sociological sense, representatives of a division between human persons as slave or free that was as much taken for granted in the ancient Mediterranean world as distinction according to sex or age (see Aristotle, *Politics* 1.2.1–23 [1253b–1255b] and Wiedemann, *Slavery*, pp. 15–21). The basic cell of the ancient body politic was the household "and the household in its perfect form consists of slaves and free men . . . and the primary and smallest parts of the household are master and slave, husband and wife, father and children" (Aristotle, *Politics* 1.2.1 [1253b]). The philosophers debated the question whether human beings were slaves by nature (*physis*) or by legal convention (*nomos*). Regardless of the issue of this debate, however, in society at large, Hellenistic or Roman, Jewish or pagan, many men and women were property, technically "living tools," belonging to other, free persons. A few small Jewish communities may have acted on the conviction that "no human being is naturally a slave" (Philo, *Spec. leg.* 2.69; 3.137; *Quod omn. prob.* 79 [on the Therapeutae]; see Bartchy, *Slavery*, p. 54; Balch, *Code*, pp. 34, 55). Their practice was, however, as exceptional as the handful of negative criticisms of slavery that remain in Greek and Latin sources (Balch, *Code*, p. 34; Wiedemann, *Slavery*, pp. 224–251). As S. S. Bartchy has noted (*Slavery*, pp. 63–65), the Hellenistic and Roman worlds suffered from armed rebellions of slaves between 140 and 70 B.C.E., but those revolts never aimed at abolishing slavery and did not abolish the institution when they succeeded (see pseudo-Menander, 698K, quoted in Jaekel, *Sententiae*, p. 92, "Slave, be fearful when you are the slave of a man who once was a slave, for the bull that does not have to work, forgets the yoke").

Slavery was a fact of ancient life, and the philosophical questioning of it produced no more than the legal admission that it involved an ownership that was against nature (*contra naturam;* see Wiedemann, *Slavery*, p. 15). The slave legally remained property, not a person. He or she had, by and large, no rights and consequently no duties in ancient society (which of course was run by those who were free). The slave was incapable of marriage; the children of slaves were the property of the master. Because the slave was not a citizen, he could not enter Roman military service and bear arms. Yet it became the regular Roman practice (in the face of Greek complaints) to manumit slaves in order to have them serve in the army as well as to increase the free population of the republic (see the texts in Wiedemann, *Slavery*, pp. 64–72). For a perversion of this practice in the last days of the First Temple, see Jer 34:8–22. Thus ancient slavery, like the society of which it was an essential part, could and did vary from place to place and from generation to generation, as well as according to the needs and aspirations of the slaves themselves.

The human, legal structures that fettered these men and women threw into high relief their status before the gods. "God is the same to all, free or slave, if you look into the matter," one of the dramatists said (perhaps Menander, cited by Clement of Alexandria, *Paedagogus* 3.12.92 [O. Stählin; Leipzig: Hinrichs, 1905, 1.287]). In Roman eyes the slave was a person (not simply property) in matters of religion (Bömer, *Religion der Sklaven*, p. 117 n. 18). The obverse of this relationship is that all human beings are equally free (or equally subject) before the gods. Hence the proverb, doubtfully attributed to Menander, "Be a slave freely, then a slave you shall not be" (857K; see Bartchy, *Slavery*, pp. 65–67 for other texts). This inner freedom of the mind and heart engaged the attention of Greek authors (thus, "Virtue has no master [*adespoton*]," Plato, *Republic* 10.617E), including the Jewish Philo (see *Quod omn. prob.* 17 et passim) and the former slave Epictetus (*Discourses* 2.1.21–28; 4.1.1–177), who saw this freedom expressing itself in the pursuit of the virtues. Their reflections were summarized in paradoxes such as "Every bad man is a slave" and "Every good man (*asteios*) is free" (Philo, *Quod omn. prob.* 1). According to this view the slave, the living tool, could be the subject of virtue. Even the inexorable logic of Aristotle had wavered momentarily at this juncture as he, perhaps grudgingly, admitted that there is a real difference between a slave as a slave and as a human being (*anthrōpos; NE* 8.11.6–7). Yet this concession occurred in a context in which the general principle was that slaves had no share in genuine happiness (as distinguished from bodily pleasures) or a life of free choice (cf. *NE* 10.6 [1177a8] with *Politics* 3.5 [1280a32]). The Christian gospel, announcing a God who made no distinctions among human beings (see Rom 2:11; Acts 10:34), before whom slave and free were equal (1 Cor 12:13; Gal 3:28; Col 3:11, 25), called both the slave and the master to abandon evil and pursue goodness of life. A share in genuine happiness, a life in which they could freely choose virtue, a manumission of the spirit was the hope given by the apostolic preaching to the slaves who heard it.

The "masters" (note the plural) in the context of this household code might be any of the free persons, old or young, male or female (cf. 2:5 with 1 Tim 5:14), who have preceded. There was a ratio of five slaves to one free person throughout the Roman Empire, perhaps three to one in Rome. Even a lower-middle-class household could have a staff of eight (W. G. Rollins, "Slavery in the NT," *IDBSup*, p. 830). The whole household in question here is Christian, and thus the conduct of its members to their slaves is included in the paraenesis directed to them (cf. 2:2 with Sir 4:30; 7:21; 33:31–32). Accordingly, these slaves can be directed "to be subject . . . in all matters," with the presumption that the Christian master or mistress would not command unchristian acts. This passage stands in some contrast to the provisions for slaves in the domestic code of 1 Tim 6:1–2, which takes into account the master who is not a believer. Theoretically, a slave could belong to several masters (thus Spicq, *EP*, p. 625), only one of whom might be a Christian. This code ignores such possibilities. The Greek term for the "masters," *despotai*, suggests unqualified ownership and the right to dispose of a particular property without answering to anyone. It contrasts with the Greek *kyrios*, "master, ruler, lord," which designates one who has the governance and use of property but not necessarily an absolute title to it. The arbitrary and legally limitless power of the *despotai* gave credibility to the scathing rhetoric of Seneca against the arrogant brutality of some masters:

> Then there is that proverb . . . that we have as many enemies as we have slaves. They aren't our enemies unless we make them so. I shan't mention some other cruel and inhumane ways in which we would be maltreating them even if they were dumb beasts instead of human beings—when, for instance, we lie down to dine, and someone has to clear up the vomit, while another stands at the bottom of the couch to remove the leavings of the drunken guests. There is someone whose task it is to carve expensive fowl. He guides his well-trained hand around the bird's breast and rump as he carves it up; he has no personal motive for doing this whatsoever. What a wretch, to live for no other purpose than to carve up fattened birds skillfully—unless the man who teaches someone this skill because it is going to give him pleasure is more to be pitied than the slave who has no choice but to learn it! Another pours the wine; he is dressed like a woman and has great difficulty in not betraying his age. (*Epistulae morales* 47 in Wiedemann, *Slavery*, pp. 233–236)

Yet Cicero speaks for Roman practical common sense when he observes that it is not a bad rule to treat slaves as if they were employees (*mercenarii*), in other words, to require work of them and to give them just recompense (*iusta; De officiis* 1.13.41; see Sir 33:24–25 for much the same sentiment in a Hellenistic Palestinian milieu). The investment in the slave, if nothing else, would dictate discretion and restraint in all but the most irresponsible owners.

The virtues of the Christian slaves in this code are five, two positive, then two negative, and a concluding characteristic that expands with a *hina* clause in a pattern that has become familiar. Note the five qualities recommended to Titus in 2:7 as well as the five prerequisites for the Jewish-Christian presbyter in 1:6. The list here leads off with "to be subject," an imperatival infinitive that uses the same verb as the one designating the young wife's offering herself and her service to her husband (2:5). As in that passage, the emphasis here is on the order (*tassein, taxis*) that ought to prevail in human relationships, not on a *sub*mission, *sub*jection, or *sub*ordination designated by the prefixed *hypo-* (see Statius, *Silvae*, 3.3.43–55; J. H. Elliott, *Home*, p. 139, citing L. Goppelt).

The masters are not commanded to make their slaves submit any more than husbands are directed to make their wives subject to them. This free acceptance of a social order as incomplete and fragile as the human relationships that constitute it is not to deny another transcendent order in which all men and women are subject to the one God. The tension between these orders finds typical expression in Luke's first use of *hyptassein* as he narrates Jesus' continuing to be subordinate to his parents while belonging to another house, to another Father (Luke 2:51).

The second positive quality urged on Christian slaves is "to please" (literally, "to be pleasing to," *euarestous*) their masters. All of the other Christian uses of *euarestos* in the first century indicate that this admonition would be heard theologically, if not christologically. Thus for slaves to be pleasing to their Christian masters is to be pleasing to God and Christ. Behind their earthly masters in the Christian household stands the unseen Master (see 2 Tim 2:20–21), whom ultimately they are to please. Dibelius and Conzelmann observe that *euarestos* here accents values that were cherished by contemporary Hellenistic society (see MM, s.v.) and by the "bourgeois ethic" that produced the secular paraenesis inserted by the author of the PE at this point. The line of development is complex, however, because the author of the PE is drawing on a source that is already Christian, which he cited not because of the secular values it included but because of the authority of an ecclesial tradition that had assimilated such values and knew how to integrate them into explicitly Christian paraenesis (as in Col 3:23; Phil 4:8; Eph 6:6). The laconic character of the entries into a household code such as this one in Titus ought to be evaluated in the light of an admonition of Gerhard von Rad: "The peculiarly trite diction of the (OT) wisdom writers has often led to a serious failure on the part of exegetes to recognize the intensely concentrated nature of their theology" (*Hexateuch*, p. 247). The popularity of the wisdom writings in first-century Christian teaching and moral formation hardly needs documentation, and those Scriptures were involved in transmitting "the wisdom of the home" for the sake of a family's successful growth (C. Westermann, *Blessing,* p. 38). Sirach even offers a household code of sorts (7:18–28; Crouch, *Haustafel,* pp. 74–75), in which the master of a faithful and devoted slave is admonished (7:20; see 33:30–31). Accordingly, the exegete must reckon with the possibility of a Hellenistic Jewish composition that was "according to the Scriptures" and that preceded the Jewish-Christian source cited here.

J. E. Crouch (*Haustafel,* pp. 117–119) notes that neither Stoic nor Jewish ethical compositions regularly addressed themselves to the duties of slaves as such (the case of the Jewish master with a Jewish slave is another matter). Occasionally, as in Philo, *Deca.* 165–167, a Jewish author evinces an interest in the relations of slaves to masters in which the former give "an affectionate loyalty to their masters" (*eis hypēresian philodespoton*). His comparison of the relation of the mind to the philosophical disciplines with Sarah doing what is pleasing to herself (using *euarestos*) in relation to her slave is also notable (*Cong.* 156–157; cf. *Spec. leg.* 1.201 on the mind as *euarestos* to God and the most religious of sacrifices). A fragmentary line of a Black Sea synagogue inscription recording the emancipation of slaves uses *euarestoi tēi/m* . . . , but it is unclear whether this is the adjective or a form of the verb (*CII* 684.12). In any event, one surmises that Hellenistic Jewish apologetic compositions may have expressed a concern about the virtuous qualities that a slave ought to cultivate. In a Jewish-Christian setting, such an interest may have received stimulus from an enthusiastic interpretation of the implications of unity in the Lord for the baptized ("neither slave nor free," cf. Gal 3:28 with 1 Cor 12:13; Col 3:11; Crouch, *Haustafel,* pp. 120–129). Still, unity is not totally synonymous with equality, and the Jewish-Christian household, in which all including slaves were one in Christ, saw slaves and free persons alike bound by duties and responsibilities within that household. The order within the community of believers and their complementary obligations to care for one another, which Paul had illustrated with his elaborate metaphor of the many members in the one body (1 Cor 12:12–26), is here given concrete form in the qualities prescribed for all the members of the household church. If some of the Christian slaves in the typical Jewish-Christian household were of pagan origin (see CD 12:10–11 and Schiffman, "Non-Jews," pp. 379–380, 388, for some of the Jewish legal background for such a situation), then the specialized prescriptions at this point in Titus become more understandable. Such slaves (even more than the young wives above) would not only be more susceptible to enthusiastic and unrealistic expectations about their new Christian status, they would also need more practical instructions about moral conduct than a slave of Jewish origin who already shared in a monotheistic moral tradition that prescribed the way he ought to be treated (e.g., Exod 21 passim; Lev 25:39–55; Deut 15:12–18; Job 31:13–15; Strack-Billerbeck 4.698–716, and the articles "Slavery in the OT" by I. Mendelsohn, *IDB* 4.383–391 and W. Zimmerli, *IDBSup,* pp. 829–830). The duties or virtuous acts incumbent upon Jewish slaves are scarcely alluded to in the OT, however, though the situation in which they love their master enough to remain in slavery is taken into account (Exod 21:5; Deut 15:16–17). The explicit listing here in Titus of the moral duties of slaves, even Jewish ones, is, according to this interpretation, an innovation proper to the Jewish-Christian household code.

The first of the pair of negative imperatives aimed at Christian slaves, "not to oppose" their masters, follows smoothly from the preceding pair, which in the Greek was introduced by an alliteration with *p* that reappears at the end of the list. In this translation the rhetorical effect has been preserved by sandwiching alliterative terms between these two points. The participial imperative *antilegontas* designates contradiction, that is, verbal opposition (see 1:9), in contrast to (*mēde*) the action of thievery, the second of the prohibitions at this point. "To pilfer" represents a current Hellenistic Greek usage of *nosphizomenous* (see MM s.v.; Spicq, *Lexic.* p. 584). The slave stealing from his master was proverbial in the ancient world, whether Jewish (e.g., *Aboth* 2.8, *apud* Strack-Billerbeck 4.732), Greek (Xenophon, *Memorabilia* 2.1.16; Menander, *Aspis* 397–398), or Roman (Dionysius of Halicarnassus, *Roman Antiquities* 4.24.4; Pliny the Elder, *Naturalis historia* 33.6.26–27, who was pining for the good old days when slaves were few and nothing around the house had to be sealed with the master's signet ring). The runaway slave Onesimus, for whom Paul interceded, had apparently stolen from his master (Phlm 11, 18–19). The PE advert to stealing once again in 1 Tim 1:10, with its reference to slave traders who kidnap or purchase human persons to sell them into bondage.

In contrast (*alla*) to bad conduct in word and deed, the fifth and final characteristic of the service of Christian slaves is summed up with an imperatival, "they are to give . . . good evidence of complete reliability." This version takes up the juridical nuance of *endeiknymenous* (see Rom 2:15), a nuance that has appeared in other parts of this paraenesis (e.g., "irreproachable" in 2:8). The Greek *pistis* was heard as "reliability" or faithfulness in this list, as in the list of what constitutes "the harvest of the Spirit" in Gal 5:22. The same sense appears in the church order for widows in 1 Tim 5:12. This "reliability" is to have the widest possible extension (in the now familiar use of *pasan*), and the possibility of misunderstanding, which such an injunction may have prompted, is precluded by qualifying *pasan pistin* with *agathēn*, "good," in the emphatic position at the end of the whole phrase. There are limits to the loyalty that a Christian slave shows to his Christian master. If the latter commands his slave to do something evil, the performance of it is not "good evidence of complete reliability," literally, "all good loyalty." Blind obedience in slaves is not the aim of this paraenesis.

The purpose for this thoroughgoing, verifiable reliability is missionary in character. The lives of Christian slaves, like the behavior patterns of their Christian mistresses (2:5), are to make credible "the message of God" or "the instruction of our savior, God," the latter referring to Paul's apostolic interpretation of the OT scriptures about slavery (see 1:9). The one God of Israel who rescued his people (note the first-person plural; contrast 2:8) from slavery cares for the slaves who are numbered among his people (cf. Deut 5:14–15 with 15:12–14). The slaves' response of reliable loyalty to the master and mistress who share their faith is a shining ornament for the Jewish-Christian household "in every way." That final phrase in this fifth and last member of the paraenesis for slaves (which is in its turn the fifth and last section of this household code) recalls the same phrase in the opening of this section (2:9) and suggests that all of the previously named qualities add attractive luster to the Pauline teaching. It is striking that the slaves, the last and least in the social order of the ancient world, are the only ones in this *Haustafel* who are described as positively ornamenting the apostolic teaching and eliciting esteem for it (contrast 2:5; see Spicq, *EP*, p. 626 and *Lexic.*, pp. 444–445). The Pauline apostolate, including those who share in it, has called this Jewish-Christian household into existence under God, and the first-person plurals from this verse through 3:7 include Paul with Titus in the community to which they minister.

II.B.2. THE FAITH, MATRIX OF CHRISTIAN LIVING (2:11–14)

2 ¹¹Revealed was the grace of God for the rescue of all human beings. ¹²It disciplines us to disown godlessness and worldly lusts, and to live in a sensible, honest, godly way in this present age ¹³as we wait for the blessed hope revealed in the glory of Jesus Christ, our great God and savior. ¹⁴He laid down his life for us, to set us free from every wrong and to cleanse for himself a people of his very own, enthusiastic for fine deeds.

NOTES

2:11. *Revealed was the grace of God.* The formally passive *epephanē* (also in 3:4), its initial position, and the periphrastic phrase referring to God give a Septuagintal (cf. Gen 35:7 with Zeph 2:11; 3 Macc 6:39) and hence "biblical" tone to the single, solemn periodic sentence that extends in Greek to the end of v 14. In v 13 the cognate noun, *epiphaneian*, "appearance," signals the further development of the concept introduced by this verb. Otherwise in the NT, forms of *epiphainein* occur only in Zechariah's hymn about "the Dawn from on High" shining over those huddled in darkness (Luke 1:78–79; Fitzmyer, *AB Lk*, pp. 387–388; Brown, *Birth*, pp. 373–374), and in Acts 27:20 of the despair that gripped those on the tempest-tossed ship with Paul, lost in the darkness "when for days on end neither sun nor stars appeared." The LXX uses forms of *epiphainein* most frequently of the Lord's face (*prosōpon*) being revealed to his worshipers (LXX Num 6:25; Pss 30:17; 66:2; 79:4, 8, 20; 118:135; Theod. Dan 9:17 (of the sanctuary); 3 Macc 6:18). Because the phrase "the grace of God" is non-Septuagintal, but at every turn those who believe in Yahweh "find favor (*charin*) before him" (LXX Gen 6:8; 18:13 et passim), or in his eyes (2 Kgdms 15:25), and thus before his face, it is possible that the grace of God is meant to suggest his *prosōpon*, that is, his personal appearance. In the Ap. Frs. only the prayer of *1 Clem.* 59.4 and 60.3 takes up the Septuagintal *epiphainein*. Similarly *1 Clem.* 8.1 and 55.3 alone use the articular phrase "the grace of God" (though the anarthrous phrase appears regularly in Ignatius; see esp. Ign. *Magn.* insc., "blessed in the grace of God the Father [*en chariti theou patros*]"). The primitive Indo-European links of "grace" with the burning light of dawn may not be far from the surface of the phrase here (see Friedrich, *Aphrodite*, pp. 196–198; *pace DELG*, s.v.). On the usage of *charis* in both secular and Jewish Greek, which prepared for its frequent NT meaning of "a tangible power at work in the believer," see Nolland, "Grace," pp. 26–31.

for the rescue. This phrase presumes the reading of the anarthrous adjectival *sōterios* in S^c, A, C*, D*, and 1739; the *sōteros* of S* is a reflex to the common *sōter* of the preceding verse in preference to a term that appears otherwise in the NT only in the Lukan corpus and then as a noun (see Excursus V, "The PE on Salvation"). In LXX Amos 5:22 (not in the MT) Yahweh says, "I will not accept (*prosdexomai;* cf. Titus 2:13) these [holocausts], I will not look upon your appearances as guaranteeing safety (*sōtēriou[s] epiphaneias; lect. dub.*)." See BDF §113.1.

of all human beings. The Greek *anthrōpos*, like the English "anthropology," does not ordinarily suggest differentiation according to sex (contrast *anēr*, "man," in 1:6 and *arsēn*, "male," as in *arsenokoites*, "homosexual," in 1 Tim 1:10). The connotation of *anthrōpos* is illustrated by a saying of Apollonius of Tyana, "One must endure poverty like a man (*hōs andra*); one must be humane (*hōs anthrōpon*) when he is rich" (*Epistle 22*, in Robert J. Penella, ed., *The Letters of Apollonius of Tyana* [Leiden: Brill, 1979]; cf. Clement of Alexandria, *Paedagogus* 1.4.11–16, citing Menander [Koerte 19]).

Beginning with Titus 1:14, the PE use *anthrōpos* a score of times, occasionally with some ethical qualification for the person in question (see 3:10 on "the divisive man" and 1 Tim 6:11; 2 Tim 3:17 on "the man of God"). Only of Christ Jesus do the PE use an unqualified *anthrōpos* in the singular (1 Tim 2:5). The plural *anthrōpoi* (except at 3:8) contrasts mere human beings to God (1 Tim 2:5; 6:16, and see *DELG*, p. 90); when qualifications appear they generally emphasize the moral debility of human beings (see 1:14 above and 1 Tim 5:24; 6:5, 9; 2 Tim 3:2, 8, 13). Only 2 Tim 2:2 refers to "trustworthy men." No adjective more frequently qualifies *anthrōpoi* in the PE than *pantes*, "all" (3:2; 1 Tim 2:1, 4; 4:10), which signals the importance that the PE attach to the universality of the offer of salvation.

12. *It disciplines us.* The PE also employ *paideuein* in 1 Tim 1:20 and 2 Tim 2:25. For the cognates *apaideutos,* "undisciplined," and *paideia,* "training," see 2 Tim 2:23 and 3:16. In the two other Pauline uses of the verb it designates the effects of grievous illness and life-threatening trials (1 Cor 11:32; 2 Cor 6:9). Hebrews 12:5–11 (using LXX Prov 3:11–12) exploits the *paideuein/ paideia* terminology in its apologetic for Christian suffering (see Rev 3:19). The most vivid example of what the term popularly suggested to the Hellenistic reader appears in Luke 23:16, 22, where it refers to the scourging of Jesus (see also LXX 3 Kgdms 12:11–14; 2 Chr 10:11–14); yet in the Hellenistic biographical language of Acts 7:22 and 22:3, this verb emphasizes intellectual activity rather than the buffets that accompany it (see Unnik, *Tarsus,* p. 28 = *Sparsa* 1.281–282 and the many citations from the *corpus hellenisticum* in this study). The LXX regularly translates the *ysr* of the MT as *paideuein.* Thus Deut 8:5 (taken up in 4Q 504.1–2.iii.6: DJD 7) speaks of Yahweh's humbling and testing Israel as a father disciplines his son (cf. Deut 21:18 with 22:18). Although in LXX Esth 2:7, Mordecai "brought up *(epaideusen)"* Esther in precisely the sense of Menander, *Aspis* 293, the regular Septuagintal usage dominates *1 Clem.* (certainly in 56.3–5, 16; 57.1; probably in 59.3, which ought to be read with the following section; in 21.6 the tribulations of youthful learning are no more than implicit [see Pol. *Phil.* 4.2]). The rare uses in Hermas also correspond to the predominant sense in the LXX (*Vis.* 2.3.1 and 3.9.10). In the epilogue of Tatian's *Oratio* 42 (see D-C, p. 143), the intellectual aspect of education is emphasized, but there is no trace of the influence of Titus (which Tatian rejected in any case). The Hellenistic intellectual and cultural conception of *paideuein* also influences Jewish Greek articulation of the meaning of "education" for Israel (*Ep. Arist.* 121, 287, 321; for Philo, see Mott, "Ethics," pp. 31–35; see also Hengel, *Hellenism* 1.65–83). Yet even Philo does not dilute the uncongenial directive in Deut 21:18 about a parent chastising a stubborn, rebellious son (*Spec. leg.* 2.232; *Ebr.* 14; cf. *Post.* 97), and Josephus also eventually makes place for it (*Ant.* 4.260–265).

to disown godlessness and worldly lusts. For "disown" see 1:16. See Excursus III, *"Eusebeia* and Its Cognates in the PE" on "godlessness," *asebeia,* which recurs in 2 Tim 2:16 (see 1 Tim 1:9 for the cognate adjective). "Lusts" *(epithymiai),* only in the plural in the PE, recurs in 3:3, as well as in 1 Tim 6:9 and 2 Tim 2:22; 3:6; 4:3. As in the remainder of the NT as well as in the Ap. Frs. and *T. 12 Patr.,* the plural always has a pejorative sense, a phenomenon that is regular in the LXX (but not universal, as LXX Prov 13:19 illustrates; see also Theod. Dan 9:23; 10:11, 19; and 10:3 in both the LXX and Theod.). The singular in the biblical tradition regularly has a neutral or good sense (though cf. Gal 5:16 with 24), especially of the craving for food, and the same is true of the cognate verb *epithymein* (cf. LXX Num 11:4 with Luke 22:15). This verb appears only once in the PE, in 1 Tim 3:1b, of the man who craves, in a good sense, the fine work of the episcopate.

The disparaging sense of the plural "lusts" is reinforced with an adjective in the PE (even in the hendiadys of 3:3). Here they are "worldly," *kosmikai*, an adjective undocumented in the LXX and occurring otherwise in the NT only in the phrase of Heb 9:1 describing the "earthly sanctuary" (in a neutral if not a good sense, as in *Did.* 11.11; cf. Josephus, *War* 4.324). A faintly derogatory nuance is present in the "worldly glory" of *T. Jos.* 17.8, unlike the single occurrences in Philo (*Aet.* 53) and Josephus (above). This shade of meaning is just beneath the surface of *2 Clem.* 5.6 (note *epithymein* in the context) and quite explicit in 17.3, which seems to be quoting "worldly lusts" from Titus. A fragment of Justin (*PG* 6.1580), along with *Mart. Pol.* 2.3, Athenagoras (*Legatio* 24.5 [*PG* 6.948]), and Clement of Alexandria, (*Paedagogus* 3.2 [O. Stählin; Leipzig: Hinrichs, 1908, 241.15]) show the continuing depreciation of *kosmikos* in Christian parlance and the semantic power of the precedent initiated here in Titus.

and to live in a sensible, honest, godly way in this present age. For "to live" see Excursus IV, "The Terminology for Life in the PE"; for "sensible," Excursus V, "The PE on Salvation"; for "godly," Excursus III, *"Eusebeia* and Its Cognates in the PE." This is the only use of the adverbial *dikaiōs* in the PE (see 3:5, 7 for the usage of the **(a)dik-* cluster). At this point, the rhetorical resemblance between the trio "holy and honest (*dikaiōs*) and blameless" in 1 Thess 2:10 is as notable as the semantic equivalence to the usage in Titus. There is no verbally exact precedent in Hellenistic Greek (biblical or otherwise) for the adverbial triad in Titus, though *dikaiōs* is paired with other adverbs in the Ap. Frs. (*1 Clem.* 51.2; 62.1; *2 Clem.* 5.6). For similar secular Hellenistic texts see Spicq, *EP*, pp. 638–639; and *Lexic.*, p. 870 n. 3.

The almost formulaic "in this present age," *en tōi nyn aiōni,* is treated in Excursus IV, "The Terminology for Life in the PE." *Aiōn* will reappear in 1 Tim 1:17 (*tris*) and 6:17 (in this same phrase); and in 2 Tim 4:10, 18 (*bis*). The term occurs 114 times elsewhere in the NT and almost 30 times in the other Paulines. The apocalyptic connotations of *aiōn* are signaled already by its 26 uses in Revelation. The LXX employs this noun very often, particularly in the sapiential literature, and in no book more often than the Psalms, a phenomenon that suggests why this term in particular became a fixed part of the language of prayer and worship in Christianity (e.g., *Did.* 8.2; 9.2–4; *1 Clem.* 20.12; 32.4; etc.). For "present," *nyn*, which will recur four times in the correspondence with Timothy, see Excursus IV, "The Terminology for Life in the PE."

13. *as we wait for the blessed hope revealed in the glory.* Literally, "awaiting the blessed hope and appearance of the glory." "As we wait for" translates the participial *prosdechomenoi*, which occurs only here in the PE. The two other Pauline uses refer to receiving or welcoming persons (Rom 16:2; Phil 2:29). The rest of the NT occurrences are mainly in the Lukan corpus, and they refer not only to the act of waiting to welcome a person (Luke 12:36, "like men who are

waiting for their master (*kyrion*)," even sinners (Luke 15:2), but also such realities as "the consolation of Israel" (Luke 2:25), "the redemption of Jerusalem" (Luke 2:38, materially parallel with Heb 11:35), "the kingdom of God" (Luke 23:51 = Mark 15:43), even a Roman tribune's promise (Acts 23:21). When Paul is before Felix he declares that, like a sect among his countrymen, he too has "a hope (*elpida*) in God (*eis ton theon*) which they themselves wait for (*prosdechontai*), and that there will be a resurrection of both the just and the unjust" (Acts 24:15). Jude 21, describing those who are "waiting for the mercy (*eleos*) of our Lord Jesus Christ unto life eternal," is conceptually parallel to Titus 2:13. The paradoxical expression in Heb 10:34 and the handful of occurrences in the Ap. Frs. offer no parallels to the usage in Titus. The LXX, however, has several phrases with *prosdechesthai* that are evocative of the concepts here in the PE (e.g., welcoming/waiting for "my face," Gen 32:21; "the hope of my salvation," Job 2:9a [not in the MT]; "him who saves me," Ps 54:9 [not in the MT]; "the salvation of the righteous," Wis 18:7; and "hope upon hope," Isa 28:10 [where the MT is misunderstood]). In Philo, *Spec. leg.* 2.218, God himself welcomes the prayer of the oppressed.

See Titus 1:2 on *elpis*, "hope," meaning "the one hoped for." Here it is "blessed," *makarios*, a qualification that the PE otherwise apply only to God (1 Tim 1:11; 6:15), who is never thus described in the forty-seven other NT uses of this adjective, not to mention the LXX and the Ap. Frs., which employ the term regularly for persons.

The LXX *makarios* always translates a form of the Hebrew *ʾašrê* and is to be distinguished from *eulogētos* and its cognates, which are not found in the PE. The Hebrew term is preeminently a liturgical acclamation belonging to the language of prayer (see Pss passim). It is applied only to human beings, never to God or to nonhuman objects. The reason is not far to seek. A person is recognized and acclaimed as blessed because he has received a gift from God, a gift that the one who offers the blessing prayer or macarism envies and desires for himself (see Janzen, "ʾĀŠRÊ," pp. 224–226 and H. Cazelles in *TDOT*, 1.445–448). The Greek *makarios* bears this connotation on occasion also (thus Aristophanes, *Wasps* 550–551; Epicurus, *Sententiae vaticanae* 17; Theocritus 7.83–85). The LXX exploited this nuance in translating the Hebrew Scriptures (see LXX Ps 31:1–2 = Rom 4:7–8), and Greek-speaking Judaism and Christianity remained reluctant to apply *makarios* to God. Their choice was probably reinforced by the practice from Homer onward of designating the Greek gods as *makares* (the blessed ones) and then *makarioi* (see Spicq, *Supp. Lexic.*, pp. 436–446). In Aristotle's phrase, "The whole life of the gods is blessed (*ho bios makarios*)" (*NE* 1178b27). Philo's elaborate descriptions of God as *makarios* seem to protest too much (*Leg.* 5; other texts in D-C, pp. 25–26), and even Josephus appears reserved (*Ant.* 10.278, quoting an Epicurean phrase; *Apion* 2.190, where in Greek the adjective is conspicuously distanced from God, *ho* [s.v.l.] *theos*). The PE (and the traditions assimilated by them) are innovative but cautious (see *monos* in 1 Tim 6:15) in their use of *makarios* not only for God but also here in Titus for "hope." *Elpis* is never thus qualified in the rest of the NT, LXX, or Ap. Frs. Very rarely is anything other than a person designated "blessed." A martyr's death and the age to come are *makarios* in 4 Macc 10:15 and 17:18. In *1 Clem.* 35.1 the "blessed and wonderful gifts (*dōra*) of God" are, first of all, "life in immortality" (see *2 Clem.* 19.4). That is the hope to which Titus 1:2 and 3:7 refer, "a hope of life eternal." See Spicq, *Supp. Lexic.*, pp. 436–446.

revealed in the glory. Literally, "and appearance of the glory," completes the hendiadys introduced by the preceding articular phrase (the cursive 33 has repeated *tēn* before *epiphaneian*, which is otherwise arthrous in the NT; 2 Tim 4:1 was probably still in the copyist's memory). *Epiphaneia* occurs in the NT outside of the PE only in 2 Thess 2:8, "the appearance of his presence (*parousia*)." Similarly in the PE it always has one or more attached (pro-)nouns that refer to Jesus: "of our Lord, Jesus Christ," 1 Tim 6:14; "of our savior, Christ Jesus," 2 Tim 1:10; "his revelation," 2 Tim 4:1, 8. The only appearances of *epiphaneia* in the Ap. Frs. refer to the coming "day of revelation" of the God of Israel in judgment (*2 Clem.* 12.1; 17.4, commenting on LXX Isa 66:18). Most of the dozen Septuagintal uses of this noun designate tangible divine interventions in battle and occur in 2 and 3 Macc; *epiphaneia* designates the appearance or arrival of a human being only in Amos 5:22 (cited at 2:11 above) and Esther 5:1c, of the king "seated on his royal throne, arrayed in all his splendid attire (*pasan stolēn tēs epiphaneias;* cf. 1a), all covered with gold and precious stones —a most formidable sight" (Moore, *AB Dan. add.* pp. 216, 218 and the literature cited there). For the religious use of the *epiphan-* cluster in Hellenism, where it is particularly associated "with datable events and with a cult," see R. Bultmann and D. Lührmann in *TDNT* 9.8–9, who also analyze the usage of Philo and Josephus.

The Semitic turn of phrase, "appearance of the glory (*doxēs*)" (see BDF §165), is parallel to the preceding, more Hellenistic "blessed hope." In profane Greek, *doxa* means human opinion, with all of the uncertainties therein implied; the LXX chooses the term often to translate the Hebrew *kābôd*, the visible, powerful self-manifestation of Yahweh in behalf of his people; and this Hebraic sense passes into Jewish and later Christian Greek (thus G. von Rad and G. Kittel in *TDNT* 2.233–253). The NT and the Ap. Frs. do not employ *doxa* with the sense "opinion." The PE use *doxa* six times, regularly of God, as in 1 Tim 1:11 (also a Hebraic genitive), 17; 3:16; 2 Tim 2:10, and of Christ the Lord in 2 Tim 4:18. Almost half of the remaining 160 NT occurrences are in the other Paulines, with the Hebraic genitive no less than half a dozen times (see esp. 1 Cor 2:8). The relatively fewer Lukan uses (17, with only 4 in Acts) offer notable parallels to the PE (see below).

of Jesus Christ, our great God and savior. Literally, "of the great (*tou megalou*) God and savior of us, Jesus Christ." The Greek admits of two meanings, taking God and savior together and predicating both of Jesus (as does the version above), or distinguishing between "the great God" and Christ the savior, as between two separate persons. The latter sense would be certain if "savior" had the Greek definite article; it remains possible because popular Greek at this time did not demand the repetition of the article to distinguish between paired substantives (Moule, *Idiom*, p. 109; BDF §276.1–3, comparing 2 Pet 1:1). The Greek manuscripts betray no nervousness about the interpretation. Augustine may transmit a Western scruple (see Ambrosiaster, *PL* 17.502), and the Palestinian Syriac certainly records an Eastern one (see J. K. Elliott, *Greek Text*, p. 187, though not following him on the reading of S). The solution must be sought in the text as it stands. It is anachronistic to explain what the author of the PE had to mean in terms of the fourth-century controversies that surrounded Nicaea. The "great God" of 2:13 need not be the same person who is called "God" in v 11, any more than the "savior" of v 10 must designate the same person as "savior" here (see 1:3–4). Moreover, in secular and Jewish Greek *theos kai sōtēr* is a formulaic bound phrase that applies to one divine person; it was never parceled out between two (for the texts and literature, Spicq, *Agape*, 3.31 n. 3; much abbreviated in the E.T. 2.399). The addition of the name "Jesus Christ" to this formula excludes its being taken to mean "the Father." See M. J. Harris, "Titus 2:13," whose full review of the literature to date and detailed analysis of the text have been used at every turn in this summary.

Since F. J. A. Hort (*James*, pp. 47, 103–104), the possibility has been debated in various forms that this text is designating Jesus himself under the title, "the glory of the great God." Thus the meaning could be ". . . and revelation of the great God's glory, namely (epexegetic *kai*), our savior, Jesus Christ" or ". . . and revelation of our great God and savior's glory, Jesus Christ." Thus far these versions have failed to win the day. The striking point is that there are very few NT passages calling Jesus "God," and there is not one that clearly calls him "the glory of God." The Johannine use of *doxa* verges on this sense (see John 1:14; 2:11; 17:5, 22, 24), and Ralph P. Martin (*Carmen*, p. 111 n. 3; "NT Hymns," p. 41) and Nigel Turner (*Words*, pp. 187, 198) read Acts 7:55 with an epexegetic *kai*, so that Stephen "saw the glory of God, that is (*kai*), Jesus standing at the right hand of God." The title does not appear in the Ap. Frs., but it does in Origen (*De oratione*, *PG* 14.820; cf. Cyril of Alexandria, *PG* 68.768).

For "Jesus Christ, our savior," see Excursus V, "The PE on Salvation." "Great (*megalou*) God" occurs only here in the NT and Ap. Frs., but the feminine form appears as the title of the Ephesian Artemis (Acts 19:27–28, 34–35). The LXX describes not only the God of Israel as *ho theos ho megas*, "the great God" (Deut 10:17; LXX 2 Esdr 5:8; 18:6; 19:32 [= MT Neh 4:14; 8:6; 9:32]; Isa 26:4; Dan 2:45; 9:4) but also makes it clear that this is the title for the pagan gods (cf. LXX Ps 76:14 with 85:10), the popularity of which is witnessed in papyri and inscriptions (see LSJ and BAGD s.v. as well as Spicq, *EP*, pp. 249–

251, 640 for the references). A tantalizing occurrence appears in *T. Sim.* 6.5 (s.v.l.; see Charlesworth, *OT Pseud.*, 1.787). In the first century of the Christian era a Jewish inscription from Egypt has a dedication "to the great God (*theoi [me]galo[i]*) who hears prayers" (*CII* 2.1432 = B. Lifshitz, *Donateurs*, p. 76 §86.3–4). See also *Sibylline Oracles* 3.656 (Charlesworth, *OT Pseud.* 1.376). A pagan inscription from Caesarea reads *theoi megaloi des[potei]*, as restored by B. Lifshitz, "Cesarée," p. 56 §1.

The PE employ *megas* of "the mystery of godliness" (1 Tim 3:16) and the gain from godliness (1 Tim 6:6) as well as of the parabolic house in 2 Tim 2:20. For all of the hundreds of occurrences of this term in the NT, there are only five uses in the other Paulines. Luke–Acts employ forms of *megas* more than fifty times, and no book of the NT uses the term more often than Rev (eighty times). Hence in P. S. Minear's title it is "An Apocalyptic Adjective" ("Apoc. Adj.," pp. 218–222).

Instead of "Jesus Christ," S*, F, and G, as well as the Bohairic Coptic, Armenian, and a few old Latin versions (see *VL* 25. [2].909) read "Christ Jesus." The text of 1739 omits "Christ," but this reading is most unlikely to be original, for the PE never otherwise use the name "Jesus" alone (thus J. K. Elliott, *Greek Text*, p. 198). The variant order may be due to liturgical usage or other accidents in transmission. The source cited here and the author of the PE probably wrote "savior of us" and then immediately added "Jesus" as the name of the one who gave that phrase its Christian meaning (cf. 1:1 with 4 above).

14. *He laid down his life for us.* Literally, "who gave (the aorist *edoken*) himself," which reappears in 1 Tim 2:6 with the aorist participle *dous*. An already formulaic use of the phrase occurs in Gal 1:4 (cf. 2 Cor 8:5; 2 Thess 3:9; and contrast Acts 19:31). In 1 Macc 6:44 Eleazar's fatal heroism in battle is summed up, "So he gave himself (*edoken heauton*) to save (*sōsai*) his people (*laon*) and to win (*peripoiesai*) for himself an everlasting name." The Semitic background of the phrase is quite clear in 1 Macc 2:50, when the father of the Maccabees exhorts his sons, "now, my children, show zeal (*zēlōsate*) for the law and give your lives (*dote tas psychas hymōn*) for (*hyper*) the covenant of our fathers." To give oneself is ultimately to give one's life (*psychē*) for the sake of a good that one esteems more. The aged martyr Eleazar of 4 Macc 6:29 prays for his people, "Make my blood their purification (*katharsion*) and take my life (*psychēn*) in exchange for theirs (*antipsychon autōn*)." Similarly in the gospel tradition, Mark 10:45 (= Matt 20:28; *SFG* §263) has Jesus say that the son of man came "to give his life (*dounai tēn psychēn*) as ransom (*lytron*) for (*anti*) many." In Attic Greek, by way of contrast, Thucydides has Pericles eulogize the Athenian soldiers "who gave their bodies (*ta somata didontes*) for their own common good" (*History of the Peloponnesian War* 2.43.2; in distinction from "they gave themselves" in 2.68.7; see Luke 22:19). The Ap. Frs. rarely employ the phrase "to give oneself" (Ign. *Smyrn.* 4.2; *Herm. Vis.* 4.1.8), but "to give one's body/life" never occurs.

"For us," *hyper hēmōn*, occurs only here in the PE, but the preposition appears in the church order of 1 Tim 2:1–2 and 6 of prayer "for all human beings . . . all in high station," and of "Christ Jesus, who gave himself as a ransom for all." Of the dozen appearances of *hyper hēmōn* in the rest of the Paulines, the most notable uses are in the already formulaic allusions to Jesus' sufferings in 1 Thess 5:10; Gal 3:13 (cf. 1:4; 2:20), and Rom 5:8 (cf. 8:31–34). There are four other NT uses of *hyper hēmōn*. The phrase refers to the object of Jesus' priestly intercession in heaven in Heb 6:20 and 9:24. In 1 John 3:16 the sign of Jesus' love is "that he laid down his life (*tēn psychēn autou ethēken*) for us" (where *psychēn tethenai* is a more Semitic way of saying *didonai heauton*). The NT prefers to designate the effect and goal of Jesus' passion with a *hyper* formula instead of a phrase introduced by *peri* or *anti* (see J. Jeremias in *TDNT* 5.710 n. 435 for the texts). In the Ap. Frs. the phrase *hyper hēmōn* is reserved for the passion of Jesus (*1 Clem.* 21.6; 49.6; Ign. *Rom.* 6.1; *Smyrn.* 1.2; Pol. *Phil.* 9.2). The LXX regularly employs *hyper* for the object of prayer, individual and corporate, in words and in sacrificial acts (thus 1 Kgdms 1:27; 1 Esdr 7:7–8; 8:63; Ps 31:6; 2 Macc 12:44). This object embraces all of the needs of Israel, the people of God (see 2 Macc 1:26), particularly the need for forgiveness of sin (see Ezek 45:17, 22, 23, 25) and for liberation from oppressors (cf. Ps 104:14 with 1 Chr 16:21). Yet the LXX never uses the phrase *hyper hēmōn*. The *T. Reub.* 6.12, however, does speak of the Maccabean(?) kings from Levi's progeny who die *hyper hēmōn* in visible and invisible battles (see *T. Benj.* 3.8 for the death of a spotless, sinless one for the sake of the lawless [*hyper anomōn*] and ungodly). Sacrificial worship on behalf of the whole nation is expressed with *hyper* in *T. Reub.* 6.8 and prayer for an individual in *T. Gad* 7.1 and *T. Jos.* 18.2.

to set us free from every wrong. The verb *lytroun* occurs only here in the Pauline corpus; in the rest of the NT it occurs only in Luke 24:21 and 1 Pet 1:18. The Ap. Frs. employ the term of ransoming slaves (thus *1 Clem.* 55.2; 59.4) as well as of Jesus redeeming God's people (thus Ign. *Phld.* 11.1; *2 Clem.* 17.4; *Barn.* 14.5–8). The LXX has about a hundred uses of *lytroun* but relatively seldom speaks of an emancipation from sins, as does LXX Ps 129:7–8, "For with the Lord is mercy and plentiful redemption (*lytrōsis*) is with him; and he will redeem (*lytrōsetai* [cf. the reading of Titus 2:14 in P]) Israel from all its sins (*pasōn . . . anomiōn*)." See also LXX Dan 4:27. "From every wrong" (*apo pasēs anomias*) echoes the same psalm. *Anomia*, only here in the PE, appears otherwise in the Paulines only in Rom 4:7 (citing LXX Ps 31:1); 6:19; 2 Cor 6:14; 2 Thess 2:3, 7 ("the man/mystery of wrong"). Hebrews 1:9 and 10:17 use the term in citing LXX Ps 44:8 and LXX(?) Jer 38:34. The remaining five NT uses of *anomia* are in Matt (see Guelich, *Sermon*, p. 402) and 1 John 3:4 (see Brown, *AB Epistles*, pp. 398–400). Ten of eleven occurrences in *1 Clem.* appear in citations of the OT. Among these 18.9, citing LXX Ps 50:11, "Blot out all (*pasas*) my wrongs" recalls "from every wrong" here in Titus. *Testament of Dan* 3.2 and *T. Naph.* 4.1 also speak of "every wrong," the latter reminding one of the apocalyptic usage of *anomia* in Enoch's epistle (*Enoch* 97.6; 98.1, 5; 99.15) and *3 Apoc. Bar.* 8.5 (see Charlesworth, *OT Pseud.* 1.673).

The cognate adjective *anomos,* "lawless," occurs in the PE only in 1 Tim 1:9. Otherwise in the Paulines 1 Cor 9:21 uses this adjective four times in the sense of "without the (Mosaic) law" (see the sole NT use of the adverb in Rom 2:12). In 2 Thess 2:8 the apocalyptic enemy of Christ is *ho anomos,* "the Outlaw par excellence," who cannot be understood apart from "the man/mystery of wrong" that has preceded. In Luke–Acts a further nuance appears as Luke 22:37 cites Isa 53:12 (LXX? see *1 Clem.* 16.13) as an apology for Jesus' crucifixion between outlaws (Marshall, *Luke,* p. 826). In Acts 2:23, however, the "lawless" are the Roman Gentiles whom Jesus' countrymen use to crucify him (see Haenchen, *Acts,* p. 180). In its last NT use, the "works" of the Sodomites, not the persons, are called "lawless" (2 Pet 2:8), and in the Ap. Frs., *Barn.* 4.9 can describe the present time as "lawless." The author of *1 Clem.* uses the adjective as he did the noun, in citing or referring to the OT (18.13; 35.9; 45.4; 56.11). The LXX often employs *anomos* of persons who are sinning, but on occasion their acts are *ta anoma* (thus LXX Job 34:8; 35:14; Prov 1:19) and Wis 15:17 writes of "the lawless hands" that fashion an idol. For *T. Benj.* 3.8, see above on "for us." The notable number of occurrences of the **anom-* cluster in citations of and allusions to the OT signals already the problem with which this terminology confronted the Christian believer, namely, his relation to the Law of Moses.

and to cleanse for himself a people of his very own, enthusiastic for fine deeds. This verb "to cleanse," *katharizein,* occurs only here in the PE (cf. *ekkatharein,* 2 Tim 2:21) but thirty times otherwise in the NT. It appears elsewhere in the Paulines only twice, however: in 2 Cor 7:1 believers are to cleanse themselves of impurities because they are God's people (cf. 2 Cor 6:16); in Eph 5:26 Christ himself cleanses his church in the baptismal rite (cf. 1 Cor 6:11 with Acts 22:16). The synoptics usually speak of the cleansing of persons with leprosy (with its suggestion of Levitical verification), but passages in Luke–Acts, adduced in the NOTES and COMMENTS on Titus 1:15, speak of the cleansing of the Gentiles by faith in Jesus. The Letter to the Hebrews (9:14, 22–23; 10:2) and 1 John (1:7–9) link the internal cleansing of believers with the sacrificial blood of Jesus crucified (in contrast to the external cleansing conferred by the animal sacrifices of Levitical worship). Ignatius (*Eph.* 18.2) explicitly broaches the baptismal aspect of this language when he explains that Christ "was baptized so that water might be cleansed by his passion (*tōi pathei . . . katharisēi*)." *First Clement* takes up *katharizein* in citations of the OT, at 16.10 (Isa 53) and 18.3, 7 (LXX Ps 50:4, 9, where the parallels with washing and sprinkling are notable). Hermas frequently employs this verb; and in *Sim.* 5.6.3, when he describes the redemptive work of the Son of God, he writes that the Son "cleansed the sins of the people (*laou*)." Although the LXX more than a hundred times, especially in Lev and Ezek (see 37:23), uses *katharizein,* one must go to LXX 2 Esdr 22:30

(MT Neh 12:30) to read that priests and Levites "cleansed the people (*ton laon*)" (see Jdt 16:18 for the passive).

Only in Titus in the NT are the "people" qualified as "his very own," *periousios*. The LXX uses this adjective with *laos* in a series of passages that normally translate the *'ăm səgullāh*, referring to Israel as "the people peculiarly his own" (Exod 19:5; 23:22 [not in MT]; Deut 7:6; 14:2; 26:18), as distinguished from all other nations. The closing invocation of *1 Clem.* 64.1 uses the phrase precisely as Titus does, of the Christian people. The Septuagintal meaning for this adjective and the cognate *periousiasmos* (LXX Ps 134:5; Eccl 2:8 for *səgullāh*), namely, a private possession or a special treasure, is not the meaning of the terms in the **periousi-* cluster in nonbiblical Greek, where the reference is to riches, abundance, and surplus of goods. The papyri and inscriptions (see MM s.v.) hardly bring us farther than Jerome, whose inquiries among contemporary philologists unearthed no profane text containing *periousios* with the meaning it has here (*On Titus, PL* 26.587). Once a married man is described as "chosen" in P Geneve 11.57. In the MT *səgullāh* also appears in 1 Chr 29:3 (LXX *ho peripepoiemai;* see this verb in 1 Tim 3:13) and Mal 3:17 (LXX *eis peripoiēsin,* as in 1 Pet 2:9; see BDF §113.1). No evidence has emerged thus far that the Qumran sect used this term.

The term "people," *laos,* occurs only here in the PE and 141 times otherwise in the NT, almost always in the singular. All 11 Pauline uses are in quotations from the OT, 8 of them in Rom. The lion's share of the NT usage belongs to Luke–Acts with 84 occurrences, which range in meaning from a crowd of people or a nation, specifically Israel, to the Christian people, whether Jewish in origin or not (see Acts 15:14; 18:10; and H. Strathmann in *TDNT* 4.50–54 for further texts). In the Ap. Frs., *1 Clem.* uses *laos* 12 out of 13 times in quotations or paraphrases of the OT; in the great concluding prayer at 59.4 he asks God to bring back those of his people who have wandered, and even this may be a paraphrase of LXX Ezek 34:16. Hermas employs *laos* as often as *1 Clem.,* but the links with the OT are of a more allusive character. The identity of the people of God is a central concern of *Barn.,* and none of the Ap. Frs. uses *laos* more often, quoting key passages from the LXX as well as reflecting on the meaning of the consecrated biblical terminology in the light of the problem of the relation of the Christian *laos* to that of the OT. The LXX speaks of the *laos* about 2,000 times, almost always to translate the Hebrew *'ăm* and usually to designate Israel as Yahweh's own flock, the people of God (cf. *periousios* here as well as H. Strathmann in *TDNT* 4.29–39 and Good, *Sheep,* for what follows). The term *laos* belongs to the oldest tradition of Greek poetry and is not at all common in Greek prose. To Greek ears *laos* was a dignified and lofty word to designate a united group of free men and women, as distinguished from their ruler or leader to whom they subjected themselves. Regularly in the *Iliad* this term means the men in the army as distinguished from their chieftains, and this nuance appears in Pindar's description of the Sicilian cavalry host as *laos hip-*

paichmos (*Nemean* 1.16–20). Thus *laos* served admirably to convey the sense of the Hebrew *ʿam*, a union of free persons in the service of the one God (the *ʿam yhwh* is the tribal league in military formation), who led their armies and won the victories against their foes. The Hebrew ideology of the holy war (see Vaux, *Israel*, pp. 258–267) entered Greek-speaking Judaism and the LXX through *laos*, as Jdt strikingly illustrates, where *laos* designates Israel (apart from 16:22) or the armies (*Kriegsvolk*, Strathmann) mobilized against God's people. In the *T. 12 Patr.* the Septuagintal usage appears when *laos* designates the tribes of Israel (*T. Reub.* 6.11; *T. Judah* 25.3, 5[?]) or an army with its chieftain (*T. Judah* 3.1, 2; 9.2; perhaps *T. Sim.* 6.4). *Enoch* 20.5 describes the Archangel Michael as the leader set over the virtuous of the people (*epi tōn tou laou agathōn*), in other words, over the army of Israel.

enthusiastic for fine deeds. Literally, "zealot(s) (*zēlōtēn*) for attractive works (*kalōn ergōn*)." The noun *zēlōtēs* appears nowhere else in the PE. Of its seven other NT uses, two are in Paul and four in Luke–Acts. When the apostle directs the Corinthians to be "zealots for the spirits," that is, the spiritual gifts (1 Cor 14:12; cf. 14:1), his frame of reference intersects not only with Titus but also with 1 Pet 3:13 on "zealots for the good" (*agathou;* cf. Sir 51:18). A darker nuance appears when Paul described himself, before his conversion, as a zealot for the Law (Gal 1:14; cf. Phil 3:6 and 2 Macc 4:2 with 4 Macc 18:12); and thus Acts 22:3 remembers him as "zealous for God." Yet even Jewish Christians are "zealots for the Law" in Acts 21:20. In Luke's list of the Twelve (Luke 6:15; Acts 1:13) there appears "Simon the zealous" or "the Zealot," a translation of the title *Kananaios*, which Mark 3:18 and Matt 10:4 (*SFG* §49) have transliterated from the Aramaic *qanʾānāʾ* (see Fitzmyer, *AB Lk*, p. 619; Marshall, *Luke*, p. 240; *pace* MM, p. 320). The rare uses of *zēlōtēs* in the Ap. Frs. are in contexts that at least imply that one can be a zealot in a bad cause as well as a good one (*1 Clem.* 45.1; Pol. *Phil.* 6.3, *peri to kalon*). In *Did.* 3.2 the term means a jealous man in a thoroughly bad sense (see COMMENT). Yet in the LXX Yahweh himself is *zēlōtēs*, translating the Hebrew *qannāʾ*, "the zealous one" (Exod 20:5; 34:14; Deut 4:24; 5:9; 6:15; Nah 1:2), and his worshipers are so described in a good sense in the latest strata of the Greek Bible (but only twice; see above). In Philo God is not called *zēlōtēs*, but human beings may be zealots for righteousness or evil (see COMMENT). According to Josephus, *War* 2.651 and 4.160–162, a faction of "bloodstained polluters" inside Jerusalem as the Romans moved up for the final siege during the Jewish revolt were the first to designate themselves as "Zealots" (contrast the usage in Josephus, *War* 2.444, 564, where the noun is not a party title). This technical usage gave a sinister political nuance to *zēlōtēs* that was new and difficult for Jews and Jewish Christians to ignore thereafter. In secular Greek inscriptions the phrase *zēlōtai tōn kalliston*, "enthusiasts for the finest things," is not uncommon (Spicq, *EP*, p. 643; D-C, p. 143 n. 13; MM s.v.). For the specifically Christian phrase, proper to the PE, "fine deeds," see the NOTES on 1:16 and 2:7.

COMMENT

2:11. *Revealed was the grace of God for the rescue of all human beings.* The domestic code for Christian living in the household of the one God now opens into a confession of the faith that generates that life, a confession that Clement of Alexandria cited (with 3:3–5) in his description of "the new song" (*kainon aisma*) that the incarnation introduced into human life (*Protrepticus* 1.4.3–1.7.3 [O. Stählin; Leipzig: Hinrichs, 1908, 1.5–7]).

The Greek *gar*, "for," represented in this version by the inverted word order, serves both to link and to distinguish what has preceded from what is to follow (see 1:7, 10; 3:3, 9, 12). The recurrences of the first-person plural, the repetitions of the terms *pasin*, "all," and "God," and the play on *sōtēros/sōtērios*, "savior/the rescue of," reinforce the hermeneutical connection of this confession with the code preceding. All Christian life, all activities of every age, sex, and state of life, find their taproot in the revelation of "the grace of God," the *charis* that is one of the heart-words of the Pauline gospel (see 1:4). At this point in Titus, as well as in 3:7, a fully conscious, theological use of *charis* appears, as the articular *tou theou*, "of God," makes clear (note "God's was the grace" in 3:7). The Greek article here indicates that *theos* is a personal name or title for the Father (see 1:1), and so it is his "grace" (see 1:4) that is singled out and then qualified with the instrumental *sōtērios*, literally, "saving."

That "saving grace" is not quite personified at this point (but see 2:13) where the emphasis is on the revelation of the Father's gift, a revelation that has appeared (cf. *epephanē*, as in 3:4, with the *epiphaneian* of Christ to come in 2:13). In the correspondence with Timothy a similar confession proposes a link between God's gracious design (literally, "purpose and grace"), "given us in Christ Jesus," which "has now been made clear (*phanerōthesan*) through the revelation (*epiphaneias*) of our savior, Christ Jesus" and the commission of Paul as "herald and apostle and teacher" (2 Tim 1:9–11). In 1 Tim 1:14 the thanksgiving prayer extols (for the only time in the PE) "the grace of our Lord," that is, of the risen Jesus who converted and called Paul to "his ministry." Titus in this letter is the one through whom the apostolic *charis* of Paul (see 1:4) illumines persons who are physically far from the apostle (cf. 2 Tim 1:9 with 2:1–2). "The grace of God," which began to dawn on humankind in the birth, death, and resurrection of the Savior, Jesus, changed the life of the apostle. It ought to change the life of his coworker (2:7–8) and the actual, historical lives of all who put their faith in the Pauline preaching and teaching, whether old or young, women or men, free or slave. Ultimately this grace is for "all human beings." The apostle, his coworkers, the community that has responded to this gift of God (see the first-person plural of the verse following), all exist to bring "the grace of God" to every human being. God's will and plan to save all men and women, universally and without exception, is a controlling theme in the PE (note the various uses of the phrase "all human beings" in 1 Tim 2:1, 4 and 4:10). The creedal fact serves as the basis for the Christian's attitude "to every person" (3:2).

The phrase *pas anthrōpos*, in singular and plural, appears a dozen times in Paul outside of the PE, in the context of his most profound teaching (thus Rom 5:12, 18; Col 1:28) as well as in polemic that can scarcely be pressed scientifically (1 Thess 2:15). The phrase in the plural is unknown to the gospel tradition, except in the "woe" of Luke 6:26 and in a reference to "all persons dwelling in Jerusalem" (Luke 13:4, a usage that does not resemble the PE). In Acts 17:30, however, a striking variant on the phrase occurs in the climax of the Areopagus speech, "God overlooked the times of ignorance but now he commands all human beings everywhere (*tois anthrōpois pantas pantachou*) to repent." In the second account of Paul's conversion Ananias announces that the risen Jesus has appeared to reveal "the will" of the God of Israel, asking that Saul be a witness "to all human beings" (*pros pantas anthrōpous*) of what he has seen and heard (Acts 22:14–15). The conception of the Pauline mission and preaching is notably similar to that of the PE. This verse of Titus suggests further that just as the one sun and its light are for all human beings and their life, so the Father's grace ushers in the light of a new day for every human being without distinction. The light imagery reaches full intensity in the description of the "revelation," *epiphaneian*, in 2:13.

12. *It disciplines us to disown godlessness and worldly lusts, and to live in a sensible, honest, godly way in this present age.* The Father's gift, which appeared (aorist in Greek) in a given moment of the past, has a continuing educative function (present participle, *paideuousa*). Nonetheless, one must be on guard against anachronistically reading into this term the twentieth-century American concept of enthusiastically motivated and spontaneous learning activity in a permissive atmosphere. A more refined and no less misleading exegesis simply equates the technical Greek philosophical use of *paideia* with popular Hellenistic understanding of *paideuein* and its cognates (see Mott, "Ethics," pp. 30–35 and the authors cited there). The education or schooling of the young designated by this cluster of terms was in the Hellenistic world so closely associated with whipping and cudgeling the refractory student that *paideuein* popularly designated corporal punishment as well as what a modern would call "education" (see Marrou, *Education*, pp. 158–159). Aristotle submitted as self-evident that learning occurs with pain (*meta lypēs gar hē mathēsis, Politics* 8.1339a29; cf. Hesiod, *Works and Days* 218, *pathōn de te nēpios egnō*, "When suffering the infant [or the senseless] comes to know"). Seneca and Quintilian are *extra chorum* in the Roman world as they argue with custom and the received wisdom against the flogging of students (*De clementia* 1.16.3; *Institutio oratoria* 1.3.13–17; cf. Martial, *Epigrams* 9.68.1–12; 10.62.1–12; and Bonner, *Education*, pp. 141–145). This is not to deny the cultural and intellectual content of teaching

the young as the ancients conceived it (see Acts 7:22; 22:3); it is to emphasize that teaching the young was practically inconceivable apart from externally inflicted suffering. The first-century Christian did not set out to abolish corporal punishment in teaching any more than to abolish slavery. He did employ both social institutions as theological and christological paradigms, uses that in turn had an eventual, drastic effect on the model itself. Similarly, the first believers did not set about abolishing crucifixion, but eventually their belief about what had occurred in the crucifixion of Jesus, who bore "chastisement (*paideia*, LXX Isa 53:5) for our peace," made that "most cruel and most revolting punishment" (Cicero, *Against Verres* 5.64.165) simply inconceivable for even the most heinous crimes (see W. Westermann, *Slave*, p. 156).

Thus when "the grace of God" the Father "disciplines us," it is in a school of suffering and chastisement, of blows and scourges. Paul and his coworker are part of a family (thus the first-person plural) that is in the school of the cross (see 2:14). The leadership that Paul and his colleagues exercise in this family is not primarily the packaging and transmission of an abstract theological system, dogmatic or moral, but a sharing first of all of their own experience in the school of the cross. Hence the emphasis in the PE on the sufferings of Paul and his coworkers (see 1 Tim 6:11–16; 2 Tim 1:8, 12, 16; 2:3–6, 8–13; 3:10–12; 4:1–8). Hence too the emphasis here on virtuous actions, not "wisdom," as the aim of this schooling.

The purpose (*hina*) of this education is articulated in a negative, then in a positive formulation. The former ("to disown") looks to a definitive act in the past (aorist); the latter ("to live") to an ongoing ecclesial way of life in the present (note the first-person plural). These are the negative and positive poles within a phenomenon that can be designated as Christian conversion (for the Platonic and Hellenistic conception of conversion, see Nock, *Conversion*, passim, and Jaeger, *Paideia* 2.295–300). The preceding verse suggests that it is a turning from darkness to light, a darkness now specified as "godlessness and worldly lusts." The passage out of the night of these vices was a once-for-all act of solemn, public renunciation (see 1:16) in the personal, historical life of believers who had turned to the grace of the Father, a grace that had appeared in human history with the incarnation and was now appearing in their personal history. "To disown" suggests in Greek the repudiation of relationships with another person, the breaking with vices that are practically personified as Satan's agents. The day of Christian baptism involved such a public "apostasy" from the prince of darkness (see Riesenfeld, *"Arneisthai,"* pp. 216–217) and a corresponding profession of faith in Christ (for *homologein* see 1:16 and 1 Tim 6:12). The most primitive form of Hippolytus's *Apostolic Tradition* had the baptizand's renunciation of the devil in vigorous, direct address, "I renounce you, Satan, and all your service and all your works," followed by the profession of faith in the three Persons in the one God (Cuming, *Hippolytus*, §21; *Essays*, p. 57). If some such liturgical scene is presupposed by this text in Titus, then the first part of v 12 summarizes negatively what the baptismal event has meant for a Pauline church ("us"); a lengthier and more positive description of the baptismal life as such follows then through v 13.

"To disown godlessness" (*tēn asebeian*) contrasts both verbally and conceptually with the following "to live in a . . . godly way" (*eusebōs*). In 2 Tim 2:16, "godlessness" spreads like gangrene among certain Christians. Here in Titus, however, *asebeia* characterizes the condition before conversion to Christ. Is it possible to discern whether the "godlessness" of this confession refers to pagans or to Jews? Paul used *asebeia* of the former and then of the latter when he wrote to the Romans (1:18; 11:26 citing LXX Isa 59:20; see 4:5 and 5:6 for the adjective). If the Letter to Titus envisions a Jewish-Christian house church, then the "godlessness" could characterize the members' way of life before their conversion. Still, it would be quite appropriate for a confession in the Pauline tradition to use the term inclusively, designating the universal sinfulness of Jew and pagan before the one God whose grace appeared "for the rescue of all human beings." The *asebeia* of Israel was its rejection of "the grace of God" that was "revealed" in Christ Jesus; the "godlessness" of pagans consisted in their worship of many deities instead of the one God of Israel, a godlessness that in the Jewish sapiential critique issued inevitably into every kind of vice (Wis 14:8–29), the "lusts" that are enumerated at length in the appalling catalog of Rom 1:18–32. Here in Titus the one term "worldly," *kosmikos*, condenses all of the reasons for the convert's repudiation of merely human cravings. In the light of Greek usage at large, which did not hear *kosmikos* in a bad sense, it may be significant that in Rome at the end of the first century Martial twits a perfumed dandy who thinks he is *cosmicos*, "cosmopolitan" (transliterating the Greek adjective into Latin [*OLD* s.v.]; contrast the *mundanus* in Cicero, *Tusculan Disputations* 5.37.108) by noting that *cosmica . . . tam mala quam bona sunt,* "as many worldly things are bad as good" (*Epigrams* 7.41.1–2; see the name Cosmus in 1.87.2; 3.55.1; etc.). The confession in Titus perhaps has picked up and capitalized on a shade of meaning for *kosmikos* that was in the air in Rome before 90 C.E. In any case, the meaning of "worldly lusts" here in Titus ought to be compared to 2 Pet 1:4 and 1 John 2:16, "For all that is in the world (*kosmoi*) —human nature full of desire (*epithymia*), eyes hungry (*epithymia*) for all they see, material life that inflates self-assurance—does not belong to the Father; all that belongs to the world (*kosmou*)" (see Brown, *AB Epistles*, pp. 293, 325–326). The dawn of God's grace in the world puts all human appetites in a new light. In the Pauline tradition represented here, these cravings are to be taken in a bad sense. They include avarice and sexual license and more (cf. 1 Tim 6:9; 2 Tim 2:22; 3:6 with Rom 1:24; 6:12; 13:13–14; Eph 2:3; Col 3:5; 1 Thess 4:5), though there appears to be a growing emphasis on abuses of sexual power (*1 Clem.* 30:1; Ign. *Pol.* 5.2; Pol. *Phil.* 5.3, who writes of "being cut off from the lusts in the world [*en tōi kosmōi*]"), an emphasis that appears also in the Jewish tradition. The *T. 12 Patr.* regularly use the singular *epithymia* to mean the sexual appetite.

The moment that marked the abjuration of "godlessness and worldly lusts" was also the beginning of a life. All turns on the verb "to live" in this second, positive part of the purposive clause under analysis. The "grace of God" and his discipline are intended to create a passage from the death of infidelity and vice to a new way of living. The conversion being described with an ingressive aorist starts a vital process, a *zōē* that is not to be confused with material human existence, a *bios*. This *zōē* is the "life eternal" of 1:2, which will figure again in the formulation of the Christian message adduced in 3:7 (see Excursus IV). It is conceived as unfolding in the historical order, "in this present age" (see 1 Tim 6:17), though ordered to and belonging radically to another sphere or order, that of "the age to come" (see 1 Tim 4:8), as the verse following here makes clear. This vital process or dynamic is described with an adjectival triad the elements of which are closely drawn together with the thrice-repeated adverbial ending in -ōs and with the polysyndetic *kai*, which also suggests the rich abundance and extensiveness of the life in question (BDF §460.3). The assonance with seven-fold *ō* in the last half of this verse reinforces the centering of its thought on what constitutes Christian "living."

The form of the adverbial triad, the individual terms, and the way of life being signified are unabashedly Hellenistic (see Malherbe, *Cynic Epistles*, pp. 260–261). This confession assumes that really living, in other words, living as a Christian, "in this present age," involves assimilating much of what Hellenistic culture valued in human life. When Luke applied the sower parable to ecclesial life, he had the seed of "the word of God" (i.e., the gospel) planted "in a heart, fine and good (*kalēi kai agathēi*)," and "bearing fruit in patience," that is, in a person who possessed and showed all of the qualities that the Greek world prized (Luke 8:11, 15; *SFG* §124; Fitzmyer, *AB Lk*, p. 714; but see Marshall, *Luke*, p. 327 for reservations). Similarly in this confession in Titus, "the grace of God" has shone on the field of this world, vivifying it, producing appropriate harvests. The sun that brings life to one kind of crop in Palestine produces other fruits in other lands.

The order of Greek adverbs, *sōphronōs, dikaiōs, eusebōs*, "in a sensible, honest, godly way," bears attention. In 1:8 the cognate adjectives "sensible, upright" appear in the same order as here, followed by "devout," which to a considerable extent coincides semantically with "godly" at the end of this triad. The baptismal confession cited here is perhaps the source for the qualifications adduced in 1:8. The initial position of *sōphronōs* gives emphasis to a personal balance and self-mastery that the Greek world valued most highly. Greek is the medium for these letters, and the author obviously wanted to speak to believers who were at home in the Hellenistic world. The adverbs single out virtuous qualities on which Jews and Romans put a premium; for the just man, honest and upright, is the ideal of OT teaching and prayer, and the man who is *pius*, "reverent," is the Roman ideal (see Excursus III).

The triad as a whole, however, would designate qualities that were appreciated and distinguished from one another by Greeks. Schematically, each would refer to giving what was due: *sōphronōs*, to one's self; *dikaiōs*, to fellow human beings; *eusebōs*, to the gods (see Xenophon's final sketch of the virtues of Socrates in *Memorabilia* 4.8.11, "so *religious* [*eusebēs*] that he did nothing without counsel from the gods; so *just* [*dikaios*] that he did no injury, however small, to any man . . . ; *self-controlled* [*egkratēs*] . . . *wise* [*phronimos*]").

Is the triadic form employed here related to a fourfold canon for what the patristic age started to call the cardinal virtues? In the *Seven Against Thebes* 610–611, Aeschylus describes Teiresias as *sōphrōn, dikaios, agathos, eusebēs anēr, megas prophētēs*, "a sensible, just, good [= brave?], godly man, a great prophet" (see Pindar, *Nemean* 3.70–76 and Ferguson, *Values*, pp. 24–52 on these and what follows; also Dover, *Morality*, pp. 66–67). This tetradic pattern appears in Plato, where his ideal society is "wise, strong, sensible, just," *sophē, andreia, sōphrōn, dikaia* (*Republic* 4.427E), with only two virtues coinciding with the list in Aeschylus. Moreover, even in Plato, the fourfold schema can replace one virtue by another. Thus, "The sensible man (*sōphrona*) being honest (*dikaion*) and brave (*andreion*) and devout (*hosion*) must by all means be a good man (*agathon andra*)" (*Gorgias* 507C; cf. *Phaedo* 69C; *Laws* 1.631C). "There is no [fourth-century B.C.] evidence either of popular fourfold division or of an immediately accepted normative exposition," as John Ferguson (*Values*, p. 27) remarks, though when the schema finally became current it was under the Platonic aegis (see Diogenes Laertius 3.80). Thus with regard to form alone, the triad in Titus obviously does not correspond to the tetrads of secular Greek authors; furthermore, the fluid order and the terminology within the tetrads never precisely coincide with the order and terms in Titus. Philo, who uses the fourfold form regularly, admits godliness, *eusebeia*, to the list (cf. *hosiotēs*, "holiness," in the fifth place in Plato's list in *Protagoras* 349B), and a few times the order and terminology within a tetrad correspond to Titus (thus *sōphrosynē, dikaiosynē, eusebeia* in *Det.* 73, 143 but contrast 18, 24).

The question that remains is, Why a tetradic pattern? What did it mean? S. C. Mott ("Ethics," pp. 26–27) contends that from Plato on (*Laches* 199C–E; *Gorgias* 507A–C; etc.) the writers of the Academy and Stoa used a fourfold form "to indicate virtue par excellence and the unity of virtue," in other words, the ethical qualities that are the very best cohere inseparably with one another. But on this analysis there is little philological basis for a comparison of the triad in Titus with a tetrad of "cardinal virtues." *Andreia*, "fortitude," is missing for reasons suggested in 2:2; the terminology for "wisdom," *sophia, sophos*, k.t.l., is not found, probably because the tradition was influenced by the Pauline critique of the Hellenistic wise man (see Rom 1:22; 1 Cor 1:18–2:13; 3:18–20); and the terminological coincidences that remain hardly show more than that this language was in the air of the Hellenistic world and was part of the rhetoric for ethical discourse (the ninefold list of Lucian's *Somnium sive vita Luciani* 10 opens with *sōphrosynē, dikaiosynē, eusebeia*).

Is the comparison of triad with triad more fruitful? Plato did marshal virtues in threefold lists (*Protagoras* 325A; 329C; *Meno* 78D), and in the second century B.C. the Jewish Alexandrian philosopher Aristobulus writes of the Law as a complete training in godliness, righteousness, and self-control (*eusebeia, dikaisynē, egkrateia, apud* Eusebius, *Praeparatio evangelica* 13.12 [*PG* 21.1101]). Philo marshals similar triads, such as good sense, endurance, and righteousness (*phronēsis, karteria, dikaiosynē* in *Det.* 157; *Post.* 93), but none corresponds in terminology or order with that in Titus (*pace* Mott, "Ethics," p. 28). The same must be observed of the adverbial triad in Dio Chrysostom 23.7 about living justly, prudently, and sensibly (*dikaiōs, phronimōs, sophronōs*). From the absence of a source for the precise language and order found in Titus one could infer that the Christian tradition here was discriminating in its assimilation of Hellenistic ethical values. Some were adopted; some were put on hold; some were modified to the point of rejection. As with the fourfold form above, one must inquire what the triadic form itself suggested. A threefold schema for virtues has already surfaced in 1:6 and 2:2b, and other forms of it will reappear in 1 Tim 1:5, 13 (for vices), 17 (for divine attributes); 3:8 (vices); and 2 Tim 1:7 and 2:21b. The triadic form for citing virtues was probably a pre-Pauline catechetical device and certainly figured in the Pauline tradition (see 2:2b and NOTES above). Here the assonance, the rhyming *-ōs* of the adverbs, the polysyndeton, the adverbial usage, together conspire to suggest that one can distinguish but cannot separate the "sensible, honest" and "godly" in Christian living. In this respect the triadic form here (as with the fourfold form discussed above) is a cipher that stands for that fullness of the virtuous life which "the grace of God" generates in his family (see Mott, "Ethics," p. 29). The "rescue" or salvation that he offers here is from vice, which is implicitly death, in contrast to living "in a sensible, honest, godly way in this present age."

The past and present have framed the development of the confession thus far. The future dominates the next stage in v 13, *as we wait for the blessed hope revealed in the glory of Jesus Christ, our great God and savior.* The life of the Christian community, which expressed itself in conduct appreciated by the Hellenistic world, is at this point characterized by that kind of constant (note the present participle) eschatological expectancy which marked the oldest Jewish Christian communities (see Jas 5:7–9). The Monteverde inscription (*CII* 476) illustrates how a Latin-speaking Jewish couple in Rome at the beginning of the second Christian century similarly linked virtuous conduct in this life with hope for the resurrection. The husband of the deceased Regina says,

Again she will live, again return to the light, for she was able to hope (*sperare*) because she would arise to the life (*aevom*) that has been promised. This is an authentic assurance (*vera fides*) for the worthy and the devout (*piisque*). This has merited possessing a place in the awesome country (of Paradise). Devotion (*pietas*) has bestowed this on you; a chaste life has bestowed this on you; love of family (*generis*) also has bestowed this; observance of the Law has bestowed this; the worthiness of the marriage whose glory was your concern has bestowed this. For these deeds the things that are to come ought to be your hope (*speranda*). From them also a sad husband seeks comfort.

The "sensible, honest, godly way" of Christian life does not derive from Greek ethical demonstrations; it does not hope for that knowledge (*phronēsis*) of the good which the philosophers promised. The consolation and release that believers expect are bound up with the coming of the risen Lord and their own resurrection, literally, "the blessed hope and manifestation (*epiphaneian*) of the glory of the great God and our savior, Jesus Christ." "Hope" in the PE means the person hoped for (see 1:2), Jesus, hidden for the time being but certain to appear.

In both the Greek and the Roman worlds, the terminology for hope (*elpis/ spes*) had an ambivalence that must be marked if "the blessed hope" of this confession is to be understood. "Hope" in the Hellenistic world suggested not only optimistic expectation of a better future but also the self-deluding desire of what was simply unattainable. The sole remaining occupant of Pandora's box was far from an unmixed blessing (Hesiod, *Works and Days* 96–99); it was not without reason that hope had been sealed away with all the rest of the plagues and evils that make humankind miserable. Hope indeed sustains men and women, but it can be a hallucinogenic and an anesthetic (see the texts in Pindar and Euripides cited in Walsh, *"Spes,"* p. 33 and Clark, *"Spes,"* p. 102 n. 21, for the current literature; what follows is dependent on these authors and their references).

The Romans tended to have a more optimistic evaluation of *spes*, though there is no dearth of individual texts that speak about "empty hopes" (thus Quintilian, *Institutio oratoria* 6, *prooemium* 12; *CIL* 6.7578, in Gordon, *Epigraphy*, pp. 140–141; the pagan Caecilius in Minucius Felix, *Octavius* 8.5 on *fallax spes*) or *spes* playing games with human beings. There is some justification for the Pauline characterization of pagans as "having no hope and 'godforsaken' (*atheoi*) in the world" (Eph 2:12).

The positive evaluation of hope appears in Roman life above all in the "public" texts, that is, the governmental acts and their ideology as represented in the coinage and inscriptions. Here *spes* is "the power or operative influence inherent in a supernatural being," who bestows on the Roman people and those under their governance the benefit (*utilitas*) of confident trust in their leaders (see Fears, "Virtues," pp. 832–833, citing Cicero, *De natura deorum* 2.60–62). A divine hope for the continuing material benefits of a good government is embodied in the charismatic leaders of the Republic, and it is practically hypostatized in Augustus and in his successors. Statius (*Silvae*, 4.2.15) hails Domitian as "magne parens . . . spes hominum . . . cura deorum" ("mighty sire . . . hope of human beings . . . care of the gods"). Indeed the focus of the *spes Augusta* is the perpetuation of peace and prosperity in the households of the Roman world precisely through the continuance of the imperial household. Hope becomes personified in the legitimate son and heir of the emperor (see Clark, "*Spes*," pp. 81, 101 nn. 5, 6).

Against this background of the Roman imperial ideology, new contours appear in the confession of "the blessed hope" that God the Father offers in Jesus, his Son (a title that the PE never use) and "our great God and savior." The qualification of this hope as "blessed" unmistakably removes it from the realm of delusive desires (cf. LXX Isa 28:15; 31:2; Jer 13:25 with *Barn.* 16.2) and already suggests that it is to be conceived as personal and even as belonging to a divine order (see LXX Jer 17:5, 7). The broader Greek meaning of *makarios*, suggesting the happiness proper to the gods, has not quite been taken up by the Jewish-Christian congregation that fashioned this confession in Titus. But the congregations in which converts from paganism form a significant part explicitly describe and invoke the one God of Israel as *makarios* (1 Tim 1:11; 6:15). The meaning of the Hebrew *'ašrê*, which had dominated Jewish and Christian use of *makarios* up to this point, begins to fade in these texts. If "the hope" that the Father has revealed in his Son can be acclaimed as *makaria*, then the Father who bestowed this hope can also be acclaimed as "the blessed God."

Reading hope and revelation (*epiphaneia*) in hendiadys amounts to saying "hope revealed." Thus personified, hope will become visible in literally "a revelation of the glory of our great God and savior." The tension within the hendiadys becomes apparent when one recalls the Pauline teaching that "hope that is seen is not hope" (Rom 8:24; cf. Heb 11:1). The unseen focus of the present hope of believers is the risen Jesus, whose glory will become visible at the end of human history. He is the link between the present expectation that believers have of resurrection and the future consummation of life eternal. In Acts 23:6 the way in which "hope" is joined in hendiadys to "the resurrection of the dead" is parallel conceptually to what the confession in Titus means by "the hope and revelation of the glory." Revelation is the object of "the blessed hope," and it is further specified as a revelation "of the glory," a genitive that can be read qualitatively to mean "glorious revelation" or objectively to mean "glory" as the content of "the blessed hope revealed" (cf. BDF §163 with 165). The former is more Lukan and Semitic (BDF, preface to §162); the latter may have been the meaning of this confession as it stood in its source. In any case, the addition of "glory" perhaps serves to distinguish this "epiphany" from that of the incarnation (2 Tim 1:10). In a word, there is a single revelation of Christ that began with his birth and continues to the final Day of the Lord, when it will reach its glorious climax.

The "epiphany" is furthermore a theophany, for Jesus' "glory" is synonymous with that of his Father (*ho theos*). The final, tangible, powerful manifestation of Yahweh in human history will reveal that "the blessed hope" of Christians is himself "the great God and savior," a phrase that in Greek forms another hendiadys, perhaps equivalent to divine savior or saving God and parallel to the preceding "blessed hope and revelation." As *makaria* there suggested a liturgical acclamation, so *megas* here reinforces the eschatological orientation of this confession (see Acts 2:20, citing LXX Joel 3:4 on "the great and manifest [*tēn megalēn kai epiphanē*] day of the Lord") while suggesting its triumphal, public character (see 1 Tim 3:16). An even greater conceptual tension exists in this hendiadys between "God" and "savior" than in the preceding "hope" and "revelation." In the Greek these tensions are finally resolved with the naming of Jesus Christ, who in his person reconciles hidden, present hope with a visibly glorious future appearance, the invisible God of history with a present personal rescuer of his people.

14. *He laid down his life for us, to set us free from every wrong and to cleanse for himself a people of his very own, enthusiastic for fine deeds.* The terminology and the style of the confession change abruptly at this point. The translation represents this shift with a new sentence. In Greek an adjectival clause beginning with *hos*, "who" (referring to Christ) unfolds in three, gradually lengthening stichs. Translated literally, they read,

> who gave himself for us
> so that he might set us free from all lawlessness
> and cleanse for himself a chosen people eager for fine deeds.

The language here is not otherwise characteristic of the PE, but it is conspicuously Septuagintal and reminiscent of the most archaic Christian formulas for expressing what Jesus had done (see Hengel, *BJP*, pp. 78–96, with his references). The initial relative pronoun and the rhythmic structure remind one of such hymnic fragments as 1 Tim 3:16 and 2 Tim 2:11–13. Yet the whole clause is so nicely joined to the preceding verse that, if in fact it is the citation of an archaic Christian hymn, it must have been made by those who originally composed the confession and not by the author of the PE.

The reason for the citation is not far to seek, for its text offers venerable kerygmatic grounds for the opening to the concepts and values of the Hellenistic world represented in vv 11–12. The lives of believers are grounded in their hope in Christ to come, who is identical with the one who was crucified for them. The theology of the cross is not outshone by a theology of glory. The saving "grace of God" that is being confessed in public worship here came definitively into human history on the day that Jesus suffered and died. The voluntary surrender to the cross and death was the only passage into "the blessed hope revealed in" his "glory." This free gift was in its turn understood in the light of the sacrificial worship of Israel, a light refracted through the already archaic formula "for us," which unfolded in the apostolic kerygma that "the Christ died for our sins according to the scriptures" (1 Cor 15:3). Behind both expressions the description of the work of the Isaian Servant can be discerned (Isa 53:4–12), not to mention the pregnant variations of the phrase that are placed on the lips of Jesus as he gives his body and blood to the Twelve before his passion "for you/for many/for the forgiveness of sins/for the life of the world" (*SFG* §311; see Romaniuk, "L'Origine . . . pour nous," pp. 55–76 and Hengel, *Atonement,* pp. 34–38).

The exceedingly dense "for us" now unfolds in the two members of a purposive clause that conceptually expand the pre-Pauline proclamation that "the Christ died for our sins." The death of Jesus took place "to set us free from every wrong and to cleanse for himself a people of his very own." His death was a public sacrificial prayer to the God of Israel for the rescue of his people, a costly rescue expressed with a Greek root (**lytr-*) that refers to ransoming slaves. D. W. Hill emphasizes (*Greek Words,* p. 70) that self-surrender is not quite the same as being compelled to pay a price. The connotations of this cluster of **lytr-* terms were vivid and deeply appealing in the Hellenistic and Roman worlds, where slavery was a major part of daily life (see 2:9–10). If the "for us" of the kerygma is explained as the freeing of slaves, the implication is that there is a sense in which all human beings (not just part of the contemporary society) are in slavery and that the death of Jesus touches all of them precisely as slaves. This universal scope of the redemption appears explicitly in 1 Tim 2:6, where Jesus is confessed as the man "who gave himself as a ransom (*dous heauton antilytron*) for all (*hyper pantōn*)." Both the terminology and the concept appear in the synoptic tradition, when Jesus is represented as saying that the Son of Man has come "to give his life as a ransom (*dounai tēn psychēn autou lytron*) for many (*anti pollōn*)" (Mark 10:45; Matt 20:28; but not in the closest Lukan parallel, *SFG* §263). Luke uses the **lytr-* cluster regularly for the Jewish hope for the redemption of Israel (Luke 1:68; 2:38; 21:28 [see Marshall, *Luke,* p. 777]; 24:21), not of all peoples. Even in Acts 7:35 Moses is *lytrōtēs,* "redeemer," for God's people in Egypt (contrast LXX Ps 18:15; 77:35). The confession here in Titus stands on the trajectory from that quite Hebraic and OT usage to the emphatic universalism of the confession in 1 Tim 2:6. The Hebrew root *gʾl* (regularly = LXX **lytr-*), with its general field of meaning, "to restore/repair," had come to designate political liberation, as the coins of the First Jewish Revolt poignantly illustrate. The *gōʾēl,* "redeemer," is the closest blood relative who stands by and defends a kinsman in trouble. For those in Israel who have no earthly helper, the widow and the orphan or the Hebrew slaves in Egypt, Yahweh himself is *gōʾēl* (see H. Ringgren in *TDOT* 2.350–355).

This OT conception of Yahweh's coming to the rescue of his helpless people becomes here in Titus the means for explaining what Jesus has accomplished by his death on the cross. He "set us free," not in a purely political sense but rather "from every wrong." The echo of the archaic kerygma "The Christ died for our sins" is evident, but here the emphasis is on the whole gamut of human sins within which men and women are caged like slaves. The universality of the liberation corresponds to the universality of persons affected. As Christ died for all, so he died to deliver them from every sin. The term used for sin here adds its own nuance, for the Greek *anomia* is literally "lawlessness," defiance of the *nomos*, which for the Jewish tradition meant defiance of the Torah, the Law par excellence. Thus the Jewish Christian heard this passage as a confession that Christ had freed believers from their violations of the Torah, and by that very fact the continuing relation of all believers to the Law's commands begins to surface. The problem becomes acute when the believers have been pagan, and thus it is addressed explicitly in this correspondence as such congregations are so instructed (see 1 Tim 1:8–11).

After the negative description of the purpose of Jesus' passion, a complementary positive description ensues, the language of which leads back into the cultic traditions of the OT and into the Exodus revelation. The theme of cleansing is not unrelated to the shedding of blood, and otherwise in the NT the terminology of "redemption" is complemented by a reference to the blood of Christ, cleansing the believer (cf. Rom 3:24–25; Eph 1:7 with Heb 9:11–15). That blood is so precious that it has emancipated every human being (cf. 1 Pet 1:18–20 with the *agorasanta*, the "purchasing" in 2 Pet 2:1 and Rev 5:9); and the apostolic church, all of those including Paul and Titus who have put their faith in and accepted this manumission, are not simply the object but also the sign and manifestation of this cleansing to those who have not yet believed. In both the Pauline and the Lukan traditions such cleansing is not simply by faith but is inseparable from the Spirit and the baptismal washing (cf. Acts 15:8–9 with 10:43–44, 47 and 11:16–17). The same elements become explicit in the confession at 3:4–8a.

The cleansing blood of Christ marks out for his own possession "a people" as a special treasure. The Greek phrase represented by "a people of his very own" goes back to the OT narratives of the creation and the deliverance of Israel during the Exodus (see LXX Deut 7:6–8 for Yahweh's redemption [*elytrōseto*] of the *laos periousios*), and ultimately it is rooted in the promise that Yahweh made to the descendants of Abraham, Isaac, and Jacob in Exod 19:5–6, "you shall be my own possession among all peoples; for all the earth is mine, and you shall be to me a kingdom of priests (LXX *basileion hierateuma*) and a holy nation (LXX *ethnos*)." In contrast to 1 Pet 2:9, the confession here in Titus focuses on one phrase of the Exodus promise, which designates a quite personal treasure that belongs in an especially intimate fashion to the person who has picked it, so that it will be with him in a way that other goods are not. Yahweh is ruler of all nations, administering them as a public trust; but Israel is his private property, his privy purse. The special relationship, like marriage, is one of special freedom and intimacy but, for that reason, one that is more demanding and even more threatening.

The mention of Yahweh's own people in a venerable phrase that evoked the election of Israel as a nation mobilized by God himself calls forth a complementary phrase for which the link with the preceding is unclear. Why should "a people of his very own" be explained by "enthusiastic for fine deeds"? In the context of Exodus (20:5), as the covenant commandments are narrated, Yahweh is confessed as "a jealous God," 'el qannā'. But it is only as the OT period is ending that the LXX describes a Jew as zēlōtēs, "a zealous defender" of what God has revealed and that Philo begins to use the term in a negative as well as a positive sense. Josephus offers the key to the changing connotations of the word in the first Christian century. Some highly visible groups in contemporary Palestinian Judaism had interpreted and acted on their interpretation of the assurance that they belonged to a special people. The "zeal" for the Torah that had given birth to Pharisaism also spawned the drastic politics of "the Zealots," fanatically intent upon "the redemption of Zion" from Roman rule at any cost to their own persons and to their countrymen, not to mention their enemies. Their devotion to complete political liberation was as unquenchable as it was irresponsible (at least according to Josephus, whose account is at best the varnished truth). Angry enthusiasts and extremists, embodying a terrifying combination of cold-blooded politics and hot-headed piety, they chose their name shrewdly so that it justified in advance every act that they would perform. Just as democracy is the concern of more than Democrats and the republic of more than Republicans, so zeal for the Torah and God was the concern of more than those who styled themselves Zealots. As Josephus remarked, with bitterness and obvious disgust, these terrorists of the mid-sixties of the first century called themselves Zealots as though they were zealous "in the cause of virtue and not for vice in its basest (zēlōsantes ta kakista tōn ergōn) and most extravagant form" (War 4.161; see 7.268–274; Schürer, HJP 2.598–606 for the literature; R. Horsley, "Zealots," pp. 159–192 for their social origins as well as Horsley and Hanson, Bandits, passim). The author of Luke–Acts seems to have favored the older meaning of zēlōtēs, declining to call the self-appointed executioners of Paul "zealots" though their tactics could have earned them the later title (Acts 23:12–22).

Thus there were zealots and Zealots, and the distinction governs the language of Titus 2:14 at this point. If believers are indeed a chosen people ready for a holy war, if they have in fact become God's own special treasure, it is so that they may be zealous in doing good. They are not to be confused with those Jewish partisans who used God's name and glory to cloak their political maneuverings and ruthless assassinations. Didachē 3.2 sounds very much as if it had been occasioned by the experience of Jewish Christians who had been lured into aligning themselves with the Zealot party, only to discover themselves involved with those who were shedding innocent blood. "Be not wrathful, for wrath leads to murder, nor jealous (*zēlōtēs*) or contentious or irascible, for from all these are murders engendered."

The deep concern of the PE for good works, *erga agatha/kala*, has already appeared in 1:16 and 2:7. In the great confessional formula cited at this point one detects not only an opening to the ethical interests of the Hellenistic world but also a repudiation of a Palestinian political activism that promised to compromise the Jewish-Christian community envisioned by the Letter to Titus. The position endorsed here has also intra-Christian repercussions, which come into sharp focus when one juxtaposes the emphasis of this confession on good deeds and the equally clear affirmation of 3:5 that God "saved us, no thanks to any upright deeds that we performed ourselves but because of his own mercy." The latter affirmation is certainly hewn from the bedrock of Pauline teaching, as is 2 Tim 1:9, describing "the God who saved us and called us for a holy life. That saving call did not correspond to our deeds (*ou kata erga hēmōn*)." As noted at 1:16, the plural *erga* (without further adjectival specification) are at best useless (1:16), if not in fact evil (2 Tim 4:14; see Luke 11:48). The PE, unlike the rest of the Paulines, never mention "the works of the law," and still the unqualified plural *erga* are taken in a bad sense. For that reason the PE, whenever they wish to speak of "deeds" in a good sense, add the qualification *agatha/kala*, "excellent/fine." With these adjectives one encounters the most basic terms for the expression of ethical values in the Hellenistic world.

The Greek *kalos*, always represented in this version of the PE by "fine," designates what is aesthetically pleasing to Greek eyes, the visibly good. The Greek, unlike the English equivalents usually proposed, suggests obligation in the ethical realm (see Owens, "*Kalon*," pp. 263–264, 273–275). Thus when the LXX translates the Hebrew *ṭôb* of Gen 1:4, 8, 10, and so on with *kalon*, it not only suggests the visible, attractive loveliness of creation (cf. LXX Prov 15:30) but also transmits the sense of the original *ṭôb*, that is to say, "good for something." With Wis 13:7, it is in the context of the danger posed by visible loveliness that the author affirms that the visible works of God are beautiful (*kala*; cf. LXX Gen 3:6 of the forbidden fruit). The world is full of the beautiful works of God. In fact, his are the only works that the LXX calls *kala* (Sir 39:16) or *agatha* ("good, excellent"; Sir 39:33). Yet they can be idolized or abused and thus made destructive.

The PE come to grips with the analogous problem in the order of Christian conduct, a world filled with God's good works, a world of visible, attractive, pleasing works created by God. But it is also a world in which one can idolize such works, abuse them, ultimately destroy oneself with them. The risk of moral visibility is that it can result in hypocrisy, the appearance only of goodness (see 2 Tim 3:5). The risk of invisible and unseen goodness is that it says nothing to other persons, whether in the Christian household or in the wider world of unbelievers (cf. 2 Cor 8:21 with LXX Prov 3:4). Inner goodness is indispensable, that moral excellence which motivates human actions and which the Greek *agathos* designates. But the *erga agatha* that God creates in the individual human heart must somehow emerge from the individual and appear before human society. The PE accordingly urge the believer to perform deeds that are both *agatha* and *kala*.

Is it possible to specify further what the PE conceived to be the content of works that are *agatha* or *kala?* It was noted at 1:16 that the singular *ergon* refers to the "work" of ecclesial ministry. The *kala erga* in 2:7 surely include Titus's works of instruction and preaching, visible, impartial, respectable, wholesome, unimpeachable. At 3:8, 14 below the generic direction "to take the lead in fine deeds" is specified in terms of the visible, material support of the apostolic missionaries who are to visit the Cretan churches. The candidate for the widows' order in 1 Tim 5:10 must have public attestation to "fine deeds" such as rearing her family; extending hospitality, particularly to traveling Christians; aiding the oppressed; in a word, the whole gamut of excellent deeds (*pan ergon agathon*). In 1 Tim 5:24–25 not only are some sins "obvious enough" but so are "fine deeds." In 1 Tim 6:17–18 the rich of this world are told "to do good" (*agathoergein;* cf. Acts 14:17, of God), which is explained in the parallel, "to become wealthy in fine deeds," specified in their turn as generosity and readiness to share their goods. Thus deeds, precisely as *kala*, are those which visibly reach out to and involve care for one's neighbors, particularly fellow Christians (see 1 Tim 6:2 on *euergesia* and Jeremias, *NTD*, p. 40).

The specific content of the *ergon agathon* (as distinguished from *kalon*) is more difficult to isolate, for it is regularly used with *pan*, "every," and thus becomes quite general. Still it is notable that such good work is that of everyday life (1:16; 3:1; see 1 Tim 5:10 for the only use of the plural phrase in the PE), a result of the way in which the master of the house chooses to use his vessels (2 Tim 2:21). As the PE conclude in 2 Tim 3:17, the OT scriptures, precisely because "inspired by God," serve to equip completely "the man of God," namely, Timothy, "for every excellent deed" in the apostolic ministry that he shares with Paul.

In summary, for the PE fine or excellent deeds, *erga kala/agatha*, are radically God's work, not "our works." The latter come under the Pauline critique of 3:5 and 2 Tim 1:9; *erga kala/agatha* are never qualified as *hēmōn* or *hymōn*, "ours" or "yours." In the deepest sense, we do not do them. Yet they are not only good but palpably, verifiably, attractively good. They are the "works of charity" and those of everyday honest living. They are a work or works that must be characteristic of those who share in the apostolic ministry (see 1:8 on the bishop as "one who likes guests, likes goodness [*philagathon*]").

In summary retrospect, liturgical and hymnic traditions seem to resonate at every turn throughout this great confession of the faith as the matrix for Christian living. Thus its pivotal proclamation about "the glory of Jesus Christ" leads one into the correspondence with Timothy and its description of what constitutes the gospel entrusted to Paul, "the good news of the glory of the blessed

God" (1 Tim 1:11), not to mention the great doxological formula that concludes the prayer to the risen Jesus in 1 Tim 1:12–17 (cf. 2 Tim 2:10 with 4:18) and the final stich of the hymnic fragment in 1 Tim 3:16. There is no controverting the typically Hellenistic language of Titus 2:11–14; still it is no less the language of the communal articulation of the Christian faith in Christian liturgical worship. The echoes of acclamation, prayer, and hymn—often leading back into the archaic Palestinian Jewish churches, with their apocalyptic fervor—may indicate here a contribution from the prophetic order within the Jewish-Christian community envisioned in Titus, a contribution that aimed to give a memorable form, intelligible to Hellenistic believers, to the apocalyptic content of the old Palestinian *didachē*.

II.B.3. THE BAPTISMAL LIFE (2:15–3:11)
II.B.3.a. OBEDIENCE VERSUS DISOBEDIENCE: PRESENT VERSUS PAST (2:15–3:2)

2 ¹⁵These are the things to speak of, Titus, in as commanding a way as possible, whether you are encouraging or refuting. Let no one slight you. 3 ¹Remind these Jewish Christians

to be subject to government authorities,
to accept direction,
to be ready to take any honest work.
²They are not to insult anyone,
    not to be argumentative.
They are to be gentle,
    to show every consideration to every person.

NOTES

2:15. *These are the things to speak of, Titus, in as commanding a way as possible, whether you are encouraging or refuting.* Literally, "Speak these things (*tauta*) and encourage and refute." The singular imperative address with the repetition of *lalei* from 2:1 marks another stage in the exposition. *Didaske*, "teach," is the reading of A at this point, specifying the sense of *lalei* that in classical Greek means "to chatter" (J. K. Elliott, *Greek Text*, p. 188). On "encourage" and "refute" see 1:9. The pronominal *tauta* is used regularly in the PE not only to refer to what has preceded (3:8) but also to introduce another step in the exposition (1 Tim 3:14; 4:6, 11; 6:2; 2 Tim 2:14).

"In as commanding a way as possible" is literally "with all command (*epitagēs*)." On *epitagē* see NOTES at 1:3; however, the phrase *meta* (*pasēs*) *epitagēs* is not documented otherwise in biblical Greek, the Ap. Frs., or the Apologists. Theodoret understands the phrase as equivalent to *syn parrēsiai*, "with open frankness" (D-C, p. 146) and the Old Latin translated *cum omni imperio*, which Jerome understood with *increpa*, "rebuke," and not with the two preceding verbs (see *VL* 25[2].911–912; *PL* 26.589). The reading *hyptagēs* (442, 463, and Syr^pal), "subordination/subordinating," is hardly intelligible Greek.

Let no one slight you. Periphronein, "slight," is not otherwise attested in the NT or Ap. Frs. In the LXX, however, it appears in 4 Macc 6:9; 7:16; and 14:1 of martyrs scorning torture. Early medieval scribes sought at times to assimilate this phrase to 1 Tim 4:12, reading "slight your *youth*" (PSI) or substituting the synonym *kataphroneitō* (P, 919, 1, 243, etc.). Jerome sensed a distinction between the verbs (*On Titus, PL* 26.589–590), noting that *kataphronein* designates contempt properly speaking (see Heb 12:2), while *periphronein* can mean contempt for another joined with an inflated notion of one's own importance. Aristophanes' usage illustrates the point, as the playwright has Strepsiades (alias Socrates) proclaim twice in the *Clouds*, "I am walking in the air and I 'contemn-plate' (*periphronō*) the sun" (225, 1503; see B. B. Rogers in the LCL *ad loc.*). The term from Thucydides to Josephus often casts a shadow of insolence (see Spicq, *Lexic.*, pp. 690–691 for texts).

3:1. *Remind these Jewish Christians*. The abrupt transition, the hidden antecedent for the pronominal "these," and the asyndetic list that follows have provoked a flurry of connective particles in the manuscript tradition of this whole verse. All of them melt away under textual criticism (J. K. Elliott, *Greek Text*, pp. 211–212, 216). The same singular imperative address, *hypomimnēiske*, recurs in 2 Tim 2:14, with perhaps a different shade of meaning (BAGD). Although the term does not otherwise turn up in the Paulines, Luke uses it of Peter being reminded of the prediction of his denial (22:61, with the genitive). The only other NT uses are in the Johannine corpus (John 14:26, of the Paraclete, with the accusative; 3 John 10) and in 2 Pet 1:12 and Jude 5. The usage of the Ap. Frs. corresponds to the "remind" of Titus (*1 Clem.* 7.1; 62.2–3; *Barn.* 12.2), and the four appearances in the LXX have this meaning too: Wis 12:2 (of the spirit); 18:22 (of Moses reminding God of the promises to the patriarchs); and 3 Kgdms 4:3 and 4 Macc 18:4, both of written reminders (see *T. Levi* 9.6–7).

to be subject to government authorities. See 2:5 on "to be subject." In Greek a septuple, asyndetic list begins at this point with *archais exousiais*, literally, "rulers authorities." The phrase is no less harsh in English than in the original (BDF §460.1). The intrusive *kai* in later witnesses is an attempt to ease the asyndeton (B. Metzger, *TCGNT*, p. 655) and a material harmonization with "the rulers and (*kai*) powers" of Eph 3:10 (cf. 6:12) and Col 2:15 (cf. Col 1:16 with correlative *eite* and the virtually plural and anarthrous uses in Eph 1:21; Col 2:10). The phrase thus read with *kai* would refer to angelic rulers (Lohse, *Col.*, ad loc.), a meaning that appears in the reference of 1 Cor 15:24 to Christ annihilating finally "every ruler [cf. Rom 8:38] and every authority and power (*dynamin*)" (with Conzelmann, *1 Cor.*, pp. 271–272 *contra* Carr, *Angels*, pp. 90–92). As will become evident in what follows, this admonition does not refer to spirits, and the *kai* is positively mischievous (*pace* J. K. Elliott, *Greek Text*, pp. 211–212).

The PE nowhere else speak of "rulers," *archai*. Eight of the ten uses in the rest of Paulines, as just noted, refer to spirits; however, it is difficult to find a trace of this meaning in the forty-four other occurrences of *archē* in the NT (but see Jude 6) or in the usage of the Ap. Frs. The plural of human beings appears only in Luke 12:11 (see Marshall, *Luke*, p. 520 and Mark 13:11 in *SFG* §289). There the evangelist adds detail about the moment "when they haul you before the (*tas*) synagogues, and the rulers and authorities (*tas archas kai tas exousias*)." Evidently here the bound phrase *archai kai exousiai* means the civil judicial authorities (see Plato, *Alcibiades*, 1.135AB) as distinct from those of the Jewish synagogues (see the more abstract singular in Luke 20:20, when Jesus' enemies sought "to deliver him over to the rule and authority (*tēi archēi kai tēi exousiai*)" of the governor. The Ap. Frs. do not employ the phrase at all, though it surfaces again in *Mart. Pol.* 10.2 as the old bishop, Polycarp, testifies to his judge, "We have been taught to give due honor to rulers and authorities." Justin uses the phrase, however, in a Pauline form to mean angelic spirits (*Dialogue* 120 *ad fin.*), as does the *T. Solomon* 20.15. The phrase is non-Septuagintal, though the language of LXX Dan 7:27 may offer a background for it (see Carr, *Angels*, pp. 25–43).

"Authorities," *exousiai*, appears only here in the PE but 101 times in the rest of the NT; by contrast, the plural is found only seven other times, usually in tandem with *archai* (see citations above) but once with angels and powers (1 Pet 3:22; cf. *Ascension of Isaiah* 1.3 with *T. Levi* 3.7–8) and once by itself in Rom 13:1 meaning "civil authorities" (for the dispute here, see BAGD s.v.; Käsemann, *Rom.*, pp. 350–354; Cranfield, *Rom.*, pp. 656–663). The Ap. Frs. never use the plural, and the LXX employs it only twice, in both instances to mean secular authorities (Esth 8.12e; Dan 7:27).

to accept direction. Peitharchein, "to accept direction," appears otherwise in the NT only in Acts 5:29 and 32, of those who accept God's direction, not men's, as well as in 27:21, of Paul's advice to winter in Crete. In the Ap. Frs. only Pol. *Phil.* 9.1 employs this verb to urge the Philippian believers "to accept the direction of the word (*logoi*) of righteousness," even to martyrdom. In the LXX Dan 7:27 (already noted several times) this verb describes the eschatological turning of the tables when all of the earth's rulers will follow the directions of "the holy people of the Most High." The only other Septuagintal uses are in

1 Esdr 8:94 (of the law) and Sir 33:29 (of a slave's duty to take his master's direction). On the etymological development of the compound meaning "to obey one in authority," see *DELG* s.v. *peithomai;* for the meanings, see Spicq, *Lexic.*, pp. 676–678; for the construction with the dative, G. Horsley, *NDIEC* 2.104 §82.

to be ready to take any honest work. The phrase comes from 1:16 with "ready," *hetoimos,* replacing "unfit" there. The PE do not otherwise use *hetoimos,* though the cognate verb occurs when 2 Tim 2:21 takes up this phrase again. Construing *hetoimos* with *pros,* literally "ready for," instead of *eis,* is rare in biblical Greek (1 Pet 3:15; Tob 5:17) and is not found in the Ap. Frs. A variation between *pros* and *eis* may pertain to current Greek idiomatic style (Moule, *Idiom,* p. 68) and may thus be conceptually of no consequence. *Hetoimos* appears in the other Paulines only in 2 Cor 9:5; and 10:6, 16. The thirteen other NT uses are closer to the usage here in Titus (see Luke 12:40; 14:17; 22:23; Acts 23:15, 21). The Ap. Frs. employ *hetoimos* fewer than a dozen times, principally Ignatius, but *1 Clem.* 2.7 may be quoting Titus (or the list that served as a source at this point) when he writes nostalgically to the troubled Corinthian church, "You were without misgiving in doing every kind of good, ready for every good work (*hetoimoi eis pan ergon agathon*)." Ignatius (in *Pol.* 7.3) expresses this concept but with some different terms when he writes, "For I believe by grace that you are ready for performing well the things (*hetoimoi este eis eupoiïan*) proper to God."

2. *They are not to insult anyone, not to be argumentative.* See 2:5 on "insult." "Argumentative" represents *amachos,* an adjective found again in 1 Tim 3:3 but nowhere else in biblical Greek (though the adverb in the variant of Sir 19:6 is for that reason notable) or the Ap. Frs. The meaning here is unusual for a Greek term that ordinarily meant "unbeatable" with some martial connotation (thus always in Philo and Josephus; cf. even Menander, *Dyscolos* 193, 775, 869–870; K334/403.6; see LSJ s.v.). A couple of sepulchral inscriptions, however, use *amachos* in the sense that it has here in Titus: for example, "I lived without fighting with friends and relatives," circa third century C.E., MM s.v. In the seventh century, Leontius Neapolitanus writes of human beings who are "as angels, not quarrelsome and judgmental" (Lampe, *PGL,* s.v.).

They are to be gentle, to show every consideration to every person. Epieikēs, "gentle," recurs in the list of episcopal virtues in 1 Tim 3:3. Similar lists are the context for this term in its other appearances in the NT (Jas 3:17 [see Dibelius, *James,* pp. 213–214]; 1 Pet 2:18, of pagans in a domestic code). The nominal use of the adjective in Phil 4:5, "Let your gentleness be known to every person," its only remaining NT occurrence, resembles the phrase about "consideration" that follows here in Titus. In the Ap. Frs., *epieikēs* occurs only in *1 Clem.* and Hermas, and only twice in the LXX, once about the Lord (LXX Ps 85:5; cf. *Ep. Arist.* 211 with *1 Clem.* 29.1) and once about a human ruler (LXX Esth 3:13b).

"To show," *endeiknymenous,* is literally "evidencing," as in 2:10. S* reads *endeiknysthai,* harmonizing the participle (understood with *einai*) with all of the infinitives in this list (J. K. Elliott, *Greek Text,* p. 189).

"Every consideration to every person." On *pros pantas anthrōpous,* literally, "for all human beings," see 2:11, *pasin anthrōpois.* The prepositional phrase here does not recur in the PE, but it is found in Acts 22:15 of Paul's witness to the risen Jesus. The particle *pros* here, as in 2 Tim 2:24, suggests a friendly, affective relationship (B. Reicke in *TDNT* 6.723).

"Every consideration," *pasan . . . praütēta,* becomes in S* *spoudēn,* "earnestness" (cf. Heb 6:11), with *ta* beginning the following line. The reading is indefensible, its origin inexplicable (for attempts see J. K. Elliott, *Greek Text,* p. 190). *Praütēs* recurs in the conclusion of the catalog of virtues for the Lord's servant in 2 Tim 2:25 (cf. *praüpathia,* 1 Tim 6:11). Six of the nine other NT occurrences are in the Paulines, once with *epieikeia,* of Christ (2 Cor 10:1; cf. *Diog.* 7.4), more often in lists of Christian virtues (Gal 5:23; Eph 4:2; Col 3:12). *Didache* 5.2 (see *Barn.* 20.2) also uses *praütēs* in a list, as do *1 Clem.* 21.7 (with *epieikēs*) and 30.8 (with *epieikeia*). Of the ten Septuagintal uses of *praütēs/praotēs,* LXX Ps 44:5 lists this noun between truth and righteousness (cf. *T. Judah* 24.1), and Sir has it in tandem with faith (1:27; 45:4) and mercy (36:23). The **praü-/praö* cluster in the LXX, when it has a Hebrew equivalent, corresponds to some form of *ʿnh/ʿnw* in the MT and the Hebrew fragments of Sir. The Semitic root denotes a lowly person, without property, who makes his living by serving others; the Greek root (both etymologically and semantically related to the English "friendly") covers the same field of meaning as *hēmeros,* namely, humane, civilized, even tamed (*DELG,* s.v.).

COMMENT

2:15. *These are the things to speak of, Titus, in as commanding a way as possible, whether you are encouraging or refuting. Let no one slight you.* This transitional sentence initiates another stage in the paraenesis of the epistle. The repetition of the imperatival "speak" from 2:1 refers the reader to the immediately preceding teaching for diverse groups within the household of believers; the phrase about "encouraging or refuting" is verbally reminiscent of the charge for presbyter-bishops in 1:9 and the summary description of true versus false teaching that occupies the remainder of that chapter, in which Titus himself is to refute the Jewish Christians who contradict Pauline doctrine (1:13) as he is himself to encourage believers (2:6). Five uses of the singular address in this verse and the following (surpassing even 1:5) serve to emphasize the person of *Titus* (whose name has been added to the translation in order to bring out this point). The emphasis of the text at this juncture reminds the reader that Titus functions literarily as an ideal or paradigmatic figure in his relation to Paul (as the apostle's "child," 1:4) and in his relation to the Jewish-Christian household that he teaches and guides (as "a pattern in fine deeds," 2:7).

In the INTRODUCTION to this volume, with the help of Benjamin Fiore's analysis, two characteristic features of Hellenistic epistolary paraenesis emerged in the PE: directives to junior executives about the way in which they and their charges ought to think and act; then, prescriptions for conduct that would harmonize with the practice of a particular philosophical tradition or school. Ideal figures from the past ground such paraenesis in history; the paraenesis itself professes to preserve and hand on the teaching of these persons to another generation. Because paraenesis presupposes the irrefutable character of its traditional guidance, it gives rise to questions about the authority of Paul's "child" to transmit such guidance. Hence, at precisely this point in the Letter to Titus, the continuity of his authority with that of Paul receives dramatic emphasis. There is to be no appeal to the apostolic father over his son's head.

The authorization of Titus derives from the "slave of God, yet apostle of Jesus Christ" (1:1), who has in his turn imposed these tasks by virtue of his own commission "at the order of our savior, God" (1:3). The imperial authority, the *imperium* of God (thus the evocative translation of the Old Latin here as well as at 1:3 and 1 Tim 1:1 [*VL* 25(1).392, (2).854, 911]) through Paul, enters the ecclesial household in the teaching and direction of Titus. He stands in the assembly with Paul's letter as if he were a Roman consul with the Senate's brief. He is to brook no contemptuous dismissal but to challenge the opposition to a clear decision. The confrontation between Popilius Laenas and Antiochus Epiphanes in 168 B.C. outside of Alexandria in Egypt was a commonplace in the ancient historians (see Livy 45.12.1–6; Polybius, *Histories* 29.27.1–6; Appian, *Roman History* (*Syrian Wars*) 11.66; Diodorus Siculus 31.2.1–2). The Roman consul handed the Senate's letter to the Syrian king, who asked for time to consider its proposal at leisure. Popilius with his staff drew a circle in the sand around the royal adventurer and said, "Think about it here." Antiochus promptly abandoned his foray into Egypt. Some such conception of and confident conviction about the hegemony of the apostle and his coworker stand behind the phraseology of this epistle, as the author here stamps its paraenesis with the cachet of apostolic authority.

3:1. *Remind these Jewish Christians to be subject to government authorities, to accept direction, to be ready to take any honest work.* With the fifth and final imperative address that opens this verse, the reason for the emphatic reaffirmation of apostolic power at the opening of this transitional paragraph (2:15–3:2) becomes more easily recognizable. The traditional chapter division at this point made the reference to "these Jewish Christians" (represented in Greek by the pronoun *autous* alone) somewhat clearer. The household code with its liturgico-catechetical summary that occupied 2:1–14 is now formally set aside, and the exposition returns to the Jewish-Christian opponents who were refuted as "refractory (*anypotaktoi*)" and "disobedient abominations, counterfeiters of all excellent deeds (*apeitheis . . . pros pan ergōn agathōn*)" (1:10, 16). As in that passage, so here Titus himself is to confront the opponents. Whereas he refuted them there (1:13), now he is to inculcate positive attitudes and acts that are verbally opposite to vices previously scored ("to be subject, to accept direction, to be ready to take any honest work" represent the Greek *hypotassesthai, peitharchein, pros pan ergon agathon . . .*). This rhetorical flashback, somewhat abrupt for modern tastes, has its precedents in Paul himself (thus Rom 9:30–10:21 divide the remainder of Rom 9 from 11; similarly, 1 Cor 13 on charity divides 1 Cor 12 from 14 on the charisms).

The present imperative "remind" has an iterative nuance, as if to say "keep reminding" these Jewish-Christian opponents of an ethical commitment as well as of a creedal one that they share with the Pauline tradition. They have known their duties long since, and the septuple list that begins in 3:1 is adduced as a tradition that the opposition will recognize to be one that they had received as authoritative. The content thus requires no further demonstration or argument.

A tentative origin may be inferred for such a catechesis. Its acceptance by Jewish-Christian opponents of the Pauline teaching appears to confirm its Jewish-Christian origin. The fact that insubordination to "government authorities" heads the list suggests that the original audience for this moral formation (not to mention the present opponents of the Pauline teaching) were Jewish converts whose sympathies and even convictions had been with the Palestinian revolutionaries in A.D. 66–70. It is notable in this connection that the household code cited in the previous chapter, though it had an already conventional wisdom about "liberation movements" on the part of women and slaves (2:5, 9), has nothing to say about those who wanted at any cost to be free of the Roman *imperium*. The case is otherwise with the oblique reference to "zealots for fine deeds," which climaxes the creedal confession of 2:11–14. The hint there comes into sharper focus in this traditional list.

Paul had certainly dispensed counsel to the Roman Christians on the subject of civil obedience in the late fifties (Rom 13:1–7); Ernst Bammel ("Rom 13," p. 370) has suggested traces of Zealot agitation in some groups there (cf. the "insurgents" of Rom 13.2 with the divisive people in 16:17; Benko, "Criticism," pp. 1060–1061). Yet this list in Titus has hardly two words in common with Rom (*exousiais hypotassesthai/-thō*). There is even less verbal correspondence with the conceptually similar paraenesis in 1 Pet 2:13–17. Accordingly, it looks as if the author of the PE, for all his veneration for Paul and Paul's teaching, cited at this point not the actual text of the apostle but an already traditional list of Jewish-Christian origin. The brief intersection of this list with Rom in the words "to be subject to authorities" is precisely the sort of didactic "bumper sticker" that passes down in catechesis and exhortation without having a firm anchor in a text. It is conceivable that the original list read *archais hypotassesthai*, "be subject to governors," and that a redactor glossed *archais* with *exousiais* to harmonize it with the familiar Pauline slogan. He did not join the terms with *kai* lest they be confused with the bound phrase that in the Pauline tradition referred to angelic spirits.

The Jewish-Christian converts to whom the admonitions of this list were originally directed would have been already closely identified with the synagogue. There would have been as little point in reminding them to be subject to its rulers as in reminding them to be subject to the angels. Nonetheless, if after the debacle of the Palestinian revolt displaced and disillusioned rebels, many of them sold into slavery, felt the attraction of the Christian messianic faith of their Jewish confreres, then a group appears on the historical scene who would not readily forget their former activities in the cause of national liberation. They may have conceived themselves as changing allegiance from one apocalyptic movement to another, and their unchanged nationalistic zeal held them on a collision course with the Roman *imperium*. Thus their catechesis immediately had confronted them with "be subject to" governors. There was to be no mistaking the reference to authorities in general (as the asyndeton suggests) and to those of this world.

Where is the place for such a meeting of established and uncompromised Jewish-Christian congregations with Jewish colleagues tainted with rebellion? The city of Rome appears most likely, probably in one of the more conservative Jewish-Christian house churches (see INTRODUCTION), possibly in what is now Trastevere, where Philo knew there was a large Jewish population (as many as fifty thousand). They were mostly descended from persons captured and enslaved by the Roman legions in Asia but by Augustus' time were Roman citizens who sent yearly tithes to Jerusalem, who met for study and worship in special buildings, who received monthly food and support from the imperial bounty (with special treatment when that distribution fell on the sabbath; see Philo, *Spec. leg.* 155–158). Devout Jews with such a history would hardly turn their backs on the waves of their Palestinian countrymen, "numberless thousands" (*infinita milia captivorum*, Jerome, *On Jeremiah* 6.18.6 [CCL 74.307]) captured and enslaved after the fall of Jerusalem in A.D. 70 and brought to Rome. Seven hundred were brought to ornament the triumph of the Flavians alone (see Josephus, *War* 6.417–418; 7.118, 138). Perhaps many more were purchased by Roman Jews who remembered their own history in the city, not to mention Deut 15:12–15. In any case, their countrymen must have sought out and consoled this pitiable addition to their diaspora, inviting them to join their religious assemblies (see Smallwood, *Jews*, pp. 327, 367, 519–520).

The Roman Jewish community does not appear to have had central coordination as the Christian era opened (see Brown and Meier, *Antioch/Rome*, p. 101; Bammel, "Rom 13," p. 368). Thus Jewish-Christian house churches, particularly the more traditional ones, would have found it simple to step forward with their Jewish confreres to offer assistance to this first wave of a new diaspora of their fellow Jews. It is in some such setting that the list of virtues in 3:1–2 could have originated, as Roman Jewish-Christian hosts sought to assuage the despair, shame, and anger of their disillusioned compatriots. With minimal adjustments the catalog continued to prove useful, and the author of Titus intended it to be used generally in Jewish-Christian congregations of the second apostolic generation, as they continued to deal for decades with these displaced persons.

The second entry in this catalog, "to accept direction," *peitharchein,* echoes the *archais,* "rulers," of the first admonition in the original list. But *peitharchein* suggests a willingness to listen to the directions of a leader and openness to persuasion to serve the common good according to his guidance. Thus Menander's Sostratos, told to dig the soil like a poor farmer, replies in a phrase that resonates with this part of Titus, *hetoimos panta peitharchein,* "I'm ready to do all I'm told" (*Dyscolos* 370). In Aeschylus, *Persians* 374, the oarsmen respond to their captains' orders *peitharchōi phreni,* "with a heart ready to obey."

The two verbs that have opened this list complement each other in meaning, and their emphatic position indicates what the original list, as well as the author of Titus, considered the virtues most needed by new waves of Jewish-Christian converts. Because the author of Titus has composed this message for and addressed it to Jewish Christians on "Crete," perhaps the addressees are meant to infer that this obedience extends to bad governors and governments as well as good, for the Cretan constitution and political life prompted one ancient historian to remark that it was almost "impossible to find . . . personal conduct more treacherous or public policy more unjust than in Crete" (Polybius, *Histories* 6.47.5; see 6.46.1–47.6).

The third admonition, "to be ready to take any honest work," suggests in its context that there are other jobs or works that these converts are quite ready for but which are not being encouraged (as the assassins in Acts 23:15, 21 are "ready" but for no good deed). The phrase here designates a spontaneous, voluntary readiness for any kind of good activity, over and above accepting and carrying out the directions of public authorities. Thus the catechesis forestalled a legalistic recalcitrance that would interpret the admonition to be subordinate and open to direction as if it meant that one had to wait for commands and instructions for any good activity. No warrant is given here for indolent aloofness. The new diaspora is not a nobility in exile. Honest work of whatever sort is not beneath them.

2. *They are not to insult anyone, not to be argumentative. They are to be gentle, to show every consideration to every person.* The catalog centers on a pair of complementary negative admonitions, which would again be peculiarly apt for Jews who had been partisans in the Zealot cause. In this connection particularly, the suggestion that some of these slaves had been Essenes is attractive (Hinson, "Essene Influence," pp. 697–701). The careful delimitations on hatred in their rules suggest that it was a problem for the members of the sect (see Sutcliffe, "Hatred," pp. 349–352). Even more than the unbelievers of 2:5 and 1 Tim 6:1, they are touchy and aggressive, looking for trouble; flaring up at any

criticism, real and imagined; scorching anyone in range of their insulting mockery. More than the congregation of believers is imperiled by such divisive language (see 1 Tim 1:20; 6:4), for these vanquished patriots wanted to heat up the fires more, bringing the Jewish Christians on any pretext into a blazing confrontation with the Roman authorities. The congregation that originally designed this catechesis had been intent on putting out such fires for obvious political reasons, not simply because of their specifically Christian ethos. Those who had once insulted everybody now, as Christians, "are not to insult anyone," not even those who have hurt and insulted them. The author of Titus has a further reason for retaining this admonition, a Pauline reason. The apostolate to pagans was and remains the will of the risen Jesus. It is being endangered by disaffected malcontents who think that they run the control board for the end of history and the consummation of the kingdom of God.

It is notable that the author of this letter did not recognize (or at least was not disturbed by) any inconsistency between what he urged here and the polemic with which he had scored the same opponents in 1:10–16. Such inconsistency is of course no monopoly of this author; it appears earlier in the Paul of history (contrast 1 Cor 4:12; Rom 12:14 with Gal 5:12; Phil 3:2, 19) and later in letters emanating from the community of the beloved disciple (see Brown, *AB Epistles*, p. 808, under "Love, narrowness"). It is a reminder that even the apostolic work and teaching come in and through human work and teaching, marked by human limitations and sin.

As the preceding phrase implied picking a fight verbally, its complement, "not to be argumentative," recommends being a noncombatant (see Aelian, *Tactica* 2.2; eds., H. Koechly and W. Rüstow, *Griechische Kriegsschriftsteller*, vol. 2.1; Leipzig: Engelmann, 1855) in speech. The "wranglings about the Law" in 3:9 may be in view here.

These men, whose working model of fortitude was a rudeness that rode roughshod over friend and foe alike, are urged "to be gentle, to show every consideration to every person," a pair of positive complementary phrases that contrast with the preceding negative pair. The attitude being inculcated seems to belong to a traditional paraenesis, already exploited by Paul. Here in Titus, the language does not suggest that those being addressed are superiors. Rather, as Ragnar Leivestad ("Meekness," pp. 157–164) has shown, gentleness or lenience is in the biblical tradition a virtue for the weak as well as for the powerful. Similarly, "consideration," for all its profane application to divine and human authorities, is not employed thus in biblical Greek. Rather, with telegraphic density these terms may have suggested (at least for the author of Titus) the Pauline appeal "through the gentleness and consideration of Christ" to refractory Corinthian believers, an appeal to the humbled and weak Messiah of the apostolic kerygma (2 Cor 10:1). Paul's proclamation was meant for every human being; so the conduct of Jews and pagans alike who put their faith in it must mirror Jesus' own attitude in suffering.

The succinct "to be gentle" is complemented by a leisurely and solemn embolism devoted to "consideration." Such an expansion has marked the style of these lists before (1:9; 2:4, 6, 10); still, in this case the formal resemblances to 2:10 are striking. Note the repetition of *endeiknymenous*, the forms of *pas* that introduce and conclude the clause, the alliteration with *p* (more conspicuous here). Perhaps the author of Titus is of set purpose alluding to the previous directives for slaves, delicately reminding the recipients of his catechesis about their current status. In any case, it looks as if a Pauline redactor's hand has appeared in the missionary vision of the closing phrase as it emphatically extends "every consideration to every person." The partisan, divisive strategy of the Zealots is to give way before the ecclesial mission valued highly by the Pauline tradition and the PE, a mission that is visible not only in the words of the apostolic heralds but also in their lives and in the lives of all who take their words to heart.

II.B.3.b. THE BAPTISMAL EVENT
(3:3–8a)

3   ³After all, we were once

fools ourselves,
disobedient,
deluded,
slaving for diverse lusts and pleasures,
in malice and jealousy spending our days,
detested,
hating one another.

⁴"When the humane munificence of our savior, God, was revealed, ⁵he saved us, no thanks to any upright deeds that we performed ourselves but because of his own mercy, saved us through a washing of regeneration and of renewal from the Holy Spirit ⁶that he poured out lavishly on us, through Jesus Christ, our savior. ⁷God's was the grace that made us upright, so that we could become heirs with a hope of life eternal." ⁸ªThat is the Christian message, meant to be believed.

NOTES

3:3. *After all, we were once fools ourselves, disobedient, deluded.* "After all, we were once . . . ourselves" translates a cumbersome but emphatic Greek *ēmen gar pote kai hēmeis.* Scribes sought to streamline the phrase by writing *kai hēmeis pote* (P, PSI, 81, etc.) or by omitting *kai* altogether (1319), but the gangling original stands (see J. K. Elliott, *Greek Text*, pp. 190, 212). The enclitic particle *pote*, "once," occurs nowhere else in the PE but nineteen times in other Paulines. In the Lukan corpus, Luke 22:32 alone uses the particle, but of the future.

"Fools, disobedient" represent an opening pair of alpha privatives, *anoētoi, apeitheis*, in an asyndetic septet; scribes have attempted to soften its relentless staccato by inserting *kai* at various points (J. K. Elliott, *Greek Text*, p. 212). On *apeitheis* see 1:16. *Anoētos* qualifies "lusts," *epithymiai*, when it recurs in 1 Tim 6:9 (cf. *anoia* in 2 Tim 3:9). Paul applies the word only to his non-Greek converts (Gal 3:1, 3; Rom 1:14). In its one other NT occurrence, in Luke 24:25, Jesus thus scores some of his Jewish disciples. The LXX uses the term seldom, but the occurrences in the sapiential strata are notable (thus LXX Prov 15:21; 17:28; Sir 21:19; 42:8). Three of the four uses in the Ap. Frs. are in *1 Clem.* and Hermas. Particularly suggestive is *1 Clem.* 21.5, "Let us rather offend men who are thoughtless and foolish (*anoētois*) and arrogant and boastful."

"Deluded" represents *planōmenoi*, which will recur twice in 2 Tim 3:13 of "charlatans . . . deluding and deluded" (cf. *planos* in 1 Tim 4:1 and *apoplanasthai* in 1 Tim 6:10). The other Paulines know the verb only in the warning, "Be not deluded" (1 Cor 6:9; 15:33; Gal 6:7). The one use in the Lukan corpus (Luke 21:8) is similar. Matthew and Rev share between them almost half of thirty-three other NT uses (see Brown, *AB Epistles*, pp. 206–207, who notes the links to false prophets and surveys the usage of the LXX, Qumran, and *T. 12 Patr.*). In the Ap. Frs., Ignatius normally uses (with slight variants) the Pauline phrase cited above; however, Ign. *Magn.* 8.1, "Do not be deluded by heterodoxies," is not far from the usage of the PE; neither is *Did.* 6.1, "See 'that no one makes you err' (*planēsei;* Matt 24:4) from this Way of the Teaching (*tēs didachēs*), for he teaches you without God." Of the occurrences in *1 Clem.*, the most significant is the petition in the list of intercessions in 59.4, "Bring back those of your people who have strayed (*planōmenous*)." The ethical sense of *planan* (which basically refers to physical wandering, as in the original sense of the term *planet*) occurs in secular Greek. Thus in Menander's *Perikeiromenē* 268–269, Moschion says to Davos of the unfounded rumors that he has brought on other occasions, "You are a braggart (*alazōn;* see 2 Tim 3:2) and an enemy of the gods. Now, however, if you're misleading (*planais*) me," to which Davos retorts, "Hang me on the spot if I mislead (*ei planō*)" (contrast *Epitrepontes* 486). In the Greek *Enoch* 19.1 and then in the epistolary appendix of that work, *planan* and its cognates have both a doctrinal and an ethical sense (97.10; 98.16 [see 98.15, *planēsis*]; 99.8 [see 99.1, *planēma;* 99.7, *planē;* 99.14, *planēsis*] 99.10 *bis;* 104.9).

Slaving for diverse lusts and pleasures. Douleuontes, "slaving," is cognate with *dedoulomenas* in 2:3, of older women "who have been enslaved" by drunkenness. *Douleuein* occurs once more in the PE in 1 Tim 6:2, where it has its normal secular, sociological sense, "to do a slave's work," a meaning comparatively rare in the almost two dozen other NT uses of the verb (see, e.g., Rom 9:12; Eph 6:7). In the Pauline tradition a Christian ethical sense predominates. In a good sense one "slaves" for Christ the Lord, for the gospel, for God, for fellow believers (see Rom 12:11; 14:18; Col 3:24; Phil 2:22; 1 Thess 1:9; Gal 5:13). Already in Romans an ethical dialectic has developed, contrasting slaving for "the law of God" or for "Christ our Lord" with enslavement to the flesh or the belly (Rom 7:25; 16:18). Slavery to God stands in contradiction to slavery to sin (Rom 6:6; cf. 7:5–6), to say nothing of slaving for false gods (Gal 4:8–9).

Outside the Pauline tradition, the ethical sense of *douleuein* is taken up in the Lukan tradition when the author incorporates the parabolic logion of Jesus about the choice that has to be made between slaving for God or slaving for money (Luke 16:13 = Matt 6:24). This dialectic appears to bracket Paul's self-description in Acts 20:18–19 and 33, as he begins by telling the Ephesian presbyter-bishops that he had lived among them "slaving for the Lord with all humility and with tears and with trials" and closes by asserting, "I lusted after nobody's silver or gold or garments." The secular sense appears in the parable of the prodigal when the elder son invidiously calls his work for his father "slaving" for him (Luke 15:29; see also Acts 7:6–7).

For *"lusts"* see 2:12. S* added *en* before *epithymiais*, possibly by dittography (J. K. Elliott, *Greek Text*, p. 190). In 2 Tim 3:6 the "lusts" are qualified as "diverse"; here in Titus the adjective *poikilais* follows the phrase "lusts and pleasures." *Poikilos* never appears otherwise in the Paulines (though see Eph 3:10 for the wisdom of God as *polypoikilos*, "manifold"). Those afflicted "with various illnesses *(nosois poikilois)*" are brought to Jesus for a cure in Luke 4:40 (see Mark 1:34; Matt 4:24). The word qualifies "strange teachings" as well as miracles in Heb 2:4 and 13:9. Both Jas 1:2 and 1 Pet 1:6 thus qualify "trials," but in 1 Pet 4:10 it is "the grace of God" that is *poikilē*. The variety designated in most of these instances (diseases, lusts, pleasures, odd doctrines, trials) is not particularly attractive. Yet the semantic pattern is not consistent. There are more than two dozen uses of the adjective in the LXX, mostly in Gen and the Maccabean corpus, where *poikilos* qualifies a wide range of objects, from tie-dyed clothing to prayers. In *T. 12 Patr.*, similarly, the term can be used pejoratively of "fancy foods" (*T. Iss.* 4.2) but in a neutral if not good sense of "spotted rods" (*T. Zeb.* 1.3). In the Ap. Frs. only Hermas employs *poikilos* and the cognate noun. Thus he calls his sins *pollai . . . kai poikilai*, "numerous and varied," in *Man.* 4.2.3. The *Mart. Pol.* 2.4 thus qualifies tortures, as do 4 Macc 17:7 and 18:21. In none of these instances is the term used of *epithymiai* or *hēdonai*.

"Pleasures," *hēdonai*, only here in the PE, does not recur in the Paulines. Otherwise in the NT, in Luke's interpretation of the sower parable there is a distinction between "cares and wealth" and "the pleasures of life" (Luke 8:14;

see Mark 4:19, *epithymiai, SFG* §124). In Jas 4:1 and 3 this distinction is not clear (see Dibelius, *James,* pp. 215–217, nn. 40, 41, 47, with texts from Plato and Philo). In 2 Pet 2:13 the reference is to the "pleasure" (the only NT use of the singular) of overindulgence at the banquet table. In each of these instances, the connotations of *hēdonē* are ethically bad. The LXX usually speaks of "pleasure" in the singular. The word appears mostly in the latest strata, with no Hebrew equivalent. In Wis 7:2; 16:20 (cf. LXX Num 11:8; Prov 17:1) the pleasures of sexual intercourse and eating are viewed positively. The ten remaining uses of the term are in 4 Macc, where pleasure and pain are discussed as the sources of the emotions, and the ethical ambivalence of pleasure is described thus: "In pleasure there exists even a malevolent tendency, which is the most complex of all emotions. In the soul it is boastfulness, covetousness, thirst for honor, rivalry, and malice; in the body, indiscriminate eating, gluttony, and solitary gormandizing" (4 Macc 1:25–27; cf. 2 Tim 3:2–5 and Philo, *Sacr.* 32–33; for Philo on the vices in this verse, see Mott, "Ethics," pp. 35–36). Used in the plural, *hēdonai* once refers to the pleasures that come from virtue (9:31); otherwise, a bad sense dominates (1:33; 6:35), and once a variant occurs on the phrase here in Titus, "pleasures and lusts" (5:23). In *T. 12 Patr., hēdonē* and *philēdonia* regularly suggest that which is evil, and they are often linked with sexual pleasure (see the only use of the plural in *T. Judah* 14.2). In the Ap. Frs., *hēdonē* in the singular has a good or neutral sense (*2 Clem.* 15.5; *Herm. Man.* 10.3.3; 12.5.3; *Sim.* 6.5.7) unless explicitly characterized as "evil pleasure" (Ign. *Trall.* 6.2; *Phld.* 2.2). The plural, however, has only a bad connotation (Ign. *Rom.* 7.3; *Herm. Sim.* 8.8.5; 8.9.4).

in malice and jealousy spending our days. Kakia, "malice," appears in the PE only here, but half of the other ten NT uses are in the Paulines (1 Cor 5:8; 14:20; Eph 4:31; Col 3:8). In the vice list of Rom 1:29, *kakia* concludes one division and *phthonos,* "jealousy," begins another (see also the list in 1 Pet 2:1). In the Lukan writings, the sin of Simon Magus is stigmatized as *kakia* (Acts 8:22). The rest of the NT occurrences are in Matt 6:34; Jas 1:21; and 1 Pet 2:16 (where the freedom of the believer is not to be an excuse for *kakia*). The LXX uses *kakia* often, but only LXX Ps 49:19 and Zech 8:17 are taken up in the Ap. Frs. (*1 Clem.* 35.8; *Barn.* 2.8). In *1 Clem.* 45.7, the persecutors of Daniel and his companions are *"detested (stygētoi:* see below) and full of *malice."* In the screed of *Did.* 5.1, *kakia* figures between pride and stubbornness (see *Barn.* 20.1). The four remaining occurrences in the Ap. Frs. (Ign. *Eph.* 19.3; *2 Clem* 10.1; *Herm. Sim.* 9.29.1, 3) are not as pertinent to this passage in Titus. Only at the end of the *T. 12 Patr.,* with their frequent use of *kakia,* does one encounter a passage in which "malice" and "jealousy" are joined in a list: "But you, my children, run from *malice, jealousy,* and hatred of brothers" (*T. Benj.* 8.1).

"Jealousy," *phthonos,* recurs in the PE in the vice list of 1 Tim 6:4. Of the seven other NT occurrences, Rom 1:29 is cited above; in Gal 5:21, "jealousy" is listed among the most divisive "works of the flesh" (note *zelos* in 5:20); in Phil

1:15 there are Jewish Christians who proclaim Christ "from jealousy and rivalry (*erin*)." The Lukan writings do not know the term (somewhat surprisingly, in the light of Mark 15:10; Matt 27:18; *SFG* §339). The use in 1 Pet 2:1 has been noted already. The only other NT occurrence is in the baffling citation of "Scripture" in Jas 4:5 (see Johnson, *"Topos,"* pp. 330–331, 341–346). *Phthonos* appears four times in the latest strata of the LXX: Wis 2:24, of "the devil's jealousy"; 6:23, of "sickly jealousy"; 3 Macc 6:7, of "the slanders of jealousy"; and in the eulogy of the Romans in 1 Macc 8:16, "There is no jealousy or envy (*zēlos*) among them." This last phrase appears to have influenced the only uses of *phthonos* in the Ap. Frs., in *1 Clem.* 3.2; 4.7, 13; and 5.2, which reaches its climax in attributing the deaths of Peter and Paul to "envy and jealousy." For the inscriptions and the rare uses in the papyri, see Spicq, *Lexic.*, pp. 919–921.

"Spending our days" represents the Greek participle *diagontes*. In the PE *diagein* reappears in the phrase "to spend a quiet and tranquil existence (*bion*)" in 1 Tim 2:2. There are no other NT occurrences, but the LXX does use the term and on occasion of time (Sir 38:27; 2 Macc 12:38 of the sabbath; 3 Macc 4:8). The absolute use here in Titus is similar to Josephus writing of the Spartans who "spent their life (*diēgon*) in the city" (*Apion* 2.229) or of the charge against him that he "lived in luxury (*en tryphais diagontos*)" (*Vita* 284; cf. the Western reading at Luke 7:25 and *T. Jos.* 3.4).

Ignatius, in the only use in the Ap. Frs., uses *diagein* for living in Christ (see COMMENT). *T. Jos.* 9.3 writes of one who "lives in control of himself (*en sōphrosynēi diagōn*)."

detested, hating one another. Even in secular Greek *stygētoi* is an uncommon adjective (Aeschylus, *Prometheus* 592, of Io "detested by Hera"; later OxyP 433.28 and Heliodorus, *Erotici* 5.29.4 (in *Les Éthiopiques*, eds., R. M. Rattenbury, T. W. Lumb, and J. Maillon; 3 vols., second edition; Paris: Les Belles Lettres, 1960) of *eros*, "sexual passion"). The occurrence here is unique in the NT and the LXX (though see the vice lists of Rom 1:30 for the *theostygeis*, "God-haters" and *1 Clem.* 35.5, *theostygia*, "hatred of God"). In the Ap. Frs. only *1 Clem.* uses *stygētoi*, in 35.6 of evildoers as "detested by God" and in 45.7, cited above. The single occurrence in Philo brands the adulterer's act as *stygēton kai theomisēton*, "detested and hated by God" (*Deca.* 131).

"Hating one another" in Greek is *misountes allēlous*, or "detesting one another" (as in Menander, Koerte 779/718K). For the phrase, see Matt 24:10, where it is paired with "betraying one another," perhaps designating Jewish Christians in the days preceding the destruction of Jerusalem (see *Did.* 16.4).

The verb *misein*, "to hate or detest," appears forty times in the NT but only here in the PE and in the Paulines only in Rom 7:15; 9:13 (LXX Mal 1:2–3); and Eph 5:29. In the Lukan writings *misein* occurs seven times but in the gospel only. Luke 6:27, "Love your enemies; do good to those who hate you," illustrates how *agapan* was heard as the opposite of *misein* in the NT generally (see Brown, *AB Epistles*, p. 269, on the Johannine usage). As the passages from Romans listed above and Heb 1:9 (LXX Ps 44:8) show, the usage went back through the LXX (where *misein* occurs frequently) to the Hebrew. Even so, as Menander, *Epitrepontes* 432–433 (F. Sandbach; see also *Samia* 330–331) illustrates with its "I hoped for love (*erasthai*) but the man hates me with a superhuman hatred (*theion de misei misos*)," a similar opposition also occurs in Greek. Some of the almost two dozen uses in the Ap. Frs. appear in the COMMENT below. In *T. Levi* 17.5, "All Israel shall hate each one his neighbor" closely parallels the phrase in Titus. There are ten other uses of *misein* in *T. 12 Patr.*, and *T. Gad* is devoted to warnings about hatred.

4. *"When the humane munificence of our savior, God, was revealed."* For *epephanē*, "was revealed," see 2:11; for "our savior, God," see 1:3, 2:10, and Excursus V, "The PE on Salvation." The temporal *hote*, "when," occurs otherwise in the PE only in 2 Tim 4:3 (with the future). Seventeen of the 101 remaining NT uses are in the other Paulines; 22 are in the Lukan writings.

"Humane munificence" represents *hē chrēstotēs kai hē philanthrōpia*, literally, "the generosity and the kindness." The phrase is undocumented in biblical Greek or the Ap. Frs. But it occurs often, in various forms, in profane texts, which have been assembled in Spicq, *Lexic.*, pp. 924–925 and 972–973.

All ten NT uses of *chrēstotēs* are in the Paulines (but in the PE only here), and half of them are in Rom (2:4; 3:12 = LXX Ps 13:3; and 11:22 *tris*). Most of these, including Eph 2:7 with its use of *charis*, refer to God's "kindness." In 2 Cor 6:6, Gal 5:22, and Col 3:12 "kindness" appears in the list of Christian virtues, paired several times with *makrothymia*, "forbearance." Fifteen of eighteen Septuagintal uses are in the Pss, and two-thirds of these clearly refer to God's *chrēstotēs*. In the five appearances in the Ap. Frs., the term refers to God (e.g., *1 Clem.* 9:1) or Christ (e.g., Ign. *Magn.* 10.1). The Hellenistic esteem for this quality appears in Menander's dictum, "The greatest good is kindness with intelligence" (Koerte 435/788K; see also 531/785K; 407/472K), though he censures the "bleeding hearts" of that age too (Koerte 548/579K). For further detail see Spicq, *Lexic.*, pp. 971–976 and the studies cited there.

The second term in the Greek phrase translated by "humane munificence" is *philanthrōpia*, a word that occurs otherwise in the NT only in Acts 28:2 (see 27:3 for the adverb). The application to God here in Titus is unique in biblical Greek, for all five Septuagintal uses of the noun refer to human beings, particularly kings (thus LXX Esth 8:12k; 3 Macc 3:15) who claim their kindness extends "to all" (2 Macc 14:9; 3 Macc 3:18). *Philanthrōpia* does not appear in the Ap. Frs. or *T. 12 Patr.* But Philo devotes a short treatise to this virtue (*Virt.* 51–174) and applies the term to God (see COMMENT), as does Josephus, *Ant.* 1.24. The first Christian use of *philanthrōpia* after Titus is by the apologists Justin (*Trypho* 47 [*PG* 6.577]), apparently citing this passage, and Theophilus of Antioch (*Ad Autolycum* 2.27 [*PG* 6.1096]). For the rich documentation, see Ferguson, *Values*, pp. 102–117; Spicq, *Lexic.*, pp. 922–927; G. Horsley, *NDIEC* 1.74–75, §26; 87–88, §47; 2.157, §97.

5. *"he saved us, no thanks to any upright deeds."* For "he saved us," see Excursus V, "The PE on Salvation." "No thanks to any upright deeds that we performed ourselves" is literally, "not by reason of works (*ex ergōn*) that [were] in righteousness, [works] that we did ourselves." For *erga* (*agatha/kala*) see 1:18 and 2:14. The phrase "in righteousness" recurs in 2 Tim 3:16 and in the other Paulines in an expanded form in Eph 4:24; 5:9; see also Luke 1:75; Acts 17:31, as well as 2 Pet 1:1 and Rev 19:11. The phrase appears forty-four times in the LXX, especially in the Pss (sixteen times) and Isa. In the Ap. Frs. *1 Clem.* 42.5 takes up part of LXX Isa 60.17, and *Barn.* 14.7 cites LXX Isa 42.6; expansions of the phrase predominate the eleven other uses. Thus also *T. Judah* 24.1 reads, "And a man shall arise from my posterity like the Sun of righteousness, walking with the sons of men in gentleness and righteousness (*en praotēti kai dikaiosynēi*)"; but *T. Asher* 1.6 ("If a soul wants to follow the good way, all of its deeds [*pasa praxis*] are done in righteousness") uses the phrase, as does this passage in Titus (but with a good sense).

The term "righteousness," *dikaiosynē*, also appears in the PE in 1 Tim 6:11 and 2 Tim 2:22 in a phrase translated as "pursue upright conduct"; and in 2 Tim 4:8 on "the crown of the upright life." The cognate verb appears in "the grace that made us upright" in v 7 below. The adjective *dikaios*, "upright," appeared in the virtue list of 1:8; the adverb *dikaios*, "in an honest way," in 2:12. *Adikia*, "wickedness," appears in 2 Tim 2:19. This terminological cluster coincides in large part with that of the other Paulines as well as of other strata in the NT, not to mention the LXX (for the details and documentation, see the indexes in Reumann, *Righteousness*) and the Ap. Frs.

"that we performed ourselves." The relative *ha*, "that," refers to *ergōn*, "deeds," but it is not attracted into the genitive (as in Atticistic *hōn* of D^b, C^b, etc.) because of the preceding nominal modifiers (BDF §294.1; J. K. Elliott, *Greek Text*, p. 63) and its own importance. "Performed," from *poiein*, recurs in 1 Tim 1:13 (of Paul's persecuting believers); 2:1; 4:16; 5:21; and 2 Tim 4:5 (of the *ergon*, "the work of one who announces the gospel"). The NT uses this verb more than 560 times, in every book except 2 John. The Lukan writings particularly favor *poiein* (156 times). There are more than 3,200 occurrences in the LXX, many times of God performing an action. This usage appears also in Paul, notably in passages that emphasize God's faithfulness (thus, 1 Thess 5:24; 1 Cor 10:13, both with *pistos;* Rom 4:21). The PE, however, use *poiein* only of human action, a practice that resembles that of Ignatius and Polycarp in the Ap. Frs.

"but because of his own mercy." The unusual word order, *to autou eleos* becomes *to eleos autou* in a few witnesses (D*, E, F, G). The PE do not insert *autou* between article and noun elsewhere; hence the more difficult reading was eased, but without sufficient reason, as 1 Pet 1:3 shows (see BDF §284.3). The resulting *to eleos autou* resembles Luke 1:50, 58, and may be more Semitic, but the frequent liturgical use of Mary's canticle probably contributed to normalizing the reading here in Titus (*pace* J. K. Elliott, *Greek Text*, p. 191). The whole

phrase here in Titus does not appear in precisely this form in the rest of the NT, the LXX, or the Ap. Frs., though there are some close parallels that will be adduced in what follows.

"Mercy," *eleos*, appears elsewhere in the PE in the short prayers of 1 Tim 1:2; 2 Tim 1:2, 16, 18. Of the twenty-two remaining uses in the NT, five are in the other Paulines, six are in Luke's gospel. Seventy-five of the roughly two hundred appearances in the LXX are in the Pss. Less than a dozen times one encounters the phrase *kata to mega/poly eleos sou* or *kata to plēthos (tou) eleos sou/autou*, "according to your great/abundant mercy" or "according to the abundance of your/his mercy." The phrase occurs without an adjective but with a second-person possessive, *sou*, only in LXX Pss 108:26; 118:88, 124, 149; and in 1 Macc 13:46 (addressed to the high priest Simon). The Ap. Frs. have almost a score of uses of *eleos*, regularly of God or Christ and in contexts of prayer (thus *1 Clem.* 9.1; 18.1–2; 50.2; Ign. *Trall.* 12.3; *Smyrn.* 12.2; Pol. *Phil.* inscr.). The *T. Zeb.* deals with compassion and mercy but the phrase *kata to poly autou eleos* appears in *T. Naph.* 4.3. See Spicq, *Supp. Lexic.*, pp. 250–258.

"*saved us through a washing of regeneration and of renewal by the Holy Spirit.*" Literally, "through a bath (*dia loutrou*) of regeneration (*paliggenesias*) and of renewal (*anakainōseōs*) of the Holy Spirit." Before *loutrou* A reads the article, probably in order to harmonize this phrase with the preceding *to eleos autou*. A variety of Western witnesses (D*, F, G, L, b, d, g, Lcf., Ambst., etc.) read "through (*dia*) the Holy Spirit" (see 2 Tim 1:14), possibly under the influence of the preceding *dia loutrou* as well as *dia Iesou Christou* in the verse that follows. The reading would insure that the final terms of this chain of genitives would be read in an instrumental sense (see J. K. Elliott, *Greek Text*, p. 191).

"Through a washing": The instrumental *dia* here is parallel in meaning to *dia Iesou Christou* in the next verse. For the dozen uses of *dia* in the Timothy correspondence, see 1 Tim 2:10, 15; 4:5, 14; 2 Tim 1:1, 6, 10², 14; 2:2; 3:15; 4:17. "Washing," *loutron*, occurs otherwise in the NT only in Eph 5:26 of Christ "having cleansed [the church] by the washing (*tōi loutrōi*) of water with the word." In the LXX *loutron* means the bath for cleansing sheep (LXX Cant 4:2; 6:6) and the Jewish ritual washing after touching the dead in Sir 34:25. The word does not appear in *T. 12 Patr.* or the Ap. Frs., but Justin uses it in alluding to this passage in Titus or its source (*Apology* 1.61 [*PG* 6.420–421]; see Irenaeus, *Adversus haereses* 5.3 [*PG* 5.15.3]; Theophilus of Antioch, *Ad Autolycum* 2.16 [*PG* 6.1077]).

"Of regeneration" represents the noun *paliggenesia*, found elsewhere in the NT only in Jesus' saying to the Twelve, "in the regeneration when the Son of Man shall sit on the throne of his glory, you who have followed me shall also sit on twelve thrones, judging the twelve tribes of Israel" (Matt 19:28; adjusted in Luke 22:30 for apologetic considerations; see Derrett, "*Palingenesia,*" pp. 51–58 for many of the texts cited hereafter). The LXX and *T. 12 Patr.* do not use the term, but it does appear in *1 Clem.* 9.4: "Noah, found faithful (*pistos*) in his service, proclaimed regeneration to the world, and through him the Master saved (*diesōsen*) the living creatures which entered in concord into the ark."

Philo, who first uses *paliggenesia* in Hellenistic Judaism, also had written that Noah and his family, after they emerged from the ark, "became leaders of the regeneration (*paliggenesias . . . hēgemones*), inaugurators of a second cycle . . . embers to rekindle humankind" (*Mos.* 2.65). Most of the dozen other Philonic uses of the word are in his critique of the Stoic cosmology with its teaching about the final combustion and regeneration of the universe in *Aet.* (9, 47, 76, 85², 93, 99, 103, 107). Once he speaks of the survival of the human soul after bodily death as *paliggenesia* (*Cher.* 114; see Burnett, "Philo," pp. 447–470). He significantly qualifies the term when he applies it to Seth giving "regeneration so to speak" to murdered Abel (*Post.* 124) or the emperor awakening his petitioner "as if by regeneration" (*Leg.* 325).

Josephus has the Jewish exiles "celebrating the recovery and regeneration of their land" due to the benevolent Persian monarch, a usage that reminds one of Cicero calling his return from the provinces *paliggenesia* (*To Atticus* 6.6.4). As a Pharisee Josephus believed in the survival of the human soul and the resurrection of the body (see *War* 3.374). In *Apion* 2.218 he wrote that "God has granted renewed existence (*genesthai te palin*) and, in the revolution of the ages, a gift of a better life" to those who observe his law unto death. "To come to be again" is cognate with *paliggenesia*. *Qua* soul a human being survives death; *qua* body, God brings him into existence again. The link of this regeneration with a belief that issues in a way of conduct is notable.

From mid-second century Christian authors apply *paliggenesia* to the resurrection of the body (see Justin, *De resurrectione* 14 [*PG* 6.1581]; the letter about the martyrs of Lyons quoted by Eusebius, *Church History* 5.1.62–63; Origen, *De oratione* 25 [*PG* 11.500]; Lampe, *PGL*, s.v.). Clement of Alexandria describes an extraordinary example of Christian repentance as "a great means of recognizing *paliggenesia*, a trophy of resurrection (*anastaseōs*) that can be seen" (*Quis dives* [*PG* 9.649]). Minucius Felix has the pagan Caecilius bitterly mock the Christian faith in the resurrection, asserting, "They say they are born again after death (*renasci . . . post mortem*) from cinders and ashes, and with a confidence that cannot be accounted for they believe their lies to one another. You would think that they already had come back to life (*revixisse*)" (*Octavius* 11.2). Jerome (*On Matthew* 3 [*CCL* 77.172–173]) and Augustine (*City of God* 20.5 [*CCL* 48.704–705]; *De peccatorum meritis* 2.7 and *Against Pelagian Letters* 3 [*PL* 44.156 and 591]) among the Latin Fathers are particularly emphatic about the term in Matthew meaning the final resurrection.

For centuries before this Christian usage, the Stoics employed *paliggenesia* along with *ekpyrosis*, "conflagration," in articulating their hypothesis on the periodic destruction and renewal of the cosmos (see von Arnim, *SVF* 2.190–191, §627; Cicero, *De natura deorum* 2.118; and the Philonic texts cited above). By the first century C.E. the technical Stoic meaning had rivals. Varro wrote of fortunetellers who taught "that men are destined to be reborn (renascendis), which the Greeks call paliggenesia" (see Ovid, Fasti 3.153–154, on Pythagoras). After a certain time, "the same soul and the same body which were formerly in a human being shall again be rejoined" (apud Augustine, City of God 22.28 [CCL 48.855–856]). In the middle of the first Christian century, the Greek novelist Chariton of Aphrodisias uses paliggenesia whimsically in a context that shows he understood it of a resurrection (Chaireas and Callirhoe 1.8.1). Plutarch used the term for return to life of dismembered divinities as well of the transmigration of human souls into animal bodies (thus Moralia 364F, 379F, 389A, 438D, 996C, 998C). Lucian, Muscae laudatio 7, ironically supplements the Platonic doctrine about the immortality of the soul, by observing that ashes sprinkled on a dead fly cause it to rise up (anistatai) "and a kind of regeneration (paliggenesia) occurs and another life (bios) starts. This should completely convince anybody that the fly's soul is immortal, because after leaving the body it comes back again (palin) and recognizes it and makes it rise up." Thus from Varro through Lucian paliggenesia suggested bodily resurrection in the conversation of the educated.

The discourse on regeneration in Corpus Hermeticum 13 illustrates how paliggenesia entered religious speculation from the second century C.E. (see Nock, EGC, pp. 13–15). The term may also have entered the language of those who had been initiated into the ancient mystery cults, though "it is to be noted that paliggenesia is not a characteristic mystery word" (Nock, ERAW, p. 342 = JBL 52 [1933], p. 132). In the mid-second century, Apuleius uses a qualified language of rebirth to describe the restoration of his hero, Lucius, to human form in the setting of the mysteries (quodammodo renatus, Metamorphoses 11.16, 21; cf. 11.18, 24). Later still, the "Mithras Liturgy" has the initiate pray, "O Lord, while being regenerated (palingenomenos), I am passing away; while growing and having grown, I am dying; while being born from a life-generating birth (apo geneseōs zōogonou genomenos), I am passing on, released to death— as you have founded, as you have decreed, and have established the mystery (mystērion)" (Meyer, "Mithras," p. 21; cf. pp. 5, 15). In 376 C.E. a man who had received the blood bath of the taurobolium announces that he has been in aeternum renatus, "forever reborn" (CIL 6.510.17ff.; see Nock, ERAW, pp. 102–103; Conversion, pp. 69–71). Although these late texts cast very uncertain light on first-century usage, they show how the language of regeneration stayed in circulation in religious as well as literary circles for centuries. Thus an ordinary citizen of the Hellenistic world, if he heard or read this text of Titus, would have noted the "approximation to the phraseology of the world around, a lessening of the feeling of isolation, and an increase in intelligibility" for a listener like himself (Nock, ERAW, pp. 342–343).

"And of renewal" represents the anarthrous anakainōseōs. If paliggenesia has a secular and a religious (Jewish as well as pagan) history antedating Christianity, the same cannot be said for the noun with which it is paired here, for *anakainōsis* has still to appear in a secular or biblical text antecedent to Rom 12:2, where Paul urges that church, "Do not be conformed to this age but be transformed by the renewal of the mind (*tēi anakainōsei tou noos*)." He alone uses the cognate verb in 2 Cor 4:16 when he writes, "Though our outer nature is wasting away, our inner nature is being renewed (*anakainountai*) every day" (also Col 3:10). After this passage in Titus one must wait until *Herm. Vis.* 3.8.9, with its mention of "the renewal of your spirits," for its appearance in the second century (and again in a Roman *Sitz im Leben*). The use of *anakainizein*, "restore," in Heb 6:6 and in *Herm. Sim.* 8.6.3 and 9.14.3 shows a similar pattern.

The anarthrous *pneumatos hagiou* (literally, "of Holy Spirit") marks the first explicit (see 1:12) mention of the Holy Spirit in the PE. The omission of the article could indicate that the "Holy Spirit" was heard as a name at this point in Titus (and in the source cited; see N. Turner, *Insights*, pp. 18–19). The same phrase (governed by *dia*) reappears in 2 Tim 1:14 (see BDF §257.2; 474.1 as well as Wallace, "Adjective," p. 153 on the attributive character of *hagion* in this anarthrous phrase). In the remainder of the NT one reads of the Holy Spirit regularly (except in 2 and 3 John), and the phrase is particularly frequent in Luke–Acts (see Fitzmyer, *AB Lk*, pp. 227–231, 266–267) and the remaining Paulines. In the LXX, however, *to pneuma to hagion* appears only in LXX Ps 50:13, "And your holy spirit take not from me," and LXX Isa 63:10–11, "But they were disloyal and exasperated his [the Lord's] holy spirit and he was turned into an enemy for them and he himself fought against them. And the one who brought up from the land [of Egypt] the shepherd of the sheep remembered the days of old. Where is he who put his holy spirit on them?" (see LXX Num 11:25–26, 29). In both places *to pneuma to hagion* is the spirit of the Holy One of Israel; it is once linked with the salvation of an individual sinner, once with the salvation of the sinful nation. The Ap. Frs. regularly use the phrase. The closest that the *T. 12 Patr.* come to it is in *T. Levi* 18.11, *pneuma hagiōsynēs estai ep' autois*, "The spirit of holiness shall be upon them."

There are five other uses of *pneuma* in the PE. Three appear in the "piece in pause" in 1 Tim 3:16–4:1, where *pneuma* stands in contrast to *sarx*, "flesh," and then *tode pneuma* utters an oracle (the only time in the PE in which the Spirit is the subject of a sentence). Within the oracle *pneumasin planois*, "specious spirits," are scored. The remaining occurrences are in 2 Tim, where an anarthrous *pneuma* that Timothy receives through the imposition of Paul's hands is modified by a series of nouns in the genitive (2 Tim 1:7); then the closing blessing of the letter is for Timothy's "spirit," *to pneuma sou* (2 Tim 4:22). There are hundreds of occurrences of *pneuma* in the NT and the LXX, not to mention the Ap. Frs. and *T. 12 Patr.*

In the PE, *hagios*, "holy" qualifies not only *pneuma* but also the Christian vocation (2 Tim 1:9), and in 1 Tim 5:10 the term is used nominally for the Christian travelers whom a devout widow welcomes. Again, as with *pneuma*, there are hundreds of other appearances of the term in biblical Greek and in the early Jewish and Christian literature. Worthy of note is that Luke–Acts and the other Paulines use *hagios,* more than seventy times in each body of literature.

6. *"that he poured out lavishly on us, through Jesus Christ, our savior."* The relative *hou* has been attracted into the genitive of its antecedent, *pneumatos.* A few witnesses read *ho* (D*, 1739, 326) to preclude visual confusion with the negative *ou.* J. K. Elliott (*Greek Text,* pp. 63, 191) defends the authenticity of *ho* on the ground that the author of the PE characteristically avoided such attraction. But the evidence for this is meager, the witnesses few and unimpressive, and the confession that is being cited need not follow the author's style. On "Jesus Christ, our savior," see Excursus V, "The PE on Salvation." For the minor variants on this phrase, see J. K. Elliott, *Greek Text,* pp. 191–192.

"He poured out" represents *ekchein,* only here in the PE. Of the fifteen other uses in the NT, Luke uses this verb only of the Holy Spirit (Acts 2:17, 18 [= LXX Joel 3:1–2], 33); once in his half-dozen uses of the cognate *ekchynesthai* he describes the amazement of Jewish Christians that "the gift of the Holy Spirit had been poured out even on the Gentiles" (Acts 10:45; see Rom 5:5). In the Ap. Frs. *ekchein* appears five times, perhaps most notably in *1 Clem.* 46.6, "Or do we not have one God and one Christ and one Spirit of grace poured out on us?" (cf. 2.2, "a full outpouring (*ekchysis*) of the Holy Spirit happened to all of you"). *Barnabas* 1.3 has "The Spirit has been poured out upon you from the Lord's rich spring (*apo tou plousiou tēs pēgēs kyriou*)," which suggests the baptismal waters (see *Did.* 7.3, "Pour [*ekcheon*] water three times on the head" when running water for immersion is not available).

The LXX, which regularly uses *ekchein* for the pouring out of blood (as well as of the soul), only writes of the pouring out of the spirit in LXX Joel 3:1–2 and in LXX Zech 12:10, "I shall pour out . . . a spirit of grace and pity." In the *T. 12 Patr.,* *T. Judah* 24.2 writes of a messianic outpouring of a spirit of blessing and of grace and a Christian interpolation in *T. Benj.* 9.4 has "The Spirit of God will move on to all nations as a fire is poured out."

"Lavishly," *plousiōs,* will recur in 1 Tim 6:17, again in a positive sense as in its other NT uses (Col 3:16; 2 Pet 1:11) and its one appearance in the Ap. Frs. (*Barn.* 9.7). This adverb does not appear in the LXX or *T. 12 Patr.*

7. *"God's was the grace that made us upright, so that we could become heirs with a hope of life eternal."* Literally, "So that made upright by the former's grace. . . ." For "the grace" (of God) see 1:4 and 2:11. *Dikaioun,* "to make upright," is the last instance of the **dik-* cluster in Titus (*dikaios,* 1:8; *dikaios,* 2:12; *dikaiosynē,* 3:5). This verb reappears in the hymnic fragment of 1 Tim 3:16; in the rest of the Paulines, twenty-three of twenty-five uses are in Rom and Gal (see the chart for the cluster in Reumann, *Righteousness,* p. 42). The seven instances in the Lukan corpus climax in the usage of the speech placed on the lips of Paul in Acts 13:39. Otherwise in the NT *dikaioun* appears only in Jas 2:21, 24, 25, and in Matt 11:19 (Q, see Luke 7:35); 12:37.

The Ap. Frs. employ *dikaioun* fourteen times, citing not only the LXX (*1 Clem.* 8.4; 16.12; 18.4; *Barn.* 6.1) but also Paul himself (Ign. *Rom.* 5.1 = 1 Cor 4:4). For *1 Clem.* 32.4 and other passages, see the COMMENT that follows.

The forty-five Septuagintal uses of *dikaioun* cluster in Sir, Isa, and the Pss. The links of the verb with inheritance in LXX Tob 6:11–12 (S) and Esth 10:3i are notable in the light of the "heirs" here in Titus. The two appearances of *dikaioun* in *T. 12 Patr.* illustrate the variety of meanings that this verb assumes in Jewish Greek (*T. Sim.* 6.1; *T. Dan* 3.3).

For "a hope of life eternal," see 1:2 and Excursus IV, "The Terminology for Life in the PE." "With a hope" represents *kat' elpida*, literally, "with the goal/purpose of hope" as in 1:1, 4, "for the faith" (see BAGD, pp. 406–407, §II.4). Otherwise in the NT only Phil 1:20 uses *kata* to govern the compound phrase *apokaradokian kai elpida*, as Paul in prison writes of a rescue "according to my eager expectation and hope." In the LXX, Ap. Frs., and *T. 12 Patr., kat' elpida* is not found.

"So that we could become" renders *hina . . . genēthōmen*. The correctors of S and D as well as the scribes of PSI, K, L, and many Byzantine witnesses found the first aorist passive of *ginesthai* unattractive and wrote the second aorist *genōmetha* (which appears in Paul, e.g., in 2 Cor 5:21).

Ginesthai reappears in the letters to Timothy eight times. The verb is very frequent in the NT outside of the PE (661 times), not to mention the LXX and the Ap. Frs. To "become heirs," *klēronomoi*, is a phrase otherwise undocumented in the PE, which do not employ any of the *klēr-* terminology. Hebrews 11:7 alone in the NT uses the phrase to describe how Noah "became an heir of the righteousness that is *kata pistin.*" The noun *klēronomos* occurs in the gospel tradition only of the beloved son sent to the parabolic vineyard (Mark 12:7; Matt 21:38; Luke 20:14; *SFG* §278). The ten remaining NT uses are Jas 2:5 (plural); Heb 1:2 (of the Son); 6:17 (plural); and in Paul (see COMMENT below). There are scarcely five uses of the noun (none with *ginesthai*) in the Ap. Frs., notably *Barn.* 6.19; 13.6 and *Herm. Sim.* 5.2.6 (of the beloved Son). *Klēronomos* appears five times at the most in the LXX, never with *ginesthai* and with no particular relevance to this passage in Titus. In *T. 12 Patr.* and the Greek fragments of *Enoch* the term does not appear.

8a. *That is the Christian message, meant to be believed.* For the individual terms "message," *logos*, and "meant to be believed," *pistos*, as well as the phrase as a whole, see 1:3, 9 and Excursus I, "*Pistis* Terminology in the PE." The phrase will reappear four times in the correspondence with Timothy, in 1 Tim 1:15; 3:1; 4:9; and 2 Tim 2:11. It does not appear elsewhere in the NT, the Ap. Frs., or the LXX, and it is very rare in Greek otherwise (see Knight, *Sayings*, pp. 4–6 and COMMENT).

The term *pistos* appears about seventy times in the LXX, but only a few passages coincide significantly with the meaning in the PE. Thus, LXX Ps 144:13, "Faithful (*pistos*) is the Lord in all his words (*logois*)"; Sir 33:3, "The law (*nomos*) is as dependable (*pistos*) as an oracular inquiry" as well as 37:22, 23, of a wise man, "the fruits of his understanding are dependable (*pistoi*) on his lips"; and Prov 14:5, "A dependable witness (*martys pistos*) does not lie." In their use of *pistos*, the Ap. Frs. offer no parallel to its meaning as it is used in this phrase. The term does not appear in *T. 12 Patr.* or *Enoch.*

COMMENT

3:3. *After all, we were once fools ourselves, disobedient, deluded, slaving for diverse lusts and pleasures, in malice and jealousy spending our days, detested hating one another.* The transition, emphatic in its prolixity, and the reappearance of the first-person plural (see 2:8, 10) signal the approaching ecclesial confession of 3:4–7, with its half-dozen such plurals (see 2:11–14). This confession is in its turn "the message meant to be believed" (3:8a). The transitional phrase offers a bridge between the septuple list of virtues that had been urged on Jewish-Christian converts in 3:1–2 and the antithetical sevenfold catalog of vices that is adduced here. The previous list had urged what a Jewish Christian ought to be; the following, what they all (including the apostle Paul) had been before conversion to Christ. The confession of 3:4–7 articulates the single, adequate ground and reason for the resolution of this dialectic, namely, the grace of God that in Christ and through the Spirit had touched and changed their personal histories, their lives and conduct.

The opening phrase, "we were once . . . ourselves," emphatically includes Paul himself in the situation of those addressed in 3:1–2, as if the author of this letter were saying, "We Jewish Christians . . . ," perhaps in implicit contrast to Titus, the Gentile convert, whom this letter addresses. Paul's "zealotism" had once issued in arrogant, ruthless persecution. He regarded that existence as something from which the risen Jesus had delivered him (see 1 Tim 1:12–17 and 2:14 above). Precisely as a Jew Paul now identifies with his "kinsmen by race" (Rom 9:3), so that they who have followed the apostle into faith in Christ will follow him in thoroughly abandoning the vices of their past. All alike have been "zealots" in a bad sense. The Christ who had led one man out of that kind of zeal can lead a people out of it. The apostle to the Gentiles is not without a message and a role for his Jewish brothers.

The catalog of vices adduced here has—as its parallel with the previous septuple list already implies—a certain formal character that distances it from the actual life of a particular Jewish Christian (including Paul). The list is not biographical, much less autobiographical. The group is conceived (and the plural is notable) as having individual members who at one time or another practiced one vice or another of those which are schematized and typified in this list of "seven capital sins." The paraenesis is not scientific, in the sense that it is not based on confidential questionnaires or sociological surveys. Nevertheless, it is not a complete abstraction or a stereotype, automatically adduced and applied without regard for the situation of the intended audience. The items of this vice catalog are not vices as such; they are adjectival of persons.

It was not the regular practice of the Paul of history to accuse himself of the vices that he was adducing in a list (see 1 Cor 6:9–11, "And such were some of you"; Rom 2:1–24 versus Eph 2:3). At times the rhetorical *topos* as such seems to exclude the use of the first-person plural. At other times it is possible that the writer was aware of (and intended to avoid) any "autobiographical" interpretation of the catalog, whether as a whole or for a particular item. What does weigh heavily in the rhetorical purpose of such a list is what K. J. Dover (*Morality*, pp. 50–51) calls "the relational aspect" of the use of moral terms, by which their utterance shapes "the relationship between speaker and hearer . . . [who] offers or withdraws affection and respect, and implies the probability of similar offer or withdrawal on the part of others." He continues, "Furthermore, the use of a moral word is a declaration of alignment; by my judgment on a particular act I associate myself with one category of people and dissociate myself from another." Finally, "by far the most important use of moral words . . . is the manipulative or persuasive use, in which the speaker tries to bring into being . . . an emotional orientation, favourable or unfavourable, towards particular persons, acts and events." He notes that such use of moral language is akin to its use in prayer, entreaty, and incantation. We aim to make persons be what we call them.

These relational purposes dictate the shape of this catalog of vices in Titus. The apostle is conceived to be identifying with the lives of a new wave of converts from Judaism, identifying his own journey to belief in Christ with theirs. They have left behind only what Paul had abandoned, a life of vice. They have become associated and aligned with the people who believe in Jesus. The language of this list intends to complete the conversion of its hearers from a viewpoint and a way of living that run counter to what faith in Christ involves. Their response involves their relationship with Paul and, through him, with the church that speaks in his person. This way of arguing for ethical conversion may have been part of a contemporary Hellenistic Jewish tradition with a link to Philo, who had fashioned an opening for Hellenistic ethical philosophy in arguing for the conversion or change demanded of one who believed the Jewish law (see the vision of the conversion of Israel at the conclusion of *Praem.* 162–172; Mott, "Ethics," pp. 43–48).

The septet of vicious qualities has its own formal, rhetorical arrangement. A pair of alpha privatives signal its opening; the rhyming endings in -*oi* link the first item with the third and sixth, thus framing the central chiasmus (the translation reproduces this effect with the repetition of *d* sounds in the second, third, sixth, and seventh items). An expansive conclusion has characterized other lists in Titus; here instead the elaborate chiasmus is the rhetorical centerpiece, introduced and concluded by the alliteration and rhyme of *douleuontes* . . . *diagontes*.

The opening of the catalog reminds the reader that the group of Jewish Christians whom the apostle is addressing had already in 1:16 been characterized as "disobedient." That they had been "fools" in their pursuit of national liberation reminds the reader of the stinging rebuke that Luke placed on the lips of the risen Jesus for those who had "hoped that he was the one to redeem Israel" (Luke 24:21, 25; see Acts 1:6). Josephus remarked similarly that when he returned from Rome to Palestine just before the outbreak of the revolt of 66 C.E. and found the country seething with sedition, "I warned them not to risk the very worst for their homeland, their families, and themselves, recklessly and quite foolishly (*anoētōs*)" (*Vita* 18). Those revolutionaries had talked a good fight, but events had indeed proved them utterly senseless. They and their sympathizers had earned a title that belongs to the oldest sapiential strata in Israel, that of the fool, the *ˀewil*, of whom it was typical that his words produced no corresponding effects. The fool acts at the wrong time and ruins his life. He is like a stubborn adolescent whose folly is intractable. He refuses to "know" Yahweh and his righteousness (see the texts collected by H. Cazelles in *TDOT* 1.137–140). From such a senseless existence, their conversion to Christ had delivered the Jewish Christians addressed here in Titus.

If such an existence had been led in folly and disobedience, it was because these Jews had been "deluded," *planōmenoi*. The Pauline encouragement or prophetic *paraklēsis* that they are receiving at this point (see *parakalei* in 2:15) stands implicitly in contrast with the false prophecies that had driven the firestorm of revolution over Palestine. The **plan-* cluster of terms in the LXX and Jewish Greek regularly characterized what the authors considered spurious prophecy (see the texts and bibliography in Horbury, "False Prophecy," pp. 492–507, on this subject and what follows here). The claims of such oracles were regularly thinly disguised calls to sedition against Rome, from Theudas who "said he was a prophet" (Josephus, *Ant.* 20.97: cf. Acts 5:36), through the Egyptian charlatan (*goēs*) and prophet with whom Paul was confused (Josephus, *War* 2.261–263; Acts 21:38). "Deceivers (*planoi*) and imposters, under the pretence of divine inspiration (*theiasmou*) fostering revolutionary changes, they persuaded the multitude to act like madmen, and led them out into the desert, intending God to give them there signs of liberation (*sēmeia eleutherias*)" (*War* 2.259). Their frenzy grew even in the last ghastly stages of the revolt. "Many were the prophets at this time who were suborned by the tyrants to deceive the people by proclaiming that they should await help from God. . . . Thus it was then that deceivers and pretended messengers of the deity misled the wretched people" (*War* 6.286, 288, cf. 312–313; see Hengel, *Charismatic*, p. 42; Aune, *Prophecy*, pp. 127–129, 137–138, with its cautions for taking Josephus neat). Although some Zealots may indeed have been prophets, it must be admitted that not all of the politically motivated prophets of the first century C.E. shared the specifically Zealot program (see Aune, *Prophecy*, pp. 106–107, qualifying M. Hengel and J. Becker). Hence the politicized Jewish converts posited here in Titus need not have been themselves prophets or have listened to prophets who were Zealots.

The oracle of Jesus peculiar to Matt 24:10–12 may transmit an experience analogous to the one presupposed at this point in Titus. The evangelist writes, "And then many will take scandal and they will betray one another and they will hate one another (*misēsousin allēlous*, as at the end of this list in Titus) and many pseudoprophets will arise and they will delude (*planēsousin*) many. And because wrong (*anomian*) will abound, the love (*agapē*) of many will grow cold." A similar prophetic saying appears in Matt 24:23–24: "Then should anyone say to you, 'Behold, there is the Christ!' or 'Here he is!' do not believe it, for pseudochrists and pseudoprophets will arise and show great signs and wonders, so as to delude (*planēsai*), if possible, even the elect" (see Mark 13:21–22 with *apoplanan*, *SFG* §291; cf. Mark 13:5–6 with Matt 24:4–5, *SFG* §288). The resemblances are conspicuous to the pseudoprophets in Matt 7:23, whose deeds belie their professions of faith and who are "doing wrong (*hoi ergazomenoi tēn anomian*)." The situation behind these oracles is shadowy, and clear identifications are in the nature of the case hard to come by (see the review of the literature in Hill, "False Prophets," pp. 327–333; adding Guelich, *Sermon*, pp. 390–403, 408–411 for the state of the question exegetically); but, with Aune, *Prophecy*, pp. 222–224, 274, 319, 324, one can surmise that the Palestinian Jewish liberation movement of the first century C.E., with its paroxysms of eschatological fervor, produced prophetic oracles and acts that made a bad impression in some very influential quarters in Jewish Christianity. It appears as if some of these prophets, without changing their prophetic activities and interests, became Christians and entered the Jewish-Christian congregations that Matthew was addressing. The evangelist then had to deal with these prophets, as the author of Titus is here dealing with converts from the Zealots and their sympathizers.

A further illustration of the inroads of false prophecy in a Christian congregation appears in Rev. There, in the prophetic letter to Thyatira, one encounters a pseudoprophetess, a "Jezebel," who deludes (*planai*) her coterie of Christian prophets into immorality and idolatry (2:20; her OT namesake kept a stable of 850 false prophets of the false gods, Baal and Asherah, 1 Kgs 18:19; see Aune, *Prophecy*, pp. 197, 218, 417 n. 19). As the seer of Rev warms to his theme, the eschatological pseudoprophet who "had worked the signs by which he deceived (*eplanēsen*) those who had received the mark of the beast" is hurled with the beast into a fiery, sulphurous lake (19:20; cf. 18:23). The "deluded" whom Paul addresses at this point could have met the same judgment if they had not believed in Christ; yet the trial and temptation of false prophecy continue.

Twinges recur in the scars of the deluded because the pseudoprophetic directions to which they had listened were not simply politico-theological incitements. They who had dreamed of freedom and liberation had actually been tricked into "slaving for diverse lusts and pleasures." They had once heeded false prophetic oracles which not only could have catapulted them into eschatological disaster but also lured them into an immoral existence.

Slavery to vice was not an unusual theme in Greek thought. Plato, *Republic* 10.617E has a certain prophet announce, "Virtue is not subject to a master (*adespoton*)," a saying taken up by Apollonius of Tyana, *Epistle* 15, who applies it to the person that can be bought for money and "makes for himself many masters (*despotas*)" (see R. Penella, *Apollonius*, p. 99 for other texts). Menander was thinking of the popular, contemporary hedonism when he had one of his characters question, "To what then has a man been enslaved (*dedoulontai*)? . . . does some pleasure (*hēdonē*) in companionship urge lovers on?" (Koerte 568/541K); and another assert, "All kinds of living things that behold the sun which we in common share, all these are slaves of pleasure (*doula . . . hēdonēs*)" (Koerte 737/611K), and the tartness of the final phrase becomes explicit in other sayings, "Pleasant (*hēdus*) as it may be, a base life is a matter for reproach" (Koerte 738/756K; see Plutarch, *Moralia* 21C) and "I never thought that a free man should put up with pleasure (*hēdonēn*) which has much in common with arrogance (*hybrei*)" (Koerte 613a/728K). G. Mussier (*Dio Chrys.*, p. 219) has an impressive collection of parallels to this phrase as well as to other items in v 3. On the Roman scene, Seneca observes, "Show me who is not a slave. One is a slave to lust, another to avarice, another to ambition, and all alike are slaves to fear" (*Epistulae morales* 47.17).

Jewish Greek exploits the same theme of enslavement to lust and passion in 4 Macc 3:2 and 13:2, and *T. Judah* 18.6 has the patriarch say of the man who is avaricious and sexually promiscuous, "For two passions (*pathē*) contrary to God's commands enslave (*douleuon*) him, so that he is unable to obey God; they blind his soul, and he goes about in the day as though it were night." Potiphar's wife "is enslaved (*doulōthēi*)" by the passion of evil lust (*epithymias*)" in *T. Jos.* 7.8.

The "pleasures" of taste are suggested by the **hēd-* cluster in Greek, as they are by the etymologically related *sweet* in English (see *DELG*, pp. 406–407). Again Menander writes of a gourmand who wants to die "eating and eating and saying, 'I rot for the pleasure (*hypo tēs hēdonēs*) of it' " (Koerte 23/23K); and another character is taken to task with the words, "When you get up again you stuff in food for pleasure (*pros hēdonēn*); your very life is a sleep" (Koerte, *Phasma* 37–38).

For Menander also the adjective *poikilos* can describe a richly varied lunch menu (*Epitrepontes* 609–610) or a sauce (*Phasma* 74 [F. Sandbach]) or embroideries (*Perikeiromenē* 756 [F. Sandbach]), but the term for him also suggests that which is undependable. "How unstable (*poikilon*) and delusive (*planon*) a thing is luck" (*Kitharistes*, fragment 8/288K). The incorrigible pupil in Herodas, *Mime* 3.89, is, in his distraught mother's phrase, "much shiftier (*poikiloteros*) than a hydra." This nuance of meaning may be intended here in Titus, first of all for the always shifting "pleasures" (of taste), which are immediately qualified by the term, and then for the similarly unstable "lusts," with their suggestion of sexual desires and avarice (1 Tim 6:9).

So the liberation for which these quondam Zealots and their sympathizers had passionately longed has been here reinterpreted in terms of a slavery not to human rulers but to evil, and not to extrinsic evils but to those which spring up and flourish in human hearts. These Jewish converts had indeed had a variety of masters, of tyrants, of despots, but they all were within themselves. The coincidence with the Qumran Rule (1QS 4.10) will be examined subsequently.

The second member of the chiasmus is represented in the translation by the inversion of the phrase, "in malice and jealousy spending our days." The elegantly balanced construction, in which singular nouns now correspond to the plurals in the first member, as well as the sounds of the original reinforce the impact of this central statement of the list.

The absolute use of *diagontes*, translated here as "spending our days," appears to be deliberate. *Zōntes*, "living" in the sense of 2:12, would be intolerable here; *diagontes bion* for a Christian existence, as in 1 Tim 2:2, is similarly inconceivable (see Ign. *Trall.* 2.1–2, not *kata anthrōpon zōntes*, "not living as men live but as Jesus Christ," and *en hōi diagontes*, "in whom [Christ] we exist"). For the PE to live in virtue is to live in Christ; a Christian existence is the only one worthy of the name. Time spent "in malice and jealousy" is in no sense life.

In the Hellenistic world, "malice," *kakia*, suggested pervasive badness, evil as a principle of action, just as *arete* suggested moral excellence as a quality. Although the NT never speaks of *arete*, Wis 5:13 contrasts *arete* with *kakia*, when the ungodly say, "We had no token of virtue (*aretēs*) to show but in our wickedness (*kakiai*) were utterly consumed." A fragment of Menander illustrates at more than one point the terminology and the thought of this passage in Titus, as he has one of his characters say: "My boy, you don't seem even to suspect that everything rots by reason of its own badness (*kakias*). All that defiles is from within. That is the case, if you'd only look into the matter, with rust on iron, with moths in mantles, with termites in timbers. So jealousy (*phthonos*), the very baddest of all the bad (*to kakiston tōn kakōn*), the impious impulse of an evil soul, has made you—makes you—will make you waste away" (Koerte 538/540K). In another fragment a misogynist catalogs the "bad desires (*epithymiai kakai*)" that follow on marriage. Pride of place goes to "the grimmest of diseases, jealousy (*phthonos*)" (Koerte 718/535K). For the scrawny, skeletal personification of jealous envy, choking on his own pent-up malice, see K. Dunbabin, *"Invida,"* pp. 7–37, plates 2–4. For the Hellenistic *topos* on envy and its links with hatred, wars, and murder, see L. T. Johnson, *"Topos,"* pp. 334–346. When, as here in Titus, *phthonos*, "jealousy," is coupled with *kakia*, "malice," the whole phrase clearly suggests that which saps and destroys trust and solidarity among human beings. In the situation constructed as a background for this passage, the reference is to the divisive "malice and jealousy" that the Zealots and their sympathizers had poured like acid into Palestinian Jewish life.

After the chiastic centerpiece, the next item in the list, the recherché and solemn-sounding *stygētoi*, harks back to *planōmenoi* (an effect sought by the alliteration of "detested" with "deluded"). The unique repugnance generated by the evil ways and attitudes of the Zealots is compressed into this unusual term.

The seventh and final item in this catalog, "hating one another," caps all of the previous. The mutual hatreds within this seditious party surpassed even the hatred that they had evoked. The heavy accent on Jewish hatreds as this list concludes presumes that those who heard this catechesis would recognize what these animosities had brought about. As the rabbis later taught, the Temple was destroyed by fratricidal hatred as well as by lust, idolatry, and avarice (texts collected by O. Michel in *TDNT* 4.688). The Roman perception of the Jews as "inflexibly loyal to one another and always ready to show mercy, but showing everybody else hostile hatred" (Tacitus, *Histories* 5.5) was not altogether accurate. The rancors were internecine as well.

The symptoms of these endemic animosities in intertestamental Judaism appear in *Pss. Sol.* 12.6, "May the Lord preserve the quiet soul that hates the unrighteous," and in the Qumran texts that prescribe that the sectaries "love all that which God has chosen and hate what he has rejected" (1QS 1:3–4), doing what God prescribes, "that they may love all the sons of light . . . and that they may hate all the sons of darkness, each according to his fault" (1QS 1:9–10). The instructor of those entering the Qumran community has to discern the spirits that motivate the aspirants and discriminate among them accordingly. "And as his love is, so shall his hatred be" (1QS 9:16). A little later, the Rule inculcates "the norms of conduct for a man of understanding in these times, concerning what he must love and how he must hate. Everlasting hatred in a spirit of secrecy for all the men of destruction!" (1QS 9:21–22; see A. Leaney, *RQM*, pp. 231–232). In the Damascus Document punishment awaits those who apostatize from the community, "because they did not depart from the way of traitors, and because they defiled themselves in the ways of lust and in the riches of iniquity, and because they took revenge and bore malice each towards his brother, and because each man hated his fellow" (CD 8:4–6). One recalls in this connection the closing hymn in the Rule, where an ethic of nonretaliation and goodness to fellow Jews is followed immediately by complete disassociation from those who rob and pillage their fellows (the resemblance to the activities of the Zealots is notable; see A. Leaney, *RQM*, p. 249). Judgment is left to God but the faithful sectary declares, "Nevertheless, I will not retract my wrath from men of iniquity. . . . I will not keep wrath against those returning from transgression but I will be merciless to those who have turned aside from the way" (1QS 10:17–21).

The dualistic ethic, presupposed by the preceding quotations, is based on a love/hate dialectic that resists systematic explanation. It has no lack of OT precedents (see Sutcliffe, "Hatred," pp. 345–349; Ringgren, *Faith*, pp. 132–139). Distinctions between the sin and the sinner do not appear commonplace in the ancient Jewish world, for which sin was not so much an object as the irresponsible action of a person, an action from which he could not disassociate himself. In Israel only God can forgive sin as only God can create. Accordingly, the sectary keeps his anger with sinners to himself, "in a spirit of secrecy," and abstains from outwardly hostile acts, even does good to those whom he holds in contempt (see A. Leaney, *RQM*, p. 249).

The *T. 12 Patr.* show that the way in which the Rule at Qumran resolved the tension between love and hate in ethical practice was by no means universally accepted. If a form of the *Testaments* circulated within the Qumran community, perhaps the Rule represents a "minimalist" guideline accommodating an approach that began to dissolve the love/hate dialectic by advising even internal goodwill in relation to enemies. As noted above, *T. Benj.* 8.1 exhorts "But you, my children, run from malice, jealousy, and hatred of brothers," and the *T. Gad* explicitly submits that "the spirit of hatred . . . is evil beyond all human deeds" (3.1), abhorring God's repeated commands about love of neighbor (4.1), desiring to exterminate "those who have committed the slightest sin" (4.6). The author urges his children, "Each of you, love his brother. Drive hatred out of your hearts. Love one another in deed and word and inward thoughts. . . . Love one another from the heart therefore" (6.1, 3). The internal practice inculcated here is far more demanding than that of the Qumran Rule and coincides notably with the love commands of Jesus, "Bless those who curse you, pray for those who abuse you . . . and you will be sons of the most High; for he is kind to the ungrateful and the selfish. Be merciful, even as your Father is merciful" (Luke 6.28, 35–36). The *Did.* appeals to the Lukan teaching in 1.3 (see 2.7), and *2 Clem.* also cites it, adding pointedly that this splendid teaching astonishes the pagans "but when they see that we not only do not love those who hate us but that we do not even love those who love us, they jeer at us and the Name is blasphemed" (13.4; cf. the jibe of Tacitus against the Jews already cited). The innovation of Jesus, at least as it was understood by those who believed in him, was the universal extension of the love command to every human person, regardless of age or sex or status or nationality or religion or attitude about the believer. Hatred, as a Christian response, was left for deeds and attitudes that displease God (see *2 Clem.* 6.6; 17.7; *Did.* 4.12; *Barn.* 4.1, 10; 19.2; *Herm. Man.* 12.1.1).

The abrupt conclusion of this septet of vices accents the contrast between the vicious existence just described and the act of God that is featured in the great baptismal confession beginning in the next verse. The abruptness has another effect rhetorically, for, as it brings the reader up short, it also demands a backward glance over what has preceded in order to negotiate the transition. The development thus far has been dominated by two septets that contrast present and past, virtue and vice, in the lives of the Jewish-Christian converts addressed. The contrasting lists, as well as not a few terms and concepts, coincide notably with a page in the Qumran Rule in which the operations of the spirits of light and darkness are described. The spirit of light causes

> The enlightenment of man's heart, the making straight before him all the ways of righteousness and truth, the implanting in his heart of fear for the judgments of God, of a spirit of humility, of patience, of abundant compassion, of perpetual goodness, of insight, of perception, of that mighty wisdom that is based at once on an apprehension of God's works and a reliance on his plenteous mercy, of a spirit of knowledge informing every plan of action, of a zeal for righteous government, of a hallowed mind in a controlled nature, of abounding love for all who follow the truth, of a self-respecting purity which abhors all the taint of filth, of a modesty of behavior coupled with a general prudence and an ability to hide within oneself the secrets of what one knows—these are the things that come to men in this world through communion with the spirit of truth.

A little later the contrasting list reads, "But to the spirit of perversity belong greed, remissness in right-doing, wickedness and falsehood, pride and presumption, ruthless deception and guile, abundant evil, shortness of temper and profusion of folly, arrogant zeal, abominable acts in a spirit of lewdness, filthy ways in the thralldom of unchastity, a blasphemous tongue, blindness of eyes, dullness of ears, stiffness of neck and hardness of heart, to the end that a man walks entirely in ways of darkness and of evil cunning" (1QS 4:2–6, 9–11; E.T. is Gaster[3], *DSS*, p. 49, with adjustments).

Granted that vice lists tend to be the more primitive, one infers that such items in Titus as "not to insult anyone, not to be argumentative" (3:2) may have a relation to an older catalog of vices that scored "a blasphemous tongue" (1QS 4:10, noting that LXX translates *gdp* with *blasphēm-*) and "shortness of temper" (1QS 4:10). The latter stands in contrast to the "patience" and "abundant compassion" of the catalog of good qualities in 1QS 4:3. The "fools" of Titus 3:3 remind one of the "profusion of folly" of 1QS 4:10 (*'wlt*) and by contrast the repeated emphasis in 1QS 4:3–6 on insight, perception, knowledge, "mighty wisdom," "a general prudence," and discretion. As Titus 3:3 decries the "disobedient" (who stand in contrast to those who "accept direction" in the preceding verse), 1QS 4.11 proscribes those whose ears are dull, whose necks are stiff, whose hearts are hard. A little later in the Qumran Rule, as it enjoins obedience upon the sectaries, there is an admonition that casts further light on this passage. "Let no man walk in the stubbornness of his heart to stray (*lt˓wt*) by following his heart and eyes and the thoughts of his inclination" (1QS 5:4–5; cf. 11–12). The perfect sectary intervenes by bringing "discernment to those whose spirit has strayed (*ltw˓y*), instructing in sound doctrine those who are murmuring" (1QS 11:1). The association of the "disobedient" with the "deluded" in Titus becomes clearer against this background (note that the LXX often translates *t˓h* with *plan-*). The "deluded," moreover, contrast with those who have the many forms of knowledge cited above. In the Qumran vice catalog the "abominable acts in a spirit of lewdness, filthy ways in slavery (*b˓bwdt*) to impurity" (1QS 4.10; cf. "greed" in 4:9) correspond strikingly to Titus, "slaving for diverse lusts and pleasures." Because the parallels are so conspicuous it is important to note that what the Qumran community regarded as "lewdness" and "impurity" may have only partially coincided with what the authors of the lists in Titus meant by "lusts and pleasures" (see the references in A. Leaney, *RQM*, p. 153, as well as CD 4:12–15 on the three nets of Belial). An approximate parallel to "in malice . . . spending our days" may be found in the "abundant evil" (*hnp*, "profaneness, pollution") of 1QS 4:10.

The list of the ills produced by "the spirit of falsehood" does not include parallels to the "detested, hating one another" of Titus (see above on the love/ hate ethical schema), but these evils do stand in striking contrast to the spirit that produces "abounding love for all who follow the truth" (1QS 4:5). Perhaps one detects an extension (and thus a Christianizing) of the quality endorsed by the Qumran Rule when the septet of virtues in Titus 3:2 concludes with the reminder "to be gentle, to show every consideration to every person." In any case, "consideration" corresponds to what 1QS 4:3 calls "a spirit of humility (*˓nwh*, a term that the LXX regularly translates with a form of *praü-*), of patience, of abundant compassion." When Titus commends readiness "to take any honest work," one is reminded of the "remissness in right doing" criticized in 1QS 4:9, not to mention the "arrogant zeal (*qn˒t zdwn*)" and "abominable acts" of 1QS 4:10. The Qumran Rule (like the Hebrew Bible) also knows a good sense for the term "zeal," for the spirit of truth produces "a zeal (*qn˒t*) for righteous government" (1QS 4:4). The coincidence with the opening of this paraenesis in Titus, "to be subject to government authorities," is not to be overlooked.

The nature of the evidence marshaled above permits only surmises about what brought about the coincidences between the contrasting septets of ethical qualities in Titus and the considerably longer antithetical lists in the Qumran Rule. The similarities surely imply common OT and Jewish ethical attitudes. They do not appear to be close enough to warrant positing a common documentary source or the immediate translation of the items from the Qumran Rule into the paraenesis of Titus. Possibly the coincidences are to be explained by positing a catechetical tradition in which the Jewish-Christian instructors knew or became acquainted with the sectarian features of the Jewish religious background of their neophytes. They would have then adapted this previous formation for use within a Christian setting just as they adapted the OT background that they had in common with their Jewish countrymen. If in fact the teaching of the Qumran Rule was exploited, it is notable that its schema of the two spirits and ethical dualism do not surface in these lists in Titus. The position of the Holy Spirit in the confession that follows in vv 4–7, however, signals another problematic governing this paraenesis in Titus, which (unlike Timothy) does not explicitly acknowledge unholy spirits.

3:4–6. *"When the humane munificence of our savior, God, was revealed, he saved us, no thanks to any upright deeds that we performed ourselves but because of his own mercy, saved us through a washing of regeneration and of renewal from the Holy Spirit that he poured out lavishly on us, through Jesus Christ, our savior."* With these verses begins a single Greek sentence that runs through v 7, a sentence that is characterized in verse 8a as "the Christian message, meant to be believed," *pistos ho logos.* The scribes of S, A, and P[61] began a new section with v 4, thus indicating where they thought "the message" started. G. W. Knight (*Sayings*, pp. 80–86) has reviewed the boundaries that commentators previous to 1968 had drawn for the "message, meant to be believed."

Each of these five citations in the PE appears to consist of a single sentence (1 Tim 2:14–3:1a represents special problems). Here in Titus, as in 1 Tim 3:1 and 4:9, the formula *pistos ho logos* concludes the citation (with S versus A); in 1 Tim 1:15 and 2 Tim 2:11, the formula precedes. The materials cited appear in various literary forms, ranging from the hymnic 2 Tim 2:11–13, through the homiletic liturgical charge of 1 Tim 2:14–15, the epitome of the Gospel in 1 Tim 1:15, and the ethical catechesis of 1 Tim 4:9. *NTG* [26corr] (unlike *GNT* [3corr]) prints the text of Titus 3:4–7 in a format that suggests a poetic source for the sentence. In a literal English version the poem would read,

4   When the generosity and the kindness appeared
     of our savior God,
5   Not by reason of works that are in righteousness
     which we performed ourselves
    But in accord with his own mercy
     he saved us through a bath of regeneration
    And of renewal of the Holy Spirit,
6   which he poured out on us lavishly
    Through Jesus Christ our savior,
7   so that made righteous by the former's grace
    We might become heirs according to hope of life eternal.

For a somewhat different format, see Joachim Jeremias (*NTD*, p. 74), who also suggests (because he posits Pauline authorship) that verse 5a is a Pauline interpolation in a hymn of praise that thanks God for the grace of baptism. When

M. Boismard analyzed the hymnic character of 1 Pet 1:3–5, he submitted that a parallel hymn at this point in Titus constituted a "re-reading" of the primitive baptismal hymn cited in 1 Pet (Boismard, *Hymnes*, pp. 15–23; cf. *DBSup* 7.1415–1455, esp. 1422–1423). R. P. Martin (*Carmen*, pp. 19, 292) classifies this passage in Titus among "sacramental" hymns. In the light of the more objective criteria commonly proposed for isolating hymnic passages in the NT (see Barth, "Traditions," p. 10), the first-person plural designating the congregation is notable, as well as the third-person singular aorists leading into a purposive clause and the chain of anarthrous genitives in v 5. Still, there is no introductory formula, no word of praise or thanks for the God who is explicitly named, no regular pattern of syllables or accents per stich, a soft parallelism between the stichs, and no obvious chiasmic features, "ring-composition," or the like.

If there was a baptismal hymn behind this passage (and the resemblances to 1 Pet have suggested this hypothesis), it has been freely reshaped in the tradition, probably the liturgical tradition for baptism, to form a prose, didactic prayer (an *oratio*, as the Roman rite called such compositions in Latin liturgy). The author of Titus cited the rolling cadences of a single sentence from that prayer, which in its turn may have taken up and amplified a prior hymnic confession by the church assembled for baptism (the schema that remains to this day in the Easter Eve baptismal eucharist in the Roman rite is Scripture reading, hymnic response, oration). The insertion of another *pistos logos* into the center of the great thanksgiving prayer of 1 Tim 1:12–17 may be modeled on the prayer context suggested for this passage in Titus. G. Cuming ("ΕΥΧΗΣ," p. 81, discussing an elusive phrase in Justin, *Apology* 1.66.2) has proposed that *logos* in that phrase means "a form/pattern of words" proper to a particular prayer of thanksgiving (see 1.13.1). A. Gelston (*"Euchēs,"* pp. 172–175) has reservations about other aspects of Cuming's evidence, but a prayer formula cited here in Titus would support Cuming's case. In any case, the practices of ancient formal rhetoric adequately account for the form of the citation in Titus without recourse to a much more problematic poetic source (see Lash, "Hymn-Hunting," pp. 293–297, with its reference to Marrou, *Education*, p. 197).

Was there an intervening stage between the baptismal *oratio* and the citation here in Titus? *Logos* in the formula *pistos ho logos* may designate a verbal composition in an oral as well as a written medium (see Knight, *Sayings*, pp. 14–18). The fact that there are five texts, each of which the PE call "the message meant to be believed," may well point to a preexistent collection or enchiridion of ecclesial aphorisms, culled from various catechetical and liturgical sources. This collection the author of the PE would have commended, as he did a parallel collection of "the wholesome sayings that come from our Lord, Jesus Christ" (1 Tim 6:3; a collection that would resemble the one from which the author of Acts 20:35 cited "the words of the Lord Jesus"; see Moule, *Birth*,

p. 284). C. H. Roberts has suggested that papyrus tablets for recording the directives of Jesus (on the model of the papyrus notebooks used by Jews for recording prescriptions of the Mishna, the oral law) appeared among the Antiochean Christians engaged in the mission to the pagans sometime before 100 C.E. (Roberts and Skeat, *Birth*, pp. 58–60; see the INTRODUCTION). If this is the case, the congregation from which the PE emanated (the Roman Christians, on the hypothesis favored in this commentary) adopted the Antiochean innovation early on, copying its papyrus tablets with Jesus' *logia*, assembling other protocodices of local liturgical and catechetical materials, which the author of the PE cites as "the message that is meant to be believed, according to the teaching" (1:9).

The quotation marks that open the translation at 3:4 serve to set off and contrast "the message meant to be believed" with respect to the ethical lists of vv 1–3. This function is performed by the postpositive *de* in the original, a particle that may be the redactor's insertion into the text that he is citing. The text itself has been fashioned out of very archaic (even Palestinian) *didachē*, traditional Pauline doctrine, and terminology that plugs into the thought currents of the Roman Hellenism. The analysis that follows proposes to identify these elements.

The aorist *epephanē*, represented by "was revealed" in the opening temporal clause, has a tenuous link with the Lukan corpus but none with the remainder of the Paulines (in contrast to *phaneroun*, 1 Tim 3:16). The **phain-* cluster of terms was from Homer's time associated with the bodily appearances of deities (see *Iliad* 20.131, "For the gods are hard to behold when they appear bodily"; *Odyssey* 16.161). As C. Mohrmann (*Études* 1.249) has noted, the Greeks recalled an appearance of a god on its anniversary as the god's birthday (the reading of this passage from Titus on the Christmas feast in the Roman rite still recalls this view). As in 2:11, so here the incarnation at a particular moment in human history is conceived as an epiphanic act "of our savior, God," that is, an act of the Father. The trinitarian development of the thought continues in v 5, where "the Holy Spirit" is named, and in v 6, where "Jesus Christ" receives the savior title that was God's as Father (the third recurrence of a pattern that has appeared before in the brief compass of this letter in 1:3–4 and 2:10–11). In the other Paulines, "savior" is not used of God the Father (and only once of Jesus, in Phil 3:20). If a baptismal hymn lies somewhere behind the tradition cited at this point, it bears noting that Luke–Acts designate the Father as "savior" in a hymnic context (Luke 1:47; cf. the doxology of Jude 25) and Jesus as "savior" in kerygmatic contexts (2:11; Acts 5:31; 13:23). The baptismal setting presupposed at this point in Titus suggests that the three names here have some link with the baptismal rite. The absence of the titles "Father" and "Son" at this point may indicate a rite in which a sacramental hymn by the congregation or the creedal expression of trinitarian faith in a formulaic, threefold question addressed to the one being baptized (or less probably a declarative formula pronounced by the baptizer) did not yet highlight these titles (the baptismal formula "in the name of the Father and of the Son and of the Holy Spirit," absent in the *Apostolic Tradition* of Hippolytus, appeared in the Roman rite only after 700 C.E.; see Whitaker, "Formula," pp. 1–12 and "Baptism," p. 58).

The original baptismal setting of Titus 3:4–7 reminds the reader that the sharp, even abrupt contrast with the preceding verse is more than a matter of words, more than a matter of concepts. Two different orders of human existence are juxtaposed here. The *logos* cited here does not explicitly mention faith, but that throws into relief the force of *pistos;* the "message" cited is "meant to be believed," and it comes from the unique moment of initiation into the life of faith that is described in the citation. An existence without faith in Christ, an existence that was verifiably foolish and hateful, stands in antithesis to a divine intervention that offered a new existence to Jews and Gentiles who put their faith in Jesus Christ.

"The humane munificence" of God the Father represents two feminine nouns followed by a singular verb, a construction that suggests that the pair are closely coordinated and conceived to be a unit (see BDF §135.1b). Thus "humane munificence" here is synonymous with "the grace" of 2:11 (see Demosthenes, *Against Meidias* 21.148, questioning whether a wrongdoer "deserves pardon or kindness or any kind of favor" [*ē philanthrōpias ē charitos*]). The phrase in the translation represents the psalmic and Pauline *chrēstotēs,* "generosity," and the biblically rather unusal *philanthrōpia,* which to Latin ears meant *humanitas,* "kindness" (see *VL* 25[2].919; *OLD* s.v.; Schadewaldt, "Humanitas Romana," pp. 43–62). The Roman Christians may have acquired their predilection for the former term from Paul's letter to them. There God's *chrēstotēs* (along with his forbearance and patience) are meant to lead the Jew and the pagan alike to repentance and faith (Rom 2:4; cf. 11:22). *Chrēstotēs* in secular Greek was used only of persons, and it may be significant that *chrēstos,* "good," could in the first Christian century be heard as the title *Christos,* due to the nearly identical pronunciation of *i* and *ē* in *koine* Greek (see K. Weiss in *TDNT* 9.484, 488–489; W. Grundmann in *TDNT* 9.579 n. 546; Brown and Meier, *Antioch/Rome,* pp. 100–101). Thus here the mention of the savior God's visible *chrēstotēs* prepares the way verbally for the description of the savior *Christos/ chrēstos* (see Benko, "Criticism," pp. 1057–1058, and how the LXX Ps 33:9, *chrēstos ho Kyrios,* "the Lord is good," becomes for the scribe of the P[72] 1 Pet 2:3, *Christos [XC] ho Kyrios,* "Christ is the Lord"). The LXX does speak of God as *chrēstos* in Wis 15:1 and 2 Macc 1:24. The importance of the "Christ" title in Titus is thrown into relief by nonuse of the title "Lord" as well as "Son" in this letter.

The attribution of *philanthrōpia* to God in this citation in Titus is as striking in its way as the first appearance of this terminology in Greek literature; for it is in the shattering opening of Aeschylus's *Prometheus* 11, 28 that we for the first time read of the *philanthrōpos tropos,* a way of being on the side of humanity, that dooms the divine Titan to everlasting torture, spreadeagled on a wintry crag (see Ferguson, *Values*, pp. 102–103, 111 and passim for what follows). The cluster of **philanthrōp-* terms suggest "gifts and services to the community" (J. Ferguson), but they also carry a nuance of condescension (as that of royalty and persons in power) that sharply differentiates them from *agapē*, "loving care," and its congeners. Menander's saying, "Being rich can also make us humane (*philanthrōpous*)," illustrates the point, though his "To refrain from any wrong-doing makes us humane" was likewise proverbial (Koerte 19, 398/19, 463K; see also *Aspis* 395 and *Samia* 35). From Aristophanes (*Peace* 392) to Plutarch (*Moralia* 1051E, 1075E), Greek deities are *philanthrōpoi*. In Septuagintal Greek the closest approach to this usage is that of Wis 1:6 and 7:23, where God's wisdom possesses "a humane spirit." But in Philo the God of Israel has *philanthrōpia* (*Virt.* 188), the loving kindness of a father (*Virt.* 77; *Prov.* 2.6) as well as that of a king (*Cher.* 99). The confession in Titus shares this Hellenistic Jewish conception of the *philanthrōpia* of God as Father.

What in the Jewish and then in a Jewish-Christian milieu (in Rome) elicited this solemn assertion of the *philanthrōpia* of the God of Israel and the God of Christians? The answer may lie in the contemporary pagan Roman perception of the Jewish religion and those who claimed to worship the one God. Tacitus, in his description of the Neronian persecution of the Roman Christians in 64 C.E., notes that they were condemned "not so much for the crime of arson as for hatred of the human race (*odio humani generis*)" (*Annales* 15.44; see Keresztes, "Imperial Government," pp. 247–257). The latter charge was leveled by Hellenistic authors against Jews as early as Hecataeus of Abdera (300 B.C.E.) but became popular under the influence of a polemical work about the Jews by the first-century B.C.E. rhetorician, Apollonius Molon, who taught Cicero and Caesar on the island of Rhodes. Josephus quotes him calling the Jews *misanthrō-pous*, "misanthropes," and "unwilling to have anything in common with people who have elected a different kind of life" (see Stern, *Authors on Jews*, pp. 26, §11; 155–156, §49–50 for the texts cited here and in what follows; Benko, "Criticism," pp. 1062–1065; Bruce, "Tacitus," pp. 38–40). Diodorus Siculus (first century B.C.E.) writes of the Jewish tradition of *to misos to pros tous anthrōpous*, "hatred for human beings," and of *ta misanthrōpa . . . ethē*, "their misanthropic ways," *tēn misanthrōpian pantōn ethnōn*, their "misan-thropy for all nations," and *ta misoxēna nomima*, "their laws which hate strang-ers" (Stern, *Authors on Jews*, p. 182, §63). Lysimachus has Moses instructing his nation "to show goodwill (*eunoesein*) to no human being," and Apion has all Jews swear "to show no goodwill to any other nationality, particularly to the Greeks" (Stern, *Authors on Jews*, pp. 383, §158; 413–414, §173). Quintilian asserts that "the founder of the Jewish superstition . . . drew together a people bent on the destruction of others." Tacitus himself, in his implacably bitter description of the Jews, asserts that "They regard all the rest [of mankind] with the hatred normally kept for enemies" (*adversus omnis alios hostile odium,*

Histories 5.5). According to this construction, his description of the victims of Nero would fit particularly Jewish Christians in Rome in 64 c.e., despised by their pagan neighbors, rejected and perhaps betrayed by fellow Jews, whether Christian or not (Benko, "Criticism," pp. 1067–1068, 1070).

The Jewish Christians of the first generation, even in Palestine, had experienced persecution at the hands of their countrymen, not least at the hands of Paul; and later the apostle himself took up the pagan caricature of his fellow Jews to stigmatize them as "opposed to every human being (*pasin anthrōpois enantiōn*)" (1 Thess 2:15; on other grounds the Pauline authorship, strictly speaking, has been questioned and reaffirmed; see most recently, Schmidt, "Interpolation," pp. 269–279 and Donfried, "Paul," pp. 242–253, with their references to the literature). In an ironic turn the Christians were perceived by their first-century pagan contemporaries as Jews, and there was an undeniable accuracy about the observation, for their founder, their leadership, and many of their number in that generation were of Jewish origin, had been committed to the Jewish religion, and continued to use the sacred books of the Jews as well as to maintain a good deal of Jewish religious praxis. Because of this pagan perception of their identity, which perdured well into the second century, as Galen and Celsus witness (Benko, "Criticism," pp. 1098–1108), they were tarred with the same brush as their Jewish confreres and contemptuously dismissed as haters of the human race.

Philo early in the first century (as Josephus at the end) had countered the popular pagan slander against Jews by extolling the *philanthrōpia* of the God of Israel. Jews were devoted to the God who loved humankind; they could not reasonably hate what their God loved (on the benevolent virtues of God in Philo, see Mott, "Ethics," pp. 36–46). The Jewish Christians who fashioned the baptismal confession quoted here in Titus countered the same pagan perception with basically the same insight, but adding that Jesus, the savior, was the visible, historical revelation of God's *philanthrōpia* to all human beings. That vision of the baptismal profession became in its turn the antithesis to the vicious existence that converts from extremist Jewish sects had once led. They had formerly been "detested, hating one another." Now, in faith, they have seen "the humane munificence of our savior, God, . . . revealed." They have no longer any basis for hating those whom God, their Father and savior, has loved.

The language and conceptualization of the baptismal confession thus far, even the use of *philanthrōpia* with its precedents in the language and thought of Philo, fit snugly into an archaic Jewish-Christian tradition. With the antithetically balanced clauses that open v 4, "he saved us, no thanks to any upright deeds that we performed ourselves but because of his own mercy," the terms and the thought of this "message meant to be believed" become strikingly Pauline. The clauses seek to articulate the reasons that could have called forth "the humane munificence" just cited. The negative former clause clears the ground. There is no appreciating God's saving work until men and women have demolished root and branch any presupposition about having earned this rescue because of the good things that human beings have first done for their God. The vice list of v 3 was a summary of what "we were once," as sinners in a people who awaited the revelation "of our savior, God." It was Paul's contention that no human being, not even the people of Israel, was made upright "from the works of the Law" (see, e.g., Rom 3:20, 27–28, 4:2; 9:11). The "deeds that we performed ourselves" (note the emphatic *hēmeis*) did not proceed from any basic uprightness in us, and hence our so-called "upright deeds" were radically no better than their authors, and the authors were bad persons. Thus God's rescue of men and women was in no sense owed to human beings. In the seven other NT uses of forms of *en dikaiosynēi*, the phrase refers to the works of God or Christ or the human being already made upright by God. In the crabbed Greek of this passage in Titus, "deeds" are qualified with the Septuagintal *en dikaiosynēi*, "in uprightness," but not with the Pauline "of the Law." The righteousness in question is biblical, that is to say, righteousness as the OT and first-century Judaism conceived it, an obedient performance of the commands of the one God (see 2 Tim 3:15–16 and the references in Reumann, *Righteousness*, p. 234, §433). The performance of such works, precisely as our own, merely human response to the divine will, emphatically did not bring God's salvation to his people. That had always been the faith of Israel (see Deut 9:5–6), and it was emphatically reaffirmed in first-century Palestinian Judaism. Thus 1QM 11:3–4 reads, "You delivered us many times by the hand of our kings, by virtue of your mercies (*bᶜbwr rḥymkh*), not for our own deeds (*bmᶜśynw*), which we have done wickedly, nor for our sinful actions." Again, according to 1QH 4:30–32, "And I, I know that righteousness lies not with a human being nor perfection of conduct with mortals. Only with God on High are all works of righteousness; and never can a human being's conduct be firm except by the spirit which God has fashioned for him, to bring unto perfection the conduct of mortals" (Gaster, *DSS* modified). This concept was foundational for OT belief and prayer (see the parallels cited by Yadin, *War*, pp. 309–311), and it was probably praying the psalms that shaped the language in Titus. The mentality envisioned here was not altogether alien to the Hellenistic world, which cherished the lines of Xenophanes about the first duty of persons being to pray to an unnamed god for the power to do right things (*euxamenous ta dikaia dynasthai prēssein;* cited in Athenaeus, *Deipnosophistai*, 11.462e–f; see Meijer, "Philosophers," pp. 232–233).

In v 7 below the Pauline teaching about and terminology for uprightness will recur in this confession. Meantime, the text now expounds positively how God's rescue reached those who were incapable of reaching him. As opposed to the specious reason that has just been rejected, the genuine one is now seen all the more clearly and forcefully. The only possible reason for God's saving intervention is to be sought in God the Father himself. "He saved us . . . because of his own mercy." The accusative *hēmas*, "us," stands in sharp antithesis to the nominative *hēmeis* of the preceding phrase. In the salvation of human beings God is wholly subject, men and women are wholly objects. Salvation appeared in the person of one whose name means "savior," one through whom the Father's righteousness and mercy touch and heal inwardly those who believe and are baptized. The language again suggests a congregation whose prayers were the psalms, and the coincidence with 1 Pet 1:3 is the first of a number that suggest a tradition of baptismal liturgy shared by Titus. That the tradition is emphatically Jewish Christian is suggested by the prayer canticles and other material in Luke's infancy narrative, where the theme of the saving mercy of the God of Israel is conspicuous (Luke 1:50, 54, 58, 72, 78; in Luke 10:37 *eleos* refers to human mercy).

The term *eleos* in the examples cited in the NOTES almost always translates the *ḥesed* of the MT, and thus this word became the bridge over which much of the OT faith about the covenant love, the *ḥesed* of Yahweh, passed into Hellenistic Jewish congregations and through them into Jewish-Christian belief. The process has been summarized in the maxim *lex orandi lex credendi*, the law that establishes how one ought to pray is the same law that establishes how one ought to believe. As the Hebrew tradition understood and spoke of God's acts occurring "because of Yahweh's covenant love," so the prayer here taken up in Titus explained the Father's saving intervention as "because of his own mercy."

The archaic Jerusalem kerygma had explained the brute fact of the cross as "for our sins, according to the scriptures" (1 Cor 15:3). The tradition cited here in Titus further unpacks this kerygmatic summary, explaining that "for our sins" means "no thanks to any upright deeds that we performed ourselves." Then this tradition (as also 1 Pet) draws from the scriptures a motive for the death of the Lord. It is the *ḥesed* of Yahweh, his *eleos*, which was the compelling reason adduced by the OT for God's initiating a covenant bond with his people. That same divine mercy is now adduced as the motive for initiating a new covenant with his people. This archaic, Jewish Christian use of *eleos* apparently did not prevail in the first Christian century; yet it was authoritative enough to resist displacement by the *agapē* cluster of terms used by Paul and John for the Father's and the Son's love of human beings (Gal 2:20; John 3:16).

The means by which God's saving mercy intervened are now specified: he "saved us through (*dia*) a washing of regeneration and of renewal by the Holy Spirit." The aorist represented by "saved" implies that a specific intervention by the Father in the historical lives of those who had come to believe brought them into a community (*hēmas*), a church that included the apostle and Titus, the congregations now addressed in this epistle, along with those who originally used this "message meant to be believed." That intervention was certainly in baptism, and thus sacramental (to use the terminology of a later age). It is the Father who is the principal agent, not Christ (as in Eph 5:26), and the process of "washing" or bathing is qualified perhaps in the Semitic manner with two adjectival genitives which could be paraphrased, "a regenerating and renewing bath" (Spicq, *EP*, p. 653). Instead, the genitives may be objective and mean, "a bath that brings about regeneration and renewal," as when Philo writes of the soul "that has washed away its defilements and made use of baths and purifications that bring about understanding (*tois phronēseōs loutrois* . . . *kai katharsiois* [s.v.1.]; *Mut.* 124; see 2 Cor 3:7–9 on "the ministry of death / of the Spirit / of condemnation / of righteousness").

The meaning of the chain of genitives that follows "through a washing" is ambiguous when examined closely, and the terms are patient of several translations (see BDF §168; Bratcher, *Translator*, pp. 121–122). Schematically, they are

through a washing . . .
1. that belongs to (see BDF §162 on origin, relationship)
2. that leads to (see BDF §166 on direction, purpose, result)
3. which consists in (see BDF §167 on appositive)
4. that effects (see BDF §163 on objective)

. . . *regeneration and renewal.*

The first possibility appears to be conceptually anomalous in early Christian Greek; the second resembles the usage in the phrase "baptism of repentance" (Mark 1:4; *SFG* §13), and is conceptually possible. The third is possible grammatically and conceptually; its probability will be discussed below. The fourth appears probable grammatically and conceptually. Before settling on this last possibility, one must come to a decision on how to interpret "of the Holy Spirit."

The difficulties with the first option above appear to compound when various possibilities for the understanding "of the Holy Spirit" are added. With the latter three options, the following possibilities present themselves:

A. *through a washing* that leads to *regeneration and renewal*
   1. which lead to the Holy Spirit (direction, purpose, result)
   2. which consist in the Holy Spirit (appositive)
   3. which belong to the Holy Spirit (origin)
B. *through a washing* that consists in *regeneration and renewal*
   1. which lead to the Holy Spirit
   2. which consist in the Holy Spirit
   3. which belong to the Holy Spirit
C. *through a washing* that effects *regeneration and renewal*
   1. which lead to the Holy Spirit

2. which consist in the Holy Spirit
3. which belong to the Holy Spirit.

An interpretation that involves "regeneration and renewal" leading to or being the equivalent of "the Holy Spirit" (A.1–2, B.1–2, C.1–2) appears anomalous and conceptually indefensible. Some Western scribes surely wanted the genitival "of the Holy Spirit" to mean "through (*dia*) the Holy Spirit." Apparently they were deliberately excluding the possessive meaning of A.3, B.3 and C.3, a meaning that the shorter and more difficult reading allows. Yet the longer Western text, harmonizing with the preceding *dia loutrou* and the following *dia Iesou Christou*, raises more conceptual problems than it solves, for it seems to regard the washing, the Spirit, and Jesus as instrumental in the same sense.

Granted then that the text understands the Spirit to be in some sense the origin and possessor of "regeneration and renewal," which of the interpretations of their relation to the "washing" is most probable? The appositional sense (B) appears to be most difficult to justify, for it explains *ignotum per ignotius* or, better perhaps in this case, a known process, "washing," through a phrase about unknown factors that demand explanation. The interpretation of the "washing" as "leading to" or "resulting in" regeneration and renewal (A) raises the very question that exercised the Western scribes and provoked their insertion of *dia*. Their indefensible solution does not invalidate their intuition of the problem. It is possible that the author of this tradition meant to imply that the process of washing in baptism produced a rebirth of which the Spirit was the origin in another sense (the "from" in the translation is deliberately ambiguous). But this may be to put too fine a point on the rhetorical construction of the tradition, which stems from liturgical prayer rather than theological analysis. The objective interpretation of the genitive (C) in which the process of "washing" produces or effects "regeneration and renewal," which in their turn belong to the Spirit (thus "from" in another sense), seems best to preserve the development of the thought in the passage, which is concerned with a visible, tangible process that has invisible, intangible effects in another order or sphere, which is properly that of the Spirit.

Still another possibility for reading the genitival chain presents itself. Perhaps "through a washing of regeneration" should be read independently of the Spirit's renewal, which in its turn becomes a second, distinct effect produced by the baptismal bath. The reference on this reading might be to the sealing with the Spirit (Confirmation in a much later terminology) that followed the baptismal washing. The text then would refer to salvation "through a washing of regeneration and [through] renewal from the Holy Spirit." Another option for separating the phrases would involve taking *kai* epexegetically and translating "through a washing of regeneration, *that is*, renewal from the Holy Spirit." Both possibilities appear rhetorically forced and inappropriate, but the anarthrous character of the whole phrase makes it impossible altogether to exclude them.

Before addressing the question of the nature of "regeneration and of renewal from the Holy Spirit," the unusual *loutron* for "washing" needs some elucidation. This *pistos logos* and the PE themselves never use the **bapti-* cluster of words to describe initiation into the Christian life. It is suggestive that Paul, for all his other uses of **bapti-* words, used this cluster only once in writing to the Romans (6:3–4). Indeed, Heb 6:2 and 9:10 may indicate the normal understanding of this terminology in the Roman Jewish-Christian churches. *First Clement* does not employ the terms, and Hermas does so only in *Vis.* 3.7.3.

The term *loutron* (in contradistinction to *baptisma*) suggested in the Roman world at large a place, even a building, available to the public for bathing at a nominal charge. As every Greek town worthy of the name had a theater, so a Roman town had at least one heated bath. Rome itself eventually had, in the imperial period, about nine hundred baths, including monumental public structures called *thermae*, the first of which was given to the people of Rome by Augustus's great lieutenant, Agrippa, about 19 B.C.E. Then Nero and the Flavians continued the practice, which reached its apogee in such stunning complexes as those of Caracalla and Diocletian. The buildings themselves were surrounded with formal gardens, courts for exercise, colonnades for strolling, all from the humane munificence of the reigning emperor. Such structures were meant as centers for the people, and they provided not only physical refreshment but also cultural formation. The heating systems for air and water still stagger the imagination, but it is easy to overlook the fact that these vast complexes came to contain shrines, libraries, theaters, club rooms, classrooms for philosophers and poets, and art treasures from the conquered Hellenistic world, as well as sumptuous marble mosaics and paintings from the artisans of the city (see Lucian, *Hippias;* Seneca, *Epistulae morales* 86.1–13; Statius, *Silvae* 1.5). The Roman bath was an entry into a vast new world that existed for the ordinary people in the middle of the stench and filth of ancient urban life (see Carcopino, *Rome*, pp. 277–286). The baths were "the most important buildings of the Romans" (*OCD*, s.v.), so when this tradition in Titus calls the Christian baptismal rite a *loutron*, the turn of speech is an unusually evocative innovation, for it makes a standard fixture of Roman social life into a parable for a cleansing and purification of the human body that are more than bodily, as in fact the Roman baths were understood to be more than hygienic conveniences.

The "washing" by which "the humane munificence" of God "saved" his people introduced them into a new world "of regeneration and of renewal from the Spirit." What did the author of Titus and his source mean by that phrase? As the NOTES above indicate, in the first Christian century and not least in the Roman ambience, *paliggenesia* popularly meant a return after death to one's own bodily life, a "resurrection" (note the translation for this term in Matt 19:28 in LSJ, s.v.). Probably the "washing of regeneration" here means a bath that effects bodily resurrection, in other words, a rite through which the merciful God brings believers into the mystery of the death and resurrection of Jesus and sets them on a course that culminates at last in the bodily resurrection of all human beings, with its accompanying judgment. The emphasis here on the resurrection of Jesus and the faithful would give a specifically Christian cachet to "regeneration," about which there were differing conceptions in other quarters of first-century Judaism. Thus in Philo's philosophical view *paliggenesia* had nothing to do with judgment and referred to the incorporeal existence of the immortal soul alone (see Burnett, "Philo," p. 470).

In circles in which Jewish apocalyptic flourished, the concept of the eschatological renewal of creation forms a likely conceptual background for the way "regeneration" is understood here in Titus. Texts from Isa such as, "For behold, I create new heavens and a new earth" (65:17, LXX *estai gar ho ouranos kainos kai hē gē kainē;* 43:19; 48:6–7) were the core that energized such diverse apocalyptic fallout as one encounters in the books of *Enoch* (thus 91.16), *Jub.* (1.29), and some of the Qumran documents, not to mention the targums (on all of these and what follows see Le Déaut, *Nuit,* pp. 239–257).

Particularly tantalizing in this connection is the concept of "renewal" at Qumran. After the description of the two spirits battling in human hearts, the Rule asserts that "God has apportioned these [spirits] in equal measure until the final age when he makes new" (*w'śwt ḥdšh;* 1QS 4:25). Significantly, it is in texts of hymns and prayers that the contours of this "renewal" start to appear, as in 1QH 13:11–12, where the meditation on God's creation leads to reflection on the time he will bring these things to an end "by creating things that are new, by setting aside what was formerly established." The sect believes that "the new covenant" is beginning among them (CD 6:19; 8:21; 19:34; 20:12) and will be irrevocably established by the future "Prince of the Congregation" (1QSb 5:21). On the Feast of Weeks (Pentecost), the sectaries prayed thus: "And you [God] have appointed them [the Qumran congregation] to be set apart from all the people as a holy thing for yourself, and you renewed (*wtḥdš*) your covenant, by the vision of your glory [on Sinai] and the words of your Holy [Spirit], by the works of your hands" (1Q34 bis 3:2.6–7; DJD 1.154; see also the fragmentary daily prayers of 4Q503 3:2; 8:9; 11:2 [DJD 7.105–117] and the puzzling fragment of 6Q 20:5 [DJD 3.136–137]). Another document from Cave Four deals with the epochs fixed by God for human history, in the course of which the author observes, "in accordance with the tender mercy of God, in accordance with his goodness and with the wondrous manifestation of his glory, he has granted to some of the sons of the earth to gain admittance to the congregation of the holy, to be reckoned among the community of angelic beings who are with him, to have station there for life everlasting (*lḥyy 'wlm*) and to be in one lot with his holy ones" (4Q181 3–4, but as corrected and interpreted by Strugnell, "Notes," pp. 254–255, and Milik, "Melki-sedeq," pp. 109–124; E.T.

here is Gaster, *DSS* modified). The immediately following lines of the text seem to paraphrase Dan 12:2, referring once again to "life everlasting."

The brief hymn of thanksgiving in 1QH 11:3–14 (see Kittel, *Hymns*, pp. 112–116) is particularly intriguing. After two stanzas with elaborate lists of the attributes of God, the closing refrain and stanza (lines 9–14) may be translated as follows:

[Refrain] For you made them know your dependable counsel, and through your wondrous mysteries you have enlightened them.

[Stanza C] For your glory's sake you cleansed man from transgression, so that he may consecrate himself to you; (you have cleansed him) from all impure abominations and guilt of evil doing, to unite him [with] your dependable sons and in a lot with your holy ones. (This was your purpose.) To lift from the dust the worm that is man [see Isa 41:14] into the counsel [of eternity], (to lift him) from a crooked spirit to [your] divine [holy] understanding and to station him before your face, with the eternal host and the spirits [of eternity], and to be renewed (*wlthds*) with everything else that is and with those who know in a common exultation.

Similarly, after a description of the wars that usher in the final judgment, 1QH 6:34 declares, "And those who lay in the dust have hoisted the banner and the worm of mankind has raised up an ensign [. . .]." The worm-eaten flesh of the faithful dead will return to life to participate in the renewal that will occur at the end of time.

Initiation into the community of the "new covenant" is certainly one of the events that belong to this period, but more may be at stake than a "present, realized resurrection" due to knowing God's mysteries (*pace* Cavallin, *Life*, pp. 64, 68 nn. 36–38; G. Nickelsburg in *IDBSup*, p. 350). The Qumran cemetery lay beside the dwellings in which these hymns were read and perhaps even written. The physical death of their colleagues appears not to have troubled the beliefs and hopes of the survivors. The dead were still part of this community, which expected a new act by the creator God that, for its cosmic and salvific dimensions, could be compared with a new birth (1QH 3:7–10) and a new creation (see Le Déaut, *Nuit*, p. 245). The knowledge of this mystery of renewal involved, at least for some members of the sect, a revelation of the resurrection that would usher in the divine judgment and cosmic renewal. All of this is the object of a lively hope for a future containing realities that human beings have not experienced (thus a *new* creation). These realities in turn are expressed in a hymnic genre and doxological language that resist close, systematic analysis. Because the hope for personal immortality and even the resurrection of the flesh was cherished in some quarters (but not universally) in intertestamental Judaism (see Mansoor, *Hymns*, pp. 84–89), it appears in the light of the texts adduced difficult to rule out the acceptance of such hopes by some members, even influential ones, of the Qumran congregation.

A principle that is presupposed in the language of regeneration and renewal in Jewish (see 1QH 12:4–11, esp. 7–8) and Christian sources alike is that the end time of the world mirrors its beginning. "The Lord says, 'See, I make the last things as the first (*ta eschata hōs ta prota*)' " (*Barn.* 6.13). One can probe the mysteries of the end of the world by analyzing its beginnings. Thus Genesis corresponds to the Apocalypse, the *genesis* of human history will culminate in a *paliggenesia*. The one whom God raised from the dust in a living body at the beginning he will raise from the dust at the end. The gospel tradition remembers Jesus appealing to this principle to set aside Moses on divorce (Mark 10:3–9; Matt 19:4–8); it underlies his refutation of the Sadducees by appealing to the God of the patriarchs in Gen, "the God not of the dead but of the living" (Matt 22:32; cf. Mark 12:18–27 with Luke 20:27–39; *SFG* §281), in order to drive home his point that there is indeed a final resurrection of the dead that lies beyond their conceptions. The striking denial of sexual activity to men and women who have risen from the dead in this passage may indicate why the term *paliggenisia* was used for "resurrection" not only in Matt 19:28 but also in this passage of Titus. "Regeneration" does not suggest sexual generation, so it does not immediately pose the difficulties that inhere in language about being born again (cf. 1 Pet 1:3, with its explicit mention of the resurrection, with John 3:3–8). The difficulty of Nicodemus was not endemic to Judaism, it was the difficulty of the Hellenistic world, nowhere posed more acutely than in Epicurus's axiom, "We were born once, there is no being born twice; rather we must forever be no more" (*Sententiae vaticanae* 14). The language of "regeneration" outflanks biological caviling about the parabolic language of rebirth and confronts the hearer with the eschatological vision of the God who, according to the Scriptures, created human beings and thus has the power and will to re-create them. Whoever denies this, knows "neither the scriptures nor the power of God" (Mark 12:24; Matt 22:29 but not in Luke).

There is a further reason that *paliggenesia* was precisely the term to articulate the hope of Christians for their vindication in the final resurrection and judgment to be ushered in by their Lord. This Christian hope was a new patch on the old apocalyptic garment popular on the Palestinian scene among Zealot guerillas and Qumran sectaries. Their fervor eventually found an outlet in the suicidal frenzy of the revolt of 66–70 C.E., which was supposed to usher in a cosmic divine intervention and victory over all who oppressed God's people. Among Jewish Christians who had lived through those days, even from afar, there was a tendency to distance the expression of their eschatological faith from its apocalyptic kindred. Thus Jesus' cosmic intervention at the final resurrection, on a vast, public, and drastic scale (as in Matt 19:28) moved from that wide screen to the sacramental order within the community of believers, where the liturgical prayer about baptism emphasizes the internal, personal effect of

God's intervention. In this way apocalyptic enthusiasm was depoliticized. Entrance into the congregation of those who believed in the risen Jesus and the final age initiated by his resurrection meant first of all a change of heart, not a change of government.

This decaffeinated apocalyptic had its dangers too. They became apparent when influential Christian teachers proposed "that the resurrection has already occurred" (2 Tim 2:18). The internal linkage and cohesion of the death and resurrection of Jesus, the believer's death, burial, and rising with Jesus in baptism, and the final resurrection and judgment were no more self-evident in the first Christian generations than they are now (see 1 Pet 3:18–22; 2 Pet 2:5; 3:3–13, noting their link with the Roman Christians). Some Corinthian Christians, in the middle of the first century, had already collapsed the eschatological structure of Christian existence and provoked the withering reply of Paul himself (1 Cor 15). When the apostle wrote to the Romans, he presumed that those Christians believed that baptism had made them participate "in the likeness" of the death, burial, and rising of Jesus. He distinguished two aspects of participation in the resurrection, one aspect still to come at the last judgment, another that begins with the baptismal initiation into the community, "so that . . . we too might walk in newness of life" (Rom 6:4–5).

It is to that second aspect of the existence initiated through the baptismal washing that the second term in the phrase "regeneration and renewal" refers. The inseparable complement of *paliggenesia* is *anakainōsis*. Each term qualifies the other, but the second, as the NOTES show, is specific to the Pauline tradition and emphatically designates an inner, unseen, present aspect of the human person. The Pauline neologism apparently caught the ear of Roman Christians, and whoever composed the baptismal oration cited here in Titus put an unmistakably Pauline stamp and interpretation on the preceding (and perhaps very archaic) *paliggenesia* by joining it to *anakainōsis*. "Regeneration" was susceptible to misinterpretation by an apocalyptic *manqué* (that thought God was on the verge of changing everything) and by an overrealized eschatology (that thought God's intervention required no changes whatever). In either scenario, God's final judgment posed no threat for their actions. The Pauline *anakainōsis*, with its accent on the internal effect of the baptismal washing, put a definitive touch on the understanding of *paliggenesia*, interpreted as the resurrection of the flesh. In Paul's teaching, both the resurrection of the human body and the renewal of the human mind have their origin in the Holy Spirit (see Rom 7:21 through 8:27, esp. 8:2–13). Thus here in Titus both the "regeneration" and the "renewal" are "from the Holy Spirit," in other words, the one Spirit is the origin of the resurrection to come and the renovation of the Christian heart, now set on "what is good and acceptable and perfect" (Rom 12:2). For the later Greek Fathers on this specifically Christian understanding of *anakainōsis* as referring to the internal, invisible renewal of human beings by God's word and Spirit, see Lampe, *PGL* s.v.

As one looks more closely at the explicit terminology for the Spirit in the PE, notable variations can be observed. For the first time in this correspondence the Spirit is described at this point in Titus as "Holy," and the description is evidently not a reflex formula for the author. In point of fact, *hagios*, "holy," had not previously occurred in Titus, and apart from its one later use of the Spirit in 2 Tim 1:14, the only other adjectival use of the term is the reference in 2 Tim 1:9 to the God "who saved us and called us for a holy life (*klēsei hagiai*)." The one other use of the word in the PE is as a noun, in 1 Tim 5:10, where *hagion* ("the saints") refer to living Christian travelers. For the PE, because the "Spirit" is "Holy," those called to the Christian life are holy. Accordingly, when one returns to the initial appearance of the "Holy Spirit" at this point in Titus, it seems far from arbitrary that the Spirit is described as holy precisely in conjunction with the baptismal washing that recreated and renewed a family for an eternal inheritance.

Thus, in summary, the visibility of the "washing" through which the Father's mercy rescues believers forestalls one's taking "regeneration and renewal" as simply interior and unseen; the invisibility and interiority of the originating Spirit prevents them both from being understood simply as the result of an external, visible, material operation. The Spirit who changes the human heart will change the human body, and thus the human world.

Verse 6 goes on expanding the description of the Spirit as the one that the Father "poured out lavishly on us, through Jesus Christ, our savior." The description of the coming of the Spirit in terms of a once-for-all pouring out (an aorist in the Greek) upon the faithful suggests the visible baptismal washing in which the sacramental waters had flowed over the believer. The terminological coincidences with the LXX's prophets, describing the way in which Yahweh's spirit would pour out over Israel, put the bestowal of the Holy Spirit and the baptismal act within the cadre of events that are "according to the Scriptures" and so willed by the God of Israel (note the way John 19:37 appeals to LXX Zech 12:10 to show that Jesus' death was according to the Scriptures).

Although LXX Ezek 39:29 writes of the time "when I pour out my heart upon the house of Israel, says the Lord Yahweh," and LXX Sir 1:9; 18:11 of God's pouring out his wisdom and mercy, it is the language and imagery of Joel that have left the most notable mark on the language here in Titus. "And it shall come to pass afterward, that *I will pour out my spirit* on all flesh; your sons and your daughters shall prophesy, your old men shall dream dreams and your young men shall see visions. Even upon the male slaves and female slaves in those days, *I will pour out my spirit*" (cf. Joel 2:23–24 in the MT with Isa 32:14–15; 44:3–5). The downpour of a rainstorm, bringing life and growth to a desert, is the image the prophet exploits in transmitting this oracle of Yahweh. The apostolic interpretation of the Pentecost events, after the death and rising of Jesus, opened with this prophecy (according to Luke) and closed with a repetition of the crucial verb to describe the exalted Christ who, "having received from the Father the promise of the Holy Spirit, . . . has poured out (*execheen*) this which you see and hear" (Acts 2:17–18, 33). Thus this OT prophetic text is alluded to at just those points in Luke's work that the Spirit comes upon first Israel, then, in the household of Cornelius, "upon all flesh" (10:45; NOTES). The work of the Spirit, like the work of Jesus, must be "according to the Scripture."

The "message meant to be believed" has enhanced the verb "poured out" with the adverb "lavishly," *plousiōs*. The Spirit's munificence in this text is, like the Spirit itself, radically unseen and internal, and this lavish outpouring is "on us." The first-person plural should not be heard in a monopolistic sense. Rather it designates the personal, internal experience of the Spirit that the community of believers profess together (Rom 5:5) as well as the universal goal inherent in the witness of the church as a community, which seeks and hopes to share the lavish blessings poured out "on us" with all flesh, that is, with all human beings (see 2:11–14). When this letter of "Paul" to "Titus" takes up the first-person plural of the *pistos logos*, the reader would be expected to understand the phrase of the Spirit poured out on Paul, the Jew, and Titus, the Gentile, men who, like the whole congregation of believers, are to take the lead in sharing the Spirit's gifts with all people.

The act of the savior Father, which has poured out the regenerating renewal of the Spirit upon his people, has taken place not simply "through a washing" but also "through Jesus Christ, our savior." In Titus the only uses of "through," *dia*, are in this *pistos logos*. In fact, for all of the many uses of this particle in 1 Tim and 2 Tim, the PE do not employ this phrase again (frequent as it is in the rest of the Paulines). Its only appearance in Lukan corpus is in Acts 10:36, where it also may pertain to the source being redacted at that point. Thus this turn of phrase has a Pauline cachet, while the subsequent "our savior" is peculiar to the PE. For the third time in Titus the phrase "our savior" has been applied to Jesus after it has first been used of the Father. Perhaps this pattern may have originally belonged to the style for God and Jesus in the *pistos logos* being analyzed here. The form and authority of this liturgical source in its turn influenced the terminology of 1:3–4 and even the other liturgical piece cited in 2:11 and 13, which seems to be a paraenesis that presupposes a creedal position such as the one here in 3:4–7.

7. *"God's was the grace that made us upright, so that we could become heirs with a hope of life eternal."* The unusual positioning of *ekeinou* (see also 2 Tim 2:26) in the opening phrase of v 7, represented in the translation by "God's was the grace that made us upright," is parallel to the usage *kata to autou eleos* in v 5. Hence the reference is emphatically to "the grace of our savior God," the Father, in v 4 (to whom the *charis* of 2:11 was also attributed). The reference here at the conclusion of the "message meant to be believed" to its opening phrase serves to bind vv 4–7 closely together and to set them distinctly apart from the preceding verses.

The goal and purpose of the divine, saving intervention described in this *pistos logos* are introduced by "God's was the grace that made us upright," a phrase that takes up the Pauline cause and language from the apostle's historic confrontation with his Jewish-Christian colleagues on the relation of works (of the Law) to justification. The topic was broached in v 5. Here the verb *dikaioun*, "to make upright," stands as a creedal commitment to the Pauline side in the controversy about God's righteousness and human works, and it functions in a way that the Nicaean *homoousios*, "of one substance," does in identifying the convictions of the Athanasian party in the Arian controversies of the fourth century. For the seventh and final time in this "message meant to be believed," a form of the first-person plural recurs in *genēthōmen, so that we could become*, and thus a process of change is sketched that stretches from the once-for-all events of baptism and justification to "life eternal."

The characteristic emphasis of the PE appears when one contrasts their positive teaching about uprightness (or justification), using the *dik-* cluster of Greek terms, with their single reference to "wickedness," in other words, the lack of uprightness, *adikia*, in 2 Tim 2:19. The rest of the Paulines exploit the antithetical *adik-* terminology much more often; the PE have no taste for that verbal dialectic (perhaps because the opponents themselves are exploiting it in endless quibbles over terminology; see 1:10–11; 3:9; 1 Tim 1:6–7; 2 Tim 2:14, 16). In any event, in 2 Tim 2:19 the author stonewalls the teaching of those whose conduct fails to correspond with their profession of Christian faith, those who do not "depart from wickedness."

In this perspective the emphasis of the PE on the good conduct of all classes of believers becomes intelligible. The new Pauline presbyter-bishops are to be selected for their virtues, familial and personal. They are to be "sensible, upright (*dikaion*), devout, self-controlled," as in 1:8 above. Along with Titus (2:1, 7–8) they are to instruct believers, old and young, men and women, free and slaves, to make visible in their daily conduct "the grace of God" intended for "all human beings" (2:11). That grace had dawned in the life and death of Jesus "to set us free from every wrong and to cleanse for himself a people of his very own" (2:14). The "fine deeds" (2:7, 14; 3:8, 14) of this people (along with their Pauline ministers), disciplined by this grace to "disown godlessness and worldly lusts, and to live in a sensible, honest (*dikaios*), godly way," continue to reveal in human history, "in this present age" (2:12), what the terminology for righteousness actually signifies. Genuine Christian conduct is not antinomian, and it stops the accusations of unbelievers who claim that it is (see 2:8, 10; 1 Tim 3:7; 6:1). As shown in the COMMENTS on 1:16 and 2:7, for the PE good deeds are not enough; they must be visibly good and attractive (*kala* as distinct from *agatha*). The actual conduct of believers is thus kerygmatic, that is to say, it proclaims to unbelievers the gospel of Christ's death for sins and his resurrection for our justification (see Rom 4:25).

Christian deeds precede and are the setting not for justification but for the Christian word, "the message meant to be believed," here in 3:4–7. The unbeliever is attracted by the changed conduct of those who once were as he still is. He asks why and how this happened. The answering word, the *pistos logos* here, is the ecclesial confession of faith in the gospel as Paul taught it. The formulation is certainly no quotation of an extant Pauline letter; yet it no less surely proclaims Paul's gospel on the total gratuity of the uprightness bestowed by baptism and the Spirit. With the phrase "God's was the grace that made us upright," the language and conceptualization of this confession coincide certainly with that of the Paul of Rom and Gal (see Reumann, *Righteousness*, pp. 98–102, 104–105 and my essay in the same volume, pp. 231–238, used extensively in these NOTES and COMMENT). The church that used this confession was as firmly committed to the Pauline explanation of the relation between genuine holiness and merely human acts as it was committed to the seriousness and missionary importance of the visibly good conduct that the Spirit prompted in those who had "put their faith in God" (3:8b). The Paul of history had to counter charges that his teaching about justification encouraged evil acts (Rom 3:8; 6:1, 15). The author of the PE was compelled to explain why the conduct of believers was (and ought to be) attractively good.

Granted that it takes Paul to summarize adequately the Pauline theology of justification, the second-generation attempt that one meets here, in the Lukan corpus (see Reumann, *Righteousness*, pp. 135–143, 219–220), and in *1 Clem.* 32.3–4 (see Räisänen, "Werkgerechtigkeit," pp. 79–99) is as good as what most succeeding generations have lucubrated and better than many. Such liturgical summaries as this one in Titus open a way back to the Paul of history and the apostle's understanding of the grace that he preached in the previous generation. The PE, like Luke–Acts and *1 Clem.*, do not succumb to the presumption that Paul was readily intelligible to all and sundry or to the counsel of despair that the church at large could not be expected to assimilate or to profit from the Pauline gospel (see 1 Tim 2:7; 2 Tim 1:11). The PE particularly attempt to transmit not just the Pauline apostolic teaching (important as that was) but the Pauline apostolate to churches that had forgotten, or ignored, or were embarrassed by the words and works, the life and death, of this slave who had not been above his Master. Accordingly, this correspondence portrays a Paul who teaches in the church, as a member of the church, and for the sake of the church. There was little point in transmitting Paul's teaching unless the church also perdured, living as Paul would have had it live, supervised by the apostle across the generation gap as it was once guided by Paul's emissaries and epistles across geographical barriers.

The process that began with justification has its issue "so that we could become heirs with a hope of life eternal." As with the cluster of **dikai-* terms that refer to uprightness, so with the family of words in **klēr-* that designate various aspects of inheritance one must deal with juridical terms and images. The inheritance language of this *pistos logos* may represent again a creedal crystallization of an imagery and language that Paul used on occasion, notably in

Rom 4:13–14 and 8:16–17, where (unlike here) the heirs are explicitly children (*tekna*) of the Father. For the gospel tradition, in the vineyard parable, the son is the heir and so is to be murdered to get his inheritance, *klēronomia*. The parabolic setting reminds the reader of the care necessary to interpret these legal images. Inheritances in the human, juridical order were no concern of Jesus (Luke 12:13), but he is repeatedly portrayed as answering inquiries about "What shall I do to inherit eternal life (*zōēn aiōnion klēronomēsō*)?" (Luke 10:25; 18:18 = Mark 10:17). In Acts Abraham receives no inheritance in Palestine (7:5). When Paul bids farewell to the presbyters of Ephesus in Acts 20:32, he says, "And now I commend you to God and to the word of his grace (*tōi logōi tēs charitos autou*) which is able to build you up and to give you the inheritance (*tēn klēronomian;* cf. the *klēros* of 26:18) among all those who are sanctified." The coincidences, conceptual and terminological, with *pistos logos* about the grace of the Father that makes human beings heirs suggests that the source placed under the pen of Paul here in Titus was placed on his lips in Acts.

The ones "made upright" are "heirs with a hope of life eternal." The *kata*, "with," is polyvalent and patient of several interpretations. It may signify the goal or purpose of the savior God's merciful act (see 1:1). In this case, its meaning would be parallel to the phrase of 1:2, "in hope (*ep' elpidi*) of life eternal" (see 1 Tim 1:16 with *eis* and BAGD, p. 287, *e*). As at 3:5 above (cf. 1:3), *kata* could refer to the originating cause or reason for God's intervention. Moreover, the particle can give the phrase an adjectival sense (as in 1:1b or 1 Tim 6:3). Then the meaning would be that the "heirs" are people who hope for "life eternal." Finally, the *kata* phrase could be the equivalent of a noun in the genitive, which in this instance would have to be construed objectively and so as the equivalent of the first interpretation above. The polyvalence may well be intentional and appropriate also for a formula that was intended for public use. In that case the variants with *epi* and *eis* noted otherwise in the PE understand the *kata* of an already venerable, local formula as referring to purpose. Perhaps one catches the echo of the Hebrew *k*[e] in this usage of the Greek particle and thus a Semitic background for the church that fashioned this summary confession.

The final clause summarizes the content of the eschatological hope of believers, a hope of an eternal life that involves bodily resurrection (see Excursus V, "The Terminology for Life in the PE"). That hope in its turn is grounded on the revelation that God, the Father of the family of believers, has mercifully promised this inheritance to them. The influence of this whole section of Titus on the theology of Christians has been considerable. *Diognetus* 9.1–4 is well known. Moreover, it touched Christian faith at the edge of the Roman Empire in Scythia Minor, for there an epitaph (fourth or fifth century) of a husband and wife announces, "We have come here, among the just, with hope of resurrection (*eph' elpidi*), of the enjoyment of life eternal" (as cited by G. Horsley, *NDIEC*, 2.197, §110).

8a. *That is the Christian message, meant to be believed.* What the author of the PE means by the phrase *pistos ho logos* opens the question of the origin of this formula. It appears in Greek for the first time in Rome in the latter first century B.C.E., when Dionysius of Halicarnassus in his *Roman Antiquities* 3.23.17 has a speaker submit that his (misleading) report will be believed "because I shall have made my acts correspond with what I profess" (in 9.19.3 the verb *einai* appears in the phrase; see BDF §127.5 on its omission). About the end of the first Christian century, Dio Chrysostom, again in connection with Rome, speaking of Trajan's munificence to him, remarks, "perhaps the report (*logos*) will not appear credible." Another link with the Roman scene was suggested by W. R. Oldfather and W. L. Daly ("Menander," pp. 202–204), who noted that the Roman playwright Terence, after citing a commonplace about the avarice of old people, has a character say (somewhat confusedly) "et dictumst vere et re ipsa fieri oportet" ("and it has been said truly and should be put in practice"; *Adelphoe* 955) as an idiomatic paraphrase of a line in the lost *Adelphoi* of Menander, which arguably could have read *pistos ho logos k'apodochēs pasēs axios*, a metrical form of the words that appear in 1 Tim 1:15 and 4:9. The latter part of this phrase does not appear here in Titus, though verse 8b expresses its meaning in other words.

Pistos ho logos has yet to be documented in Greek-speaking Judaism, but there is a notable parallel from the Qumran fragments of the "Book of Mysteries" (as J. Milik called it), where a section that begins with the OT formula "And this for you is the sign that these things shall take place" continues with an apocalyptic description of the final triumph of righteousness, which concludes by saying, "All who hold fast to the wondrous mysteries will be no more. The world shall be filled with knowledge and there shall be no more folly in it." Then the author concludes his narrative of the sign with the words "The word will assuredly come to pass and certain is the prediction," *nkwn hdbr lbw' w'mt hms'* (1Q 27:1.5–8 [DJD 1.103]). The sentence is not exactly parallel to the Greek formula, but it is close enough to suggest that the Greek (already in circulation in Roman ambience at the beginning of the Christian era) would be at hand for a Jewish-Christian author who wanted a formula for citing specifically Christian teachings, a formula that would at the same time have some kinship with the Palestinian, apocalyptic language with which Jewish converts (perhaps even Essenes) had been familiar before baptism.

Another factor, ultimately also Palestinian, may have made the Greek formula attractive for citing Christian teachings. Theodore of Mopsuestia noted that *pistos ho logos* is "like the saying expressed in the Gospel, 'Amen, amen, I say to you' " (*Ad Tim* 3:1; Swete, *Theodore* 2.97). Scores of times in the gospel tradition Jesus is represented as prefixing *Amēn, (Amēn,) legō hymin/soi* to his sayings, calling attention to and emphasizing his own teaching, proposing it for belief precisely because he is saying it. The *pistos ho logos* formula could well correspond in cultivated Greek to the more Semitic phrase in the gospels, with *legein* becoming *logos* and with *amēn* becoming *pistos* (see Knight, *Sayings*, pp. 12–13).

The Book of Revelation may provide another clue about the origin and core meaning of the *pistos* formula. As that work of apocalyptic prophecy opens, Jesus Christ, the faithful witness (1:5), directs John to write to the Laodicean church, opening the letter with, "These things (*tade*) are what the Amen, the witness faithful and true (*ho pistos kai alēthinos*) says" (3:14). In 19:11 the vision begins, "Then I saw heaven opened, and behold, a white horse! He who sat upon it is called Faithful and True (*pistos . . . kai alēthinos*)" and at 19:13, "the name by which he is called is the Word of God (*ho logos tou theou*)." Thus the risen Jesus is the faithful and truthful one, par excellence, for the prophet John. He who in his earthly life had prefaced his sayings with the distinctive "Amen, I say to you," is himself the "Amen," the one who is to be believed. His authority and his faithfulness stand behind the words and the writing of his prophet. In the vision of the new Jerusalem, the one seated on the throne can say accordingly, "Write this, for these words (*hoi logoi*) are to be believed and are true (*pistoi kai alēthinoi*)" (21:5; 22:6). So the faithfulness of God and his Christ and their truthfulness are at stake in the words, the *logoi*, that they and their messengers have spoken. The apocalyptic prophetic vision of Qumran is set aside as the Christian prophet proposes a completely different view of the eschatological mystery of God's righteousness entering human history. Still, although the realities differ, there appears to be a common language for articulating them.

Paul uses the phrase *pistos ho theos*, "God is faithful/to be believed and trusted," and its formal resemblance to *pistos ho logos* offers several further clues to the origin and meaning of the latter. The opening thanksgiving prayer of 1 Cor 1:9, also the typological paraenesis of 1 Cor 10:13 on temptation, conclude with an emphatic "Faithful is God" (see 2 Thess 3:2–3 for "Faithful is the Lord"). The adjective is in a predicative (not an attributive) relation to God, and therefore makes the principal point of the statement (see Knight, *Sayings*, pp. 21–22; Wallace, "Adjective," pp. 135–136). In 2 Cor 1:18 the resemblance becomes more than formal as the apostle writes, "But God is faithful (*pistos ho de theos*), that our word (*ho logos hēmon*) to you has not been Yes and No." The initial phrase here has become practically an authenticating or certifying oath (see *DELG*, p. 869 on the juridical overtones that belong to the most archaic roots of the *peith-* system). Thus the proclamation of Paul, Silvanus, and Timothy about Jesus as Son of God was a *logos* with an indisputable content on which their witness was in agreement. If the Corinthians believe God, they must believe the apostolic *logos*. Both of them are *pistos*.

Pistos in Greek generally and in the NT admits of an active translation (i.e., "believing, faithful," as in 1 Tim 4:10, where Christians are called *pistoi*). The passive sense, however, represented here by "meant to be believed," is more common (the usage in Aeschylus, *Persians* 2, 528, 681, 979 is apposite) and certainly the meaning in biblical Greek when it qualifies God or Jesus. In the whole Pauline corpus *pistos,* whether active or passive, describes persons, except in the phrase *pistos ho logos.* This phenomenon so impressed E. Walder that he proposed that *logos* in these passages was used in the personal sense as it is in John 1:1 and 14, of the Word who became flesh. W. Lock's critique rendered this position untenable (see Knight, *Sayings,* pp. 18–19 for the references). Yet there is this to be said for it: the PE as a whole and this formula in particular do conceive of the faithfulness of "the God who is without deceit" as standing behind and as present in the apostolic preaching (see 1:2–3). There is no escaping the emphasis that *pistos* brings to this citation formula.

Some have proposed that a formula for citation and one for emphasis are mutually exclusive. But this dialectic appears arbitrary when one notes that *logos* refers to the material cited, while it is the predicative *pistos* that serves to accent and specify the manner in which the hearers make "the Christian message" their own (see Knight, *Sayings,* pp. 19–20).

In summary, then, the emphatic citation formula *pistos ho logos* appears to have been adopted from Hellenistic Greek, perhaps in a Roman setting, by a Jewish-Christian congregation. The formula had conceptual and even verbal ties with contemporary Jewish and Jewish-Christian prophetic and apocalyptic phraseology, as well as an echo in the traditions of a formula employed by Jesus to introduce his teachings. Perhaps behind the repeated formula in the PE lies the title *pistoi hoi logoi* for an actual collection of authoritative texts from the liturgy and catechesis of a local church with strong Jewish ties (one is reminded of the Jewish-Christian congregation implied in the context of Heb 10:23). If the content of the citations in the PE represents the mentality of a larger collection, one could extrapolate to a community that was distancing itself from the ticking bomb of apocalyptic and moving toward a more general, inclusive, and even abstract theological vision of "the ways of God with man." In any event, this was the view of the author of this correspondence, who chose this quintet of sayings for his epistolary.

The author of the PE had this collection among his sources, and he used its materials according to his own plan as he sought to communicate the Pauline tradition to a second generation of Jewish converts whom the apostle had not himself instructed, either face to face or in letters. So the "Paul" of the PE writes to the Jewish-Christian churches envisioned in Titus through a coworker and subordinate. His apostolate can continue after his death through those whom he has designated to continue it. And it is not only individual human beings who can continue it. The sacramental usage of the churches, their confessions and prayers, their creeds and catechesis, their collections of authoritative written texts (whether Scriptural or ecclesiastical), their whole way of living, all are levied into service. Anything that bears the cachet of the Pauline apostolate helps continue that apostolate. For the author of the PE (as for Luke–Acts),

Paul has not died in any sense except the physical, and that is practically ignored.

II.B.3.c. TRUE AND FALSE INSTRUCTION (3:8b–11)

3 ^{8b}I wish you, Titus, to insist on these matters, so that those who have put their faith in God will be intent on "taking the lead in fine deeds." Activity like that is fine and is useful for people.

⁹On the other hand, steer clear of foolish speculations, of genealogies, of controversies, of wranglings about the Law. Such activities are useless and fruitless. ¹⁰Give the divisive man one warning, then a second. Don't see him again, ¹¹for you can be sure a man like that has turned sour and keeps on sinning as he brings on his own condemnation.

NOTES

3:8b. *I wish you, Titus, to insist on these matters.* "I wish" represents *boulomai*, which will reappear in 1 Tim 2:8 and 5:14 (both also in the first-person singular); and 6:9. Almost half of the thirty-three other NT uses are in Luke–Acts. Of the four other uses by Paul, three refer to the apostle's personal will (2 Cor 1:15, 17; Phil 1:12); the Spirit gives a portion to each person as he wills in 1 Cor 12:11. In the Ap. Frs. the verb is almost confined to *1 Clem.*, *2 Clem.*, and Hermas, where it frequently designates the divine will. Forms of *boulesthai* characterize the letters of Hellenistic kings (see the first-person singular in Welles, *Correspondence*, nos. 5.12; 52.27), and among the frequent appearances of the verb in the LXX for the will of God and human beings, King Antiochus writes a letter saying, "I am determined (*boulomai*) to assert my claim to the kingdom . . . and I intend (*boulomai*) to land in our territory" (1 Macc 15:3–5; Goldstein, *AB 1 Macc* version). The verb suggests a personal, deliberate decision for which the person making it has to take ultimate responsibility, for good or for ill (as the only uses in *T. 12 Patr.* illustrate, *T. Zeb.* 1.7; *T. Jos.* 4.1).

"To insist," *diabebaiousthai*, in 1 Tim 1:7, describes certain self-styled "rabbis" who boldly assert things in which they have no competence and about which they have no title to speak. This composite verb (see BDF §116), though common enough in Hellenistic Greek, appears nowhere else in biblical Greek, the Ap. Frs., or the *T. 12 Patr.* In a fragment of Papias, however, he "vouches (*diabebaiomenous*) for the truth" of the interpretations of the apostles that he had heard from the presbyters of the previous generation (*apud* Irenaeus, *Adver-*

sus haereses 5.33.4 *ut cit.* Eusebius, *Church History* 3.39.3). Jewish authors use the word for confident assertions, whether true or not (see *Ep. Arist.* 99; Philo, *Det.* 38; *Deca.* 139; Josephus, *Apion* 2.14, 288; *War* 3.314; *Ant.* 10.161). For *bebaios,* etc., in the inscriptions and papyri, see Spicq, *Lexic.,* pp. 182–185.

   so that those who have put their faith in God will be intent on "taking the lead in fine deeds." "So that" formally opens a result clause (N. Turner, *Grammar* 3.103–104), which may be construed imperatively both here and in 3:13–14, where the language coincides with this verse in other respects (Deer, *"Hina,"* p. 148). The Septuagintal verb *phrontizōsin,* "those . . . will be intent," which is not found elsewhere in the NT, leads off this clause in Semitic fashion. In the LXX the no more than fifteen uses of *phrontizein* occur mostly in the latest strata and regularly refer to providing for security (1 Macc 16:14) and for adequate clothing, food, and drink, for the common good (see LXX Prov 31:21; Sir 32:1; 50:3–4; 2 Macc 4:21; 5:21; 11:15). In the Ap. Frs. only Ign. *Pol.* 1.2 employs the verb to urge care for unity among Christians. Menander, *Perikeiromenē* 544 (Sandbach, *Menandri*), employs this verb of a slave who cares more about his lunch than about his master. For the papyri and inscriptions (esp. *CII* 722, 723) see Spicq, *Lexic.,* pp. 950–952.

   "Taking the lead in fine deeds" is in quotation marks because it recurs word-for-word in 3:14 below. See 2:14 on "fine deeds." "Taking the lead," *proistasthai,* also is used of bishop, deacons, and presbyters in the church orders being cited in 1 Tim 3:4, 5, 12 and 5:17. The appearance of forms of *kalos* with this verb in the PE is notable. The only other NT occurrences are in 1 Thess 5:12, of the leaders of the Christians in Thessalonika, and in Rom 12:8, of a local leader in the ecclesial work of charity, whether in the sense of patron or administrative officer or both (see Cranfield, *Rom.,* pp. 625–627). Hermas (in the one use in the Ap. Frs.) writes copies of his book not only for Clement to send abroad and for Grapte to use in exhorting the widows but also "in this city [Rome] you shall read it yourself with the presbyters who are leaders (*meta tōn presbyterōn tōn proistamenōn*) of the church" (*Vis.* 2.4.3). For the *proestos* in Justin, see *Apology* 1.65; 67 (*PG* 6.428–429), where he is "the one who has been placed over the brothers" to preside at the Roman Sunday eucharist (assisted by deacons and readers) in which he receives and sees to the distribution of offerings for relief of the poor and sick, of travelers and prisoners. In the eight Septuagintal uses of the *proistanai,* it is explicitly linked with terms for a household in 2 Kgdms 13:17; Prov 23:5; Amos 6:10, and in LXX Bel 8, the *proestēkotas* of the pagan temple are the *hiereis,* "priests," of Theod.

   "Those who have put their faith in God," *hoi pepisteukotes theōi,* is an unusual way for the NT to describe believers in God (or for that matter, in Christ). Romans 4:3 (cf. 4:17) and Gal 3:6 employ an articular form of the phrase as they cite LXX Gen 15:6 (as does Jas 2:23). The Philippian jailor and his household in Acts 16:34 "put their faith in God (*pepisteukōs tōi theōi*)." In Acts 27:25 Paul says, "I put my faith in God (*tōi theōi*)" with reference to the fulfillment of the prophetic vision that has just been narrated. The LXX has only a handful of instances of the expression, and of these only LXX Prov 30:1 and 4 Macc 7:21 (with *pepisteukōs theōi*) have the anarthrous phrase. Only the articular expression appears in the Ap. Frs. (*1 Clem.* 10.6, citing Gen 15:6; and of Christian believers in *Barn.* 16.7 and *Herm. Man.* 9.7; 12.6.2; *Sim.* 5.1.5). Similarly, Josephus uses only the articular phrase of those who trust in and rely upon the protection of the God of Israel (*War* 3.387; *Ant.* 2.117; 3.309; 4.5; cf. 20.48).

Activity like that is fine and is useful for people. Literally, "These are fine (*kala*) and useful for human beings (*anthrōpois*)." Later texts tend to read *ta kala* (D¹ and the *Textus receptus*), perhaps for stylistic reasons (see J. K. Elliott, *Greek Text*, p. 193). For *kala* (*erga*) see 1:16 and 2:7. For "people," *anthrōpoi*, see 2:11.

"Useful," *ōphelima*, will appear in 1 Tim 4:8, of bodily exercise and godliness, and in 2 Tim 3:16 of the Scriptures; the antonym, *anōpheleis*, appears below in v 9. *Ōphelimos* does not otherwise occur in biblical Greek or *T. 12 Patr.* but a Roman connection appears in the Ap. Frs.: *1 Clem.* 56.2 calls the admonition that he is writing "fine (*kalē*) and exceedingly useful" and, in 62.1, "most useful for those who want godly and just (*eusebōs kai dikaiōs*) direction to a virtuous way of living" (see also *Herm. Vis.* 3.6.7).

9. *On the other hand, steer clear.* Literally, "go around," a middle imperative address, that appears in this form in 2 Tim 2:16. Active forms of the verb recur twice otherwise in the NT to designate a circle of bystanders (cf. Acts 25:7 with John 11:42). The word is not used in the Ap. Frs., and the half-dozen uses in the LXX offer no parallel to the late meaning here in the PE. The earliest instances of the meaning "to shun" appear in Philodemus of Gadara, who came from Palestine to Rome to teach Epicurean philosophy in the first century B.C.E. (cf. Sudhaus, 1.384.8 with 1.8.36; 180.18–19). A similar usage and geographical trajectory appear in Josephus, *War* 2.135 (of the Essenes who shun oaths); *Ant.* 1.45; 4.151; 10.210, and in the second century C.E. links of this usage with the Roman scene continue to appear (Galen, *De usu partium* [Teubner] 10.14; Marcus Aurelius 3.2). The Atticist Lucian mocks the usage as a solecism (*Solecist* 5) but uses it nevertheless (*Hermotimus* 86). See MM s.v. for the few papyri that at this time start to use the verb to mean "shun."

of foolish speculations, mōras zēteseis. An expanded form of this unusual phrase recurs in an admonition to Timothy (2 Tim 2:23) but not otherwise in biblical Greek or the Ap. Frs. The noun *zētēsis* appears in 1 Tim 6:4, which has other points of contact with this passage in Titus (cf. *ekzētēsis* in 1 Tim 1:4). Otherwise in the NT, apart from John 3:25, only Luke writes of controversy between judaizing Christians and the apostles Paul and Barnabas as *zētēsis* (Acts 15:2, 7), and it is Festus's word for the debates that swirled about his hotly controversial prisoner, Paul (Acts 25:20; see the uses of the cognate *zētēma* in 15:2; 18:15; 23:29; 25:19; 26:3). Philo calls philosophical investigation *zētēsis* (about God in *Mig.* 76), but Josephus uses the term occasionally in a sense that appeared only in the later first century of a controversial question (see *Apion* 1.11; *Ant.* 20.132). The qualification of *zēteseis* as *mōras,* "foolish," here and in 2 Tim 2:23 indicates that a bad sense for the noun was not to be presumed.

Mōros, "foolish," appears ten times in the NT outside the PE, with the Pauline uses concentrated in 1 Cor 1:25, 27; 3:18; and 4:10 (see the cognates in 1:18, 20, 21, 23; 2:14; 3:19), where it describes the paradoxical foolishness of God and his Christians. A mirror image of this usage can be seen in Rom 1:22, of idolaters, "claiming to be wise, they became fools (*emōranthēsan*)." The "silly talk (*mōrologia*) and levity" of Eph 5:4 bear comparison with the phrase here in Titus. In the Ap. Frs., *1 Clem.* 39.1 links *mōroi* with *apaideutoi* to describe the "foolish and undisciplined" people who buck his paraenesis. There are almost a dozen uses by Hermas. Of them, *Sim.* 8.6.5 is notable, as it describes those who have introduced strange teachings into the Roman congregation, misleading the faithful with "foolish teachings (*didachais mōrais*)." Ignatius, in *Eph.* 17.2, asks in a context of following false teachers, "Why do we foolishly (*mōrōs*) perish?"

In the LXX there are about three dozen uses of *mōros,* almost always in sapiential contexts where the term suggests a religious evaluation. The lion's share of the occurrences are in Sir (see Spicq, *Supp. Lexic.,* pp. 490–495). In the relatively few instances in which a corresponding Hebrew text is extant, *mōros* translates forms of *nbl* and *skl* (both meaning "to be senseless or foolish"), which in the Qumran documents are used of a foolish word or stupid laughter (1QS 7:3, 9; CD 10:18; on the link with Eph 5:4, see Kuhn, "Epheserbrief," pp. 338–339).

of genealogies. Genealogiai will reappear in the phrase "tales and endless genealogies" in 1 Tim 1:4, but there is not another occurrence of the term in biblical Greek or the Ap. Frs. For Philo and Josephus, see COMMENT. A few manuscripts substitute *logomachias,* "quibbling about terminology," for "genealogies," probably under the influence of 1 Tim 6:4 (J. K. Elliott, *Greek Text,* p. 193).

of controversies. Ereis, literally, "contentions" (BDF §47.3). In the singular, *eris* recurs in the list in 1 Tim 6:4 (s.v.l.). The seven other NT uses are similarly in a negative sense, as in Paul, where the normal Hellenistic plural, *erides,* appears without variants in 1 Cor 1:11. For *erin* in Titus 3:9 a few witnesses read *eridas* (241, 462) but this means little more than that these scribes normalized some form that they read as plural. Due to itacism, the normal singular *erin* could appear as *erein;* the plural *ereis* could be spelled *eris.* A scribe faced with an exemplar that read *erein* or *eris* or even *erin* in a list of accusative plurals would tend to normalize the spelling in the direction of *ereis.* This is the reading of S², A, C, K, L, P, 075, 0142, Old Latin, Coptic, and others (see B. Metzger, *TCGNT,* p. 655). The singular *erin* (*erein*) was opted for by S*, D*, F, G, PSI, 999, the Ethiopic and Armenian versions, and more. J. K. Elliott (*Greek Text,* p. 92) considers the more difficult reading of the singular to be the original. Still, the precedents of the singular in Paul and particularly in 1 Tim 6:4 (which has otherwise influenced the transmission of the text here in Titus) may mean that this scribal choice is no more than a harmonization. Hence the plural of *GNT*[3corr] and *NTG*[26corr] is to be retained here.

In the Ap. Frs. all of the examples of *eris* (except Ign. *Eph.* 8.1, s.v.l.) appear in *1 Clem*. There it occurs in both the singular and the plural (as *ereis*, but note the v.l. at 14.2) and regularly in lists (3.2; 35.5; 46.5; 54.2). There are only four LXX examples of the word and only one in the plural, in LXX Ps 138:20. The remaining appearances are in Sir, twice in catalogs of afflictions and vices (40:4, 9). In *Ep. Arist.* 250, provocation *pros erin* refers to domestic strife. Philo uses *eris* a dozen times (in a list in *Mut.* 95; with *machai* in *Ebr.* 99), but the plural is never *ereis*. Josephus employs only the singular. See Spicq, *Lexic.*, pp. 288–291.

of wranglings about the Law, machas nomikas. The plural *machai* recurs in 2 Tim 2:23 (cf. *machesthai* in 2:24), and the other NT uses in 2 Cor 7:5 and Jas 4:1 are also in the plural. The Ap. Frs. do not employ *machē* though it is "Septuagintal, appearing particularly in Prov and Sir. The *T. 12 Patr.* use only the singular, *machē*, but the polysyndetic vice list of *T. Judah* 16.3 (cf. *T. Benj.* 6.4) is notable.

Nomikos, "about the Law," reappears in 3:13 to identify "Zenas the lawyer," *ton nomikon.* Six of the seven other NT uses are in Luke's gospel, and all of the references, including Matt 22:35 s.v.l., designate those who are professionally expert in interpreting the Torah (see Fitzmyer, *AB Lk*, p. 676; R. Leaney, *"Nomikos,"* pp. 166–167). This is also the meaning when 4 Macc 5:4 thus describes old Eleazar (the only Septuagintal use). The Ap. Frs. and *T. 12 Patr.* do not use the word. The unique use in Philo, *Spec. leg.* 4.64, of "a most lawful verdict" does not refer as such to the Torah, and the *nomikos* in Josephus, *War* 2.628 appears to be understood as a name (though with its meaning as an expert in the Torah still close to the surface). In the oldest extant aretalogy of Isis there is mention of "legalized violence," *tēn bian nomikon* (G. Horsley, *NDIEC* 1.10, §2.30).

Such activities are useless and fruitless. Anōpheleis, "useless," appears otherwise in the NT only in Heb 7:18, where it is used nominally with *asthenes* to describe the weakness and uselessness of an OT command about the physical descent of a priest. In the Ap. Frs., Ign. *Magn.* 8.1 warns, "Do not be led astray by strange opinions nor by old fables (*mytheumasin*) that are useless, for if we are living still according to Judaism, we are admitting that we have not received grace." In *Herm. Sim.* 5.1.3, a "useless fast" is a merely conventional, physical one at a particular time with no interior conversion. The "useless" in some contexts suggests even the harmful. Thus BAGD s.v. contrast "the violent and useless rainstorm" of LXX Prov 28:3 with the "useless things" pursued by the false prophets in LXX Jer 2:8 or the "useless murmuring" of Wis 1:11. Nevertheless, the context in the latter instances suggests that a distinction as such was hardly sensed in biblical Greek (even in *Pss. Sol.* 18.8 and *Ep. Arist.* 253). The one remaining use in the LXX, Isa 44:9–10, combines "useless" with "fruitless" in a way reminiscent of this passage in Titus. The passage reads: "All who fashion idol-images are fruitless (*mataioi*), those who make things according to their own fancies, things which do not help (*ōphelesei*) them. But all who fashion a god and carve useless things (*anōphelē*) will be put to shame."

"Fruitless," *mataios*, literally, "empty" or "futile," appears five times otherwise in the NT (for *mataiologos* see 1:10; for *mataiologia*, 1 Tim 1:6). The other Pauline uses are in 1 Cor 3:20, of the futile thoughts of the wise (citing LXX Ps 93:11), and 15:17, of a futile faith in a Christ who has remained dead and buried. In Acts 14:15, "these futile things" are idols; "the futile way of life inherited from your fathers" in 1 Pet 1:18 may include Jewish religious practice. In Jas 1:26 it is a futile religion that does not involve restraint in speech. The Ap. Frs. employ the term regularly. The "empty and futile cares" and "futile dissension" of *1 Clem.* 7.6 and 63.1 are particularly notable in view of this passage in Titus, as is *Herm. Sim.* 5.1.4, which goes on to describe the "useless fast" cited above as "futile." Among the scores of Septuagintal uses of *mataios*, the phrase *kena kai mataia*, "empty and futile" (see LXX Job 20:18; Hos 12:2), has similarities to the phrase here in Titus. Particularly notable is LXX Isa 30:7, "The Egyptians will help (*ōphelēsousin*) you in empty and futile ways (*mataia kai kena*). I have proclaimed to them, 'This appeal (*paraklēsis*) of yours is futile (*mataia*).'" The links with the worship of false gods (thus Wis 13.1; 15:8; see *Ep. Arist.* 136, 139) and false prophecy (thus LXX Lam 2:14; Ezek 13:6–9) are significant also.

10. *Give the divisive man one warning, then a second. Don't see him again.* "The divisive man" is *hairetikon anthrōpon*, literally, "a factious or partisan person." This is the only appearance of the adjective in biblical Greek or the Ap. Frs. In secular Greek, where it appears rarely and late, the sense of the term and its cognates is of exercising generally positive choices. Thus a second-century B.C.E. inscription from Seleucia in Pieria uses the adverb to mean "being well-disposed towards the city" (LSJ, *Suppl.*, p. 5; see D-C, p. 151 for other texts; Spicq, *EP*, p. 686 notes its absence in the papyri before the Byzantine era). As early as Irenaeus these verses in Titus and the term *hairetikos* designate in a technical sense a Christian heretic (*Adversus haereses* 1.16.3; 3.1.2; 3.3.4). The Old Latin versions of this verse, which simply transliterate *haereticum* (a term unknown to classical Latin), witness to this technical sense in the Christian Latin of the second century (*VL* 25[2].935). In Tertullian it is firmly ensconced (thus *De praescriptione haereticorum* 6.1–2; 12.1; 14.4). In the East, Clement of Alexandria and Origen witness to the same usage (see Lampe, *PGL*, s.v., adding Origen on this verse in Titus in *Deoratione* [*PG* 14.1303–1306]).

"One warning, then a second": *nouthesia*, an instructive "warning," has an etymological sense of putting something into a person's mind, of "reminding" him of what is to be done or avoided (see *DELG*, p. 756). In the NT this noun appears only in 1 Cor 10:11, of the Scriptures on the chastisements for Israel during the Exodus bringing an instructive warning to Christians; and in Eph 6:4, where fathers are told to rear their children "in the Lord's discipline and instructive warning (*en paideiai* [see 2 Tim 3:16] *kai nouthesiai* [see *T. Reub.* 3.8])." The latter passage reminds one of the only use of *nouthesia* in the Ap. Frs., when Ignatius (*Eph* 3.1) expresses a hope that the Ephesian Christians will anoint him for his coming contest "with faith, instructive admonition (*nouthesiai*), endurance, long-suffering." The single Septuagintal use, in Wis 16:6, reminds one of the passage cited from 1 Cor, with its appeal to Israel's desert trial by the fiery serpents "for a little while as an instructive warning." The verb *nouthetein* is found in Paul and Luke in the NT as well as in the LXX (see COMMENT). Among the Ap. Frs. only *1 Clem.*, *2 Clem.*, and Hermas use this verb (see *1 Clem.* 56.2, 6 for the cognate nouns *nouthetēsis* and *nouthetēma*).

"One warning, then a second" represents *meta mian kai deuteran nouthesian*, literally, "after one and a second warning." Some scribes were exercised by the shift from the cardinal *mia* to the ordinal *deutera*, though the loose usage is not anomalous (see Strabo, *Geography* 2.1.40; Josephus, *Vita* 32, 35–36; Justin, *Apology* 1.52 and Wikgren, "Problems," pp. 148, 152). Western texts brought *nouthesian* back to *mian* and then read *kai duo* (thus D*, L, Old Latin) or *kai deuteran* (Dᶜ, 1245, 2005) or *ē deuteran* (F, G, vg). Some omit *kai deuteran* altogether (thus 1739). In the NT generally and in 1 Tim 5:19, numbers precede the noun that they qualify (J. K. Elliott, *Greek Text*, p. 194), and thus most probably the original text is that of S, A, C, and apparently P⁶¹, adopted by *NTG* ²⁶ᶜᵒʳʳ, and *GNT* ³ᶜᵒʳʳ, and this version.

The numeral "one" reappears in the acclamation "God is one" in 1 Tim 2:5. *Deuteros*, "second," occurs forty-two times outside the PE in the NT. Acts 12:10, with its description of Peter and his rescuing angel "passing the first guard and the second (*protēn phylakēn kai deuteran*)" is notable in the light of the phrase's textual history here in Titus.

"Don't see him again" is simply the singular imperative address, *paraitou*, which reappears three times in this form in the correspondence with Timothy, who is told to reject myths and speculations (1 Tim 4:7; 2 Tim 2:23), as well as young widows who apply for admission to the widows' order (1 Tim 5:11). The verb does not appear in the other Paulines, but half of the eight other NT uses are in the Lukan corpus (in Luke 14:18–19 with the sense "to excuse oneself," and in Acts 25:11 as here in Titus). *Paraiteisthai* does not appear in the Ap. Frs., and of the half-dozen Septuagintal uses only 2 Macc 2:31 and 4 Macc 11:2 resemble the usage here (see *Ep. Arist.* 184).

11. *for you can be sure a man like that has turned sour and keeps on sinning as he brings on his own condemnation*. *Eidōs hoti*, "for you can be sure," literally, "knowing that," recurs in this form in the PE in 1 Tim 1:9 (cf. 1:8) and 2 Tim 2:23 (cf. 1:15). The phrase is found in Acts 2:30, and forms of it abound in the Pauline corpus and the rest of the NT as well as in the Ap. Frs. and the LXX.

"A man like that" translates *ho toioutos,* a nominal use of an adjective (BDF §274) that appears only here in the PE but fifty-six times otherwise in the NT. Sometimes in Paul (1 Cor 5:5; 2 Cor 2:6–7; 10:11a; Gal 6:1) as well as in Acts 22:22 the special characteristics of the person or class being described are viewed negatively.

"Has turned sour," *exestraptai,* is an unusual perfect passive from *ek-strephein.* *Exestreptai* in A, F, G, O88, and 1245 may be due to the influence of the aorist passive, *estrephthē* (J. K. Elliott, *Greek Text,* pp. 194–195). This verb appears only here in the NT, and in the Ap. Frs. only in *Herm. Sim.* 8.6.5, of hypocrites who have introduced strange doctrines about the impossibility of repentance and perverted (*ekstrephontes*) God's servants. Of the five Septuagintal appearances of the term, Deut 32:20 is notable when it calls a generation "perverted (*exestrammenē*), sons in whom there is no faith." The LXX Amos 6:12 addresses Israel with, "You perverted judgment into whimsy and the fruit of justice into bitterness."

"And keeps on sinning," *kai hamartanei,* is used of sinning presbyters in 1 Tim 5:20 (for the noun, *hamartia,* see 5:22, 24; 2 Tim 3:6, and for *hamartōlos,* 1 Tim 1:9, 15). The verb appears otherwise in the NT forty-one times. Fourteen of the fifteen Pauline uses are in Rom and 1 Cor (Eph 4:26 is a citation of LXX Ps 4:5). The prodigal son in Luke 15:18 and 21 says, "Father, I sinned against (*eis*) heaven and before you," and in Luke 17:3–4 the brother who sins does so against another brother. When Paul, in Acts 25:8, declares, "I sinned in no way against the law of the Jews or against the temple or against the emperor," the sociological rather than the theological sense of the verb comes to the fore in the last phrase. Even to do an inadvertent wrong is *hamartanein.* A character of Menander can say, "Anthrōpos ōn hēmarton. Ou thaumasteon" ("Being human, I made a mistake. You shouldn't be surprised"; Koerte 432/499K; see Herodas 5.27, in *Mimiambi,* ed., I. C. Cunningham; Oxford: Clarendon, 1971). Thus among the Ap. Frs., *1 Clem.* 2.3 speaks of sinning unwillingly (*ei ti akontes hēmartete;* see LXX Job 14:17, *ei ti akōn parebēn*). Hermas employs the verb frequently, as do the LXX and other Jewish Greek documents, including *T. 12 Patr.*

"As he brings on his own condemnation" represents one word, *autokatakritos,* literally, "self-condemned." The term is not found otherwise in biblical Greek or the Ap. Frs., but it does occur once in a fragment of Philo cited by John Damascene (see D-C, p. 151 for text and a version). As early as Irenaeus, as cited above, the word appears in other Christian documents (see pseudo-Justin, *Epistola ad Zenam et Serenum* 17; Lampe, *PGL,* s.v.).

COMMENT

3:8b. *I wish you, Titus, to insist on these matters, so that those who have put their faith in God will be intent on "taking the lead in fine deeds." Activity like that is fine and useful for people.* The opening of this verse and the phrase *pistos ho logos* look back to the baptismal oration of vv 4–7 and explicitly set that citation in the context of ecclesial faith. With *peitharchein* and *apeitheis* in vv 1 and 3, *pistos* completes a verbal inclusion around "the message meant to be believed." In the remainder of this verse the author looks forward to "fine deeds" or works as the complement to that faith. Creedal confession is to have practical application in the life and teaching of the Jewish-Christian churches.

The more personal tone of the first-person singular and second-person singular address, represented in this translation by adding the word "Titus," last appeared in this letter in 1:3 and 5. It now gives some relief from the imperatival address that has dominated the body of the epistle thus far (except for the creedal confessions). The reader is thus prepared for vv 12–15 and the *personalia* with which this letter closes. There the four-times-repeated forms of the first-person singular restore some faint warmth and intimacy to a type of composition that has resembled a memorandum in its brusque staccato of directives.

Perhaps 8b is a second fragment of an original, much shorter note that was traced through 1:5 above. On that surmise the pronominal phrase *peri toutōn*, "on these matters," could refer to *ta leiponta*, "the remaining matters," in 1:5. If we pursue this hypothesis, the original note would have amounted to a letter of authorization for Titus in his organizational work, a specimen of the letters missive or patent (note the plural address of 3:15) that were a familiar feature of Roman imperial administration. The author of Acts was not unaware of such brief dispatches in both secular Roman (Acts 23:26–30, 33–34) and Jewish religious affairs (Acts 9:1–2; 28:21). The author-redactor of the PE may have selected the epistolary form as eminently appropriate to his purpose precisely because he had a dossier that contained notes to men whom Paul in the previous generation had authorized publicly to share his apostolic work and authority.

The terminology of this verse coincides sufficiently with the rest of the Paulines to make it reasonable to suggest that it came from the apostle's entourage, perhaps in the sixties (see the INTRODUCTION). By the same token, the language is by no means alien to Luke–Acts, and it would have been congenial to one familiar with that literature as he set out to compose or redact this sentence.

The wish of the apostle is an executive order for his coworker, who is made responsible, in the second-person singular address, for emphatically vouching for the Pauline origin and character of the directives and doctrine that have preceded. "These matters" must refer, in the redactor-author's mind, not only to the citation of the baptismal confession but also to the paraenesis that began in 2:15, with the same formal structure encountered here, namely, a summary reference to what had gone before, followed by a hortatory opening of the new subject. The reference probably does not include the previous block of material in 1:10–16 on the problems with certain Jewish Christians, problems that will be explicitly addressed in 3:9.

The positive result of the Pauline directives transmitted by Titus is "that those who have put their faith in God will be intent on 'taking the lead in fine deeds.'" As the preceding "message" was "meant to be believed," attention now turns to those who responded to that message with a biblical faith and remain faithful (note the perfect tense) to the God of Israel (note the anarthrous *theōi*), whose historical initiative and sacramental intervention in their lives have been articulated in the baptismal confession cited in 3:4–7. The commentator ought not to presume that the author of the PE should have written "those who put their faith in Christ" (perhaps under the influence of the equally unusual phrase in 2 Tim 1:12; cf. Acts 18:8). Although D-C, p. 151, notes correctly that the phrase corresponds with *hoi hēmeteroi*, "our own people" in v 14 and thus means Christian believers, that still leaves open the question whether these Christians had been Jews or pagans. The perfect participle construed with the dative in this verse in Titus denotes persons who have believed in the God of their father, Abraham, and still believe in him as Jewish Christians.

A difficulty arises for this interpretation from the confession that was cited in 2:11–14. There the articular *theos*, which had been the rule in Titus from 2:1 and will recur in 3:4, is not only a personal title for the Father but also part of a title for Jesus. But this is the usage of the traditions that are being cited, the language of which the redactor-author of the PE respected. The difficulty eases notably when one observes that in 1:16, the close of the previous section on Jewish-Christian troublemakers, the author has said, "God they profess to know," using an anarthrous *theon* and evidently referring to the God of Israel. Here at 3:8, returning to some of the matters addressed in that section, he varies the previous expression to describe those Jewish Christians who have really put their faith in the God of Israel.

Such a sound Pauline baptismal faith gives Christians a heart for a visibly attractive Christian life, "intent on 'taking the lead in fine deeds.'" If verse 8b is not an actual fragment of the original letter of commendation, then at least the words in quotation marks are a citation from the original dispatch, and they serve to generalize what had applied to "our own people" in 3:14. The sense of this verb in Titus is still nontechnical, unlike the uses in 1 Tim, where it designates aspects of leadership in the Christian ministries. Still, the suggestion of the household and its responsibility for providing for the material needs of the extended family are part of the case being made here. All members of the Christian family are to set their hearts on "fine deeds" (see 2:14), as exemplified and taught by Titus himself (2:7; 3:14). As 1:7–8 indicates, the presbyter-bishops for the Jewish-Christian churches visualized in Titus are to be chosen on the basis of qualities and actions characteristic of Christian men who are already "intent on taking the lead in fine deeds." A terminology that is still somewhat undifferentiated and flexible in its application in Titus becomes technical and specific to the leadership offices in the churches envisioned in 1 Tim (see 1 Tim 3:4–5 for the discussion of this subject and references to the literature).

But is there any clue to what specific activities the phrase "taking the lead in fine deeds" refers? The dispatch from which the phrase is cited (or of which 3:8b is an integral part) furnishes some answers. The Christian people, following Titus's and Paul's teaching, are to contribute "the urgent necessities of life" (3:14)—food, drink, clothing, money—to those who lack such things. In the context, the Pauline emissaries are such persons and ought to be the object of the "fine deeds" of the churches that they visit in their apostolic ministry.

Verse 8b concludes with "Activity like that is fine and useful for people." The sentence is awkwardly, even harshly phrased. The reference of *tauta*, literally, "these things," is not altogether clear. The version here, under the influence of the repeated *kala*, "fine," refers to the "fine deeds" of the preceding sentence, but it is conceivable that *tauta* refers to the antecedent of *toutōn* in "on these matters." The author has lost control of his references before (1:3) and will do so again (1 Tim 1:3). The banal correctness of the version here seemed preferable to foisting further obscurity upon the text with no compensatory gains in understanding the author.

In any case, the repeated "fine" reinforces a major theme in Titus, the attractive visibility of the response that the Christian believer makes to his God. Now the further qualification appears that "fine works" do people good, that they are "useful for people." The phrase was far from trite for those who first read it here in the PE, which—along with Clement and Hermas—understand this usefulness as extending beyond the good of the individual who has or who does something that is thus qualified. *Ōphelima* here is no synonym for *agatha*, though their meanings partially coincide. Some "good things" are "useful" too; some are not. Some "useful things" are "good"; some are not (*contra* Zeno, *apud* Spicq, *EP*, p. 657). Just as *kala*, "fine," means Christian faith and conduct that are visibly attractive to people, so *ōphelima* adds the new note that they are useful as well. As before (2:5, 7–8, 10–11; 3:2), the PE are not concerned with "fine deeds" for their own sake. Good works are done for the sake of other people, for those who have not yet seen or believed in "the humane munificence of our savior, God" (3:4). Basic to this attitude is an ineradicable optimism about the power of God to reveal himself through the limitations and frailties of human goodness. This optimism is of a piece with that affirmation of the goodness of all creation which the PE champion (see 1 Tim 4:4–5). Although this has periodically occasioned theological dyspepsia, good actions belong as much to the realm of God's creation as the other good things with which he has adorned his cosmos.

9. *On the other hand, steer clear of foolish speculations, of genealogies, of controversies, of wranglings about the Law. Such activities are useless and fruitless.* In contrast (*de*) to "the Christian message meant to be believed" and the "fine deeds" energized by it, the paraenesis now turns from these useful matters to teachings and activities that are stigmatized as "useless." Titus is directed not to confront but to "steer clear" of four areas, which are specified as speculations, genealogies, controversies, and wranglings. A polysyndetic *kai* (translated with the repeated "of") suggests emphatically an exhaustive enumeration (BDF §460.3).

The paraenesis now appears to be the opposite of the one given in 1:10 and 13, where Titus and the presbyter-bishops are told to muzzle and refute the refractory, judaizing opposition. It is conceivable that two different sources have been reproduced but not brought into harmony. It is possible that a source is adduced in 1:10–16 and that the author-redactor here deliberately submits another strategy to meet a different situation. The text is, however, not in formal contradiction with itself, and the opposition is only apparent. In 1:10–16, the presbyter-bishops and Titus are to refute erring persons; here Titus alone (like Timothy in 2 Tim 2:16) is to shun four activities that are taken together (in Semitic fashion) as a definition and identification of the preoccupations and praxis of the party that is being combated. The paradigmatic character of the list is evidenced by the fact that almost every term in it recurs in related contexts in 1 and 2 Tim. The dense core of the resistance to the Pauline apostolate, as the author-redactor of the PE conceived it, has been brought to a head in this definition. Elements of the infection are to be found elsewhere, but this is the boil to be lanced.

The atmosphere in the two sections is markedly different. The overheated polemic of personal confrontation and denunciation in the former passage has changed to a chillier attitude of contempt for and avoidance of the activities of the judaizers. This attitude in its turn issues into an administrative procedure for discerning whether the representative of Paul is dealing with the common and remediable frailty of the flesh or an obstinate and incorrigible fixation in beliefs and actions that are radically unchristian. The former section stopped short of excluding the troublemaker from the church. This section proposes a procedure and grounds for precisely that, and the initial usage of "steer clear" suggests a Roman setting for the directives.

Leading off the list of activities that the coworker with Paul is to avoid are "foolish speculations," which in the correspondence with Timothy characterize those whose teachings differ from Paul's, people whose instruction is not grounded either in Jesus' words or in those of the OT. The "speculations" of such persons are synonymous with "quibbling about terminology," *logomachiai* (note the *machai nomikai* here) and issue in controversy (*eris*), among other things (1 Tim 6:3–4). Such speculations are, in 2 Tim 2:23, not only "foolish" but undisciplined, and "they breed only wranglings (*machas*)." In 1 Tim 1:4, *ekzēteseis* are lucubrations that involve strange teachings about tales and endless genealogies. One infers, particularly after examining *zētēsis/zētēma* in Acts (see Wright, *Midrash*, p. 40 n. 22) that this cluster of terms was on the way to becoming technical in certain second-generation Christian circles, and that it designated questions about the interpretation of the Bible, which meant at this point the OT (see Culpepper, *School*, pp. 291–296). The debates need not have involved a clean split along the lines of the Jewish or pagan origins of the converts. Jewish Christian could well have been pitted against Jewish Christian; Gentile against Gentile. Whatever the line of division, the person of Paul, including his apostleship and his teaching, appears to be the sign of contradiction. The authority of the Pauline hermeneutic of the OT and its application to Christian living is being prescribed by some Christians and proscribed by others. For the author of the PE, speculations that ignore or attempt to discredit Paul are "foolish."

"Genealogies" are listed, with a polysyndetic *kai*, after "foolish speculations," specifying a typical direction taken by the repellent researches (see 1 Tim 1:4). If the Melchizedek exegesis of Heb 7:3 may be taken as an indicator, a Jewish-Christian community (in Rome?) has to be reminded of the theological irrelevance of genealogical speculations about the priestly nature and work of Christ. This leaves open the question whether genealogical inquiries were in order about other subjects. In any event, one encounters here an interest and concern that are more characteristic of converts from Judaism than of converts from paganism.

The Jewish interest is traceable to the great *toledoth*, lists of the "generations," which the priestly editors incorporated into the Torah (see also LXX 1 Chr 5:1). Philo thus described the Pentateuch as consisting of two parts, the historical and the legislative (*Praem.* 1–2). The historical is in turn subdivided into what concerns the origin of the world and what concerns the "genealogical," *genealogikon.* The latter is about the ways in which the good are rewarded and the evil punished (*Mos.* 2.46–47) and practically means personal histories or biographies, a sense attested among secular Greek rhetoricians and grammarians (see the note by F. H. Colson in the LCL *Philo* 6.606, adding a reference to "genealogies and myths" in Polybius, *Histories* 9.2 and to Josephus's irritable remarks on the "genealogies" of the Greek historians in *Apion* 1.16). Such biography had for Philo a practical, moral purpose (*Mos.* 2.48; cf. *Cong.* 44; *Abr.* 31).

The Philonic interest has its counterpart in Qumran, where "all of the sons of light," the members of the community, are to be taught "about the generations (*btwldwt*, i.e., the "natural history") of all of the sons of men, about all their different spirits with their signs, about their deeds in their lifetimes (*bdwrwtm*), and about the visitation of their chastisements, together with their final rewards" (1QS 3:13–15, adapted from A. Leaney, *RQM*, p. 143). As Leaney explains (pp. 146–147), these are "typical men" who become the vehicles for the encouragement and instruction of a later generation, whose "fathers" they are by their experiences and example as well as by physical generation. The 1QapGen, with its embellishments of the Gen narratives, appears to be the type of literature that such interests produced. The presence of fragments of the *Jub.* and of forms of the *T. 12 Patr.* in the Qumran library also illustrate the interest in "genealogies" in this special sense of edifying biographical narratives about the forefathers of the intended readers.

These compositions resemble haggadic midrash (see 1:14; Spicq, *EP*, pp. 101–103). Addison Wright (*Midrash*, pp. 35–36, 40) has noted that the Hebrew root *drs*, "to seek, to study" and eventually "to interpret" (whence *midrash*, "interpretation"), often becomes a form of *zētein* in the LXX but never with the meaning "to interpret/interpretation." The use of the nouns in the sense of interpretation, and regularly with links to the interpretation of the OT (and possibly with *midrash*), appears for the first time in the PE and Acts.

The talmudic parallels that have been adduced for the "genealogies" in the PE are thin at best (see Sandmel, "Myths," p. 158 and 1:14 above) and at least once removed from the Judaism of the first century c.e., for certainly at this point in Titus, as in chap. 1, the controversies involve Jewish Christians. What kind of genealogies were *they* proposing to their second-generation Jewish-Christian colleagues and interested converts from paganism? Sandmel contends that they were genealogies of Jesus Christ ("Myths," pp. 161–162 with his references), examples of which have survived in Matt and Luke (see Falconer, *PE*, pp. 49–50). They are lacking, perhaps significantly, in Mark and John. Hebrews, as noted above, proposed a theological reason to exclude such constructs from its argument for the priesthood of Jesus. The Pauline misgivings about the life of Jesus "according to the flesh" (2 Cor 5:16) are well known, though precisely what the apostle means is controverted. Thus at this point in Titus one encounters an attempt to obviate a waste of time and energy on the construction and perhaps the harmonization of the various genealogies of Jesus circulating in Jewish-Christian circles in the latter part of the first Christian century. If Jerome is to be credited, a convert from Judaism in Rome at the end of the fourth century was worrying the naïve with such genealogical questions (*On Titus, PL* 26.595).

If the preceding observations on the meaning of "generations," *toledot*, hold (see Thompson, *Origin*, pp. 62–71), "genealogies" here designates not only bare lists of ancestors but also biographical *topoi* about the Jesus of history, the little narratives of his words and deeds that the first generation had fashioned and begun to collect for its own purposes. The PE represent an attitude of resistance to the further multiplication of such materials and a mistrust of the exercise of religious imagination necessarily involved in such compositions. The attitude appears in other words in Rev 22:18–19, where both excisions from and additions to the prophetic oracles are severely censured.

The author of Luke–Acts had fashioned a great, composite, unified work for the second Christian generation, using many narratives of the previous generation (Luke 1:1–2). He had chosen what he considered trustworthy and edifying, including a genealogy in the modern sense of the term (Luke 3:23–38) as well as a redaction of compositions about Jesus' deeds and words (Acts 1:1). If the PE were the epistolary appendix to those two volumes (see the INTRODUCTION), the author of Luke–Acts in the name of Paul asserted that further questions and disputes about the merits and demerits of competing accounts are "foolish." Perhaps at this very time in another sector of the church the Gospel according to Matthew was taking shape, using a different genealogy with other biographical materials, to address another second-generation audience. The product was different enough from the Lukan synthesis to bring them into a collision course; yet it was authoritative enough to have survived. The opposition between them was quickly dissolved by the expedient of separating Luke's work into its component parts, joining his gospel in a codex alongside one or more of the other gospels. The PE, like Acts, then circulated independently, and the "genealogies" of which they spoke no longer had an identifiable antecedent. Yet nothing had been added to or excised from documents already received as sacred and authoritative for the churches.

With the mention of "controversies, of wranglings about the Law," the elements that have made the "speculations" and "genealogies" odious to the author of this correspondence come into sharper focus. Speculation and genealogies have spawned strife and bitter battles among Christians. The PE share with Paul and the catechetical traditions from which the apostle himself drew a deep concern that the community of believers be purged of that contention and strife which are the works of the flesh (see Gal 5:20; Rom 1:29; 1 Cor 1:11; 3:3; 2 Cor 12:20). If speculations and genealogies are fueling such controversies and wranglings, then the apostolic leader is to shun them and thus provide an example for the community that he leads.

The confrontations implied by "controversies" escalate in intensity to produce the "wranglings" that climax this list, reminding one of Philo's remark, "Controversy is the mother of anger" (*Leg. all.* 3.131). The other NT references about such battles lead one to suspect what the adjectival "about the Law" makes explicit. These angry, intramural Christian quarrels are about the interpretation of the Scriptures that all Christians (whether of Jewish or of pagan origin) share with Judaism. The adjectival "about the Law" here surely suggests that the battles are about the interpretation of the Law par excellence, the five books of Moses. Still, it is quite possible that the qualification was not intended to be restricted to the Torah as such but was understood of the Jewish Scriptures as a whole. It is conceivable in the light of 1 Tim 1:8–9 (the only use of *nomos* in the PE) that even a system of regulations apart from the OT (though not necessarily opposed to it) could be thought of as law and could generate legal "wranglings."

If the suggestions I have made about the content of the "genealogies" hold, then the "wranglings" here may be about the passages of the Jewish Scriptures that were taken to refer to Jesus, as well as the way in which the commandments of the Law were to guide Christian life. It is not the OT as such that is to be shunned. In the correspondence with Timothy it is "useful (*ōphelimos*) for instruction" (2 Tim 3:16). Furthermore, there is no suggestion about abandoning the principle that the apostolic kerygma was "according to the Scriptures." Rather, wranglings with Jewish Christians about the application of the OT, whether to Jesus or to Christians, are to be avoided as "useless."

The negative, summary conclusion of v 9, "Such activities are useless and fruitless," contrasts with the positive conclusion of 8b, in which *ōphelima*, "useful," stands in antithesis to *anōpheleis*, "useless," here. "Fruitless," *mataioi*, is then to be construed as the opposite of "fine," *kala*, in 8b. Visibly and really good acts are in antithesis to the things just listed here, which, for all their specious attractiveness, are as empty and powerless as pagan worship. The masculine *mataioi*, "fruitless," is unexpected because the nouns in the preceding list are feminine in gender. Still the usage would not be anomalous (see BDF §§134, 138; N. Turner, *Grammar*, 3.21–22, 311–312), and the author's rhetoric tends to close the gap between the activities that are being scored and the persons who perform them. *Mataioi* qualifies not simply the speculations, the genealogies, the controversies, and the wranglings, conceived as abstract cases (see N. Turner, *Grammar*, 3.27–28), but also recalls "the Jewish Christians . . . spouting nonsense (*mataiologoi*)" of 1:10.

10–11. *Give the divisive man one warning, then a second. Don't see him again, for you can be sure a man like that has turned sour and keeps on sinning as he brings on his own condemnation.* The preceding verse offered a descriptive definition of aberrant activities peremptorily to be avoided. This verse turns from the activities to the procedures for dealing with the person, *anthrōpon*, here stigmatized as "divisive," *hairetikon*, who engages in them. There is somewhat more leeway for dealing with the erring individual who is presented in the singular as an individual (not as a sect or party), pitted against the apostle and Titus and, only by implication, against the Jewish-Christian community. Has *hairetikon* become a technical term meaning "heretic" at this point? To the extent that the term designates one who has just been descriptively defined as given to foolish speculations, genealogies, controversies, and wranglings about the Law, it could be considered technical for the PE, even though it lacks the nuances and developments of later centuries. Heretics, like bishops, must be understood in their historical context if they are not to be misunderstood. Both have recognizable antecedents; neither can simply be identified with them.

A description of the usage of the noun *hairesis*, cognate with *hairetikon*, is helpful for understanding the usage here in Titus. In secular Greek *hairesis* signifies, with a good, neutral, or bad sense, a group or school that holds certain distinctive philosophical (see Cicero, *Epistolae ad familiares* 15.16.3) or medical doctrines in common. Heinrich von Staden has "the impression that Greek medicine is the more significant early nurturing ground for *hairesis* as a doctrinal group designation" ("Hairesis," p. 81; the article has been used for what follows here).

Although the LXX does not use *hairesis* in the sense of a group, Josephus so designates the religious parties of Judaism, sects as varied as the Zealots, the Essenes, the Pharisees, and the Sadducees (see *War* 2.118–119, 137; *Ant.* 13.171; *Vita* 10). The earliest NT uses of the noun are Pauline and in a negative sense: thus 1 Cor 11:19 and the vice catalog of Gal 5:20, where the term occurs between "dissensions" and "jealousies" and shortly after *eris*, "controversy." The latest use of *hairesis* in the NT, in 2 Pet 2:1, occurs in the description of "false teachers . . . who will secretly bring in destructive heresies (*haireseis apōleias*)." Here the noun designates groups of persons who are more than factious; their parties espouse heterodox doctrinal systems, which recognizably coincide with what a later generation called heresy (see Ign. *Eph.* 6.2; *Trall.* 6.1).

Acts speaks of *hairesis* in several shades of meaning. The term designates only religious parties within first-century Judaism in the more or less neutral sense already noted in Josephus (Acts 5:17; 15:5; 26:5). When various speakers use the word of the Christian Way, however, *hairesis* means a sect to which the speakers cited are opposed (Acts 24:5, 14; 28:22; cf. Justin, *Trypho* 108 [*PG* 6.725]).

The redactor-author of the PE has not used the collective noun at all, perhaps not willing to number the Christian congregations with the other parties of contemporary Judaism (including the Zealots) as well as not wanting to give any group status to the aberrant movements among Christians. The author and perhaps also his source here have made use of an unusual adjective, *hairetikos*, and given it an even more unusual sense, which has much in common with the Pauline (and perhaps pre-Pauline) Christian attitude to "options" and the consequent divisions or parties among believers. The usage appears to be less technical than that in 2 Pet and Ignatius, but the bad sense is more pronounced than in Acts.

The apostolic minister envisioned here is dealing with fellow Christians as individuals with their frailties and limitations. The procedure submitted ensures a hearing and "due process" as well as forestalling wasting time in pointless argument. Already in the miscellany of sayings intended for teaching the disciples in Luke 17:1–10 there is a directive placed on Jesus' lips, "If your brother does wrong (*hamartēi*), warn (singular, *epitimēson*) him, and if he repents (*metanoēsē*), forgive (singular, *aphes*) him" (Luke 17:3; *SFG* §170; see Marshall, *Luke*, pp. 641–643 for the background and literature). This looks like the simplest and most archaic form of a dominical directive that, in the Matthean church, became a three-step, ecclesial procedure for dealing with a person who did wrong to a brother Christian (perhaps conceived to be one who exercised an apostolic ministry to the church; see Matt 18:15–18). The careful, explicit, detailed process outlined in Matt is probably the precipitate of a generation and more of Jewish-Christian ecclesial life. Pride of place is given to Christian love of neighbor, for the first admonition is to be "between you and him alone" (see Lev 19:17–18; Sir 19:13–17). If the first is fruitless, the second is to take place before two or three Christian witnesses, thus fulfilling the Deuteronomic laws of evidence (see Deut 19:15). Only then is "the church" to be informed and to issue its call to obedience or else.

Are there models in pre-Christian Judaism for the attitude to and procedures about erring members of the community witnessed to by Matt and Titus? A process similar to the one in Matt appears to have been known in Qumran (see Forkman, *Limits*, pp. 47–70, 127–128 for this and what follows). The Community Rule prescribes for the sectaries,

> Their spiritual attitudes and their performance are to be reviewed however year by year, some being then promoted by virtue of their (improved) understanding and the integrity of their conduct, and others demoted for their waywardness. When anyone has a charge against his neighbor, he is to prosecute it truthfully, humbly, and humanely [see Lev 19:17–18]. He is not to speak to him angrily or querulously or arrogantly or in any wicked mood. He is not to bear hatred [toward him in the inner recesses] of his heart. When he has a charge against him, he is to proffer it on the selfsame day and not render himself liable to penalty by nursing a grudge. Furthermore, no man is to bring a charge against his neighbor before the public assembly except he prove it by witnesses. (1QS 5.23–6.1 *apud* Gaster *DSS* modified; see A. Leaney, *RQM*, pp. 176–180, also CD 7:2–3; 9:2–8, 16; 10:3)

The procedures are based on the same OT texts that undergird the Matthean process; they also presume three steps that resemble but are not quite identical to those in Matt (thus the mention of the "selfsame day," the variant descriptions of the functions of the witnesses).

The procedure outlined in Titus resembles that in Matt and Qumran in containing three steps that deal with an erring individual, but it differs from both on several notable counts. It is far less detailed (and so closer to the Lukan logion). The procedure mentions no witnesses, no ecclesial confrontation with the "divisive man" or ratification of the process against him. The silence of course does not prove that witnesses and the congregation played no part; it does mean that one is encountering here a different level or aspect of the process for excluding a troublemaker from the church. The directive in Titus confines the whole process to encounters between the apostolic minister and the "divisive man." Specifically, this text is concerned about how the Pauline apostolic minister, precisely as a Pauline leader, is to deal with a heterodox Jewish Christian (see COMMENT on *elegchein* in 1:9). He is not peremptorily to eliminate such a person. Rather, he must give two distinct warnings. Whereas the Matthean process ends in completely cutting off the wrongdoer from the community, though not from repentant return (see Forkman, *Limits*, pp. 129–132), in Titus the procedure concludes with the apostolic minister alone being told "Don't see him again" after the two warnings. The final rupture is accordingly not quite so final in Titus. Whereas the leader is to break off official relationships with the "divisive man," the members of the church are not so instructed.

The two separate warnings by the apostolic minister enjoined in Titus appear to be a distinct variant on the Deuteronomic laws for multiple witnesses, a variant that has a parallel in the Damascus Document rather than in the Community Rule at Qumran. Basically the problem is this: What should be the procedure when an act of wrongdoing has been witnessed not by two or three men simultaneously but by a single witness on several occasions? Is it possible to fulfill the Deuteronomic laws of witness by adding up the separate occasions to produce the witnesses required for a valid judgment? In *CD* 9:16–20 that problem is solved thus: "For every infringement which a man commits against the Law, and which his fellow has seen, being alone, if it is a matter liable to capital punishment, reproving him (*bhwkyh*), the witness shall denounce the culprit in his presence to the overseer (*lmbqr*); and the overseer shall inscribe him with his own hand, waiting until he commits another (violation) before one person alone, and the latter again denounces him to the overseer. If he relapses and is caught in the act (for the third time) before one person alone, his case is juridically complete" (Dupont-Sommer, *EWQ*, p. 150 modified; see also Forkman, *Limits*, pp. 48–51; Schiffman, "Testimony," pp. 603–612 for what follows). The *halakah* of the rabbinic traditions does not envision such an accumulation of single witnesses to separate acts of wrongdoing. Yet the apostle Paul apparently presumes some such procedure in 2 Cor 13:1–2 when he, like the overseer of the Damascus community, gives in writing a second warning, before he arrives to convict the erring Corinthian Christians publicly on charges that "must be sustained by two or three witnesses." Perhaps the background for such a procedure appears when the apostle appeals to the Roman Christians "to take note of those who create dissensions (*dichostastias;* cf. Gal 5:20) and stumbling blocks, in opposition to the doctrine (*tēn didachēn*) which you have been taught; avoid (*ekklinete*) them" (Rom 16:17). In any event, the process outlined here in Titus coincides at several points with that detailed in the Damascus Document and is complemented by it. The position of the apostolic minister represented by Titus corresponds to that of the overseer, the *mbqr*, of an Essene community outside of Qumran. Both are to deliver two warnings to a wrongdoer in the community. The Damascus Document would make it clear that the violation of the congregation's law had been witnessed by one person on two separate occasions instead of by two persons on one occasion. It would also imply that the apostolic minister, like the overseer, had made a record of the denunciation, which would give permanence to his reception of the deposition by the single witness in the presence of the wrongdoer and his consequent warning. The procedure in the Damascus Document may issue in a death sentence (though the *mbqr* is not said to pass it); in Titus the process results in the apostolic minister's shunning the "divisive man" (see 2 Tim 2:23–24 and 1QS 9:16 cited there). The resemblances suggest that the procedure in Titus originated in a Jewish-Christian milieu that drew on legal traditions used by the Essenes as well as by Paul himself. The differences suggest that charity as it was conceived of by Christians gentled the procedure, which left room for the reconciliation of the disaffected whom the congregation as such had not expelled.

Is it possible to infer more specifically the content of the repeated "warning"? The Pauline and Septuagintal usage would suggest a fatherly, that is, an authoritative but affectionate, correction (see the verb in 1 Cor 4:14) that cited scriptural precedents, particularly from the trials that befell those who resisted Moses, the appointed leader of the people of God, as he brought them to freedom (see 2 Tim 3:8–9; Josephus, *Ant.* 3.311). In the Paulines the cognate verb designates the apostle's instructive warning (Col 1:28; thus also Acts 20:31, the only NT use of the verb outside of Paul). But not only are leaders of the congregation to admonish believers (1 Thess 5:12), but also the faithful are expected to admonish one another (1 Thess 5:14; 2 Thess 3:15; Rom 15:14; Col 3:16). In this setting of believers who are expected to be instructing and admonishing one another about how to live their belief, the intervention of a community leader and even of an apostle can be expected when a particularly knotty dispute emanates from an instructive warning to a Christian brother or sister.

The Pauline apostolic minister who has followed the process outlined in v 10 is presumed to have administered the formal warnings sympathetically, even "with tears" for the one he was admonishing (cf. Acts 20:31 with Phil 3:18). The procedure is not self-evident or prescribed by a word of Jesus but one based on familiar Jewish practices. As a legal channel for ensuring the charity that the Lord had commanded, it is expected to leave the apostolic leader with misgivings about "divorcing" himself from the troublemaker (Josephus, *Ant.* 20.147 and Plutarch, *Moralia* 206A use *paraiteisthai* in this sense). Thus v 11 now proposes reasons that are intended more to comfort the administrator than to reconcile the "divisive man," who is now contemptuously dismissed as "a man like that."

With a typically Pauline "for you can be sure" addressed to the paradigmatic Titus, the Pauline apostolic minister is assured that the person who has refused a hearing and belief to the Pauline warnings, personally delivered, is actually beyond human help, even that of an apostle. "A man like that has turned sour," literally, "has been perverted," in a sense that is vividly illustrated in the ancient texts on medicine and alchemy that refer to drastic changes

(Spicq, *EP*, p. 687; LSJ s.v.). The meaning here is that permanent, irreversible damage had occurred before the "divisive man" encountered the apostolic minister. The well had been poisoned, and nothing could now sweeten it.

After noting that the factious man's condition is irreparable, it is next observed that he "keeps on sinning," with the present tense accenting a wrong action continuing in spite of the repeated warning. Perhaps a distinction is beginning to appear between what was wrong and what makes it personally blameworthy or sinful, that is, ignoring an instructive admonition (see Philo, *Spec. leg.* 1.227, 235 and D-C, p. 151).

Finally, the "divisive man" is stigmatized as one who keeps bringing (note the present participle *ōn*) on "his own condemnation," *autokatakritos*. The recherché term makes the closing observation sound important and technical. The sense clearly is that the very refusal to accept the apostolic admonition is to pronounce one's own sentence of condemnation. The concept is by no means alien to the NT. Thus Paul said that Peter "stood condemned (*kategnōsmenos ēn*)" for adopting Jewish meal practices in the mixed church at Antioch (Gal 2:11; see Betz, *Gal.*, p. 106). In Luke 19:22 the returning master says, "I will condemn you out of your own mouth, you wicked servant" (see LXX Job 15:6). The continuing refusal to heed the Pauline teaching is to be continually condemning oneself.

III. PERSONAL NOTES (3:12–15a)
III.A. DECISIONS AND DIRECTIVES (3:12–14)

3   ¹²As soon as I send Artemas to you, Titus, or perhaps Tychicus, do your best to come to me at Nicopolis, for I have decided to spend the winter there. ¹³Do all you can to speed the journey of Zenas the lawyer, and Apollos, with all their needs satisfied. ¹⁴Thus let our own people too learn what it means "to take the lead in fine deeds" with regard to the urgent necessities of life, so that they will not be fruitless.

III.B.   GREETINGS (3:15a)

3   ¹⁵ᵃAll who are here with me join in greeting you affectionately, Titus. Greet those who in faith are friends of ours.

IV. FINAL PRAYER (3:15b)

3   ^{15b}Grace be with all of you.

NOTES

3:12.   *As soon as I send Artemas to you, Titus, or perhaps Tychicus.* The initial phrase, *hotan pempsō*, with its future indicative is postclassical (see Luke 13:28 v.l. and BDF §382.4). *Hotan* with the subjunctive appears in 1 Tim 5:11. The particle occurs twenty-one times in the rest of the Paulines and one hundred times otherwise in the NT, with twenty-nine occurrences in Luke but only two in Acts. It is common in the Ap. Frs., taking the future in *2 Clem.* 12.2 and 17.6, as it does in LXX 1 Kgdms 10:7.

Pempein, "send" appears only here in the PE but seventy-eight times otherwise in the NT. Fourteen of these uses are in the other Paulines; twenty-one occur in Luke–Acts. This verb is common in the Ap. Frs. for sending church representatives and documents. Particularly notable is *1 Clem.* 63.3, "And we have sent prudent and trustworthy men who have lived blamelessly among us from youth to old age, and they shall be witnesses between you and us." These men are named in 65.1 as Claudius Ephebus, Valerius Vito, and Fortunatus (see the comments on Tychicus below). In the LXX *pempein* does not appear often and only in half a dozen places out of twenty-six is there a Hebrew original (usually a form of *slh*).

The name Artemas, a shortened form of Artemidoros, "Gift of Artemis," is of pagan origin (BDF §125.1), and it does not otherwise appear in biblical Greek or the Ap. Frs., not to mention Josephus or *CII.*

"Tychicus" will reappear in 2 Tim 4:12. In Acts 20:4 the name is given to a man described as "Asian," in other words, from Ephesus (see the reading of D and Haenchen, *Acts,* p. 581). In Col 4:7 and Eph 6:21 a Tychicus is "faithful servant *(diakonos)*" and "the beloved brother" of Paul as well as "fellow-slave *(syndoulos),*" distinguished from the Jewish Christians noted in Col 4:10–11 and thus apparently of pagan origin. The name certainly was of pagan origin, deriving from the goddess of luck, Tyche (or Fortuna in Latin, whence the Roman name Fortunatus). The English sobriquet "Lucky" corresponds to these ancient precedents. The name "Tychicus" does not appear in the LXX or the Ap. Frs., but *1 Clem.* does mention a messenger named Fortunatus (see above). Roman Jews bore forms of the names too (*CII* 240 has Fortunianus; 412, a father and son, Eutychis and Tychicos).

do your best to come to me at Nicopolis. Literally, "hasten," *spoudason;* this word occurs again in 2 Tim 2:15 and, with *elthein,* in 4:9 and 21. Otherwise in the NT there are seven appearances of the verb; three are in the Paulines (Gal 2:10; Eph 4:3; 1 Thess 2:17), three are in 2 Pet (1:10, 15; 3:14), and one with *eiselthein* in Heb 4:11. The term is used thirteen times in the Ap. Frs., but only the variant reading in Ign. *Eph.* 1.2 parallels the usage of the PE. In the dozen Septuagintal uses, generally of physical haste, not moral effort, there is likewise no parallel. For the adverb *spoudaiōs* see 3:13. The adjective *spoudaiōs* occurs in the NT only in 2 Cor 8:17 (of Titus; cf. the noun in v 16), 22. See Spicq, *Lexic.*, pp. 816–825.

"To come," *elthein*, is frequent in the NT (636 times) and in Paul. Forms of the verb appear eight times in the correspondence with Timothy, usually of the goings and comings of Paul and members of his entourage (1 Tim 3:14; 4:13; 2 Tim 4:9 [also with *pros me*], 13, 21). A pregnant theological usage appears when it is employed of the incarnation (1 Tim 1:15) and coming "to full knowledge of the truth" (1 Tim 2:4; 2 Tim 3:7).

Nicopolis appears only here in biblical Greek and the Ap. Frs. There was many a "Victory City" in the Hellenistic world (see Stillwell, *PECS*, pp. 302, 625–626; J. Finegan in *IDB* 3.548–549; Schoder, *Hellas*, pp. 154–157). Josephus, *War* 4.659, mentions the one founded by Augustus in Egypt in 24 B.C.E., and he alludes to the Nicopolis previously founded in memory of the victory at Actium in 31 B.C.E. (*War* 1.425; *Ant.* 16.147; see Strabo, *Geography* 7.7.5–6; 10.2.2; Dio Cassius, *Roman History* 50.12.1–8; 51.1.2–3). This Nicopolis in Epirus, with its double harbor, was the largest city at that time on the western coast of Greece. Augustus built and organized it as a Greek *polis*, using the preexisting villages in the neighborhood to form a new provincial capital (see the contemporary verses in *Greek Anthology* 9.553). The city issued its own coins and fielded quadrennial games on a par with those of Olympia. The remains of the stadium are still visible, along with those of a bath and a spacious theater. Roman roads go east from Nicopolis across central Greece and north to the Via Egnatia and Dyrrachium. It is about two hundred miles by sea from Nicopolis, toward the northwest across the Adriatic, to Brindisi, on the heel of the Italian boot. There one picks up the Via Appia, which terminates in Rome. When Domitian in 94 C.E. banished philosophers from Rome and Italy, the Stoic Epictetus reassembled his school in Nicopolis (Aulus Gellius, *Noctes atticae* 15.11.3–5).

for I have decided to spend the winter there. Literally, "I have judged," from *krinein*, which recurs in the phrase "to judge the living and the dead" in 2 Tim 4:1. The verb occurs elsewhere in the NT 113 times. Romans and 1 Cor share 35 of the 39 other uses of the verb in Paul, where the sense here in Titus appears also in Rom 14:13b; 1 Cor 2:2; 7:37; 2 Cor 2:1 (with *elthein*). Luke-Acts has 28 uses of the verb (see Acts 27:1, "When it was decided that we were to set sail for Italy"; also 3:13; 20:16; 25:25). Of more than a score of uses in the Ap. Frs., the sense here is most closely paralleled in *Herm. Man.* 12.3.6, "Since you have already decided for yourself that these commandments cannot be kept by a human being." The LXX uses *krinein* often, particularly to translate the *špṭ* terminology of the Hebrew Bible. But it is usage in the Maccabean corpus particularly (see 1 Macc 11:33; 2 Macc 11:25, 36; 3 Macc 1:6; 6:30) that parallels this passage of Titus.

"To spend the winter," *paracheimasai*, is found otherwise in the NT only in 1 Cor 16:6, where the apostle tells his Corinthian converts, "Perhaps I will stay with you or even spend the winter, so that you may speed (*propempsēte;* see 2 Cor 1:16) me on my journey, wherever I go"; and in Acts 27:12 and 28:11, where there is explicit reference to the necessity of interrupting seafaring from November 10 through March 10, the *tempus clausum,* the "season closed" by the storms of the Mediterranean winter. The verb does not appear in the LXX or Ap. Frs. In secular Greek the verb occurs sometimes in a context of seafaring; thus, Demosthenes 34 (*Against Phormio*) 8; 56 (*Against Dionysodorus*) 30; see also *cheimazein* in Dio Cassius, *Roman History* 40.4.1.

Ekei, "there," appears 105 times in the NT but only here in the PE and in the rest of the Paulines only in Rom 9:26 (citing LXX Hos 2:1) and 15:24, where Paul writes, "I hope to see you en route as I journey to Spain and to be sped on my way (*propemphthēnai*) there (*ekei*) by you, once I have enjoyed your company a little." Luke–Acts share 27 uses of the term, which appears regularly in the Ap. Frs. (see esp. Ign. *Eph.* 21.2; *Rom.* 6.2; *Phld.* 10.1) and hundreds of times in the LXX.

13. *Do all you can to speed the journey. Spoudaiōs propempson,* literally, "diligently send on their way." The adverbial *spoudaiōs* (also in 2 Tim 1:17) recurs in the NT only twice: in Phil 2:28, where Paul is "the more eager to send (*spoudaioteros . . . epempsa*)" Epaphroditus back to Philippi to allay anxieties about his health; and in Luke 7:4, where it qualifies the urgency of the petition of the Jewish elders on behalf of the centurion at Capernaum. The adverb does not appear in the Ap. Frs., but there is one use in the LXX, in Wis 2:6, where the godless say, "Come then, let us enjoy the good things at hand and make use of creation with youthful zest (*spoudaiōs;* AB)." See Spicq, *Lexic.,* pp. 818–822.

Propempein, "to send on a trip," occurs eight times elsewhere in the NT. Romans 15:24 and 1 Cor 16:6 (with a reference to 2 Cor 1:16) have been quoted above. Paul solicited a like "sendoff" for Timothy in 1 Cor 16:11. Luke used this verb to recall the way in which Paul and Barnabas were sent off by the Christians of Antioch to the Jerusalem meeting (Acts 15:3) or the way in which Paul was put on the boat to Palestine by the Ephesian presbyter-bishops (Acts 20:38) and by all the Christians of Tyre (Acts 21:5). The identical, almost technical, use appears in 3 John 6, as well as in Pol. *Phil.* 1.1 (see Brown, *AB Epistles,* p. 711). The verb appears in the latest strata of the LXX of those sent with letters for safe conduct (1 Esdr 4:47; 1 Macc 12:4 [see Malherbe, *Social Aspects,* pp. 106–107]; cf. *Ep. Arist.* 172) and with provision for their journey (Wis 19:2). The escort in Jdt 10:15 is honorary, however, and the use of Eleazar's being sent off to the underworld is, at the best, ironic.

of Zenas the lawyer, and Apollos. Both names are of pagan origin, Zēnas from Zenodorus, "Gift of Zeus," and Apollōs from Apollodorus, "Gift of Apollo," or from Apollonius (see the D reading in Acts 18:24 and BDF §125.1 as well as the Maccabean literature and Ign. *Magn.* 2.1) or even from Apollonides (see MM s.v.). On the various spellings of the accusative here (Apollō, -ōn, -ōna) see BDF §55.1g and J. K. Elliott, *Greek Text,* pp. 195–196. The name Zēnas, possibly suggesting servile background (G. Horsley, *NDIEC*, 2.89; §57), does not appear otherwise in biblical Greek or the Ap. Frs., but a Jewish woman from Rome had the name Marcia Zenodora (*CII* 43). It is important to note that Jews could bear pagan names (like Mordechai in Esth) and that quite commonly, particularly in the Diaspora, Jews had both a pagan and a Jewish name. By contrast, pagans appear not to have adopted Jewish names. For *nomikos,* here "the lawyer," see 3:9.

Apollōs in this form is not found in the LXX, but there are notices of an individual with this name in both 1 Cor (1:12; 3:4, 5, 6, 22; 4:6; 16:12) and Acts (18:24; 19:1). *First Clement* 47.3 refers to the individual described in 1 Cor. All of these notices refer to the same person, a Jewish Christian of Alexandrian origin with notable skills in interpreting the OT and communicating what he learned. In Acts he appears at Ephesus in the early fifties C.E. and goes on to Corinth with a letter of introduction to the Pauline congregation there (see BAGD, s.v. and Haenchen, *Acts,* pp. 549–552, with the literature cited there, as well as Conzelmann, *1 Cor.,* pp. 33, 85, 297). A party of Corinthian believers lionized him, though he personally remained loyal to Paul. For his identity with the Apollos here in Titus, see COMMENT.

with all their needs satisfied. Literally, it reads "so that nothing may be lacking to them." For the present subjunctive *leipēi* (as in A), some scribes read the second aorist subjunctive *lipēi* (as in S, D*, PSI, 81, etc.). J. K. Elliott (*Greek Text,* pp. 162–163, 196) favors the aorist as characteristic of the PE. If this passage, however, belongs to a source that predates the PE, the present subjunctive appears more likely. For the verb *leipein,* see 1:5.

14. *Thus let our own people too learn what it means "to take the lead in fine deeds" with regard to the urgent necessities of life.* The adjective *hēmeteroi,* literally "our," appears eight times in the NT, including 2 Tim 4:15, but it is used nominally meaning "our own people" only here (see the variant *to hēmeteron* in Luke 16:12). A similar number of uses of *hēmeteros* in the Ap. Frs. contains one variant reading that resembles the meaning here in Titus (Ign. *Smyrn.* 11.3). In *Mart. Pol.* 9.1, however, the narrator says of a voice that sounded from the sky, "Those present from our people heard the voice (*tōn hēmeterōn hoi parontes*)." The usage has a few Septuagintal precedents (Josh 5:13 in the singular; 3 Macc 1:27 in the plural; Esth 8:12b, the neuter plural meaning "our part"). In secular Greek, see Philodemus of Gadara, *Volumina rhetorica* (Sudhaus 1.12, 47; suppl. p. 8 and the papyri cited in Spicq, *EP,* p. 692; *Lexic.,* p. 77 n. 1). In the first Christian century possessive pronouns

were being used less often, and G. D. Kilpatrick ("Possessive," pp. 184–186) has noted a curious phenomenon in the NT: the Paulines (without the PE) and Acts use these possessives only attributively, whereas the third Gospel uses them only predicatively or pronominally (as here in Titus).

"Learn what it means," *manthanetōsan,* occurs two dozen times otherwise in the NT, six times in the correspondence with Timothy (1 Tim 2:11; 5:4, 13; 2 Tim 3:7, 14) and nine times in the other Paulines (see COMMENT). In the Lukan writings the verb appears only in Acts 23:27. *First Clement* 8.4 quotes LXX Isa 1:17, "Learn to do good," and counsels that children "learn what strength humility has before God" (21.8) and that the factious at Corinth be subordinate (57.2). Ignatius writes to the Romans, "In chains now I am learning to set my heart on nothing" (4.3) and to the Magnesians, "Let us learn to live according to Christianity" (10.1; in contrast to Judaism). *Barnabas* employs *manthanein* ten times, generally in an imperative address to heed the Christian interpretation and application of the OT. In the LXX there are almost fifty uses of *manthanein,* usually translating the Hebrew *lmd,* but none parallels the usage here in Titus as closely as the Isaian passage cited in *1 Clem.* (but see LXX Jer 12:16). In the *T. 12 Patr.* the verb designates a learning that comes from God; see *T. Gad* 5.8; *T. Jos.* 4.4 (*logon Kyriou*); 6.7.

"To take the lead in fine deeds": see the analysis of the phrase in 3:8b.

"With regard to the urgent necessities of life" is, literally, "for the necessary needs," *eis tas anagkaias chreias,* a phrase documented in Hellenistic literary, inscriptional, and papyrus texts (see Spicq, *Lexic.,* pp. 77–80; *EP,* p. 693) but found only here in biblical Greek or the Ap. Frs.

The individual terms of the phrase, however, occur regularly, particularly *chreia,* which appears, aside from this one occurrence in the PE, four dozen times in the NT. Of the thirteen uses in the other Paulines, several clearly refer to provision for the necessities of life, food, drink, shelter, clothing (Rom 12:13; Phil 2:25; 4:16). A similar meaning appears in Luke 10:42; Acts 4:35; 6:3; 20:34; 28:10, not to mention Matt 6:8; Mark 2:25; and 1 John 3:17. In the Ap. Frs. only the *Did.* uses *chreia* (and only 1.5 of the necessities of life). Of more than fifty appearances in the LXX, a few in Sir refer to the basic human needs, particularly 39:26, "Basic to all the needs of man's life are water and fire and iron and salt and wheat flour and milk and honey, the blood of the grape, and oil and clothing" (RSV; see 13:6; 29:2; 39:33; 42:23). The fisherman Zebulon in *T. Zeb.* 6.5 says, "If anyone were a traveler, or sick, or aged, I cooked the fish, prepared it well, and offered to each person according to his need, being either convivial or consoling."

The adjective *anagkaios,* "urgent" but literally "necessary," appears only here in the PE and seven times elsewhere in the NT, four times in the other Paulines and twice in Acts. None offers a notable parallel to the usage here, and the same must be said of the two occurrences in the Ap. Frs., in *1 Clem.* and Ignatius. Of the six LXX uses, however, Wis 16:3 writes of Egyptians losing an "urgent appetite" for food because of "the hideousness of the creatures sent against them" (Winston, *AB Wisd.*, p. 292). Here the sense of that which is physically pressing is clear.

so that they will not be fruitless. The adjective *akarpoi* occurs only here in the PE. Of the half dozen other NT uses, there are only two in Paul (of the mind that is unproductive in glossolalia [1 Cor 14:14] and of the "fruitless works of darkness" [Eph 5:11]); and none in Luke–Acts. In the Ap. Frs. one must wait until Hermas for its appearance (*Sim.* 2.3; 4.4; 9.19.2). The LXX uses the term only three times: of "a waterless and sterile land" (Jer 2:6); of the sterile labor of those who paint idols (Wis 15:4); and of "the fruitless nurturings" that the mother of the Maccabean martyrs never had to regret (4 Macc 16:7). See Spicq, *Lexic.*, pp. 57–58 and, for the positive, nominal *karpos*, 2 Tim 2:6.

15a. *All who are here with me join in greeting you affectionately, Titus.* Literally, it is "All those with me greet you" (singular). "With me," *met' emou*, which appears again in 2 Tim 4:11, also occurs in Acts 20:34 but not in the other Paulines, which prefer *syn emoi* (cf. 1 Cor 16:4; 2 Cor 9:4; Gal 1:2; 2:3; Phil 4:21 with 1 Cor 15:10; Phil 2:22). The present indicative of *aspazesthai*, to "greet," becomes the aorist imperative in the latter part of this verse, a characteristic Pauline variation (see Furnish, *AB 2 Cor*, p. 582). This order is reversed when the same verb occurs in the conclusion of the correspondence with Timothy (2 Tim 4:19, 21). Most of the other fifty-five uses of *aspazesthai* in the NT are in epistolary formulas for greeting. Thus the rest of the Paulines use this verb thirty-six times; twenty-one of these uses are in Rom 16. By contrast, the term does not appear in Gal (see MM s.v.), Eph, or 2 Thess (perhaps for literary reasons). The greeting includes not only words of welcome or appreciation but also the friendly embrace and kiss on the cheeks that is common in the Mediterranean world to this day (see Rom 16:16; 1 Cor 16:20; 2 Cor 13:12; 1 Thess 5:26; perhaps to be presumed in Luke 1:40; 10:4; Acts 18:22; 20:1; 21:7, 19; 25:13).

The technical "epistolary" sense for the verb predominates in the Ap. Frs., where twenty-two of twenty-six uses are in the Ignatian letters (the other four in Hermas). In the LXX *aspazesthai* appears six of thirteen times in the Maccabean corpus, and in 1 Macc 12:17 the greeting accompanies a letter. In *T. Gad* 3.3 the person filled with hate welcomes slander.

Greet those who in faith are friends of ours. For "greet," see above; the scribes of A and b read a plural imperative address here, probably under the influence of the plurals in 15b. For "in faith," see Excursus I, "*Pistis* Terminology in the PE." "Friends of ours" is literally "those who love us," *philountas hēmas. Philein* appears only here in the PE. Otherwise in the Paulines it occurs only in 1 Cor 16:22 in a formulaic liturgical phrase about one who is no friend of the Lord. Similarly, the only uses in the Lukan corpus refer to the scribes who like greetings (*aspasmous*) in public places and Judas showing his affection for Jesus (Luke 20:46; 22:47). Thirteen of twenty-one other NT uses of *philein* are in the Gospel according to John. The one certain occurrence in the Ap. Frs. is in the admonition of Ign. *Pol.* 2.1, "If you have affection for fine disciples, it is no credit to you." In the LXX the verb, in its more than thirty uses, often designates an affectionate kiss between members of a family (Gen 27:26–27; 29:13; 33:4; 48:10; 50:1; Exod 18:7; cf. *T. Benj.* 1.2) or in courtship and marriage (Gen 29:11; Tob 10:12 [cf. *aspasamenos* in S]; Cant 1:2). It should also be noted that the meaning extends to a liking for a dish of wild game (Gen 27:4, 9, 14) or wine and oil (Prov 21:17).

15b. *Grace be with all of you.* On *charis*, "grace," see 1:4. Some scribes read "grace of God/of the Lord," probably an expansion that derives from liturgical usage, as does the closing *amēn* of many witnesses (see J. K. Elliott, *Greek Text,* pp. 197, 104; B. Metzger, *TCGNT,* pp. 655–656). The combination of liturgical usage and the actual text of 2 Tim 4:22 have led to "with your [singular] spirit" in 33 and "with you all and with your [singular] spirit" in 81.

Various subscriptions in the manuscripts testify to the opinions current at the time and place of their writing about the origin and destination of the preceding document. "To Titus" appears in many. Some add that the letter was written from Nicopolis (in Crete, according to one); another, from Macedonia. Many state that Titus was appointed the first bishop of the church of the Cretans. The Bohairic Coptic notes that the letter was sent by Artemas; the Peshitta, by Zenas and Apollos (see B. Metzger, *TCGNT,* p. 656; Spicq, *EP,* pp. 307–308).

COMMENT

3:12. *As soon as I send Artemas to you, Titus, or perhaps Tychicus, do your best to come to me at Nicopolis, for I have decided to spend the winter there.* There is no transition from the preceding section. Very abruptly the redactor-author turns to a series of personal notes containing Paul's decisions and directives for his coworker. These notes are closely linked with one another by a series of verbal repetitions; thus *pempsō* corresponds with *propempson* in the following verse; *spoudason* with the following *spoudaios; hoi hēmeteroi* in v 14 with *hēmas* in v 15; *aspazontai* and *pantes* in the first part of v 15 with *aspasai* and *pantōn* later. The emphatic return of the first-person singular (three times in v 12 and once in v 15) takes one back to the equally emphatic repetition in 1:3 and 5. Thus the author signals formally that this concluding section is to be read, not with the immediately preceding directives on true and false instruction, but with the opening verses of the letter. Once alerted to this compositional "envelope" for the body of the letter, one can detect other, more subtle correspondences (e.g., the *leipēi* of 3:13 continuing the *apelipon, ta leiponta* of 1:5; the *en pistei* of 3:15 taking up the *kata koinēn pistin* of 1:4; or the *charis* of 3:15b resonating with that term at 1:4b, 5).

This "letter envelope," when read apart from the intervening three chapters of Titus, combines memorandums that resemble the Pauline form for the dispatch of an apostolic emissary (see Funk, "Parousia," pp. 255–258) with the form for a letter of introduction, an *epistolē systatikē*, for Apollos and Zenas, carried by them from Paul (and his entourage) to Titus (and Christian congregations) on Crete (see Kim, *Recommendation*, whose analysis is used below).

The note greets Titus and describes summarily a specific and apparently temporary task for which Paul had left him on Crete when the apostle and the rest of his entourage had embarked. Now Paul wants to dispatch another coworker and have Titus rejoin him as he moves toward winter quarters. The implication is that this dispatch was sent in autumn, before the sea lanes closed for the winter. The dispatch envisions Artemas and Tychicus as accompanying Paul at the time it was sent; Zenas and Apollos are certainly there to receive this letter of recommendation, but they need not have been part of the circle traveling with Paul. Rather, their route had intersected with that of Paul, and he has engaged them to carry a hurried letter for Titus, which will at the same time assure them welcome and help on a journey that is taking them through Crete (perhaps on the way to Alexandria).

Greek rhetoricians when they discussed types of letters included the *epistolē systatikē*. The pseudo-Demetrius (second century B.C.E.–third century C.E.) proposed no less than twenty-one kinds of letters, among which was the

> commendatory type which we write on behalf of one person to another, mixing in praise, at the same time also speaking of those who had previously been unacquainted as though they were (now) acquainted. In the following manner: So-and-so, who is conveying this letter to you [singular] has been tested by us and is loved on account of his trustworthiness. You will do well if you deem him worthy of hospitality [*apodochēs*] both for my sake and his, and indeed for your own. For you will not be sorry if you entrust to him, in any matter you wish, either words or deeds of a confidential nature. Indeed, you, too, will praise him to others when you see how useful he can be in everything. (Malherbe, "Theorists," p. 31; see also material on pseudo-Libanius, p. 71)

As Chan-Hie Kim has noted (*Recommendation*, pp. 2–3), such theoretical, rhetorical models had minimal influence on surviving letters of recommendation between actual persons (see his Appendix III for eighty-three texts; also G. Horsley, *NDIEC* 1.64–66, §21).

The form and structure of Greek letters of recommendation, in Kim's analysis, distinguish this type of private correspondence (i.e., letters that were not written with an eye to publication) from other ancient letters between individuals. Five consecutive divisions can be isolated:

THE LETTER TO TITUS

1. Salutation
2. Background for the one recommended
3. Request from the recipient
4. Appreciation
5. Closing

Within these divisions, further elements characteristic of the form and structure of the letter of recommendation appear, and many of them coincide with form and structure of the "letter envelope" for Titus. Thus in the salutation the order of the greeting, *"A to B, chairein,"* becomes "Paul to Titus, grace and peace," which in turn contains a specifically Christian and Pauline variant on the wish for the recipient's good health. Paul's describing himself as slave and apostle as well as his identifying Titus as "his true child" parallel somewhat the language of respectful and familial relationships found in the other letters of recommendation in the Roman Hellenistic age. After the memorandums for Titus, one meets in 3:13–14 the request from the recipient and the background of those recommended. The reversal in the order of the elements is due to the intervening directive for Titus, which attracts the request from the recipient to its present position.

The imperatival address, "Do all you can to speed the journey," has some precedents in the secular letters of recommendation but is regular in Christian ones. The generic character of the assistance requested is typical, and the circumstantial *spoudaiōs*, "diligently," reminds one that a verb that could have been expected here would have been *spoudason.* The purposive clause with *hina*, here translated "with all their needs satisfied," is regularly the third and final element in the request.

The background for those recommended, Zenas and Apollos, again follows the regular Hellenistic pattern, with the explicit naming of the persons recommended. Zenas is further identified by his occupation (which is not usual in the secular or later Christian practice, both of which prefer the terminology of familial relationship). Apollos is named with no further identification, which is equivalent to saying that he is the well-known Apollos (see Kim, *Recommendation,* p. 52). After the naming, the background needed to obtain the favor asked is supplied.

14. *Thus let our own people too learn what it means "to take the lead in fine deeds" with regard to the urgent necessities of life, so that (hina) they will not be fruitless.* The Greek *de,* which is represented by the opening "thus" in 3:14, is the commonest connective transition at this point in the secular recommendations, where its meaning is not adversative but simply explanatory (ibid., pp. 56–57). Even the final, somewhat awkward purposive clause (*hina*) may be due to the influence of the normal pattern in commendations that had a request end-

ing with such a clause in this position in the letter instead of in the background of the ones recommended.

In the secular letters of recommendation, as in the later Christian ones, the expression of appreciation is found rarely or omitted altogether. This is the case here in Titus, where the closing of the letter follows immediately after the background of the recommended. The secular form regularly ends with a stereotyped *errōso*, "farewell," but it may simply break off abruptly. Occasionally, however, it ends on a note of affectionate familiarity, which reminds one of the friendly phrases in 3:15a. Later Christian letters of recommendation resemble Titus at this point (ibid., p. 114). The closing prayer of blessing in 3:15b may be regarded as a Christian variant on the stylized wish for good health in the closing of some secular letters.

On the whole the letter of recommendation framing Titus is closer in form and structure to its secular counterparts than to the relatively few Christian letters of this type that have survived from the third to the fifth centuries. The Paul of history knew about such Christian letters of recommendation (see Furnish, *AB 2 Cor*, pp. 179–183, 192–196, on 2 Cor 3:1–3) and wrote one himself, to Philemon about Onesimus. The Pauline form, as Kim has noted (*Recommendation*, p. 134), is indistinguishable from the form he used to dispatch emissaries. There is an introduction of the request, a presentation of credentials, and an action that is requested (the latter two may be reversed, as in Phil 4:2–3). The form here in Titus is not typically Pauline, though it combines both the dispatch of an emissary and a recommendation. Rather, one encounters here a christianization of the form and structure of typically Hellenistic letters of recommendation. The later Christian letters of this type do not thus depend on the secular form, as Kim has noted (ibid., p. 117).

This letter envelope in Titus does not quite fit the picture that has been filled out in the intervening chapters, in which the process of formation and reformation that the apostle's coworker is to direct can scarcely be conceived as occurring within the month or two envisioned in this dispatch. The frame in this instance may well have preexisted the picture and have been considered by the redactor-author of the PE as worth preserving for its own sake. An authentic, brief dispatch from Paul in the mid-sixties of the first Christian century would, according to this reconstruction, serve to frame a reworking and reapplication of Pauline traditions twenty years later. If in fact Luke was the redactor-author of the PE as well as a member of Paul's entourage in the apostle's last years, one would need to look no further for the one who had drafted and then preserved a copy of such a memorandum, Pauline in its content, Hellenistic in its form. Luke's intimate connection with the origin of this dispatch and letter of recommendation would have warranted his later and different use of it.

In any case, both Paul (thus 1 Cor 4:17; 2 Cor 9:3; in Acts 15:22, 25 he is the one sent) and Luke can say that the apostle *sends* coworkers as here he debates whether to send Artemas or Tychicus. The former name is typical of a slave or freedman. Varro (*De lingua latina* 8.21) describes how the name of a slave purchased at Ephesus may be derived from the name of the one who sold him, and thus Artemas, the slave, from Artemidorus, the slave dealer. The link of both names with the worship of Artemis at Ephesus is more than a coincidence. The person in question here in Titus is probably a convert from paganism, perhaps of Asian origin; and one could speculate that he is being considered to replace Titus, who was certainly a convert from paganism (Gal 2:3), because he was to represent Paul in an area in which Jewish Christians were numerous and posing troublesome questions. Perhaps the hesitation evinced here has something to do with the actual situation on Crete in the late sixties C.E. If all is proceeding smoothly, a relatively unknown and even inexperienced coworker may be quite adequate. If not, the more practiced and versatile Tychicus is called for.

Although the name "Tychicus" was common enough in antiquity, it seems hypercritical to deny that the NT texts that mention the name intend to refer to one person (though that would not ipso facto authenticate the historical accuracy of placing that one individual in each of the scenes envisioned). All of the other strands of NT evidence link him in some way to the province of Asia and Ephesus. Perhaps this dispatch presumes that Paul's entourage is in the province of Asia and near Ephesus at this juncture (see 1 Tim 1:3; Quinn, "Captivity," pp. 289–299), though the names "Artemas" and "Tychicus" are only hints at this. As Tychicus is Timothy's peer in 2 Tim 4:12, he is Titus's peer in this passage, quite capable of taking up his predecessor's task *in persona Pauli*. The mention of his name in second place, as an alternate for Artemas, may reflect the apostle's reluctance to part with an especially valuable lieutenant.

Particularly if Tychicus must be sent, Titus is to be "quick to come" to Paul. *Spoudason* is formulaic in Hellenistic correspondence but is nevertheless appropriate here as a directive from a dynamic and enthusiastic apostle who valued such qualities in his coworkers (2 Cor 8:16–17, 22). As in Menander, *Dyscolos* 148, the accent of the verb lies not on speed but on determination, "bent on business" (Gomme and Sandbach, *Commentary*, p. 159; cf. *Kitharistes* 100; Koerte 644, 745/555K, 562K); hence "do your best." As early as Jerome (*PL* 26.598) the Nicopolis in Epirus, on the northern side of the Ambracian Gulf, a few miles north of modern Preveza and its strait into the Ambracian Gulf (modern Arta), was singled out, from other cities with the same name, as the place in which Paul wanted to meet Titus and to spend the winter (see D-C, pp. 152–153 and J. Finegan in *IDB* 3.548 reviewing the sites). To this day the area has the highest rainfall on the coast, and the winters in the mountains of Epirus are proverbially cruel. The port was frequented in the Roman period by the great commercial boats that sailed between the eastern Mediterranean and Italy. The large numbers of Corinthian coins that have been discovered around the site point to a long and regular association with Corinth and perhaps hint (as does the verb for "to spend the winter") that Paul had in mind coming to the city by sea rather than overland (see Hammond, *Epirus*, pp. 18–19, 62–63, 724–725). At such a crossroad for the sea traffic up and down the Adriatic as well as between northern Greece and southern Italy, the apostle planned for his entourage to winter. The opportunity for several months of contact with travelers from many different places, confined temporarily by the weather and ready to listen to something new, would mean no halt in the Pauline apostolate (see Rom 15:19). If indeed Paul at this point was under sentence of exile from Rome and Italy (see *1 Clem.* 5.6; the INTRODUCTION; and Quinn, "Seven Times," p. 574), then he would be as close to Italy as he could legally be.

13. *Do all you can to speed the journey of Zenas the lawyer, and Apollos, with all their needs satisfied.* The letter of recommendation proper begins at this point, with the formal variants noted above due to its telescoping out of the dispatch of an emissary. The two persons named are not only the carriers of the dispatch (as Theodore of Mopsuestia already remarked; Swete, *Theodore*, 2.256) but also the ones recommended to Titus and the Christian congregations he is guiding. Apollos is apparently so well known to Titus that he needs no further identification. Zenas, however, is introduced by name as well as by his occupation as "the lawyer." Because from the point of view of the form one expects a somewhat more intimate identification, even in a familial terminology, it is probable (as Chrysostom noted, *On Titus* [*PG* 62.696]) that *nomikos* here designates a Christian skilled in the Law par excellence, the Torah, even the whole OT. In another context Paul himself used an identification by profession in an intimate sense. Thus "Luke, the beloved physician" (Col 4:14) means "my own beloved doctor" (cf. "our sailor" in the letter of introduction cited by G. Horsley, *NDIEC* 1.64–65). The case of "Erastus, the city treasurer" (Rom 16:23) is anomalous (see 2 Tim 4:20; Theissen, *Setting*, pp. 75–76).

Some have contended that the pagan name, Zenas, and attitude of the PE to the Jewish Law and its teachers tips the probabilities toward *nomikos* meaning one trained in the civil, that is, the Roman, law (thus D-C and Spicq). But the pagan name could be borne by a man, even of Jewish origin, who had become a Christian, as in fact is the case with the name of Apollos. Zenas could even have been a slave of pagan origin who converted to the Judaism of the master who owned him and eventually freed him. In any case, his identification in terms of his skill in the Jewish Law would serve to accredit him with the Jewish Christians among those to whom he is being introduced. Identification as a civil lawyer hardly is a recommendation to a Christian congregation, whether Jewish or pagan in origin, and there is no hint that Zenas stands in an intimate relation to Paul—as if he were "Zenas, the beloved lawyer"—or that he would be useful in matters of the Roman law with which the new churches had to come to terms (*pace* Hasler, *Timotheus*, p. 99).

As to the attitude of the PE about the Law and its teachers, the "wranglings about the Law" (*machas nomikas*) that are censured in 3:9 do not discredit the

Law itself any more than the self-styled "rabbis" (*nomodidaskaloi*) of 1 Tim 1:7 compromise the indisputable principle in 1 Tim 1:8 that the Law is a fine thing (*kalos ho nomos*), much less the teachers who instructed the Pauline minister in "the sacred letters" from childhood (2 Tim 3:14–15). In fact, the meaning of *nomikos* in Titus 3:9 leads one to suspect that at least the redactor of Titus used the same term in 3:13 as designating a Christian trained in the OT and particularly in the interpretation of the Torah. There is a healthy, profitable Pauline hermeneutic for the OT, and Zenas is here identified as one equipped with it. His pagan name may constitute the very reason for the explicit identification as one skilled in the Jewish Law. If Jewish Christians on Crete had even in the latter sixties C.E. been troublesome, there would have been still more reason to emphasize this qualification of Zenas, which would place him on par with Apollos, already well known as one whose skillful Jewish-Christian interpretation of the OT Paul trusted (see 1 Cor 4:1–2, 6).

The historical setting of the original letter of recommendation poses no basic difficulty for recognizing the Apollos named here as the Alexandrian Jew whom both Paul and Acts link with Ephesus and Corinth. He apparently did not regularly travel with the Pauline missionary entourage, any more than Cephas did. The letter of recommendation here presumes that he was personally known to Titus but not to the Christians of Crete (except perhaps by reputation). In the fifties there are glimpses of his movements on an axis between Ephesus and Corinth. This letter suggests that he and another Jewish-Christian OT scholar (who needed explicit identification as one versed in the Torah) had encountered Paul, Artemas, Tychicus, Luke(?), and Timothy, perhaps in the neighborhood of Ephesus, where Timothy was to be left (1 Tim 1:3). The two were evidently on a missionary voyage that recommended them to the hospitality of the Christian congregations they visited en route. They intended or were easily persuaded by Paul to make a stop in Crete. Their ultimate destination is unspecified, but in the light of the southerly course taken along with the place of Apollos's origin, it is conceivable that they were heading for Alexandria in Egypt. In any case, as a pair of Jewish-Christian witnesses versed in the interpretation of the OT about Christ and for Christians, their testimony as a pair (in accord with the deuteronomic law for witnesses) would have no little impact on the Cretan Jewish Christians, who were remembered by the author-redactor of the PE as looking down on the convert from paganism, Titus, whom Paul had left with them (2:15). In the laconic note of Theodore of Mopsuestia, they were sent to help Titus and to correct others (Swete, *Theodore*, 2.256).

The stay of Zenas and Apollos on Crete was not to be lengthy. Titus is instructed with a vocabulary that is all but technical for the NT authors to do all he can to speed their voyage (see Malherbe, *Social Aspects*, pp. 65–68, 94–103, on this and the following). The well-known interest of Luke in hospitality is particularly interesting in the light of his possible connection with the origin of this letter of recommendation. In any case, one encounters in the directive about Zenas and Apollos an actual example of the institutional framework for facilitating the travels between the churches of more or less official missionaries (see 1:8 as well as 2 Cor 8:23 with its "representatives [apostoloi] of the churches"). Their Christian role was public and recognized. They were accredited by the congregation (or the apostle) who sent them. They were to be received hospitably by and to minister to the congregations they visited. After their visit (which was often brief, as this letter also presumes), their journey to the next Christian church was to be made easier by the Christians whom they had just served. There were gatherings for prayer, for ancient highways and seaways had their perils also (see Acts 13:3; 20:36; 21:5). Letters of introduction and recommendation were drawn up. Guides and routes were furnished. Suitable food, means of transportation, and money were placed at the disposal of the missionaries. It is this Christian hospitality that Paul is directing Titus to provide for Zenas and Apollos. They are to be sent on their way "with all their needs satisfied," a delicate allusion to the underwriting of their expenses.

14 (*bis*). *Thus let our own people too learn what it means "to take the lead in fine deeds" with regard to the urgent necessities of life, so that they will not be fruitless.* Titus is not dispensed from generosity himself (as "too," *de kai*, suggests). Yet he is also a traveling missionary and does not have extensive resources at his personal disposal. He is accordingly to urge the Cretan congregations to be generous (a task that was congenial to the Titus of history, as 2 Cor 8:6, 16–17, and 23 suggest).

The unusual description of at least some of the Cretan Christians as "our own people" implies, with its first-person plural, that they stood in an identifiable relation to Paul and Titus, one that distinguished them not only from pagans and Jews but also from Jewish Christians on Crete who opposed the Pauline apostolate (the memory of such an opposition, which dated from an appearance of Paul and his colleagues on the island, appears to lie behind 1:10). Perhaps some of "our own people" are Paul's converts from Judaism and paganism. Others may be Jewish Christians who antedated the Pauline mission but who welcomed the apostle and his converts. All of them, regardless of origin, if they have an authentic relation to Paul, are to learn how to support the Pauline mission with their hospitable charity for the traveling missionaries whom Paul recommends. Pauline congregations must learn to show their identity and unity in the support that they give to such men as Zenas and Apollos. Titus, the Pauline leader, must make such learning possible by urging and organizing concrete acts of fraternal care and service.

The use of "learn" here is in the style of Phil 4:9 and 11, where the apostle first writes, "What you have *learned* and received and heard and seen in me, do (*prassete*)." Then a little later he adds, "Not that I complain of want; for I have *learned* in whatever state I am, to be content." The learning urged here is no abstract, theological systematization. It is learning charity by acting charitably (see Malherbe, *Social Aspects*, p. 67). Thus, the Pauline congregations here in the PE are to follow the lead of Titus himself (again, note "too," *de kai*) as they "take the lead in fine deeds." The material needs of Christian missionaries for food, shelter, and money become an occasion for uniting believers in the work of fraternal charity, a kind of parable for the "leadership" that the apostolic minister and the Christian community are to exercise in a society that has not yet believed, a leadership in sacrificial charity. The visibly attractive works are here further specified as those ordered "to the urgent necessities of life," a phrase with Lukan as well as Pauline resonances. Philippians 4:16 and 19 are notably close to the sense here, as the apostle rehearses the long-standing generosity of his Philippian converts in supplying his needs and promises that "my God will fill every need (*chreian*) of yours according to the wealth that is his in glory in Christ Jesus."

If the missionaries are sent on their way "with all their needs satisfied," then the Jewish-Christian congregations on Crete "will not be fruitless." The tree itself has no use for its fruit; the latter is meant to support the life of others. So the fraternal charity of the Cretan Christians helps sustain the life and missionary work of others for Christ and his church (see 2 Tim 2:6). An emphasis on good works as the fruit of the Spirit and *agapē* is Pauline (Gal 5:22, 25; 6:8–10), as is the use of the term "fruitless." The latter is undocumented in the Lukan corpus; when it occurs in the gospel tradition (Mark 4:19; Matt 13:22; *SFG* §124), Luke 8:14 changes the Markan *didachē* about the "fruitless" word, saying instead that certain persons "do not produce mature fruit (*telesphorousin*)."

15a. *All who are here with me join in greeting you affectionately, Titus. Greet those who in faith are friends of ours.* With this closing greeting, which goes back to the end of the original dispatch and the Pauline apostolate, the whole (*pantes*) apostolic entourage comes into focus (see 3:12 and, for a parallel instance, 2 Tim 4:11, as well as the closing of the papyrus letter of recommendation cited by G. Horsley, *NDIEC* 1.65–66, §21). They are emphatically Paul's men, at his side (in a phrase that is Lukan), sharing his apostolic work. They now, as a group, greet Titus alone (note the singular address), numbering him with themselves, supporting him in a task that isolates him from them as well as from the congregations that it is his duty to correct and direct (see 1:5). The repeated forms of *aspazesthai*, here translated as "greet (affectionately)," serve to bridge those gaps verbally with an epistolary formula that underlined the apostolic *parousia*, the "presence" that the letter effected and that Titus is in turn to communicate in the name of Paul to the Cretan Christians who are devoted to the apostle and his coworkers. The first-person plural "friends of ours" emphatically joins Titus with the Pauline entourage: to be devoted to the apostle's coworker in the midst of the local church is to be devoted to Paul and all those with him. The phrase "in faith" serves to christianize a set epistolary formula (see G. Stählin in *TDNT* 9.137 n. 214; Spicq, *Agape*, E.T. 3.227–228). This friendship and affection take their origin from the faith, the true faith as

Paul teaches it. What a later theology would identify as collegial communion is presumed in this christianization of a standard closing greeting.

15b. *Grace be with all of you.* As Titus opened with a greeting that mentioned faith and grace (1:1, 4), so it now closes with a blessing that occurs verbatim in Heb 13:25 and without *pantōn*, "all," in 1 and 2 Tim. The character of the original dispatch as an open letter of instructions for Titus and of recommendation for its bearers, Zenas and Apollos, becomes explicit with the plural address, "all of you." The Cretan congregations were intended to hear both Paul's recall of Titus and Paul's authorization of Titus's successor (Artemas or Tychicus). The original communication was a personal letter with a public function, and thus the apostle's blessing prayer goes out to all who hear it read out to them (for the plural implies that an assembled group has heard the letter). The reason for this public reading, signaled by the abrupt appearance of the plural address, may lie in the request for material support that is the burden of the *epistolē systatikē*. Such requests are embarrassing, particularly for those who need the help. The public reading of an open letter of recommendation to the whole congregation takes the burden of the request off the apostolic co-worker and the missionaries, but it calls for Paul to thank (*charis*) personally those who have listened as a group. His thanksgiving takes the form of an apostolic blessing for the believers assembled to hear his letter.

The closing blessing, like the opening one (1:4), has the form of a prayer. The mention of "grace" is typical of the closing blessing in the Pauline epistolary; the other NT letters (except Heb) do not employ *charis* in their concluding blessings but *eirēnē*, "peace," if anything at all. The latter is more Jewish and reminds one of the fundamental character of a letter as a substitute for a conversation or a speech. The apostolic letter comes to the house church as a substitute for the visit in person of the apostle, one whom the risen Jesus has sent as he had once dispatched disciples in his historical ministry as that was transmitted by the gospel tradition. Thus Luke has Jesus instruct the seventy as he sends them two by two to bear witness that the kingdom of God has arrived: "Into whatever house (*oikian*) you enter, first say, 'Peace (*eirēnē*) to this household (*tōi oikōi toutōi*)' " (Luke 10:5; see Matt 10:11–12, *SFG* §177, which has, "As you enter the house (*oikian*), greet (*aspasasthe*) them," which includes gestures as well as words; also Marshall, *Luke*, p. 419). As Claus Westermann (*Blessing*, pp. 94–97) has pointed out, these itinerant preachers bring the gospel into settled, domestic lives where blessing has its characteristic link with the life and growth, the health and wealth, the strengthening and prosperity of God's family. Blessing stands at the intersection of the apostolic mission and the growth of Christian communities that remain settled. It belongs to an almost ritual framework around a visitor's arrival and departure, which, in this instance, occurs in a Pauline letter. The closing blessing bears his personal cachet as he substitutes *charis* for the formulaic Jewish *eirēnē*.

The form of a closing blessing in the NT regularly consists in the designation of that which is prayed for, then the divine source of such a blessing, and finally the recipient (Mullins, "Benediction," p. 60). In the closing blessings of the PE there is always mention of the first, using *hē charis;* and the last, using the plural address in the phrase, *meth' hymōn.* The divine source is never specified in the closing blessings of the PE. Nonetheless, the opening blessings always refer to God the Father and Christ Jesus our savior (or our Lord) as the source of blessings being prayed for, and one infers that the "grace" of this final benediction is that of the Father and Jesus, with perhaps a special emphasis on the latter (see 1 Tim 1:14), who was the revelation of "the grace of God." Conceptually, the language here is close to Paul's promise to the Roman house churches, "I know that when I come to you I shall come in the fullness of the blessing (*eulogias*) of Christ" (Rom 15:29). That blessing is no less than the apostolic gospel itself (see the variant readings) about the grace of God in Christ, a gospel of which the "proclamation . . . brings about the growth, prosperity, and strengthening of the community" (C. Westermann, *Blessing,* p. 99). So here in Titus the "grace" of the closing blessing is not so much the revelation of what the Father has accomplished in Jesus or even in justification (see 2:11; 3:7, "God's was the grace that made us upright") as it is a designation of the effect of Christ's work.

EXCURSUSES

♦

EXCURSUS I

Pistis Terminology in the PE

	Titus	1 Tim	2 Tim	PE/Paulines	Luke/Acts	NT
pistis	6	19	8	33/109	11/15	243
faith, faithfulness, pledge, reliability						
apistia	0	1	0	1/4	0/0	11
unbelief						
pistos	3	11	3	17/16	6/4	67
faithful, to be believed						
apistos	1	1	0	2/14	2/1	23
unbeliever						
pisteuein	2	3	1	6/48	9/37	241
to believe, entrust, put faith, receive in faith						
apistein	0	0	1	1/1	2/1	8
to be faithless						
pistoun	0	0	1	1/0	0/0	1
to become convinced						
total	12	35	14	61/192	30/58	594

For previous studies and the literature, see Merk, "Glaube," pp. 91–102 and Kretschmar, "Glaube," pp. 115–140.

The terminology that derives from **pist-* in the PE is predominantly substantival and adjectival. The verbal terminology is relatively uncommon and more differentiated. This profile the PE share by and large with the remainder of the NT, including Luke but not Acts. The negative terminology for unbelief occurs relatively seldom in the PE, and again that is characteristic of the rest of the NT, except for the use of *apistos* in the other Paulines.

The teaching of the PE regarding faith is sketched in Titus and developed more fully in 1 Tim. Little that is new appears in 2 Tim, except for the uses of the verbs in 2:13 and 3:14, and the use of *dia pisteōs* in 3:15.

The most frequent setting for the **pist-* vocabulary in the PE is personal. The apostle and his coworker have as their goal and purpose "the faith of God's elect," "the faith all share" (Titus 1:1, 4). Behind this purpose stands the act of a personal God entrusting the apostle with the proclamation of the gospel (cf. *episteuthēn* of Titus 1:3 with 1 Tim 1:11). The apostle himself responds with trust (2 Tim 1:12) in the one God who has trusted him, and becomes "a model of those who are going to believe in (*ep'*)" Jesus Christ (1 Tim 1:16), who in the archaic hymnic fragment of 1 Tim 3:16 "was received in faith, in the world (*episteuthē en kosmōi*)." In Titus 3:8 the Jewish Christians, "those who have put their faith in God" (*hoi pepisteukotes theōi:* anarthrous, see Tit 1:16), in a way that corresponds to the Pauline teaching (as the PE conceive it), are to show this in their actions. The possibility of believers failing in faith (see below) is explicitly broached in the *apistoumen,* "we are faithless," of 2 Tim 2:13. The exhortation to Timothy to "persevere in the things you . . . became sure of (*epistōthēs:* 2 Tim 3:14)" stands in contrast to such infidelity.

The prologue to the PE, Titus 1:1–4, firmly links the apostle and his coworker with faith. Four times in Titus 1:5–16, the section entitled "For Ministry and Magisterium," forms from **pist-* recur. As Paul and Titus, the one who shared his work so intimately that he was "his true child," existed for the sake of the faith of the church, so do the men whom Titus is commanded (cf. Titus 1:5 with 1:3) to appoint to an apostolic ministry in the churches on Crete. For the parallel command to Timothy, see 2 Tim 2:2. It is precisely because such a ministry exists for the faith that the man picked for it must first himself be trustworthy and responsible, that is to say, ready to answer for the grace that has been committed to him as an unimpeachable manager (see Titus 1:6–7). This trustworthiness is to be verifiable even from his family life with one spouse and from the children whom he has reared as believers (*pista*). These faithful children of a man's own home are a parable and pledge for the faithful to whom he will minister as a presbyter-bishop (see 1 Tim 3:4–5).

In the PE, *pistos* designates both an individual who believes in Christ (1 Tim 5:16 of a woman; contrast the *apistos,* "unbeliever," of 5:8) and the body of believers or groups within that body (1 Tim 4:3, 10, 12; 6:2 *bis*). In such cases the adjective has become a technical term, but its use of Christ (2 Tim 2:13), of Paul (1 Tim 1:12), and of men (2 Tim 2:2), women (1 Tim 3:11), and children (Titus 1:6) indicates that it was not strictly technical but really belonged to the persons so designated (cf. 2 Tim 2:2 with 1 Tim 1:12).

That personal and subjective nuance in the use of *pistos* in the PE can be contrasted with those half-dozen passages in which the term qualifies not persons but (*ho*) *logos,* the message with which Paul was entrusted (Titus 1:3) and which presbyter-bishops are to retain (Titus 1:9). The faithful are not the same as the credulous. They are not ready to believe anything. An apostolic *logos* has been addressed to them and has controlled their postbaptismal formation (see *didachē,* "teaching," in Titus 1:9). They are *pistoi* because of what they believe, because of the one in whom they believe. They can lapse from this commitment and again be numbered with the (Jewish?) *apistoi,* "unbelievers" (Titus 1:15; 1 Tim 5:8). Five times the PE return to this question of contents of belief, always using the formula *pistos ho logos,* unique to this correspondence, to identify the formulations adduced (Titus 3:8; 1 Tim 1:15; 3:1; 4:9; 2 Tim 2:11). The materials have been drawn from diverse settings, baptismal confession, creedal statements, midrashic applications of Scripture to the order for Christian worship assemblies, paraenesis for moral living, and a prophetic hymn (cf. the prophet who is to be believed, *prophētēs pistos,* in 1 Macc 14:41). All appear to have had a link with the public worship. The encounter within which these *logoi* of apostolic revelation (which is itself the *logos*) were articulated was the liturgy. *Lex orandi lex credendi.*

A closer definition of *pistis* and *apistia* in the PE calls for observations on their use (and nonuse) of the Greek article, as well as on their predicative use of these terms, particularly with prepositions. In its polemical sketch of the Jewish Christians and their sympathizers who pit themselves against the teaching of the presbyter-bishops picked by Titus, the "True and False Teaching" section of the letter to Titus (1:10–16) directs the recipient himself "to refute them sharply," so that they recover their health (imagery that the PE favor; see Titus 1:9 on "wholesome instruction"). *Hē pistis* in Titus 1:13 is the first of fifteen occurrences in the PE of *pistis* with the article (the eighteen anarthrous uses begin with Titus 1:1, 4). The unique occurrence of *apistia* in the PE (1 Tim 1:13) is anarthrous (in contrast to the other Pauline uses in Rom 3:3; 4:20; 11:20, 23). In the PE the appearance of the article with *pistis* does not signal the faith in terms of content (cf. Titus 2:2; 2 Tim 3:10 with 1 Tim 6:11; 2 Tim 2:22), and the anarthrous *pistis* does not designate simply the personal act of believing (cf. 1 Tim 2:7). The appearance (or absence) of the article has far more to do with the grammatical and rhetorical patterns of Hellenistic Greek than with systematic theological distinctions.

More significant for describing the meaning of *pistis* and *apistia* in the PE is another grammatical phenomenon: these nouns are never the subject of a sentence. For this correspondence *pistis* requires no definition, needs no verbal predicate, though it can on occasion be qualified by adjectives (Titus 1:4; 2:10; 1 Tim 1:5; 2 Tim 1:5; 1 Tim 5:12). At the same time, *pistis* is frequently the object of verbs: all kinds of human persons, men and women, slaves and free, apostle and apostate, are described as giving evidence of or breaking *pistis* (Titus 2:10; 1 Tim 5:12); as having it (1 Tim 1:19), pursuing it (1 Tim 6:11; 2 Tim 2:22, cf. 3:10 with dative), or keeping it (2 Tim 4:7); as abandoning, denying, or overturning it (1 Tim 4:1 with genitive; 5:8; 2 Tim 2:18). Genitival phrases designate "the mystery of the faith" (1 Tim 3:9); for other uses see 1 Tim 4:6; 6:12; and the Pauline recollection of Timothy's "unfeigned faith" (2 Tim 1:5).

In Hellenistic Greek generally, anarthrous prepositional phrases have a "qualitative force" (Moulton, *Grammar* 1.82), and this holds true of those ten instances in the PE of *en pistei/apistiai* (though Titus 1:13, cited above, employs the article). Less often observed is the relational character of all of the prepositional particles and thus the relational and personal character involved when *pistis* is governed by a preposition. Accordingly, the closing instructions of Titus 3:15 direct the recipient of this letter, "Greet those who in faith (*en pistei*) are friends of ours." The apostle and his coworker, as this letter opens, exist "for the faith all share" (Titus 1:1, 4); as the letter closes, the affectionate attachment that the members of the community have with the apostle and his collaborators (note the collegial first-person plural) is based on something beyond simply human contact or personal acquaintance with Paul and his colleagues. They are united precisely *en pistei*, that is to say, as persons sharing a belief (Titus 1:4).

The full implications of this phrase are drawn out in 1 Tim, especially where *en pistei* occurs immediately in conjunction with other terms. Thus 1 Tim 2:7, *en pistei kai alētheiai*, "in faith and truth," emphasizes the solid knowledge in which belief issues, whereas in 1 Tim 2:15; 4:12; and 2 Tim 1:13 it is linked with *agapē*, "charity" (as well as with holiness and purity), and thus with a choice and election that transcend a purely intellectual grasp of reality. With *en pistei* the PE designate the dimension within which both the apostolic ministry and the church operate, a dimension as real as those in space and time, the ambience or atmosphere of ecclesial life (see Spicq, *EP*, p. 279).

As in the other terms derived from **pist-*, a further question remains about the phrase *en pistei:* Believing *in what?* On two occasions in the PE that query is explicitly answered. In 2 Tim 1:13, the apostle exhorts his colleague to cling to the Pauline words, literally, "with (*en*) that faith and charity which are yours in Christ Jesus." More clearly in 1 Tim 3:13 the author asserts that the ministry of deacons brings "a right to speak out for (*en*) the faith that is theirs in Christ Jesus." In both cases the final adjectival phrase specifies the object of the belief. This is confirmed by the description of Paul, zealously Jewish but still unconverted to Christ, as acting *en apistiai* (1 Tim 1:13). For the PE, *en pistei* is practically equivalent to *en Christōi*. The passages cited, as well as 1 Tim 1:2 and 4, illustrate this when compared with the phrases of 1 Tim 1:14 (*meta pisteōs*) and 2 Tim 3:15 (*dia pisteōs*).

In the PE there are several other prepositional phrases with *pistis* besides those already adduced (*kata, en, meta, dia*). Of these the commonest is *peri tēn pistin*, used in a pejorative context, of those who have made a shipwreck in regard to faith (1 Tim 1:19), who have missed the point in it (1 Tim 6:21; cf. 1:6), or who have counterfeited it (2 Tim 3:8). A similar context is found in the only use of *apo tēs pisteōs* in 1 Tim 6:10, writing of the avaricious who "have strayed off from the faith." Similarly when 1 Tim 1:5–6 describes *agapē* as arising "from (*ek*) a clean heart and from a clean conscience and from a faith unfeigned," the text immediately turns by contrast to persons who "have deviated from these."

Faith in Jesus is ultimately for the PE what differentiates and identifies God's elect (Titus 1:1) among their unbelieving fellowmen, whether Jews or pagans. Can this be related to the conceptions, particularly the Pauline ones, of the first Christian generation? A corrective for some rooted modern misconceptions can be inferred from Paul's description of Palestinian Christian reaction to his conversion, in Gal 1:23. "He who once persecuted *us* [the churches of 1:22] is now preaching *the faith* he once tried to destroy." The parallel with Gal 1:13, "I [Paul] persecuted *the church* of God violently and tried to *destroy* it," implies that "the faith" was very early defined in terms of the persons ("us") who constituted the church (or churches) of God (see Betz, *Gal.*, p. 81 and the literature cited there). Thus eventually Ignatius writes of "the faith of God (*pistin theou*) for the sake of which (*hyper hēs*) Jesus Christ was crucified" (Ign. *Eph.* 16.2). In the even more daring phrase of Ign. *Trall.* 8.1, faith is "the flesh of the Lord" as charity is his blood. Polycarp speaks of faith as "the mother of us all" (Pol. *Phil.* 3.2–3; see Gal 4:26); and a martyr companion of Justin, when asked to name his parents, replied that "our true father is Christ and our faith in him is our mother" (Recension B, 4.22–23 of the acts of Justin and his companions in Musurillo, *Acts*, pp. 50–51). Thus "Mother Faith" anticipates the later phrase "Mother Church" (see Plumpe, *Mater*, pp. 18–22; Bisbee, "Acts of Justin," pp. 154–155). The faith thus conceived is audible and visible, and so vulnerable, in the persons who publicly professed it. The Paul who had savaged the assemblies of his fellow Jews who confessed their special relationship to Jesus became one of their number and proclaimed what had made them an identifiable group in the first place: the faith.

The reality that the **pist-* terminology enables a Christian to articulate has a polarity built into it. Already in the PE one meets a cautious attempt to probe it theologically. Faith must take account of both the person who believes (subjective faith/*fides qua*) and the person in whom he believes (objective faith/*fides quae*). Faith in the Pauline usage is at the same time both subjective and objective. In this connection, Günther Bornkamm aptly observes, "Faith always means faith in . . . or faith that" (*Paul*, p. 141), but a further nuancing is in order: dichotomizing *fides qua* from *fides quae* and absolutizing that quite legitimate scholastic distinction does in theology what a similar dichotomy has done for the soul–body distinction in theological anthropology (cf. Lührmann, *Glaube*). Christian faith is always a response to a person who has taken the initiative and chosen to speak, act, reveal himself as a person to the one addressed.

In the earliest Jewish-Christian congregations in Palestine (one would infer from the *pistis* of Gal 1:23) the objective pole, the new content of the Christian "way," the person of Jesus as Lord, was emphasized. After all, the Jews were by definition a believing people from the day Abraham received the divine promise.

Thus the subjective aspect of the faith process was presupposed and was to remain relatively unexamined among Jewish Christians. Into this situation came Paul, first as persecutor, then as apostle. As persecutor he had isolated and evaluated precisely the specifically new element in the lives of his coreligionists, namely, their confessed belief in Jesus as their Lord. As apostle to the pagans, in other words, to persons who were perceived as having no *torah* (see Jervell, *Paul*, pp. 39–43) and no salvation history, and who consequently did not really know what believing in God meant as a personal act, Paul could not take for granted the subjective aspects of belief but was compelled to probe into the way this new element in Israel's faith perfected and fulfilled the subjective response that God's people were to make to his word to them. The Paul who used the *pistis* terminology in its more objective sense (see 2 Cor 13:5; Phil 1:27; Col 2:6–7; Eph 4:4–6) was recognized by his characteristic emphasis on the subjective "obedience of faith," for which the risen Lord had given him "grace and apostleship" for sake of the pagans (Rom 1:5; 16:26; cf. 2 Cor 10:5).

With the PE the Pauline churches in the Hellenistic world have a history in Christ. They have a generation of belief in its subjective sense behind them. For these Christians believing is not new, whether their roots were in Judaism or elsewhere. They are simply *hoi pistoi;* and the PE, in the name of Paul, intend to center the belief of the churches precisely in the Christ as Paul had confessed and heralded him. The intervening years had seen not only men and women continuing to come to faith in Christ but also Christians falling away from the Pauline gospel and the demands it made on them. The PE, with their renewed emphasis on the objective pole in belief, are nothing less than a program for renewing the Pauline apostolate in a new generation.

EXCURSUS II

Truth and *epignōsis alētheias* in the PE

	Titus	1 Tim	2 Tim	PE/Paulines	Luke/Acts	NT
alētheia truth	2	6	6	14/33	3/3	109
alēthēs truthful	1	0	0	1/3	0/1	26
alēthinos true	0	0	0	0/1	1/0	28
alēthōs truly	0	0	0	0/1	3/1	18
alētheuein to tell the truth	0	0	0	0/2	0/0	2
totals	3	6	6	15/40	7/5	183

A survey of the terminology for truth and its recognition (*epignōsis*) in documents outside the PE must precede analysis of this language in the correspondence itself. Supplement the survey of the Hebrew and Septuagintal words for truth in *TDNT* 1.232–251 (G. Quell, G. Kittel, and R. Bultmann) with A. Jepsen ("*ʾaman*," *TDOT* 1.292–323, esp. 309–316) and Ignace de la Potterie ("Truth," p. 619).

As the table above indicates, almost half of the Pauline uses of *alētheia* occur in the PE, where the usage on the whole corresponds with the rest of the Paulines, in which truth is not simply knowledge in a generic sense but "the opening up of the divine world and its claim" (Käsemann, *Rom.*, p. 38 paraphrasing R. Bultmann in *TDNT* 1.243). With this sense of the revelation of God (as in Rom 1:18–19; 2:8, 20; 3:7) compare the PE below on resistance to the truth (Titus 1:14; 1 Tim 6:5; 2 Tim 2:18; 3:8; 4:4) as well as on the positive function of an apostolic church and its ministry (1 Tim 2:7; 3:15; 2 Tim 2:15).

Luke–Acts stand in contrast to all of the Paulines, with five of the six uses of *alētheia* confined to the non-Pauline phrase *ep' alētheias*, "truly, really" (see Mark 12:14, 32); in Acts 26:25 Paul speaks "words of truth and prudence," in other words, "the sober truth" (RSV). Moreover, the Lukan corpus has no predilection for the other *alēth*- terminology, and the uses that do occur are largely stereotyped (but cf. Acts 12:9 with Titus 1:13).

Of the twenty NT uses of *epignōsis*, fifteen are in the Pauline epistolary. The four uses of *epignōsis* in the PE are with *alētheias* and governed by *eis* or *kata*. Although other Pauline texts do not mention *epignōsis alētheias*, they do speak of the recognition (*epignōsis*) of God; of his Son, Jesus Christ, who is the mystery of God and of his will and of all that is good (thus Eph 1:17; 4:13; Col 1:9–10; 2:2; Phlm 6). No less significantly, Rom 3:20 mentions "recognition of sin." Outside the PE, however, only Heb 10:26 in the NT uses the articular phrase *tēn epignōsin tēs alētheias*, in describing the effects of sin "after receiving the knowledge of the truth." *Epignōsis* occurs otherwise in the NT in 2 Pet of the recognition of God and of the Lord, Jesus Christ. *First Clement* 59.2, alone among the Ap. Frs., speaks of this kind of knowledge when describing the elect called "from ignorance to recognition (*eis epignōsin*) of the glory of his name" (see *Mart. Pol.* 14.1 and *Diogn.* 10.1, both of the Father).

Epignōsis occurs no more than eight times in the LXX and never with *alētheias*. It does, however, designate recognition of God in Jdt 9:14; LXX Prov 2:5; and Hos 4:1, 6; and 6:6.

In the Jewish literature after 100 B.C. the phrase "knowledge of the truth" appears in Greek in Philo, *Quod omn. prob.* 74, describing the goal of the researches of the Persian magi as *epignōsin tēs alētheias*. See *Leg. all.* 3.48, of the good man who returns "to the knowledge (*epignōsin*) of the One [God]," thus winning "a noble race and proving victor in this grandest of all contests," and 3.77; *Mos.* 2.97 (where he apparently glosses the term *cherubim* as *epignōsis*); *Spec. leg.* 1.64 (of God's giving "knowledge of the future" to the godly). Josephus once writes of "recognition by voice" (*tēn . . . dia boēs epignōsin,* War 6.138), but he does not mention "recognition of the truth."

The phrase *eis/pros epignōsin tēs alētheias* appears late and seldom in secular Greek (Epictetus, *Discourses* 2.20.21; Diogenes Laertius, *Vitae* 8.42) and refers to the means at human disposal for recognizing or discovering the truth (see Potterie, *Ver. S. Jn.* p. 541 n. 12).

Although *epignōsis alētheias* appears rarely in Greek (in pagan, Jewish, or Christian texts), it is associated with certain more or less well-defined groups ("Hebrews"; magi; Stoics) when it is used. These references suggest a context for the usage in the PE, for Titus 1:1 opens with a description of the apostle, sent "for the faith . . . and for full and godly knowledge of the truth." Before describing what the Christian community who received the PE understood by *epignōsis alētheias,* the survey of the usage of *alētheia* in the PE ought to be continued. The Letter to Titus returns to the subject of *alētheia* after the greeting. In the apostolic commission to his coworker, in the section entitled "True and False Teaching" (1:10–16), the terminology for truth appears in 1:13–14. Members of a Jewish-Christian movement (1:10), convicted on the "truthful (*alēthēs*) testimony" of a pagan poet as unsound "in the faith" (*en tēi pistei:* 1:13), are scored as "doting on Jewish tales and commandments of people who are abandoning the truth." Second Timothy 4:4 exploits the same contrast of the truth with tales. The truth referred to here is the very opposite of certain halakhic and haggadic materials that seek to bridge the gap between Jewish Scriptures and the life of the Jewish-Christian congregations. The bridging in question contradicts the Pauline gospel; such commentaries and directives are vitiated by the atrophying faith of their authors (see Titus 1:14–15). The apostolic gospel is emphatically "according to the Scriptures" (1 Cor 15:3–4); but not every interpretation of the Scripture of Israel is according to Paul's gospel (see 2 Tim 2:8), and the Pauline gospel ultimately judges its hermeneutic and not vice versa.

First Timothy, again after the phrase *epignōsis alētheias* of 2:4, has Paul write, in 2:7, "For that testimony I was appointed a herald and apostle—it is a fact (*alētheian legō*) though it sounds incredible—the Gentiles' teacher in faith and truth." If apostolic proclamation is, in fact, the last court of appeal, one can still ask, "What is an apostle?" or "Was Paul really an apostle?" The riposte of 1 Tim here is an echo of another, offered by the historical Paul (see Rom 9:1). No room remains for a wedge between the apostolic gospel (1 Tim 2:5–6) and its transparently honest herald (see also 1 Tim 1:15). Distinctions can, however, be made among the groups to whom the apostles were sent, and Paul's mission was to the pagans (as distinguished from the Jews). For them he was the "teacher in faith and truth," in both their subjective and objective aspects. In this hendiadys *alētheia* emphasizes the revelation that has been offered for belief, and the collocation of faith with truth recalls Titus 1:1.

In 1 Tim 3:15 "the truth" can be defined more clearly, for it is conceived as ensconced upon "a pillar and pedestal," as the image of a ruler or god was enthroned in the Hellenistic Roman world. Whether that column is the apostolic coworker himself or the church, local or universal, "the truth" is the personal revelation of God, publicly, visibly, even dramatically set out before his people. The figure suggests a reciprocal and solid relationship, yet still a subordinate one between believers and "the truth," namely, the person in whom they put their faith and whom they offer for belief to all. This "truth" is "the mystery of the faith" (see 1 Tim 3:9), the person of the Son, incarnate and risen, who is hymned in 1 Tim 3:16.

Are there antitheses to these conceptions of "the truth?" First Timothy 4:1–5 describes the "lying frauds" who "apostatize from the faith" and issue irrelevant dietary and sexual imperatives about the good things "that God created for believers (*pistois*) and persons who have recognized the truth (*epegnōkosi tēn alētheian*)." The latter phrase reproduces in adjectival forms the *kata pistin . . . kai epignōsin alētheias* of Titus 1:1, though the focus of *epignōsis alētheias* shifts from the conversion experience to Christian life as such (see below on 2 Tim 2:25–26; 3:6–7). As the apostasy of 1 Tim 4:1 was from faith in the person of Christ (see Excursus I), so in 4:3 "believers," that is, the faithful (*hoi pistoi*), are defined as having come to know, precisely and profoundly, "the truth," again the person of Christ. To have deviated in belief (1 Tim 6:21: *peri tēn pistin ēstochēsan*) is synonymous with missing the truth (*peri tēn alētheian ēstochēsan*) about the resurrection and overturning the faith (2 Tim 2:18). In 1 Tim 6:5 the harvest of heterodoxy climaxes in "the incessant bickerings of men whose minds (*noun*) are a shambles and who have been robbed of the truth (*apesterēmenōn tēs alētheias*)." A subjective/objective schema underlies this description, and the objective part includes the teaching of Jesus and his apostle (see 6:3). Moreover, as regularly in the passages cited here, inner links are posited between truth and virtue, error and vice. The theme has roots in the sapiential traditions of Israel (Spicq, *EP*, p. 90). Ignorance of the truth issues in wrong conduct; rejection of it issues in sinful conduct. Thus the PE usually speak of the truth as opposed to both intellectual and moral error, with (mis-)conduct in a symbiotic relationship with (mis-)understanding. For the significance of ignorance in such a problematic, see 1 Tim 1:13.

In contrast to these mistaken men stands "Timothy," the apostolic coworker, "who clears the way for the message of the truth (*ton logon tēs alētheias*)" (2 Tim 2:15). Granted a link between vice and error, the conversion from the former will involve receiving the truth, a process that the PE summarize in the phrase *epignōsis alētheias*, when they describe an apostle as sent "for full and godly knowledge" (Titus 1:1), when they describe God as one "who wants all human beings to be saved and to come to full knowledge of the truth" (1 Tim 2:4). The phrase certainly has something to do with conversion, as the *metanoia* of 2 Tim 2:25 indicates (see D-C, p. 41; Spicq, *EP*, pp. 364, 267; and Murphy-O'Connor, *PQ*, pp. 213–214). The "conversion" can be the one that precedes baptism; it can also be a postbaptismal repentance (see below on 2 Tim 2:25–26 and 3:6–7 with Heb 10:26). Already Col 1:6 has described the moment of conversion to Christ as the day on which "you heard and experienced (*epegnōte*) the grace of God in truth." Such expressions certainly prepared the way for the formulaic usage of the PE and perhaps Heb (see Dupont, *Gnosis*, p. 12 n. 1; Murphy-O'Connor, *PQ*, p. 213; Lohse, *Col.*, p. 21).

But there are precedents behind the usage of the PE in both the Hebrew and Greek scriptures as well as in the Qumran documents. Thus Ignace de la Potterie (*Ver. S. Jn.*, 2.539–547) has verified the suggestion of L. Bouyer that the verbal phrase *ginōskein tēn alētheian*, surprisingly rare in secular Greek, came out of sapiential and apocalyptic circles within Judaism. Moreover, Tob 5:14 (BA; cf. 12:7, 11) associates the *alētheia* terminology with the revelation of a heavenly mystery, and the link reappears in the epistolary appendix of the Greek *Enoch*, as it speaks of the truth (104.9–13; 106.12) and the mysteries that *Enoch* had come to know (104.12). This apocalyptic and sapiential usage links *epignōsis alētheias* with Greek Jewish thought.

In Qumran texts *da'at 'emet*, the Hebrew equivalent of *epignōsis alētheias*, has turned up in four places. When the Community Rule (1QS 9:12–26) assembled directives for "the recruitment and formation of new members" (see 1QS 1:11–12 and Carmignac and Guilbert *apud* Murphy-O'Connor, *PQ*, p. 214), which A. R. C. Leaney (*RQM*, p. 228) titles "Guidance for the Instructor of the Pioneer Community," there was a series of guidelines for daily communal living and for engaging in religious discussions with both colleagues and those who disagreed with the sectaries (1QS 9:12–21; Gaster, *DSS*, pp. 64–65). The latter are to be ignored (see Titus 3:9). "With those, however, who have chosen the [right] path (*drk*), everyone is indeed to discuss matters pertaining to knowledge of truth (*d't 'mt*) and to discernment of righteousness (*mšpt ṣdq*)" (1QS 9:17–18; Gaster, *DSS*, p. 64 adapted). The notion of the community as a forum for rehearsing the divine truth is notable (Potterie, *Ver. S. Jn.*, p. 543). Jerome Murphy-O'Connor has further observed that the Hebrew phrase means more than "exact knowledge," because *'mt* for the sectaries meant the revelation itself, the hidden, divine mysteries that dictated their conduct (see 1QS 9:18–19). Thus the trajectory in *'mt* runs from revelation through community knowledge into communal action. A text on heavenly worship (4Q Sir Sabb 1:1, 18 [*VTSupp* 7.322; Gaster, *DSS*, p. 290]) seems to confirm this interpretation when it refers to the fourth angelic prince who "will bless all the godly ones who exalt knowledge of [his] tru[th] (*d't 'em[tw]*) with seven words of justice for the mercies of [his glory]." Here blessings of the divine order are the counterpart of those given in this world for carrying out God's revelation. In the Qumran Hymnal *d't 'mt* occurs in a fragmented context (1QH 10:20, 29). The hymnist describes himself, saying: "You, O Lord, have enlarged his inheritance through the knowledge of your truth (*bd't 'mtkh*) and according to his knowledge [he shall be glorified]" (1QH 10:29; Murphy-O'Connor, *PQ*, p. 216; see Gaster,

DSS, p. 185, and Dupont-Sommer, *EWQ*, p. 235). Then 1QH 10:21 continues, "my heart rejoices in your covenant and your truth delights my soul." The parallelism of "truth" with "covenant" (the combination here meaning "the true covenant") suggests that the Torah was par excellence and irreplaceably the revelation of God's will for his people. The Torah on this reading becomes synonymous with the "truth" (see Murphy-O'Connor, *PQ*, p. 216). A total commitment, in practical living as well as in thinking, to the Torah is "knowledge" of the Torah and ultimately "knowledge of God," as Israel regarded "knowledge" (see Hos 4:1–6; 6:6 and McKenzie, "Knowledge," 22–27; Mal 2:6–7). Such a commitment implies for any human being a conversion, though it is notable that only in 1QS 9:17–21 is that concept close to the surface.

The use of *d't 'mt* at Qumran is the closest extant parallel to the distinctively Christian use of *epignōsis* (*tēs*) *alētheias* in the NT. The distinctiveness of the Christian usage goes back to the understanding of *alētheia* as the person of Christ, who has thus replaced the Torah as "truth." Furthermore, as 1 Tim 2:3–4 makes explicit, God is not simply *"our savior"* (i.e., savior of Paul, Timothy, the church at prayer) but he "wills that all human persons be saved and come to full knowledge of the truth." Just as the reality designated as faith in the PE coincided partially with *epignōsis alētheias* (Titus 1:1), so this "knowledge of truth" coincides to some extent with the phenomenon the PE describe using the terminology for salvation (see Titus 1:3–4; 2:11–14; 3:4–7 and Excursus V, "The PE on Salvation"). Paul as apostle is sent "for full and godly knowledge" (Titus 1:1) and because this offer of saving "knowledge of the truth" is universal, Paul has been sent to the pagans (cf. 1 Tim 2:4 with 7). In such contexts, "knowledge of the truth" acquires a kerygmatic nuance that Ignace de la Potterie (*Ver. S. Jn.*, p. 546) has noted, with a suggestion of the conversion elicited by the kerygma.

That kerygmatic connotation may not be involved in 2 Tim 2:25–26 and 3:6–7. In the former passage the content deals with those who had fallen away from genuine faith in Christ (2 Tim 2:17–18), and Timothy's ministry as "the Lord's slave" (2 Tim 2:24) is directed toward erring believers. He is to teach such refractory persons gently "just in case God may grant them a change of heart (*metanoian*) that will lead back into full knowledge of the truth" (2:25). For such opponents, however, the blistering polemic of 2 Tim 3:1–9 has been written. The gullible women victimized by the erring Christian teachers are probably not the object of a mission to the pagans. Rather they are lapsed believers. Their time for repentance has almost run out while they are "ever learning and never turning to full knowledge of the truth." With a plume from that midrashic learning which perhaps a Hymenaeus and a Philetus (2 Tim 2:17) had flaunted, the author declares, "Just as once Jannes and Jambres defied Moses, so too these numbskulled counterfeiters of the faith are defying the truth (*tēi alētheiai*)" (2 Tim 3:8). What the Egyptian magicians had been to

God and Moses, these opponents are to Christ and Paul. They obstruct the people of God on their way to real knowledge of the truth.

As noted above, Ignace de la Potterie (*Ver. S. Jn.*, pp. 543–545) has called attention to *Sophia Jesu Christi* 94.1–4 (*NHL*, p. 209); the *Gospel of Truth* 17.15–17; 18.18–21 (*NHL*, p. 38); and the *Gos. Thom.*, logion 78 (*NHL*, p. 127). In addition, in *Thom. Cont.* 2.138.10–15 (*NHL*, p. 189), the risen Jesus says to Judas Thomas, "you had already understood that I am the knowledge of truth." In the *Gos. Eg.* 3.64.4–9 (*NHL*, p. 203), the great Seth, who has put on "Jesus the living one," has armed "those who are brought forth and taken away" "with an armor of the knowledge (*sooun*) of this truth (*alētheia/me*) with an unconquerable power of incorruptibility" (see Böhlig and Wisse, *G. Egypt.*, pp. 146–147, 191–194: in Coptic *sooun* may mean either *gnōsis*, as in the *Gos. Eg.* 3.60.24 = 4.72.6 or *epignōsis* as in the Coptic versions of Col 1:9 [Crum, *CD*, p. 370]). Finally, in the *Apoc. Adam* 83.9–20 (Robinson, *NHL*, p. 263, not clearly Christian) the nations exclaim, "Blessed is the soul of those men because they have known God with a knowledge of the truth: They shall live forever, because they have not been corrupted by their desire, along with the angels, . . . they have stood . . . in his presence in a knowledge of God like light that has come forth from fire and blood." The knowledge of the risen Jesus (see J. D. Turner on *Thom. Cont.* in Krause, *Essays NH*, pp. 113–114) or of God is a knowledge that in turn leads the one who knows into an incorruptible existence. For all the material coincidence of *epignōsis alētheias* in the PE with "knowledge of the truth" in the Nag Hammadi texts, the thought of the gnostic texts seems to respond to the Johannine, not to the Pauline, tradition.

EXCURSUS III

Eusebeia and Its Cognates in the PE

	Titus	1 Tim	2 Tim	PE/Paulines	Luke/Acts	NT
eusebeia	1	8	1	10/0	0/1	15
godliness						
eusebein	0	1	0	1/0	0/1	2
to revere(nce)						
eusebōs	1	0	1	2/0	0/0	2
godly						
eusebēs	0	0	0	0/0	0/2	3
devout						
theosebeia	0	1	0	1/0	0/0	1
godliness						

(continued)

	Titus	1 Tim	2 Tim	PE/Paulines	Luke/Acts	NT
asebeia godlessness	1	0	1	2/2	0/0	6
asebein to be ungodly	0	0	0	0/0	0/0	2
asebōs godlessly	0	0	0	0/0	0/0	0
asebēs godless	0	1	0	1/2	0/0	9
totals	3	11	3	17/4	0/4	40

This profile can be compared with the following schema for the rest of the *seb/m*-root, with its final bilabial, nasal or not:

	Titus	1 Tim	2 Tim	PE/Paulines	Luke/Acts	NT
sebesthai to be devout/worship	0	0	0	0/0	0/8	10
sebazesthai to worship	0	0	0	0/1	0/0	1
sebasma object of worship	0	0	0	0/1	0/1	2
sebastos Augustan, Augustus	0	0	0	0/0	0/3	3
semnos serious	1	2	0	3/1	0/0	4
semnotēs reverent	1	2	0	3/0	0/0	3
totals	2	4	0	6/3	0/12	23

The profile of the twenty-three uses of the *seb/m*- cluster within the PE, arranged consecutively, appears as follows:

Titus	1 Timothy	2 Timothy
1:1 *eusebeia*	1:9 *asebēs*	2:16 *asebeia*
2:2 *semnos*	2:2 *eusebeia; semnotēs*	2:16 *asebeia*
2:7 *semnotēs*	2:10 *theosebeia*	3:12 *eusebōs*
2:12 *asebeia; eusebōs*	3:4 *semnotēs*	
	3:8 *semnos*	
	3:11 *semnos*	
	3:16 *eusebeia*	
	4:7 *eusebeia*	
	4:8 *eusebeia*	

Titus	1 Timothy	2 Timothy
	5:4 *eusebein*	
	6:3 *eusebeia*	
	6:5 *eusebeia*	
	6:6 *eusebeia*	
	6:11 *eusebeia*	

Eusebeia occurs in the NT outside the Paulines and Luke–Acts only in 2 Pet, which also has *eusebēs*. The *aseb-* language is found otherwise in the NT in both 1 and 2 Pet as well as Jude.

Notable features include (a) the concentration of the NT usage within the relatively brief compass of the PE; (b) the faint traces of a relationship running from the *aseb-* cluster into Rom alone of the other Paulines and from the *euseb-* cluster into Acts (but never into the third Gospel); and (c) the way that 1 Tim glosses at length the few occurrences of the **seb/m* cluster in traditional materials in Titus.

In the Ap. Frs. the *euseb-* cluster of terms is documented only in *1* and *2 Clem.* Apart from *Mart. Pol.* 11.2 and the half-dozen uses of *asebēs* in *Barn.*, the *aseb-* terminology is also confined to *1* and *2 Clem.* Moreover, *semnotēs*, *semnos*, and *semnos* occur only in *1 Clem.* and Hermas; *theosebeia* and *theosebēs* only in *1* and *2 Clem.* (but cf. *Mart. Pol.* 3.1).

The whole complex of **seb/m-* terminology appears, on the basis of the data extending from the Letter to the Romans to the *Shepherd* of Hermas, to have been particularly congenial to the Roman church from the middle of the first Christian century and into the second.

The **seb/m-* stem in Greek "always denotes awe" (W. Foerster in *TDNT* 7.169) and frequently suggests religious devotion and respect, even if directed toward a human person (cf. Menander, *Samia* 274 and *Geōrgos* 35–39, where an *agron eusebesteron*, "a very godfearing plot of ground," pays back its sower *orthōs kai dikaiōs*, "fair and square," F. Allison, LCL). Practically the whole cluster of **seb/m-* terms (W. Foerster in *TDNT* 7.168–196) was used to articulate the reverence felt by pagans toward the gods (see Menander, *Dyscolos* 449).

Hellenistic Judaism was not particularly eager to take up the terminology, as its rare use in inscriptions witnesses (*CII* 500 [cf. 731e of Prolegomenon, p. 89, and 2.748], 683, cf. 690b of Prolegomenon, p. 69), though it is notable that forms of the personal name "Eusebios" occur nine times among the hundreds of names in European Jewish inscriptions. The oldest strata of the LXX show a similar reluctance, though the negative *aseb-* words became more popular, particularly in the sapiential literature.

With the advent of the Roman principate, the color of the **seb/m-* terminology altered. The imperial title *augustus*, which the Roman Senate conferred on Octavian in 27 B.C. (W. Foerster in *TDNT* 7.174–175), became, in Hellenistic Greek, *sebastos* (see Acts 25:21, 25 of Nero; 27:1 of a cohort of the Roman army), and Philo, nervously playing on the **seb/m-* terminology (see *Leg.* 48, 143, 148–151, 316–317, 319), "is going as far as he can" (Nock, *ERAW* 2.564 n. 23) when he notes that the Jews show *eusebeia* to their Roman benefactors (*Flacc.* 48) and that their synagogues are the real "headquarters of the religious veneration (*hosiotētos*) [of the Jews] for the Augustan (*Sebaston*) house" (*Flacc.* 49, cf. 50), for there they gather to offer their thanks to God for the benefits provided by the Roman *imperium* (*Flacc.* 48).

The mixture of paganism and politics in the first-century c.e. usage of the **seb/m-* cluster had a number of explosive potentialities, and the earliest Christian documents regularly avoided the terminology in its positive form. This avoidance did not, however, continue in the second Christian generation; the PE, along with Acts and 2 Pet, are obviously prepared to use such language. A. D. Nock (*ERAW* 1.342–343) found in Christian adaptations of pagan religious language "an approximation to the phraseology of the world around, a lessening of the feeling of isolation, and an increase in intelligibility to the ordinary contemporary man." Still one can ask of the **seb/m-* terminology, Why does it appear in texts linked with the Roman church? Did that church, already in the first century, find this cluster of words congenial? Can reasons still be unearthed that that congregation found persuasive, even compelling, for departing from the earlier Jewish and Jewish-Christian practice of avoiding this terminology, an avoidance that should have been reinforced by the political adaptation of *sebastos?*

The "Scriptures" of Hellenistic Judaism and of Greek-speaking converts to Jesus, whether Jewish or Gentile, were the LXX; and that venerable congeries of translations and original works still shows traces of the philosophico-religious trajectory that the **seb/m-* terminology was traveling from 250 b.c.e. into the first Christian century. The noun *eusebeia* translates the Hebrew of three texts. In Isa 11:2 and 33:6, this Greek term stands for the Hebrew phrase *yir' āt yhwh*. In Sir 49:3 it renders *ḥsd* (Barthélemy and Rickenbacher, *KHS*, p. 131).

The great Isaian oracles on the Davidic messiah (Isa 6–11: see Dodd, *Acc. Scr.*, pp. 78–83) surround Isa 11:2, with its sonorous list of six gifts from the Spirit of Yahweh resting on the anointed son of David. The final pair are "a spirit of knowledge and fear of Yahweh," which the LXX renders *pneuma gnōseōs kai eusebeias* (without *pros ton Kyrion*) and which Titus 1:1 recalls in *kata . . . epignōsin alētheias tēs kat' eusebeian*. This passage, along with Isa 33:6 with its *epistēmē kai eusebeia pros ton Kyrion*, represents a serious attempt to translate the Hebrew phrases *da'at Yahweh ('elōhîm)*, "knowledge of Yahweh (God)," and *yīr'āt yhwh*, "fear of/awe at Yahweh," which in their turn are paraphrases that designate realities to which modern languages apply one term "religion." In fact, ancient Greek—like Hebrew—offered no single term that meant "religion" in our sense of the word. "*Eusebeia* approximates to it, but in essence it means no more than the regular performance of due worship in the proper spirit" (Nock, *Conversion*, p. 10), though the emphasis may fall on motivation as much as on action. This motivational emphasis appears in these Isaian passages (see also *eusebēs* in LXX Isa 24:16; 26:7 and cf. 32:8 with 33:6).

The one other instance in which the LXX *eusebeia* renders a Hebrew text illustrates the active aspect of the noun. The Hebrew of Sir 49:3, in its eulogy of King Josiah's reforms of divine worship, remarks that "in the days of wickedness (*ḥms*) he kept covenant loyalty (*'śh ḥsd*)." There the Greek translator (about 132 B.C.E. in Egypt) rendered *ḥsd* (which with *'emet* constituted still another of those phrases that stood for all that Hebrews meant by "religion") by *tēn eusebeian* (he regularly translated forms of *ṣdyq* with the adjective *eusebēs*). Josiah had restored the Passover, repaired the Temple, practiced his religion. He had "set his heart wholly upon the Lord" (49:3; see Deut 6:4–5 and note "virtue" in Di Lella, *AB Sir.*, p. 540). *Eusebeia* translated that program quite fairly. Similarly LXX 1 Esdr 1:21 (RSV, 23) summarized the Josianic reform of worship with, "And the deeds of Josiah were upright in the sight of his Lord for his heart was full of godliness (*eusebeias*)." This usage reappears in 2 Macc 3:1, where *eusebeia* and the antithetical *misoponeria*, "hatred of evil," characterize the high priest Onias. Even in 2 Macc 12:45 *eusebeia* characterizes death in battle for the temple and worship in the temple (cf. the *v. 1.* for *euprepeia*, "beauty," in 3 Macc 1:9). In 3 Macc 2:31–32 *eusebeia* designates the practice of the Jewish religion as contrasted with apostasy to pagan worship.

When *eusebeia* appears in the sapiential strata of the LXX (see H-R s.vv. for the cognates as well) it serves to explain what the wisdom writers meant by the phrase *yīr' āt Yahweh*. The Hebrew text of Prov 1:7 announces the theme of the whole collection that follows with, "The fear of Yahweh is the beginning of knowledge; // fools (*asebeis*) despise wisdom and instruction." The LXX inserts at //, "Good is the intelligence of all who act wisely (literally, do this [wisdom]): the beginning of perception (*aisthēseōs*) is respect for God (*eusebeia . . . eis theon*)." Again in LXX Prov 13:11 the one who gathers wealth *met' eusebeias* (i.e., with respect for God's laws: note, e.g., *met' anomias* in parallel and Lev 25:36–37) will prosper (the Greek freely supplements an idiomatic Hebrew text). In Wis 10:12 wisdom teaches Jacob that "godliness (*eusebeia*) is more powerful than anything." At this point the sense is generic and not evidently concerned with carrying out the externals of worship; *eusebeia* may be understood as doing all that God commands. The connotations are those of the internal and personal Isaian usage already noted.

It is 4 Macc that serves as the watershed for the *euseb-* terms in the LXX, with as many as five uses of *eusebein*, eleven of *eusebēs*, the only Septuagintal use of *eusebōs* (s.v.l. 7:21), and forty-seven of *eusebeia*. This Jewish diatribe, composed in Greek (note, e.g., the play on *semnē-eusebeia* in 17:5–7), originating in the middle of the first Christian century, perhaps in Antioch (Charlesworth, *Pseud.* 1.151–152; *NOAB*, p. 309), is a defense of the role of godly reason (*ho eusebēs logismos*, 1:1, cf. 7; *ho tēs eusebeias logismos*, 7:4; 8:1; etc.) over all human affections. It is, moreover, *eusebeia* (which here means "our Jewish religion": see W. Foerster in *TDNT* 7.179) that informs and governs reason itself, and reason in turn dictates the total conduct of one's life (see 7:16–8:1). In this problematic, godliness is and gives knowledge. In contrast, it was an axiom of the Hellenistic philosophy of the age that "knowledge of God is or produces piety" (Nock, *Conversion*, p. 119: cf. Cicero, *De natura deorum* 2.153). This Hellenistic problematic continued in gnostics of the second and third centuries; it was not the line taken by the Hellenistic Judaism of the LXX crystallized in 4 Macc. Neither was it the line chosen by the PE. The "truth" (Titus 1:1) and the "instruction" (1 Tim 6:3) of the PE are *kat' eusebeian*, that is, they are defined by godliness, not vice versa.

Could the Septuagintal use of *eusebeia* and its cognates, particularly in the sapiential and Maccabean texts, hope for a sympathetic hearing outside Jewish circles? For Hellenism at large *eusebeia* was not simply external ritual. In secular Greek the term was understood of an internal intent that expressed itself in external activity, and that intent was not always explicitly cultic (see W. Foerster in *TNDT* 7.177). This "inside" of godliness seems to have been linked with the spirit in LXX Isa 11:2 (cf. LXX Susanna 63; 2 Macc 12:45; 4 Macc 14:6, *hypo psychēs athanatou tēs eusebeias*, "with a deathless spirit of godliness"); and 2 Tim 3:5 distinguishes "the appearance of godliness" from "its dynamic." Hellenistic philosophers proposed understanding *eusebeia*, along with *dikaiosynē* and *sōphrosynē* (see Titus 2:12), in terms of what a human being owed to the gods, to his fellowmen, and to himself (Xenophon, *Memorabilia* 4.8.11; see W. Foerster in *TDNT* 7.176, for other texts). *Eusebeia* was thus a matter of justice, of giving heaven its due with respectful reverence.

No Jew would take exception to the principle that man's first duty was to God and that the first debt to be paid was that of totally loyal worship (thus the *Shemaʿ* of Deut 6:4–5: Quinn, *Ap. Ministry*, pp. 481–482). The *euseb-* terms noted above in connection with the cultus and the temple corroborate this point (see Philo, *Mos.* 2.66). The great church order that opens in 1 Tim 2:1–2 presupposes that public prayer is the primary forum for expressing Christian *eusebeia*. But giving God his due in worship is inextricably bound up, in Jewish tradition, with giving human beings their due. The one God who can command total loyalty to himself, as an intrinsic part of his worship, forbids also every form of injustice among men and women. The faith of Israel is accordingly laminated into the actual conduct of human life. For some of the Jewish apologists of Alexandria and elsewhere (the authors of the Maccabean corpus and Philo) the *euseb-* terminology helped to articulate the common ground between the Hellenistic philosophical concern for human conduct and the Jewish way of life. For many civilized persons of the Hellenistic age their ethical philosophy was their religion; for the contemporary Jew his religion was his philosophy. In the area of actual daily human conduct both parties found themselves urging the same kind of actions for different kinds of reasons. The *euseb-* language, for all its pagan and eventually political resonances, offered the Hellenistic Jew a means for explaining and expressing himself to contemporary society (see W. Foerster in *TDNT* 7.180–181 on Philo). The antithetical *aseb-* language simultaneously offered a terminology for critiquing paganism precisely as paganism, where a godliness *manqué*, a misplaced *eusebeia*, spawned and justified the very conduct scored by the philosophers (see the critique of idolatry in Wis 14 as well as Rom 1:18–32 and 2 Pet 2).

The Hellenistic background makes quite understandable both the distrust and the adoption of the **seb/m-* cluster in the NT; one is left wondering why the most conspicuous transplant of the language has been into the PE (twenty-three times) and, further, why the Roman church favored this terminology into the second century. The Hellenistic Jewish concerns about the use of this language certainly surface in the links that the PE forge at every turn between godliness and virtue. The concern for good morals is parallel to the concern for teaching a sound ethic, true *eusebeia* (see Titus 2:2, 7, 12; 1 Tim 1:9; 2:10; [C. Spicq in *DBS* 10.228–230]; 3:4, 8, 11; 5:4; 6:11; 2 Tim 3:12). Often the same passages (e.g., Titus 2:12; 2 Tim 2:16) presuppose a link between ungodliness and vice. The **seb/m-* language frequently occurs in traditional materials, for example, in the virtue list of Titus 2:2–7; the vice list of 1 Tim 1:9–10; the baptismal confession of Titus 2:11–14; the church order of 1 Tim 2:1–3:13, where it figures particularly in the lists of virtues for the ecclesial ministers; the ordination homily quoted in 1 Tim 6:11–16, where "godliness" occurs second in a list of virtues (see also 2 Pet 1:6–7); and the *pistos logos* of 1 Tim 4:8 (see C. Spicq in *DBS* 10.223–228).

One infers that this terminology was taken for granted in the worship and catechesis of the Christian community from which the author of the PE derived these materials. That community would understand that the "mystery of godliness," summarized in a hymnic fragment (1 Tim 3:16), was synonymous (D-C, p. 61) with "the mystery of faith" (1 Tim 3:9). If "the faith" in the PE is often practically equivalent to "Christianity" (cf. R. Bultmann in *TDNT* 6.213–214, though he takes *kata pistin* in Titus 1:1 and 4 adjectivally as meaning "Christian"), then "godliness" denotes the whole Christian life, Christianity in practice, or as H. J. Cremer put it (*BW* s.v.), "the sum of Christian behavior." The adoption of the **seb/m-* language by witnesses linked with the Roman Christians may document precisely their own continuing attempt to address and relate to the specific human society around them. At Alexandria and Antioch the *euseb-* terminology had become "biblical" in the later strata of the LXX in an attempt to translate what Israel had meant by fear of Yahweh. Now that precedent was taken up as a Greek-speaking Christian church sought the right words to describe and justify their whole way of life. Further data suggest that this church was in the city of Rome, where the native language and mentality were Latin.

The Roman who spoke Latin and acquired Greek heard the whole **seb/m-*

cluster in terms of the Latin *pius, pietas, pie* "reverent, reverence, reverently" versus *impius, impietas, impie,* "wicked, wickedness, wickedly" (see *Res gestae divi Augusti* 6.20 = 18.6 and *CII* 262). The **pi-* words belonged to the terminology for Roman religion as distinct from—and opposed to—the myths, the mysteries, the sects that had rolled in over Rome from Greece and the whole Near East. The native Roman cults have struck observers, from ancient times to our own, as a "centralized, oligarchic legalism" (Nock, *ERAW* 2.964), an unspeakably pedestrian, caviling, all-embracing, and austere complex of attitudes and acts in the presence of the divine (see Polybius, *Histories* 6.56.6–12 and Cumont, *ORRP*, pp. 28–29). The Roman people, who tenaciously believed in these cults (as they never did in the myths and rituals of Greece and the Near East) were at bottom convinced that the survival of every part of their colossal society hinged on these rituals (Palmer, *RRRE*, pp. viii–ix). The archaic rites were their natural duty and that was precisely the concept at the root of the **pi-* terminology, which designated what a man owed others *morally* (as distinguished from legally; bibliography in Fears, "Virtues," p. 844). "*Pietas* consists in conformity with normal, traditional, indisputable relationships . . . which exist between people of the same blood and the same *civitas*, between neighbors, between allies, and between contracting parties; or, without reciprocity [?], between the individual and that which is superior to him—his country, the gods, and finally humanity" (Dumézil, *ARR*, pp. 132–133: cf. Spicq, *EP*, pp. 486 n. 3; 489 n. 5). Thus Vergil sang of *insignem pietate virum*, "a man marked out by reverence" (*Aeneid* 1.10), *pius Aeneas* (see Spicq, *EP*, pp. 486 n. 3, 489 n. 4). Even Juvenal had no sarcasm to pour over the frugal old Roman rites and the local deities (see Weiss, "Pagani," pp. 45–50; Apuleius, *Apologia* 56.4–6).

From the start the Latin translators of the PE rendered every occurrence of *theosebeia/eusebeia/eusebōs* with *pietas/pie* and of *asebeia/asebēs* with *impietas/impie*. In contrast, the Jewish community in Rome adopted the Latin terminology of piety with even less eagerness than they had the Greek (*CII* 476.7, 9 quoted on Titus 2:13: see 262, 641, 642, which appear to be the only evidence from Italy). The **seb/m-* language of the PE marks a continuing attempt of Roman Christians to identify themselves in terms of the society in which they lived, a city that had temples to personified Pietas (Livy, 40.34.4) and to Spes in the *forum holitorium*, as well as a temple for Fides (cf. Dumézil, *ARR* 2.398). To the old Roman terminology and mentality the Roman Christians brought a new content and meaning for *pietas* (not to mention for faith and hope; cf. Titus 1:1–2). The PE are missionary documents produced by a missionary religion, and the use of **seb/m-* terminology support this view. The values grounded on *pietas* in pagan Rome offered a point of departure for showing what Christians meant by *eusebeia*, and they took up the **seb/m-* language to explore that area.

In this connection, the usage of Acts is notable (see the table at the beginning of this discussion). In the description of Paul in Athens the verb *eusebeite* is placed on the apostle's lips (Acts 17:23) to designate precisely the Athenian worship of that unknown god whom Paul proclaims (in contrast to the neutered *sebasmata* noted there, and used otherwise in the NT only in 2 Thess 2:4). Here the *euseb-* language furnishes common ground between Athenian philosophers (17:18) and the gospel.

In Acts 3:12 Peter's disclaimer that the cripple's healing had come from "our own power or godliness" (*dynamei ē eusebeiai:* cf. 2 Tim 3:5) is balanced by his assertion that it had occurred because of faith in Jesus' name (Acts 3:16). The crabbed Greek of the latter affirmation sidles away from saying explicitly that power and godliness inherited in Jesus (cf. Heb 5:7 of Jesus' *eulabeias,* "reverence"). The sidling may have been occasioned by the fact that in Greek one who is divine does not show *eusebeia,* he *evokes* it. A Roman reader would not have been put off, however, by attributing *eusebeia/pietas* to Jesus, for the gods too had *pietas* to men (see Vergil, *Aeneid* 5.688; 12.839).

A Roman citizen and centurion of the Italian cohort and one of his unit, in Acts 10:2 and 7, are designated *eusebēs* (otherwise in the NT, only 2 Pet 2:9), and the adjective is parallel to and defined by *phoboumenos ton theon* (cf. 10:35), in other words, sharing the genuine religion or religious sensibility of Israel. The quality is emphatically that of the whole little community led by this officer, Cornelius (*syn panti tōi oikōi autou,* cf. 10:7), and his almsgiving as well as his prayer make it manifest. The link of the *euseb-* language with constant prayer (*deomenos . . . dia pantos*) recalls 1 Tim 2:1–2. The man who is *eusebēs* is generous to the poor, and particularly to the people of God (see Luke 7:2, 5), who are by definition poor, suffering, and in need of relief; this had not been noted in the LXX, though obviously 1 Tim 5:4 refers to properly motivated material support for a widowed mother and 1 Tim 6:5 (cf. 10) scores the greedy who make godliness pay (cf. also 2 Tim 3:2–5). In evaluating the impact that the story of a Roman citizen-soldier would have had on a Roman reader, one should note not simply that *eusebēs* means *pius,* but further that a Roman is "interested in a story only if it has some connection with Rome, if it presented 'Roman history,' justifying some detail in the organization of the city, a positive or negative rule of conduct, a Roman conception or prejudice" (Dumézil, *ARR,* p. 116). The narrative in Acts 10 is tailor-made to that description.

The **seb/m-* language of the PE and Acts has proved to be rooted in materials that are or profess to be traditional, materials that aim at forming the conduct of the believer according to a model that will also be persuasive for those who have not yet put their faith in Christ. The terminology and the whole way of life that it designates are together witnesses to the missionary convictions of the congregation that adopted it for worship and catechesis. In this connection one recalls the Pauline exhortation to the Philippian converts to think over the true, the honorable (*semna*), the just, the pure, the lovely, the gracious, the excellent, the praiseworthy (Phil 4:8). Is this in fact a Roman Christian catechetical list reflecting these very convictions, which Paul accordingly averred were part and parcel of his own missionary catechesis (Phil 4:9)?

EXCURSUS IV

The Terminology for Life in the PE

	Titus	1 Tim	2 Tim	PE/Paulines	Luke/Acts	NT
zēn to live	1	3	2	6/53	9/12	140
zōiogonein to keep alive	0	1	0	1/0	1/1	3
zōgrein to keep alive	0	0	1	1/0	1/0	2
syzein to share (someone's) life	0	0	1	1/2	0/0	3
anazēn to come to life (again)	0	0	0	0/1	1/0	2
anazōpyrein to rekindle	0	0	1	1/0	0/0	1
zōē life	2	4	2	8/29	5/8	135
[zōē aiōnios eternal life	2	2	0	4/5	3/2	43]
psychē life	0	0	0	0/13	14/15	103
anapsychein to revive	0	0	1	0/0	0/0	1
bios life	0	1	1	2/0	4/0	9
total	3	9	9	21/98	36/36	399

The Greek terms *bios/psychē/zōē*, all of which English may translate with "life," pose problems similar to the English "love" in relation to the Greek *eros/philia/agapē*. The circles that produced the LXX were already sensitive to the semantic pressures among these terms, as a glance at their distribution suggests. *Bios* simply does not occur in the Pentateuch or the Prophets. When it does appear, in the sapiential literature and the Maccabean corpus, it translates Hebrew *ḥāyyîm*, "life," only once (LXX Prov 4:10). Again, *psychē* appears more than a thousand times, in every stratum of the LXX, but scarcely six times for Hebrew *ḥāyyîm/ḥāyyā*. These Hebrew words are in the vast majority of instances translated by the Greek *zōē;* a majority of the 278 occurrences of *zōē* are found in the latest strata of the LXX (G. Bertram in *TDNT* 2.852 n. 154; Hill, *Greek Words*, pp. 171–175). It is finally *zōē* alone that can be qualified as *aiōnios*, never *bios* or *psychē* (though *eusebeia* has a "deathless spirit," *psychē athanatos*, in 4 Macc 14:6).

What did a Greek speaker mean when he referred to life now as *bios*, then as *psychē*, and still again as *zōē?* With *bios* he designated regularly tangible, measurable aspects of an individual life nourished by food and drink, supported and extended through a certain length of time in physical and social contexts (cf. English "biology," "biography"). *Psychē* designates life as an unseen and internal principle of individual movement and growth that can include the principle of human understanding and volition.

What did Greek designate as *zōē?* A commonplace in the Hellenistic world was the line of Menander, *tout' esti to zēn, ouch heautōi zēn monon* (Koerte 646/507K), "This is living, not to live only for oneself." The teleological and personal concerns of Greek culture gathered around the *zēn/zōē* terminology for life, which included all that *bios* and *psychē* suggested and yet designated something more. The *why* of human existence was not answered by citing man's physical generation. The nature of man was not explained by weighing him or his works (even his books). Really living (*zēn/zōē*) involved the way in which one spent *bios* and *psychē* with (and for) others. "How sweet is life (*zēn*) when it is with the persons one chooses" (Menander, Koerte 440/506K and cf. Sandbach, *Menandri*, p. 333, lines 135–137, for a similar statement from an unidentified comedian). "The time of life (*biou*) is something brief and we really live (*zōmen*) a scant part of that" (Koerte 340/410K and cf. Hill, *Greek Words*, p. 170). Dio Cassius (*Roman History* 69.19) cites an epitaph from Trajan's day: "Here lies Similis who lived (*bious*) for such and such a number of years but really lived (*zēsas de*) for seven," the number spent quietly retired in the country. The aspects to which we point when we are asked, "What is life really for?" are preeminently *zōē.* This transcends the particularity of *bios/psychē,* to define life in terms of a person's relations with others. *Bios* and *psychē* did not regularly suggest this societal orientation of life. *Zōē* did, so it came to suggest also a kind of secular eschatology.

Hellenistic Judaism, and in particular those circles which produced the latest strata in the LXX, use *zōē* of the moral and qualitative aspects of religious life in preference to its earlier, quantitative use for the length of life (though a long life remained a good and a value). *Zōē,* gift of the God of Israel, was increasingly understood of a reality that was to be returned to him in worship and obedience even at the cost of (premature) death (see 4 Macc 7:19; 16:25; 18:19; cf. 9:8). That part of life which was destructible might well be lost for the sake of that which remained indestructible. Thus 4 Macc 17:12, "The prize [for the martyrs] was indestructibility (*aphtharisia*) in a life exceedingly long (*en zōēi polychroniōi*)." It was apparently the tension between what was destructible in the reality called life and what was indestructible that led to the qualification of *zōē* as *aiōnios* (see R. Bultmann in *TDNT* 2.864 n. 272) as early as Dan 12:2, where the LXX translates *lᵉḥāyyē ʿōlām* with the phrase *eis zoēn aiōnion.*

In that passage too the future bodily resurrection of the dead is explicitly linked with life eternal (Di Lella, *AB Dan.,* pp. 308–309). The circles that produced the Maccabean literature shared in varying degrees belief in the final resurrection and the "everlasting renewal of life" (see 2 Macc 7:9, 11, 14, 23; 12:44–45; 14:46). They also linked life eternal with godliness (*eusebeian,* 4 Macc 15:3; cf. 16:13). The post-Maccabean *Pss. Sol.* declare, "They that fear the Lord shall rise to life eternal" (3:12; see 13:11 and Hill, *Greek Words,* p. 173).

Still, significant segments of the Palestinian Jewish community in the first centuries B.C.E. and C.E. ignored or resisted belief in the resurrection and understood "life eternal" as something less than personal immortality. Thus the Hebrew of Sir 37:26, "and his name stands in (ever-)lasting life (*wšmw ʿmd bḥyy ʿwlm*)," becomes the LXX "and his name will live for ages (*zēsetai eis ton aiōna*)." Here the unspecified length of *ʿwlm* is handled as in *Enoch* 10:10, where a long life of five hundred years is apparently equated with the Aramaic *ḥyy[ʿlm]* in 4QEnᵇ 1.iv.7 and with *zōē aiōnios* in the Greek version (see 25:5–6). The very few Qumran texts that refer to (ever-)lasting or perpetual life (*ḥyy nṣḥ* in 1QS 4:7 and CD 3:20 and *ḥyy ʿwlm* in 4Q 181:14, cf. 6, a work that may be related to 1QS and CD on other grounds [see Strugnell, "Notes," p. 255]) may indeed refer to immortality; they need not refer to bodily resurrection (see Josephus, *War* 2.154–155; *Ant.* 18.18; Hill, *Greek Words,* pp. 183–185; G. Nickelsburg in *IDBSup,* p. 350; Vermes, *DSS,* pp. 186–188, 196–197; *pace* E. Lohse in *TDNT* 9.636). The Sadducees were actively opposed to belief in the resurrection (see Josephus, *Ant.* 18.16; Luke 20:27; Acts 23:6–8).

All parties in Judaism were united in their belief that the God of Israel was the living God who gave and sustained life and who demanded that his people give it back in obedience and worship (cf. LXX Deut 30:15, 19, 20; 32:47). That latter complex of relationships was preeminently *zōē* for Israel. A Greek tradition could affirm that really living was not to live only for oneself. The Israelite religious tradition believed that really living was to live only for God. The question, "What is life really for?" the Israelite answered with his confession of the one Lord. With Philo he might even say, "Is not life eternal (*zōē aiōnios*) to take refuge in him who is?" (*Fug.* 78).

Bios by contrast was for Hellenistic Jews, in the last analysis, short and painful (see Job, Prov, Wis passim; Sir 40:29 for a *bios* that cannot be considered *zōē*); *psychē* was a spiderweb before the God who alone could bring it *eis zoēn* (cf. LXX Ps 38:12–14 with 65:9).

The NT documents take up and develop the usage of *bios/psychē/zōē* and their cognates in Hellenistic Judaism. Thus for Luke 8:14 (43 s.v.1.); 15:12, 30; and 21:4 (= Mark 12:44), *bios* denotes human life as an economic reality, in which material goods are produced and consumed (see cognates in Luke 21:34; Acts 26:4). Paul found it incongruous that believers would resort to civil litigation about such matters, mere *biōtika* (1 Cor 6:3–4). For the Johannine tradition, the rich may have the life of this world (see *ton bion tou kosmou*, 1 John 3:17), namely, the goods prized by human society, but they are no more than the ground for arrogance (*hē alazoneia tou biou*, 1 John 2:16) unless shared out with the poor.

The *psychē* terminology appears more than a hundred times in the NT traditions for a life that, for all its value, is somehow to be lost for Jesus' sake (see E. Schweizer in *TDNT* 9:637–656 on the individual passages). The Paulines rarely treat *psychē*, and this term is altogether absent from the PE, which only once employ even a cognate expression, the *anapsychein* of 2 Tim 1:16, for the refreshment that Onesiphorus brought the imprisoned Paul (*TDNT* 9.663–664).

The previous Jewish usage of the *zōē* cluster of terms was taken up by the first Jewish Christians who added their confession of the risen Jesus to the confession of the one God of Israel (see the use of *zōē aiōnios* in Luke 10:25; 18:18, 30; Acts 13:46, 48). In the risen Lord, they believed, the hope of Israel for life eternal had come into sharp focus. If among their Jewish colleagues the options still remained open on precisely what human existence beyond the grave involved, after the resurrection of Jesus those who believed in him found themselves on the side of their coreligionists who conceived of eternal life through bodily resurrection.

Within this context the usage of *zōē* terminology in the PE can be approximately assessed. This correspondence opens with the explicit affirmation that the apostle works and believes "in hope of life eternal" (Titus 1:1–2). There is no analogy for this phrase outside the PE, whether in the LXX, NT, or Ap. Frs. It recurs in the sacramental catechesis of Titus 3:4–8a, where the climactic goal of God's saving grace is "so that we could become heirs with (*kat'*) a hope of life eternal" (Titus 3:7).

This catechesis appears to be the vein that has been quarried for Titus 1:2 and 1 Tim 1:16, and it is not surprising to discover that a number of the other appearances of the *zōē* terminology in the PE are in materials that have been identified as preexistent compositions: thus 1 Tim 4:8 (ethical instruction); 6:12–13 (an ordination charge); 2 Tim 1:10 (a creedal confession); 2:11 (a hymn); 4:1 (the emerging formula "to judge the living and the dead"); and so on. The appearance of *zōē* in the already stylized opening of 2 Tim 1:1 illustrates the traditional character of the term as well as the importance of the concept of life eternal for the author.

What does the *zōē* cluster of terminology signify in the PE? The last chapter of this correspondence opens (2 Tim 4:1) with a solemn adjuration that invokes "Christ Jesus who is going to judge the living and dead (*zōntas kai nekrous*)," an inchoate formula in the second Christian generation (see Acts

10:42; 1 Pet 4:5; and note the earlier variation on it in Rom 14:9). The precedents in Jewish and Christian usage can be traced into LXX Isa 8:19 and Tob 5:10 (S) as well as the dominical logion referring to "the God not of the dead but of the living" (Mark 12:27 par. *SFG* §281); almost the precise phrase is documented in a Jewish source, *Ep. Arist.* 146 (*nekrous te kai zōntes*). In the PE, the verbal expression *zōntōn* designates living humans in a generic but not in a simply biological sense. The living are bound for the judgment of Christ as much as the dead. There is an aspect of the process of living (*zēn*) that comes under divine judgment even if one has entered the ranks of the dead. That this aspect is ethical, that is, bound up with one's personal conduct, can be verified in the description of the voluptuous widow of 1 Tim 5:6 who "has died while still living" (*zōsa tethnēken*). Self-indulgence makes human living and dying completely relative (see Rev 3:1–2). What a man or woman does turns what is to all appearances life into what is actually death and vice versa (see Luke 15:24 *anezēsen*, 32, "This brother of yours was dead [*nekros*] and has come to life [*ezēsen*]," and 2 Tim 1:6, *anazōpyrein*, "to rekindle").

Paradoxically, this drastic redefinition of life and death makes the conversion of the sinner conceivable, for while he is at least apparently alive, there is still space for repentance. In fact, that is why sinners remain alive. "God may grant them a change of heart that will lead back into full knowledge of the truth. Then their heads would clear and they would find their way 'out of the snare of the devil in which he has been keeping them alive (*ezōgrēmenoi*)' and into the will (*to . . . thelēma*) of God himself" (2 Tim 2:25–26). The text is as tortured as any in the PE, but the source being cited seems to envision sinners as caught in Satan's nets but still "alive" like fish in a seine; the only other NT use of the verb, in Luke 5:10, is also a figurative application of the term to the fisherman Simon Peter, who is henceforth to catch human beings. Sinners in the PE are prisoners of war (see LXX Deut 20:16; 2 Kgdms 8:2; 2 Chr 25:12; cf. Num 31:15, 18); the final battle remains to be fought. If they are still apparently alive it is because the divine will (2 Tim 1:1) is to save all humankind (see 1 Tim 2:3–6).

The favored usage of *zēn* in the PE appears in the programmatic, traditional material cited in Titus 2:11–14. This chapter of Titus prescribes the conduct for every order among believers. The warrant for those prescriptions is the divine grace that "disciplines us . . . to live (*zēsōmen*) in a sensible, honest, godly way (*sōphronōs kai dikaiōs kai eusebōs*) in this present age" (Titus 2:12). In the text of the PE this is the first occurrence of the verb *zēn*, and its only use in Titus. It is, moreover, set between the two references in this letter to "life eternal" and in paraenetic material that is cited as familiar and authoritative (see Titus 2:15). For this author "to live" is above all and essentially to give what one owes to oneself, to one's neighbor, to God, and to do it now, in spite of the suffering that it must entail. Thus in 2 Tim 3:12 Paul is presented as recalling the harassments of his apostolate in Pisidian Antioch, Iconium, and Lystra, and inferring accordingly, "Moreover, all who want to live in a godly way (*eusebōs zēn*) in Christ Jesus will be persecuted." Living "in this present age" has here become living "in Christ Jesus."

Certainly for the PE the actual conduct of human life reveals that one is, in fact, living, but life, *zōē*, is more than behavior. What is *zōē* for the PE? It is certainly not the life (*bios*) mentioned in 1 Tim 2:2 and 2 Tim 2:4. In the former passage, the great church order of 1 Tim 2–3 opens with a Pauline command for Christian prayers "for all human beings" and specifically political leaders. "Our purpose is to spend a tranquil and quiet existence (*bion diagōmen*) in an altogether godly and reverent way (*eusebeiai kai semnoteti*)." The final phrase refers to that living in a godly way seen above (contrast Titus 3:3). Here it is placed in conjunction with another "living" (*bion*), which depends on the goodwill of those who govern the state. The language of the source that the author of the PE is redacting at this point may be very close to the surface in the phrase *bion diagōmen;* the combination is otherwise undocumented in the LXX, the NT, or the Ap. Frs. (though Josephus uses it half a dozen times). The other NT texts that employ *bios* qualify it only by *pas* or *holos;* here, perhaps because of the materialistic connotations of *bios* alone it is defined as "tranquil and quiet," again a phrase not otherwise documented in the LXX, NT, Ap. Frs., or Josephus (similarly "a virtuous life," *enareton bion,* in *1 Clem.* 62.1, and Josephus, *Ant.* 11.219, "and so let us lead our lives in peace," *met' eirēnēs hēmin ton bion diagein*). The whole phrase here in 1 Tim 2:2 is evidently not characteristic of Jewish or Christian religious expression. The terminology is, however, not recondite or recherché; it is the formal Greek of pagan Hellenistic society, meant to be quite intelligible to the rulers of this world (see BAGD s.vv.; C. Spicq in D-C ad loc.). This is no petition for their conversion but one for a blessing on their proper work because they exist for the common good of the people whom they lead, a good here described in terms of a peaceful existence. Such a prayer ought not be taxed as selfish parochialism. Rulers are not being asked to provide salvation, eternal life. This prayer is concerned with what rulers can and at their best want to provide. One must pray to God for what only God can give; one may also pray to him for what men can and ought to give, "a quiet and tranquil existence."

The one other occurrence of *bios* in the PE is at the beginning of the Pauline testament to Timothy in 2 Tim 2:4. There Timothy is exhorted to suffer along with Paul as one of Christ's soldiers. The comparison prompts the observation, "No one on active duty in the military gets involved in the business of civilian life (*tais tou biou pragmateiais*). He avoids this to please the man who called him to arms." Evidently "the business" of making a living is given low priority here. The NT does not use the noun *pragmateia* elsewhere (see Luke 19:13 for the cognate verb, again a NT *hapax*). Although *bios* in 2 Tim 2:4 resembles 1 Tim 2:2 in designating the external circumstances of human existence, it resembles far more closely the gospel usage cited above (see especially

Luke 21:4 = Mark 12:44), which refers to the material necessities of life. The society that needs the protection of the soldier must provide his livelihood, his food and shelter, which are understood as a relatively small recompense for the rigors of military life.

Understanding the relation of *bios* to *zōē* can be enlarged by adducing the teaching on the Christian's use of riches to which 1 Tim returns in 6:17–19. There "the wealthy of the present age" are admonished to humility and generosity with an eye to a future (see 1 Tim 4:8) that offers "the life which deserves that name." The present age is the temporal, spatial scene for living "in a sensible, honest, godly way" (Titus 2:12). Precisely what that means for wealthy believers is here detailed. To live in the present age is one thing; to love it is quite another (see 2 Tim 4:10 and Pol. *Phil.* 5.2; 9.2), for all that it contains is by definition ephemeral, contingent, mortal, offering in the end neither security nor hope. Thus livelihood (*bios*) is not life (*zōē*), and this charge to the wealthy reaches its climax by an appeal to a future in which believers at last "can lay hold on the life which deserves that name (*tēs ontōs zoēs*)." There is a Christian *zōē* that so transcends its secular counterpart that the latter seems less than real and authentic (cf. the *ontōs* of real widows in 1 Tim 5:3, 5, 16). As vicious conduct turns what human society considers living into death itself, so the unselfish conduct that proceeds from faith makes relative what the world, even at its best, considers life.

The life that the PE prize and that they always designate as *zōē* spans two orders, the present time and the future world for which believers are bound. The traditional catechetical materials incorporated into 1 Tim 4:8 teach that "Godliness (*eusebeia*) is useful for everything, because it contains the promise of a life that is now and that is going to be." In 2 Tim 1:1 this vein of material is tapped to describe Paul as an apostle "for the sake of the promise of life that is in Christ Jesus," a theme on which Titus 1:1–2 further enlarges with its description of Paul as one sent "for the faith of God's elect . . . in hope of life eternal which the God who is without deceit promised from all eternity." The terminology of hope and promise is Pauline (see Rom 4:16–21) and makes explicit the intrinsic momentum into the future that is suggested for the PE by the noun *zōē*. The catechesis cited here describes such life as one "that is now (*nyn*) and that is going to be (*mellousēs*)." The traditional verbal description of living "in this present age (*en tōi nyn aiōni*)" in Titus 2:12 here appears as the nominal "life that is now." This nominal *nyn* has a Septuagintal resonance (*apo tou nyn*) and is characteristic of the Lukan corpus but not of Paul (G. Stählin in *TDNT* 4:1107, 1113–1114). Here in the PE it is to be understood with the adverbial *nyn* of the creedal confession of 2 Tim 1:10 (see below), where God's gracious design, previously hidden in eternity, "has now (*nyn*) been made clear through the revelation (*epiphaneias*) of our savior, Christ Jesus. He broke the power of death. He made life and immortality (*zōēn kai aphtharsian*) shine forth through the gospel." The now, this present age, is the eschatological age that began with the life and, above all, the risen life of Jesus. For the PE, *zōē* "now" is life in the last age, in the time between the resurrection of Jesus and joining the Lord in the age that is going to be (cf. 1 Tim 6:19 with Acts 24:25).

The one life is now and is to come. *Zōē mellousa*, "the life that is going to be," is a phrase otherwise undocumented in the LXX, NT, and Ap. Frs. Because *nyn* preceding the phrase is a variant on *en tōi nyn aiōni* (Titus 2:12), *mellouses* here is to be understood in the sense of *ho aiōn mellōn*, "the age to come"; the same contrast occurs in 1 Tim 6:17 and 19. The Lucianic text tradition renders the phrase *'ebî 'ād*, "everlasting father," in Isa 9:5 with *patēr tou mellontos aiōnos*, "father of the coming age," evidently taken here as a reference to the messianic age. Josephus (*Ant.* 18.287), in contrast, uses *ho aiōn mellōn* to refer simply to the distant future. Christian usage settled on the more abstract sense. *Second Clement* 6.3 even writes of "this and *ho mellōn*" as enemies of each other. In the Pauline tradition Eph 1:21 writes of Christ's exaltation "above every name that is named not only in this age but also in that which is to come (*en toi [aiōni] mellonti*)." Matthew 12:32 (*SFG* §118) expands the dominical logion on the sin that will not be forgiven "in this age or the age to come (*en [tōi aiōni] mellonti*)." In both places the emphasis on that which spans both present and future is notable; when Heb 6:5 writes of "the powers of the age to come (*dynameis te mellontos aiōnos*)," it is because believers have already actually experienced them in this life.

The transfer of the eschatological qualification to *zōē* as "the life that is going to be" can probably be traced into a variety of traditions that predate the PE. Chief among them are the sayings of Jesus with their paradoxical promise of life now and in the future for his followers who have left the persons and things that extend and enrich human existence. They will have compensation a hundredfold "now in this time" and they will have "in the age to come (*en tōi aiōni tōi erchomenōi*) eternal life" (Mark 10:30–31; cf. Matt 19:29; Luke 18:30; *SFG* §255). The catechesis of 1 Tim 4:8, summarizing that promise as "the promise of a life that is now and that is going to be," thus bonded with a Pauline theological term into an evangelical tradition the language of which was ultimately that of apocalyptic.

The hymn cited in the catechetical material of 2 Tim 2:11–13 reminds one that, behind the more technical, theological definitions and descriptions surveyed thus far, there lies the living worship of Christ by his followers. In him they had found and continued to experience the life that prompted them to sing,

. . . for if we shared in his death (*synapethanomen*),
we shall share in his life (*syzēsomen*).

This torso of a hymn for which the introduction has been lost comes out of the first Christian generation. The hymn seems to be presupposed by Rom 6:8 as a formulation of the baptismal faith already well known to the recipients of that letter, part perhaps of the "standard of teaching" (Rom 6:17) they had received from God; such a hymn may have come with the authority of God's word out of the prophetic order. Paul paraphrases the hymn as part of the tradition of a church with a faith that is known throughout the world (see Rom 1:8); the PE prefer to quote the text itself. The first-person plural underlines the communal character of both the experience and the response that it evokes, and the repetition of *sy*(*n-*) emphasizes the solidarity of this community with Jesus Christ (see the paraphrase and expansion in Rom 6:8). These believers have been plunged sacramentally into his death and burial and are now on the way to their resurrection with him (see Rom 6:3–5), for the life that they believe they will share is that of "Jesus Christ, risen from the dead, from the line of David" (2 Tim 2:8). The verb *syzēn*, "to co-live," is in the NT uniquely Pauline, found only here in 2 Tim, as well as in Rom 6:8 and 2 Cor 7:3. In each of these instances it is preceded by a form of (*syn*)*apothanein*, and the first-person plural in each context underscores the ecclesial quality of the life hoped for. The "co-living" is precisely that of sharing Jesus' life for his Father (Rom 6:10b–11; cf. 2 Cor 5:15 and Menander, Koerte 646/507K, cited above). Just as that life of his appeared in a history that passed through human death into a risen life with the Father, so the believer's co-life with Christ begins when his own mortal existence is joined to Christ's death. With that union a life of love of God and neighbor begins, which issues into life with God and the resurrection. In this perspective, the individual human death of a believer has been as relativized as a merely human life (*zōē*) before faith and baptism. The only "real" death was the death of Jesus for our sins; the only "real" life is the one that he led and leads and shares with those who have died with him (see Gal 2:19–20). Thus the present life of the community of believers can be inseparably united with the life to come (see R. Bultmann in *TDNT* 2.869).

Important as all of the vocabulary of life is, the privileged phrase in the PE for designating life in its specifically Christian sense is *zōē aiōnios*. The adjective *aiōnios* is frequent in the LXX, often qualifying "covenant" (*diathēkē*) or "commandment" (*nomimon*); it qualifies *zōē* only twice (Dan 12:2, both LXX and Theod.; 4 Macc 15:3; see 2 Macc 7:9). In the Qumran documents, see *ḥyy ῾wlm*, "life everlasting," in 4Q 181:4, 6; and *ḥyy nṣḥ*, "life perpetual" in CD 3:20. In forty-three out seventy-one NT uses of the adjective it does modify *zōē*. In the remaining twenty-eight instances it applies to fire, torment, sin, and judgment as well as things unseen, including salvation, redemption, the covenant, the inheritance, kingdom, gospel, the Spirit, and God himself. This adjectival usage is heavily eschatological (N. Turner, "NT Vocab.," p. 157), as even the "everlasting tents" of the parable of the dishonest manager (Luke 16:9) illustrate.

The usage in the PE is consistent with other strata in the NT. Thus Titus 1:2 (see also 2 Tim 1:9) writes of *chronoi aiōnioi*, literally, "eternal times," linked thus with the preceding "hope of life eternal." In 2 Tim 2:10 the present suffering of the apostle is to issue in the salvation of the elect "in Christ Jesus with eternal glory" where *doxa*, "glory," is almost synonymous with *zōē*. In the closing doxology of the hymnic acclamation in 1 Tim 6:16, "might eternal (*kratos aiōnion*)" belongs to "the only one who possesses immortality (*athanasian*)," "the God who keeps all things alive (*zōiogonountos ta panta*)" (1 Tim 6:13). Insofar as the adjective *aiōnios* is more and more frequently employed to qualify a reality and an order that belong immediately to God and are remote from human existence, it finds its definition in the God of Israel as he revealed himself (see LXX Ps 101:13, 25–26). Thus when the one to be ordained in 1 Tim 6:12 is charged to "lay hold on eternal life (*tēs zōēs aiōniou*)," the life being designated cannot be divorced from the subsequent description of the person of "the God who keeps all things alive," uniquely immortal and eternally strong.

A prayer is also the context for the mention of eternal life in 1 Tim 1:16, the thanksgiving prayer of the apostle that his own passage from aggressive infidelity to faith will in the future give evidence of Jesus' patience with other sinners "who are going to believe in him for eternal life." Just as in Titus 1:1–2 the apostle is called "for the faith of God's elect . . . in hope of life eternal," so also in Titus 3:7 the baptismal catechesis on rebirth and renewal, "so that we could become heirs (*klēronomoi*) with a hope of life eternal," is "the Christian message, meant to be believed (*pistos ho logos*)" (Titus 3:8a). Faith in Christ Jesus is indispensable for passage into eternal life. Those who believe the Christian message and who are reborn in baptism thus become heirs of life, a figure of speech that captures both the already and the not-yet aspects of a form of living that has actually begun but has not reached its goal. Similarly, in 1 Tim 6:12, the charge to the one to be ordained to take hold of eternal life continues, "You were called (*eklēthēs*) into that life and for it you made that fine profession before the eyes of many witnesses." The calling vocabulary is the language of invitation, particularly to share a banquet and life-giving food with the wealthy, generous host (see the invitation parables of Luke 14:7–24 and the beatitude of Rev 19:9). Here the man of God has received such an invitation, from a host whom he acknowledges as his king, and he is on his way to the promised meal.

Can the nature of eternal life, as the PE conceive it, be still further specified? The prayer of thanksgiving that opens 2 Tim contains as its generative core a creedal confession, partially cited above, to which one must return at this point. The apostle is appealing to "the God who saved us and called us" (2 Tim 1:9; see 1 Tim 6:12 above). He continues, "That saving call did not correspond to our deeds. It corresponded with his own design, his own grace, given us in Christ Jesus from all eternity (*pro chronōn aiōniōn*). That gracious design, however, has now been made clear through the revelation of our savior, Christ Jesus. He broke the power of death. He made life and immortality (*zōēn kai aphtharsian*) shine forth through the gospel" (2 Tim 1:9–10). The resurrection of Jesus has nullified and made inoperative human death, the horizon of human existence. He sank below that horizon and then returned, so to speak, from the opposite direction, revealing the hidden shape of our world. That return, the resurrection, made the old horizon obsolete, insignificant. Easter revealed that real life is "immortality (*aphtharsia*)."

What then is *aphtharsia?* In the NT this term and its cognates are concentrated in the Pauline and Petrine correspondence. But the noun occurs only here in the PE, and their sole use of the adjective "immortal, incorruptible" is for a divine attribute in the doxology of 1 Tim 1:17 (see Rom 1:23). The recherché *aphthoria*, "open-handedness," in Titus 2:7 designates moral incorruptibility in teaching. In 2 Tim 1:10 the Pauline usage of *aphtharsia* is presumed, above all that of Rom 2:6–7, with its description of God rendering "to every person according to his works: to those who, by patience in well-doing, seek for glory and honor and immortality (*aphtharsian*), he will give eternal life (*zōēn aiōnion*)." What from the human viewpoint is called *aphtharsia* is from God's viewpoint *zōē aiōnios*. The usage in Eph 6:24, as the letter concludes, is an isolated and complex problem, on which see Spicq, *Agape* 1.296–298; Barth, *AB Eph.* 2.812–14; G. Harder in *TDNT* 9.105.

In 1 Cor 15:42–57 this immortality is nothing less than the final bodily resurrection of believers, the "incorruptible wreath" (1 Cor 9:25) at the end of their race. The contest/*agōn* metaphor also figures in the Hellenistic Jewish tradition. It is said of the Maccabean martyrs that the prize for enduring challenges to faith was "immortality in a long-lasting life (*aphtharsia en zōēi polychroniōi*)" (4 Macc 17:12; cf. 9:22), but neither this composition nor the Wisdom of Solomon in 2:23; 6:18–19 (cf. 12:1; 18:4 for the adjective) defines *aphtharsia* as involving bodily resurrection (see G. Nickelsburg in *IDBSup*, p. 350). In Wis 18:4, what is imperishable is the light of the Mosaic law that Israel transmits to humankind; the resurrection is not envisioned. Hellenistic Greek texts, including Josephus (*War* 2.163) and the Wisdom of Solomon (12:1) describe the *psychē* as *aphthartos* (see G. Harder in *TDNT* 9.96, 100). In contrast, Christian writers refer to *sarx*, "the flesh," in this connection: *2 Clem.* 14.5 writes of how "great a gift of life and immortality (*zōēn kai aphtharsian*) this flesh (*hē sarx hautē*) has the power to receive, if the Holy Spirit be joined to it." For Ignatius "the gospel is the consummation of immortality (*apartisma . . . aphtharsias*)," and the gospel includes "the coming (*parousia:* see *epiphaneia* of 2 Tim 1:10) of the Savior, our Lord, Jesus Christ, the passion, the resurrection (*tēn anastasin*)" (*Phld.* 9.2; see *Pol.* 2.3; *Eph.* 17.1; *Magn.* 6.2).

Is it possible to define more precisely the ultimate source of eternal life in the risen flesh, as the PE understand it? The answer is suggested by 1 Tim 4:8–10. After relating "the Christian message, meant to be believed" on godliness as containing "the promise of a life that is now and that is going to be," the apostle avers of himself and Timothy "that we have fixed our hope on the living God (*epi theōi zōnti*), savior of all." The hope for resurrection and life is grounded ultimately in a God who is living. There are more than 1,300 uses of *theos* in the

NT; only a dozen times is that noun qualified with *zōn*, and half of them are in the Paulines, including 1 Tim 3:15 and 4:10. The proportion is similar to the LXX, where *(ho) theos zōn* occurs less than two dozen times in more than 2,600 uses of *theos*. The Pauline usage intersects with the Septuagintal tradition when Rom 9:26, citing LXX Hos 2:1, speaks of both Jewish and Gentile believers as destined to be "sons of the living God" (see 3 Macc 6:28). This phrase, perhaps the prophet's "own creative formulation" or his revival of an ancient phrase (Wolff, *Hos.* p. 27; Andersen and Freedman, *AB Hosea*, pp. 206–207), is the font for his prophetic teaching that it is the one God of Israel who bestows life in all its forms (cf. LXX 2:8–11; 6:2; 9:11–14; 13:14 [quoted in 1 Cor 15:54–55]; 14:8). The lurid pack of local fertility deities have nothing to do with life. In fact, they precipitate men and women into condemnation and death (LXX 2:5; 5:9–12; 9:16–17; 13:1–9). By contrast, the living God makes Israel his child (11:1–4) and the people into brothers and sisters (2:3). Their own "fathers" (9:10–14) have generated death; the God who gives life is the real father of Israel, and they find life in worship of him alone.

The prophetic passage cited by Paul is in fact the key for understanding the comparatively rare phrase "the living God" (LXX Pss 41:3; 83:3). He is where the ark is (LXX Josh 3:10). Above all the temple is "the house of the living God" (LXX Dan 4:22; 5:23 and see LXX Isa 37:4, 17 = 4 Kgdms 19:4, 16), a theme that will surface again in the NT.

When the NT authors use the phase "the living God," it is to contrast his worship with idolatry and apostasy (1 Thess 1:9; Heb 3:12; 9:14; 10:31). He is the object of worship beyond this world (Heb 12:22; Rev 7:2–12); even now the believer's heart is God's temple and his ark (2 Cor 3:3; 6:16); the worshiper receives life from the one who is really his Father in the temple (Rom 9:26, after LXX Hos 2:1 and perhaps 1 Pet 1:23). The ultimate meaning of the phrase "the living God" appears when Matthew (16:16; 26:63) places its articular form on the lips of Peter and Caiaphas. For the latter Jesus is the blasphemer who mocks the temple as he makes himself the Son of God. For Peter he really is "the Christ, the Son of the living God." The PE do not write of "the living God" with Matthean intensity, but the Pauline (and Septuagintal) emphases appear in 1 Tim 3:15: "Still, if I do delay, this letter will let you know how a person has to behave in God's house, which is the church of the living God." The PE in this notable passage understand a congregation of believers, a church, as a house-hold, on the broad familial model of the ancient world. The family life of the bishop or presbyter-bishop is to be a parable of the life of the church in which he is a steward (see Titus 1:5–7; 1 Tim 3:2–5), and in which God is himself the father of the household. "God's house" is in the LXX "a fixed term for the sanctuary" (O. Michel in *TNDT* 5:120), and thus 1 Tim 3:15 adds here a nuance to the meaning of *oikos*, which up to this point in the PE had referred to human households and their inner relationships. That shade of meaning is further drawn out when this sanctuary is defined as "the church of the living

God." What the LXX had called "the house of the living God" is in the PE the church, which is now God's family, in which he is truly known by faith (cf. Gal 6:10) and given genuine worship (cf. Mark 11:17 and parallels: John 2:16–17; SFG §25). God is "living" as the father who gives life to this family, which his love has called into existence and which he sustains.

At this point one must return to the ordination charge to "lay hold on eternal life" (1 Tim 6:12) and its adjuration, "Before the eyes of the God who keeps all things alive (enōpion tou theou tou zōiogonountos ta panta) and of Christ Jesus who publicly attested to the fine profession before Pontius Pilate I charge you to keep the apostolic command beyond blemish, beyond reproach, until the revelation of our Lord, Jesus Christ" (1 Tim 6:13–14). The PE seldom designate God as God the Father (Titus 1:4; 1 Tim 1:2; 2 Tim 1:2); here in 1 Tim 6:13 the articular ho theos is to be taken as the personal name of the Father, a name that is explained by the following phrase, "who keeps all things alive," with its unusual verb zōiogonein, which occurs otherwise in the NT only in Luke 17:33 and Acts 7:19. Although one can distinguish in English between giving life and sustaining it, this Greek verb always included both of those aspects (cf. teknogonein, "to bear and rear children," in 1 Tim 5:14). In the eleven Septuagintal uses, even in the one in which God is the subject (1 Kgdms 2:6), it refers to a return from grave illness and death's door. Thus the meaning extends beyond "giving life" to "keeping life" (for the terminology for giving life only see LXX Deut 32:39 and 4 Kgdms 5:7). In 1 Tim 6:13 this Septuagintal and Lukan usage continues with the invocation of God as the one who makes and keeps all things alive. An older creedal schema about God the creator/ Christ the redeemer may stand behind the solemn adjuration in the present text (2 Tim 4:1). The emphasis specifically on life as God's creation reminds one of the standard Israelite formula for an oath (e.g. LXX 1 Kgdms 14:39, 45), which can be used by Yahweh himself (LXX Num 14:21, 28; Zeph 2:9; Isa 49:18). All of these lines lead out from a radical conviction that life in every sense (cf. panta, "all things"), in its origin and in its continuance, depends on one who is alive without qualification, the one God of Israel.

Thus for the PE the living God who gives all life is the one who bestows a share in his own endless life upon those who believe in and worship him. In that faith and worship believers have begun to live as God's children. Their just, devout, and temperate conduct in the flesh is already a revelation of the eternal life that involves the bodily resurrection of the dead.

EXCURSUS V

The PE on Salvation

	Titus	1 Tim	2 Tim	PE/Paulines	Luke/Acts	NT
sōizein to save	1	4	2	7/22	17/13	106
sōtēr savior	6	3	1	10/2	2/2	24
sōtēria salvation	0	0	2	2/16	4/6	45
sōtērion rescue	0	0	0	0/1	2/1	4
sōtērios rescuing	1	0	0	1/0	0/0	1
asōtia debauchery	1	0	0	1/1	0/0	3
asōtōs dissolutely	0	0	0	0/0	1/0	1
total	9	7	5	21/42	26/22	184
diasōizō to save	0	0	0	0/0	1/5	8
eksōizō to bring safely	0	0	0	0/0	0/1(s.v.l.)	1
sōphronein to use common sense, be in one's right mind	1	0	0	1/2	1/0	6
sōphronizein to spur on	1	0	0	1/2	0/0	1
sōphronismos discretion	0	0	1	1/0	0/0	1
sōphronōs sensibly	1	0	0	1/0	0/0	1
sōphrosynē sensibleness	0	2	0	2/0	0/1	3
sōphrōn sensible	3	1	0	4/0	0/0	4
total	6	3	1	10/2	1/1	16

The basic *sō(s)- cluster of terms, the first seven words listed in the table, is a feature that the PE share with the rest of the Paulines and with Luke–Acts. But the other Paulines and the Lukan corpus favor the words sōizein and sōteria. The second roll of Luke's work ends with the solemn reference to to sōtērion tou theou (Acts 28:28), as his first volume begins (Luke 2:30; 3:6) with such references (Fitzmyer, AB Lk, pp. 222–223). Moreover, in the other Paulines the *sō(s)- terminology occurs regularly in a future perspective. This is not the rule in Luke–Acts (Throckmorton, "Sōzein," pp. 515–526); like them, the PE emphasize the present aspects of salvation while adverting to its links with the past and the future (e.g., Titus 2:10, 13; 3:4–6; 1 Tim 4:16; 2 Tim 1:9; 4:18; see S. Wilson, Lk PE, pp. 20–22; Beasley-Murray, Bapt. NT, p. 208). The PE opt for the personal title sōtēr ten times, more than Luke–Acts and the other Paulines put together.

Luke's use of sōtērios as an instrumental substantive meaning "rescue, salvation" (see Eph 6:17) reflects the usage of a community that had assimilated the typical practice of the LXX Pss. The only one of the Ap. Frs. who uses the substantival sōtērion is Clement, who after citing LXX Pss three times (1 Clem. 15.6; 18.12; 35.12) designates Jesus Christ as sōtērion hēmōn ("our salvation," 36.1). The PE certainly know this personal understanding of *sōs- terms, but they are not limited to it. For example, the baptismal paraenesis presupposed by Titus 2:11–14 opens with the declaration, "Revealed was the grace of God for the rescue (hē charis . . . sōtērios, literally, "the rescuing grace") of all human beings." This adjectival use of sōtērios—only here in the NT, undocumented in the Ap. Frs., and occurring not half a dozen times in the LXX—makes charis sōtērios a notably fresh expression for the unprecedented, universal gift from "our savior, God" (Titus 2:10), namely "Jesus Christ, our . . . savior" (2:13). This grace, through which God has rescued a people for himself, is for all practical purposes synonymous with Jesus Christ who appeared and died "for us" (Titus 2:14).

More basic for the PE is the verb sōizein. A baptismal paraenesis later in Titus contains the only use of this verb in the letter. It describes how "our savior, God . . . saved us, no thanks to any upright deeds that we performed ourselves but because of (kata) his own mercy, saved us through a washing of regeneration and of renewal by the Holy Spirit that he poured out lavishly on us, through (dia) Jesus Christ, our savior. God's was the grace (tei ekeinou chariti) that made us upright" (Titus 3:4–7). For the PE the action of saving is ultimately an act of God as ho theos, the Father (cf. 1 Tim 2:3–4 with 2 Tim 1:8–9). Precisely because of the relationship in which Jesus stands to the Father, he too can be the subject of sōizein (1 Tim 1:15; 2 Tim 4:18).

Against this background of the priority of the acts of God and Jesus in saving people, it is at first glance disconcerting to read the summary exhortation to Timothy: "Pay attention to yourself and to your instruction. Persevere in these activities; for, if you do this, you will save (sōseis) both yourself and the persons listening to you" (1 Tim 4:16). If God and his Christ saved human beings, in what sense does the apostle's coworker save them now? In fact, how can the historical Paul write, "I have become all things for all people, so that I might by all means save (*sōsō*) some" (1 Cor 9:22)? The problem is analogous to the relation between the ineffectual, hollow works we do in Titus 3:5 and the fruitful works of 1 Tim 4:16. God's saving initiative (Titus 3:5) is the horizon and ground for Timothy's saving himself and those who listen to his teaching. The aorist *esōsen* designates a saving act of God that was antecedent to all human works; the future tense of *sōseis* in 1 Tim 4:16 points to the eschatological culmination of this divine act. The initial act of God has issued in a variety of saving actions with which believers at last appear "before the judgment seat of Christ, so that each may receive good or evil, according to what he has done in the body" (2 Cor 5:10).

The passive usage of 1 Tim 2:15, as distinct from the vexed grammar of this theologoumenon, requires this same way of conceptualizing the saving action of God. "A person will be saved rearing children" means that the God who has saved the Christian mother and father will finally bring their salvation through (*dia*) their parenting. In the NT, *dia* regularly occurs with the passive of *sōizein* and thus the question of instrumentality is explicitly raised. In the other Paulines, believers are to be saved not only *by* the crucified Christ but also *through* the Pauline *kerygma* and the gospel (1 Cor 1:21; 15:2). Acts 15:11 has Peter's intervention in the Jerusalem council culminate with, "But we believe that we shall be saved through (*dia*) the grace of the Lord Jesus." In 1 Pet 3:20–21 sacramental baptism saves now as once Noah's family "were saved (*diesōthēsan*, i.e., by God; see Acts 27:44; 28:1, 4) through (*dia*) water." The only NT example of the active *sōizein* with *dia* is the reference to the baptismal washing in Titus 3:5.

The references in Titus and 1 Pet in particular, as they link God's saving act with the tangible sacramental act of baptism, furnish a key to the unparalleled and highly original association of the rearing of children with salvation in 1 Tim 2:15. The passage is explained as a quotation from a paraenetic charge at a Christian marriage. The teaching that links salvation to the daily activity of Christian family life is modeled on the way God saves through the instrumentality of baptism.

Whereas the subjects of the active uses of *sōizein* disclose who are, for the PE, the agents of the saving activity, the objects of the verb help specify the sort of rescue involved. The paraenesis of Titus 3:5, as well as that of 2 Tim 1:9, declares that God saved "us," *hēmas*. The first-person plural designates the congregation or community of believers (including the apostle, 2 Tim 4:8, 18) who together acknowledge their common rescue. In the thanksgiving prayer of 1 Tim 1:15 that once-for-all intervention is summarized in still another citation of an authoritative doctrinal formula: "Christ Jesus came into the world (*eis ton kosmon*) to save sinners (*hamartōlous sōsai*)." It is assumed here that the human community as such, the *kosmos,* needs rescue; what had occurred in the life of every Christian in baptism, through which he passed from his sins into a new life (Titus 3:3–7), is in this theologoumenon formulated in terms of what happened to humankind in the incarnation. The life and death of Jesus for the sins of all (cf. Titus 2:11 with 14) are not just chronologically but also theologically prior to the apostle's proclamation by which he brings a new community to baptismal birth "in the world" (see 1 Tim 3:16; Titus 2:14). The emphasis in 1 Tim 1:15 is not on the rescue from sins but on the rescue of sinners. Human beings are not here said to be saved from specific consequences of their acts; they have been rescued from themselves.

To the universal character of human sinfulness corresponds the universality of the act of God that has saved the race. This universality becomes explicit in 1 Tim 2:3–4, where prayer for all human beings is said to be an "excellent thing and welcome in the eyes of our savior (*sōterōs*) God, who wants all human beings to be saved (*sothenai*) and to come to full knowledge of the truth." Here for the only time in the PE God is the subject of *thelein,* a usage common in the Lukan corpus (thus Acts 18:21) and rather more frequent in the other Paulines. On the only occasion that *thelei sōsai* appears in the gospel tradition (Mark 8:35; see *SFG* §160), the phrase describes the futility of the human wish to save one's own life (*psychēn*). Here in 1 Tim 2:4 the contrary affirmation is proposed; God wills to save all human persons, for none can expect to save himself. Behind the once-for-all acts of the man Christ Jesus stands the enduring will (present tense) of the one God for all to "be saved and to come to full knowledge of the truth." The latter phrase brings the requisite human response to the divine offer of salvation into focus (see Excursus II, "Truth and *epignōsis alētheias* in the PE"). As "Christ Jesus *came* into the world to *save* sinners," so God's will to *save* all has, as its present complement, that all also *come* by faith and baptism to the recognition of who Jesus really is.

The way by which human beings come to such faith brings one again to 1 Tim 4:16, where Timothy's transmission of the Pauline teaching saves the teacher himself and the persons listening (*akouontas*) to him. Listening here is practically synonymous with believing, that is, hearing and accepting the word of another in lieu of the visible, tangible experience. Both physical hearing and an internal understanding and acceptance are implied here (cf. Hebrew *sᵉmaᶜ,* "to listen," better "to hearken," and so, in Deut 6:4, implying "to believe"). Timothy is to be believed because he has listened to Paul (2 Tim 1:13; see 4:17 of all of the pagans listening to Paul's proclamation). What Timothy has heard he shares in turn with those who hear him (2 Tim 2:2). In 2 Tim 2:14, the PE score a listening that subverts the hearers, the very opposite of hearing the saving instruction of 1 Tim 4:16.

Against this background of the use of the verb *sōizein* in the PE, it is notable that the correspondence speaks only twice of *sōtēria* (contrast the rest of the Paulines and the Lukan corpus). Yet at every turn the personal noun *sōtēr* appears in the PE. The volume of the PE opens with the emphatic designation of God and then Christ as *tou sōtēros hēmōn*. At the end of Acts, the Roman Jews are said to have resisted (28:24–25), in fact not to have listened (28:26) to the Pauline *kerygma* and *didachē*. In contrast, the community of Jewish Christians in Titus 1:3–4 have accepted the one God and the one Christ as "our savior," literally, "the savior of us." The Jewish-Christian apostle and his Gentile-Christian colleague, Titus, have in common belief in the God of Israel and in his Christ (see Titus 1:4 on *kata koinēn pistin*). They share this faith with others with whom they are to be identified, to whom they belong, and who belong to them (see Titus 3:14, *hoi hēmeteroi*). The savior is inconceivable apart from the body or community of persons whom he has rescued; hence the PE write nine out of ten times *"our* savior." In the one case in which *sōtēr* is used predicatively and without *hēmōn*, in 1 Tim 4:10, it is in a summary statement of the relation between God's will to save all human beings (see above on 1 Tim 1:15; 2:3–4) and the community of those who have responded to it.

Why do the PE return repeatedly to the title *sōtēr?* In the ancient Greek world *sōtēr* was commonly applied to a person whose achievements (Plutarch, *Lives, Coriolanus* 11.2) had benefited a community, whether defined politically, sociologically, or economically (see Nock, *EGC*, pp. 36–39; *ERAW* 2.720, 724, 727–728; R. Wilson, *"Sōtēria,"* p. 408). Thus the chorus of Aeschylus's *Libation-Bearers* addresses Orestes and Electra, "O saviors (*sōtēres*) of your father's hearth" (264; see his *Suppliants* 980–982 and Nock, *EGC*, p. 26; *ERAW* 2.720–721, 726). Thirty-six times the LXX adopted *sōtēr* to describe the persons through whom Yahweh had rescued Israel as a corporate entity from physical peril and death. Thus, for example, LXX Judg 3:9 and 15, and compare 12:3 in B with 2 Esdr 19:27; see R. Wilson, *"Sōtēria,"* pp. 409–410, 412; Cullmann, *Christology*, pp. 239–240; and LXX 1 Kgdms 10:19, *hymōn sōtēr;* and perhaps 1 Chr 16:35, *ho theos ho sōtēr hēmōn (s.v.1.)* in a prayer; Isa 25:9, *epi tōi sōtēri hēmōn (s.v.1.).* In the LXX the term is not limited to human beings. In LXX Ps 78:9 God is "our savior" even from sins. The two other LXX uses of *sōtēr hēmōn* are also in the Pss (64:6; 94:1). The *Pss. Sol.* 8:33; 17:3 (cf. 3:6; 16:4–5) invoke God as *kyrie, sōtēr hēmōn,* for his goodwill to his holy ones. They depict the community declaring, "We hope in God, our savior" (17:3, *epi ton theon sōtēra hēmōn*). Esth 5:1a describes a prayer to "the all-seeing God and Savior," which contrasts sharply with 8:12n, where Mordecai is, in the language of Artaxerxes' decree, "our savior (*ton te hēmeteron sōtēra*) and perpetual benefactor (*euergetēn*)."

In the LXX, as in profane Greek, though *sōtēr* is a title suitable for the deity it also can be bestowed on humans without implying that they have become divine. The reverse is also true: the god who is *sōtēr* need not be or have been human. *Sōtēr* hypostatizes the action of *sōizein* and serves to articulate the gratitude and honor emanating from those who have experienced that rescuing activity.

EXCURSUSES

The reciprocal relationship created between public and hero on the reception of a benefit belonged to the social fabric of the Hellenistic world. The primary obligation of the person or community benefited was the public expression of gratitude (as numerous ancient inscriptions bear witness); it was understood that this acknowledgment would generate further benefits. The relations between gods and men were expressed in terms of this paradigm, which involved the notions of philanthropy and benefaction (see the texts assembled by Mott, "Benevolence," pp. 60–72). In the NT it is only Luke–Acts and the PE that take up the terminology for benefaction (*euerg-*), whether ironically of secular rulers (Luke 22:25) or of the healing ministry of Jesus (Acts 10:38) and his apostles (Acts 4:9) or of the kindness to be shown by masters to their slaves (1 Tim 6:2).

Within this horizon of reciprocal benevolence, a person could be acclaimed *sōtēr*, once or repeatedly. The acclamation "was one thing when used to express the gratitude or hopes or promises of a moment, another thing when accorded or assumed as a constant epithet" (Nock, *ERAW* 2.721–722). The PE accord the title to God and Jesus; 2 Pet gives it only to Jesus. The PE resemble the rest of the NT in restricting the term to those two. In Titus each of the three uses of the title for God is followed by a use of it for Christ. The alternation is certainly deliberate (Berge, "Savior," p. 138) and appears in still another form in the Timothy correspondence, where 1 Tim uses *sōtēr* only of God, 2 Tim only of Christ. The first volume of Luke's work begins with the same alternation (Luke 1:47; 2:11).

The alternation may have its explanation in the way that the OT employed *sōtēr*, for this noun, used normally of God but also for human rescuers, is never a title for a "Messiah" in the LXX or the intertestamental literature, including Qumran (see D-C, p. 101). The tendency was emerging in these documents to hypostatize God's saving action or its result (see W. Foerster in *TDNT* 7.1013–1014 for texts; and Brownlee, *Qumran*, pp. 196–203 on 1Q Isa^a 51:5 etc.), but the NT documents are the first explicitly to designate the Christ as savior, beginning with Phil 3:20 (otherwise in the Paulines, only Eph 5:23). Along with Luke–Acts, the PE take up the uniquely Christian usage. By placing it regularly in tandem with both God and Christ, these texts are doing with *sōtēr* what had been done with *kyrios* in the first Christian generation. Jesus the Christ is to be addressed by the same titles as those which could be given to the God of Israel. The established role of *kyrios* and the newness of *sōtēr* are suggested by the fact that Titus, which contains the lion's share of the **sō(s)-* terminology and doctrine of the PE, is the only Pauline document that never uses *kyrios*. For the PE the title *sōtēr* is the key for unlocking the understanding of God and his Christ; it is, further, the common denominator for understanding the titles that will surface later in this correspondence.

The question remains why *sōtēr* has become a title of preference for God and his Christ. The parallels from the cult offered to Hellenistic kings and the

Roman emperors as *sōtēres*, the titles and concepts current in the Hellenistic mystery religions, the usage of Hellenistic Judaism (LXX, intertestamental literature, Josephus, Philo) have all been combed out (see D-C, pp. 100–103; Nock, *EGC*, pp. 35–44; *ERAW* 2.728–735; Mott, "Deliverance"). Only minimal similarities with the usage of the NT have been found in the documentation for the imperial cult and the oriental mysteries, though they were, possibly from the beginning and surely eventually, rivals of Christianity (Cullmann, *Christology*, p. 240). The Jewish practice already noted of describing and invoking the God of Israel as *sōtēr* (*hēmōn*) certainly illustrates a pre-Christian tendency to "personalize" God's saving activity (*yšʿ*). The application of that title to God in the PE (but not in the other Paulines) and in Luke–Acts is easily explained in terms of the OT practice (see Wis 16:7), for such usage was "according to the Scriptures." The problem centers around the reason for favoring the term for Jesus (Titus 1:4). Paul, in Phil 3:20, had first used *sōtēr* with this meaning, perhaps taking it up from a Roman tradition (Cullmann, *Christology*, p. 244; Bultmann, *Th. NT* 1.79). The title is there applied to Jesus as the one who will come in glory.

The reason for this aspect of the usage may be closer to hand than at first appears. The personal name "Jesus" (*Iesous*, a short form of the earlier *yhwš[w]ʿ*, *yehošuaʿ*, "Joshua" [BAGD, s.v. and W. Foerster in *TDNT* 3.284–286, 289–290]) was a common one in Judaism until the second century C.E., and it was popularly treated as a form of the Hebrew **yšʿ*, "to save or rescue" (see Sir 46:1 and *Iesous de sōtēria kyriou*, Philo, *Mut.* 121). This understanding surfaces in the NT, in the earliest traditions about the mockery of the crucified (Mark 15:30–31, *SFG* §345; cf. Mark 9:38–39, *SFG* §167) and in the later explanation of the name of *Iesous* given by Matt 1:21 (see Brown, *Birth*, pp. 130–131; Cullmann, *Christology*, pp. 242, 244–245). In a word, God's salvation is "personified" in Jesus of Nazareth; as the Semitic meaning of his name began to fade from consciousness in a Greek-speaking world, the sense of the name of the one through whom God brought salvation had to be preserved. Luke–Acts already offer evidence of this process, for example, in the *sōtēria* of Luke 19:9 and the explicit link of a unique *sōtēria* with the name of Jesus in Acts 4:7, 10–12; 2:38; 3:6, 16; and 19:13–17. In the Hellenistic world one recalls that theology was constructed through etymology, as in the work of Cornutus.

The PE of set purpose begin their exposition of the Pauline teaching about Jesus (and no personal name comes near occurring as often as that of Jesus Christ in this correspondence) by translating that name. Complementing the emphasis on the **sō(s)*- terminology in Titus, the term *Iesous* occurs relatively few times in this initial letter. A similar staging occurs with the noun *sōtēria*, which does not appear in the PE before the last testament of Paul in 2 Tim. There the apostle under arrest explains his shameful condition as "for the sake of the elect. . . . My purpose is that they too reach the salvation (*sōtērias tychōsin*) which is in Christ Jesus with eternal glory" (2 Tim 2:10). The last clause unmistakably defines *sōtēria* in terms of the relation of the elect to the person of Jesus. The phrase *sōtērias tygchanein* is not otherwise documented in the LXX, NT, or Ap. Frs., but the verb is used as it is in Luke–Acts and not as in the other Paulines. The sufferings of Paul serve to target others for a salvation (cf. 1 Tim 4:16) that is ultimately reached in the person of Jesus and life with him (see 2 Tim 1:1) "with eternal glory" (2 Tim 2:10, cf. 4:18). The apostolic mission has as its ultimate goal a salvation that lies beyond the horizon of human history.

A similar affirmation is made of "the sacred letters which have the power to make you [Timothy] astute in attaining salvation (*eis sōtērian*) through faith (*dia pisteōs*) which comes from union with Christ Jesus (*tēs en Christōi Iesou*)" (2 Tim 3:15). In this passage the letter of the OT is for salvation, as the trials of the apostle are for salvation in the former citation. The unusual *sōtērias tychōsin* of 2:10 is conceptually the equivalent of the rather more Hebraic and Septuagintal *eis sōtērian* of 3:15 (see LXX Exod 15:2; Num 6:14; 2 Kgdms 10:11; 1 Chr 19:12; 2 Chr 12:7; etc.). The relation between salvation and the person of Christ Jesus is further defined by explicitly noting at this point personal adherence to Jesus "through faith" (a phrase not found otherwise in the PE but regularly in Paul [cf. Gal 3:26 with Rom 3:22]). Thus on the only two occasions that the PE speak of salvation in nominal form, it is inseparable from the specifically Christian relation to the person of Jesus.

If, in fact, the name and person of Jesus "define" the terms "savior" and "salvation" (as they also define the term "Christ"), then their meaning is to be traced through what believers were convinced he had done and taught. Jesus had saved or rescued those who had invoked him and by that very invocation asked for salvation (Harnack, *Mission*, pp. 101–103, though controverted by P. Wendland, cited in Cullmann, *Christology*, p. 241 n. 3). In what ways did he respond? Some of the earliest traditions of Jesus' ministry describe his response as involving both word and action. He was remembered as healing persons, not just limbs (W. Foerster in *TDNT* 7.990), as healing both unseen sins and visible paralysis (Mark 2:1–12; *SFG* §92). The complementary visible and invisible aspects of Jesus' activity are not simply juxtaposed. What human beings can see and hear is a parabolic act of God, which has an aspect that they cannot sense. Yet the seen and the unseen are related, not by any intrinsic bond between illness and evil, but by the deliberate act and word of Jesus who revealed one by means of the other. The visible healing that Jesus gives becomes a window into that inner world in which God forgives. The saving activity of the unseen savior God has visibly appeared (see Titus 2:11; 3:4–5) in the man who bore the name that means salvation (see Luke 1:69, 71; 19:9), and salvation includes at its hidden center the forgiveness of sins (see Luke 1:77–79; 19:10). The author of Acts emphatically links the healings bestowed through Peter with salvation in Jesus' name (see esp. Acts 4:12) and, when further healings heighten the persecution of the apostles, Jesus is explicitly called their "leader and savior, [the one] to give repentance to Israel and forgiveness of sins" (Acts 5:31 s.v.1.). The savior title reappears in Acts 13:23 (cf. 26, 47) as the Pauline *kerygma* announces Jesus with the words, "Through this man forgiveness of sins is proclaimed to you" (Acts 13:38; cf. Acts 22:16 of Paul himself calling on Jesus' name while receiving baptism and forgiveness).

In the PE the *$sō(s)$- terms (including the cognate compounds in *$sōphro(n)$- and even, from a negative view, the *asōtia* of Titus 1:6) designate realities, both present and to come, that are ultimately invisible, a deliverance or healing of human persons that occurs now in the internal, moral order but with an orientation toward a goal that is also unseen. "Christ Jesus came into the world to save sinners" (1 Tim 1:15; see above on Titus 3:3–7; 2 Tim 1:9–10).

God offers deliverance to all because all stand in need of it (1 Tim 2:3–4; 4:10). He alone offers it because he alone is God; he offers it only through Jesus because Jesus alone is its mediator (1 Tim 2:5). The PE are not innovative in this use of the terminology for salvation. It was already traditional in Christian worship and catechesis, as the preceding citations illustrate. Nonetheless, the focus on internal, religious and moral deliverance is not present in the OT or the Qumran texts. The tendency had been growing within Hellenistic Judaism to explain God's salvation in terms of an inner, moral conversion and a deliverance for a higher life, a development illustrated by as many as forty Philonic texts studied by S. C. Mott, "Ethics," pp. 44–46 (e.g., *Praem.* 163). Some new Christian congregations took up that tendency as they reflected on the person and name of Jesus "who died for our sins" (cf. 1 Cor 15:3 with Titus 2:14; 1 Tim 2:6) and publicly formulated their gratitude by acclaiming him in worship as *sōtēr hēmōn*, along with God himself. The PE assumed that terminology and its sharp focus on inner ethical deliverance and salvation.

W. Foerster has suggested that an antignostic polemic prompts this concentration on moral renewal (*TDNT* 7.1017). The data will bear a different—indeed opposite—reading. The Ap. Frs., writing in the decades after the PE, did not further exploit that emphasis (Sachot, "Salut," pp. 54–70). Certainly Valentinian and his followers in the mid-second century favored the salvation terminology and the savior title for Jesus (which was systematically substituted for Lord: cf. Irenaeus, *Adversus haereses* 1.1.3; W. Foerster in *TDNT* 7.999–1001; 1019–1020). The singular emphasis on the inner, unseen aspects of salvation in the PE may have offered a foothold for later gnostic speculations on salvation as a completely internal and invisible rescue of the human mind and spirit, trapped in the coils of matter. A gnostic had no interest in the bodily healings by Jesus as effective signs of the internal healing of diseased souls.

The secondary character of these gnostic speculations becomes evident on examining the line of development that the PE have in fact taken. That line took its origin from Jewish and Jewish-Christian theology of the Name, that is to say, systematic reflection upon and probing of the personal names, titles, and epithets for the God of Israel and for the one whom Christians believed to be the Messiah (see H. Bietenhard in *TDNT* 5.242–283; Daniélou, *TJC*, pp. 147–163; Longenecker, *Christology*, pp. 41–46). The biblical authors, like the many other writers of the ancient world, liked to emphasize the meaning of a personal name, particularly when later developments stimulated speculation about that particular person. The exceedingly archaic and specifically Jewish-Christian and Palestinian origin of this type of theological inquiry has left its precipitate in that highly select group of proper names which have received special treatment as *nomina sacra* in the copying of the earliest Christian manuscripts that have survived, as well as in such a passage as *Barn.* 9.7–9, with its arithmetical extrapolations from the name of Jesus, taken as a number written with the Greek abbreviation *IH* (Roberts, "P. Yale I," pp. 25–28; *Manuscript*, pp. 26–48; Roberts and Skeat, *Birth*, pp. 57–59). The Greek letters *CP* for *sōtēr* are another of these privileged abbreviations, and, if Roberts is correct, *CP* goes back to a Jewish-Christian theological interest, and ultimately a Palestinian one. The traditions employed by Acts that trace the **sō(s)-* terminology and interest in Jesus' name back into the earliest Jerusalem congregation may well be accurate. In any case, the PE employ a theology of the name (see *onoma tou theou/kyriou* in 1 Tim 6:1; 2 Tim 2:19) in which the meaning of the names and titles for Jesus is of fundamental importance, and the most basic of all for the PE is *sōtēr*. Even the *kyrios* title, which makes its appearance in the PE in 1 Tim 1:2 and predominates thereafter, has been introduced by the *sōtēr* of the preceding letter in this collection, and *sōtēr* accordingly grounds the meaning of *kyrios* in the Timothy correspondence.

When salvation is an internal, ethical phenomenon, does the link with healing and health in the most archaic gospel traditions completely vanish? In the PE it does not. Healthy instruction, health in faith, wholesome preaching, healthy words (Titus 1:9, 13; 2:1–2, 8; 2 Tim 1:13; etc.) are constantly projected as the sign and paradigm of the inner moral deliverance, the salvation, effected by baptismal rebirth into God's grace (Titus 3:4–8; for another way of arguing this point, see Donelson, *Pseudepig.*, pp. 135–154, on salvation in the PE). Good deeds are thus coordinated by the PE with sound teaching, whereas vicious conduct emanates from gangrenous teaching (cf. 2 Tim 2:16–18 with 3:1–9). Later Christian thinkers, not least Clement of Alexandria and Origen, elaborated this comparison of the healing ministry of Jesus as *sōtēr* with the healing brought to a diseased world by the Christian faith and its sacraments (for the texts, see Harnack, *Mission*, pp. 103–124).

The way in which the PE use and understand the **sōphro(n)-* terminology for virtue illustrates how the health bestowed by salvation is linked to the internal moral character that emanates from that healing. The passages already cited develop their thought by variations on the **sō(s)-* terminology itself. For example, God is *sōtēr;* Jesus is *sōtēr* (Titus 1:3–4); the savior God saved through the savior Jesus (Titus 3:4–6); the savior God wants all to be saved (1 Tim 2:3–4); and the power of God saved us through our savior Christ Jesus (2 Tim 1:8–10).

313

In no passage of the PE is this more conspicuous than in the baptismal paraenesis cited in Titus 2:11–14, which moves from the savior God (2:10) and his saving (*sōtērios*) grace to the glorious parousia of "our savior Jesus Christ." This saving grace (2:11) "disciplines us to disown godlessness and worldly lusts (*tas kosmikas epithymias*) and to live in a sensible (*sōphronōs*), honest, godly way in this present age" (2:12). The play on *sōterios/sōphronōs* could be dismissed as an accident of the source being employed, but it is no accident in the redaction before us. The paraenesis is cited precisely to relate the whole preceding instruction on the character and conduct of believers (Titus 2:1–10) to baptismal faith as the matrix for Christian living. The **sōphro(n)-* terminology recurs in that instruction at 2:2, 4, 5, and 6. The adverbial *sōphronōs* of 2:12, unique in the NT (and unique in the LXX in Wis 9:11) then grounds the way of living inculcated by this language in the *charis sōterios* of the savior God. Even the brief list headed by *sōphronōs* reminds one that the **sōphro(n)-* terms in the PE are always in lists and codes (cf. the list in 4 Macc 15:10). Thus the qualities listed for the bishop or presbyter-bishop include his being sensible (*sōphrona:* Titus 1:8; 1 Tim 3:2). In 1 Tim 2:9, 15; 2 Tim 1:7, *sōphrosynē* and *sōphronismos* occur along with one to three other virtues.

The etymological source of **sōphro(n)-* is the compounding of **sō(s)-* with *phren*, "mind, heart." This base was adverted to from Plato (*Cratylus* 411E) and Aristotle (*NE* 6.5.4–6; 1140b 11–14) to Philo (*Virt.* 14), who remarks that the term used for the health (*hygeia*) of the soul is *sōphrosynē*, which he calls *sōterian tōi phronounti tōn en hymin apergazomenē*, "the virtue that makes one's thinking sane."

The English *sanity* catches some of the nuances of internal equilibrium and sense of balance, the mental health that the **sōphro(n)-* cluster designated in Greek. When Festus has accused Paul of raving, Acts 26:25 has Paul defend his gospel as "words of truth and sanity (*sōphrosynēs*)" (cf. 2 Cor 5:13). The unique use of *sōphronein* in the gospel tradition, to describe the cured demoniac in Mark 5:15/Luke 8:35 (*SFG* §137), illustrates this meaning dramatically; note particularly the Lukan addition that it was "at the feet of Jesus" that the Gerasenes found the man "in his right mind (*sōphronounta*)." The relationship with Jesus is precisely the concern of the author of the PE as he refracts the **sōphro(n)-* language of Titus 2:1–10 through the paraenetic baptismal confession in which the chapter culminates (cf. the **phron-* language in Rom 12:3). What Col 3:18, 20 and Eph 6:1 s.v.1. have done by inserting "in the Lord" into the traditional domestic codes, the author of Titus has done by subjoining 2:11–14 to his domestic code as its climax. The PE have gone about this task more extensively than the earlier Paulines.

Who among believers are characterized by the *sōphro(n)-* language in the PE? The domestic code of Titus 2:1–10 uses the terms of the old men and women as well as of young adults; women in general and a married woman in particular are thus characterized (1 Tim 2:9–10, 11–15, noting how *sōthesetai* is picked up in the closing *meta sōphrosynēs*). Timothy, as one who shares the Pauline apostolate, is to have along with Paul a spirit of discretion or discipline (*sōphronismou;* 2 Tim 1:7); as noted already, the bishop and presbyter-bishop of the PE must be sensible (*sōphrona*). The terminology is not used, however, of Christian slaves, perhaps because of the simply material, instrumental definition of slaves in the Hellenistic world (Titus 1:1; 2:9–10; 1 Tim 6:1), though Menander has a slave becoming *sōphronesteras* because of having good masters (Koerte 722/Sandbach, *Menandri*, p. 322). This Hellenistic definition will eventually be overridden by the paraenesis addressed to all believers in Titus 2:11–14.

The meaning of the **sōphro(n)*- terminology in the PE varies not only as different words are used of different persons but also as the terms are used in different literary genres: lists, domestic codes, sacramental paraeneses, church orders, and prayers. The flexible usage of the PE in turn mirrors the complex significance that the *sōphro(n)*- language enjoyed in formal Hellenistic composition; the terms are, for example, relatively rare in the papyri (Spicq, *Lexic.,* p. 867). They signal here in the PE a deliberate and reflective integration of Christian life with some of the qualities that Hellenistic society and its educated spokesmen considered most important in human life. The author of the PE has the widest conceivable application for the **sōphro(n)*- language. The internal equilibrium that it designates belongs everywhere (Titus 2:6–7). The contrast in Titus between "worldly lusts" and a "sensible" life reminds the reader that *sōphrosynē* refers even to an inner control of one's physical appetites (see Aristotle, *NE* 3.10.3; 1118a) that partially corresponds with what English calls "temperance." For the Greek to live sensibly was giving what one owed to oneself, as distinguished from what one owed to other human beings (*dikaiōs*) and to the deity (*eusebōs;* Titus 2:12). The savior in the PE has touched and healed all of the internal human powers on whose exercise depend the virtues prized by Hellenistic society.

The salvation proposed by this correspondence is the internal, ethical deliverance, the moral change that has been identified in the Jewish tradition represented by Philo (Mott, "Ethics," pp. 22–48); this tradition (perhaps an Alexandrian one) was used by Wis and 4 Macc as well as by Titus. The absence of the whole **sō(s)*- cluster from Jewish inscriptions (the single occurrence in *CII* 728 seems to refer to a physical healing) may indicate from another perspective that the Alexandrian initiative did not find a response in Hellenistic Jewish parlance elsewhere. The welcome that certain early Christian texts gave to this language would accordingly be a deliberate missionary opening to certain ethical values that the surrounding culture cherished (see Excursus III, *"Eusebeia* and Its Cognates in the PE").

ANCIENT AUTHORS AND WORKS

♦

Aboth, 149
Acta Alexandrinorum, 51
Aelian, *Tactica,* 186
Aelianus, *Varia Historia,* 135
Aeschylus: *Libation Bearers,* 308; *Persians,*
    185, 231; *Prometheus,* 191, 213; *Seven
    Against Thebes,* 167; *Suppliants,* 308
Alcaeus, 100, 121
Ambrosiaster, 3, 156
Ammonius, 68
Apocalypse of Adam, 282
Apollonius: Molon, 214; of Tyana, 151, 204
Appian, *Roman History,* 182
Apuleius: *Apologia,* 289; *Metamorphoses,* 196
Aquinas, Thomas, 1
Aristides of Athens, 140
Aristobulus, 168
Aristophanes: *Clouds,* 130, 138, 178; *Knights,*
    119; *Peace,* 214; *Thesmophoriazusae,* 120;
    Wasps, 154
Aristotle: *Nicomedean Ethics,* 60, 79, 133,
    145, 154, 314, 315; *Politics,* 60, 144, 145,
    163; *Rhetoric,* 9, 107; *Topics,* 119
Artemidorus Daldianus, *Onirocriticus,* 141
Ascension of Isaiah, 179
Athenaeus, *Deipnosophistai,* 130, 216
Athenagoras, 140, 153
Augustine: *Against Pelegian Letters,* 195; *City
    of God,* 196; *De peccatorum meritis,* 195;
    Letters, 67
Aulus Gellius, *Noctes atticae,* 79, 129, 255

Barnabas, 54, 57, 59, 82, 98, 103, 108, 113,
    119, 122, 127, 158, 159, 170, 178, 181,
    190, 193, 198, 199, 207, 223, 235, 258, 313
Baruch, Third Apocalypse of, 158

Callimachus, *Hymn to Zeus,* 108
Carphyllides, 79
Chariton of Aphrodisias, *Chaireas and
    Callirhoe,* 196
Cicero: *Against Verres,* 164; *De natura
    deorum,* 169, 195, 287; *De officiis,* 90, 131,
    132, 133, 147; *De senectute,* 131; *Epistolae*

ad familiares, 249; *Orator,* 131; *To Atticus,*
    195; *Tusculan Disputations,* 165
Clement: *First,* 51, 52, 54, 55, 56, 58, 59, 67,
    68, 78, 80, 81, 90, 99, 102, 104, 118, 120,
    121, 122, 124, 126, 127, 128, 131, 133,
    137, 142, 151, 152, 153, 155, 158, 159,
    160, 161, 165, 178, 180, 181, 188, 190,
    191, 192, 193, 194, 198, 199, 228, 235,
    236, 237, 238, 239, 240, 254, 257, 258,
    265, 277, 296, 305; *Second,* 52, 81, 100,
    103, 104, 120, 124, 153, 155, 158, 190, 207,
    254, 298, 301
Clementine Homilies, 55, 111
Clement of Alexandria: *Paedagogus,* 140, 145,
    151, 153; *Protrepticus,* 162; *Quis dives,* 195;
    Stromata, 79, 95, 107, 121
Constitutiones Apostolorum, 84
Corpus Hermeticum, 196
Cyril of Alexandria, 156

Demosthenes: *Against Dionysodorus,* 256;
    Against Medias, 213; *Against Phormio,* 256
Didache, 57, 80, 103, 122, 124, 127, 153, 161,
    174, 181, 188, 190, 191, 198, 207, 258
Dio Cassius, *Roman History,* 255, 256, 292
Dio Chrysostom, 168, 204, 230
Diodorus Siculus, 181, 214
Diogenes Laertius, 167, 278
Diogenetus, 181, 229, 277
Dionysius of Halicarnassus, 87; *Roman
    Antiquities,* 111, 135, 149, 230

Enoch, 57, 159, 161, 188, 221, 280, 293
Epimenides of Crete, 12, 107
Epictetus, *Discourses,* 132, 141, 145, 278
Epicurus, *Sententiae vaticanae,* 154, 223
Epistle of Aristeas, 81, 118, 124, 152, 180,
    234, 237, 238, 239, 256, 295
Eugnostos, 55
Euripides, 108; *Andromache,* 94; *Bacchae,* 60;
    Heracles furens, 120; *Ion,* 60; *Orestes,* 55,
    60, 121; *Phoenissae,* 94, 120
Eusebius, *Church History,* 140, 195, 234;
    Praeparatio evangelica, 168

Recent Authors

◆

RECENT AUTHORS

INDEX OF SCRIPTURAL REFERENCES
OUTSIDE OF THE PE

◆

324

INDEX OF SCRIPTURAL REFERENCES

327